Translator's Preface

Richard Muther's German Book Illustration of the Gothic Period and the Early Renaissance, covering the period from about 1460 to 1530, is a classic contribution to the history of the book.

It has been reprinted but the mid-nineteenth century German is not easy going even for the reasonably competent reader of German and, in spots, particularly when an occasional typo occurs, as the fates decree in almost every book, it is all but undecipherable. Furthermore, as was the German scholarly style of the period, Muther is verbose and repetitive in many places, and at times, instead of staying strictly with his subject, which is the history of book illustration as such, he tells us the story in the book, which frequently has little direct connection with its illustrations as identifying the printer, edition, period, etc. These asides, which are not material to the exciting story of the revolution in book illustration, which Muther covers so well, tend to dilute its message and were, therefore, omitted. In many cases Muther limited his listings and descriptions of illustrations in a particular book to the ones that identified it from other printings, editions, artists, printers, etc., or steps forward in the art, and in these cases the translation includes them in full detail.

This is, therefore, an edited translation, which attempts to sharpen the contribution made by Muther's study, without losing any of the material or detail that is of significance to the purpose of the book, i.e., the coverage of one of the important facets of the history of the book during one of its most exciting periods, when artists of the caliber of Dürer and the two Holbeins made illustration of books a respectable branch of art instead of a mechanical trade.

Volume 2, which is almost entirely illustrations, is copied as is, except for the limited changes in format or size required for efficient production.

In order to preserve the detailed and excellent indexes, it is important to note that there are two kinds of citations in volume I. There are the customary footnotes, and in the original these start over again with each page of text. These have been renumbered consecutively for each chapter and are identified in the text by parentheses. The notes appear at the end of each chapter.

Muther also used marginal numerical notations which referred, generally, to the line on which the index citation is found. This is a consecutive series throughout the first volume, numbered from 1 to 1822. The Artists' Index, the Printers' Index and the Book Index refer to this marginal number rather than to the page numbers of the book. It should be noted that the Artists' index has the artists filed by their first names, followed by the titles they illustrated, in chronological order, accompanied by their insignias (where applicable). The Printers' index arranges the printers alphabetically under their surnames, followed by the titles they published, in chronological order. The Third Index, the Book Index, is an interfiled title and author index, with the author normally filed under his forename, if Latin, or his surname, if German. The titles are arranged alphabetically under the author. When there are multiple editions of one book these are arranged chronologically under the title. Also, a number of authors were published in Latin as well as in German, and in that case the German titles are listed first, followed by the Latin, with titles in the same kind of array in both cases.

As noted above, it is important to remember that all the citations in the general indexes to volume 1 cite the numbers that appeared in the margins rather than page numbers. Unfortunately when several editions are indexed on one line the citation numbers on the margin, which are printed only one to a line, may run for five or more lines in some cases, so they are not always specific. It is very wasteful of space to put these specific line citations in the margin, thus narrowing the type block and bulking up the book. Since they are not invariably specific, in any event, the decision was made to put them into the text preceding the material cited (though the same number may be found in the indexes under author, title, and illustrator or printer). These index numbers are identified by being enclosed in square brackets. This differentiates them from the notes (in parenthesis) which will be found at the end of each chapter. Since multiple editions are cited by different numbers in the index, the numbers in the original are not all on the same line with the specific items cited. We have, therefore, in cases such as that, grouped the index reference numbers and those referring to a batch of editions appear at the beginning of the batch of editions, enclosing the whole series within one set of square brackets. It is hoped that the bracketed citations referred to on each page can be listed at the top of each page aligned with the center margins, to make for easy reference, while the conventional page numbers could be given at the outer margins.

It should be noted especially, as indicated by Muther, that his listing of illustrated incunabula is more complete than that for 16th century works, since the latter are listed fairly completely elsewhere.

One of the factors in determining whether there has been more than one edition of an illustrated book (even when the illustrations are apparently the same throughout the work) is the size of the illustrations. Muther indicates the size of the illustrations in most cases, whether there has been more than one edition or not. He does this in two different ways. Most generally, he indicates the height and breadth of the illustrations within parentheses. Sometimes he puts them in the text. The sizes are invariably given in millimeters and the height is invariably given first. When the size is included in parenthesis; i.e., it reads (h. 190, br. 114 mm). Since this is always in the same order and is always in mm there appears to be little point in repeating the letters h. or br. or mm hundreds of times. So, in this translation, when the size of illustrations is given within parenthesis we shall use, to cite the example stated above (190 x 114). When the size of wood cuts is given in the text without parenthesis, and this is most commonly done when there are variations in size of the wood block used within one book, the above conventions are not followed strictly. Sometimes Muther gives the width first and sometimes the heigth. For example, one of his descriptions of woodcuts states "the woodcuts vary in width from 112-118 mm, and their height may be 190 or 160 or 130 mm." In cases such as this the details of the dimensions will be written out in full.

<u>Orthography:</u> The spellings in the original for the same thing are frequently highly variable. For example, the word for "chronical," used in the title or referring to the title of the particular book being discussed, may be spelled: Cronica, or chronica, or Kronik, or cronik or Kronich,

as well as in other ways. Similarly, in sequential lines or other pages, we may find the same title referred to as Ritter von Thurm or Ritter von Turm, or Ritter von Turn. In a few cases there are outright errors or what appear to be outright errors in the original titles. However, when we consider that much of what is cited consists of titles ranging back, in some cases, 500 years or more, it is not impossible that the original might use the word "fur" without the umlaut instead of with the umlaut as has been customary for a long time. In practically all these cases, which have existed in the original German edition for some 80 years without reducing its usefulness, and which really do not cause any confusion now, since the title or name to which each refers is clear, and there is no similar title or name to cause confusion, the spelling given in the original is followed, except that we have started the title with a capital letter throughout. In a few cases of personal names, such as "Marc Airer," later spelled "Marx Ayrer" or "Lirer," which is sometimes spelled "Lirar," the spelling in the index is used.

Similarly, Muther has not been consistent in his footnote references (here given at the end of chapters) but, again, where they do not cause confusion, the titles in citations are copied as given in the original.

Ralph R. Shaw

Honolulu, 1971

Author's Preface

I hope that this work will make a useful contribution and will improve access to a field that has been little worked to date. It has recently been shown again, and correctly, how important a role woodcuts played in German printing art and how full of gaps is our knowledge of this branch of the art. The significant master artists of our Fatherland have had a predilection for the block cut in producing individual plates of their own, which, to be sure, presented their deepest and noblest thoughts, as well as in illustrating outstanding classic literature. Dürer, Burgkmair, Cranach and Holbein all served as illustrators for the great printers of their time and a great many of their woodcuts, which we now admire as individual plates, were originally book illustrations.

While there could be little question about the justification for a work dealing with German book illustration of the 15th and 16th centuries, there remained the problem of how it might best be arranged. Three methods of handling this presented themselves. The first was an approach from the point of view of cultural history. One could take the major printed works of the 15th and 16th Century, group them according to their content, and investigate the position of the individual artisans who did the illustrations, how they did them and how they interpreted the works in artistic reproduction. As a second approach one could put major emphasis on the history of printing, the advances in techniques, and the differences among the individual artists and schools of block cutting, and indicate the characteristics of the illustrations done by individual masters.

The third method of handling it, finally, was the bibliographical approach, which was the one that I have, after much deliberation, made the basis for this work. While I chose this approach in spite of many misgivings, I was supported in my decision by the thought that my book is intended not only for the art historian but also for bibliophiles. The work of Panzer, Hain and Ebert, aside from parts of Weigel's Lagerkataloge were, until now, the only aids that the collector and friend of old woodcuts had available. My primary purpose was to replace these with a usable, systematic reference book. I therefore had to consider not only book-art history, narrowly construed, but had to attempt bibliographic completeness as well. This left place of publication and publisher as the only possible arrangement. Even though it leaves many questions in the history of art in the background, it provides a sound basis for a coherent approach to the history of book illustration, based on recorded sources. I should be pleased if my book also makes some contribution to the history of art and clarifies in some degree the confusion that exists with reference to the work of a number of artists.

The second volume of this work should be especially welcome, as it presents a selection of the outstanding book woodcuts of the 15th and 16th centuries in true facsimile reproduction. This second volume came into being primarily because of the services of my friend and printer, Georg Hirth, who gave my book the same care and self-sacrifice that is exemplified in his other publications on the history of art.

I have placed heaviest emphasis on incunabula and believe that the first 160 plates of this volume present a substantially complete review of the development of the art during the 15th Century. The first quarter of the 16th Century is covered by a smaller sample because many of the illustrations by Dürer, Burgkmair, Schäufelein and Holbein are already available in Hirth's Kulturgeschichtlichem Bilderbuch. I could therefore limit my selection to the rarer and unpublished plates, and especially to those that give a more exhaustive overview of book illustration of the early renaissance. Those who want encyclopedic coverage of book illustration of the early renaissance are referred to the illustrations in the original works rather than in this text. The reproductions in this work are distinguished by the fact that without exception they are given in the original size and on hand made paper so as to give them the greatest possible perfection. [Translator's note: this last statement is not true of this edition since some change in size was required in certain cases to fit the printing page sizes currently in use; and while this edition is printed on permanent/ durable paper it is not printed on hand made paper.]

Dr. G. Hirth, with his broad knowledge and practical skills, helped me very greatly in the preparation and editing of this work. In addition, I should like to give special thanks to Mr. A. F. Butsch, the honored compiler of Bucherornamentik der Renaissance, who gave me much valuable advice and information, as well as to Drs. Laubmann and Frommann, who gave me unlimited access to the Royal Bavarian Palace and State Library as well as to various German museums. I should also like to express my appreciation to my respected teacher, Professor Anton Springer, who first awakened my interest in these studies.

Dr. R. Muther

Munich, June 22, 1884.

CONTENTS

PART I:

THE GOTHIC PERIOD

INTRODUCTION

Germany has seldom achieved as magnificent a period of development as it did during the 15th Century. The invention of the art of book printing, in a single stroke, freed the intellect from the limitations it suffered in the middle ages and opened a new era. The intellectual world was inspired and animated by the idea of the deep need for education of the general public.

However, Gutenberg's achievement was not only of the greatest cultural significance; it was also epoch-making for the history of art. In the light of hindsight, it was book printing which brought the woodcut to a developing and flowering art.

Practically every period has had reverence for the book as the conveyor of the current culture; it provided dissemination for their intellectual works, even though it was costly.

Even in the beginning of the middle ages, the Roman Codices appeared in dazzling color and pomp. Whole pages were covered with ornaments; gold and silver was spread over the writing and illustrations, and the costliest material, the finest parchment, was used for the whole thing.

These books, however, rarely gave an impression of artistic unity. While the ornaments showed complete mastery of the materials, the pictures were bizarre.

This changed during the Gothic period, which followed. While the magnificence and costliness of the materials as well as the ornamentation continued at the height of the previous period, the illustrations became artistic achievements under the Gothic painters and sculptors. As in the previous romantic period, the Benedictine Order continued to lead in decorating codices in the early Gothic period. The monastery was the place where art and learning in general, as well as book illustration, found its chief nurturing (1).

This period came to an end all too soon. New orders, including the Dominicans and Franciscans, followed, and they were wrought on a completely different basis. They were basically against pomp and richness in the church; so they minimized artistic production of codices. In spite of this, if one searches, he will find some books that are artistically ornamented--although such searches usually turn out poorly. At the peak of the Gothic period there was no differentiation between art and handwork: the monks who transcribed the books simultaneously did the art work, but in the later Gothic period this changed. Painters went their own way. The production of books was handled only by a lower order of artisans who also did the book illustration. They worked so mechanically that this kind of work was generally considered a purely mechanical craft.

The search went on for a medium which could produce text and illustration simultaneously, in multiple copies, and the wood block was chosen for this purpose. This was a process that people had been using for a long time in other fields. Since it was easier to reproduce pictures than text in wood or metal, pictures played the chief role in all the old block books. The text to clarify the illustrations was made up of letters cut individually into the wood or the metallic material, as in the so-called <u>Biblia pauperum</u>, and there were rarely whole pages of text. By and large, one cannot compare these woodcut books with the miniatures of the ancient codices. Only occasional works such as the noble special edition of the Ars moriendi, the Canticum canticorum, and the special edition of the Biblia pauperum portrayed the work of artistic wood cutters of the greatest technical achievement. In general, even if the artisans knew how to give their work artistic character, this was lost in its translation into the wood because the wood-cutting technique was quite young and had, to this time, been experimented with only for Holy pictures and playing cards. Before the discovery of true book printing, therefore, nobody could believe that the decaying art would have a new life.

Gutenberg's achievement, despite its almost immeasurable importance in other respects, meant little in relation to woodcuts at first; it was only very slowly that the modern book developed from the codices of the middle ages and the wood block prints. As in the case of the block book, they continued to print the title as an insert, in different type in the margin at the beginning of the text, rather than as a separate page in the front.

Even though the text was no longer entirely on a wooden block but was printed with movable letters, the external appearance of the book changed very little. The pictorial presentations, it must be admitted, no longer played the chief role, but they received an important position for a different reason. Through the whole of the 15th Century, it was thought that pictures were one of the chief means of teaching and of intellectual contribution since they spoke a language which could be understood even by those who could not read. In the Ars moriendi it said specifically, "Sed ut omnibus ista materia sit fructosa, tam literis tantum literato deservientibus quam ymaginibus laico et literato simul deservientibus cunctorum oculis obicitur." Similarly, the scholar Sebastian Brant said, as late as the end of the 15th Century, "Illustrations are essential for learning." The more popular a work was intended to be, the more freely it had to be provided with pictures which would not be merely decoration but would teach. Coloring the illustrations continued to be done, as in the ancient codices. The woodcuts served to print the outlines which were then filled in with colors by the illuminators of miniaturists--whether they were good or poor. Cross-hatching (or shading) was not used, but the contrasting areas were to be differentiated by color; cloth, earth, drops of blood, and the like, were inserted into the cut-out parts of the block.

However, change did gradually occur and the combination of the newly developing book printing art with woodcuts opened completely new and heretofore unthought of kinds of usefulness for the woodcut. From the limited sphere of holy pictures, calendars, and playing card production, the woodcut was drawn into a circle of much broader usefulness (2).

While many of the early books were produced by one person who served as printer, binder and wood block cutter, these functions gradually separated. The painter supplied the printer with the drawings, some of which were developed as illustrations for a particular book and some as reproductions of the work of important artists. The woodcut specialist transferred these drawings into the wood. In the block books the art work served as interpretive illustrations of the text, but now it began to improve border embellishments and stamps, initials and printers' marks, etc., and they began to receive the same kind of care as was given to illustrations. In the course of just a few decades this changed woodcuts from their crudest beginnings to a significant art form.

The development of this art form was especially effective in Germany. While Italy in very early times produced classic illustrated works such as Turrecremata's Meditationes (Rome, 1467) and Valturius, De arte militari (Verona, 1472), it did not have a continuous development of the art. In Italy practically everything that was done in the way of book illustration was limited to the period from 1465 to 1510; in Germany, starting with the year 1460, the art of book illustration had uninterrupted development.

The first illustrated German books were not, as one might suppose, produced in Mainz in the office of the inventor of printing. The first who fitted his product with imaginative reproductions was the document printer, Albrecht Pfister of Bamberg. We know of four illustrated books that he produced, of which two appeared in second editions. The Armenbibel appeared around 1460. The first that appeared with his name printed in it was Buch der vier Historien von Joseph, Daniel, Esther und Judith, which was printed in 1462. The third, which did not bear his name, was dated 1461; this was Boner's Edelstein. The fourth, undated, was the Rechtsstreit des Menschen mit dem Tode. The illustrations in all four of these books are very primitive. The contour lines of the individual figures are in thick angular strokes and there is no shading. It is very difficult to study Pfister's works in the original since they are scarce and are scattered at widely separate places. There are two known copies of his Buch der vier Historien, three of von Boner's Edelstein, three of the Armenbibel, and only two of the Rechtsstreit des Menschen mid dem Tode.

The illustrations published in 1470 do not appear to be better artistically than the older Pfister illustrations.

The first city that became distinguished through its magnificent illustration work was Augsburg and that occurred in the 1470's. The first illustrated German bible, which was printed in Augsburg in about 1470, had 55 woodcuts, each filling a column, and all in color. The use of the selfsame pieces of wood for similar subjects continued on an extensive scale. An old man wearing a turban and long robe, sitting in a room at a table, with his hand on an opened book, had to serve for the whole series of prophets. A young figure with long blonde hair and wearing a crown represents varied kings. A third man serves as an apostle or evangelist type. The woodcuts appear close to the playing card technique, with the figures presented only in outline and with the intention that everything further would be done by hand.

By 1470 the work done in neighbouring Ulm was better. To be sure, the earlier works, which were published by the first printer in Ulm, Ludwig Hohenwang, do not present the characteristics of the Ulm school. It was he who, around 1470, printed the first edition of Flavius Vegetius Renatus' Vier Büchern der Ritterschaft. The 64 woodcuts contained therein were produced by various establishments and do not represent original compositions produced in Ulm; rather, they are copies of old manuscripts. The first illustrations produced in the city itself were provided by the second printer in Ulm, Johannes Zainer, who also began his work there in 1470. These illustrations are to be found in Boccaccio's Buch von berühmten Frauen, which Zainer published in 1473, and they cover the famous women of world history from Eve up to the procession for the female pope, Joan. The designs are adroit, the contours are finely rounded, and in many cases one finds shading within the figures even at this early date. The presentation of faces developed to the point that one can see a definitely human impression on them. The background is not commonly provided. However, where it appears it is flawless.

Cologne was the third city which played a great role in even the earliest days of illustrated book printing. It cannot be determined certainly when the first illustrated book appeared there. However, one of the earliest has been established as the world history which was published under the title Fasciculus temporum, with which the Cologne playing card producer, Werner Rolevink, endowed us.

The woodcuts themselves are among the crudest that have been preserved and are especially naive in the way in which the most non-pertinent illustrations were presented to the reader. One little picture which is scarcely a centimeter high, and which has a pair of towers, is presented on various pages as representing different cities ranging from Rome and Athens to Jerusalem. The illustrated works which were produced in Cologne by the printer Heinrich Quentel were of much greater importance. He exerted a most beneficent influence on intellectual work of the region for half a century. He produced the Cologne Bible around 1480. This is one of the most magnificent works of the 15th Century and its value can best be seen by comparing it with the Augsburg Bible. The woodcuts of the latter were a few centimeters high, quite in the playing card tradition, and were limited to reproduction of outlines. The individual wood blocks were repeated in a most tedious manner and there was no attempt to make illustrations which were closely related to the subject matter. Here in the Cologne Bible, for the first time, the Bible was illustrated with woodcuts including multiple figures, none of which were repeated, and we encounter a completely new philosophy of illustration. Concerning the masters whose works served as the original for the plate maker, it is indicated that they are "Just as they have been painted in the churches and cloisters from earlier periods." While various attributions have been given to the sources of these illustrations, no one has been able to come to any really firm conclusions about them.

Tremendous development in the work of illustration occurred from 1480 on. Augsburg, which in the 70's excelled the other cities in productiveness, had Anton Sorg, who in Ulrich von Reichenthal's Beschreibung des Concils von Kostnitz, which appeared in 1483, provided a product that was outstanding from the points of view of both history and art. He was joined by Hans Schonsperger and Erhard Ratdolt, who had lived in Venice from 1475 to 1485 and were particularly noteworthy because they brought Italian initial ornamentation to Germany. He also brought the best workmen available for completion of the forms and illustrations, especially for the artistic decorations of missals and breviaries which he produced for the Augsburg diocese and other places.

As in Augsburg, illustrated books improved greatly in the 1480's. Two highly skilled printers, Ludwig Hohenwang and Johannes Zainer, came to Ulm around 1482 and with the help of Leonhard Holl did the Kosmographie des Ptolemäus, the first book printed with large maps cut in wood. Of even greater importance to Ulm's progress was its second printer, Conrad Dinkmuth who, in 1486, published Thomas Lirer's Schwabische Chronik. The unknown master whose pictures appear therein appears to be the first to endow landscape with artistic significance.

Comparable to the Lirer Chronik, and closely related to it, is a magnificent work which appeared in the same year (1486) in Mainz, which was printed and illustrated by the painter Erhard Reuwich, who came from Utrecht. This was the Breidenbach's Reise nach dem heiligen Grabe. The woodcuts of this book quickly caught the attention of art critics, one of whom declared it, "Worthy of Canaletto's brush." They were outstanding illustrations to which Germany could point with pride. The views of cities and the pictures of the folk life of the Orient indicate authenticity and trueness to nature which was attained by very few travel writers of later times.

A few years later the eyes of contemporaries turned from Augsburg, Ulm, Cologne and Mainz towards Nuremburg, where Anton Koburger not only showed his own great skill but also brought the Nuremburg painters Michel Wohlgemuth and Wilhelm Pleydenwurf into his printing establishment. The first work produced by Koburger which had illustrations by Wohlgemuth was the Schatzbehalter oder Schrein der wahren Reichthümer des Heils und ewiger Seligkeit, which was printed in 1491 and had large woodcuts of biblical occurrences. The illustrations of this book must have received great acclaim. Just two years later, Koburger was able to issue an even more broadly and magnificently illustrated book, the Hartman Schedel Weltchronik, in a Latin edition in 1493 and in German in 1494, which contained a profusion and range of woodcuts such as were presented by no book long before or after. It is divided into six periods and in each the major historical occurrences are illustrated with large compositions that are full of figures. In addition to these large pictures the book has countless smaller ones. Under each epoch it illustrates the cities founded during the period or achieving a special flowering. The part concerned with the 15th Century included portraits of all of the people dealt with. The quality of the woodcuts is variable. Koburger had his own wood cutting establishment for execution of the woodcuts and it was under the supervision of a very skilled master who did the finishing work on each form.

At the same time Lübeck achieved fame with its Bible in 1494. Here, in the work of a great North German artist, is one of the most significant publications of book illustration of the entire period. G. Hirth devoted a separate publication to honor it.

While the great printed works were coming from Anton Koburger's press in Nuremburg, there was simultaneously a significant development in Basel. It is natural that illustrations can be greatly improved when they are supported by a good author. The Basel book printer found one such in Sebastian Brant who, from the beginning of the 90's until 1498, was producing works of literary merit, which had illustrations that made a major contribution to his works. What the Bible did for Cologne, what the Konzilienbuch did for Augsburg, what Lirer's Chronik did for Ulm, what Breidenbach's Reise did for Mainz, and what Schedel's Weltchronik did for Nuremberg, is what Sebastian Brant's Narrenschiff did for Basel when it was published in 1494 by his friend Johannes Bergmann von Olpe. Brant achieved an entirely new relationship of the story to the pictures of this masterpiece because he not only gave the engraver a description of the individual pictures but also gave him sketches showing how the individual pictures were to look. The craftsmanship of the woodcuts is great. The feeling is free and natural, perspective is not neglected, and the appearance of the faces is strikingly true to life. The cuts appear to be made by three or four artisans of unequal skill and vary in the effectiveness with which they transmit the thoughts of the artist. No other book in German during that period had such a tremendous success as Brant's Narrenschiff. Almost immediately, it was reprinted with the same woodcuts but in smaller size. The art would have certainly developed much more widely in Basel if Sebastian Brant had stayed in the city longer. What Basel lost in 1498, the neighboring city of Strassburg gained when he moved there.

Even though many illustrated works were published in this latter city as far back as the

80's, they were of low artistic quality. In most cases the illustrations were raw copies of pictures that appeared in other books, and they were rarely completely original drawings. The first to give Strassburg's craftsmanship in illustration matters an artistic stamp was Johann Grüninger, who, at the end of the 1490's, used woodcuts in all of his publications freely and well. Two of the earliest illustrated Grüninger works, a Terenz of 1496 and a Horaz of 1498, failed to indicate the impetus which illustration work achieved for a short period through his work. The illustrations contained in these were sub-standard and were selected arbitrarily. This was completely changed when Sebastian Brant returned from Basel to his home town in 1498. Almost immediately these two talented men entered into unflagging cooperative work and this resulted in the publication in 1502 of the masterpiece of the Grüninger establishment, the edition of Virgil supplied by Brant which contained not less than 214 large woodcuts. Brant was, also in this case, active in the production of the illustrations and apparently not only gave the engraver written instructions about what should be contained in the engraving, but a sketch of the way he wanted each engraving to appear. The fact that the whole of the Virgil was poorly translated did not prohibit the supervision of its illustration by a scholar. Whoever has read Homer and the Romans but has not seen a Greek work of art cannot have any understanding of the majesty and grace of the classic Gods. All that Brant is believed to have understood is that the Gods were not clothed. A naked man who wears a crown on his head and has a scepter in his hand is, if he is sitting on a stool in the clouds, Jupiter. He is Neptune when he stands half in the water. The Goddesses have no article of clothing other than the type of grotesque coiffures which the elegant ladies of Strassburg considered fashionable at that time. This is, however, all that shows in the classic philology. Aside from this, there is no break with the time-honored ancient origins. Unfortunately, we have no knowledge about the engraver, who was particularly outstanding in the presentation of landscape.

If one compares this Virgil with one of the old Pfister printings, he will see the tremendous development which the art of illustration achieved within forty years. When Pfister produced his first illustrated books around 1460 he had the greatest difficulties to overcome. The cutting of figures into woodcuts was limited to holy pictures and playing cards. The art of painting developed greatly in the second half of the 15th Century, as was shown in the works of Martin Schongauer, Bartholomaus Zeitblom and Michel Wohlgemuth. The woodcut of their time, as soon as it was used for widespread production of such paintings, developed its technique with unbelievable speed. Thus, in the beginning of the 16th Century there was only one more step to be taken to bring illustration to its loftiest heights.

Since the 13th Century, art and artisanship had traveled different paths. Also, the true artist only rarely applied his skills to the graphic arts. The first of the important artists who did not disdain drawing for woodcuts was Erhard Reuwich, who was soon joined by Michel Wohlgemuth. But in general, the better artists left the drawings for woodcuts to lower grade technicians who could do quite intelligent work but normally simply made imperfect copies of the pictures or copperplates of greater masters. It was not until the turn of the 16th Century that there came a great change. The work of illustration freed itself from crude manual craftsmanship and became a true art which not only was raised to a height that had not been anticipated before but attained a level that was never achieved again. It was Albrecht Dürer whose dedicated perception and example, even though his work in this field was limited, had a widespread effect (3). Under the sunshine of Dürer's work there was put in motion, gradually, a whole series of planets of famous artists.

Augsburg, where so much splendid work appeared in the 15th Century, continued to be one of the main centers of book illustration in the 16th Century and this is attributable chiefly to the artistic interests of Kaiser Maximilian. Maximilian, like every proper renaissance man, was of the opinion that of all earthly possessions fame was the greatest. Throughout his whole life, he strove to insure his fame in the most permanent way, and appears to have found the means to achieve this purpose through his unwavering literary drive and his great love of art which, naturally, resulted in epic-making masterpieces. The three illustrated books which the Kaiser sponsored in addition to Burgkmair's Heiligen des Hauses Habsburg, and the Triumphzug, were the Theuerdank, the Weiskunig and the Freydal.

Augsburg was his favorite city and his friend, Dr. Konrad Peutinger, who could understandingly undertake the entire practical supervision of these undertakings, worked there. There also lived his banker, Hans Baumgartner, who was always prepared to help if his Kaiser overestimated the money available for the task. Augsburg thus achieved first rank for outstandingly magnificent work. The printer whom the Kaiser picked was Hans Schönsperger the Elder, who was installed as the chief book printer as early as 1508. As illustrators he selected Hans Burgkmair, one of Augsburg's outstanding painters, and Hans Schäufelein, who was trained in Dürer's workshop. In addition, with Jost Dienecker, who was brought in from Antwerp especially for this purpose, they set up a woodcutting school, under the guidance of Dienecker, in order to be able to transform the drawings of these two masters into woodblocks. Unfortunately, of the three great artistic works, only the Theuerdank, whose illustrator was Hans Schäufelein, was completed during the lifetime of the Kaiser. Schäufelein's illustrations rendered the restless and dangerous life of the heroes in such a lifelike manner that the scholars of that time found the book really amazing and it went through many editions.

As against this good luck of the Theuerdank, the Weisskunig seems to have achieved oblivion; it was as though it had been pursued by some fiendish fate from the very beginning. After the death of the Kaiser in 1519 its production stopped and it was first published in Vienna in 1775 by Joseph Kurzbockens. Through the efforts of this diligent publisher, the pictures were fitted into the text to the extent that they were pertinent. The notes in the Kaiser's own handwriting were inserted when they were legible, but few of them were, and those that could not be deciphered were added as an appendix to the work. In retrospect, the power of attraction which the individual illustrations exert upon us is as great as in the case of the Theuerdank. The one upon which Maximilian placed the greatest value, the presentation of his battles, leaves us cold. The artistic presentation of the Weisskunig is not as homogeneous as that of the Theuerdank. Of the 237 woodcuts in the former, about 160 were done by Burgkmair, 70 by Schäufelein, and the rest by Springinklee and minor artists.

The third majestic production, the Freydal, can be attributed to Augsburg only on the basis that the preparation of the illustrations was begun there. The Kaiser had included in Freydal the races, jousts, battles and masquerades which he had held at various times and in various places. To this he added his love poems to Marie of Burgundy; and he wanted the whole to be presented artistically just as he had gathered together the tale of his trip to Burgundy and in the telling converted it into a poetic picture in the Theuerdank. The Freydal, like the Weisskunig, was only very partially completed during the lifetime of the Kaiser, and it lay forgotten. It was first made available, two years later, in an attractive book published by Quirin von Leitner. Chief credit for the work should go to Martin Trummer, who did the costumes. Artistically, the pictures are of highly variable quality. To us, the most interesting part of the work was the lifelike and sumptuous dress used lavishly to make a gorgeous work of art.

Art life in Augsburg in this period was very active. The magnificent illustrated books sponsored by Maximilian stood by themselves at the beginning of the 16th Century. Increasingly, Hans Burgkmair and Hans Schäufelein were responsible, in the most active way, for all of the important works turned out in the Augsburg shop. Among the works that can be identified as joint efforts of these two artists are the collected poetic works, Leidens Christi, composed by Wolfgang Mann who was chaplain of Kaiser Maximilian. This was published in a splendid edition by Hans Schönsperger the Younger, in 1515. Its magnificent types, most attractive marginal illustrations, and superb pictures make it one of the most beautiful typographic products of the 16th Century.

Book illustration in Nuremberg did not achieve as high a quality as it did in Augsburg, even though a large number of excellently produced books were done there. And to be sure, the educational prayerbooks, Hortulus Animae, printed in Nuremberg as well as in Strassburg and in other places, displayed a large number of illustrations and artistic materials produced in Nuremberg. The Hortuli are small octavo books and the pages are normally bordered with four attractive border illustrations. The initials are ornamented with foliage and masks and there are many woodcuts of God, the Christ family, the Apostles and the Evangelists; they also presented the male and female saints as well as the various sacraments. The production of such illustrated Hortuli became the speciality by 1516 of the Nuremberg printer, Johann Koburger; some of them were produced in the Nuremberg office and some by Johann Clein in Lyon. Dürer's students, Hans Springinklee and Erhardt Schön, soon distinguished themselves as illustrators of these works.

In addition to Augsburg and Nuremberg, Basel continued to be an important printing center in the 16th Century. The first important artist who supplied the printers there with illustrations was Urs Graf who was born in Solothurn between 1485 and 1490 and who, in his later years at least, was overshadowed by the brothers Holbein.

Hans Holbein, especially after 1522, gave the German bibles which Adam Petri and Thomas Wolft produced, their incomparable artistic distinction. Ambrosius Holbein, who died in 1519, is to be thanked for three little books, the Nollhard, a comedy by Pamphilus Gengenbach, Utopia by Thomas More, and the Gauchmatt by Thomas Murner. In elegance of type and careful execution these Basel products excelled anything produced elsewhere at the time.

Furthermore, the books done in Strassburg at this time are of importance in a different way. In the 15th Century, Sebastian Brant was in the forefront because of his large illustrated publications. At this period a priest at Munster, Geiler von Kaisersperg, was able to get the cooperation of outstanding book printers and illustrators. The first of these artists, Hans Wächtlin, is known through only two books: one, produced by the printer, Johann Knoblouch in 1508, was the Leben Christi; the other, the Feldbuch der Wundarznei, was by Hans Gersdorfs and was printed by Johann Schott in 1517. The former is more like an illustrated book of the 15th Century, while in the anatomical pages of the Feldbuch der Wundarznei there are some presentations which can be recognized as belonging to a later period.

Just as in the case of Urs Graf and both of the Holbeins, Wächtlin must, in his later years, have changed over to the younger circle of artists which had Hans Baldung Grien as its center. The Buch Granatapfel, by Geiler von Kaisersperg, appeared in 1510; a Hortulus animae was published by Martin Flach in 1512; and Grüninger's Auslegung der zehn Gebot, which appeared in 1516, was done in close cooperation by these genial master artists. Only the content of these books is religious, the pictures are worldly. With Baldung's voluptuously sensual women as ornamentation, the Hortulus no longer provides the general spiritually esthetic impression which was expected of it in the 15th Century. Similarly, the illustrations for the Zehn Geboten contributed more to enjoyment of the beauty of the human body than to religious experience.

To these old printing centers of Augsburg, Nuremberg, Basel and Strassburg, another was added in the 16th Century that had not been operative before. Wittemberg became a printing center and it owed its importance to Martin Luther and Lucas Cranach. As early as 1509, Cranach submitted the so-called Wittemberger Heiligthumsbuch to be printed by Johann Grunenberg. This was a book of 44 pages, with 119 woodcuts which presented the holy places, churches and holy relics that were preserved in Wittemberg. In 1521, he illustrated the Passional Christi und Antichristi, in which Luther counterposed the humility of Christ and the arrogance of the powerful on earth. After 1522, when Luther published his translation of the Bible, the Wittemberg artists gathered in large numbers in Cranach's plant and found plenty to do there in providing the necessary illustrations for the various editions of the New and Old Testaments.

To a certain extent, the active rival of Wittemberg in printing was Cologne. The Catholic Church set up the translation of Hieronymus Emser, with outstanding illustrations by Anton von Worms, and had it printed in Cologne. To counter Lucas Cranach's Wittemberg Heiligthumsbuch, Markgraf Albrecht von Brandenburg had the Hallische Heiligthumsbuchlein prepared by his chief artist, Mathias Grünewald. It presents, in 234 woodcuts, the relics to be found in the church at Halle.

German book illustration of the Gothic and the Early Renaissance eras is of great interest because of the artists whom we meet in this period, but over and above that it is of even greater interest in tracing the history of German woodcuts. While in considering broadsides one has had the problem of determining the locale and their chronology, when woodcuts are found in books which give a determined place and time, then one can generally assume that they originated in the same place in which the book was printed and were completed at approximately the same time as the book. One has only to establish whether the work was done for the book in hand or whether it had previously been issued in some other source (4).

Mostly one had to watch, therefore, the truly popular books of the 15th and 16th Century which appeared in the most varied editions and in various places. As soon as an illustration cycle was established for such a mass-produced book, it was maintained in all of the following stereotyped reprintings. When Johann Knoblouch printed the eighth edition of Guido de Columna's Histori von der Zerstörung der Stadt Troia in Strassburg in 1510, he used in it the same woodcuts which Zainer prepared for the first edition, which was produced in Augsburg in about 1470.

In the twelfth edition of Eusebius's Geschichte des grossen Alexander, translated by Johann

Hartlieb, which Mathias Hupfuff brought out in Strassburg in 1514, one finds the identical illustrations which Johann Bämler had prepared for his 1473 Augsburg edition. The same sort of thing is true of the various editions of the Hortus sanitatis, the Meisters Elucidarius, the Vierundzwanzig Alten, the Rolevink Fasciculus temporum, the Spiegels der menschlichen Behaltniss, the Belial and many other popular books of the 15th and 16th Centuries. Only rarely were the old woodblocks re-worked, as for example, Heinrich Steiner in Augsburg did in 1541 when he issued the fifth edition of Boccaccio's Compendium de praeclaris mulieribus, or as he did in 1536 in a revised edition of Ulrich von Reichenthal's Beschreibung des Concils von Kostnitz. Practically never were new compositions done completely for later editions.

The fact that it is often not easy to determine positively the relationship between illustrations of earlier and later editions is exemplified by the Bible. The Bible was printed in German seventeen times before Luther (14 times in High German and three times in Low German). Of these seventeen editions, only the first two lack woodcuts, the fifteen others are richly illustrated with them. The first illustrated German Bible appeared around 1470 in Augsburg (by Pflanzmann); the second around 1472 by Frisner and Sensenschmid in Nuremberg; the third by Günther Zainer in Augsburg in 1473 to 1475; the fourth in the same place in 1477; the fifth by Anton Sorg in Augsburg in 1477; the sixth in the same place in 1480; the seventh by Heinrich Quentel in Cologne around 1480; the eighth by Anton Koburger in Nuremberg in 1483; the ninth in Strassburg in 1485; the tenth by Schoensperger in Augsburg in 1487; the eleventh in the same place in 1490; the twelfth by Arndes in Lübeck in 1494; the thirteenth by Johannes Othmar in Augsburg in 1507; the fourteenth by Sylvan Othmar in 1518; the fifteenth by Trutebul in Halberstadt in 1520. As with all frequently printed books, the woodcuts from one edition of the Bible were transferred to the other editions. This was true of the illustrations in diverse groups. Leading the first group is the Pflanzmann Bible of 1470, whose woodcuts were used by Sorg in his edition of 1477. The first printing of the second group was in the Sensenschmidt Bible of 1472, whose illustrations are to be found copied in Zainer's editions of 1473 and 1477 as well as in Sorg's edition of 1480. The third group, which had the broadest circulation, originated in the Cologne Bible of 1480. Its woodcuts were used in the same size by Koburger in Nuremberg in 1483 and by Trutebul in Halberstadt in 1520, in reduced size in the Strassburg Bible of 1485, and in both of Schoensperger's editions of 1487 and 1490, as well as both the Othmar editions of 1507 and 1518. A fourth group is in the Lübeck Bible whose woodcuts have not been found duplicated.

The woodcuts of the first group are crude, with the plates produced completely in the playing card style. In the second grouping the woodcut initials are fitted carefully into their spaces. The third series introduces, for the first time, woodcut compositions which are larger and have more figures. The woodcuts of the Lübeck Bible, finally, are still more finished and interesting, particularly because they add a droll and comic concept.

In the years 1522-1524, the Bible translation by Luther not only provided the story in German but also made the illustrations fit it. The illustrations in its various parts fail to show any relationship with those of the pre-Lutheran Bibles and it appears clear that Luther intended it to be that way. While they are only partially of artistic value, yet they are of the greatest importance on another basis. Just as before Luther the woodcuts of the Cologne Bible could be found repeated, so with the Luther Bible, practically every reprint copied the illustrations. This was true especially of the New Testament. Not only Hans Schäufelein, for Schoensperger in Augsburg, but also Hans Burgkmair, for Othmar, and Hans Holbein who illustrated the New Testament for Petri and Wolft in Basel, stayed very close to the Wittemberg originals. The problem of the illustration of the Old Testament, which Luther did illustrate richly, was more difficult. It was necessary to go back to the 15th Century illustrations. In Augsburg the artist tended to work in very closely with the Wittemberg pictures. In Basel, Thomas Wolff began a new edition with smaller copies of the Wittemberg pages, while Petri, for his edition, used the Cologne illustration cycle with revision. In Nuremberg, Fr. Peypus made a collection of woodcuts which, while unchanged, served a completely different purpose than that of the Lyon Vulgate illustrations. In Strassburg, Johannes Knoblouch began a reworking of the Cologne woodcuts but mostly copied the Wittemberg pictures. In the Zurich Bibles, we find collections of pages which come partly from the Cologne and partly from the Wittemberg cycle. The extent of error which is possible if one is not careful is shown, for example, in the tenth chapter of Woltmann's Holbein. Woltmann presents these as Holbein's illustrations and refers to those for the Petri editions of the Old and New Testaments as original works of the Master when they were, in fact, merely revisions of the pages of the Cologne and Wittemburg editions (5).

The woodcuts of such widely printed books must, therefore, always be approached with the greatest caution since they commonly originated in a much earlier period and in an entirely different place from those in which they are found.

Furthermore, one must be particularly careful in examining the books of small print shops. The small print shops were very rarely able to provide new illustrations for their publications and they almost always borrowed the blocks from the larger print shops. Even the larger printers often went to others for illustrations. Grüninger, in Strassburg, in the last twenty years of his book production, almost invariably used woodcuts which he had used in the 15th and early 16th Centuries for his major publications. Similarly, Heinrich Steiner, in Augsburg, and Burgkmair's and Schäufelein's Illustrationen zum Petrarka and Theuerdank were used in the 17th Century in the various print shops in Frankfurt. Determining whether the cuts are newly prepared or whether the material is reused in a different context requires careful visual examination. Only the works which have newly prepared woodcuts are important for our study.

Finally, there is a third point that is especially important currently for the study of illustrated works of art of the Gothic and Early Renaissance period. Our time, like the 16th Century, is a period of production of art books. All inhabited and uninhabited countries of the world have been subjected to art books. Shakespeare, Schiller, and Goethe are issued as illustrated by "the best German artists." Countless periodicals which are full of illustrations find acceptance and acclaim.

Anyone who has considered a book of the Gothic or Early Renaissance periods and then takes a currently illustrated book in hand will feel the tremendous difference between them. It is not only the illustrations that make this difference, because we have known for a long time that we now have no Dürer, Holbein or Cranach illustrating our books; it is the entire method and way in which the print and illustration (the whole assembly of the book as such) is presented. I know nothing more pertinent to say here than what Dr. Georg Hirth wrote when I showed him the plan of my book:

...But it is not simply interest in art history and antiquarianism that develops my sympathy for your undertaking. For years I have been miserable in my attempts to reform book printing. And I tell myself that the small progress I have made as a practitioner cannot make the connoisseur happy. And it is pretty much the same with the majority of my colleagues in the "art." The basis of this is not so much in the lack of good intentions but in the whole development of the book trade, which does not permit one to have an artist at the head of a publishing house. The underlying degeneration, and the complete separation from art, which printing of books has undergone in the course of the last century, are still little realized. As in the case of all many-faceted arts, the book as a work of art permits the recognition of a skilled, artistic craft. This is, in fact, the essence of the charm that we feel in incunabula that came from hundreds of different printing plants. The works that were produced bore character.

And this is no different with the relatively undistinguished woodcuts of that golden age which reproduced the hand of the artist stroke for stroke, after which the work of illumination and coloring was performed. Paper and binding consummated the art masterpieces of these old books, which are worthy of respect. If I may say so, the decline started in the 16th Century and now one no longer says he prints it as if it were written, but he writes as if it were printed. This means that one prints and the other writes, without art and without character. The woodcut has been a virtuoso of the black art since it allows for the fantasy of the viewer and for the art of the illuminator. So I consider your publication, which has long been needed, as a contribution. It stands, quite apart from its scholarly importance, as a highly welcome member in the series of those publications which I have started with my friend Butsch and which, properly understood, will in time make for appreciation of the influence of typographic practice.

Notes

1) Huttler, M. Das Buch als Gegenstand des Kunstgewerbes. Vortrag gehalten im Kunstgewerbevereinslocale zu München am 6. December 1881; Falcke, J. von. Einleitung zum Stuttgarter Weihnachtskatalog von 1882; Lippmann, "Aufsatz über die Anfange des Formschnittes," im Repertorium fur Kunstwissenschaft; Bucher, Geschichte der technischen Künste, Stuttgart, 1874/76 (see the Chapter on wood block carving.)

2) Woltmann, Holbein und seiner Zeit, Chapter 10.

3) Springer, Der altdeutsche Holzschnitt und Kupferstich, Bilder aus der neuen Kunstgeschichte, Bonn, 1867, No. 6.

4) Essenwein's introduction to his collection, Holzschnitte des 14. und 15. Jahrhunderts im Germanischen Museum.

5) Voegelin, Salomon, "Ergänzungen und Nachweisungen zum Holzschnittwerk Hans Holbein's," Repertorium fur Kunstwissenschaft II, p. 102 and 312, V, p. 179. Muther, Richard. Die ältesten deutschen Bilderbibeln, bibliograpisch und kunstgeschichtlich beschrieben. München, Literarisches Institut von Dr. Max Huttler, 1883.

[1-2]

Chapter I

THE BEGINNINGS: PRE-1470 (1)

The early printers who liked illustrations were mostly those who had been document printers, who were accustomed to the finishing of xylographic works and therefore were prepared in the skills necessary to utilize text letters that had been cut into wood.

Albert Pfister of Bamberg filled these requirements. Whether he originated the combination of cast letters and wood blocks in book printing, or whether he was an assistant to Gutenberg who moved to Bamberg in 1455, when the firm of Fust and Gutenberg dissolved, is not certain. Very little is known of his origins. Jaeck found an Ulrich Pfister and a Seitz Pfister, whose names appeared in the Bamberg Town records in the first half of the 15th Century, and on that basis decided that Albrecht came from a Bamberg family. Pangkofer and Schuegraf, in their history of the book industry in Regensburg (2), found many similar names for printers in the Regensburg City Directories. They considered these as descendants of Albrecht and attempted to prove that he was a native of Regensburg. However, the appearance of the names in the town book do not permit a conclusion as to his origin. The name Pfister was at that time apparently as common as the name Becker, which has the same general meaning, is now.

Pfister was not given any special recognition by his contemporary typesetters. Only Paul von Prag had, in a confused way, reported on the numerous and extraordinarily fine operations he noted at Pfister's plant.

Even though the origin of Pfister remained uncertain, his original work as a document printer has been established positively. There are a number of remaining fragments of works done by Pfister and the document printer is revealed in his typographic works as well. Practically all these are popular books in the local language and nearly all of them are illustrated with a multiplicity of woodcuts.

We know four illustrated books that he produced, of which two were produced in several editions; two are dated, one in 1461, the other in 1462. The latter includes his name, and it is an excerpt of the biblical story [1] Buch der vier Historien von Joseph, Daniel, Esther and Judith (3). It is a small folio and has 61 woodcuts, of which a few are duplicated. Fourteen deal with the story of Joseph, eighteen with the story of Daniel, fourteen with that of Judith, and fifteen with Esther. There are two known copies of this work, one in Paris and the other in Althorp at Lord Spencer's.

The other [2] illustrated book by Pfister, which does not carry his name, is dated 1461. It is Boner's Edelstein (4), which has 101 woodcuts.

Pfister did two editions of this work, of which only one is dated. They differ in still another respect. The woodcuts which relate to fables do not fill the width of the page, and on the left side of each fable woodcut there is a picture of a man in full figure of the same height as the fable woodcut, which is printed from a separate block of wood. The undated edition has three different such lead pieces which are interchanged and repeated throughout the book. The man either has a hood on his head and a writing tablet in his hand, on which three columns of writing are indicated, or he holds a blank sheet of paper, or he has a hat on his head and a book in his hand. It is not known whether this figure was supposed to represent the different authors or was just intended to fill up the space. In the dated example the figure is none of these and remains the same throughout the book. One can assume from this that Pfister found the dated edition's limited woodblocks too monotonous and, therefore, in the undated second edition, permitted three new figures to be made in order to get more variation. A second theory is that the three pieces used to fill out the left margin were not related to the fable woodcuts themselves, and that they were therefore not taken care of so well, so that when the second edition was needed they had been lost. Because of this, he used a single figure in the second edition. According to the former theory, the first edition was undated. According to the latter theory, the dated edition came first. The first was illustrated by Schoenemann and the second by Sotzmann. The Sotzmann copy is probably the first edition because in the undated edition the woodcuts are still fresh and sharp, while in the dated edition they have been worn down. Accordingly, the Berlin copy has the claim to being the first edition while both dated samples (the one in the library of the Duchy of Wolfenbüttel, the other in the National Library in Paris) get second place.

It is not possible to date the other two books firmly. In any event, they appeared before 1462 and around 1460.

One of these, the [3] Armenbibel (5), like Boner's fables appeared in two editions, one Latin and one German. The only known copy of the Latin edition is in the possession of Lord Spencer and, of the two examples of the German edition, one is in Wolfenbüttel and the other is in Paris. The woodcuts are the same in both, with only the first and sixth illustrations showing slight variations in the individual copies.

The other undated book is [4] Pfister's Rechtsstreit des Menschen mit dem Tode (6), which was also titled Der Ackermann aus Böheim (Gespräch zwischen einem Wittwer und dem Tode). Its 24 sheets in small folio contain five woodcuts which fill the full length of the page. Two complete examples of this book are known. One is in Wolfenbüttel, the other in Paris. There are also two incomplete copies known: one of four sheets, sheets 21 to 25, [sic] in Bamberg, and one, consisting of the final sheet, which is part of Lord Spencer's collection. Pfister's woodcuts totaled 201, of which 61 appeared in the Buch der vier Historien, 101 in Boner's Fabeln, 34 in the Armenbibel and five are in the Rechsstreit ... mit dem Tode. They are all very primitive. Only the outlines of the individual figures are given in angular strokes and there is no shading within these outlines. The drawings stand at the low point in artistic value to which graphic art had sunk since the separation of the art from the craft. On the question of whether Pfister remained in Bamberg until his death, there is no evidence.

In addition to these four products which are unquestionably attributable to Pfister there is a fifth which forms a bench mark in printing and which appears to have been part of his work [5, Pl. 1] because the type which had been used by him is used here in noticeably worn form. This fifth book is the one that Stoeger publicized, and it is preserved in the Munich Government

Library. It is the Leiden Christi (7), which included 19 woodcuts. The woodcutting technique in this book is one which was frequently used in earlier times. The outlines of the figures were not left above the level of the block, with the superfluous material cut out, but as with copper plates, the outlines were indented. These then came out white, and the background and the filling in of the figures came out black. The background, however, was not left entirely black but was ornamented with all sorts of white flowers and arabesques.

[6, Pl. 2] The following book, which originated much later, at the earliest at the end of the 1460's, still belongs in this series because it was produced by people working with Albrecht Pfister's son, Sebastian. It is the first edition of Otto von Passau's Vierundzwanzig Alten (8). In the foliage illustration on the first sheet one finds the letters S. P. which represent the signature of Sebastian Pfister, and in the initial letter "S" of the text the initials P. A., which is the reversed signature of Albrecht Pfister, are cut in. The title page illustration, which is 180 x 125 mm, shows Christ as the King of Heaven. The equally large woodcut on the verso of the page presents the youthful blond-haired John in a long pleated robe.

In the body of the book there are 24 illustrations of aged men, before whom a queen represents a particular topic, all of which had to be represented by two 140 x 125 mm woodblocks.

Notes

1) Sprenger, Aelteste Buchdruckergeschichte von Bamberg. Nuremberg, 1800; Jaeck, Denkschrift für das Jubelfest der Buchdruckerkunst zu Bamberg. Erlangen, 1840; see v. d. Linde, Gutenberg. Stuttgart, 1878, p. 68; "Sotzmann: Briefmaler und Buchdrucker," in Raumer, Historischem Taschenbuch; "Ueber die ersten Boner'schen Fabeln Sotzmann" in Serapeum, VI, p. 321 ff., 1845; Against this view, see: Schoenemann, Hundert Merkwürdigkeiten der herzogl, Bibliothek zu Wolfenbüttel, Hannover, 1849, p. 66 ff.; Stoeger, Zwei der ältesten deutschen Druckdenkmale, München, 1833.

2) 1840, 8°.

3) Steiner, in Meusel Historisch-literarischem Magazin No. 5; Camus, Notice d'un livre imprimé à Bamberg en 1462, lue à l'institut national. Paris, An. VII; Panzer, Supplemente, p. 30; Dibdin, Bibliotheka Spenceriana, Tom. II, p. 94.

4) Lessing, Sämmtliche Werke, Bd. 18, p. 186-216; Bd. 19, p. 87-129, 130-144; Eschenburg. Denkmäler altdeutscher Dichtkunst, VII, p. 189-208; Hain, No. 3578.

5) Lessing, Sämmtliche Werke, V. 18, p. 359; Camus, p. 9-14; Heinecken, Nachrichten von Kunstlern und Kunstsachen, II, p. 117-156; Sprenger, p. 32-33.

6) Steiner, in Meusel's Magazin V, p. 25-26; Hain, No. 73; Sprenger, Buchdruckergeschichte von Bamberg, p. 27, reprinted from v. der Hagen, 1824, in Frankfurt by Varrentrapp; The lower half of the last page is illustrated in Dibdin, Bibliotheka Spenceriana, Vol. I, p. 104.

7) Stoeger, Zwei der ältesten deutschen Druckdenkmale. München, 1833.

8) Fol. s. l. e. a. Hain, No. 12127.

Chapter II

AUGSBURG, 1470-1480 (1)

There is a gap in the history of book illustration from 1462 to 1470. Albrecht Pfister stands alone in this early period, and it was not until 1470 that continuous development started.

The first center during this period was Augsburg. Conditions were especially favorable there since, during the second half of the 15th Century, it had a larger number of card manufacturers and illuminators than any other city (2). However, not all of these found book illustration to be the easiest way to make a living.

It is not possible to point to any one as the earliest printer of illustrated books in Augsburg.

Through the efforts of the Augsburg notary, [7, Pl. 3] Jodoc Pflanzmann, we know that Albrecht Pfister appeared in the tax records from 1470 to 1497.

Around 1470 he produced The first illustrated German Bible (3), which had 55 illustrations, each taking up a column, and ordinarily 105 x 80 mm. The first capital letter in each book was a carefully done woodcut.

It is like the work done in the middle ages, in rose-red, with towns complete with towers, and there are rocks, trees, a harbor and, quite clearly, in a red jacket and blue trousers, the first person. In the picture of the creation of Eve the same town of the middle ages, with its walls and towers, is used. And it is reused repeatedly for other towns.

This device of using one woodcut to represent a generic type was widely used. An old man with a turban and long robe, who sits in a room at a table with his hand on an open book, must serve for the whole series of prophets. The differentiation is shown only by coloring. A young figure with long blond hair and a crown on his head represents the various kings. A man who sits on a yellow throne in a green mountainous landscape in front of a wall that is painted rose-red, holding a book in his right hand and pressing it to his chest, represents the apostle or evangelist type. The woodcuts are completely in the style of playing card production, with the figures shown only in outline with the intention that everything else is to be added by hand.

The second illustrated book is the first German edition of the frequently reprinted [8, Pl. 4 & 5] Histori von der Zerstörung der Stadt Troia (4), which Guido of Columna, in 1262-1289, took from the earlier VI libri de bello Troiano, which appeared under the title Historia belli Troiani, in the twelfth century and which was translated and disseminated in German very early.

Of the 93 woodcuts which illustrate the book (78 x 117), 16 deal with the Argonauts, six cover the first destruction of Troy, numbers 23-43 treat occurrences before the Trojan war, and the last 50 deal with the Trojan war.

Altogether, the woodcuts are quite crude. The same woodcuts were reused for similar conditions. For example, in the battles one always sees knights who are at each other. An armored figure lying in a coffin is used for the dead Patroclos as well as for Hector and Achilles. The woodblock which originally presents Jason and Medea's departure from Oetes is later re-used for the abduction of Helen. The fact that Menelaus, standing near the ship, quietly allows his wife to depart is not supposed to bother the beholder.

A third very early book which may be considered an Augsburg product is the first edition of the later frequently reprinted [9] Sieben weisen Meister (5) or the Histori aus den Geschichten der Römer.

The woodcuts are at about the same level as those of the Trojan War, the figures are produced in outline only and there is no cross-hatching. The cutting is stiff and awkward.

The first edition of the frequently reprinted [10] Lucidarius (6), was also printed in Augsburg. Of the five woodcuts, two deal with the relationship of the moon to the sun and the others are illustrative of the stars in the sky. It was printed s. l. e. a.

The following illustrated books are attributable to the first Augsburg book printer, Günther Zainer (1470-1478).

The earliest [11, Pl. 6-8] is the Speculum humanae salvationis, der Spiegel menschlicher Behaltniss (7), which was printed around 1470. This typographic work, which appeared in Augsburg in its first edition and later was to be reproduced in many other editions, is not to be confused with the well-known xylographic "Speculum" described by Heinecken in his Nachrichten II, p. 122 ff., or with the general idea which is described in Meermann's Origin. typogr. Vol. I, p. 98 ff. This book deals with the story of the redemption of mankind through Christ.

There is a woodcut on sheet 3b of [12] the Spiegel des Sünders (8), which was also published around 1470.

The 93 woodcuts that were printed about this time [13] by Zainer in the second edition of the Histori von der Zerstörung der Stadt Troia (9) are mostly identical with those used in the first edition. A few new, smaller, cuts (75 x 85) were added to the larger ones, which were 80 x 117 mm. In these smaller woodcuts the cutting is finer, cross-hatching is more frequent and the engraving is surer-handed.

The series of the dated works by Zainer begins with the [14, Pl. 9] Heiligenleben (10) which appeared in 1471. At the beginning of each of the 234 biographies, there is a small (generally 77 x 70) woodcut, each of which shows a scene dealing with the life of that saint. When the same saint had endured multiple martyrdoms, the identical woodblock was used for each. One illustration which is very well done shows the execution of two saints, one of whom has already been beheaded, while the other is shown praying to heaven while awaiting the death stroke from the executioner. Most of the woodcuts have double margins and are very crude in certain respects. The scene is always a landscape.

The 55 woodcuts that also appeared in the first edition of [15, Pl. 10 & 11] of Rodericus Zamorensis' Spiegel des menschlichen Lebens (11), which was also published in 1471, were much better. The first, which gives the family tree of the families of Austria, occupies a whole page; the others fill the width of a page and are a third of its length.

Zainer published the first German edition [16, Pl. 12 & 13] of Belial, processus Luciferi contra Jesum Christum Judice Salamone (12), in which the prophet Jeremias Sachwalter is the advocate of the devil and the philosopher Aristotle is the advocate of Christ. It includes 32 woodcuts which are the full width of the page. One relatively adroit handling of nudes is provided in No. 12. In the same year, Zainer printed [17] a second edition.

Ingold's [18] Guldin spil, unter dem begriffen sind siben spil, durch welche die hauptfünd, die auch an der czal siben seynd, erklärt werden (13), which Zainer printed in 1472, had 12 woodcuts which occupied the full width of the page, and which portray various amusements.

As early as 1472 Zainer began to use woodcuts for illustration of scholarly books.

[19] The Isidorus Hispalensis Etimologiarum libri XX (14) has a very large table of cognate ideas and a very skilfully made series of smaller illustrations, such as the way the ocean sea surrounds the globe, showing Europe, Africa, Asia, etc. It has a monthly calendar and a sky map. It also illustrates the zones of the world that are habitable and uninhabitable. It shows the four elements and the way that climate and time of year are determined, as well as the planets and the fixed stars.

The figures in another book by Isidorus Hispalensis, also printed by Zainer in 1472, [20] De responsione mundi et de astrorum ordinatione (15), are similar. Here one finds seven circles which are supposed to explain the change of seasons, the paths of the stars, and the winds.

In 1474 he followed this with [21, Pl. 14] the Plenarium (16), with 54 woodcuts which are closely related to the content. The woodcuts in the Zainer edition are 80 x 85 mm and continue the playing card technique with little shading and frequent repetition. Nevertheless the book is worthwhile as the first of its type and its woodcuts were copied in many later editions.

In the years from 1473-75, there followed, under the title [22] Gancze heylige geschrifft Altes und Neues Testament, Zainer's first German Bible (17). It was the fifth in the series of Bibles in German and the third illustrated German Bible. The 73 woodcuts, of which 23 are in the first part and 50 in the second, are initials and are similar to those which appeared in the fourth of the series, around 1471, in Nuremburg in a Bible published by Frisner and Sensenschmid.

In his [23] German Bible of 1477 (18), Zainer used the same 73 woodcuts and added to these at the end of both parts, his escutcheon--a wild man with hairy body stepping out to the left, and holding in his right hand a shield with a snarling heraldic lion.

In 1477 Zainer also published [24, Pl. 15 & 16] a moral-allegorical book about the game of chess which the Dominican monk, Jacobus de Cessolis of Rheims, compiled around 1270 under the title Liber de moribus hominum et officiis nobilium super ludo scacchorum and which was soon translated into German under the title Der Schachzabel. Das Buch menschlicher Sitten und der ambt der edlen (19). It has 15 colored woodcuts (85 x 120) which represent the various human stations in life. The woodcuts are all made with great diligence and the scene is always set in an open space.

Around 1477 [25] Gunther Zainer may also have issued the Johannes Damascenus work which appeared without place or date, entitled Chronica von Josaphat und Barlaam (20), which is a mythical spiritual story. This book is rarely found in a perfect copy. It contains around 60 woodcuts (88 x 119). They are very crude, generally include various scenes, and the chief persons are always identified by name.

It is not yet possible to determine the time of production of [26] Gunther Zainer's reprint of Aesopischen Fabeln (21) which Johannes Zainer had first printed in Ulm. As in the Ulm edition, the title page shows Aesop telling his fables. The handsome initials of the Ulm edition are omitted. The remaining woodcuts are the same except No. 11, in which Aesop serves two guests of his Lord a tongue which he had cooked with garlic. This was new in the Zainer edition but was manufactured in Ulm.

A third of the publications issued by Zainer at this time is the [27] second edition of Tuberinus' Ermordung des Knaben zu Trident (22) which was first published in Germany by Creussner in Nuremburg.

It is not known who did the woodcuts for Zainer's publications. Murr stated in his Journal, without giving his sources, that at that time Zainer and Schüssler, the printer who worked for him, were both involved in controversy with the woodcutters, and conflict with the scribes and card manufacturers about the illustrations in his books. These guilds appealed to the Prelate of St. Ulrich, Melchior von Stamham, asking him to forbid all printing by Zainer and Schüssler. The Prelate, a learned man, permitted them both to continue production of books but he gave them the choice of discontinuing the use of capital blocks and woodcuts or of obtaining these from the local producers. Zainer preferred the latter and Schüssler the former. This indicates that Zainer could not himself be the producer of the woodcuts in his books but that he obtained these from the playing card producers or letterers.

Günther Buchdrucker lived in the local cloister during 1474 and 1475 and with him lived Kropsenstein, an amanuensis. In 1478 (after Zainer's death) Kropsenstein himself emerged as a printer and had a lettering artist living with him. This Kropsenstein may have been the illustrator of Günther Zainer's publications, but that is not certain.

Zainer's chief contribution was that he had brought a certain amount of new material to book illustration. The Speculum humanae salvationis, die Legenda aurea, der Spiegel menschlichen Lebens, der Belial, das Plenarium, which later were reprinted in practically every print shop, were produced by him in their first editions and were provided by him with woodcuts of such quality that his method became almost standard. Zainer developed book illustration to the level where it could be compared with great painting.

Günther Zainer was followed (1472-1492) by Johann Bämler, whose greatest activity likewise fell within the '70s. He started making separate title pages and [28] Summa confessorum, by Johannes Friburg (23), printed by him in 1472, had, on the page following the Table of Contents, a page showing Mary with the Jesus Child.

The [29] first publication in 1472 (24) and reprint in 1488 (25) editions of [30] Johann Nider's 24 Goldene Harfen has, after the Table of Contents, a large woodcut which fills the entire page and which shows David with the harp.

On the title page of [31] the 1473 printing of Chronik vom Berge Andechs (26), one sees an elliptical frame, bounded by four angels, in which the Monstrance stands.

In the edition [32] published in 1473 (27) and repeated in the edition published in 1476 (28) of the [33] Gregorius Dialogen, the title page shows Gregor speaking with Peter Diaconus.

The beginning of the truly illustrated book was made by Bämler's [34] Histori von den sieben weisen Meistern (29) in 1473.

It is the second edition of the book and has the same woodcuts as the first edition, which appeared without indication of place or year.

The 34 (78 x 110) woodcuts in his edition of [35] Belial, which was published in 1473 (30), are the same as those used by Zainer in 1472.

On the other hand, [36] Bämler used new materials in another book published in 1473 and these showed development on a par with much later publication. Alongside the Trojan epic cycle, the Alexander epic cycle played a great role in the second half of the 15th Century. Much of this was written in prose form by the well-known doctor and palmist Johann Hartlieb in Munich, ostensibly based on Eusebius, in honor of Duke Albrecht of Bavaria and his spouse, Anna, of Braunschweig, and was issued in 1444. This book, the Histori von dem grossen Alexander nach Eusebius, had been printed by Bämler in 1472 without illustrations. In 1473 he published it for the first time in an illustrated edition (31). The woodcut on the verso of the title page (195 x 145) shows, behind an opening in a fence, a bust of the bishop Eusebius. Of the text illustrations, only one, that of the besieging of a burning town, is 100 x 123 mm; the other 25 illustrations are 80 x 115 mm. Several are repeated and a few battle pictures have been taken from Histori der Zerstörung der Stadt Troia. There is no remarkable advance over the Zainer products in these illustrations. Here, too, only the outlines are given. The illustrations are small and are drawn badly, the figures are gross and the eyes are long slits.

Bämler's [37] Plenarium of 1474 (32) has 56 woodcuts. The 54 smaller ones are taken from Zainer's edition of 1474, and the two which occupy whole pages are new.

Bämler's edition of [38] Histori von der Zerstörung der Stadt Troia (33), of 1474, is third in the whole series of editions of this book. It is the first one to be dated and woodcuts were those used in it from the beginning.

He produced the 1474 edition of [39] Buch von den sieben Todsünden und dem sieben Tugenden (34) independently, and [40] the second edition (35) in 1479, with a [41, Pl. 17-20] third edition in 1482 (36). The woodcuts are 78 x 115 mm.

Bämler's [42] Melusine (37) (which was published in 1474), even though Hain calls it the third, may be considered the first illustrated German edition of the book. It has 70 (80 x 115) woodcuts which are attributable to various people. The illustrations are of varying artistic quality. Some have fine shading, others are executed in outline only.

In 1475 Bämler did the first edition of the frequently later reprinted [43] Buchs der Natur (38) which Conrad von Megenberg, who was apparently one of the intellectual and spiritual leaders in Regensburg in 1349, translated into German from the Latin of an unknown compiler.

The woodcuts of the eleventh book (which deals with rocks) is carved with special care and shows holy Ulrich in bishop's dress, holding a fish in his right hand and a crooked rod in his left. In his second edition [44] of Buchs der Natur (39) which was published in 1478, and in the third [45] in 1481 (40) Bämler reused these woodcuts.

Könighoven's [46, Pl. 21-23] Chronik von allen Königen und Kaiserin (41), which he published in the first edition in 1476, has only a single title page picture at the beginning of each individual part. However, these pages are among the most important that had been published in Augsburg up to that time. The first is 205 mm high and 145 mm wide, the others are 185 mm high and 120 to 130 wide.

The first edition of the [47] Geschichte des Königs Apollonios von Tyrus (42) was also published in 1476. It was very popular and was widely read at that time. It is supposed to have been available in Greek as early as the 11th Century with Latin manuscript translations found as early as the 12th Century, and was later reworked by Shakespeare into his Pericles. It is illustrated with 34 woodcuts, which, with the exception of the title page, which is 90 x 97 mm, are all 73 x 85 mm.

From 1475 to 1477, Bämler published [48] Leben der Heiligen, the third edition of this book (43) which, like the fifth edition [49] in 1480 (44), used the same woodcuts which Zainer had used.

[50] Jakob Sprenger first published [51] Statuten der Rosenkranzbruderschaft, s. l. e. a. (45) and it was published a second time by Bämler in 1477 (46). Both have a woodcut 125 mm high and 90 mm wide.

The [52] Buch der Kunst, dadurch der weltliche Mensch mag geistlich werden (47), first printed in 1477, has 107 prints that are the full width of the page (82 x 95). The woodcuts are made by various hands and were not all done for this book. The Augsburg school is easily identified and only the better and the later woodcuts can not be identified with Augsburg. Bämler repeated the woodcuts [53, 54] in his later editions of 1478 (48) and 1491 (49). However, he added a few new ones.

In 1479 he published the third edition of Rodericus Zamorensis' [55] Spiegel des menschlichen Lebens (50), which used the same woodcuts that Zainer had used.

The book by Rupertus a Santo Remigio, which appeared in 1482, [56, Pl. 24-26] Historie von der Kreuzfahrt nach dem heiligen Land und dessen Einnahme durch Gottfried von Bouillon (51), presents the first illustration of the crucifixion. The illustration on the verso of the title page is 100 x 120 mm. The other 46 woodcuts of the book are 90 x 120 mm. The woodcuts are not all new. A few of the smaller ones (80 x 115) are taken from the Histori der Zerstörung der Stadt Troia. Many have fine shading, others give only outlines.

His 1482 edition of Petrarch's [57] Griseldis (52) is the fourth in the whole series of illustrated editions of the book and reuses the woodcuts from the first Ulm edition.

The 12 illustrations in his 1482 edition of [58] Historia der Sigismunda (53), also came from Ulm.

The title page picture in [59] his Regiment der Gezundheit (54), which was published in 1482, comes from the Buch der Natur, published in 1475.

In the final years of his operations Bämler did nothing but new editions of books that he had published earlier. If we credit the regulations of his Guild, then Bämler himself would have been the illustrator of his printed works. He was originally an amanuensis, that is to say, a producer of letters and an illustrator of manuscripts. Thomas Burgkmair served as one of his apprentices in 1460. Bämler first appears as an amanuensis in the tax records, under the location of Vom Thore, in 1453. He lived there until 1462 and then for a year lived in St. Katharine Street. From 1463 to 1473 he is recorded as being at the Guild Chambers. He is listed under the location "Von Predigern" from 1474-1503. In 1477 he was recorded as a printer for the first time. He appears to have died in 1504 since in that year Mrs. Hans Bämler is recorded as paying the taxes.

The third Augsburg printer, Anton Sorg (1475-1493), really belonged only partially to this early period.

His earliest works were mostly books published without any indication of place or date.

The first of these [60, Pl. 27] Ars memorativa (55) seems almost entirely a xylographic work. The title page illustration (118 x 90) shows an old man wearing a turban who sits under a canopy in a walled space and counts something on his fingers; before him kneels a youngster with a book. This is followed by twelve pages, each imprinted with five woodcuts which represent abstract ideas very naively. The woodcuts are among the earliest and crudest that have been found in printed books.

The 60 woodcuts in Sorg's [61] Cronica von Josaphat und Barlaam (56), which was published without location or date, are the same that Zainer used in 1471. Sorg's edition of Petrarch's [62] Griseldis (57) is the third in the series of illustrated editions of this book. The ten woodcuts are identical with those in the first edition which was published in Ulm.

Sorg also issued the first edition of a widely-read [63] Reisenbeschreibung by Johann Schildberger (58), of Munich, who had been in Turkish captivity from 1395 to 1417. It contains 15 woodcuts (85 x 110).

His fifth undated book is illustrated with 32 woodcuts which are 82 x 110 mm. It is [64] the Historie Herzog Ernsts von Oesterreich (59). The title page illustration is taken from the Schachzabel.

[65] Sorg published a second edition of this book (60), which was undated.

[66] Melusine (61), which Sorg published without location or date, is second in the series of editions of this book. The 70 woodcuts are 60 x 82 mm. They were not reduced copies of the Bämler edition, but were freely modified. They are very low in value as works of art.

The last of the publications issued by Sorg without place or date was the book entitled [67] Historie von St. Brandon (62). It has 20 (80 x 110) woodcuts.

The series of Sorg's dated books begins in 1476 with the appearance of [68] Buch der Kindheit unseres Herrn Jesu Christi (63). It has 79 woodcuts of which 7 (No.'s 1, 2, 3, 4, 5, 53 and 70) are the full width of the page. The others are only the width of a column. Those in the first group are 82 x 110 mm. The others are 82 x 60 mm. The woodcuts were made by various people. In part they were copies of copper plates. The second edition of the book, [69] published in 1491 (64), used the same illustrations.

Sorg's edition of [70] Spiegels menschlicher Behaltniss (65) of 1476 is the fifth in the series of editions of this book. The woodcuts are 85 x 110 mm and none of them copy those in Zainer's edition. The figures are stouter and have the spiritless expression and the long slitted eyes that were conventional in the Augsburg School. They total 190. The Sorg edition has 15 additional woodcuts of the Passion, of which 12 are 85 x 112 mm and three, which belong to an earlier hand, are only 80 x 57 mm. The scenes presented are the usual ones.

The 76 woodcuts in Sorg's [71] Deutscher Bibel, which was published in 1477 (66), come from the Pflanzman Bible, but a few are new.

The ten large (180 x 115) colored illustrations which appeared in [72, Pl. 28-30] Büchlein das da heisset der Sele trost (67) provide the first illustrations of the ten commandments. The woodcuts were prepared especially for this book, but they were produced by various people.

Sorg's two editions of [73] the Sieben weisen Meister, which he published in 1478 (68), and [74] in 1480 (69), are the third and fourth in the series of editions of this work. The woodcuts are the same as in the first edition.

[75-78] The Leben der Heiligen, which was first published by Zainer in 1471, was published by Sorg four times: in 1478 (70), in 1481 (71), in 1486 (72), and in 1488 (73). His editions are the fourth, seventh, eleventh and twelfth in the series of editions. Unlike the others, which were folio, his were quarto. The first woodcut is 75 x 80 mm, the others are 78 x 67 mm. These others are the same scenes as in the earlier editions, but they are newly prepared for this work and are almost as crude as those done for the Zainer edition; the landscapes are far in the background, the ground is bare, and only outlines are provided for the figures.

[79-82] The Histori des grossen Alexanders, which was first produced by Bämler, was reprinted four times by Sorg: in 1478 (74), in 1480 (75), in 1483 (76), and in 1486 (77). His editions were the second, fourth, fifth and sixth of the editions of this work. The title page illustration (190 x 132) is different from that in the Bämler edition. The rest of the illustrations (80 x 115) are the same as those in the Bämler edition, with some using Bämler's woodcuts and some being copied into wood anew.

[83-85] During this period Sorg did three editions of the Plenarium: one in 1478 (78), another in 1480 (79), and the third in 1481 (80). The woodcuts were those used by Zainer.

[86-87] The Historie der Konigs Appolonius, which was first published by Bämler in 1476, was reprinted twice by Sorg, using the same woodcuts--first in 1479 (81) and again in 1480 (82).

[88-89] The 32 woodcuts in the Sorg 1479 (83) edition and in the 1481 edition (84) of Belial were those used by Zainer nine years earlier. From time to time, small changes are noticeable. For example, in the woodcut showing "Christ in Limbo," in both books Christ stands with his foot on the doorway to hell. However, in the Zainer edition the doorway lies flat on the ground, while Sorg shows, under the doorway, a little devil which Christ tramples.

His edition of [90] Lucidarius of 1879 (85) is the second publication of this book.

In 1479 he reprinted Johannes Zainer's edition, published in Ulm, of Steinhöwel's translation of [91] Boccaccio's Compendium de präclaris mulieribus (86). The woodcuts vary only slightly from those of the first edition. For example, the first initial is different and the Sorg edition has the usual type of woodcut (75 x 115) instead of the shaded cut that appeared in the Zainer edition at the head of the chapter on Eve. The other woodcuts are copies of those in the Ulm edition except that they are 75 x 115 mm instead of the 80 x 110 mm size in the Ulm edition.

In his early period Sorg published a very large number of illustrated books, as soon as he could get access to the works of his predecessors.

There are, for that reason, still two books from the late 1470's which we can not determine definitely as coming from Bämler's press or from Sorg's press.

The fourth edition of [92] Histori der Zerstörung der Stadt Troia (87), which appeared in Augsburg in 1479 without indication of publisher, has the same woodcuts as the earlier editions.

A German [93, Pl. 31-35] Kalender (88) which appeared in Augsburg around this time provided the prototype for all later calendars in the 15th Century. In general its illustrations are commendable.

Reviewing what was done in Augsburg during the ten years from 1470-1480, the amount of work done is astounding. Rarely did they limit themselves to just an illustrated title page or a moderate number of illustrations, and often the woodcuts were provided in hundreds. This mass production, however, resulted in routine craftsmanship. Only a few books, like Zainer's Spiegel des menschlichen Lebens and Bämler's Buch der natur, were really executed with care. What Augsburg neglected in this regard was made up by the second city to become a center for book illustration: Ulm.

Notes

1) For general biographical information see the tax records in the Augsburg city archives; For book catalogs: Zapf, Augsburg's Buchdruckergeschichte nebst den Jahrbüchern derselben. Part I, 1468-1500. Augsburg, 1788; Panzer, Ausführliche Beschreibung der ältesten Augsburgischen Ausgaben der Bibel. Nuremburg, 1780; Metzger, Augsburg's Älteste Druckdenkmale und Formschneiderarbeiten, welche in der vereinigten Kreis und Stadtbibliothek daselbst aufbewaren werden. Augsburg, 1840; Kraenzler, Die deutschen und lateinischen Incunabeln der Kreis -und Stadtbibliothek in Augsburg. Augsburg, 1880; Choulan, "Botanische und anatomische Abbildungen des Mittelalters." In Naumann's Archiv für die zeichnenden Künste. 3:188-345, 1857.

2) The tax records list as card makers: Trechsel (1464 and 1470 at "Vom Thore"; and at the same place Hans Gogel (1465, 1469-70, 1478, 1481, 1483, 1486, 1490-92 and in 1493-1495 it gave his location as "Below the Laundry"; Hans Riss in "Vom Thore" (1477, 1480, 1483, 1486, 1491-92); Christoph (1478). Stephan is located on Schongauergasse in 1460 and 1464, then in Judenberg in 1499; Hans Müller in the "Guild Hall" (1476-77, 1483, 1486, 1490-2, 1494 & 1499); Gabriel at the "Fish Market" (1490-91); Utz "Below the Laundry" (1490); Ulrich Kempler, in Schongauergasse (1491); Jörig, under the sign "Blacksmith" (1494).

Book 2 shows those working in this field as Hans Preying (1494); Blesy (1493) is in v. 23; and Hans Hegner at the blacksmith's (1490) and at "Vom Thore" (1493-96).

Those listed as illuminators were Jörg, at "Leopoldsbad" (1474) and at Bächim Hof (1481); Michael Müller is located at "Kapenzipfel" (1490-93) and at "Streiflinger Thor" (1495); Jörg Beck at "Sixth Street" (1483, 1486, 1490-92, 1493) and 1495 at "Judenberg."

3) Third German edition. Large folio, s. l. e. a; Hain I:417, No. 3131.

4) Hain. No. 5512, s. l. e. a.

5) Panzer. 1:54.

6) Hain. No. 8803. Quarto.

7) Ebert. No. 21581. s. l. e. a. Folio: Hain, 2:343. No. 14929; Panzer 1:6. No. 5; The first two woodcuts are reproduced in Heineken, Idée Générale, p. 463.

8) Hain, No. 14946. Folio. s. l. e. a; Geffcken, Der Bilderkatechismus des 15. Jahrhunderts. Supplement: No. 4: page 47.

9) Hain, No. 5513.

10) Hain, No. 9968. Folio.

11) Heinecken. Neue Nachrichten 1:252; Hain, No. 13948.

12) Panzer, Vol. 1, no. 11. Folio.

13) Ebert, No. 10515. Folio; Hain. Second Series 1:130. No. 9187; Panzer 1:65. No. 13; Four numbers copied by Essenwein, Die Holzschnitte des germanischen Museums, Pl. 63.

14) Hain, 2:141, No. 9273. Folio.

15) Hain, No. 9302.

16) Kraenzler, p. 4, No. 22.

17) Hain, Ser 1, 1:418, No. 3133, Large Folio; Panzer 1:14, No. 12; Panzer, Literarische Nachricht von den allerältesten gedruckten deutschen Bibeln. Nuremberg, 1777, p. 40. No. 4; Muther, Die ällesten deutschen Bilderbibeln, Munich, Huttler, 1883. No. 3.

18) Hain, No. 3134; Panzer, Literarische Nachricht p. 51, No. 5; Muther. Bilderbibeln. No. 4.

19) Ebert, No. 3939. Folio; Hain I (2):94 No. 4895; Panzer 1:96 No. 75 and Supplement, p. 37, No. 75.

20) Ebert, No. 1657, Folio.

21) Hain, No. 331. Folio. s. a.

22) Hain, No. 15658. s. a.

23) Hain, No. 7367.

24) Hain, No. 11847.

25) Hain, No. 1852.

26) Hain, No. 971.

27) Hain, No. 7970.

28) Hain, No. 7971.

29) Panzer vol. 1, No. 34; Ebert 1:82.

30) Panzer vol. 1, No. 24. Folio; Ebert, 10667. Eight numbers copied by Essenwein, Pl. 72 and 73.

31) Hain, No. 785. Folio.

32) Folio. Is not in the bibliographies; Kraenzler, Verzeichniss der Augsburger Incunabeln. No. 51.

33) Hain, No. 5514. Folio; Three items are copied in Essenwein, Pl. 58. They are: Hekuba, who is shown in a dream of a flaring battle; Jason, who kills the fire-spewing dragon, and

Paris by the shepherd.

34) Hain, No. 15534.

35) Hain, No. 15535.

36) Hain, No. 15536.

37) Hain, No. 11064.

38) Panzer 1:83. Folio; Zapf 1:32; Ebert, No. 3092; Hain, 4041. Choulant, p. 306; Numbers 1-9 reproduced in Essenwein, Pl. 75-80.

39) Trew, Catalog II, No. 1. Folio; Panzer 1:105; Zapf 1:47; Ebert, No. 3092; Hain, 4042; Choulant p. 307, No. 2.

40) Panzer 1:119. Folio; Zapf 1:57; Ebert, 3092; Hain, 4043; Choulant p. 307, No. 3. Folio.

41) Hain, 9792.

42) Hain, No. 1295. Folio.

43) Hain, No. 9970.

44) Hain, No. 9972.

45) Hain, No. 14961.

46) Hain, No. 14962.

47) Hain, No. 4036.

48) Hain, No. 4037.

49) Hain, Part I 1:564, No. 4038; Panzer 1:190, No. 314.

50) Ebert, No. 19240. Folio; Hain, Part II 2:226, No. 13949; Panzer 1:109, No. 102.

51) Hain, No. 8753.

52) Hain, No. 12820.

53) Panzer 1:131, No. 162.

54) Hain, No. 13743.

55) Hain, Part I 1:227, No. 1827. Quarto. s. l. e. a.

56) Ebert, No. 1657. Folio; Hain, Part I 2:224, No. 5916; Panzer 1:23, No. 26; 1:97, No. 76. Four reproductions in Essenwein. Pl. 83.

57) Hain, No. 12815.

58) Hain, No. 14515.

59) Hain, No. 6672.

60) Hain, No. 6675.

61) Hain, No. 11062.

62) Hain, No. 3718.

63) Hain, No. 4057. Folio.

64) Panzer 1:260. Folio.

65) Hain, No. 14942.

66) Hain, No. 3135. Folio; Panzer, *Literarische Nachricht den alleraltesten gedruckten Bibeln.* p. 56, No. 6; Muther, *Deutsche Bilderbibeln.* No. 5.

67) Hain, No. 14582; Geffcken, *Der Bilderkatechismus der 15. Jahrhunderts.*

68) Panzer, No. 97.

69) Panzer, No. 118.

70) Hain, No. 9972.

71) Hain, No. 9975.

72) Hain, No. 9979.

73) Hain, No. 9980.

74) Hain, No. 786.

75) Hain, No. 788.

76) Hain, No. 789.

77) Hain, No. 790.

78) Hain, No. 6728.

79) Hain, No. 6729.

80) Hain, No. 6731.

81) Hain, No. 1296. Folio.

82) Hain, No. 1297. Folio.

83) Panzer, No. 101. Folio.

84) Panzer, No. 127. Folio.

85) Hain, No. 8804.

86) Hain, No. 3335.

87) Hain, No. 5515.

88) Hain, No. 9728.

Chapter III

ULM, 1470-1480 (1)

In Ulm, as in Augsburg, the external conditions for early development of book illustration were very good.

In the second half of the 15th Century, Ulm had a population of more than 5,000 and was, in addition, a very extensive center of trade. It had unbroken and very close ties with Italy and at all times one would find merchants and citizens of Ulm in the market of Venice, where they could exchange their wares and handle other transactions.

The fact that material wealth goes hand in hand with spiritual and artistic growth is indicated by such names as Amandus Suso, Martin Schoen, Bartholomaeus Zeitblom and Martin Schaffner.

The Ulm tax records show the names of a large number of amanuensi and woodcutters. In 1434 Hans Wachter lived there. In 1463 Lorenz Schurner moved to Nordlingen. The wood carvers listed there were an Ulrich in 1398, a Peter von Erolzheim and a Jorg in 1441, a Lienhart in 1442, a Claus, a Stoffel and a Jos in 1447, a Wilhelm in 1455 and an Ulrich in 1470, as well as a Michel, Hans, Kunz and Lorenz in 1476.

Thus, the soil was particularly fruitful for development of book illustration in Ulm.

The earliest illustrated book, which came from the shop of Ulm's first printer, Ludwig Hohenwang [94, Pl. 36-37], is not really of the Ulm school. It is the first edition of Des durchleichtigen wolgebornen Graven Flavii Vegecii Renati kurczer red von der Ritterschaft zu dem grossmächtigeten Kaiser Theodosio seiner Bücher vierer (2), and it was printed in 1470. It had 64 woodcuts on 32 sheets, illustrating various besieging devices, which are from a much earlier source and were composed in a much earlier period than that of the Hohenwang volume. The fact that they were not prepared for the Vegetius is illustrated by the large number of guns that are in the illustrations but which have no direct connection with the Vegetius text, and were taken from other books. It is very difficult to determine their source. Heinecken's surmise that they were from the Italian edition of Valturius, Verona, 1472 (cf. Ebert, No. 23369), is incorrect. These woodcuts are from an undated German edition as is evidenced not only by the fact that many of the artists are quite skilled, but also in individual features that show many differences. Both, however, stem from a common source in that they are both copied from manuscripts. As Essenwein first pointed out, some of the illustrations in the Ulm edition appeared as early as the Cod. germ. 734, in the Munich State Library, as part of weaponry books. Johannes Formschneider, whose mark appears on some of the woodcuts for this Codex, became a citizen of Nuremberg in 1440. The drawings for the woodcuts of the Ulm edition are not of the 1470's but go back to the period around 1440. It would appear that Hohenwang himself did the woodcuts, since he says, in the Table of Contents, "since ... there is no really clear information in the text, and illustrations were required, I have set the fifth book with illustrations pertinent thereto."

The first woodcuts that were produced in the City itself were done by the second Ulm printer, Johannes Zainer, who also started printing in Ulm in 1470. Whether he was the brother of Gunther Zainer is uncertain. It has been determined only that they both came from the same place and that they belonged to the same family, since each identified himself as Zainer from Reutlingen. Furthermore, they both used the same escutcheon--the wild man with a club--that was printed by Gunther Zainer in his German Bible of 1477 and by Johannes Zainer in the fragments of his calendars that remain. Johannes was one of the martyrs of the new art; he found himself forever in the wrong. He appears for the last time in the Ulm town books of 1523.

The first illustrated book that was issued by his press was Boccaccio's [95-96, Pl. 38-41] Compendium de praeclaris mulieribus, which he published in two editions, one in the original Latin text (3) and the other in German translation (4). The translation was supplied by Dr. Heinrich Steinhöwel of Ulm, who was equally skilled in the history of the German language and in book illustration. The Latin edition appeared in 1473 and the German edition is undated, but it probably was issued simultaneously, since both have the date 1473 on their 24 woodcuts.

At the beginning of the preface, there is a beautiful initial with the Bavarian coat of arms; a second initial, very rich in imagination, is at the beginning of the first chapter, about Eve. The capital S of the initial ends in the head of the snake, which holds an apple in its mouth. Eve, standing below it, reaches for it and in her right hand she has a second apple, which she offers to Adam, who is standing below her. The illustrations themselves are 80 x 110 mm.

Boccaccio's book for women plays the same part in the history of book illustration in Ulm as was played by the Pflanzmann Bible in that of Augsburg. This very first Ulm product clearly displays the difference between the two schools. Shading is used and is better than anything that was produced in the 70's in Augsburg. We do not find the Augsburg type of crude outlines in thick strokes; in Ulm the outlines are fine and rounded, and in most cases shading is provided within the figures. The presentation of faces in Ulm had advanced so far that they have a definitely human appearance. The landscape is, to be sure, not frequently presented, but when it is, it is flawless. The same wood blocks are not reused. In the determination of individual scenes, Steinhöwel himself may have sat alongside the engraver.

In the same period [97], still a second, later much reprinted book, was issued by Zainer's press. It was the story of Griselda, the wife of Margrave Walther von Saluzzo. Petrarch had written this book long ago, before he became acquainted with Boccaccio's Decameron. He wrote it under the title De obedientia et fide uxoria and it was published in many German translations under the title Ain epistel Francisci Petrarchae von Grosser Stätigkeit einer frawen Grisel geheissen (5). Zainer's edition had ten 80 x 110 mm woodcuts. This edition is undated but the woodcuts are identical in size and style with those of his Boccaccio and they were produced in the same year (1473).

In the Pelagius [98] De Planctu ecclesiae libri II (6), which Zainer printed in 1474, there is only one woodcut of any importance and it is on sheet 8A before the initial. It is repeated at the beginning of the second part.

In the [99] Quadragesimale (7), which was printed by Johannes Gritsch in 1475, on sheet

26A the same woodcut is found as in Pelagius except that the man who is sitting in the foliage has a normal hat instead of a fool's cap, which appears in Pelagius.

Zainer made a new and exceedingly important contribution to book illustration in Heinrich Steinhöwel's translation of Aesop's fables, which was printed under the title [100, Pl. 42-48] Das Buch und Leben des hochberühmten Fabeldichters Aesopi (8). Eleven editions of this book were published by 1498 by various printers. The woodcut on the verso of the title page (190 x 114) shows Aesop himself; a bloated man with a large head and deformed large feet, who is standing on a low hill in a landscape, and is counting something on his fingers. The individual fables were primarily decorated with animal pictures. There are a total of 189 woodcuts in the Aesop. According to the index, there was, as a supplement, the Historia Sigismunde, Tochter des Fürsten Tankredi von Salernia, with 11 woodcuts, making a total of 200 woodcuts. These are of the same quality as those in the Boccaccio. Nude female bodies appear twice: once in No. 63, in the fable of the wolf, and the other in No. 94, in the fable of the woman and the peacock. Both are skillfully done. The woodcuts in Historia der Sigismunde were outstanding. The landscape stands out more than is customary in Ulm products of this period.

Johannes Zainer did not provide a completely independent work in the second edition of the Rodericus Zamorensis [101] Spiegel des menschlichen Lebens, which he published in 1472. The woodcuts are the same as those that appeared in Gunther Zainer's edition of 1471.

One other publication may be attributed to [102, Pl. 49-62] illustrated books of Hohenwang and Zainer, although to be sure, no one has any direct evidence that either of them did it. However, it can be established with certainty as a very early Ulm product. It is the: s. l. e. a., which appeared around 1470, Gaistliche usslegung des lebens Jhesu Christi (9). The four colored woodcuts are surrounded by 8mm-long cross hatchings. The size of the individual illustrations varies. The width varies from 112-118mm and the height may be 190 or 160 or 130mm. They illustrate the life of Christ in 92 pictures. The fact that the book is an Ulm product can hardly be doubted. The presentation of purgatory is copied with no substantial change in the Seelenwurzgarten produced by Conrad Dinkmut in 1483. Here, as in all Ulm products, the landscape is greatly suppressed and the human expressions are brought to the fore, with the faces being among the most lovely that 15th Century art produced. Those who have attributed the woodcuts to Martin Schoen have probably gone too far. Many of the illustrations in the book are reminiscent of Martin Schoen, and if not by him are certainly done by one of his more talented students, who, now and then, used the master's works and transferred much to his own. In addition to this one, there was a second artist who was greatly differentiated from the first one. The first always made pleats in garments, always showed grass on the soil, and loved to draw hair and shading. The hair drawn by the other is always dropping limply, he paints only the necessary folds in garments, and never draws either grass or shading.

Ulm artistic activity of the seventies cannot be compared with the quantity produced in Augsburg. Whereas the Augsburg illustrated books totalled around 100, there were only about 10 in Ulm. However, what was lacking in quantity of illustrated books in Ulm was richly made good by the skill of their execution.

Notes

1) Hassler, _Buchdruckergeschichte Ulms zur vierten Säcularfeier der Erfindung der Buchdruckkunst geschrieben._ Ulm, 1840.

2) Hain II:471, No. 15916; Hassler, No. 3.

3) Hain, No. 3329. Folio; Panzer III:528; Ebert, No. 2596; Hassler, No. 21.

4) _Der kurcz sin von etlichen Frowen von denen Johannes Boccaccius in latin beschrieben hat und Doctor Hainricus Stainhöwel getütschet;_ Hassler, No. 66. Folio; Hain, No. 3333.

5) S. a. around 1473 is not in Hain; Hassler, No. 68.

6) Hassler, No. 27. Large folio.

7) Hain, No. 8063. Large folio; Panzer III:531, No. 11; Hassler, No. 30.

8) Hain, No. 330. Folio; Hassler, No. 64.

9) Weigel IV. No. 18337. Folio; Panzer Pt. I, 1:20, No. 20; Hain Pt. I, 1:268, No. 2146.

Chapter IV

THE OTHER CITIES (PRIOR TO 1480) (1)

During the seventies all other German cities were of lesser importance in book illustration than were Augsburg and Ulm.

It was about 1471, at the earliest, when book illustration started in Nuremberg.

Johann Sensenschmidt was Nuremberg's first printer. He began to develop the craft in cooperation with Heinrich Kefer of Mainz and in 1470 they joined with Frisner of Nuremberg. They issued the [103] Zweite illustrirte deutsche Bibel (2) in 1472. Whereas the first (Pflanzmann's) Bible had the woodcuts of the large initial letters standing out separately, in this second edition the empty space around these large initials of the individual books were filled in with figures. This arrangement of little figures within the outline of the initial letters limited the format of these illustrations, and they were all very narrow. Nevertheless, they are very numerous and only a single picture was used twice.

The first illustration, before the prologue of Hieronymus, has within a letter B, a bishop and an abbot, jointly holding a book. The individual figures were, as usual, identified by name. Genesis has a large independent illustration which is 125 x 185mm.

In 1475, Sensenschmidt [104] published the second edition of Lebens des Heiligen (3), which had first been published by Zainer in Augsburg in 1471. The woodcuts are related to those in the Zainer edition, but they show some differences. The first illustration appears to be the same; however, the other woodcuts are wider, (80 x 80), than those in the Zainer edition and are surrounded by a double border. The landscape, which in Zainer's case was still very neglected, was given more space by Sensenschmidt, and each individual woodcut has more figures than in the Zainer edition. The number of woodcuts is the same and the use of the same blocks was repeated, as in Zainer. There is little difference in style. The Nuremberg edition retained the playing card tradition in the woodcuts. Only the outline is provided and it is intended that the coloring of the figures is to be done later.

The printing house founded in Nuremberg by Johannes Regiomontanus in 1472 issued very few illustrated books.

The [105] Kalendarium novum (4), which he printed in 1476, had a number of astronomical figures, such as solar eclipses, lunar orbs, and the like.

The [106] Philalethes (5), by Vegius Maphaeus, which was also published by Regiomontanus, has a full page woodcut illustration as its title page.

The third Nuremberg printer, Friedrich Creussner, 1472-1496, is credited only with the s. l. e. a. edition [107] of Tuberinus' Ermordung des Knaben zu Trident (6), which may have been printed around 1476-1477. It has a 90 x 380mm illustration at the end of the book.

The fourth Nuremberg printer, who was Marc Ayrer, published the first German edition

[108] of Collationes inter Salomonem et Marcolphum, in 1477, under the title Frag und Antwort (7). In his edition he used woodcuts that were very similar to those in the first Latin edition.

Eight of the ten popular poems of the Nuremberg surgeon Hans Folz, who printed them himself, belong to this period. Four were printed in 1479 and three in 1480; the first three being undated. Each had a woodcut at its beginning.

The woodcut for the first poem [109], Gute Lehre von allen Wildbädern (8), is 90 x 60mm. The woodcut for the second poem, [110] Von Branntwein (9), is 75 x 125. The cut for the poem [111] Berechnung des Wuchers der Juden (10), is larger (90 x 185). The woodcuts for the next three poems, which appeared in 1479 [112-114]: Von ein griechischen Arzt (11); Von einem Bürger von Strassburg der gen Rom zog (12); and Von einem faulen-Hurensohn der sich auf Büberei verlegt (13), are all very crude. The woodcut for [115] Krieg des Dichters wider einen Juden (14) was 65 x 95 mm. The other three poems were published in 1480. The woodcut for the first of these, [116] Von drei Studenten, die um eine Schöne Wirthin buhlten (15), is 65 x 95 mm. That for the second, [117] Von einem kargen Reichen, der ainen Armen eines Fasttags einlud (16), is 65 x 95 mm. The woodcut for the third of the poems published in 1480, [118] Wie Adam und Eva nach der Vertreibung aus dem Paradis gelebt (17), shows Adam and Eve sitting naked in a crude hut.

This is all that was produced in Nuremberg in the 1470's.

The entry of Cologne into the history of book illustration can not be dated positively. The only illustrated book by the prolific printer Ulrich Zell, of Hanau, who set up the first printshop in Cologne in 1466, must have been produced in the early '70's at the latest. It was the [119] Horologium devotionis (18), which appeared without citing its printer, place of publication, or year. It contained 630 small woodcuts which deal with the life of Jesus. Since eight of the large woodblocks were repeated, the number of woodblocks was 28. They fall into two classes. Thirteen (Numbers 1-7, 10, 11, 33-36) are 66 x 48 mm and these show the same technique that we described in the first chapter as occuring in the Leiden Jesu. The lines are white and the background and the spaces between the lines are all black. They are all surrounded by scroll work, which in every case goes back to very old times, and they make an awkward, stiff impression. Their kinship with the woodcuts in the Leidens Jesu is great. The 23 other blocks (8, 9, 12-32) demonstrate the customary technique, i.e., the lines are black and the background is white. They obviously belong to a later period than the smaller ones and are approximately at the level of development of the Augsburg products of its time.

Another book than can be specifically attributed to Cologne is the world history, under the title Fasciculus temporum, which Werner Rolevink produced. Of the 11 editions of this book published up to 1480, three give no place or date, seven are designated as published in Cologne and one in Speier. It may be assumed that the three first s.l.e.a. published editions (19) were done in Cologne. The book has ten small woodcuts which appear in all of its editions.

The first dated edition, [120-129], which is fourth in the whole series (20), was published by Nicolaus Götz in Cologne in 1474; the fifth (21) was likewise issued in 1474, but by Arnold Ter. Hörnen. The sixth was published by Conrad Winter von Homburg in 1476; the seventh by Johann Veldener in 1476; the ninth (22) by Nicolaus Götz in 1478, the tenth by Heinrich Quentel in 1479, who also published the eleventh edition in 1480 (23). The woodcuts are always the same except that Quentel has added the adoration of the king. They are among the crudest woodcuts that have been preserved. The outlines of the individual figures are presented in a most unattractive way. A little picture that is barely one centimeter high, which has a pair of towers, will in one case represent Rome and in other cases may be Athens or Cologne or Jerusalem, etc.

About 1474, the first illustrated book appeared in Speier where Peter Drach set up his printing plant in 1471. It is the fourth [130] s. l. e. a. edition of the Spiegels menschlicher Behaltniss (24). The 276 woodcuts are quite significant and are very different from those in the first edition by Zainer, even when relating the same thing. The nude is always well executed and the area between the outlines is always finely shaded.

Drach's edition of Rolevink's [131] Fasciculus temporum of 1477 (25) is the eighth in the series of editions of this book and the woodcuts are all reused from earlier editions.

In 1475, the eminent Hanseatic State of Lübeck entered into the history of book illustration.

The first of these illustrated works was produced by Lucas Brandis, Lübeck's earliest printer (1475-1499). It was the [132, Pl. 63] Rudimentum Noviciorum (26), which is not only a work of art in its typography, but is illustrated with many woodcuts (of which some, to be sure, are reused). The first ten pages provide genealogical tables. The book itself begins with a large illustrated initial B. The woodcuts vary in size, but are ordinarily 80 x 70 mm. The individual cuts are frequently reused so the number of different cuts is not as large as appears at first. The woodcuts are done quite skilfully. One of the truly distinguished illustrations is that of the child Jesus being held forward by Mary and Joseph. In this cut the engraver overcame all difficulties; the facial expression of the young woman is so charming that one is led to believe that he is looking at an illustration produced towards the end of the late nineties.

The Lucas Brandis [133] Passional von Jesus und Marien levende (27) was printed in 1478, in low German, and does not list its printer. It has 144 (75 x 57) woodcuts, of which 80 have a single border and 44 a double border. Most of these are reduced copies of the illustrations in the edition of the Buch von der Kindheit Jesu Christi, which was printed in Augsburg by Sorg in 1476, whose illustrations, in turn, were copies of Zwott's copperplate Passion (Weigel & Zestermann No. 425).

The first illustrated book printed in Basel was done by the local printer Bernhard Richel in 1476.

It is the fifth edition of [134, Pl. 64-66] Spiegels Menschlicher Behaltniss (28). The woodcuts are 125 x 90 mm. Each has a broad black border and all are less crude than Heineken alleges. The woodcuts differ greatly from those of the earlier editions. Even though they have little shading, when their early production is considered they are outstanding.

In February, 1480, Richel printed a [135] Missale Basiliense, with a well drawn but crudely cut illustration.

Richel is less independent in both the two other illustrated books that he produced. One of these is a German translation of Rolevink's Fasciculus temporum which he published in 1481 under the title [136] Bürdlin der Zeit (29), and the other was the fifteenth edition of the [137] original Latin edition of Fasciculus (30) which he published in 1482. The woodcuts in both of these were taken from the first Cologne edition.

Richel published [138] the Fortalitium fidei contra Judaeos, Saracenos et alios christiani nominis hostes (31). It was undated and it had only one woodcut.

In 1481 there appeared in Basel, without the name of the printer, the second edition of the book that was first published in Augsburg by Sorg [139], the Historie von St. Brandon (32). Twenty of the 21 woodcuts are the same as those in the first Augsburg edition. Only the last one differs from that of the Augsburg edition.

In 1477 two new cities entered into the history of book illustration: Esslingen and Strassburg.

In Esslingen Conrad Fyner began his activities in 1477 by publishing the book by Peter Schwarz [140], Stern Messias (33), which had two woodcuts (153 x 100), both of which are repeated at the end of the book.

Fyner published his undated [141] second edition of Ackermanns aus Beheim, or the Rechtsstreites des Menschen mit dem Todt (34).

Strassburg, which had printing from movable type as early as 1466, became a part of the history of book illustration in the same year as Esslingen. The earliest printed book produced in Strassburg that contained woodcuts [142] is the Burgundische Reimchronik über Carls des Kühnen Feldzüge von Erhardt (35). It consists of 25 sheets and has eight crude woodcuts. As a colophon it states, "Printed in Strassburg in 1477." It was apparently produced in the print shop of the second Strassburg printer, Heinrich Eggestein.

Heinrich Knoblochzer's woodcuts in his editions of [143-145] Belial from 1478 to 1483 were of equally poor quality. He issued three editions of Belial: the first in 1478 (36), the second in 1482 (37) and the third in 1483 (38). These illustrations are not copies of the Zainer originals; there are many new woodcuts and all were changed. The 53 smaller woodcuts are 60 x 75 mm and towards the end of the book Knoblochzer added two larger ones, 95 x 135 mm. The woodcuts, as compared with those done in Augsburg six years earlier, represent a giant retrogression. The faces are crude, the figures are drawn far too thick and tall, and the eyes are either drawn as long slits or are opened up like round spheres.

In addition, Hain designates the 1478 edition of Petrarch's [146] Griseldis (39), which was published without indication of place, as a Strassburg imprint. The illustrations, which are surrounded by broad borders, are ten in number and are 100 x 110 mm free copies of those in the original Ulm edition of 1473.

In 1483, Knoblochzer did a reprint [147] of Jakob von Cassalis' Schachzabel (40), which was first printed by Zainer around 1477, and he reused the original woodcuts.

Würzburg's first printer was Georg Reyser. A very early illustrated book, the typefaces of which indicate that it came from the Reyser shop, is the s. l. e. a. [148, Pl. 66] Defensorium immaculatae conceptionis Mariae (41), which could hardly have appeared later than the second half of the 1470's. The first two woodcuts illustrate the Annunciation; the first is 60 x 80 mm and the second is 123 x 80 mm. Individual woodcuts (usually 60 x 75) represent the various people involved and the illustrations total 54, all of which are primitives. Nevertheless, in one picture with the title "If a person can become a hard rock, then can not the young woman Mary give an immaculate birth?" there is a nude female figure which is not badly drawn.

A second illustrated book that is attributed to Reyser by Hain is the first edition of [149] Verzückungen des Tondalus (42), which had 20 woodcuts and was later frequently reprinted. The title page illustration is larger than the others, and all the woodcuts are as crude as those of the Defensorium.

Reyser's printing of Missals played a more important role in the history of book illustration than did these two books with woodcuts, since his Missals were the earliest books in which copper engravings are found.

The first [150] Missale diocesis herbipolensis (43), which he printed in cooperation with Stephan Dold and Johann Beckenhub in 1479, has two copper engravings. The execution of the copper engravings is very clumsy and it appears to be the work of a goldsmith who took on the work of engraving.

In the second [151] Missale (44), which appeared in 1481 and which Reyser printed alone, the content of the copper plates is the same but the execution is better.

The third [152] Missale, which was done in 1484 (45), has copper plates of the same quality as the second edition, but the content is varied somewhat and at the bottom, center, it bears the initials, A. G. (Albrecht Glockendon).

This completes the information about the other cities that is available for the period up to the 1480's. They all ventured freely and surely into this field in the last fifteen years of the century.

Notes

1) Seelen, Nachricht von den Ursprungs und Fortgange der Buchdruckeri in Lübeck. 1740; Deecke, Nachrichten von dem 15. Jahrhundert in Lübeck gedruckte niedersächsischen Büchern. Lübeck. 1840; Welzenbach, Geschichte der Buchdruckerkunst in ehemaligen Herzogthume Franken. Würzburg. 1858; Becker, "Die mit Kupferstichen versehenen Missalen des ehemaligen Hochstifts Würzburg aus dem 15. Jahrhundert," in Naumann's Archiv f. d. zeichn. 2:184-89, 1856; Weigel and Zeitermann, Die Anfänge der Druckerkunst in Bild und Schrift.

2) s. l. e. a., Panzer, Suppl. 2, p. 13. Folio; Ebert, No. 2165; Kehrein, p. 37; Panzer, Literarische Nachricht von den allerältesten gedruckten deutschen Bibeln; p. 30 ff.

3) Hain, No. 9969.

4) Kalendarium novum quo promuntur coniunctiones verae atque oppositiones luminarum itemque ecclipses eorundem figuratae ac alla plurima scitu iucundissima. Roeder Catalog No. 457. Folio; Will Gelehrt. Lex. III:280, illus. by Essenwein, Pl. 82.

5) Hain, No. 15925.

6) Legende vom heil. Kind und Märtyrer Simon. s. a. Hain, No. 15658.

7) Hain, No. 14257.

8) s. a. Hain, No. 7205.

9) s. a. Hain, No. 7207.

10) s. a. Hain, No. 7209.

11) Nuremberg. 1479.

12) Nuremberg. 1479.

13) Nuremberg. 1479; Hain, No. 7214.

14) Nuremberg. 1479; Hain, No. 7215.

15) Nuremberg. 1480.

16) Kargenspiel; Nuremberg. 1480.

17) *Leben und Buss Adams und Evas.* Nuremberg. 1480.

18) s. l. e. a. Hain, No. 8930. 12 mo.; Ennen. *Katalog der Incunabeln der Stadtbibliothek zu Cöln.* No. 135.

19) *see* the article, "Fasciculus," by Hain.

20) Ennen, No. 223. Folio.

21) Ennen, No. 147. Folio.

22) Ennen, No. 221. Folio.

23) Ennen, No. 287. Folio.

24) Ennen, No. 288. Folio.

25) s. l. e. a. Hain, No. 14935.

26) Hain, No. 4996. Large Folio; Panzer 1:524, No. 1; Ebert, No. 19548.

27) Weigel und Zestermann v. 2. No. 525; German. Mus., No. 28263. Sixteen are copied by Essenwein in his "Holzschnitte des 14. und 15. Jahrhunderts in germanischen Museum." Weigel and Zesterman list 25 of the illustrations as metal and 119 as woodcuts; Hain, No. 4061 is the 1482 edition.

28) Hain, No. 14936; Panzer 1:85, No. 176 ff.; Stockmeyer und Reber, *Baseler Buchdruckergeschichte* p. 3, No. 4; Heinecken, *Idée générale*, p. 470.

29) Stockmeyer und Reber. p. 23, No. 8.

30) Stockmeyer. p. 24, No. 10.

31) Stockmeyer. p. 21, No. 3. Large Folio.

32) Hain, No. 3720.

33) Panzer 1:95. No. 73. Quarto; Zapf, *Buchdruckergeschichte Schwabens.* p. 164, No. 4; Hain, No. 11886.

34) Hain, No. 74.

35) Hain, No. 6664.

36) Panzer, No. 89.

37) Panzer, No. 98. Folio.

38) Panzer, No. 172. Folio. (Panzer falsely dates additional editions in 1477, 1478 and 1483).

39) Hain, No. 12819.

40) Hain, No. 4897.

41) Hain, No. 6084 and 6085.

42) Hain, No. 15540.

43) Hain, No. 11308.

44) Hain, No. 11309.

45) Hain, No. 11310.

Chapter V

AUGSBURG AFTER 1480 (1)

Augsburg, which exceeded all other cities in the number of illustrated books it produced in the 1470's, continued its great activity in this field in the last 20 years of the 15th Century.

Anton Sorg, who issued a large number of illustrated books in the first five years of his operations, achieved his truly great productivity in the last 20 years of the century.

In his (eighth) [153] German Bible of 1480 (2), which was the sixth illustrated edition, Sorg used the same initial cuts that adorned the editions of both the Zainers.

The edition [154] of 1480 of the Spiegel des Sünders (3) has a 115 x 90 mm woodcut on its title page.

His [155-159] Passion nach dem Text der vier Evangelisten of 1480 (4), of 1482 (5), of 1483 (6), 1486 (7) and 1491 (8) had 26 colored woodcuts (120 x 90), each with a red border. The text is always at the left, and the right side of the page is filled in with the illustration.

The 26 woodcuts of Sorg's second edition of [160-161] Otto von Passau's 24 Alten (9), which was first published in Bamberg by Sebastian Pfister around 1470, are different from those in the Pfister edition. Both of the first two illustrations are 180 x 120 mm, as in the first edition, but they differ substantially. The 24 smaller ones are 120 x 90 mm and the number of blocks is increased from two to six. The third edition, which Sorg issued in 1483 (10), was the same as the 1480 edition.

Sorg's 1480 edition [162] of Chronik by Jakob von Königshoven (11) has two full-page illustrations (195 x 120). They are almost as crude as those in the Bämler edition of 1476.

Sorg first printed [163-164] the Lebensbeschreibung Leupolds und seines Sohnes Herzogs Wilhelm von Oesterreich (12) and he reprinted it in 1491. It had 53 woodcuts (85 x 120). All of these blocks were prepared especially for this book and they are always captioned. These do not display any advance in style.

Sorg's 1481 printing of [165] Buch der Landfahrers Marcho Polo (13) had only a title page woodcut (180 x 112).

In addition, the year 1481 brought the first edition of a book that was to be frequently reprinted in later years. This was [166, Pl. 67-69] the Reise des englischen Ritters Moundeville ins heilige Land (14). The picture on the title page is 190 x 115 mm. Since the book is full of the most varied fables, the woodcuts are very naive in content. The illustrations in the book total 116, all of which are 75 x 80 mm; and only No. 97 occupies a full page (195 x 120). The woodcuts are all of the Augsburg school. The nude, when it occurs, is not badly handled.

Sorg's 1482 edition [167] of the Histori von der Zerstörung der Stadt Troia (15) is the fifth in the series of editions of this book. The illustrations are pretty much the same as those of the earlier editions except that here, for the first time, there is the full page illustration

(175 x 120) in which Hecuba, who bore Paris, sees a burning torch in a dream. Through the doorway there is a view of the burning houses of the town.

In 1482 there appeared, in addition, the 16 illuminated woodcuts in Heinrich Sufo's [168, Pl. 70-71] Der Seusse (16). Five of these fill the entire page and the others are the full width of the page and half its length.

Sorg's 1482 edition of [169] Lebens der Altväter (17) is the third in the series of its editions; both of the first two appeared without indication of place or year. It has 282 small, rectangular, illuminated woodcuts, which give characteristic scenes from the lives of the patriarchs. Their small size differentiates this edition clearly from the first two. Only the first illustration is 105 x 80 mm; the rest are all only 75 x 55 mm. There is no relationship between its illustrations and those of the earlier editions. In 1492 Sorg did [170] another edition of the book (18) in which he reused the old woodcuts.

In his [171] Buch der Natur, published in 1482 (19), he went back to Bämler. Only a single one of the 11 woodcuts, the capital initial for the chapter on rocks, is original.

Sorg's last 1482 publication was [172] Andreas Hispanus' Buch ovidii, die Liebe zu erwerben, auch die Liebe zu erschmehen. Von Dr. Hartlieb verteutscht (20). It has 14 (85 x 118) woodcuts which are among the most attractive of the woodcuts coming from Sorg's press. Sorg reprinted [173] this edition in 1484 (21).

Nevertheless, the year 1483, in which he published [174] Ulrich von Reichenthal's Beschreibung der Kostnitzer Concils (1414-1418) (22), was Sorg's most productive year. Not only does this set have reproductions of the coats of arms of all 1145 persons who had any relation to the Council, it also has 45 large illuminated woodcuts, most of which are full page.

In addition to this massive publication, Sorg published three other illustrated books in 1483:

The translation by Dr. Hartlieb, of Munich, [175] of the Historie des grossen Alexander nach Eusebius (23) had the familiar woodcuts of this frequently reprinted book.

The woodcuts in the second edition of the [176] Seelentrostes (24) were the same as those used in the first edition of 1478.

Those of his edition of the [177] Schachzabels (25) are like those of the first Zainer edition.

The [178] Himmelsstrasse (26), by Stephan Lanzkranna, which he published in 1484, has only a full page title illustration.

The [179] Auslegung der heiligen Messe (27), which was published in the same year, had two illuminated woodcuts, each of which occupied a full page.

When Peter Schöffer published the first edition of the small [180] Hortus sanitatis in Mainz on March 28, 1485, Sorg got out a reprint during the same year (28). While the size of the full page woodcut on leaf lb is identical to that on page lb of the Mainz edition, the scroll of Augsburg pine above and the shading show that it is a new woodcut. The woodcuts of the plants and animals are the same, mostly reversed, though some are cut without reversal; still, the drawings are often changed and the cutting is lighter. Most copies are illuminated.

None of Sorg's later works is illustrated with such charm as the Kostnitzer Concilienbuch.

The eleven woodcuts in the 1488 Sorg edition of [181] Bernhard von Breidenbach's Reise nach dem heiligen Land (29) are reduced and inferior copies of those in the original Mainz edition.

The woodcuts in his two editions [182-183] of the Plenarien in 1488 (30) and in 1493 (31) are no longer those in Zainer's edition of 1474 and Sorg's editions of 1478, 1480 and 1481, but are copied from those that first appeared in the Schobfer edition of 1487.

His [184] Horologium devotionis of 1489 (32) had 35 (87 x 58) woodcuts which were prepared for this edition and were all Augsburg products. However, they are very crude and are not comparable in quality to those produced in Creussner's Horologium at the same time.

In 1490 he printed the [185] Buch der natürlichen Weisheits (33) which had a full page title page illustration and 66 small woodcuts which were the width of a column.

In addition, the translation [186] of Boccaccio's Decameron (34) was issued in 1490. Here, too, there is a full page title page illustration while the 82 woodcuts in the text are only the width of one column. They are not important illustrations.

In 1491 there followed [187] the Geschichte des Wilhelm von Orlens (35), by Rudolph von Ems; in 1492 he published the second edition of [188] Alanus de Rupe's Psalter und Rosenkrans unserer lieben Frau (36), which had a number of small round carvings surrounded by a garland of roses. In 1493 [189] Imitatio Christi (37) was issued with a decorated title page woodcut.

The Augsburg tax records give an indication of the master who was responsible for the woodcuts emanating from the Sorg print shop. Anton Sorg was a member of a cardprinting family. His father, who was named Anton Sorg or Sorg Kartenmacher, appeared in the tax records under the location "vom Thor" in 1451; in 1464 he is listed as being at the guild hall and he lived there without interruption until 1492. In the later years he was entered as Anton Sorg, the elder, to differentiate him from his son Anton. He apparently died in 1492. Anton Sorg, the younger, the book printer, did not outlive his father very long, since his name appears in the tax records for the last time in 1494, and after that the records listed only a Jorg Sorg. Since the father and son lived during practically the same period, cooperative work may be assumed and it would appear that the elder, the cardprinter, supplied the woodcuts for his son's books.

During Sorg's time there were a number of smaller print shops operating in Augsburg. These, as a rule, borrowed the woodcuts they needed from the larger printers, especially Zainer and Sorg, but a number of them produced their own.

The first of these was Peter Berger. His 1488 edition of [190] Rodericus Zamorensis' Spiegel des menschlichen Lebens (38), was the fourth in the series of editions of this book. The illustrations go back to Zainer's.

The 213 colored woodcuts in the 1488 edition of [191] Leben des Altväters (39) are the same as those in the Sorg edition of 1482.

In 1489 he printed the sixth edition [192] of the Spiegels der menschlichen Behaltnis (40). This edition bears for the first time the 190 x 120 mm title page illustration, which appeared frequently in later editions, showing with five interlaced spheres. The woodcuts in the text are 95 x 75 mm and in general are newly copied from the edition done by Peter Drach at Speyer, but there are a few that are much older, which have the long slitlike eyes of the Augsburg school.

Berger's undated publication [193] Bruder Claus (41) has original woodcuts. The title page illustration is 63 x 95 mm, and in the book proper one illustration is 140 x 97 mm and six additional pictures illustrate charitable works. Then there is the final one, 140 x 115 mm. The drawings are very crude and awkward.

The second printer is Johann Blaubirer. His edition [194] of Buchs der Geschichte der grossen Alexanders (42) is third in the series of this book and it has the same illustrations as the earlier edition.

In 1481 he printed a [195-196] Kalender (43) with astrological notes and rules for health, which he republished in a new edition in 1483 (44), reusing the same woodcuts that had been published earlier in a s. l. e. a. calendar.

Herman Kästlin [197] produced the third edition of Lucidarius (45) in 1481 and in 1482 Thomas Rüger produced an edition of the [198] Vita Christi (46) with the usual illustrations.

More illustrated books produced by Johann Schobser are available. He published, undated, the second German edition of the book first published by Reyser in Würzburg [199] the Verzückungen des Tondalus (47). While the 20 (60 x 82) woodcuts illustrate the same things as in the Reyser edition, they were produced anew and belong to the Augsburg school.

[200-201] Schobser's 1485 edition of the Historie des-grossen Alexanders nach Eusebius is the seventh in the series and his edition of 1487 is its eighth publication.

He published [202-204] Evengelienbücher three times: in 1487 (48), in 1490 (49), and in 1497 (50). The 1487 edition is the eleventh in the series of this book and it is very different from the earlier editions. It is begun with a very good (190 x 130) title page illustration of Christ on the Cross. The other 54 woodcuts are 70 x 60 mm and they are not copies of the earlier editions, but are much finer and are frequently shaded. The illustration of the three kings worshiping the Child is particularly charming.

In 1488 he produced the eighth edition [205] of Meister Elucidarius (51) and he reused the same five blocks that appear in the earlier editions.

The [206] Walfart oder bilgerung unser lieben Frauwen (52), printed in 1489, is the second German translation of this book which was first published in Ulm by Johann Reger under the title Itinerarium beate marie virginis. The many good woodcuts are copies of those in the Ulm edition.

In 1490 Schobser published the third edition [207] of Versehung von Leib, Seel Ehre und Gut. This first appeared s. l. e. a., and then was published in Nuremberg in 1489 (53). The woodcut for the title page (135 x 98) is the same in content as that in the Nuremberg edition. Nevertheless there are differences. In this edition the dead man is on the left instead of on the right as in the Nuremberg edition, and the 1490 edition does not have the maidservant coming in the door.

In 1490 Schobser published, under the title [208] Red und Widerred (54), the second German edition of the widely read popular novel Salomon und Marcolph. The woodcuts are not those that appeared in the first Latin edition, which appeared s. l. e. a., but were produced anew. The title page illustration is 120 x 85 mm and most of the others are 57 x 85 mm, with a few occupying a full page. Altogether it has fifteen woodcuts, which are all crude.

In 1494, Schobser's edition of the [209-210] Heiligenlebens (55) contained woodcuts identical with those in Sorg's edition. This was followed in 1496 by the Büchlein von Melibeus und Prudentia (56).

About this time Hans Sittich issued, sans date, [211, Pl. 74] his Ringenbüchlein (57) which, with its 21 full page woodcuts (185 x 130), advanced the art. In one case, on No. 11, there apears on the trousers a capital A with a horizontal stroke over the Ā, and this may be the artist's monogram. The woodcuts are well done, and they could have been done towards the late 1480's.

The printer Hans Schauer produced seven illustrated books. The [212] Probleumata Aristotelis tütsch (58), which he printed in 1493, has an illustration under the title that shows a teacher with a student sitting before him.

The [213] Büchlein der Lehre des Haushaltens (59) which appeared in 1494, has on the verso of the title page a 115 x 90 mm woodcut. The woodcut is soundly executed and is very interesting because of the various mechanical devices it illustrates.

In 1496 Grünbeck's [214] Tractat von dem Ursprung des bösen Franzos (60) has a title page illustration of Mary with the Child and this illustration is repeated on the verso of the title page.

Also in 1496, Schauer published [215] Vocabula pro penitentibus (61) with a 125 x 85 mm illustration on the title page, which is also repeated on the verso.

The woodcuts in Schauer's [216] Kalender of 1496 (62) are those that had been used by Blaubirer in 1481 and 1483.

[217] The Danielis somniorum expositoris veridici libri (63), which he published in 1497, has one (120 x 84) woodcut illustration.

His publication of Metlinger's [218] Regiment der jungen Kinder (64) in 1500 has a title page illustration, which, however, had appeared earlier elsewhere.

More illustrated books by Lucas Zeissenmair are available. His undated edition [219] of Chronik vom Berge Andechs (65) is the third edition of this book. Its title page woodcut is similar to the one that was used by Bämler in his edition.

His 1494 edition of [220] Tondalus (66) is the third German edition of this work; the illustrations are the same as those in the Schobser edition.

In 1495 he published the fourth edition of [221] Alanus de Rupe's Psalter und Rosenkranz unserer lieben Frau (67), in which he used the title page illustration from the Ulm edition and the remaining pictures from the Sorg edition. In the same year he did an edition of [222] Spiegel des Sünders (68) using the same title page illustration as appeared in the Sorg and Schoensperger editions.

In 1497 he printed [223] Kaiser Sigmunds Reformation (69) in which he reused the woodcuts that Bämler had used.

In 1499 he followed this with [224] Geiler von Kaissersperg's Predigt vom Pilgrim (70) which has eighteen (77 x 77) very primitive woodcuts, of which six are repeated.

[225] Jämmerlich und erschrockenen Klag eines weltlichen sündigen sterbenden Menschen (71), which has a picture on the title page, was printed by Zeissenmair in 1501.

He produced an edition of [226] Lanzkranna's Himmelsstrass (72) in 1501. Its title page woodcut is different from that of the Sorg edition of 1484.

His 1501 edition of [227] Savonarola's Beschauliche Betrachtungen (73) has a title page illustration, 100 x 90 mm, which is divided into two parts. It is well shaded and is pertinent to the text.

His 1502 publications were [228-229] Himmlische Offenbarung St. Brigittae (74), with two illustrations, and the Psalter unserer lieben Frauen (75) with five woodcuts.

Zeissenmair then moved to Wessosprunn, where he continued to be productive.

While Johann Froschauer must be counted as a sixteenth century printer in terms of dates, in terms of style his book illustrations belong in the 1480's.

His work started with two undated folio sheets [230-231] of which one is a Gebet (76) and has a title woodcut of Mary and the Child; the woodcut of the other, the Gedichtes auf St. Sebastian (77), shows an archery range with a saint tied to a tree.

Froschauer produced the third and fourth editions [232-233] of the Historie von St. Brandon in 1497 (78) and 1498 (79). The woodcuts differ only slightly from those in the original Sorg edition. Only numbers 2, 4 and 6 were prepared anew for these editions.

His [234] Regimen Sanitatis (80) of 1502 has the title page woodcut that had previously been often used for this book. His editions [235-236] of the German Kalenders of 1502 (81) and 1510 (82) contained a title page woodcut and the familiar 46 larger and 34 smaller calendar woodcuts.

In 1503 he issued the third edition [237] of the Buchs von der Kindheit unseres Herrn (83), which had first been published by Sorg in 1478, and he reused Sorg's old woodcuts.

His edition of [238] Aesopus in 1504 (84) had the woodcuts that appeared in the original Ulm edition, and he also repeated the Ulm title page woodcut in his edition of [239] De fide concubinarum (85), by Wimpfeling, which he issued in 1505.

In Valzen's [240] Himmlischer Fundgrube (86), which he printed in 1506, the title page woodcut he used was from an earlier work.

He produced editions [241-242] of Maister Elucidarius in 1507 (87) and 1509 (88), in which the woodcuts are repeated from earlier editions.

In the other three books that he published in 1507 [243-245], Trostspiegel (89) has a crude title page woodcut and the same is true of Küchenmeisterei (90) and Talat's Arzneibüchlein (91).

In 1508 he produced an edition of [246] Verzückungen des Tondalus (92), which he repeated [247] in 1515 (93). In both of these he used old woodcuts that had been used to the point where they were practically unrecognizable, touching them up a bit.

The title page picture and the 27 smaller woodcuts in his [248] Deutschen Passion of 1509 (94), similarly, are to be found thirty years earlier.

To these Augsburg publications we must add a few illustrated works whose publisher has not been identified.

In 1484 there appeared [249] Wie lang die kaiserlich Stadt Augsburg vor langen jahren ihre Ursprung und Anfang gehabt (95). The 145 x 98 mm title page woodcut shows the towers of the city. This is followed by a number of (70 x 70) woodcuts of the martyrs, etc. These are very crude.

In 1484 [250] the tenth edition of the Lebens der Heiligen (96) appeared without the name of its printer.

The first edition of the [251] Geschichte von Pontus und Sido (97) appeared in 1488. It has forty-six 75 x 128 mm woodcuts, all of which are of the Augsburg school.

In the 1491 and 1494 editions [252-253] of Versehung des Leibs (98), there is an illustration of the God-Father on the verso of the title page. In addition, before each month there is a woodcut that presents what is supposed to occur during that period.

The printing plant of Hans Schoensperger the Elder, which was founded in 1481 and achieved very great fame during the 16th century, was not any more distinguished than any of the smaller printers named above during the fifteenth century. Furthermore Schoensperger practically never produced an independently illustrated book; rather, he almost always depended upon the work of his predecessors, whether from Augsburg or elsewhere.

After the [254-257] undated appearance of the Leben Christi (99), the first illustrated book he issued was the 1481 edition (100) of the Sieben weisen Meister, which he reprinted in 1486 (101) and again in 1497. His editions are the fifth, sixth, and seventh in the series of editions of this work. The woodcuts were those used from the very beginning of this book; only numbers 21 and 43 can be differentiated from the older ones since their size is different (87 x 117) and they were done by another hand, which belonged to the Strassburg school rather than to Augsburg. Their shading is better and they are newer than the others.

The [258] Plenarium which he printed in 1481 (102), in cooperation with Thomas Ruger, had a title page woodcut (190 x 120) which he used repeatedly in later works. The 54 woodcuts in the text are 80 x 100 mm in the Schoensperger edition, and are, therefore, not copies taken from earlier editions. In general they are similar to those that Sorg used but differ in size. Their source is uncertain. Even though they were all the same size, all of them appear to have been used previously in various books. Many have fine shading and fine cutting that is reminiscent of the Ulm products, while others are cruder than those in the Zainer edition of 1474. In his later editions of [259-262] Plenarium in 1483 (103), 1489 (104), 1493 (105), and 1498 (106), Schoensperger reused these illustrations.

In 1482 he published the second edition of [263] Reise des Ritters Montevilla (107), which was first published by Sorg in 1481. His edition lacks the title page illustration which appears in the Sorg edition and also lacks Sorg's full page illustration of the Khan of Cathay sitting at the table with his wives. The other 114 illustrations are not the size of those in the Sorg edition (75 x 80) but are 80 x 60 mm. Nevertheless, they are copied from the Sorg edition.

He also printed [264-268] an edition of Leben der Heiligen in 1482 (108) which he reprinted in 1489 (109), 1494 (110), 1496 (111), and 1499 (112). His editions are the ninth, fourteenth, fifteenth, seventeenth and eighteenth of the series of editions of this book, and they differ considerably from the earlier editions. The title page illustration, to cite one example, is divided into two parts and is 195 x 130 mm. All the text woodcuts are narrower than those of the earlier editions (82 x 62) which made them the width of the column of text and made Schoensperger's format easier to produce.

The woodcuts in his 1482 edition (113) of [269] Buchs der Natur are like those in the Bämler edition.

In 1482 he also published [270] the Spiegel des Sünders (114) which was a copy of the Zainer edition of 1470. It is headed by a crude woodcut.

The last book that he published in 1482 [271] was the second edition of the Kindheit unseres Herrn which was published by Sorg in 1476.

In 1483 he first printed [272-274] the Passion (115), which he repeated in two editions in 1498 (116).

His 1484 edition of [275] Buchs der Beispiele des alten Weisen (117) is fifth in the series of editions of this book. It has the same scenes that illustrated the first edition done at Ulm, but the woodcuts are changed freely in content and in style. The title page illustration (188 x 115) is much the same in content as that of the Ulm edition. The other woodcuts are 85 x 120 mm and are the products of various hands. Only those that are cut roughly, accenting the outlines and with slight use of shading, are Augsburg products. The finer illustrations, especially the title page, appear to be the product of a Basle engraver.

Editions of [276-277] Meister Elucidarius were produced by Schoensperger in 1484 (118) and in 1491 (119), using the woodcuts that had been used earlier.

The [278-280] Seelenwurzgarten, which was published by Conrad Dinkmuth in Ulm in 1483, was reprinted by Schoensperger three times: in 1484 (120), in 1488 (121), and in 1496 (122). The title page illustration (192 x 125) was copied from the Ulm edition. The other 42 woodcuts are smaller (82 x 120) and vary considerably from those of the Ulm edition. The woodcuts appear to have been prepared for these editions and are better than the general Augsburg products of their time. The 1488 edition corresponds to the 1484 edition throughout and there appears to have been only one new woodcut (188 x 120) prepared for the 1496 edition; this was its title page illustration.

The smaller [281-286] Hortus sanitatis, which was first produced by Peter Schöfter in Mainz in 1485, and was also issued in that same year by Sorg in Augsburg, was printed six times by Hans Schoensperger: in 1486 (123), 1487 (124), 1488 (125), 1493 (126), 1496 (127), and 1499 (128). The full page woodcut illustration on the verso of the title page shows the same figures as in the title page illustration of the Mainz original and the Sorg editions, but in reversed order. The text woodcuts are smaller and poorer than those of the Mainz edition. The reader is referred to Choulant for the slight differences that appeared in the illustrations of Schoensperger's six editions.

The 108 woodcuts in Schoensperger's [287-288] Deutschen Bibelausgaben of 1487 and 1490 (129) are reduced copies of those found in the Cologne edition. They are two columns wide and not quite half a page high. The closing woodcuts of the first and second volumes bear the Monogram Hb, which is not in the Cologne Bible and can refer only to the artist who drew and reduced the woodcuts for Schoensperger's editions. Nagler, Mon. III:653, attempts to attribute these to Hans Bämler. However, since the monogram did not appear in any of Bämler's publications, which is the place they should be sought first, this finding is very improbable.

Schoensperger's editions of [289-291] Belial in 1487 (130), 1490 (131), and 1493 (132) are the ninth, tenth and twelfth of the series of editions of this book. The 37 woodcuts are reduced copies of those used by Zainer. They are 62 x 82 mm. The only full page illustration appears on the verso of the title page. As compared with the Zainer originals these woodcuts represent a backward step, and what Zainer achieved 13 years earlier by loving devotion was lost in these later editions through routine manual work.

In the three [292-294] calendars which he produced in 1487 (133), 1490 (134), and 1492 (135) under the title, Ein Buch von den 12 Monaten, 12 Zeichen des Gestirns und ihrer Kraft, von den 7 Planeten, von den 7 Temperamenten, vom Adlerlassen, von den 4 Winden, the woodcuts are all the same as those in the first calendar, which appeared without place or date around 1479, and in the calendar that Blaubirer printed in 1481.

In 1488 he produced his first edition of the [295] Reformation der Statuten und Gesetze der Stadt Nürnberg (136), which had first been published by Koburger in Nuremberg in 1484. The title page woodcut (185 x 115) is just a reduced copy of the one in the Nuremberg edition. Before the index one finds the same coat of arms and, below that, a view of the city of Nuremberg. In the second printing [296] which Schoensperger issued in 1498 (137) the woodcuts are the same.

Also in 1488, he printed a second edition of the [297] Geschichte von Pontus und Sido, the first edition of which had appeared in 1485 without the name of the printer, and he used the same woodcuts (138).

The [298] Histori von der Zerstörung der Stadt Troia, which he also issued in 1488 (139), is the sixth edition of this book. The content of the 93 illustrations is the same as those in the Bämler edition of 1474, except that the style was reworked and improved. One of these, which is differentiated from the others by its size (90 x 120) is completely new. It is so freshly conceived and so simply executed that it may be considered among the best that were produced during this century.

The book Summa, by Johannes Friburgensis, [299-300] which was first printed by Bämler in 1472, was produced by Schoensperger in 1489 and 1495 (140). The title page illustration (190 x 120) shows care in production of the woodcut.

His 1491 edition of [301-303] Buch des hochberühmten Fabeldichters Aesopis (141) was followed by his new editions of 1496 (142) and 1498 (143). The Schoensperger editions are the ninth, tenth, and eleventh in the series of editions of this book. Its title page illustration goes back to the Ulm original edition. So far as the rest of the illustrations are concerned, the woodcuts are all either exact or reversed copies of older ones. A few of the woodblocks are so worn that they are unrecognizable. The Ulm origin of these books can not be denied even in this bad presentation.

His last work to appear in 1491 [304, Pl. 72 & 73] is Das Heldenbuch oder der Wolfdieterich (144). It is a combination of a number of parts. The first poem treats of the sea voyage of Kaiser Otnit, and it has twenty 57 x 65 mm woodcuts. This first poem is followed by the much larger Wolfdieterich, which is illustrated by 146 woodcuts. The third poem treats the Rosengarten zu Worms. The title page illustration (86 x 120) presents the queen of Worms with her two sons and daughters, and there are 41 woodcuts in the text. The closing poem, which is the Rosengarten König Laurin's, has a title page woodcut that is 89 x 122 mm and there are 18 small woodcuts in the poem. The entire book contains 222 illustrations.

Schoensperger's 1492 edition (145) of the [305] Spiegels menschlicher Behaltniss is the eighth in the series of editions of this work. The content of the woodcuts in this edition is the same as that of the earlier editions but they are smaller and poorer in quality. These illustrations are 82 x 62 mm and they are reduced versions, some reversed, of those in Drach's edition. The number of illustrations is the same as in Drach's Speier edition.

In 1493 he published the copiously illustrated [306] Ritterlichen Thaten des edlen Wigoleis vom Rade oder mit dem Rade (146).

In 1493 Schoensperger also published [307] the Versehung von Leib, Seel, Ehre, und Gut (147), which had illustrations that had been used in earlier editions.

When Brant issued his Narrenschiff in Basel in 1494, Schoensperger promptly came out with a reproduction of it in octavo [308] in 1495 (148), in which he repeated the 114 woodcuts of the original work, but in reduced size.

The [309-311] Schedel'sche Weltchronik, which was published by Koburger in Nuremberg in 1493, was reprinted three times by Schoensperger: in 1496 and 1500 in German (149) and in 1497 in Latin (150). Here, too, the illustrations are smaller and are not as good as those of the Nuremberg edition, and there was very little significant change in them.

His 1497 edition [312] of Cato cum glosa et moralisatione (151) contains the woodcut of the teacher and two students with the inscription, "Accipies tanti doctoris dogmata sancti," which Moser has discussed (152). Nevertheless the woodblock is different from those used by other printers. The same woodcut is found in [313] Regulae grammaticales antiquorum cum earundem declarationibus (153) which Schoensperger published without date, and which also appeared in three books published without location, which Moser believes are Schoensperger publications because of the similarity of the type faces. These are [314-316]: 1) Esopus moralisatus cum bono commento, of 1497, which is falsely attributed to Heinrich Quentel in Cologne by Panzer, 1:315, No. 287, and by Hain, No. 316; 2) Elegantiarum viginti praeccepta, of 1497, which is listed by Hain, No. 6575 as s.l., quarto; and 3) Secreta mulierum ab Alberto magno composita, which is listed by Hain, No. 557 as s.l.e.a.

The 51 small (65 x 54) woodcuts in [317] Postila Guilielmi super epistolas et evangelia (154), which Schoensperger also printed in 1497, belong to a much earlier period. The full page title page illustration appears to be new.

When, in 1497, Grüninger in Strassburg printed [318] Hieronymus Brunschweig's Buch der Chirurgia it was once again Schoensperger who produced a reprint immediately (155). The many woodcuts are good copies of the Strassburg edition. The skeleton reproduced in the Strassburg edition is lacking.

His 1497 edition of [319] Buchs der Kunst geistlich zu werden (156) contains the woodcuts that Bämler had used.

The [320] Leben der Altväters (157), which Schoensperger printed in 1497, is the sixth in the series of editions of this work. He added a 190 x 120 mm title page woodcut which is attractive. Aside from that he changed the larger Sorg illustration of Hieronymus in his study and reduced its size to 75 x 60 mm. The rest of the woodcuts are taken from Sorg's 1482 edition.

The title page illustration of [321] Imitatio Christi, which he published in 1498 (158), is the same as the one that Sorg had used in his 1493 edition. In 1498 he also copied the [322] Ritter vom Turm (159), which had first been published by Furter in Basel.

The edition of [323] Conrad von Megenberg's Buch der Natur, which Schoensperger issued in 1499 (160), is sixth in the series of editions of this work. It has 14 illustrations as compared with 12 in its predecessors; however, the first two of these have little relation to the book. The title page illustration was taken from Brunschweig's Chirurgia of 1497. The second illustration also comes from that source. The 12 that belong with the Buch der Natur, aside from a few slight changes in the sketching, are a few mm taller and wider than those of the older editions. The drawing is, in general, better than the cutting, and is at its best in numbers 1, 3, 6, 8, 11 and 12, in which the expressions are lifelike and the scenes are true to nature.

At the very close of the century he produced, undated, the second edition of Bämler's 1473 production of [324] Chronik vom Berge Andechs (161). The woodcut on folio 2a is different from that in Bämler's edition, as are those on folio 2b and on the last page.

This review indicates that Schoensperger's performance in the fifteenth century does not give any indication of the heights to which his printing house would soar in the second decade of the sixteenth century. In this earlier period he practically confined his work to reprinting of older works, and in the process turned the good woodcuts of the earlier editions into bad copies, and among the larger Augsburg printers of the fifteenth century he was certainly the least important. Zainer printed the Spiegel menschlichen Lebens and the Belial; Bämler produced Konigshoven's Chronik and the Buch der Natur; Sorg gave us the Costnizer Concilienbuch. In the case of Schoensperger, one searches in vain for a single independently produced book with illustrations that were up to the standard of the times.

The story of Augsburg book illustration in the fifteenth century is completed with Erhard Ratdolt. He was a member of an Augsburg family and his father, who was also named Erhard, first appeared in the city tax records in 1439. Erhard and his brother lived in their father's house until 1474. From 1475 to 1485 he is not listed in the tax records because during this time he was in Venice. There, in cooperation with Peter Loslein from Langenzenn and Bernhard Pictor from Augsburg, he established a press. He reappeared in the Augsburg tax records in 1486 and lived there for 20 years. He apparently died in 1528, since in that year the tax for the Erhard Ratdolt family was paid by his son Jorg (162).

The evidence at hand indicates that Ratdolt played a greater role in book ornamentation than he did in the history of book illustration. He had purchased his printing equipment in Venice and worked with it after his return to Augsburg. As a result his type faces and his initial ornaments and his special ornaments were quite different from those customary in Augsburg. On the other hand, he had no Italian artists to illustrate his books and he turned to local artists for his book illustrations. But here too he used only the best.

Some of his books published in Venice, perhaps illustrated under the guidance of his comrade Bernhard Pictor, showed up well against their contemporaries.

A book printed by him in Venice in 1483, [325] Breviarium Benedictinum (163), had pictures of the saints and other figures as well as gilded initial letters.

His 1484 and 1485 editions published in Venice of [326-327] Werner Rolevink's Fasciculus temporum (164) are the fourteenth and fifteenth in the series of this famous publication and are differentiated from the others by their more abundant and better pictures of cities.

The [328] Poeticon Astronomicon by Hyginus (165), which he produced in Venice in 1485, has 46 star maps and planets, done by a very original master.

> Translator's note. It is difficult to understand why Dr. Muther chose to begin his list of illustrated books produced by Ratdolt in Venice, with a 1483 publication, disregarding one of Ratdolt's most important contributions to book illustration, Euclid's Elementa, which which he published in Venice on May 25, 1482. In this work he first solved the technical problems of producing the essential marginal diagrams together with the text, which had hitherto prevented the printing of Euclid. This was a giant step forward in book illustration. Douglas McMurtrie, in The Book (Oxford University Press, 1943, p. 283-285), says of the Euclid, "The result of Ratdolt's effort was not only successful, but brilliant." A page of the Euclid is reproduced on p. 285 of McMurtrie. S. H. Steinberg, Five Hundred Years of Printing (London, Penguin, 1955, p. 54), says, "The ornamentation of books ... reached a height, rarely surpassed, in the prints of Erhard Ratdolt. When he returned to his birthplace in 1486, he had already gained renown as a printer in Venice where, among his other books, the first edition of Euclid's Elementa Geometrica (1482) stands to his credit...." The Euclid is included in the Catalogue of an Exhibition of Fine Printing at the British Museum, London, 1963, in which it is item 23. The annotation states: "... Ratdolt here solves the technical problem of producing the essential marginal diagrams together with the text, which had hitherto prevented the printing of Euclid. ... Ratdolt ... was one of the most original and accomplished of the early printers."

The first illustrated book produced by Ratdolt after his return to Augsburg [329, Pl. 75-78] was Chronica Hungariae, by Johannes de Thwrocz, which had 66 illuminated woodcuts and was issued in 1488 (166). It is of little importance. Two woodcuts are page size. Of the 64 smaller illustrations the three best are: the crowning of Stephan, the first King of Hungary, by angels; Saint Ladislaus riding on an armored horse; and Queen Maria sitting on the throne.

The [330-332] Kalendarium of Regimontanus, of which he issued undated editions in 1489 and 1496 (167), had only astronomical woodcuts.

In 1490 [333] Ratdolt printed the Ars oratoris ars epistolaris et ars memoriae, by Jacobus Publicius (168). This contains two woodcuts that should be mentioned, one of a nude man and one of a nude woman, which are supposed to show the difference between the bodies of man and woman.

In 1495 he followed this with [334] the Evangelienbuch, with the woodcuts that are usually used in this work (169).

The best illustrations found in books printed by Ratdolt are in a few ecclesiastical works.

His [335] Missale Augustanum (170), published in 1491, has on the verso of the first sheet an illuminated title page woodcut.

His [336] Breviarum Frisingense of 1491 (171) has on the verso of the title page a (130 x 80) illustration. The intellectual appearance is produced well, but the hands and legs of the child are quite primitive.

His [337-338] Breviarium Augustanum, which he printed in 1493 (172) and reprinted in 1495 (173), has the same full page title page woodcut at the beginning of each of the two parts, and it is similar to one used in his Missale of 1491. The execution of the faces and of the broad folds of the clothing are especially attractive in this woodcut.

Ratdolt's [339-340] Missale Pataviense of 1494 (174) and 1498 (175) have two woodcuts. The first one (260 x 165) appears before the title page and the second one comes after the Scriptural Canons; it is 250 x 160 mm. Both of these, and especially the latter, are very well done.

The title page woodcut of the non-ecclesiastical work, [341] Buch der Lehenrecht (176), by Jodoc Pflanzmann, which is 197 x 133 mm, is equally good.

In his [342] Breviarium Ratisbonense of 1496 (177) he has a title page woodcut that is 120 x 80 mm.

In his 1505 printing of [343] Missale Constantiense, he provides another very attractive woodcut, which is 250 x 160 mm.

The title page illustration of his 1510 [344] Missale Augustanum nuper accuratissime emendatum (178), on the other hand, is simply a repetition of the Missale issued in 1491, except that the escutcheon of Bishop Friedrich von Zollen is, in the 1505 edition, interchanged with that of Bishop Heinrich IV von Liechtenau. Weigel, who attributes the composition to Hans Holbein the younger, did not apparently think of the fact that it had already been published in 1491. Since Nagler (Monogrammisten III:1038) attributes it to Hans Holbein, the elder, the matter is still unresolved.

In any event, one must believe that a very important master was involved in the production of this last mentioned woodcut, and it shows signs of the heights that were to be achieved in the next 20 years because of Kaiser Maximillian's love of art and the genius of Hans Burgkmair (179).

Notes

1) See the literature listed in note 1 of Chapter II.

2) Hain, No. 3136; Muther, Deutscher Bilderbibeln, No. 6.

3) Hain, No. 2740.

4) Hain, No. 12441.

5) Hain, No. 12442.

6) Hain, No. 12444.

7) Hain, No. 12445.

8) Hain, No. 12447.

9) Hain, No. 12128.

10) Hain, No. 12129.

11) Hain, No. 9793. Folio.

12) Hain, II No. 3245.

13) Hain, No. 10041.

14) Hain, No. 10647. Folio.

15) Hain, No. 5516.

16) Panzer 1:124. No. 144.

17) Hain, No. 8605. Folio.

18) Hain, No. 8607.

19) The fifth in the series of editions of the book; Panzer 1:126, supplement 47; Zapf 1:60; Hain, No. 4045; Choulant, p. 308, no. 5.

20) Hain, No. 994. Folio; Panzer 1:131, No. 163.

21) Panzer 1:154, No. 213; Hain, No. 995.

22) Ebert, No. 5083. Folio; Hain I, part 2, p. 187, No. 5610; Panzer 1:142, No. 187 and supplement, p. 50, No. 187; Zapf, p. 65; Vogt, p. 266.

23) Hain, No. 789.

24) Ebert, No. 23133. Folio; Hain II, part 2, p. 305, No. 14583; Panzer 1:139, No. 177; two pages copied by Essenwein, Plate 103.

25) Hain, No. 4896.

26) Panzer, 1:146. Folio; Not in Hain; see Murr, Journal II, p. 347; Zapf 1:72; Graesse 3:280.

27) Hain Pt. I, 1:268, No. 2144. Folio; Panzer 1:144, No. 193.

28) Hain, No. 8949. Folio; Pritzel, No. 11885; Choulant, p. 243, No. 2.

29) Hain, No. 3960.

30) Hain, No. 6737.

31) Hain, No. 6741.

32) Hain, No. 8935.

33) Hain, No. 4047; Panzer 1:18, No. 288.

34) Hain, No. 3281.

35) Not found in bibliographical works.

36) Hain, No. 14040.

37) Hain, No. 9117.

38) Hain, No. 13950.

39) Hain, No. 8606. Folio; Panzer 1:171, No. 255; Six illustrations copied by Essenwein on Plate 102.

40) Hain, No. 14937.

41) Hain, No. 5379.

42) Hain, No. 787.

43) Hain, No. 9731. Quarto; Literar. Museum II:271.

44) Hain, No. 9735.

45) Hain, No. 8805.

46) Hain, No. 4059.

47) Hain, No. 15544.

48) Hain, No. 6735.

49) Hain, No. 6739.

50) Hain, No. 6744.

51) Hain, No. 8811.

52) Weigel, No. 8503. Quarto. Hain, No. 9326.

53) Panzer 1:186, No. 298.

54) Panzer 1:187, No. 303.

55) Hain, No. 9984; Meusel, Neueste Literatur der Geschichtskunde II:89.

56) Hain, No. 11050.

57) Hain, No. 13916.

58) Panzer 1:206, No. 362.

59) Panzer 1:211, No. 378, Quarto; Hain, Part 1, 1:374, No. 2878.

60) Heller, Serapeum 4:303 (Bamberg Library); Quarto.

61) Not found in bibliographical works in Munich.

62) Hain, No. 9747.

63) Hain, No. 5928.

64) Weller, No. 159.

65) Hain, No. 970.

66) Hain, No. 15545, Quarto; Panzer 1:212, No. 385.

67) Hain, No. 14043.

68) Hain, No. 14951.

69) Hain, No. 14730.

70) Hain, Part II, 1:215, No. 9767, Quarto; Panzer 1:238, No. 467; According to Hain, No. 9766 an edition, without location, appeared as early as 1494.

71) Panzer 1:252, No. 511.

72) Panzer 1:251, No. 516; Geffcken, Bilderkatechismus, Supplement, p. 106.

73) Panzer 1:244, No. 488.

74) Weller, No. 214.

75) Weller, No. 32.

76) Weller, No. 85.

77) Hain, No. 3721.

78) Hain, No. 3722.

79) Weller, No. 240.

80) Panzer 1:258.

81) Weller, No. 231.

82) Panzer 1:326.

83) Panzer 1:260.

84) Panzer 1:267, No. 552.

85) Weller, No. 4070.

86) Weller, No. 353.

87) Weller, No. 4086.

88) Weller, No. 4086.

89) Weller, No. 393.

90) Weller, No. 394.

91) Weller, No. 416.

92) Panzer 1:291.

93) Weller, No. 954.

94) Weller, No. 505.

95) Hain, No. 1942.

96) Hain, No. 9978.

97) Hain, No. 13288.

98) Panzer 1:191, No. 322. Octavo.

99) Hain, No. 10007.

100) Panzer 1:122.

101) Panzer 1:163, No. 233.

102) Hain, No. 6730.

103) Hain, No. 6732.

104) Hain, No. 6738.

105) Hain, No. 6742.

106) Hain, No. 6744.

107) Hain, No. 10648.

108) Hain, No. 9977.

109) Hain, No. 9982.

110) Hain, No. 9983.

111) Hain, No. 9985.

112) Hain, No. 9987.

113) Fourth edition; Panzer I:126. Folio; Ebert, No. 3092; Hain, No. 4044; Choulant, p. 307, No. 4.

114) Hain, No. 14948. Quarto. Geffcken, Bilderkatechismus, Supplement, p. 48.

115) Hain, No. 12444.

116) Hain, No. 12448 and 12449.

117) Hain, No. 4032.

118) Hain, No. 8808.

119) Hain, No. 8811.

120) Hain, No. 14585. Folio.

121) Hain, No. 14586. Folio.

122) Hain, No. 14587. Folio.

123) Hain, No. 8951. Folio; Pritzel, No. 11887; Choulant, p. 245, No. 6.

124) Panzer 1:166; Trew, Catalogue II, No. 4, item 19; Choulant, p. 245, No. 7.

125) Trew, Catalogue II, No. 4, item 3. Folio; Panzer 1:174; Hain, No. 8953; Pritzel, No. 11889.

126) Hain, No. 8954. Folio; Pritzel, No. 11890; Choulant, p. 246, No. 11.

127) Hain, No. 8955. Folio; Pritzel, No. 11891; Choulant, p. 247, No. 12; Weigel, No. 18413.

128) Panzer 1:240. Folio; Hain, No. 8956; Pritzel, No. 11892; Choulant, p. 247, No. 13.

129) Panzer 1:182, No. 285; Muther, Deutsche Bilderbibeln, No. 10 and 11.

130) Panzer 1:252. Folio.

131) Panzer 1:287. Folio.

132) Panzer 1:346. Folio.

133) Hain, No. 9738.

134) Hain, No. 9743.

135) Hain, No. 9745; The last edition appeared in 1498.

136) Hain, No. 13717.

137) Hain II, p. 195, No. 13718; Panzer 1:233, No. 452; Will, Part I, 2:34, No. 954.

138) Hain, No. 13289.

139) Hain, No. 5517.

140) Hain, No. 338. Folio.

141) Hain, No. 339. Folio.

142) Hain, No. 340. Folio.

143) Hain, No. 8420.

144) Hain, No. 7376.

145) Hain, No. 14939; Panzer 1:193, No. 329; Heinecken, Idée générale, p. 473; Zapf 1:104.

146) Hain, No. 16161.

147) Hain, No. 16021.

148) Hain, No. 3744.

149) Moser, the woodcut with the inscription, "Accipies tanti doctoris dogmata sancti." Serapeum 4:252.

150) Hain, No. 14511 and 14512. Folio; Panzer, Annales typ. 1:125, No. 155; Ebert, No. 4147; Zapf 1:120; Hupsauer, Druckstücke aus dem 15. Jahrhundert. Augsburg, 1794. p. 191; Brunet, ed. 5, 1:1860; Graesse II:139.

151) Hain, No. 14509; Weigel, No. 8506.

152) Hain, No. 4736.

153) Hain, No. 13839.

154) Hain, No. 8296.

155) Panzer 1:227. Folio; Hain, No. 4019; Choulant, p. 268, No. 4; Weigel, No. 21114.

156) Hain, No. 4039.

157) Hain, No. 8608.

158) Hain, No. 9118.

159) Hain, No. 15515.

160) Panzer 1:240, Supplement 88. Folio; Zapf 1:130; Ebert, No. 3092; Hain, No. 4046; Choulant, p. 308, No. 6.

161) Hain, No. 969.

162) Excerpt from the Augsburg tax records.

163) Hain, No. 3803.

164) Hain, No. 6928. Folio; Panzer, Annales typogr. 3:161; Ebert, No. 7357; Zapf 1:157; Weigel, No. 8562.

165) Ebert, No. 10428; Hain, Part II, 1:116, No. 9063; Panzer 3:214, No. 830; 12 are copied by Essenwein on plages 106-107.

166) Hain, No. 15518. Quarto; Zapf 1:84; Panzer, Annales typogr. 1:114, No. 79; Ebert, No. 4142; Dibdin, Bibl. Spenceriana, 4:480; Brunet, ed. 5, p. 852, No. 26514.

167) Hain, No. 13786-88.

168) Hain, No. 13546.

169) Hain, No. 6743.

170) Panzer 6:138, No. 51.

171) Hain, No. 3842.

172) Hain, No. 3793.

173) Hain, No. 3794.

174) Hain, No. 11349.

175) Hain, No. 11350.

176) Panzer 1:201, No. 354. Folio.

177) Hain, No. 3885.

178) Panzer 6:138, No. 51.

179) Note: Even at this time there was some xylographic work done, but that is outside the scope of this book.

Chapter VI

ULM AFTER 1480 (1)

Like Augsburg, Ulm, which so brilliantly entered the history of book illustration in 1470, continued to raise its standing in the following decades.

Ludwig Hohenwang and Johannes Zainer were joined by the printing house of Leonhard Holl in 1482. He had owned a playing card manufacturing plant up to that time, and his business must have been large because he shipped his wares to Venice, Constantinople and other cities. About 1482 he exchanged his earlier occupation for the new venture in printing and in a short time he went bankrupt. In that same year [sic] he was exiled from the city, but they must have let him come back since in 1492 he was exiled again. [Trans. note: the date of his first exile, above, must be an error since he is shown below as publishing in Ulm in 1483 and 1484.]

He issued two illustrated books. The first of these was very comprehensive but since it had no pictures of people it is of little interest in the history of book illustration. It is [345] Cosmographia (2), by Claudius Ptolomaeus, which he published in 1482, and it is the first book with woodcut maps. It has 32 of these maps and on the first one there is the inscription, "The carvings are by Johann Schnitzer of Arnszheim."

In 1483 he printed a book that was much reprinted later, [346, Plates 79-81] and [347-349] the Buch der Weisheit der alten Meister von Anbeginn der Welt von Geschlecht zu Geschlecht (3), which he simultaneously published s. l. e. a. (4) and reprinted in the same year with a third edition (5), followed by a fourth edition in 1484 (6). It contains 224 woodcuts which, with the exception of the title page illustration, which is 220 x 150 mm, are all 185 x 157 mm. Only a few of the illustrations, however, deal with human life and most are related to animals. They are among the Ulm books illustrated by a very important master who appears repeatedly, and who did his most excellent work here. It is characteristic that the background is suppressed, and that the architecture is handled casually.

Simultaneously with these two books, and with illustrations by the hand of the same artist, there appeared an s. l. e. a. [350, Pl. 82-84] third German edition of Melusine (7). This same artist had, indeed, done the woodcuts for the first Bämler publications, but he excelled these in his later work. As in the Buche der Weisheit... with which this agrees in style, the 65 woodcuts, 165 to 170 mm high and 135 mm wide, each fill a full page. The landscape is neglected, but as compensation one finds magnificent male faces and women of charming appearance.

Book illustration achieved an even greater flowering under the aegis of the second of the printers active from 1482, Conrad Dinkmuth. He appears to have worked originally in Hohenwang's or Zainer's plant since he is listed in the tax records as early as 1476, whereas his own dated books start with 1482. He had immediately to compete for a living with the tragic Loos Holl. He appears as a debtor for the last time in 1495 and he left Ulm at the end of the century (in 1499).

His [351] Regimen Sanitatis of 1482 (8) has only one illustration, which appears after the index on its own page. It is a large but not very significant woodcut.

His [352, Pl. 85-87] Seelenwurzgarten (9), published in 1483, and which was later frequently reprinted, is much more important. It has 16 woodcuts (192 x 125) which are reused 110 times.

His 1485 edition [353] of Buches der Weisheit (10) is the sixth in the series. Holl published it originally in 1483. The woodcuts are those of the original edition but are changed in size; that is, they are no longer 180 x 145, but are 190 by 135 mm.

The year 1486 marks the highpoint in Dinkmuth's work. During this year there appeared the first dated edition of Thomas Lirer's Schwäbischer Chronik [354-355, Pl. 88-89], which appears to have been accompanied by his simultaneously published undated edition (11). The undated edition has 19 woodcuts and the dated edition has 21 that occupy the full page, 185 x 120 mm. Part 2, the attached Chronikbüchlein, has only a title page illustration. The woodcuts divide into two classes: landscapes and people. The unknown artist understood, for the first time, how to give landscapes artistic significance. As compared with the pictures in Breitenbachs Reise of the same time and the later Schedel'schen Chronik, these are the only significant landscape pictures of the fifteenth century. In the pictures of people, however, the landscape is surpressed, as in all Ulm products.

Almost more characteristic than the Lirer Chronik are the 30 (190 x 123) woodcuts in the second book published by Dinkmuth in 1486, [356, Pl. 90-93] the Deutschen Uebersetzung des Eunuchus des Terentius (12). While up to this time it was customary to give only the slightest indication of the background, in this book, for the first time, the people appear in properly delineated surroundings. The scene is always set on the street. The artist took a very elevated position and gives almost a bird's eye view of large complexes of houses. The people are drawn correctly and shading is used within the borders. The houses are no longer simply presented symbolically, as they were earlier, but are so well done that it appears that the people can really go into them. The conception of the individual scenes is very good and, in their proper presentation, the artist was greatly aided by Hans Nythart, who was the book's translator. The only similarity to the old-time illustrations is that the persons are identified by inscription of their names next to them.

Dinkmuth's 1487 edition of the small [357] Hortus sanitatis (13) is the eighth in the series of editions of this book. The 392 woodcuts are smaller than those in the Schöffer original edition and the Sorg reprint of 1485, but they differ from the even smaller ones that Schoensperger used in his two editions of 1486 and 1487. The title page illustration, which occupies the full page (220 x 145), is new.

In 1489, Dinkmuth printed [358] the Frauenpsalter, by Alanus de Rupe (14), in which a number of illustrations demonstrate the mysteries presented by the three-fold garlands of roses. Dinkmuth reprinted this [359-360] book in two editions in 1492 (15).

Dinkmuth's 1493 edition [361] of Zeitglöcklein des Lebens und Leidens Christi (16) is third in the series of editions of this book and has a number of woodcuts of various sizes.

There are also some illustrated books available from the fifth Ulm printer, Johannes Reger of Kemnat in the upper Pfalz. At first he printed with Leonhard Holl's types and then printed independently until he left Ulm in 1499.

His 1486 edition [362] of the Claudii Ptolomaei Cosmographia (17), is a reprint of the Holl edition of 1482, with the same maps. As a colophon it has a white heron in a black background, with the initials J. R. (Johannes Reger).

In 1487 he printed [363] the Walfart oder Bilgerung unser liben Frauen (18), which he also published s. l. e. a. [364] as Itinerarium seu peregrinatio beate virginis et deigenitricis Marie (19), which was later frequently reprinted. Here, too, the illustrations are very significant. The title page illustration (140 x 80) is divided into two parts. The 19 text woodcuts are all 140 x 80 mm.

In 1496 there followed two works [365-367] by Guilielmus Caorusin. In the one, the Stabilimenta Rhodiorum militum (20), there are 20 woodcuts and finally a picture of Caorusin. The other, with the title, Opera ad historiam Rhodiorum spectantia (21) is a collection of nine different but coherent small writings, with the title of the first one, Obsidionis Rhodie urbis descriptio, often cited as the title of the whole work. It has 26 (210 x 125) woodcuts. The title page woodcut shows Caorusin handing over the manuscript, and the last illustration shows him writing at the lectern. The landscape is neglected, as was customary, but the figures are very good.

Only a [368] Deutscher Kalender (22) of 1498 remains to represent the work of the last Ulm printer of the 15th Century, Hans Schäffler, and it has the familiar calendar woodcuts. It is uncertain whether the 1490 edition [369] of Chiromancie (23), by Aristotle, and the 1495 edition of [370] Historie des Apollonius are his.

Both of the first printers of Ulm, Ludwig Hohenwang and Johannes Zainer, continued to publish interesting books around the beginning of the new century.

Zainer's edition [371-373] of Maister Elucidarius (24), published in 1496, was reissued by him in 1497 (25) and again in 1517; all with the woodcuts of the earlier edition.

His 1499 [374] Historie von St. Brandon (26) is the fifth in the series of editions of this book. The 21 woodcuts are the same as those of the Sorg original edition in content only; they have been reworked in a different style and are smaller (60 x 87). However, these do not stand at the apex of the other Ulm products.

In 1499 [375-376] he issued the second edition of Johann Sittich's original Augsburg publication of the Tractats von der Bereitung der Weine, by Arnoldus de Villanova (27), and the fifth edition of Historie des Königs Apollonius.

In 1500 [377-379] he printed Aristotle's Chiromancie (28) and in 1502 produced Schrick's Abhandlung von den gebrannten Wassern (29), which was followed by a sixth edition of Historie Brandons (30).

Hohenwang's work was much more important. The first book he produced was still quite in the spirit of the middle ages, and its woodcuts, in terms of their composition, belonged to the period around 1450. His second book, published in 1501, show his pictures to be a product of the new times both in content and in style.

Its author was the humanist Jacob Wimpfeling and its title [380, Pl. 94-103] was De fide concubinarum (31). Hohenwang printed this and supplied 12 woodcuts for it, of which Numbers 5 and 12 are doublets. Hassler made it clear, based on their skill in perspective that the drawing and the cutting were done in Italy.

What Ulm produced up to the beginning of the sixteenth century is, therefore, very important, even though the number of works produced there was not very large. Apparently, both Conrad Dinkmuth and Leonhard Holl began, simultaneously, to published at the beginning of the 1480's. Only one illustrated work remains as a result of Holl's activities, the Buch der Weisheit. Its woodcuts excelled everything done in Augsburg. Dinkmuth was epoch-making in that respect in his publications. For the first time, landscape was handled with loving skill; and Reger closed the period with the production of fine books that were worthy of his predecessors. At the close of the period, Hohenwang, Ulm's first printer, came up with a work whose style fully met the standards of these new times.

Notes

1) Hassler, Die Buchdruckergeschichte Ulms zum vierten Säcularfeier der Erfindung der Buchdruckerkunst geschrieben. Ulm. 1840.

2) Hain, No. 13539. Large folio; Panzer, Ann typ. III:555, No. 28; Ebert, No. 1822; Hassler, p. 117, No. 99.

3) Hain, Part I, 1:562, No. 4029. Folio; Panzer, I:143, No. 189; Hassler, No. 100; Two numbers are copied in Essenwein, Plate 99.

4) Hain, No. 4028.

5) Hain, No. 4030.

6) Hain, No. 4031.

7) s. l. e. a. Hain, No. 11063.

8) Hassler, No. 104. Small folio.

9) Hassler, No. 106. Small folio; Hain, Pt. II, 2:305, No. 14584; Panzer, I:140, No. 178; Two numbers are copied in Essenwein, Plate 100.

10) Hain, No. 4033.

11) Hain, Part II, 1:267, No. 10116 and 10117. Folio; Panzer, I:38, No. 768, and page 160; Ebert, No. 12051 and 12052; Hassler, p. 123, No. 111; Brunet, ed. 5, III:1094; Graesse, IV:220.

12) Hain, No. 15436. Folio; Hassler, No. 113.

13) Panzer, I:167, Folio; Hain, No. 3952; Pritzel, No. 11888; Choulant, p. 245, No. 8.

14) Panzer I:64, No. 273b; Hain, No. 14039.

15) Hain, No. 14041 and 14042.

16) Hassler, No. 123.

17) Hassler, No. 131. Large folio.

18) Hain, No. 9325, Quarto; Hassler, No. 134.

19) Panzer IX:181, No. 206, Quarto; Hain, Part II, 1:148, No. 9322; A woodcut is reproduced in Essenwein, Plate 143.

20) Hassler, No. 138, Folio.

21) Hassler, No. 137, Folio.

22) Hain, No. 9748.

23) Hain, No. 1778, Quarto; Hassler, No. 153.

24) Hain, No. 8812; Hassler, No. 55.

25) Hain, No. 8813.

26) Hain, No. 3723; Hassler, No. 54.

27) Hain, No. 1815.

28) Weller, *Repertorium bibliographicum,* No. 138.

29) Hain, No. 14535; Weller, No. 246.

30) Weller, No. 253.

31) Fully described by Hassler, where No.'s 1 and 9 are reproduced; Weller, No. 4065.

Chapter VII

COLOGNE (1)

After the 1470's, during which Augsburg and Ulm were the places where the most important illustrated books were produced, with the beginning of the 1480's other German cities developed in this area.

Cologne, which before 1480 was of marginal significance in the history of book illustration, based such position as it had almost entirely on Heinrich Quentel.

His first publication was [381] the Summa de casibus conscientiae (2), by Astesanus, which he published in two editions in 1479. One edition has Quentel's colophon at the end (the Saviour giving the benediction with his right hand while holding the world sphere in his left hand). On the eleventh sheet, after the index, there is a small woodcut of Christ on the cross. The other edition lacks these woodcuts but has a xylographic frame on the first sheet, in which the lower part shows the adoration by the three kings, with various arabesques and comic figures around and above. The lower part of this illustration reoccurs on sheet 24 of Quentel's 1480 edition of the Fasciculus temporum (3). The same frame is found [382] on the 32nd sheet of the Destructorium vitiorum (4) by Alexander Anglicus, which was published in 1480. It occurs, finally, in the first low-German Bible, in three locations: on the first and third sheets of volume one and at the beginning of the New Testament, with different figures and arabesques on the right side in this last location.

This framing and the fact that the [383, Pl. 104-105] famous Bible (5), which used the same types as those that Quentel used in Astaxanus, in Destructorium... and in other works, indicate, despite recent Lempertz findings, that the Bible was printed by Quentel.

It is in two volumes and appeared in two editions, which differ very little. Niesert maintains that the lack of signatures, which Koelhoff used as early as 1472, indicates that they were apparently printed before 1472. Against this view there is not only the artistic execution of the woodcuts, but the fact that Quentel was not working in Cologne that early.

The opening of the work consists of the aforementioned woodcut ensemble (365 x 275), which consisted of several plates. Under the foliage that is above and on both sides, there is a bagpipe player, a dancing fool and a female figure with long hair, richly ornamented clothing and a turbanlike hat; in the lower part of the illustration there is the adoration of the kings, etc.

The Bible has 125 illustrations of which 94 are in the Old Testament and 31 are in the New Testament; however, one of those in the New Testament, in the apostolic letters, is reprinted nine times. With the exception of the large (190 x 190) woodcut at the beginning of Genesis and the oft-repeated little one in the New Testament, the rest of the illustrations are 120 x 188 mm.

As is known, the same woodcuts were reused by Koburger in his German Bible, in Nuremberg in 1483, and this has resulted in various combinations of attributions to artists.

Panzer (6) held that the woodcuts in the Cologne Bible were produced in Nuremberg, but he contradicts this in his Annalen 1:15, where he named a low-German producer. Murr (7), who held that many works of unknown artists of the fifteenth century were done in Nuremberg, suggested Michel Wohlgemuth as the presumed artist of the woodcuts in the Cologne Bible. Heller (8) goes beyond this and, without further ado, attributes it positively to Wohlgemuth. More recently, Hase (9) attempted, in his book on Koburger, to present evidence of their authorship by Wohlgemuth. Hase believes that the illustrations of the Cologne Bible were supplied by Michel Wohlgemuth and Wilhelm Pleydenwurff on the basis of an author's copy of Hartmann Schedel's Weltchronik, in which there is found a letter from Hieronymus Monetarius that, among other things, says that these are the illustrators of the Chronik.

Other bibliographers hold that the artist involved was Johann von Paderborn.

The Jesuit Harzheim (10), with whom Niesert and Lempertz agree, brings Israel of Mecheln into the act.

Whatever constitutes the work of Wohlgemuth, there is more than one uncertainty in the position taken by Hase. Certainly the quotation on which he bases his conclusion does not give a positive basis for this and, despite the lack of any conclusive evidence, it is clear that the Cologne Bible pictures are not nearly as similar to those of the Chronik and the Schatzbehalter as Hase alleges. On the contrary, it is unbelieveable that the artist could change so much in 12 years that he would prepare such basically different illustrations for the same scenes, quite apart from some external features that occur in the Cologne Bible and not in the Schatzbehalter. In practically every picture in the Bible a bird is shown flying and holding a green twig in its mouth; streams with swans or mountains with windmills recur in the Bible. Not a trace of these characteristic details is found in Wohlgemuth's work.

We know far too little of the work of Israel of Mecheln or even Johann of Paderborn to be able to trace the woodcuts to either of them with any certainty.

It is certain that the woodcuts have much more of a Cologne than a Nuremberg character. Overall, the clues indicate the influence of Eyck and the Cologne School. The way the figures are drawn and the garments are laid, the lack of perspective in the drawing of landscapes and other accessory characteristics point to the place where they originated, and one can not overlook the words in the preface: "printed in the ... city of Cologne." Thus, for a number of reasons, it would appear that the illustrations are the product of a Cologne artist. The inscription, "Joseph Broedere," on the picture in which Joseph received his brother, is further evidence of a low-German producer, since Wohlgemuth would have written, "Joseph Brueder." The decision, however, would appear to be made by the fact that the woodcut for the sixth chapter of the book of Esrah shows the chief gable builder of the Cologne cathedral with the dome hoist (11). How Wohlgemuth could have come upon the idea of drawing the Cologne Dome is quite incomprehensible.

The text of the introduction says that the pictures are included so that even those who can not read can enjoy the work, and it designates some as copies of old book illustrations. They were certainly a poor substitute for the book plates by Eyck or of the developing Cologne School of the period. The first impression is definitely negative. However, they should really be compared with the contemporary Bible illustrations rather than with book illustration. Two independently illustrated Bibles had appeared earlier; the one by Pflanzmann in Augsburg and the one by Sensenschmidt in Nuremberg. The woodcuts in the first of these were only a few centimeters high and were quite in the playing card style, limited to crude outlines and with the individual woodblocks repeated in the most boring manner. There was no attempt to relate the illustration directly to the content. In the Nuremberg Bible the illustrations of figures were confined to the space of the large initial letters and could not, therefore, be given free development. In this case (the Cologne Bible), the Bible was first illustrated with large multifigured woodcuts, with none of them repeated, and this provided a completely new motif. Thus the woodcuts of the Cologne Bible were epoch-making in the history of book illustration, and scarcely one of the later Bibles could match its influence.

In terms of technique, the illustrations of the Cologne Bible varied in quality. Those with skillfully executed borders and bold groupings of figures are among the most important and were apparently done last. The worst, technically, are numbers 7, 8, 13, and 16 which, in the bargain, were cut with very dull knives. The hideously pointed knees of Adam and Eve, in the introductory woodcut, can not be charged against the artists but against the woodcutters.

The differences between the two editions are slight. The first edition lacks the woodcuts of the Apocalypse, which appear in the second. The small woodcut with the apostolic letters (which has a person on the left who, in the presence of the Pope at Rome, hands over a letter) is used repeatedly in the first edition. It was apparently worn down to a stump in this frequent reuse and is replaced in the second edition with a reversed copy.

The Bible is the most important book produced by Quentel. In his other works, Quentel normally only has the title page picture of the teacher and two students, which was also used in Schoensperger's productions in Augsburg and by Martin Flach in Strassburg (12). The Quentel woodcut does, however, vary from Schoensperger's in a number of respects. The Latin inscription has, to be sure, the same text as in Schoensperger, but between tanti and doctoris Quentel has a comma and he spells the word doctoris correctly instead of "docioris," as in the Schoensperger; and there are other slight differences. This woodcut was used by Quentel in the following books [384-400]:

1. Expositio hymnorum, 1492. (Ennen. No. 299. Quarto)
2. Boethii liber de consolatione philosophiae, 1493. (Hain, No. 3383. Quarto)
3. Rationes breves des Rabi Samuel, 1493. (Hain, No. 14271. Quarto)
4. Expositio hymnorum, 1494.
5. Peniteas cito, 1495. Quarto.
6. Joh. Versor, Liber de anima, 1496. (Ennen, No. 306. Quarto)
7. ___ ______, Super onmes libros novae logicae, 1497. (Ennen, No. 307. Folio)
8. ___ ______, Quaestiones in veterem artem Aristotelis, 1497. (Ennen, No. 308. Folio)

9. ___ ______, Super octo libros physicorum, 1493. (Ennen, No. 320. Quarto)

10. Boetii liber de consolatione philosophiae, 1497. (Hain, No. 3390)

11. Ulricus Ebrardus modus latinitatis. s. l. e. a. (Hain, No. 6527)

12. Textus sequentiarum. s. l. e. a. (Ennen, No. 298)

13. Speculum artis bene moriendi, s. a. (Hain, No. 14911)

14. W. Occam, Dialogus de nativitate et moribus antichristi, s. a. (Not in Hain)

15. Sinthen, Composita verborum, s. a. (Hain, No. 14778)

16. _____, ________ ________, 1498. (Hain, No. 14780)

17. _____, Verba deponentialia, s. a. (Hain, No. 14786)

The Albertus Magnus Sermones (13), which Quentel printed in 1498, has as the title page illustration, the Holy Ghost, the Christ Child, Mary, Anna and the two Johns. The same woodcut [401] is found on the last page of the Viola animae (14).

In Quentel's later period this title page woodcut is in Arnoldus de Tungris' [402] Reparationes lectionum novae logicae Aristotelis (15), of 1507.

During Quentel's period there were other Cologne printers who used woodcuts in their books.

Two works with a number of woodcuts were issued by Ludwig van Reuchen.

In 1485 he printed a German Heiligenleben [403] with many colored woodcuts (16). The [404] Deutschen Evangelien und Episteln (17), which appeared in the same year, has a small woodcut before each Sunday Gospel and on the verso of the title page there is a very large Christ on the Cross, with Mary and John; in addition there is one, on leaf 107b, of Christ arising from the dead.

In 1489, Cornelius of Zürichzee, who was active from 1489-1517, printed the [405] Speculum sapientiae beati Cyrilli episcopi (18), which contains three woodcuts produced by different people. The one on the title page (40 x 34), shows Bishop Cyril, with a crook, standing in a landscape. It is quite old. The second, which is on the verso of the title page (58 x 41), is more recent and shows the young woman with the Child, etc. The third, on the last page of the book, is between these other two in artistic value.

In the same year, 1489, Cornelius produced the first edition of the book by Ulricus Molotoris, which was often reprinted later, [406, Pl. 106-107] De laniis et phitonicis mulieribus (19), containing seven woodcuts. The title page illustration is 135 x 92 mm and each of the six chapters is illustrated by a 122 x 75 mm woodcut. None of these is badly done; however, the first and the sixth are differentiated from the others by the fact that they are shaded, while the others consist solely of thick, crude outlines, and come from older works.

The [407] Historia sive evangelium Nycodemie, which Cornelius published without place or date, has a woodcut of Christ on the Cross on the title page and the same is repeated on the last page.

Johann Koelhoff, who was printing from 1471, began to print illustrated books much later. In 1489 he produced [408] the Grosse und kleine Seelentrost (20), with nine woodcuts. The illustration on the verso of the title page shows Christ with the scars, and above him there is God the Father, and the Holy Ghost. Below, there are three figures praying to them. The same woodcut is found in a limited edition produced in "Hag" by an unknown printer in a book titled Beichtspiegels (21). It can not be determined whether he copied this from Koelhoff or vice versa.

The [409] Sermonem auf das ganze Jahr (22), which appeared in 1490, has only one woodblock, which appears on sheet 45b and is titled, "The Figure of Righteousness." In addition, on sheet 60a, there are various escutcheons. The woodblock with the figure of righteousness became the property of Hermann Bongart, who used it [410-411] in the Vita S. Suiberti, which was published in 1508, as well as in his Orationes quodlibeticae, by Ortwin Gratius (23), which he published in 1507.

Koelhoff's edition [412] of the 24 Alten, in 1492 (24), is the fourth in the series of editions of this book. It has the two familiar woodcuts, of which the first is used nine times and the secone is repeated 15 times.

After the death of the father, the younger Johann took over the press [413, Pl. 108-112] and the best known thing that he published, in 1499, was the Cronica von der hilligen Stadt Coellen (25). Its woodcuts may be divided into several groups: the first group consists of pictures of the coats-of-arms of the old Cologne families and of the German cities, with the ones giving the escutcheons of the Bishops of Cologne being especially large (145 x 140). The second group is made up of small views of cities and buildings, for all of which, as was common, the self-same woodcut was used. Then there is a group of family trees. Then there are 278 small (50 x 40) pictures of various Kaisers, Popes, Kings, etc. In this group, however, eight woodcuts were used to represent all these different persons. The Chronik has 40 larger woodcuts which are frequently reused. The first illustration treats of the first parents (90 x 130). One woodcut is used to represent the towers of Babylon and then Jerusalem, Rome, Augsburg and Lübeck. The woodcuts are of various sizes, with some 135 x 90 mm, others 195 x 135 mm, others 110 x 140 mm, and still others are 225 x 140 mm. They were prepared by various people, and some of them are not worth much. The small towers had previously been used in various editions of Fasciculus temporum.

Not much is available from the younger printers.

Martin von Werden, who appears to have started a Franciscan press in 1497, had one woodcut showing the Mother of God, Mother Anna and the Christ Child, which he reused frequently. It appears on the title pages [414-415] of XIII Sermones Michaelis de Hungaria (26) and the Stimulus divini amoris, which was published in 1502.

The publications of Hermann Bongart (1493-1521) which appeared during this period [416-418] include the illustration which appeared in Jacobus de Clusa's Tractatus de apparitionibus (27), of 1496, on sheet 22a. In his 1498 edition of Manuale confessorum (28), he has a woodcut on the last page, and among the many illustrations in his 1498 edition of Epistel- und Evangelienbuches (29) there is an illustration on the last page.

If Cologne had not had its Bible, its output could not be compared with that of Augsburg and Ulm. All other books are only sparingly illustrated, conventionally with a title page illustration, and the many illustrations in the Cologne Chronik show a tremendous artistic retrogression.

The decoration of all later Bibles was influenced to some degree by the Cologne Bible. Its woodcuts were reused in the same size by Koburger in Nuremberg, in 1483, and by von Trutebul in Halberstadt, in 1520. They were reused in reduced size in the Strassburg Bible of 1485, in the Schoensperger editions of 1487 and 1490, and in the Othmar editions of 1507 and 1518. And even when Hans Holbein had to illustrate the Lutheran Old Testament for Adam Petri in Basel, in 1523, he based his full page illustrations on the illustrations of the Cologne Bible.

Notes

1) Ennen, Katalog der Incunabeln in der Stadtbibliothek zu Cöln, mit einer Einleitung über die cölnischen Buchdrucker des 15 Jahrhunderts; Especially about the Cologne Bible: Goetze, Historie der gedruckten niedersächsischen Bibeln; Goetze, Beschreibung seiner Bibelsammlung; Niefert, Literarische Nachrichten über die erste zu Cöln gedruckte niederdeutsche Bibel; Coesfeld, 1825; Lempertz, Beiträge zur ältesten Geschichte der Buchdruck- und Holzschneidekunst. No. 1. Cologne, 1839, p. 8-12.

2) Hain, I, No. 1895.

3) Ennen, No. 288. Folio.

4) Hain, No. 649.

5) Ebert, No. 2347, Large Folio; Hain, I:421, No. 3141; Panzer I:15, No. 13; Muther, Deutsche Bilderbibeln, No. 7, p. 6-13, and the bibliography therein.

6) Panzer, Geschichte der Nürnberger Bibelausgaben, p. 65, No. XII.

7) Journal zur Kunstgeschichte, Part 2, p. 132.

8) Heller, Geschichte der Holzschneidekunst, p. 71.

9) Hase, Die Koburger Buchhändler-Familie zu Nürnberg, p. 33 ff.

10) Harzheim, Bibliotheka Colon, p. 212.

11) Reproduced by Lempertz.

12) Moser, "Der Holzschnitt mit der Inschrift: Accipies tanti doctoris dogmata sancti." Serapeum IV:253.

13) Ennen, No. 313.

14) Ennen, No. 315. Quarto.

15) German. Museum, No. 28583. Quarto.

16) Ennen, No. 375. Folio.

17) Not in Hain, see Ennen.

18) Not in Hain 5903 ff; German. Museum No. 20727, Small octavo.

19) Hain, Part II, 1:456, No. 11535. Quarto; Panzer IV:332, No. 46. Three numbers copied in Essenwein, Plate 126.

20) Ebert, No. 23133. Folio; Lacking in Hain and Panzer; Grässe VI:340; Ennen, No. 215.

21) Holtrop, Confessionale ou Beichtspiegel. The Hague, 1861.

22) Ennen, No. 218. Quarto.

23) Not in Panzer VI:360 ff.

24) Ennen, No. 216. Folio.

25) Hain Part I, 2:104, No. 4989. Folio; Panzer, Annalen 1:240, No. 476; Ebert, No. 4145; Dibdin, Bibl. Spenceriana III:281 ff.; Brunet, Edition V, 1:1886; Ennen I:85; Grässe II:139.

26) Ennen, No. 401. Undated. Octavo.

27) Ennen, No. 391. Quarto.

28) Ennen, No. 399. Quarto.

29) Ennen, No. 398. Quarto.

Chapter VIII

NUREMBERG (1)

As Cologne based its fame on Heinrich Quentel, Nuremberg owed its importance almost exclusively to Anton Koburger. Book illustration, as the review of the oldest Nuremberg products has shown, was not before Koburger as satisfactory in this setting as it was in Augsburg and Ulm. Only when Koburger succeeded in drawing the Nuremberg painters into his large book-trade undertakings, did the art work and cutting blossom in Nuremberg.

By 1481 [419] his Biblia latina cum postilla Nic. de Lyra (2) contained woodcuts. The first part had 23, some of which were full page. The second part had fewer woodcuts, but among them are one that depicts the city of Jerusalem and one that gives the floor plan and elevation of the new Temple. However, these are architectural-antiquarian studies without any artistic purpose. One possible exception is the (210 x 100) figure of the high priest in part I. The face shows expression and the drawing, as a whole, is faultless.

Despite this, the Latin Bible can not be considered an independently illustrated book. One that may is the [420] Deutsche Bibel (3), which appeared two years later, in 1483. But even this one does not contribute anything new to Nuremberg printing, since its woodcuts were taken from the Cologne Bible. The only differences are that Koburger omitted the border ornaments and that, in the New Testament, instead of using the 31 woodcuts in the Cologne edition, he used only twelve of them: one at the beginning of each of the four Evangelists, and eight in the apocalypse. His Bible has a total of 107 illustrations.

The first independent title page woodcut [421] is found in the 1484 edition of Koburger's Reformation der Statut und Gesetze, die ein erbar Rat der Stadt Nürnberg vorgenommen hat (4). It has a 225 x 175 mm illustration.

In 1488 [422] Koburger published the 13th edition (5) of the Legenda Aurea, of which the first illustrated German edition was published in 1471 by Zainer. His edition, like its predecessors, had 262 woodcuts, of which 138 pertain to the summer and 124 to the winter. They differ from their predecessors chiefly in size, ranging from 85 to 90 mm in height and from 182 to 185 mm in width. It is doubtful that they were produced in Nuremberg since they are very similar to those in the Cologne Bible, and, most likely, they came from Cologne.

The first book produced by the Koburg press with illustrations that were certainly prepared under the supervision of Wohlgemuth [423] is the 1491 Schatzbehalter oder Schrein der wahren Reichthümer des Heils und ewiger Seeligkeit (6). It was attributed to P. Stephan of the Franciscan cloister at Nuremberg, who died in 1498. Its title page shows the Holy Trinity [Pl. 113-119]. Since a number of illustrations are used twice (figures 25, 39, 46, 48 and 71), in addition to one of the allegorical pictures, the book has a total of 96 full-page (252 x 175) woodcuts.

The drawings all appear attributable to Wohlegemuth, who quite often includes his mark. A richly decorated W appears on the fluttering flag on sheet 19b. On sheet 48 the W appears on both the mast pennants. On sheet 27 there is a figure which, seen from the left, looks like an M and, viewed from the right side, becomes a W. On sheet 58 there is a W on the flag of the backmost tent. No. 73 has a W on the flag born by a mercenary, and in number 80 there is a W and a crooked capital W on both the pennants at the right. To be sure the drawings are not all well done. The High Priest who sits on the altar holding the Child, in figure 13, has an excessively long arm. The shortened body of Jacob in Figure 29 is bad. The left leg of Christ in Figure 68 is awkwardly long. The worst of the lot is the illustration of the Egyptian King in Figure 69. Notwithstanding these, a book this richly illustrated with such large and carefully executed woodcuts was unheard of before. Up to this time Nuremberg obtained most of its illustrations from outside, but with this book it achieved equality with the best produced elsewhere. The cutting, since various woodcutters were used, varies in quality from bungling to accomplished work.

The illustrations of the Schatzbehalters... must have met with wide approbation or Koburger would not have come out, barely two years later, with a new illustrated work. [424-425, Pl. 120-123] This was the Hartmann Schedel'sche Neue Weltchronik, which appeared in 1493 (7) in Latin and in 1494 in German (8), and which proffered a profusion and variety of woodcuts such as never appeared in any book before or after it. The title page illustration is 377 x 240 mm. In addition to the large illustrations for each of the six ages into which the book is divided, it contains countless smaller ones. In each era there are pictures of the cities founded in that period or of cities that were otherwise outstanding. The book, therefore, presents, in addition to many imagined presentations, a whole series of views of cities which are partly geographically true, and partly not, and which may be compared with those in Lübke's Geschichte der deutschen Renaissance, p. 49-52. Besides the presentation of all historically notable places, the 15th Century demanded to see portraits of all of the key people in the tale. So, there was a second group made up of the portraits of the important persons discussed in each of the six eras.

The woodcuts are variable in quality. Among the larger compositions, that of the God Father with the enthroned Savior, as well as the sheets that treat of the life of the first humans, are outstanding. Among the pictures of cities the large views of Nuremberg, Erfurt, Strassburg, Würzburg, Venice, and Florence are originals. Among the portraits the full figure illustrations are handled with great care, while the small busts have little claim to fame. Just as in the case of the small pictures of cities, the small bust portraits reuse the same woodcut to represent various people. Only a few of the illustrations for the third and fifth eras come from the Koburg Bible of 1481. The rest of the woodcuts are so much alike in style that it is impossible to determine which were done by Wohlgemuth and which by Pleydenwurff. Koberger set up a special shop for the cutting of the forms, which was supervised by a very skillful master, who put the finishing touches on the forms.

Among the other illustrated books of the Koburg press [426-429] there are: Revelationes sanctae Brigitae (9), which was first printed in 1501 and later reprinted, some in German and some in Latin editions in 1502, 1517 and 1521. This was first printed in Lübeck by Bartholomäus

Ghotan in 1492. It has 13 woodcut plates which are made up of smaller woodcuts. They are mostly 235 x 150 mm but the first one is 230 x 145 mm. The eighth (235 x 150) is an especially pretty woodcut. All of the woodcuts are important.

The last of the Bible editions published by Koburger himself [430] was the Biblia cum concordantiis Veteris et Novi Testamenti (10). The woodcut of the title page (118 x 140) is divided into two parts.

As compared with these great undertakings of the Koburg press, the other printers fall far into the background.

Zeninger [431] printed an illustrated booklet in 1481 under the title, Onus mundi (11).

A few of the later publications of Friedrich Creussner belong in this period. He printed the undated [432] Auslegung des Amts der heiligen Messe (12). The 24 woodcuts in his [433] Horologium devotionis (13), of 1489, are particularly outstanding. They are 95 x 65 mm. All are shaded, the perspective is correct, the landscape is given a good deal of space, the drawing is surehanded and the cutting is fine. There are many similarities with the woodcuts in the Schatzbehalter and one is tempted to attribute them to Wohlgemuth. Creussner used these same woodcuts in his German edition of the Horologium, which was titled [434] the Andechtig Zeitlöcklein des Lebens Jesu (14).

A Peter Vischer, of whom nothing more is known, published [435] the first edition of the Nürnberger Heiligthumsbüchleins (15) in 1497, in which the Requiem and Ceremonies prepared in Nuremberg are pictured. The title page woodcut is 114 x 107 mm, and the second woodcut, which fills a page, is 210 x 145 mm.

Marc Airer [436-437] reprinted, once without date (16), and once in 1488 (17), Bruder Claus, which was first published in Augsburg by Peter Berger. Airer reworked the illustrations of the Berger edition in terms of style (65 x 95) but kept their content.

In addition Airer printed [438] s. l. e. a., Rosenplut's Spruch von der erlichen Regierung der Stadt Nürnberg (18), which has a title page woodcut.

Hans Mair, in 1493, did a new edition [439] of Peter Vischer's Heiligthumsbüchlein (19), using the same woodcuts. In 1498, he printed the third edition of [440-441] the s. l. e. a. Historie von vier Kaufleuten (20), and he repeated it in 1499 (21).

The woodcuts in Peter Wagner's 1494 reprint of Brant's [442] Narrenschiff (22) are reduced copies of the ones in the first Basel edition of 1494.

[443] Savanarola's Auslegung der Psalmen Miserere (23), which Wagner published without date, has, as its title page illustration, only one small (65 x 65) woodcut, which apparently had been used frequently before.

Two of the popular poems of Hans Folz belong in this period. The first one [444], which appeared in 1482, Von der Pestilenz und ihren Zeichen (24), has on the verso of the first sheet a (135 x 100) woodcut, and there are two woodcuts on the last page (135 x 50 mm).

There is one woodcut, of no artistic value, in his [445] Suptil rechnung Ruprecht Kolperger's von gsuch der judn (25), which was published in 1491. The woodcut is 90 x 57 mm.

In 1500, Ambrosius Huber [446-448] printed a Kalender (26) which used the conventional illustrations for calendars. In 1501, he supplied a title page woodcut with his Von fünf Frauen

(27) and with Von Einem Gesellen (28).

In 1504 [449] Hieronymus Huber published a Passion (29) with many (55 x 45) woodcuts. The woodcuts were very dark, but, in general, not bad.

No particular publisher can be credited with the remaining illustrated books published in Nuremberg in the 1480's and 1490's. The [450] Leben des heiligen Rochus (30), which appeared in 1484, had a quite old (160 x 95) title page woodcut. And the same is true [451] of the woodcuts in Engel's Practica auf Jahr 1488 (31).

In 1489 the second edition of [452] the Vesehung von Leib, Seel Ehre und Gut (32) was issued. The first edition was published s. l. e. a. The title page illustration (130 x 82) is the same as that in Schober's edition, and [453] is like that of the first s. l. e. a. edition, so one may assume that it originated in Nuremberg.

Among the later works [454] there is the 1491 edition, with four (105 x 68) woodcuts, of the Büchlein wie Rom gepauet ward (33). In addition to these four woodcuts the book has three escutcheons: with that of the Pope in the center, that of the Romans on the right and that of the German Kaiser at the left.

Much greater tasks than those of the smaller Nuremberg printers were undertaken around the turn of the century by Nuremberg artists for Conrad Celtes who got them to illustrate the works that he did in cooperation with the Rhine "Sodalitat." His relationship with Nuremberg, where he himself had achieved personal fame, dated from 1487.

As early as the years 1487/88 he had [455] published the Oratio Cassandrae virginis Venetae pro Berthucio Lamberto (34), with a title page woodcut 138 x 90 mm.

The title page woodcut of an ode by Celtes, that appeared early in the 1490's [456] under the title Monumentum Santo Sebaldo positum (34), in honor of his friend Sebald Schreyer, shows the Saint, with pointed shoes, set in a gothic structure.

Around 1493 he joined with Michel Wohlgemuth, intending to have a Nuremberg artist prepare mythological illustrations for Ovid; however, this undertaking was never completed.

The first woodcut that Celtes and Wohlgemuth produced jointly appears to have been the title page woodcut of the new edition [457] of the Ode an S. Sebaldus, published around 1496.

More richly illustrated books followed in the early sixteenth century: in 1501 Celtes published the works of the learned Nonne Roswitha of Gandersheim, and in 1502 he issued his Quatuor libri amorum. Among the (215 x 145) woodcuts of [458] Opera Roswithae (35), the best are the two title pages.

The eleven woodcuts in the second illustrated book by Conrad Celtes, [459], which appeared in 1502, the Quatuor libri amorum (37), are also attributable to Wohlgemuth and his school. Thausing traces back to Wohlgemuth himself the sheets that depict the city of Nuremberg and the Hymn to St. Sebaldus. The one (180 x 290) is a practically unchanged but reduced copy of the picture of Nuremberg that is found in the Weltchronik, while the other, St. Sebaldus, is very similar to the picture of St. Sebaldus that adorns the 1496 edition of Celtes' Ode. The five unimportant woodcuts must belong to the Wohlgemuth school. The three illustrated sheets of this book that are attributable to Dürer will be discussed separately later.

This book dates Dürer's entry into the history of book illustration in Nuremberg. Even though he soon left Nuremberg, Dürer's greatness was a necessary prerequisite for the development of book illustration. If it had not been for Koburger's magnificent publications, Nuremberg would not have reached the heights that it achieved by the end of the century.

While the great press of Anton Koburger was developing in Nuremberg, another German city, Basel, was undergoing tremendous development in this field.

Notes

1) Panzer, Aelteste Buchdruckergeschichte Nürnberg's oder Verzeichniss aller von Erfindung der Buchdruckerkunst bis 1500 in Nürnberg gedruckten Bücher. Nuremberg, 1789; Hase, Die Coburger. Buchhändlerfamilie zu Nürnberg. Leipzig, 1865; Thausing, Dürer, passim, especially p. 49-52.

2) Hain, Part I, No. 3166. Folio.

3) This was the ninth published German Bible. Folio. Ebert, No. 2170; Hain, Part I 1:419, No. 3137; Panzer I:113, No. 166; Vogt, p. 133; Muther, Deutsche Bilderbibeln. No. 8.

4) Hain, Part II, 2:195, No. 13716; Panzer I:149, No. 203, (also p. 160. No. 103); Will, Part I, 2:3-4, No. 954.

5) Hain, No. 9981.

6) Hain, Part II, No. 14507. Folio; Weigel II, No. 9919b; Panzer I, No. 313; Ebert, No. 20511. Two numbers reproduced by Essenwein, Plates 36 and 37.

7) Liber cronicarum. Opus de temporibus mundi. Large folio; Hain, No. 14508; Panzer, Annales typogr. II:212, No. 221; Ebert, No. 4147; Dibdin, Bibliotheka Spenceriana III:255 ff; Brunet, ed. Part V, I:1860; Grässe II:138.

8) Das Buch der Chroniken und Geschichten von Anbeginn der Welt bis auf diese unsere Zeit; Ebert, No. 4148. Folio; Hain, Part II, 2:294, No. 14510; Panzer I:204, No. 360; Vogt, p. 764; Weigel I, No. 6774. Two numbers reproduced in Essenwein, Plates 138 and 139.

9) Panzer I:256.

10) Panzer VII:439, No. 1.

11) Hain, No. 12013.

12) Hain, No. 2143.

13) Hain, No. 8934.

14) Hain, No. 16279.

15) Hain, Part II, No. 8415.

16) Hain, No. 5378.

17) Hain, No. 5380.

18) Hain, No. 13986.

19) Hain, Part II, 1:12, No. 8416. Quarto; Panzer I:200, No. 352, Suppl. p. 73, No. 352.

20) Hain, No. 8751.

21) Hain, No. 8752.

22) Panzer I:215, No. 394; Hain, No. 3737.

23) Hain, No. 14426.

24) Hain, No. 7220.

25) Hain, No. 7210.

26) Weller, No. 149.

27) Weller, No. 192.

28) Weller, No. 193.

29) Panzer, Supplement, 294 c.

30) Hain, No. 13928.

31) Hain, No. 6589.

32) Hain, No. 16019.

33) Hain, No. 11212. Small octavo.

34) *Oratio Cassandrae Virginis Venetae pro Berthutio Lamberto liberalium artium insignia suscipiente.* Nuremberg, 1487/88; Hain, Part I, 2:51, No. 4553. Quarto.

35) *Oda pro felicitate urbis Noricae s. Monumentum s. Sebaldo positum;* Hain, No. 4844.

36) *Opera Roswithae illustris virginis et monialis Germane gente Saxonia orte nuper a Conrado Celte inventa;* Panzer VII:439, No. 5. Folio.

37) Hain, Part I, 2:51, No. 4553. Quarto; Ebert, No. 3903; Panzer, VII:44, No. 17; Panzer, IX:542, No. 17; Vogt, p. 242.

Chapter IX

BASEL (1)

Basel, which had little to show in the 1470's in the way of independently illustrated works, with the coming of the 1480's produced admirable books, although it did not produce many.

There are four produced by Nicolaus Kesler, from Battwar, who became a citizen of Basel in 1480.

The woodcut of [460] Felix Hemmerlin's Variae oblectationis opuscula et tractatus (2), which he published undated, shows hornets swarming around the author. His [461] 1489 publication, the collected Werke Johann Gersons (3), assembled by Geiler von Kaisersberg, has a picture of Gerson wearing pilgrim's garb on the verso of the title page of each of its three parts. The title page woodcut of [462] Homeliarius Doctorum, which he printed in 1493, is a woodcut showing a gathering of men of differing status; and the woodcut on the second page [463] of Liber epistolarum S. Hieronymi (4), which Kesler printed in 1497, shows St. Hieronymus with the lion.

The two books printed by Leonhard Ysenhut add nothing new to the history of book illustration in Basel. The one he published in 1489 [464], Walfahrt oder bilgerschaft der allerseligsten Jungfrauen Marie (5), is illustrated with reduced copies of those in the Ulm edition; and his 1490 publication, [465] the Leben des Fabeldichters Aesopi (6), likewise, contains only copies of illustrations in earlier editions.

The printing plant of Michael Furter made a special contribution to book illustration in Basel. In 1493 [466, Pl. 124-129] he published the richly illustrated Buch des Ritters vom Thurn von den Exempeln der Gottesfurcht und Ehrbarkeit (7). The book has 45 (110 x 105) woodcuts which are so good that, as artistic works, they may be considered to be almost in a class with those produced in Ulm (8). They appear to have come from an important artist of the Martin Schön school. The artist knew that he could draw attractive nudes. Up to this time the presentation of nudes was avoided to the greatest extend possible, but in this book they are put forward strongly. In 1513 [467] Furter issued a new edition but with the same woodcuts (9).

In 1494 [468] there followed the Cursus librorum Philosophiae naturalis secundum viam doctoris subtilis Scoti (10), by Dorbellus, and it had some woodcuts.

In 1495 Furter printed [469-470] a small Quadragesimale (11), which he repeated in 1497 (12). It has 18 (100 x 72) woodcuts, of which two are printed twice. These woodcuts, like those in the Ritter von Turn, are very significant.

In addition, there are a number of other works, some dated and some undated, and without the name of the printer, which are attributable to Furter and this period.

The [471] undated Compendium octo partium orationum (13) has an illustration on the title page.

The [472] undated Postilla Guilielmi super Evangelia (14) has the conventional woodcuts of most Sunday Gospels.

The undated [473] Von sant Meinrat ein hübsch lieplich lesen, was ellend und Armut er erlitten hat (15) has 36 woodcuts, each of which fills two-thirds of a page.

The [474] Cura pastoralis pro ordinandorum tentamine collecta (16), which appeared without place or date, as well as the [475] Vegeius Maphaeus' Philalethes (17), used the woodcut previously used in the Nuremberg edition of the Philalethes.

The two illustrated works that follow can not be attributed to any identified Basel printer. The 1491 edition [476] of the Alt Herkommen der loblichen Fürsten aus dem Hause Oesterreich (18) has two woodcuts. The first is 230 x 150 mm and the second is 235 x 155 mm.

The [477] edition of Andechtig Zitglögglyn des Lebens Christi (19), which appeared in 1492, has 38 (65 x 42) woodcuts illustrating the life of Christ.

The illustrated books listed above are, however, all that appeared in Basel to the mid-1490's.

We have already pointed out the influence of particular authors. The art would not have achieved such blossoming in Ulm if it had not been for the great importance placed by Steinhowel and Nythart on the illustration of their works, and if they had not themselves worked with the artists. Basel book illustration found such a man in Sebastian Brant who, from the beginning of the 1490's until 1498, was very active in literature and who placed primary emphasis in his works on their illustration.

What the Bible did for Cologne, the Kostnitzer Concilienbuch did for Augsburg, the Lirer Chronik did for Ulm, and what the Schedel Weltchronik did for Nuremberg, [478, Pl. 130-131], Sebastian Brant's Narrenschiff (20), which he permitted his friend Johannes Bergmann from Olpe to produce in 1494, did for Basel.

It has 114 woodcuts which illustrate the individual chapters of the book. Most of them are 115 x 85 mm, and the few that occupy full pages are 165 x 105 mm. Brant worked very closely with the production of this, his chief work, and appears not only to have given the artist written instructions for the individual pictures, but seems to have supplemented these by freehand sketches. Six illustrations were repeated, so there were 108 woodcuts.

In any event, Brant put the greatest emphasis on the illustrations and gave them unstinted attention. He was guided, as he said, by the conviction that illustrations were the primary method of teaching and of intellectual communication, and that they speak a language which even those who cannot read can understand. Thus, the edition was designed from the start to make it as easy as possible for the reader to study the pictures. Up to the 74th chapter, each begins with a three-line motto, followed by the woodcut on top of the verso of the sheet. This means that the chapters, therefore, always require one or two pages of front matter, i. e., 34 or 94 lines, not one and a half (i. e., 64 lines). It is always set so that the picture is in the upper left. Indeed it appears almost as though some chapters of the book were written to fit illustrations. The rest of the book, such as chapters 76 and 82, are handled somewhat differently.

The artistic merit of the woodcuts is quite great. The motions are free and natural, the perspective is not neglected, and the expressions on the faces are surprisingly true to life. Many of the groups are very dramatic, and individual scenes are among the best caricatures that have ever been done. The carving appears to have been done by three or four artists of unequal talent; some of these do full justice to the thoughts of the artist and some do not.

No book in the German language had achieved as great popularity as did [479-484] Brant's Narrenschiff. It was reproduced immediately in practically every city, with the same woodcuts or reduced-size copies. Johannes Bergmann himself produced a new German edition (21) in 1497 and 1498, and, under the title, Stultifera navis, he issued five Latin editions translated by Jacob Locher (22), using the same woodcuts.

Bergmann printed still another book by Brant, in 1494; [485] his In laudem virginis Mariae multorumque sanctorum et varii generis carmina (23), with 14 woodcuts.

In 1495 Bergmann published [486] Brant's De origine et conservatione bonorum et laude civitatis Hierosolymae (24), with two woodcuts. They are both 132 x 95 mm.

In 1498 he printed [487] a new edition of Brant's Varia carmina, which Gruninger had published earlier in Strassburg. However, starting with 1495, we find Brant himself working with Furter.

In 1496 Furter published [488] Brant's Passio Sancti Meynhardi Martyris et eremitae (25), with a postscript to the reader by Brant in which he acknowledges the work of Furter. Its 15 woodcuts are 115 x 80 mm and are the products of various people. They can not be compared with the woodcuts in the Narrenschiff, but are, nevertheless, handled with diligence and love.

In 1498 Furter issued [489] De revelatione facta ab angelo beato Methodio in Carcere detento (26). This was a new edition, dressed up with new illustrations, of the unillustrated text published s. l. e. a. and then in a second edition by Johann Froschauer in Augsburg. In this book Brant wrote a preface, again emphasizing his special interest in illustrations. The Furter edition has 55 woodcuts, of which 5 are reused. The title page illustration is 102 x 57 mm and the others are 102 x 80 mm. Although the drawings were all well done, the uneducated could not, as Brant hoped in the preface, learn the content of the book from its illustrations alone. When Furter did a second Latin edition of this work in 1504, under a different title, and simultaneously issued a German translation, he reused these same woodcuts.

After he left Basel Brant associated himself with the production of only one more Basel imprint. This was [490] the 1501 edition of Aesopischen Fabeln (27), using the text by Laurentius Valla, which was published by Jacob von Pforzheim. Brant supplied a second part for this work, consisting of instructions prepared especially for his son, and useful anecdotes for learning good habits and philosophical maxims. Here too he was most intimately involved in the work of illustration and appears to have personally given the artist the general outlines. The woodcut on the title page is 90 x 75 mm. The 140 others are 80-85 x 115 mm.

In addition to these writings by Brant, a number of other important illustrated books were published by Bergmann and by Furter.

Bergmann published [491] one edition of Liber vagatorum (28), and in 1494 he published, s. l., [492] an edition of Carolus Verardus' Historia Baetica seu de Granada expugnata (29). It had five woodcuts (110 x 72), which are well executed both in drawing and in cutting. They show panoramas of broad stretches of land and sea.

Furter issued, s. l. e. a., but well after the end of the fifteenth century, [493] Bonaventura's Speculum sanctae Mariae Virginis (30), which is divided into eight parts, with a woodcut on the first and second pages of each part, some of which are repetitions. If this book did appear in the fifteenth century, the woodcuts are among the best produced in Basel in this period. The compositions are free, the shading is skillful and the nude is executed very naturally.

Bonaventura's [494] Psalter Mariae (31), which Furter published undated, also has a good woodcut.

In the sixteenth century [495] Peter Etterlyn brought out, in 1507, the Kronika von der loblichen Eidgenossenschaft (32), which had been printed by Furter. It has 29 illustrations, but because 17 are repeated, there were only 12 woodblocks. The title page illustration shows a young Kaiser on his throne, etc. Next comes a 232 x 175 mm woodcut showing the coats-of-arms of the various German states, below which the year 1504 is given. The rest of the woodcuts are of various times and by various people. They range from 100 to 105 mm in height and from 80 to 88 mm in width, and all originated in the 15th Century. The first four illustrations come from the Meinratlegende, and numbers 8, 13, 14, and 15 were not prepared for this book. Those that have been recut for this book are much more significant and more modern in style. The two most significant woodcuts in the book (160 x 145), were done by a great artist; one is a deep Alpine landscape and the other is of the William Tell story, set in a rocky landscape.

During this period Jacob von Pforzheim [496] printed another Missale herboplense (33), which includes the Würzburg escutcheon and a rather crude picture of the crucifixion.

Nicolaus Lamparter issued [497] a Latin edition of Brant's Narrenschiff (34) in 1509.

What was achieved in Basel in the fifteenth century was quite significant. Aside from the Cologne Bible it is hard to name another book whose woodcuts were copied as often as were those in the Narrenschiff. Basel book illustration would have reached even greater heights if the artistic and literary drive of Sebastian Brant had been available in the city longer. Basel's loss in 1498, when he left, was the gain of the neighboring city of Strassburg.

Notes

1) Stockmeyer and Reber, Beiträge zur Baseler Buchdruckergeschichte. Basel, 1840; Fechter, "Beiträge zur älteste Geschichte der Buchdruckerkunst in Basel," in Baseler Taschenbuch für 1863, p. 252; Zarncke, Sebastian Brant's Narrenschiff. Leipzig, 1854.

2) Stockmeyer, p. 53, No. 3. Folio.

3) Stockmeyer, p. 59, No. 20.

4) Stockmeyer, p. 63, No. 42. Folio.

5) Stockmeyer, p. 72. Small octavo; Hain, Part II, No. 9327.

6) Stockmeyer, p. 72. Quarto.

7) Ebert, No. 4078. Folio; Hain, Part II. 2:414, No. 15514; Panzer I:206, No. 364; Brunet, Nouv. Recherch. Suppl. du Man. I:315; Stockmeyer, p. 77, No. 3.

8) Two numbers (No's 4 and 5) reproduced by Essenwein, Plate 145.

9) Panzer I:359, No. 763; Stockmeyer and Reber, p. 84, No. 45.

10) Stockmeyer and Reber, p. 78, No. 4.

11) Quadrigesimale novum editum ac predicatum a quodam fratre minore de observantia in inclita civitate Basilensi; Stockmeyer, p. 79, No. 7. Octavo; Hain, No. 13628.

12) Hain, No. 13629.

13) Stockmeyer, p. 75, No. 2. Quarto.

14) Hupsauer, p. 347 ff.; Stockmeyer, p. 76, No. 3; Hain, No. 8250.

15) Stockmeyer, p. 77, No. 4. Quarto.

16) Stockmeyer, p. 74, No. 1a. Octavo.

17) Stockmeyer, p. 74, No. 1b. Quarto.

18) Hain, Part I. p. 95, No. 879. Folio; Panzer, Zusätze, p. 18, No. 80, also 1:46, No. 80.

19) Hain, No. 16278. Octavo; Two numbers are reproduced by Essenwein, Plate 144.

20) Ebert, No. 2922. Quarto; Panzer I:214, No. 393; Hain, Part I. 1:514, No. 3736; Stockmeyer, p. 129, No. 4; Allgemeine Biographie, p. 257, article on Brant; Two numbers are reproduced in Essenwein, Plate 147.

21) Hain, No. 3740.

22) Hain, No. 3746-3749 and 3751. Quarto; Weigel, No. 9920.

23) Hain, No. 3733 (variant). Quarto; Panzer, Annales typogr. I:176, No. 172; Brunet, ed. V, I:1202; Graesse I:520; Stockmeyer, p. 129, No. 1.

24) Hain, No. 3735. Quarto; Panzer 1:179, No. 195; Stockmeyer, p. 130, No. 5.

25) Hain, No. 12453. Quarto; Stockmeyer, p. 79, No. 9; Two numbers are reproduced in Essenwein, Plate 148.

26) Panzer VI:178, No. 29. Quarto; Stockmeyer, p. 80, No. 16 and, at the end, Furter, M. Opera et vigilantea Seb. Brant. Basel, 1498. Later editions in 1504, Quarto, and in 1516, Quarto.

27) Aesopi appologi sive mythologi cum quibusdam carminum et fabularum, additionibus Seb. Brant. Basel, Jac. de Pfortzheim, 1501; Ebert, No. 236. Folio; Panzer VI, No. 3; Stockmeyer, p. 68, No. 13.

28) Hain, No. 3016.

29) Hain, No. 15942.

30) Hain, No. 3574.

31) Hain, No. 3570.

32) Ebert, No. 6992. Folio; Panzer I:284, No. 595; Stockmeyer, p. 83, No. 38.

33) Not in Panzer VI:174 ff.

34) Brant Sebastiani navis stultifera ab J. Lochero latinitate donata; Panzer VI:181, No. 49. Quarto.

Chapter X

STRASSBURG (1)

Strassburg, which was of little importance in the 1470's, gradually developed its skills. The illustrations produced in Strassburg in the 1480's could not be compared with those done in Basel or even in Ulm. Mostly, they were crude copies of pictures that had appeared in books elsewhere. Original drawings were rare and even when they did occur were normally unskilled.

The first printing [498] by Martin Schott, who was active from 1481 to 1499, was a 1481 edition (2) of Plenarium, which he repeated [499] in 1491 (3), and he used the old Augsburg woodcuts for these. A second book attributed to him, which was set in 1480-1482, [500] was the Legende vom Ritter Herrn Peter Diemringer von Staufenberg (4), which was a short poem that had been written at the end of the thirteenth or the beginning of the fourteenth century. It included 18 small woodcuts. The illustrations are very poor and are about at the level of the earliest Augsburg products.

In 1484 Schott issued the second edition [501] of the Buchs Ovidii von der Liebe (5), in which he reused Sorg's woodcuts.

In 1488 he published the seventh edition [502] of the Buches der Geschicht des grossen Alexanders (6). The title page illustration is a reversed copy of that in the Sorg edition and the other illustrations are copied, some direct and some reversed, from Bämler. Schott published [503-504] the eighth edition of this work in 1489 (7) and the ninth edition in 1493 (8).

In 1489 he printed [505] the Histori der Zerstörung der Stadt Troia (9), with the title page illustration a reversed copy of that in the Sorg edition of 1482 and the others bad copies of those in Zainer's edition.

His 1493 edition of [506] Johannes Nider's 24 goldnen Harfen (10), is the third in the series of publications of this work. The title page woodcut is 200 x 150 mm and the 24 text woodcuts are 190 x 125, each consisting of two blocks.

Of the six illustrated books that Shott produced, four can be traced back to Augsburg.

We have more illustrated books from the press established by Johann Prüss in 1480, but they are of little importance. The first book he produced [507, Pl. 132-134], which was published without date or place, was the Buch der heiligen drei Könige, by Johannes Hildeshemien (11). It had 58 (95 x 125) woodcuts. Even though it was not important artistically and the woodcuts were very sloppy, this was the first illustrated book of any significance to be published in Strassburg.

Prüss published the third edition of [508] Reise der Ritters Montevilla in 1484 (12). It was first published by Sorg in Augsburg in 1481. The woodcut on sheet 2a shows the departure, and the other illustrations are not copies of those in the Sorg edition but are crude original work done in Strassburg. In the fourth edition [509], 1488, Prüss reworked them (13). The [510]

Martyrologium der Heiligen (14), which he also published in 1484, has a 122 x 100 mm illustration on one of the first leaves, but aside from that it has only the initial letters for each month illustrated by a (38 x 38) woodcut.

In 1485 he printed [511] the Goldne Bulle und königlich Reformation Karls IV (15), which has eleven (105 x 125) artistically meritorious woodcuts.

The two editions, 1487 (16) and 1488 (17) of [512-513] Fasciculi temporum, by Werner Rolevink, which Prüss printed, have the usual illustrations of this book which had already been printed fourteen times.

In 1488 he issued the third edition of [514] Boccaccio's Compendium de claris mulieribus (18). It has a new small woodcut in front of the chapter on Eve but he simply reused Johannes Zainer's woodcuts for the other illustrations.

In the last of the books by Prüss that belong in this period, [515] Formularen und Tischrhetorika (19), which had been printed by Heinrich Geissler in 1493, there are two unimportant Strassburg woodcuts.

Towards the end of the 1480's, Thomas Anshelm worked in Strassburg for a while, and then he later printed in Tübingen, Pforzheim and Hagenau. In Strassburg, in 1488, he printed the thirteenth German edition of [516] Plenarium (20), which is important in the history of Strassburg book illustration as well as in the history of the Plenariums. All earlier evangelical books, with the exception of that by Schott in 1481, were published in Augsburg and their illustrations were completely locked in with those of the first edition, which was issued by Zainer in 1474. Anshelm, for the first time, provided new, independent, large compositions that were rich in figures, and which really belonged more nearly to the sixteenth century than to the fifteenth. The title page woodcut is 220 x 137 mm, and is influenced by one of Schönsperger's illustrations. The text woodcuts (72 x 138) are all at a very high level, except for the last one, which is faulty. The illustrations are excellent throughout, with noble faces and faultlessly executed landscapes. The letters found on the hems of clothing in a number of cases, such as "NVOV" or "IVIIO" or "WILVIOA," appear to be merely ornamental.

Among the books published towards the end of the 1480's for which it has not been possible to identify the printer, is [517] the Zehnte deutsche Bibel (21), which appeared in 1485. It adds nothing to the history of book illustration. The 108 woodcuts that appear in its two volumes are related to those in the Bible that was printed in Cologne five years earlier. The chief difference is that these are reduced in size. For example, the first woodcut, 190 x 190 mm in the Cologne edition, is only 130 x 135 mm in this edition. The others, which are 120 x 188 mm in the Cologne edition, are reduced to 100 x 135 mm here. This resulted in suppression of details that appeared in the Cologne edition. The artist did not follow the Cologne illustrations slavishly, but the changes he made were minor, and the woodcutting in the Strassburg edition represented a great retrogression from that in the Cologne Bible.

The [518] Seelenheil (22), which was published in 1489 sans location, may be attributed to Strassburg. It has an illustration on the verso of the title page.

In 1493 and 1494 the fourth and fifth editions [519] of Petrus de Crescentiis' Liber ruralium commodorum were printed in Strassburg, without location. This was also printed in

Mainz in 1493, and the woodcuts of the fourth edition (23) are identical with those of the other 1493 s.l. Latin edition, except that rearrangement is found in books 3, 5 and 6 because in these three books the subject matter is arranged alphabetically in Latin, so the German translations had to be rearranged according to the German names. The fifth edition, which appeared in 1494 (24), is a repetition of the fourth.

The 1494 reprint [521] of Brant's Narrenschiff (25) copied the woodcuts of the original.

The 1498 edition [522] of Leben der Einsiedler Paulus und Antonius (26) has twenty-one (70 x 55) woodcuts. They are all of the Alsace school and have the haziness that frequently appears in the later illustrations published by Grüninger.

The second 1498 publication to appear in Strassburg without the name of the printer, [523] a Büchlein von Hiob (27), has a woodcut on the verso of the title page and 30 smaller and inferior woodcuts in the text.

In 1499 [524] there followed the fourth (28) and [525] fifth (29) Latin editions of Lichtenberger's Pronosticatio, with the same woodcuts as in the first edition.

[526-527] The Räthselbuch (30), appeared, s.l.e.a., with a completely insignificant woodcut; as did the second edition of the Historie Herzog Ernsts von Baiern (31), which was originally published by Sorg in Augsburg.

Only three relatively late illustrated books remain of the publications of Martin Flach, who was printing from 1475 to 1500. In 1494 [528] he issued Exercitium puerorum grammaticale per dietas distributum (32), which has the title page woodcut that had frequently been used in Cologne and Augsburg, showing the teacher and his students. However, the woodcut shows several differences from the editions issued in both the other cities. The word spacing is the same as in the Schönsperger edition, yet the dot over the letter "j" in the Latin quotation in the Schönsperger edition is lacking here, and there are a few other minor differences.

Ulrich Eberhard's [529] Modus latinitatus (33), which was printed in 1498, uses the same woodcut.

The 1500 edition [530] of Jakob Wimpfeling's Adolescentia (34) has three (100 x 95) woodcuts on the last pages. These woodcuts, particularly the first two, are very significant.

Among the printers who started later, Wilhelm Schaffner, from Ropperschwiler, played an especially important part because, so far as anyone can trace, he was the first to print [531] the Hortulus animae, a Latin prayer and devotional book. He printed it in 1498 and it met with such general approval that it was reprinted everywhere in the sixteenth century and the most important artists prepared many illustrations for it. The woodcuts that Schaffner used for Hortulus animae were closely related to the text they illustrated, and the content of this series of pictures was followed in all later editions. However, the woodcuts in the Schaffner Hortulus (35) are rather awkward and stiff and had a dirty background. He reprinted the book in 1500 (36), using the same woodcuts.

Not much was achieved in Strassburg before end of the 1490's. Martin Schott mostly reprinted books that had been done elsewhere, except for his insignificant Legende vom Ritter Diemringer. Prüss produced his Buch der heiligen drei Könige independently, but its woodcuts were worthless. Flach did practically no illustrations. The Bible of 1485 is copied from the Cologne

Bible. Only one printer, Thomas Anshelm, who did not remain in Strassburg very long, produced an important illustrated book. However, its illustrations were not of the Alsace school.

It is to the credit of Johann Grüninger that Strassburg book illustration achieved artistic character. He is first encountered as a printer in 1480 in Basel; in 1482 he bought citizenship in Strassburg and joined the guild of goldsmiths. His first book appeared in 1483. His publications covered the entire range of scholarship and literature, and practically all his works were illustrated with countless woodcuts. He could claim, with honesty, that he spent large amounts on these (37). Various artists and woodcarvers worked for him, but the most important were of the Alsace school. And it so happened that at the turn of the century, they were the most outstanding in book illustration. During this period his woodcuts were prepared anew for each book, but later, when he was thinking about an ever increasing market, this was no longer invariably true and, increasingly, he used his stock of woodcuts with little regard for the varying nature of the books.

The first illustrated book [533, Pl. 135] published by Grüninger was the Terentius cum Directorio vocabularum, Glossa interlineali, Commentariis etc. of 1496 (38). It does not foreshadow the great step forward that book illustration was shortly to take in the Grüninger plant. Its most noteworthy illustration (270 x 165) is that on the title page. Of the text woodcuts the six title pages for the individual comedies (245 x 165) are the most significant, but the illustrations within the individual comedies (85 x 30) are worthless (39). When Grüninger, in 1499, issued [534] a most unintelligible German translation of Terenz (40), he reused these same woodcuts.

His 1498 edition of Jacob Locher's edition [535] of Horaz (41) was of the same low grade. He placed special emphasis on the title page illustration (140 x 135) and, here too, the first few woodcuts are the most significant.

In 1498 and 1500 [536-537] Grüninger published the 21st (42) and 23rd (43) editions of Plenarium, which had much more significant woodcuts. The title page woodcut is 140 x 100 mm and those in the text vary in size from small ones that are only 50 x 35 mm to larger bordered illustrations that are 75 x 134 mm.

In 1497-1500 we find Grüninger working with the local surgeon, Hieronymus Brunschwig, whose widely read and often reprinted writings were first published by Grüninger. The first of these, [538, Pl. 136-137] the Buch der Chirurgia oder Handwürking der Wundartzney (44), teaches the general principles of surgery in seven tracts. It has 48 woodcuts that range from 160-180 mm in height and from 130-135 mm wide. Thirty are repeated, so that the total number of woodcuts is only 18. Where suitable, the pictures are made by combining two woodcuts that are 65 mm each. Another and greater difference is that the wounds are not cut into the wood but are always simply colored into the illustration. In the illustrations consisting of two woodcuts, normally only the half showing the patient is changed and the one representing the doctor and his group remains the same. The woodcuts are very significant. An indescribable loveliness diffuses the faces. On the title page woodcut there are the initials "E. G." and on No. 36 there are the letters "o H R," but these are not considered to be the artist's emblem. These woodcuts were reused very frequently in later years.

His second Brunschwig book [539] dealt with the art of distilling. It was first published in 1500 by Grüninger, under the title, Liber de arte distillandi de simplicibus, das buch der rechten Kunst zu distilieren die eintzigen ding (45). It was widely distributed until the second half of the sixteenth century.

His third was [540] Liber pestilentialis de venenis epidemiae (46). Its title page illustration shows a teacher and four students, and the one on sheet 2a is a sick person in bed; the other illustrations (a total of 22) are conventional.

In this same period Grüninger appears also to have produced two editions of the great Latin Hortus sanitatis, which was first published by Jacob Meydenbach, in Mainz, in 1491. These [541] were issued without place or date, but they used a number of woodcuts that were used only in Grüninger's plant.

In the first edition (47), the full page illustration on sheet 1b shows the teaching physician from the Chirurgia and the other, which is equal in size, on sheet 333b, is also from the Chirurgia. The woodcuts of the bodies are copied from the original Mainz edition but are lighter in drawing and in cut. A number of variations are introduced; for example, in the case of the pictures of animals, a landscape background is added.

In the [542] second edition (48), the doctor and the pharmacist, from the earlier edition, are used as the title page illustration and the illustration on sheet 333a is copied from the Chirurgia. The illustrations of bodies in nature which appeared in the earlier edition are reused in this one and show more wear than in the earlier edition.

Another book printed by Grüninger during this period, but undated, [543] was Melibeus und Prudentia (49), which had few woodcuts.

His 1499 edition [544] of the Goldenen Esels des Apulejus (50), likewise had few and unimportant illustrations.

The year 1500 brought two richly illustrated books, which, to be sure, did not rise to the heights of those listed above. One of these was [545] the Historie vom Metzger Hug Schapler, der König von Frankreich wurde (51). It had 33 (112 x 135) woodcuts.

The second [546-548] the Geschichte von eines Königs Tochter von Frankreich, die der König selbst zur Ehe wolt han (52) had 35 woodcuts, which mostly were no better, and, in fact in some cases, were the same as the blocks used in the ... Hug Schapler. New editions of both of these were issued in 1508.

In 1501 Grüninger printed [549-551] his first Hortulus animae (53), which he did in new editions in 1503 and 1507. The woodcuts are normally 50 x 35 mm and these editions have 98 instead of the conventional 66 illustrations.

In 1501 [552] he also did a new edition of the Buches der Weisheit (54), which first appeared in Ulm in 1483. The content of the title page illustration (134 x 137) is the same as that of the Ulm edition and the other woodcuts (90 x 138) are free copies of those used by Holl. They were usually assembled from two or three individual blocks.

Grüninger's printing achieved renewed impetus when Sebastian Brant came back home from Basel. Even while Brant was still in Basel, in 1497, Grüninger published [553] Locher's Latin translation of Brant's Narrenschiff (55), using the woodcuts that had been used in the original edition. When Brant came back to Strassburg he was at his peak and he met Grüninger, who was determined to make his printing house the outstanding one in Strassburg, regardless of cost.

By 1498 [554] they had gotten together to issue Brant's Varia Carmine (56). In 1501 they followed this with [555] Brant's Boetius de philosophico consolatu sive consolatione philosophiae (57), the woodcuts of which were even higher in quality than those of the Terenz or the Horaz. The one that follows the preface (115 x 140) shows Rome, surrounded by a round low wall, and provides a number of its special features. There are equally large and detailed title page illustrations for each of the parts. The text woodcuts vary in size from 60 x 145 mm to 57 x 90 mm. The first book has 12 text woodcuts; the second had 15; the third, 24; the fourth, 11; and the fifth had 11. All of these were prepared especially for this book and were of the Alsace school. In a few cases, but rarely, is an illustration made up of multiple woodcuts.

1502 may be considered the peak period of the Grüninger press. It is not Sebastian Brant's [556] Heiligenlebens (58) that is chiefly responsible for this, notwithstanding the importance of its 268 woodcuts (some of which may have been copied from Martin Schongauer). A few of the blocks were assembled from various pieces and others were repeated. They were cut by a Master who earlier had worked in metal, and who had also previously done work for the Hug Schapler and for the Geschichte der fanzösischen Königstochter.... They are normally 75 x 135 mm but there are a few that occupy a full page (220 x 160).

The masterpiece of 1502 was Brant's [557, Pl. 138-143] edition of Virgil (59), and the title page illustration (225 x 155) is especially meritorious. Each of the ten eclogues is illustrated by a woodcut, of which the first two are 180 x 140 mm and the rest are 115 mm high and 145-150 mm wide. The title page illustration of the "Georgicis" (175 x 245) is a landscape; it has 38 illustrations in the text, in which pastoral life is very charmingly depicted. The title page illustration for "Aeneis" (185 x 140) is, likewise, a masterpiece. The "Aeneis," as a whole, includes 142 woodcuts. It is supplemented by a number of the shorter poems attributed to Virgil, which are illustrated by 22 woodcuts, so that the book as a whole has 214 illustrations. As in the case of his Basel works, the illustrations in Brant's Virgil are completely related to the text. While there is no question of Brant's contribution to the illustrations, there has been some argument that he cut them himself. However, near the end of the book we find the monogram of the artist or woodcutter, consisting of the initials "C. A.," and it seems clear, on close examination, that more than one artist or woodcutter was involved in preparation of the illustrations in this book.

Grüninger published a book that reached the same heights as were achieved in the Virgil about two years later, 1504, in [558] Der heiligen Kirche und des Römischen Reichs Wagenfuhr, (60), by Hugo von Schlettstadt, Vicar of St. Stephan in Strassburg. The text and woodcuts for the 15 illustrations (usually 135 x 105) were both done by the same person.

Grüninger's later work, which did not put as much emphasis on artistic values, is shown in transition by a book that he assembled himself in 1505. He had printed Hieronymus Brunschwig's little Destillirbuch in 1500. In that same year Marsilius Ficinus' book, De triplici vita, de vita sana, longa et coelitus comparanda, was published by Jon Knoblouch in a Strassburg edition. Grüninger fitted together a kind of summary of Johan Adelphus' translation of the first two parts of Ficinus' book and skipped the third part. He combined this with his Destillirbuch and published this [559] under the title, Medicinarius, das Buch der Gesundheit (61). This book gives the first example of the way Grüninger ran his later publishing operations, using woodblocks out of his large stock to illustrate his later books. The woodcut for its preface (135 x 140) was reused from his Buche der Weisheit of 1501, the second illustration was reused from his Horaz, and the other 229 text illustrations are reused from the Destillirbuche, with a remarkable combination and odd mixture of woodcuts for the other illustrations. Grüninger continued to issue [560-566] the Medicinarius a number of times in later years, frequently under a different title. In 1508 he printed it as Das neue buch der rechten kunst zu destilliren (62); in 1512 (63), 1514 (64), 1515 (65) and 1521 (66) as Destillirbuchs; and in 1528 and 1531 (67) as Das neue Destillirbuch. The woodcuts remained the same in all these.

His 1507 edition of [567] Leben der Altväter (68) was the eighth in the series of editions of this book. Its illustrations were not taken from the earlier editions but were modernized in style. In addition, in 1507 he published two classical works, Cäsar and Livius. His edition [568, Pl. 144] of Cäsar (69) has 18 large woodcuts which were unquestionably done by the same artist who supplied the illustrations for the Virgil. Only one, No. 4, is taken from the Römischen Reichs Wagenfuhr. The [569] 1508 edition reused the same woodcuts.

The woodcuts for his edition [570] of Livius are not nearly as coherent a unit. Special care was given to the first woodcut, but even when the same scenes are illustrated as in the Mainz edition, the results do not appear to be at all closely related.

In 1508 Grüninger's [571] Catalogus argentinensium episcoporum, by Jacob Wimpfeling (70), had only the (85 x 95) title page woodcut.

One of Grüninger's painstaking products in 1508 was [572] the Legende der heiligen Katharina (71), by Frater Petrus. The title page woodcut (82 x 100) and the first text woodcut (70 x 90), like all the others, come from a single artist and the woodblocks are not assembled; each is cut in a single piece, as is always the case in Alsace products. The landscapes are perfect. In some illustrations the human figures leave much to be desired. They are short and compressed, the eyes are gigantic, and the lower body is too small in relation to the head.

The third book that he published in 1508 was supplied by Sebastian Brant and was republished [573] by Sebastian Wagner in Worms, in a revised edition in 1538. It was the Gedichte Freidanks (72). The title page woodcut is 79 x 90 mm and the 46 text woodcuts vary in size, ranging from 80 x 70 mm to 80 x 92 mm, with the last one 120 x 110 mm. In No. 25, within the shading, one may see the initials "A F"; in No. 35 there are the letters "H. E. V. S. R."

The difference between the illustrated Grüninger publications and those of his predecessors is tremendous. To be sure, the art work, even in Grüninger's publications, is stiff and awkward, but it is difficult to say how much of this is attributable to the woodcarver rather than to the artist. He almost invariably brings in rich backgrounds and mountains cut by rivulets, such as one would normally find in the area.

Because of the following that Grüninger achieved, his contemporary printers put more emphasis on illustration.

Johann Prüss, in his later printing, almost always went back to Grüninger. In his [574] new edition of Geissler's Tischrhetorika of 1502 (73), the title page illustration (180 x 135) is taken from Grüninger's Chirurgia of 1497.

In 1499 [575] his edition of Cato teutonice expositus (74), which had first been printed by Greif in Reutlingen in 1494, used the illustration of the annunciation as the title page illustration.

His 1502 [576] edition of Stultiferae-naviculae by Jodocus Badius (75) has seven woodcuts. The title page woodcut is 100 x 102 mm and the others are 80 x 110 mm.

The two woodcuts in Friedrich Riederer's [577] Spiegel der wahren Rhetorik (76), which Prüss printed in 1505, make no new contribution. The title page illustration (140 x 105) comes from Grüninger's Horaz of 1498 and the larger one, on the verso, is from Grüninger's Chirurgia.

In 1506 [578] there followed Surgant's Manuale curatorum (77). Prüss' [579] Hortus sanitatis of 1507-1509 (78) consists of the smaller German Hortus and its supplements, combined with a translation of the books dealing with land, air and water animals, and rocks, from the greater Latin Hortus. The woodcut titled "Physician and Pharmacist in the office" and the equally large one on the other side of the sheet come from Grüninger's Chirurgia. The text woodcuts of the first part are not those found in the usual editions of the small Hortus, but are newly cut and are better and somewhat larger, even though they are not as good as those in the original Mainz edition of 1485. Those in the second part are taken without change from the earlier editions of the large Hortus.

In 1508 Prüss issued [580] the fifteenth edition of Belial (79) with the same woodcuts as those used in the very beginning, and he also [581] issued a new edition of Aesop.

In 1509 [582] he printed the Unterrichtung eines geistlichen Lebens, by Laurentius Justinius (80). In 1510 he published [583] Weil's Translationen (81), in which the title page illustration is 190 x 130 mm (82).

Mathias Brant, who worked in Strassburg for a short time around the turn of the century, produced [584] Regimen sanitatis (83), with a 70 x 80 mm illustration on the title page.

Bartholomäus Kistler, who printed here from 1497 to 1509, is more important in the history of book illustration. In 1497 he issued [585] the fourth German edition of Pronosticatio by Johann Lichtenberger (84), which first appeared without location in 1488, reusing the original woodcuts.

During the same year he printed [586] Columbus. Ein schön lieblich lesen von etlichen Inseln, die do in kurzen Zeiten funden sind durch den Küng von Hispania (85). The woodcuts for the first and last pages (80 x 105) show a landscape in which Christ is talking with the King of Spain and his retinue, with a picture of a man in the left background.

In 1499 he published [587] the Reise des Ritters Montevilla in das heilige Land (86), which is the fifth edition of this book. The woodcuts are the same as those used by Prüss.

In 1499 or 1500 he printed [588] a Chronika von allen Königen und Kaisern (87). It has only a single woodcut (78 x 104) on the title page.

In 1500 he produced a number of small books [589-595]. One that had an illustration on its title page was Leben der Bischöfe Eucharii, Valerii und Materni (88); another, Legende von St. Anna und ihrem ganzen Geschlechte, had three woodcut illustrations; the Tractat contra pestems (89) had twelve woodcuts; and there were a number of songs that were supplied with title page pictures, including Wie sich jetzt Geistliche und Weltliche halten (90); Von des Bremberger End und Tod (91); and Von den schönen Frauen (92).

Among the most important of these illustrations are the three (100 x 115) woodcuts in the Legende von St. Anna.

His [596] Practica auf 1501 (93), which was published in 1501, has a title page woodcut and 25 illustrations in the text.

His 1502 publications [597-600] included the Wunderbarlichen geschichten von geistlichen wybspersonen (94), which had a title page illustration and six text woodcuts. His Practica auf 1502 (95) was illustrated by 19 woodcuts; the Büchlein von dem geschwinden finden der nüwen inseln (96), by Fürer, had a woodcut on its title page, and Der Türken anschläg (97) also had a woodcut illustration on its title page.

In his 1503 edition of [601] Geschichte des grossen Alexander (98), he reworked the illustrations that had been used at least ten times before into the modern style and increased their number. The title page illustration (195 x 140) is particularly characteristic of the Alsace school. Instead of the 26 woodcuts of the first edition, this eleventh edition had 74. The first of the text woodcuts is 80 x 75 mm and the others are 72 x 135 mm. Most of these are assembled from two pieces of wood. The woodcut showing Alexander kneeling before the Bishop has the letters "J. K." in the pennant carried by one of the knights. The artist appears to have had much in common with one who worked in Grüninger's plant.

Folzen's book [602], Von allen Baden, die von Natur heiss sind (99), which was printed by Kistler in 1504, had a title page woodcut.

The booklet [603] Von den peinen die do bereit seind allen denen, die da sterben in Todsünden (100), which was published in 1506, had 26 text illustrations in addition to the title page woodcut.

The group of printers who really did the bulk of their work in the sixteenth century instead of the fifteenth, begins with Mathias Hupfuff, who was active from 1492 to 1520.

His 1496 book by Johannes Trithemius [604], De immaculata conceptione virginis Mariae (101), has two woodcuts that are on the title page and its verso.

In 1498 he printed [605-606] a second edition of the little booklet, Kaiser Karls Recht (102), which was first printed by Hans Briefmaler in Bamberg, and in the same year he published the thirteenth edition of Meister Lucidarius.

In 1501 he issued [607] the sixth edition of Montevilla's Reise (103). The title page illustration is 160 x 150 mm and the other 140 woodcuts are taken from a variety of older books, though none of these was taken from the Sorg or Schoensperger editions. His [608] Cato in Latin durch Seb. Brant getütschet, which also appeared in 1501 (104), reused the picture of the teacher and students as the title page illustration. In the same year [609] his Gesetz und Ordnung der loblichen und hochberümpten freien Stadt Strassburg (105) has the city escutcheon on the title page and Mary with Child on the verso of the title page.

His 1502 publications, [610] Regiment für die Pestilenz (106) and the [611] Historie vom Leben des Bischofs Wolfgang, and his 1503 publication of [612] Valzen, Hymmelisch Funtgrub (107), had only title page illustrations. The second editions of [613] Des Endkrists leben und

Regierung (108), published in 1503, had seven large and 56 small woodcuts, and his 1504 edition (109) of the [614] Teutsche Kalender had 80. [615] Virdung's Practica of 1504 (110) likewise had many woodcuts.

In 1506 [616] he printed a Psalter with a title page woodcut (111) as well as [617] the sixth edition of Melusine (112) in which he included the 70 bad woodcuts of the Bämler original edition. In the same year, 1507, [618] he issued the booklet Von neuen Inseln (113).

His [619] Himmlische Fundgrube (114), published in 1507, had a crude woodcut on the title page and on its verso.

In his [620] Tondalus of 1507 (115) and his [621] Meerfahrt St. Brandons of 1510 (116), the woodcuts of earlier editions are reused.

Two books by Johann Schott, the son of Martin Schott, issued during this period, are his [622] 24 Alten, published in 1500, which is the fourth in the series of editions of this book (117). The title page illustration is the same as that of the first Bamberg edition. The second illustration, which was on the verso of the title page of the Bamberg edition, is not included in this one. The other woodcuts (140 x 135) are new. Two woodblocks are made to serve for all of the 24 elders, but they are well executed, beautifully shaded, and were prepared anew for this edition. His edition [623] of Boethius' Trost der Weisheit, issued in 1500 (118), has a title page illustration that is 110 x 90 mm.

The woodcuts in the two books published by Johann Wähinger are quite important. His [624-626] German Hortulus animae, which he issued in 1502 and again in 1504, and his Latin edition, which appeared in 1503 (119), are elegant small books, printed in red and black, and with many fine illustrations. There are a total of 66 woodcuts, mostly 63 x 40 mm, but with a few that are full page (78 x 50) in size. His [627] Officium (120) consists of eight quarto sheets and is likewise printed in red and black. The title page has a distinguished woodcut.

Among the books of this period that can not be attributed to any particular printer there is one that appeared in 1500 [628], the Büchleins wie Rom gebauet ward (121), which has two title page illustrations and ten text woodcuts.

The edition [629] of Drackole Waida (122), which appeared in 1500, has a very old title page illustration which is 134 x 100 mm. The [630] Büchlein von dem Rosengarten König Laurins (123), which appeared without a publisher's name in 1509, has 17 woodcuts of varying sizes which appear to have been taken from an older book. The one on the verso of the title page is full page, while the others vary from 70 to 75 mm in height and from 105 to 108 in width, and are assembled from two blocks.

The [631] Legende von St. Anna (124) has only a title page woodcut; however, the [632] Büchlein von den Peinen so do bereit seint allen denen do sterben in todsünden, which appeared in the same year, is illustrated by many woodcuts.

The number of artists who were working in the field of book illustration in Strassburg at the turn of the century and who are known by name is not large. The little known but talented painter Johann Schrotbank, of Westhoffen, is known only through one [633] book which he compiled, and which was published by Bartholomäus Kistler, in 1502, under the title Praktika (125). It is a collection of astrological prophecies. At least two of the illustrations of this peculiar book are certainly drawn by Schrotbank.

Hieronymus Greff or Groff (Graf) came to Strassburg at the turn of the century, and purchased citizenship there in 1502. In 1502 he issued a book on the apocalypse which contained 15 large woodcuts, each with explanation in German. The title [634] is *Die heimlich Offenbarung Johannis,* and it states, "Printed in Strassburg by Jheronimum Greff, the painter, 1502, 16 sheets in folio" (126). While each of the illustrations bears the monogram "J M F," they are merely copies of Dürer's apocalypse. Greff was not only the wood cutter and printer of the illustrations, he appears to have printed the text as well.

He received recognition as an artist in his guild, and in 1507 he was one of the citizens who was put in charge of arrangements when Bishop Wilhelm of Honstein visited the city (127). Nagler attributes the monogram that appeared in a book printed by Grüninger in 1518 to Hieronymus Greff.

The woodcuts do have a certain similarity with those of Grüninger's publications of the fifteenth century, but it would be peculiar that Greff should have failed to have referred to his earlier major works in view of the fact that he did claim credit for one of his later mediocre works.

There was a still unknown artist who illustrated the [635] 1504 edition of Greg. Reisch's *Margarita philosophica* (128), which was published by Johann Schott. It had fifteen woodcuts which ranged in height from 122 to 130 mm and in width from 152 to 165 mm.

In summary, it may be said that Strassburg achieved a great deal around the beginning of the sixteenth century. At first, little effort was made to achieve artistic production. Augsburg, Ulm and Cologne had achieved greatness as far back as the 1480's, and they were joined by Basel and Nuremberg in the early 1490's, while during this period Strassburg was content to copy existing woodcuts or to use crude originals. In the 80's Thomas Anshelm was the only one to have produced an artistically worthy book. It was only towards the end of the century that almost explosive development took place, as Johann Grüninger began to print in Strassburg and had the help, for a time, of Sebastian Brant, who put great emphasis on attractiveness of the woodcuts.

Notes

1) Schmidt, *Zur Geschichte der ältesten Bibliotheken und der ersten Buchdrucker zu Strassburg.* Strassburg, 1882; Fischer, "Dr. Sebastian Brant's Betheiligung bei dem Holzschnitt seiner Zeit," *Deutsches Kunstblatt* II:218, 1851; Schmidt, "Notice fur Sebastien Brant," *Revue de Alsace* III:378-83, Colmar, 1874; Marchand, *Dict. hist. typogr.* 1:289-294; Woltmann, *Geschichte der deutschen Kunst in Elsass.* Leipzig, 1876. Chapter 12, "Der Strassburger Holzschnitt."

2) Hain, No. 6731.

3) Hain, No. 6740.

4) Hain, Part I. 2:253, No. 6160. s. l. e. a.; Schoenemann, *Merkwürdigkeiten der Herzoglichen Bibliothek zu Wolfenbüttel.* Hannover, 1849. p. 69, No. 90; A new reprint, with the same illustrations reduced. Hannover, Fr. Culemann, 1849.

5) Hain, No. 995.

6) Ebert, No. 414; Hain I:87, No. 791; Panzer I:175, No. 267.

7) Hain, No. 792.

8) Hain, No. 793; Panzer I:206, No. 363.

9) Hain, No. 5518. Folio; Ebert, No. 414.

10) Hain, No. 11854.

11) Historia de gestis et trina triun regum translatione. (Based on a book done in honor of the three saintly kings); Hain, No. 9400.

12) Hain, No. 10649; Panzer I:130; Brunet, ed. V. III:1361; Graesse IV:361.

13) Hain, No. 10650.

14) Hain, Part II. No. 10874. Folio; Panzer I:146, No. 198.

15) Hain, No. 4081.

16) Hain, No. 6936. Folio; Panzer, Annales typ. I:31, No. 102; Graesse II:554.

17) Hain, No. 6937; Panzer, Annales typogr. I:35, No. 133.

18) Hain, No. 3336.

19) Heller, "Supplemente zu Panzer No. II," Serapeum VI:313, 1845. Folio.

20) Hain, No. 6736.

21) Panzer I:154, No. 214; Hain, Part I:420, No. 3138; Muther, Deutsche Bilderbibeln. No. 9.

22) Lacking in Hain, Part II. 1:215, No. 9764. Small quarto; and in Panzer, Suppl:7, No. 376; German. Mus. 1766a.

23) Hain, No. 5834. s. l., Folio; Choulant, p. 284, No. 4.

24) Hain, No. 5835. s. l., Folio; Choulant, p. 285, No. 5.

25) Hain, No. 3743.

26) Hain, No. 12474.

27) Hain, No. 9377. Quarto; Panzer I:230, No. 441.

28) Hain, No. 10084.

29) Hain, No. 10085.

30) Hain, No. 13676.

31) Hain, No. 6673.

32) Hain, No. 6770. Folio; Moser, "Der Holzschnitt mit der Inschrift Accipies tanti doctoris dogmata sancti." Serapeum IV:254.

33) Hain, No. 6547. s. l.

34) Panzer I:65, No. 371.

35) Weigel. 16, No. 14129. Small octavo; Hain, No. 8937.

36) Hain, No. 8938.

37) The Virgil of 1502, folio, which is illustrated richly with many woodcuts, states: "impressum impensa non mediocri magistri Joannis Grieninger.

38) Hain, No. 15431. Folio; Panzer, Annales typ. I:56, No. 299; Ebert, No. 22461; Dibdin, Biblioth. Spencer. II:426, ff; Brunet, Manuel ed. 5. V:710; Weigel, No. 8512.

39) Adparat. literar. III:590.

40) Terentius, Comoediae in German translation. Hain, No. 15434. Folio. (Has only an inexact title); Panzer I:241; Ebert, No. 22554; Brunet. ed. 5. V:723.

41) Horatius, Opera cum annotationibus Jac. Locheri. Hain, Part II. No. 8898. Folio; Panzer, Annales typ. I:61, No. 339; Ebert, No. 10136; Hupsauer, Druckst. aus dem 15. Jahrhundert. p. 204, ff.; Dibdin, Bibl. Spencer. II:87-95; Brunet. ed. 5. III:311; Graesse III:348.

42) Hain, No. 6745.

43) Hain, No. 6747; Panzer, p. 244.

44) Ebert, No. 3071; Hain, Part I. 1:559, No. 4017; Panzer I:226, No. 431; Choulant, Botanische und anatomische Abbildung. p. 266, No. 1.

45) Hain, No. 4021. Folio; Panzer I:246; Brunet. ed. 5. I:1301; Graesse I:556; Choulant, p. 269, No. 1; Weller, No. 135.

46) Hain, No. 4020. Folio; Panzer, Zusätze zu den Annalen. No. 496 b; Brunet. ed. 5. I:1301; Graesse I:556; Choulant, p. 269; Weller, No. 136.

47) Hain, No. 8942. Folio. s. l. e. a.; Ebert, No. 10294; Pritzel, No. 11877; Choulant, p. 250, No. 16.

48) The s. l. e. a. edition is not listed in Hain or Pritzel; Choulant, p. 251, No. 17.

49) Hain, No. 11047. s. a.

50) Histori von Apulejus in Gestalt eines Esels verwandelt; Hain, No. 1320.

51) Ebert, No. 10350. Folio; Panzer I:251; Panzer I:300, No. 626; Hain, No. 8970.

52) Ebert, No. 11501. Folio; Panzer I:251, No. 507; Weller, No. 155.

53) Weller, No. 191.

54) Panzer I:256; Weller, No. 188.

55) Weigel, No. 8515.

56) Hain, No. 3723. Quarto; Variant in Panzer, Annales Typ. I:61, No. 341; Ebert, No. 2921; Brunet. ed. 5. I:1202; Graesse, Trésor. I:520.

57) De Philosophico consolatu sive de consolatione philosophiae cum figuris ornatissimis novis expolit. ed, Seb. Brant; Panzer VI:27, No. 5.

58) Weller, No. 232.

59) Publii Vergilii Maronis opera cum quinque commentariis (Servii, Donati, Landini, Mancinelli et Calderoni) expolitissimisque figuris atque imaginibus per. Seb. Brant superadditis; Ebert, No. 23665. Folio.

60) Ebert, No. 10360. Small folio; Panzer I:266, No. 550.

61) Panzer I:269, No. 557. Folio; II:49, No. 1239; Weller, No. 311.

62) Panzer I:297; Folio.

63) Weller, No. 712.

64) Weller, No. 822.

65) Panzer I:379; Trew VI:3.

66) Panzer II:49; Trew VI:4.

67) Trew VI:4; Folio

68) Panzer I:277.

69) Ebert, No. 3307. Folio; Panzer I:298, No. 624 (for thc 1508 edition); Panzer I: 283 (for the 1507 edition).

70) Panzer VI:40, No. 112. Quarto.

71) Hain, No. 12851; Legenda de origine St. Catharinae.

72) Weller, No. 435.

73) Heller, "Supplemente zu Panzer No. II." Serapeum VI:313, 1845. Folio; Weller, No. 228.

74) Hain, No. 4748.

75) Ebert, No. 1507. Quarto; Panzer VI:28, No. 16.

76) Panzer I:202, No. 385. Folio.

77) Weller, No. 366.

78) Trew catal. II, No. IV:9 and V:5. Folio; Panzer I:283 and 311; Pritzel, No. 11894 and No. 11895; Choulant, p. 253, No. 21.

79) Panzer I. No. 604. Folio.

80) Panzer I:302, No. 635.

81) Panzer I:325.

82) It is incomprehensible how Nagler could ascribe this sheet to Hans Baldung Grün.

83) Ebert, No. 18758. Quarto; Weller, No. 168.

84) Hain, No. 10088.

85) Hain, No. 5493.

86) Hain, No. 10651.

87) Hain, Part I. 2:105, No. 4993. Small quarto; Panzer, Suppl:89, No. 475 b, s. a.

88) Weller, No. 145.

89) Weller, No. 175.

90) Weller, No. 156.

91) Weller, No. 157.

92) Weller, No. 158.

93) Weller, No. 201.

94) Weller, No. 239.

95) Weller, No. 240.

96) Weller, No. 215.

97) Weller, No. 247.

98) Ebert, No. 414; Panzer I:263, No. 540, and Suppl., p. 98, No. 540.

99) Weller, No. 274.

100) Weller, No. 354.

101) Hain, Part II. 2:431, No. 15640. Small quarto.

102) Hain, No. 4527.

103) Weller, No. 200.

104) Weller, No. 184.

105) Weller, No. 189.

106) Weller, No. 217.

107) Weller, No. 255.

108) Hain, No. 1150; Denis, _Einletung in die Bucherkunde._ Part I, p. 90-91.

109) Weller, No. 277.

110) Weller, No. 303.

111) Panzer I:271, No. 562.

112) Weller, No. 357.

113) Weller, No. 360.

114) Weller, No. 379.

115) Weller, No. 380.

116) Panzer I:322.

117) Hain, No. 12130.

118) Hain, No. 3359; Weller, No. 134.

119) Schmidt. Part I, 1:131; Panzer I:452; Weller, No. 236 and 276.

120) Schmidt. Part I. 2:131. s.a.

121) Lacking in Panzer.

122) Hain I:280, No. 6405.

123) Ebert, No. 19387. Quarto; Panzer, Suppl., p. 116, No. 658 b.

124) Panzer I:306, No. 643.

125) Weller, No. 239.

126) Weller, No. 238. Folio.

127) _Code hist. et diplomat. de la ville de Strassbourg._ Strassburg, 1843. Part 2, p. 286, cf. Schmidt.

128) Ebert, No. 18892. Quarto; Panzer VI:31, No. 44.

[636-639, Pl. 145-149]

Chapter XI

MAINZ (1)

It is strange that Mainz, which was the cradle of book printing, produced a substantially smaller number of illustrated books than the other cities which have been treated up to this point.

Of the Mainz trio, Gutenberg, Fust, and Schöffer, only Schöffer has any place in the history of book illustration.

In 1484 he produced [636] the first edition of a book that was later frequently reprinted, the Herbarius Moguntinus (2), a household remedy book for the poor, in which 150 herbs are discussed and illustrated. The illustrations of plants were done with greater skill and care than had ever been done for this type of book, though in incidentals and decoration of broadsides, lives of saints, and in copper plates, better representations of plants, by more outstanding artists, appeared much earlier. In the Herbarius... the illustrations are frequently very crude and stiff, but the the plant is frequently recognizable. Most are presented in toto, showing the stem, flowers and leaves, but some are less complete. They are represented in heavy outline and with no shading.

Schöffer's second illustrated book [637] was just as successful as his Herbarius.... In 1485 he published the first edition of the Kleinen deutschen Hortus sanitatis (3), which is fully described by Choulant.

The last of his illustrated books, which was the third Mainz illustrated book, [638, Pl. 145-147] is Conrad Botho's Chroneken der Sassen (4). Repetitious use is made of the same woodblocks to represent different things extensively. The letters that appear on sheet 54 and sheet 8b, etc., give no clues to the names of the artists.

The second Mainz printer who played a part in the history of book illustration was the painter, Erhard Reuwich, of Utrecht, who produced several of the most outstanding woodcuts of the fifteenth century. It was a particularly fortunate circumstance (5) that Bernhard von Breidenbach [639, Pl. 148-149], in cooperation with several others, decided to go to the Holy Land and to describe their travels. He selected Erhard Reuwich to accompany them as the painter who would record the outstanding things in foreign countries on the spot.

After fifteen days they arrived in Venice, where they were joined by others. Reuwich used the 25-day stay there to do a large (over five-feet long) drawing which showed the "Civitas Veneciarum" with the St. Nicholas Gate, the public hospital, the Duke's palace, and the church of St. Mark, and other features. As they traveled along, Reuwich continued to record the scenes. A warship shown in one of his illustrations is reproduced by Dibdin (6).

In 1484 the pilgrims returned to Mainz and Breidenbach began to write up his travels. Reuwich added to the drawings that were made on the voyage, a (250 x 187) masterpiece to serve as the title page.

In 1486, by which time Reuwich had added to his renown as a distinguished painter that of an equally skilled book printer, he handled the printing of the text and the cutting of the drawings. The entire work was first published by him in Latin as [640] Opusculum sanctorum peregrinationum in montem Syon ad venerandum Christi sepulchrum. In the summer of the same year, 1486, he issued a second edition in high-German [641] under the title Die heyligen reysen gen Jerusalem. In May, 1488, he followed this with a low-German edition, titled Heilige bevaerden tot dat heylighe grafft in iherusalem.

The woodcuts in Breidenbach's Reise very quickly caught the attention of art lovers. Dibdin (7) declared that they were worthy of Canaletto's brush, and Rumohr (8), after a thorough evaluation of these illustrations, said, "if they were cut out of the books and laid out by themselves, one could be incredulous that they came from such an early period." And, indeed, they are the most distinguished woodcuts that Germany could lay claim to in this period.

The third Mainz printer, Jacob Meidenbach, is known only through his illustrations in one book, the Latin [642, Pl. 150] Hortus sanitatis (9), which he issued in 1491. Choulant, to differentiate this from the first edition of the smaller German Hortus published by Peter Schöffer, termed this one the "Large Hortus." It includes, in addition to coverage of the plants in the small Hortus, books on land, air, and water animals, minerals, etc. For this reason, the number of woodcuts is also substantially larger. Some of the woodcuts appear to be based on those in the Schöffer edition (for the plants covered in both). The majority of the text woodcuts are not a full column in width and are lighter in drawing and in cut than those of the 1485 Schöffer edition; nevertheless, they are interesting because the artist understood how to present the individual botanical and zoological materials in generic groupings.

Aside from this frequently reprinted Hortus sanitatis, the second edition of [643] Lichtenberger's Pronosticativo (10), which was printed without indication of place of publication, is traced back to Meidenbach because it used the same woodcuts as the first edition, which was published s. l. e. a.

Perhaps Meidenbach was responsible for the first edition, published in Mainz in 1493, of [644] the illustrated Latin edition of Liber ruralium commodorum (11), a book on agriculture written by Petrus de Crescentiis, of Bologna, between 1302 and 1309, based largely on his own extensive experience in agriculture and partly taken from ancient authors, including Palladius, Cato, Varro and Columella. The woodcuts extend up to the 37th chapter of book 10, which deals with fishing, and they vary in quality.

Johann Schöffer (1502-1552), who was Peter Schöffer's son and Fust's grandson, was the fourth Mainz printer who was of importance in the history of book illustration. His [645, Pl. 151-153] Liviüsubersetzung, by Bernhard Schöferlein (12), was issued in 1505. It had 214 (118 x 145) woodcuts and a title page woodcut (215 x 170). The similarities between the Virgil and the Livius illustrations has already been pointed out by Fischer in his study of Brant's contributions to the woodcut. Practically all of the woodcuts are colored and it is unbelievable how much was achieved here by color and how well they understood how to reuse the same woodcut for varying scenes by varying the coloring.

In 1508 [646] Johann Schöffer printed Laienspiegel (13) by Tengler, which was first published in Augsburg, and he followed this, in 1509 [647] with Vom Teutschorden (14). Each had a woodcut illustration on the title page.

Among the products of the Mainz printer, Friedrich Heumann, [648] only the Regimen sanitatis (15) of 1509 and the [649] Reimbüchlein, in 1510 (16), are provided with woodcut illustrations for their title pages.

Thus, in terms of the number of illustrated publications, Mainz was far behind the other cities. Gutenberg and Fust illustrated nothing; Peter Schöffer printed two illustrated plant books and the Chroneken der Sassen. Reuwich did Breidenbach's travels; Meidenbach did the large Hortus sanitatis; Johann Schöffer, the Livius. However, it should be noted that all these works were independently produced, and were not, as in Strassburg, copies of works done elsewhere. The three books on plants were copied in all other cities, and the Livius may be placed on a par with the Strassburg Virgil. Breidenbach's travels, however, is unquestionably on a par with Lirer's work and the Schedel Chronik.

Notes

1) Zapf, Aelteste Buchdruckergeschichte von Mainz. Ulm, 1790; Schaab, Geschichte der Erfindung der Buchdruckerkunst. Mainz, 1830-1891. 3v.; Choulant, "Botanische und anatomische Abbildungen des Mittelalters." Naumann's Archiv III:188-345, 1857; For Breydenbach's travels see Jackson and Chatto, Treatise on wood engraving. London, 1839, p. 253; Rumohr, Zur Geschichte und Theorie der Formschneidekunst. p. 77; Lempertz, Beiträge zur älten Geschichte der Buchdrucker- und Holzschneidekunst. Cologne, 1839. No. 1:5b; Choulant, Die Anfänge wissenschaftlicher Naturgeschichte und naturhistorischer Abbildung in christliche Abendlande. Dresden, 1856, p. 40-44.

2) Herbarius cum herbarum figuris. Small quarto; Schaab. 52; Panzer VI:130; Hain, No. 8444; Pritzel, No. 11867; Allgemeines medicinische Annalen. 1829: 1158-1165; Choulant, Botanische und anatomische Abbildungen des Mittelalters. No. 1, p. 200.

3) Hain, No. 8948. Folio; Panzer I:156; Dibdin, Bibl. Spencer IV:503; Brunet. ed. 5. III:343; Pritzel, No. 11884; Choulant, p. 242, No. 1; Trew, Catal. II (4):1.

4) Hain, No. 4990. Folio; Panzer I:196, No. 338; Zapf, Buchdruckergeschichte von Mainz. p. 106; Ebert, No. 2833; Schaab I:540, No. 63; Brunet. ed. 5. I:1887; Graesse, Tresor 1:504.

5) Sanctae Peregrenationes in montem Syon ad venerandum Christi Sepulchrum in Jerusalem atque in montem Sinai ad divam virginem et martyrem Katherinam; Hain I:550, No. 3956. Folio; Panzer, Annales typogr. II:131, No. 58; Ejusd, Annalen der ältern deutschen Lit., p. 162; Clement, Bibl. cur. V:222; Masch, Beiträge zur Geschichte merkwürdiger Bücher. VIII; Stück, p. 622; Baumgarten, Nachrichten von merkwürdigen Büchern. II:233, IX:218; Zapf, p. 95; Ebert I:233, No. 2973; Schaab I:530, No. 55; Dibdin, Bibl. Spencer, III:216 ff, IV:459, VI:87; Brunet. ed. 5. I:1249 ff; Graesse I:538; There is an outstanding evaluation in Butsch, Bücherornamentik.

6) The Ship is reproduced in Dibdin I:122.

7) Bibliotheca Spenceriana. London, 1814/1815. III:227.

8) Zur Geschichte der Formschneidekunst, p. 77.

9) Panzer, Annales Typogr. II:132. Folio; Hain, Part II, I:96, No. 8944; Ebert, No. 10295; Pritzel, No. 11879; Choulant, p. 248, No. 249; Schaab, No. 62.

10) Ebert, No's 11964-69. Folio; Schaab, No. 64.

11) Hain, No. 5832. Folio; Choulant, p. 283, No. 1.

12) Ebert, No. 12134. Folio; Panzer I:269, No. 559.

13) Weller, No. 463.

14) Weller, No. 668.

15) Weller, No. 511.

16) Weller, No. 541.

Chapter XII

THE SMALLER PRINTING CENTERS (1)

In the last twenty years of the fifteenth century illustrated books were being printed in a large number of cities in addition to those that have been discussed up to this point.

In Bamberg, where Albrecht Pfister was active in the 1460's, there was great activity during the later period. Around the beginning of the 1480's Johann Sensenschmidt moved from Nuremberg to Bamberg, where he merged with Heinrich Petzensteiner, and they published religious books primarily.

There is a woodcut [650] in the 1484 edition of Breviarium Bambergense (2). The [651] Missale Frisingense (3) has a woodcut illustration at the end of the preface. The woodcut in [652] the 1490 edition of the Missale Bambergense (4) varies only slightly from that in the 1484 edition. As in the Breviarium..., there is an attractive illustration on the verso of the title page of [653] Statuta synodalia in Synodo publica per reverendissimum in Christo patrem et dominum dmn Heinricum Dei gracia Episcopum Bambergen in ecclesia Bambergense celebrata lecta et publicata (5). It is similar to that previously used, with the differences being that this one is somewhat larger (130 x 115) and that the Bishop's escutcheon is omitted. While this book was published in 1491, without indication of the printer, it was certainly produced by Sensenschmidt.

The same woodcut that appeared in the Breviarum of 1484 [654-655] was used again in the Obsequiale Bambergense (6) in 1491, and in the Reformatio judicii decantus ecclesiae Bambergensis (7) which appeared in about 1492 without indication of printer or date.

The second Bamberg printer, Hans Sporer, who had been a xylographer and had worked in Nuremberg from 1470 to the beginning of the 1490's (c.f. Murr, Journal zur K.-G. 2:134), produced a number of illustrated works. The publications that he illustrated were usually of a few sheets only; they were popular, and often were poems by master singers. Everything that he produced in Bamberg was published in 1493.

The booklet [656], Von Kaiser Karls Recht. Wie er ein Kauffmann und ein iuden macht schlecht. Von eins pfund wegen, das er aus seiner seitten um M.gl versetzt hat (8), has a crude woodcut under the title.

The [657] Histori von dem grafen in dem pflug (9), which does not indicate its printer, has a title page woodcut.

The [658] title page woodcut for Des Edeln Ritter Morgeners Walfart in Sant Thomas land (10) shows the departure of the Knight. That of the [659] booklet, Ein treffliches wunderzeichen des Heiligen zwelffpoten Sant Thome in India, wie er alle Jahr das Sacrament den leuten reichet (11), represents the miracle.

The volume, [660] Vom Kunig im pad, dem sein gewalt genumen war (12), has a title page illustration and four woodcuts in the text.

[661] Hans Rosenplüt's poem, Der Mann im Garten (13), has a title page woodcut, as do [662-664] the Erschöpfung des ersten menschen Adams (14); Mit einer grüntlichen lere von gepurt unsers herrn Jesu Christi (15a); Der Paurn lob (15b); and the undated Gedicht vom ersten Edelmanns (16).

Hans Sporer was thrown into jail in 1494 because of his pamphlets.

Johann Pfeyl, who in 1491 and 1492 worked with Johann Sensenschmidt and Heinrich Petzensteiner, later became active, by himself, as the most important printer in Bamberg, producing up to 1519.

Around 1494 [665] he printed the Reformation des Gerichts der Dechaney de Thumstifts zu Bamberberg (17), which repeated the title page illustration that first appeared in Sensenschmidt's Breviarum of 1484.

Pfeyl's [666] Breviarium Ratisbonense of 1496 (18) has a large (300 x 237) woodcut after the index, which is well executed. Since the woodcut is clearly related to the large woodcuts in the Schedel Chronik, it is probably safe to attribute it to Wohlgemuth. The faces are executed outstandingly and the clothing is handled very artistically.

The [667] Missale Bambergense (19) of 1499 repeats the woodcut from the Sensenschmidt Breviarium of 1484. The [668] Missale Bergense of 1506 adds one handsome new woodcut of Christ on the Cross to the conventional ones.

Pfeyl's chief work [669] is the Bambergische Halsgerichtsordnung (20) of 1507, which had 21 woodcuts. Most of these fill a full page (245 or 175 x 175) and many of them are assembled from two woodblocks. By and large these illustrations are all diligently prepared, but the many tag lines on each give a feeling of their being quite old fashioned.

This was followed in 1509 by [670] the Weysung und ausruffung des hochwürdigen Heilthumbs zu Bamberg nach dem rechten waren Heilthumb abgezeichnet (21), which was published without the name of the printer but can definitely be attributed to Pfeyl. On its title page Kaiser Heinrich and Kaiserin Kunigunde are shown, along with the dome, below, which is the bishop's escutcheon. The remaining woodcuts represent the saints. After Pfeyl had used the picture of Kaiser Heinrich and his wife so often as a title page picture, in 1511 [671] he pictured them in a separate book, the Legende von heiligen Kaiser Heinrich (22). This book has fourteen woodcuts, of which four are printed twice.

In Brunswick, in 1506, Hans Dorn published [672] Evengelienbuch (23), with very bad woodcuts; and his 1507 [673] Historie von St. Anna (24) is not any better so far as its illustrations are concerned.

The first illustrated book from Breslau, where Conrad Elyan started his press very early, is [674] the Legende der hailigsten Frawen Sandt Hedwigis (25), which was published by Conrad Baumgarten in 1504. The 58 woodcuts are 140 x 120 mm. These woodcuts are very good and seem related to the Nuremberg school. There is a "W" on the shield of a knight in one illustration, which could possibly be the artist's monogram or could be simply ornamentation.

At the end of the century, Hans Sporer, who had printed in Nuremberg and Bamberg, turned out a number of small works in Erfurt. [675-677] In 1498 he published, with a title page woodcut, Angesicht des Herrn (26); in 1500, Ernst's Ausfahrt (27) and a new edition of Morgener's

Wallfahrt ins heilige Land (28).

In 1505 Wolfgang Schenk published woodcut illustrated editions of [678-679] the Betrachtung der Stunden des Todes (29) and the Büchlein von der Seele (30).

In Eichstädt Michael Reyser, a brother of Georg Reyser of Würzburg, was active in the 1480's; and, like his brother, distinguished himself through his missals illustrated by copper plates. The [680] copper plate in his Missale Eystettense, of 1486, shows the escutcheons of several bishops.

In Freiburg, the first edition of the woodcut illustrated [681] Spiegel der wahren Rhetorik (31) by Riederer, was published in 1493. Towards the end of the century, Heinrich Gran brought Hagenau into the history of book illustration, but few of his books were suitable for illustration. Mostly, like [682] the Expositio hymnorum of 1493 (32) and a few textbooks of 1494 and 1495, they have the picture of the teacher on the title page, which had often been used by Quentel and Schoensperger.

In 1501 he issued [683] an edition of Stellarium coronae benedictae Mariae virginis (33), with very few woodcuts.

The 1509 edition of [684] Heldenbuch (34), which Gran printed at Knoblouch's expense, is the only one he printed with pictures in the text. Since Knoblouch bore the cost, he no doubt also supplied the 222 woodcuts, which are reduced copies of those in the Schoensperger edition of 1491. Those that occupy one column are normally 60 x 60 mm; those that occupy two columns are normally 70 x 105 mm.

Heinrich Knoblochzer, who moved to Heidelberg from Strassburg, started his printing in Heidelberg in 1490 [685] by issuing the third edition of the Ackermanns aus Böheim oder der Rechtsstreits des Menschen mit dem Tode (35). In 1491 [686] he printed the fifth edition of Melusine, using the woodcuts of the earlier editions in both of the above titles.

The [687] Der Suoszpfadt tzuo der ewigen seligkeyt (36) appeared in 1494 without indication of its printer. There are woodcuts on the title page and on sheet 4b.

In 1501, Conrad Hist printed [688] Schelling's Regiment der Gesundheit (37), with two woodcuts on the title page.

[689] In Ingolstadt, Practica, by Hans Engel (38), was published in 1497.

Leipzig, where printing began in 1481, did not produce any illustrated works until the 1490's. The [690] Praktika von Leupzig (39) has a colored title page woodcut. It was published by Johannes Virdung in 1490. The typographically produced [691-692] editions of the Ars moriendi produced in Leipzig in 1494 (40), and reprinted in 1496 (41), had 13 conventional woodcuts which had appeared in xylographic editions. However, they are reduced in size (145 x 94) and are re-worked in style.

Gregor Bötticher, in 1495, [693] published the second edition of the Historie von vier Kaufleuten, which had first appeared s. l. e. a. It had 20 woodcuts (42).

In 1495 [694] Kachelofen published Beichtspiegel (43), with a relatively important title page illustration (145 x 92).

The title page of [695] Virdung's Practica auf das Jahr 1497 (44) is 115 x 110 mm and is not without some merit.

In 1499 Melchior Lotter printed [696] Johannes Peyligk's Philosophiae naturalis compendium (45), with eleven anatomical illustrations, which have been evaluated by Choulant.

The [697] De summo bono (46), by Isidorus Hispalensis, was published without date, but before 1500, by Arnold of Cologne and it has the familiar Cologne title page woodcut of the teacher with his students.

In 1501 (47) and 1503 (48), Melchior Lotter [698-702] printed the Grammatellus, with a title page woodcut, and in 1507 he published Büchlein von Sterben (49), using the 13 woodcuts he had used in the Ars moriendi. In 1508 he produced the booklet Es tu scholaris (50) with a title page woodcut; and in 1509 he issued, similarly decorated by a title page woodcut, the Regimen sanitatis (51).

Lübeck, which appeared in the history of book illustration as far back as 1475, with Lucas Brandis, also produced a number of illustrated books in the last decades of the century. Mathias Brandis joined Lucas Brandis and they produced the 1485 low-German edition [703] of Lucidarius (52).

The second printer who was active during this period was Bartholomäus Ghotan (1480-1492). In 1484 he produced [704] the Licht der Seele (53), which had a woodcut on the title page. In the same year [705], he published Bishop Johann of Olunz's Leben des heiligen Hieronymous (54), with a number of colored woodcut illustrations. The first one, which is large, is at the beginning of Eusebius, and the same cut is used for two other saints. Of the two others, one appears on sheet 71b and the other on sheet 88a.

The [706] Speygel der dogede (55), which appeared in Lübeck without the name of the printer, in 1485, may be ascribed to Ghotan because its first woodcut, on p. IIb is taken from his Licht der Seele of 1484. The book has 26 woodcuts, of which 23 occupy a full page. However, one of these is used seven times, a second is used five times, a third three times, and a fourth, twice.

The last of Ghotan's illustrated books [707] was his 1492 Revelationes St. Brigittae de Suecia (56), the illustrations of which were copied in all later editions of the book. In 1496 he printed the book [708] in German (57), with the same woodcuts.

The third Lübeck printer of this period was Stephan Arndes, who was born in Hamburg. He was printing in Perugia, Italy, in 1481, in Schleswig in 1486, and from 1487 in Lübeck, producing a number of illustrated books there. In 1488 he published [709-711] a low-German edition of the Heiligenlebens (58), which he repeated in 1492 (59); it contained some woodcuts not found in the high-German editions. The woodcuts of his Evangelienbuch in 1488 (60) are of varying value. The pictures of the evangelists are 70 x 145 mm. Then there is one 105 x 155 mm woodcut. The rest of the pictures come from various periods. Those which measure 75 x 57 mm are quite old and probably go back to the 1470's. The others, which are 65 x 42 mm, are newer but are artistically worthless and were not prepared for this book.

In 1492 he did a [712] low-German translation of the small Hortus sanitatus (61), adding one chapter from the large Hortus, under the title "De ghenochlike Gharde der Suntheit." The illustrations of plants are the same as those in the Latin edition.

He followed this in 1494 with [713, Pl. 158-161] the first Lübeckische Bibel in low-Saxon

German, which was the last German bible before Luther that contained independent illustrations and, indeed, illustrations of very special artistic value. F. A. Butsch rightfully declared that the noble Lübeck Bible of 1494 (62) was the most beautifully illustrated German book of the fifteenth century.

In later years Arndes tended increasingly to reproduce older [714-717] books. In 1506 he did a new edition of the Evangelienbuchs (63), in 1507 a new edition of Passional (64), in 1509 a third edition of the Evangelienbuch (65), and in 1510 the second edition of Garten der Gesundheit (66).

Among the Lübeck books that can not be ascribed to any particular printer, there is [718-719] the Lübecker Todtentanz (67), which first appeared in 1489 and was reissued in a second edition in 1496. It has 59 (82 x 59) woodcuts and they are very significant.

On the other hand, [720-722] the woodcuts in the Lübeck Evangelienbuchern of 1489 (68), 1492 (69), and 1493 (70) are quite as worthless as those in the Arndes edition of 1488.

The low-Saxon-German [723] Psalter (71) followed in 1493. It has woodcut illustrations on the title page, on sheet 1b, on sheet 275b and on leaf 289. In 1496 [724] the Speygel der leyen (72) was published with 30 woodcuts of various sizes, and in 1499 [725] there was a low-German edition of the Heiligenlebens (73).

In Magdeburg, Albert Ravenstein published [726] the second low German edition of the Evengelienbuch (74) in 1484.

He was followed by Moritz Brandes who, in 1492, did [727] the first edition of Belial (75), with the familiar woodcuts, and [728] in 1501 he produced Thomas a Kempis' Bock van der navolginge christi (76), which included a woodcut illustration on the title page.

Simon Mentzer printed [729] an Evangelienbuch (77) in 1509.

Albrecht Kunne started printing in Memmingen in 1482 when [730] he issued an edition of Guilielmus' Postilla.

In 1486 he published [731] Tractatus de divina praedestinatione (78), by Felicianus, providing a woodcut illustration for the title page, and in the same year [732] Kunne printed Breviarum totius juris canonici (79), by Paulus Florentinus, and provided a picture of the compiler on the first page.

The woodcut in [733] De virtutibus herbarum (80), by Albertus Magnus, which appeared undated, in Memmingen, is even less significant than were the preceding two. It appears on the title page and its verso, as well as on the last side of the 24th sheet.

[734-736] Kunne's later books: Hieronymus Schauung of 1508 (81); Niemand, in 1510 (82); and Stopel's Auslesung (83) of 1514, all, similarly, have only unimportant title page illustrations.

Caspar Hochfeder, from Nuremberg, published in Metz [737] the first illustrated German edition of Geschichte von Flore und Blansche Flur (84), with 94 woodcut illustrations ranging from 110-125 mm in height and from 145-150 mm wide. The woodcuts are very significant and the pictures appear to belong to the sixteenth century rather than the fifteenth so far as their style is concerned. The landscapes are of especial interest and their perspective is right, with their shading very fine. The illustrations do not make an old-fashioned impression even when reused for the third time in Grüninger's edition of 1520. The second edition [738] was done by Hochfeder himself in 1500 (85).

Conrad Baumgarten worked in Olmutz towards the end of the century and then moved on to Breslau. [739] In Olmutz he produced the Geschichten von geistlichen Weibspersonen (86).

Thomas Anshelm, who had been printing in Strassburg back in 1488, worked in Pforzheim from 1500-1511. In 1502 he printed [740] Sebastian Brant's Traum (87) as well as the interesting little booklet, [741] Ars memorandi notabilis per figuras evangelistarum, in which there are fifteen (145 x 95) woodcuts and five different variations of the four Evangelist symbols. The woodcuts are very good. Anshelm reused [742] them in his 1505 edition and, in 1510, in his new edition [743] which appeared under the title, Rationarium evangelistarum omnia in se evangelia prosa, versu, imaginibusque quam mirifice complectens (88).

Michael Greyff, Reutlingen's first printer, who had been printing there since 1480, produced as his first illustrated book the s. l. e. a. [744] seventh edition of the Spiegels menschlicher Behaltniss (89).

In 1490 he printed [745] Einem hübschen Kalender mit ettlicher Zubehorung mit namen zu finden was sunntäglicher buchstab sey und wz die guldin zal sey (90), in which the usual calendar illustrations are used.

His edition [746] of Meister Elucidarius (91), issued in 1491, is the tenth in the series of this book. The title page illustration, which shows a man teaching astronomy to a boy, is repeated on the next page. All the other woodcuts are the customary astronomical-physical illustrations of other editions. His [747] Cato teutonice expositus, of 1494 (92), has the picture of the teacher and student on the title page.

In the same year [748] Greyff printed Postilla des Guilielmus (93). It has the usual title page illustration of teacher and students (76 x 51). The text woodcuts (51 x 38) are the usual ones found in evangelical books. The woodcut in [749] Expositio Hymnorum cum notabili commento (94), which Greyff printed in 1496, shows Mary with the Child in her arms, standing in a beam of light in the crescent of the Moon. In 1502 [750] he printed the Regimen sanitatis (95), providing it with two woodcuts.

In this same year Johannes Othmar issued the eighth edition [751] of Heiligenleben (96), using the familiar, unimportant, woodcuts. He also published [752] Von den Unholden oder Hexen (97), which appeared in Reutlingen without printer or year of publication, and was the second German edition of [753] Ulricus Molitoris' Tractatus de laniis et phitonicis mulieribus. The woodcuts are taken from the earlier Latin edition. To be sure, the title page illustration (130 x 82) did not appear in the Cologne edition of 1489, but it did appear in the second, s. l. e. a., edition.

The woodcut on the first page of [754] Othmar's Cato teutonice expositus (98), issued in 1495, shows a saint, and the one on its verso is the teacher and students.

The 1494 Reutlingen edition [755] of Brant's Narrenschiff (99), which did not bear the name of the printer, reprinted the woodcuts of the original edition.

Peter Drach was active in Speier until the end of the century. In 1490 [756] he published the second Latin edition of Breidenbach's Reise.

In Surse im Ergau there appeared in 1500 [757] the Chronik des Kriegs des schwäbischen Bundes gegen den römischen König (100), which was written by Nicolaus Schradin.

A book with a puzzling place of publication [758] is, according to Weigel, Hye nach volget der Curss und ampt der heiligen iungfrawen und mutter gottes marie...(101).

In 1497 the eighth edition [759] of Sieben weisen Meister (102) appeared in Klein Troyga, with one woodcut illustration at the beginning.

Johannes Othmar worked for the bookseller Fr. Meynberger in Tübingen in 1498. In 1499 [760] he published Expositio sacri canonis missae, by Gabriel Biel (103), which has a woodcut illustration on sheet 40a.

Conrad Fyner moved from Esslingen to Urach in 1481 and in that year he printed two illustrated books: a Leben der Heiligen and a Plenarium. His [761] Heiligenleben (104) is the sixth in the series of this book. The first woodcut of the Summer Part of the book is 80 x 82 mm and the one at the beginning of the Winter part is 88 x 75 mm. The 234 woodcuts in the text are of various sizes and are the products of many hands. Nevertheless they are all much better than those of earlier editions; the figures are finely shaded and the landscapes are correct and natural throughout.

The title page illustration [762] of Plenarium (105) shows Christ on the Cross with Mary and John next to Him; above and below Him are the evangelistic symbols in round medallions.

Lucas Zeissenmair worked in Wessoprunn from the beginning of the century. [763] In the Funf Liedern by Preining (106), which he published in 1503, he has a large woodcut of Mary with the Child and three worshippers. In 1505 there followed [764] an edition of Nider's 24 goldnen Harfen, with a skillfully handled (185 x 120) title page woodcut.

There is an attractive title page in [765] Chronik wie Kaiser Ludwig IV das loblich Gottshaus unser Frawen zu Etal erpawet und gestift ist (107), which was published by Zeissenmair, undated. On its last sheet there is an illustration of Kaiser Ludwig and the church.

In Vienna, where book printing started in 1482, the first [766] illustrated book appeared, undated, and was apparently the work of an itinerant printer. It is the second edition of the Legende vom heiligen Rochus (108), and its woodcut is as crude as that of the Nuremberg edition.

Johannes Winterburger, who was active from 1492 to 1519, and was the first one whose name appeared on a book printed in Vienna, was responsible for [767] the elegant 1502 edition of the Wiener Heiligthumsbüchlein (109). It has a title page illustration and four woodcuts, 160-170 mm high and 115-120 mm wide. The woodcuts are equal in quality to the best of the Basel and Ulm works.

There is only one rather late [768] illustrated book from Worms. It was printed in 1499 and was [769] reprinted in 1509. It was the Reformation der Stadt Wormbs Recht, Gesetze, Ordnung und Statuta (110). In addition to a coat-of-arms on the verso of the title page, it has one very old woodcut illustration (195 x 120).

Würzburg [770-775], which was distinguished from 1484 by its Missals with copper plate illustrations, set aside this art around 1490. The Missals which Georg Reyser published in editions that followed each other rapidly, in 1491, 1493, 1495, 1496, 1497 and 1503 (111), are decorated with woodcuts, each with coats-of-arms and crosses, in folio and grand folio, and there is no recognizable relationship between these and the earlier copper plate illustrations. Artistically, they are more like the woodcuts in Schedel Chronica since Weigel, in his description of the edition of 1495 (Large Folio; No. 16346), attributes them directly to Wohlgemuth. At the beginning of the fifteenth century Georg Reyser left Würzburg and joined his brother in Eichstadt. There was no longer anyone capable of producing Missals in Würzburg, and this type of work was continued, particularly by Jacob von Pforzheim, in Basel.

To the books enumerated above, we must add a number to which no place of publication can be assigned.

The [776] Buch des Fabeldichter Aesopi, which was first published by Johannes Zainer in Ulm and then by Günther Zainer in Augsburg, has a third, fourth, fifth and sixth edition to which no printer can be assigned. The woodcuts of the third come from the same blocks as those of the second and the edition appears, therefore, to be attributable to Günther Zainer. The only difference [777] is that the Historie der Sigismunde is omitted. In the fourth edition (113) there are likewise no [778] changes (114). The title page illustration in the fifth edition (195 x 115) is somewhat larger than that of the first edition and is much more crudely cut. The large initial D of the preface shows Aesop at his writing desk with a small boy reading beneath it (70 x 62). The other woodcuts are very poorly done reversed copies of the Ulm edition. The [779] sixth edition (115) is once again closer to the first edition.

[780-781] Die vier Angeltugenden appeared s. l. e. a. in two editions, each with six woodcuts. The woodcuts in the first edition (116) were very crude. They were reworked from 60 x 80 mm to 75 x 80 mm in the second. The first edition may have come from Augsburg around 1480, while the second probably originated in Basel around the end of the century.

A very important s. l. e. a. book [782, Pl. 154-155] is the Antichristus oder Endschrift (118) which, indeed, according to Denis and Heinecken, is considered to belong to the transitional period in the development of book printing, even though it certainly used movable type. It has been attributed also to Thomas Fröschlin at Reutlingen. The title page is 200 x 125 mm and, of the woodcuts in the text (82 x 135), the first 44 depict the life of the Antichrist and No's 45-60 give the twelve signs of the Last Judgment. These woodcuts are very important, and may have been produced in 1494.

The illustrations [783] in the s. l. e. a. Beyspiel eines guten und auch bösen Rathschlages dieser Welt (119) are unimportant.

Bonaventura's [784] s. l. e. a. Psalter Mariae has a 65 x 45 mm. title page illustration.

Brant's [785] Auslesung der wunderbaren Geburt des Kindes zu Worms (120), which was published in 1495, has a very crude title page woodcut (75 x 60).

The Schachzabel [786] by Jacob de Cessolis appeared s. l. e. a. in low-German (121), with the customary woodcuts.

[787] The Liber ruralium commodorum, by Petrus de Crescentiis, appeared s. l. e. a. in the second Latin edition (122) and [788] s. l. e. a., in the first German edition. These have the same 317 woodcut prints that appeared in the first illustrated Mainz edition.

[789] Culmacher's s. l. e. a. Regimen wider der Pestilenz has a (124 x 93) title page illustration.

Five editions [790-794] of Donatus minor (124) appeared s. l. e. a., with the title page woodcut that of the teacher with students; three (125) editions [795-797] of Donatus cum vulgari expositione were published; and there is [798] one edition of Donatus' Grammatices rudimenta.

The first s. l. e. a. edition [799] of Drackole Waida (126) has a skillful portrait of a man on its title page.

In 1499 Egkstein's [800] Practica auf 1500 (127) was published with many woodcuts.

The 1501 edition [801] of Wunderlichen Geschichten von geistlichen Weibspersonen (128), which was published without location, has a very attractive title page woodcut (154 x 100) that is of the general quality of Dürer's work.

Six editions [802-807] of the Postilla by Guilielmus, containing woodcuts, were published s. l. e. a. Their title page woodcut is generally 210 x 130 mm. The woodcuts in the text are generally 85 x 72 mm.

No place of publication can be determined for [808] the first German edition (130) of Hieronymus' Leben der Altväter. The woodcuts in [809] the s. l. e. a. edition, which is described by Hain, No. 8604, as the second edition, are much less important. The seventh edition, which was published in low-German s. l. e. a., uses the same woodcuts as the first edition (131).

The second edition [810] of Historie von vier Kaufleuten (132) was printed in Leipzig in 1495 by Gregor Böttichers, but the first edition appeared s. l. e. a.

There are four s. l. editions of the Hortus sanitatis, which was first published by Peter Schöffer in Mainz in 1485, with the second edition appearing the same year in Augsburg, printed by Anton Sorg. These s. l. editions are the third, fourth, fifth, and ninth in its series of editions. The woodcuts [811] in the third (133) edition are smaller and of lower quality than those of the first two editions. In [812] the fourth edition (134) the full page illustration on the first page is the same as that of the first two editions, except that it is reversed. The remaining woodcuts are smaller than those in the first two editions, however they appear to be more worn than those. It may have been printed in Strassburg or Mainz, but certainly not in Augsburg, since in the copying of the title page the pine kernels are omitted from the escutcheon. The [813] fifth edition (135) appears likely to have been published in Strassburg or Mainz. The [814] ninth s. l. e. a. edition (136) is most similar to the two editions that Hans Schoensperger published in 1488, and may, therefore, be considered an Augsburg publication.

The woodcuts in [815] the second edition of Johannes Hildeshemiensis' Buch der heiligen drei Könige (137), which was first published by Johannes Prüss in Strassburg, are the same as those in the first edition.

There are two editions [816-817] of Liber Vagatorum to which no place of publication can be assigned (138).

The Ringbüchlein, which was first published in Augsburg by Sittich, appeared s. l. e. a. [818] under the title Die recht Kunst und Art des Ringens (139). The content of the 27 circular pictures is the same, but they are reduced in size (120 x 90), better shaded, and reworked in the modern style. It also has a new title page illustration (125 x 103).

Around 1480, the first low-German edition [819] of the Heiligenleben (140) may have been published in Rostock. Its woodcuts may be divided into two groups: the larger ones (120 x 145), a few of which are significant, and the many smaller ones (90 x 65), which are noteworthy in that they do not portray the Martyrs, as is normally done in the high-German Passions, but rather show the individual saints with their instruments of torture, in a landscape. These woodblocks were copied very widely.

A very interesting book that was printed ten times in the 1480's and 1490's [820, Pl. 156-157], is the Pronosticatio latina anno 88 ad magnam coniuctionem Saturni et Jovis, quae fuit 84 ad ecclipsin solis anni sequentis 85 confecta ac nunc de nova emendata, in which Kaiser Friedrich III's astronomer, Johann Lichtenberger, presents his suggested reforms of church and state in the form of a prophecy. Naturally, he made every effort, in the woodcuts for the individual chapters, to illustrate enough so that the even those who could not read would receive the intended impression. The first three [821-824] Latin editions (141) as well as the first two German editions were issued, without place of publication, between 1488 and 1492 (142). The 44 woodcuts are the same in all these editions, normally 200 x 150 mm. They were very original, and were provided with either German or Latin titles.

A very unimportant attachment to Lichtenberger's Pronosticatio is the [825] s. l. e. a. Bruder Lolhard (143).

The second edition of [826] Ulricus Molitoris' Tractatus de laniis et phitonicis mulieribus (144) varies from the Cologne first edition only in its (130 x 80) title page illustration.

Ludwig Moser's [827] s. l. e. a. Bereitung zu dem heiligen Sacrament mit andechtigen betrachtungen und gebeten vor und nach (145) was probably printed by Michael Furter in Basel. It has 55 colored woodcuts, usually 65 x 55 mm. The woodcuts belong to three different periods and hands. The oldest of these (around 1470) was responsible for numbers 2 and 48; the third (around 1485) was responsible for the 70 x 55 mm illustrations, Numbers 8 and 9. The greatest number of the woodcuts were done by the second producer (around 1480).

The first Latin edition [828] of Collationes inter Salomonem et Marcolphum (146) was published s. l. e. a. It has eight woodcuts which are different from those of later editions. The first of these is 70 x 62 mm and the others are 48 x 65 mm.

Sinthen's [829-830] Composita verborum (147) and Verba deponentialia (148) appeared in various s. l. e. a. editions and always had the title page illustration showing the teacher and scholar.

[831-832] No location can be assigned for the printing of the second (149) and third (150) editions of the Spiegel menschlicher Behaltniss.

The first German edition [833] s. l. e. a. of Tondalus (151) has woodcuts that are different from those in the later editions. All of its woodcuts are 70 x 70 mm except the one that shows Tondalus at the gates of Hell, which is 110 x 70 mm.

In the half century from 1460 to 1510 book illustration developed very greatly, starting with Albrecht Pfister in Bamberg, who, in 1460, was the first to illustrate his books with crude woodcuts. About 1470 book illustration started in Augsburg where, in the ten years to 1480, a great array of illustrated books was produced. While most of the Augsburg illustrations were crude, during the same period Ulm produced some of high artistic merit. Much richer activity started in 1480. In Augsburg Anton Sorg and Johann Schoensperger produced a mass of illustrated books and Erhard Ratdolt excelled both of them through the artistic production of his books. Leonhard Holl and Conrad Dinkmuth were working in Ulm in this period and Ludwig Hohenwang, who was at the close of his activity in this field, produced his most admired book. Cologne achieved fame through Heinrich Quentel, who produced the first highly artistically illustrated Bible.

Nuremberg overtook all the other cities from the beginning of Anton Koburger's highly artistic activities, especially after he obtained the services of Michel Wohlgemuth for the adornment of his publications. Basel became recognized early for the excellence of its work and achieved enviable development through the literary work of Sebastian Brant. Strassburg did not amount to much until near the end of the century, when Johann Grüninger opened his plant and gathered skilled workmen, and this progress was aided greatly when Sebastian Brant returned to the city in 1498. Mainz cannot be compared with any of the above-mentioned cities in terms of quantity of its production, but it was here that the still unmatched Rewich drawings for Breidenbach's Reise were done. When the first printed book was illustrated, the graphic arts and the woodcarving art stood at a very low artistic level. In the fifty years from 1460 to 1510 they were both developed to such a point that when the latest books of the period were produced, both woodcarving and the graphic arts had reached their highest level.

Notes

1) Sprenger, Aelteste Buchdruckergeschichte von Bamberg. Nuremberg, 1800; Zapf, Aelteste Buchdruckergeschichte Schwabens. Ulm, 1791.

2) Sprenger, No. 12. Folio.

3) Sprenger, No. 18. Large Folio.

4) Sprenger, No. 21. Large Folio.

5) Hain, Part II, 2:355 No. 15027. Small folio; Sprenger, No. 22.

6) Agenda sive obsequiale ecclesiae Bambergensis. Quarto; Sprenger, No. 23.

7) Sprenger, No. 46. Small Folio; Hain, Part II, 2:195, No. 13715; Panzer. Suppl. p. 62, No. 259b.

8) Hain, No. 4526. Quarto; Sprenger, No. 29; Panzer I:207, No. 365.

9) Sprenger, No. 30. Quarto; Panzer I:207, No. 366.

10) Sprenger, No. 31; Panzer I:208, No. 367.

11) Sprenger, No. 32. Quarto; Panzer I:208, No. 368.

12) Sprenger, No. 33. Quarto; Panzer I:208, No. 369.

13) Sprenger, No. 34. Quarto; Panzer I:208, No. 370.

14) Hain, No. 81. Quarto; Panzer I:208, No. 371; Sprenger, No. 35.

15a & 15b) Hain, No. 2711. s. l. e. a.; Sprenger, No. 44; Panzer I:208, No. 369.

16) Hain, No. 6550. s. a.

17) Sprenger, No. 47. Small folio; Hain, Part II, 2:195, No. 13715; Panzer, Suppl. p. 62, No. 2596; Illustrated in Essenwein, Plate 124.

18) Hain, No. 3886.

19) Sprenger, No. 42. Folio.

20) Ebert, No. 9226. Folio; Panzer I:279, No. 586.

21) Sprenger, No. 55. Quarto.

22) Ebert, No. 11811. Quarto; Panzer I:328, No. 690; Sprenger, No. 58.

23) Panzer I, No. 566.

24) Panzer, Suppl., No. 579d.

25) Weigel, No. 17025. Folio; Panzer I:265, No. 547.

26) Hain, No. 1103.

27) Hain, No. 6676.

28) Weller, No. 161.

29) Weller, No. 310.

30) Weller, No. 342.

31) Hain, No. 13914.

32) Hain, No. 6785.

33) Panzer VII:66, No. 1.

34) Ebert, No. 9388. Folio; Panzer I:313, No. 659; Vogt, p. 422.

35) Hain, No. 75.

36) Hain, No. 7401; Geffken, Bilderkatechismus des 15. Jahrh. Beilagen.

37) Weller, No. 206.

38) Hain, No. 6590.

39) Hain, Part II, 1:7, No. 8371. Quarto; Panzer I:188, No. 307.

40) Hain, No. 1836.

41) Hain, No. 1837.

42) Bodemann, Incunabeln der k. Bibliothek von Hannover. Hannover, 1866. p. 93, No. 156. Not in the bibliographies.

43) Hain, No. 2745.

44) Hain, Part II, No. 8374.

45) Hain, Part II, No. 12861. Folio.

46) Hain, No. 9287. Quarto; Graesse III:432.

47) Weller, No. 190.

48) Weller, No. 260.

49) Weller, No. 378.

50) Weller, No. 434.

51) Weller, No. 500.

52) Hain, No. 8815.

53) Geffken, Bilderkatechismus des 15. Jahrhunderts, Beilagen, p. 126, No. 12.

54) Hain, No. 6723. Large quarto. This is not listed by the other bibliographers.

55) Geffken, Bilderkatechismus, p. 140, No. 14.

56) Hain, No. 3204. Folio; Panzer, Annales typ. I:527, No. 11; Lacking in Ebert; Falkenstein, Geschichte der Buchdruckerkunst, p. 176; Brunet, ed. 5. I:1259; Graesse I:430.

57) Hain, No. 3206.

58) Hain, No. 9990.

59) Hain, No. 9991.

60) Hain, No. 6750.

61) Hain, No. 8957. Folio; Panzer, p. 195, No. 337; v. Seelen, Select. litter. p. 650; Dibdin, Biblioth. Spencer. V:153; Brunet, ed. 5. III:343; Graesse, Tresor III:375; Bibl. Rivin. No. 5683; Bünemann, Catal. mss. item librorum impressor. rarior. Mind. 1732. 8:19; Haller, Bibl. botan. I:241; Pritzel, No. 11902; Choulant, p. 257, No. 29.

62) Hain, No. 3143. Large folio; Panzer, p. 209, No. 374; Goeze, Historie der gedruckten niedersächsischen Bibeln. Halle, 1775. p. 85 ff; Ebert, No. 2348; Deecke, Nachrichten von den im 15. Jahrhundert zu Lübeck gedruckten niedersächsischen Büchern. p. 20, No. 36; Dibdin, Biblioth. Spencer. 1:55 ff; Falkenstein, Geschichte der Buchdruckerkunst, p. 177; Lacking in Brunet; Graesse I:377; Weigel, No. 18770.

63) Prophezeienbuch, Evangelien und Episteln; Panzer, No. 565.

64) Panzer, No. 578.

65) Panzer, Suppl., No. 630c.

66) Panzer I:323, No. 678. Folio.

67) Germ. Museum. No. 28260, cf. Brunet; five items are reproduced by Essenwein, Plates 127-128; With reference to the second edition see: Schönemann, Merkwürdigkeiten der Wolffenbüttler Bibliothek, No. 248; Bruhns, Beiträge der kritischen Bearbeitung alter Drucke. 3:197-216, 327-360.

68) Hain, No. 6751.

69) Hain, No. 6752.

70) Hain, No. 6753.

71) Hain, No. 13519. Quarto (has the title incorrectly); Panzer I:198; Ebert, No. 18119; It is lacking in Götze, Historie der niedersächsischen Bibeln.

72) Geffken, Bilderkatechismus. p. 148, No. 14.

73) Hain, No. 9992.

74) Hain, No. 6749.

75) Panzer I:194, No. 333. Folio.

76) Bodemann, Incunabeln von Hannover. No. 49; Panzer, Suppl., No. 510c.

77) Panzer I, No. 630.

78) Zapf, p. 221, No. 9. Quarto.

79) Zapf, p. 222, No. 11. Quarto.

80) Zapf, p. 251, No. 55. Quarto.

81) Weller, No. 436.

82) Niemanis haiss ich was iederman thut zucht man mich.; Weller, No. 600. Square Folio sheet.

83) Weller, No. 855.

84) Panzer I:483; Hain, No. 7190.

85) Hain, No. 7191.

86) Panzer, Suppl., No. 512c.

87) Weller, No. 216.

88) Weigel, No. 6800.

89) Hain, No. 14938.

90) Heller, Serapeum IV:301; Hain, No. 9744.

91) Heller, "Zusätze zu Panzer," im Serapeum IV:302.

92) Panzer I:217, No. 397; Hain, No. 4746.

93) Zapf, p. 208, No. 42. Octavo; Hain, No. 8287.

94) Zapf, p. 210, No. 44. Quarto.

95) Weller, No. 243.

96) Hain, No. 9976.

97) Hain, No. 11540. s. l. e. a.

98) Zapf, p. 203, No. 33. Octavo; Hain, No. 4744.

99) Hain, No. 3739.

100) Hain, No. 14526; Weller, No. 173.

101) Weigel, No. 19429. Octavo.

102) Hain, No. 8733.

103) Hain, No. 3180. Folio; Panzer, Annales. III:55; Graesse I:422; Zapf, p. 219, No. 11.

104) Hain, No. 9974; Zapf, p. 261, No. 1. Folio.

105) Zapf, p. 262, No. 2.

106) Weller, No. 262.

107) s. a., lacking in bibliographies; German. Museum

108) Falkenstein, Gesch. der Buchdruckerkunst. p. 189; s. a.; Quarto.

109) Denis, Wiens Buchdruckergeschichte. p. 15, No. 16; Panzer I:258, No. 526.

110) Hain, No. 13719. Folio.

111) Hain, No. 11311-11315.

112) Hain, No. 332.

113) Hain, No. 333.

114) Hain, No. 334.

115) Hain, No. 335.

116) Hain, No. 1097.

117) Hain, No. 1098.

118) Hain, No. 1149.

119) Hain, No. 3025.

120) Hain, No. 3759. s. l. 1495.

121) Hain, No. 4898.

122) Panzer, Annal Typ. IV:117. s. l. e. a. Folio; Hain, No. 5826; Ebert, No. 5438; Choulant, p. 284, No. 2.

123) Hain, No. 5833; Ebert, No. 5443; Choulant, p. 284, No. 3.

124) Hain, No. 6335-6342.

125) Hain, No. 6364-6367.

126) Hain, Part I, p. 280, No. 6405. Quarto.

127) Hain, No. 6578.

128) Weller, No. 187.

129) Hain, No. 8234, 8235, 8240, 8241, 8251.

130) Hain, No. 8603. Folio.

131) Hain, No. 8608.

132) Hain, No. 8750.

133) Choulant, p. 243, No. 3. Folio; not in the bibliographies.

134) Hain, No. 8947. Folio; Pritzel, No. 11883; Choulant p. 244, No. 4.

135) According to Hain (No. 8946) this is either a Strassburg or a Mainz imprint. Folio; Pritzel, No. 11882; Choulant, p. 244, No. 5.

136) Hain, No. 8945. Folio; Pritzel, No. 11881; Choulant, p. 246, No. 9.

137) Hain, No. 9401. s. l. e. a.

138) Hain, No. 3016 and 3017.

139) Hain, No. 9802. Quarto.

140) Hain, No. 9988. Folio.

141) Hain, No. 10080. The first small folio; Panzer, Annales typ. IV:45; Ebert, No. 11960; Brunet, ed. 5. III:1071, No. 9023; Graesse IV:204; the other two are Hain, No. 10081 and No. 10083.

142) Hain, No. 10086 and 10087.

143) Hain, No. 10223.

144) Hain, No. 11536.

145) Weller, No. 101.

146) Hain, Part II:266, No. 14252.

147) Hain, No. 14778ff.

148) Hain, No. 14782ff.

149) Hain, No. 14933.

150) Hain, No. 14934.

151) Hain, No. 15544.

VOLUME I

PART 2

INTRODUCTION

While book illustration developed quickly and successfully in the fifteenth century, there was one circumstance that hindered it from reaching its full flowering. Art and craftsmanship had gone their separate ways since the thirteenth century. In the field of graphics as well, it was only rarely that a true artist would contribute his powers. The first important artist who did not disdain to prepare drawings for woodcuts was Erhart Reuwich, and a few, like Michel Wohlgemuth, who prepared the drawings for the Lübeck Bible of 1494, joined him. But, in general, the better artists avoided this field, leaving the entire field to lower order craftsmen who, no matter how diligent their performance, were not in a position to raise graphics to the level at which it would be considered true art.

It was not until the beginning of the sixteenth century that the great change occurred. Book illustration freed itself from being considered a crude handicraft and was taken over by true artists, who brought it to heights which could not theretofore have been anticipated and which were not reached again in later years.

It was Albrecht Dürer through whom this step was achieved. His [834] Apokalypse of 1498 (1) accompanies a German text taken from the preface of Koburger's Bible.

Through Pirkheimer or Schedel he became acquainted with Conrad Celtes and he supplied three pages for Celtes' 1502 publication, [835] Quator libri amorum. He did the illustration of Apollo on Parnassus for Celtes 1507 edition [836] of Guntherus Ligurinus' De gestis Imp. Caes. Frederici I (2).

In 1510 Dürer supplied three of his own poems with title pages: for the [837] 64-line poem (3) the title page was that of the schoolmaster; the [838] 76-line poem (4) had the page depicting death and a soldier; and that for [839] the 80-line poem (5) depicted Christ on the Cross, between Mary and John. In 1513, when King Emanuel, the first King of Portugal to visit Europe since Roman times arrived, as part of the celebration [840] Dürer prepared the pamphlet Rhinoceros (6). When his friend Lazarus Spengler [841] edited the biography of Saint Hieronymus according to Eusebius, and had it published by Hieronymus Hölzel in 1514 (7), Dürer supplied a woodcut of "Hieronymus in a rocky grotto" for it. In 1515, his partly ornamental and partly illustrating border drawings [842] appeared in Gebetbuche Kaiser Maximilians (8). In the [843] Eichstädter Missale (9), which was printed by Hieronymous Hölzel in 1517, one finds, for the first time, the beautiful title page woodcut of Christ on the Cross, between Mary and John, with the four angels, which was to be used frequently later. In 1521 he supplied [844] the large title page illustration for the Reformation der Stat Nüremberg (10), which was printed by Friedrich Peypus.

Despite these few demonstrations of his activity, his example had a widespread influence. Around Dürer's sun there always orbited a group of artists, and through their works German book illustration achieved its finest period.

Notes

1) cf. Thausing, 184-198.

2) Augsburg, Oegelin-Nadler, 1507; Panzer VI:136, No. 41; Zapf, p. 29.

3) Weller, No. 543; Heller, Dürer II:683; Thausing, p. 349.

4) Weller, No. 544; Heller, Dürer II:686; Thausing, p. 350.

5) Weller, No. 619; Heller, Dürer II:613; Thausing, p. 350.

6) Weller, No. 978; Heller, Dürer II:691; Thausing, p. 378.

7) Panzer II:365, No. 776; Bartsch 113; Heller 1845; Retberg 197.

8) Bartsch 56; Heller, 1633; Thausing, p. 383.

9) Panzer, No. 1235; Thausing, p. 445.

10) cf. Thausing, Dürer, p. 379, and the literature listed therein. We have not attempted comprehensive coverage of Dürer's works in this volume.

Chapter XIII

KAISER MAXIMILIAN'S ILLUSTRATED BOOKS (1)

Augsburg, where book illustration took root earliest, remained its chief place of development in the sixteenth century.

Just as every art achieves its greatest significance when it is set to great public works, book illustration reached its highest flowering under the wide-scale undertakings of Kaiser Maximilian.

Maximilian I's intent in producing his costly deluxe editions is stated straightforwardly in the Weisskunig:

> When a man dies his works do not follow him, and whosoever does not build a memorial to himself during his lifetime has no memorial after his death and is forgotten with the bells; and therefore the money that I spend this way in building my memorial is not lost.

He was striving to ensure his own posthumous fame. And with his indefatigable literary creative impulse and his great love of art, it seems natural that he saw epochmaking production of magnificent books as a suitable means for achieving this purpose.

This literary-artistic plan was best spelled out in a letter, dated October 14, 1512, that Kaiser Maximilian wrote to Siegmund von Dietrichstein, his counsel and keeper of his plate room. In this letter he tells von Dietrichstein about the progress on a couple of lesser works and says that as soon as Stabius arrives, which he expects daily, these should be finished up and sent to Peutinger, after which they will, without any question, be printed within a week; and he promises to send Dietrichstein a copy from the first batch of copies received.

He reports that, as of the previous day, he had completed his Genealogy and had had it sent to Peutinger to have it printed; that it would certainly be completed in two weeks, and he promises to have one of the first batch of these sent to Dietrichstein also. He reports that Stabius also has the Triumpfwagen well on its way, but that he had not yet reviewed it. As to the Freydal, the Kaiser reports that it is about half completed and that most of the work was done in Cologne. So far as the Weisskunig is concerned, the letter states,

> We have also the Weissen König about half completed; but the figures, because it requires so many, are not all cut as yet; which is true also of the Freydal because of the large number of illustrations--about 250 for the Freydal alone.... (2)

The Genealogy, which the Kaiser had completed and was about to send to Peutinger, as well as the Triumphwagen, the first draft of which was completed by Johann Stabius, may not be considered as printed books, in fact, because their text is so minor in relation to the pictures. However, the other three books mentioned in the letter, the Theuerdank, the Weisskunig and the Freydal were all the more important. The Theuerdank was to report the Kaiser's wedding trip to Burgundy; the Weisskunig was to cover his biography and the history of his governmental activities; and the Freydal was to detail his historical knightly activities.

Augsburg was his favorite city. It was here that he had the metallic portraits made (both forms and castings) by which he honored the historically memorable people; it was here that he had his armor made, to his great satisfaction; and it was the place he selected for the completion of the deluxe editions of books that he had in preparation. His friend Dr. Conrad Peutinger, who was knowledgeable about art, lived in Augsburg and was capable of overseeing the entire enterprise with understanding of all its various phases. Hans Baumgartner also lived in Augsburg; his purse at that time seemed bottomless, and he was always ready to help when his Kaiser overestimated the amount of money available to him.

The printer whom the Kaiser and Peutinger selected was Hans Schönsperger, the Elder, who, back in 1508, had been appointed for life by Maximilian as the Kaiser's printer (3). The Kaiser in this appointment made a provision for 100 Gulden to be paid annually to Schönsperger from the State Treasury at Innsbruck, and if he was called to the Castle, provision was made for his support and that of his helpers, plus a special honorarium for his work. And, to be sure, the Kaiser made use of his chief printer many times. Schönsperger gave up his regular work as a printer early in the sixteenth century. He was implicated in legal processes and found guilty, and in 1509 was on the point of being exiled from Augsburg. The Kaiser wrote no less than three letters--from Antdorf on January 10th; from Mecheln on March 10th; and from the Persen Castle on June 30th--to the authorities of the city, in defense of his "beloved servant" (4).

There was no shortage of illustrators in Augsburg. Hans Burgkmair had already been involved in the Genealogie and by 1510 he had prepared 92 drawings for the Kaiser. Peutinger paid 113 fl., 24 kr. to Burgkmair and the 13 others involved in cutting and preparing the forms (5). He, therefore, was the first considered for the new undertaking. Another developing talent in the Schwabian circle was Hans Scheifelin, who came from Nördlingen, near Augsburg and, at the request of the Kaiser, moved to the City.

In addition to these two, who contributed the bulk of the work, there was also Hans Springinklee, from Nuremberg, and an unknown Augsburg artist, who signed his drawing with the monogram LB, working in the group.

This great undertaking necessitated the formation of a woodcutting school of their own. To be sure, they had used two formcutters in Augsburg, back in 1510, in doing the Genealogie, but that did not work out too well. One of them suddenly left the city and there was no substitute, so that Hans Burgkmair had to help out by serving as a woodcarver as well as artist (6). This time their selection of woodcarver was especially fortunate. How the Kaiser or Peutinger happened upon Jost Dienecker of Antwerp is unknown. He arrived in Augsburg in 1512, and is entered on the tax records as "Jost, His Imperial Majesty's block carver." In a very short time it became clear that he could not possibly handle the volume of work that was involved. It was decided that two or three additional woodcarvers had to be engaged, and Dienecker himself suggested this to the Kaiser. In a letter to Maximilian, dated October 20, he wrote,

> wishing to inform his Everlasting Majesty that the work that I am to prepare would move along much better if I could have the assistance of two or three additional formcutters. I should appreciate this very much. I now know two formcarvers who have a certain amount of skill and who would be glad to work with me in the ... Kaiser's works. Therefore, if the ... Kaiser intends to add these two wood carvers, would His

> ... Majesty permit me to request from Mr. Baumgartner that he supply each of them with 100 Gulden per year in order that they be able to come and work with me ...

He then goes on to tell how he intends to arrange his work with both of these people, saying,

> I will prearrange everything for these two form carvers, and I shall, with my own hands, do the cleaning up and finishing of the forms so that all the carving, when completed, is alike in cutting and is finished by one person, and no one will be able to recognize more than a single hand in the woodcuts. And since I shall be a third cutter, as well, I am sure that we can complete six or seven good pieces each month, all in the same masterly cutting, so that Schönsperger will be able to get started on the printing. I will also exert all diligence to expedite the work and to see that it is completed in accordance with Your Majesty's desire.

In closing the letter he requests that the Kaiser assign the two additional wood carvers and himself to the same quarters so that they may work more effectively (7).

The Kaiser does not seem to have granted this last request since, according to the tax records at least, Dienecker lived by himself. His home, which he continued to use in the following years, was in the street of the Haustetter Gate, now called the red door.

They went to work with fresh energy. Unfortunately, right at the beginning there were some disagreements. The Kaiser had fixed in his mind that the Augsburg formcarvers were supposed to be working for him and for no one else. Dienecker, however, had misgivings over this requirement and complained to Peutinger about it. Then he had to take his case to the Kaiser, and in a letter dated October 27, 1512, he says "...I have never done any work other than for the ... Kaiser. Except for the portrait of Hans Baumgartner I have made nothing for anyone" (8).

Hans Scheifelin was also unsatisfied. He had already sent a number of drawings to Schönsperger, and it had been agreed that he should be paid for these. Schönsperger paid him entirely according to his own judgment, giving him "two Gulden for three figures." For this reason Scheifelin wanted to be freed from Schönsperger and to receive his pay from someone else; from Peutinger or Baumgartner or Dienecker, and preferably the last-named since he understood what was involved. He asked Dienecker to write to the Kaiser for permission to make this change (9).

As the Kaiser thought in terms of completing the Weisskunig in 1513, the number of woodcarvers was increased still further. Alexius Lindt came on to the staff and did not appear to be living very well, since the tax records state "he gives nothing."

Dienecker went on with his work diligently and Peutinger, in writing to the Kaiser on October 5, 1513, was able to advise that the work was making good progress and that Baumgartner was prepared to make further advances for paying the artists. He said he saw no need to hire more woodcarvers, and that the work should be completed on schedule (10).

The Kaiser was always very active in this himself. Since he wanted to see each new woodblock and drawing to make sure that the fineness of the drawing did not suffer in the carving, Peutinger sent him, on October 5, 1513, everything that had been completed to date, "except for three which were so badly damaged here that they have to be redone..." (11).

The year 1514 brought disappointment relating to the text of the Weisskunig. Still convinced that the work could be completed, the Kaiser had his secretary, Marx Treitzsaurwein, review it and make sure of its progress. The secretary prepared an extensive supplementary manuscript which pointed out confusion and a lack of clarity in many of the accounts, which made it impossible to go on with completion of the work. The Kaiser did not allow himself to be scared off at first, and on into the beginning of 1516 he had a part of the illustrations sent to him at Triento for review. He received six, of which three were for Freydal, one for Theuerdank and two for the Weisskunig (12).

Although completion of the text of the Weisskunig was no longer moving forward, and there was a definite slowdown in production of woodcuts, Peutinger had built the staff of woodcarvers up to nine. Jacob Rupp came to Augsburg in 1515 and Cornelius Liefrink, who had previously worked in Augsburg, came back from Antwerp in 1516.

The woodcarvers became impatient and demanded their "weekly waiting pay" when they had no work to do; and the Netherlanders, in particular, did not want to remain any longer without work to do. Stabius, who was working for the Kaiser in Nuremberg, had only one woodcarver at that time, Hieronymus Resch, so he sent the bulk of his work to Augsburg and Peutinger put five of his woodcarvers to the work for Stabius, keeping only four at work on the Theuerdank and the Weisskunig. Peutinger covered this all in a letter to the Kaiser dated June 9, 1516 (13). This was the last letter that Peutinger wrote to the Kaiser about his illustrated books.

Thus, of all the great works that he brought far along in the preparatory work, only an insignificant part was completed during the Kaiser's lifetime. In the year before his death, the Kaiser made his active co-worker, Melchior Pfinzing, Prior of St. Sebald in Nuremberg, responsible for completion of all his books and give him all the necessary directions that would enable him to complete the books after the Kaiser's death (14). The Kaiser further emphasized this in his Testament of December 30, 1518. Of the three great deluxe books that he worked on with all his energies, he lived to see only one completed in print, [845, Pl. 162-163] the Theuerdank.

The Theuerdank, which the Kaiser originally planned in 1505-1508 (15), was to present, in allegorical form, the adventures of Maximilian in his travels to the estate of the beautiful and rich Maria of Burgundy. As the correspondence with Dietrichstein indicates, by 1512 a large part of the poem was completed. Dietrichstein had even returned to the Kaiser the draft of the first part for review. A private secretary who served the Kaiser in his literary undertakings, Melchior Pfinzing, was then given the assignment of reworking the often irregular versification, and of revising the whole thing. Along with the printing, so far as can be determined from the related correspondence from Dienecker, dated October 27, 1512, Dienecker was committed, with his two helpers, to produce six or seven good woodcuts per month so that Schoensperger could begin printing in 1512. The famed first edition which appeared in 1517 bears the statement, "Printed in the Imperial City of Nuremberg, by Hans Schoensperger, the elder, citizen of Augsburg." People have tried to explain this note in various ways. Panzer surmises that, despite this note, the edition was printed in Augsburg, where the later editions were produced, and Nuremberg was mentioned only to honor Melchior Pfinzing. It is difficult to see how Pfinzing could be honored by a false place of publication. Zapf is of the opinion that Pfinzing wanted the work printed in his locality so that he could oversee the correctness of the work, and that Schoensperger, therefore, moved to Nuremberg for the duration of this undertaking. This theory is contradicted, however, by the fact that the Augsburg tax records show Schoensperger living in Augsburg, where he was a citizen and a Guild member through 1517. Thus it would have to be proved that more than the last signature was printed in Nuremberg. The only apparently acceptable theory is that Schoensperger, whose economic situation did not improve over the years, printed the edition in Nuremberg simply to get away from his creditors. Just at that time he may have been beset by his creditors, who may have been impatiently expecting that upon completion of the Theuerdank he would receive a good deal of money.

In the pressure to get the book into print only a few copies were printed. The Kaiser had expected many more so that he might distribute them to the aristocracy as a symbol of his special regard. This is indicated by King Ferdinand's instruction about reprinting the works of Kaiser Maximilian I, in 1526, in which he says, "Since the book Theuerdank was published in his lifetime and only a single small run was made, and Kaiser Maximilian expected it to be distributed more widely, six hundred copies are to be provided here in Augsburg and another three hundred are to be delivered to Treitzsaurwein, who shall take them to Vienna at our expense and shall distribute them to the Nobles and certain others in the five lower-Austrian lands as our way of honoring them" (16).

Each of the 118 chapters of the book is illustrated by a large woodcut. Here as always, one of the primary questions is that of determining the attribution of the drawings to their artists. Relatively few monograms appear in this book. Of the 118 woodcuts, only Numbers 13, 30, 39, 42, 48, 58, 69 and 70 are signed with Scheifelin's monogram, but that appears on numbers 30 and 70 in only a few copies. Necker's monogram is found on a few and is on no. 70 in just a few copies.

There is a special note about the preparers of the illustrations in the first edition, but the note does not always correspond with the illustrator. Mathaus Schultes states on the title page of each of his two editions in the seventeenth century that the Theuerdank "is illustrated by the distinguished painter Scheifelin of Nordlingen, with 117 illustrations, cut into wood, which aid in understanding of the text."

He repeats this in the preface and on the fifth page, in the biography of Maximilian I which is added to his editions. Sandrart also names Hans Scheifelin as the artist. Also naming him as the artist are: Doppelmayr (p. 193); Meusel, Neue Miscellaneen für Kunstler und Kunstliebhaber, Leipzig, 1799; and Zapf and Panzer (p. 409). It was not until the 18th century that a different point of view was presented. In the Bibliotheca Vilenbroukiana, which was published in 1729 in eight volumes, it states (1:285, No. 1351), "with 118 beautiful prints done contemporaneously by Albert Dürer, Jean Burchmeyer and H. S." Fournier, in his Dissertation sur l'Imprimerie (1758, p. 75), and Debure, in his Bibliographie Instructive, name the artists as Hans Sebalde and Hans Schäufelin. Huber and Rost, Handbuch fur Kunstliebhaber, which was published in Zurich in 1796-1808 in 8 volumes (1:140, No. 48), take the same position as the Bibliotheca Vilenbroukiana. None of these attributions appears to provide any firm evidence for acceptance. Later, Passow, in a paper in Serapeum IV:13, pointed out that Theuerdank appears in three different costumes on various pages: in full armor, in hunting clothes, and in a long monk-like coat, and he attempted to establish the artist based on the clothing on the various pages. Nagler tended to agree with him in the Monogrammisten. But this point of view likewise has no evidence based on contemporary source materials, nor is there any that establishes Scheifelin as the artist.

The one who made the greatest gain out of the edition was Schoensperger. From 30 pence his payment in 1518-1519 rose to 1 Florin, 30 farthings. However, he did not enjoy this change in his fortunes very long. In 1519, shortly after he completed the second printing of the Theuerdank, he died.

This [846] 1519 Augsburg second edition of Theuerdank had only 115 illustrations, i. e., three less than the first. It lacks Numbers 14, 31 and 40. Otherwise the illustrations and the type are the same.

The third edition [847], with the same text and figures, was published by Heinrich Steiner in 1537. The only difference between the earlier editions and this one is that the type shows normal wear and the woodcuts are worn to the point that they are unrecognizable.

In the years that followed, the woodblocks were lost so that when Egenolff, in Frankfurt, wanted to produce [848] the fourth edition in 1533 he had to have new woodcuts made for it, which he also used in [849] his fifth edition in 1563 and in [850] the sixth edition in 1589. The seventh edition, which was printed [851] in octavo, had sixteen woodcuts made for it which were very poor.

In the second half of the seventeenth century the Ulm printer, Matthäus Schultes found the old woodblocks, renewed them, and made use of them. They had, as Schultes writes in the preface of the undated edition that he issued, "been hidden away so that for 162 years no one knew much if anything about them ... until one of my close friends, quite by chance, came upon a hint as to where ... these woodcuts, but without the text, ... might be found. Upon the advice of good friends, I thought about bringing them out of their long guarded dark dungeon ... I have, therefore, undertaken this difficult project, which was not without very special cost, so that those interested in history and amateurs of art may have them see the light of day again."

Schultes published two editions. One, the eighth, [852] was issued in Ulm in 1679 with the 118 Scheifelin illustrations and an additional six old ones which are not found in the first three editions of the poem. With reference to these, Schultes writes in his preface, "Since the rediscovered Theuerdank woodblocks included another six that had unquestionably been prepared for this work but are not found included in the old editions, it seemed to the printer that it might be useful to add these six as a supplement to the work."

In his second edition (the ninth) [853] which was published undated in Augsburg, Schultes omitted these six extra woodcuts and the explanation, and the ninth edition thus had the same woodcuts as the first. Even in the washed out new printings from the worn blocks, it was possible to appreciate the fineness of the originals.

As compared with the, at least partially lucky, history of the Theuerdank, [854, Pl. 164-165] the Weisskunig appears to have been destined from the very beginning to fall into oblivion. And yet it was a twin of the Theuerdank, since the Kaiser worked with both of them simultaneously and was determined to get them both done at the same time. While the plan for the Theuerdank was being carried out by Pfinzing, the Kaiser turned over the Weisskunig for simultaneous revision by his secretary, Marx Treizsaurwein.

The Kaiser had completed half of the dictation for the Weisskunig back in 1512, as is indicated in his letter of October 14, 1512 to Sigmund von Dietrichstein. A preliminary draft was prepared by Treizsaurwein from the Kaiser's dictation and other material that had been gathered for this purpose by Christmas of 1514, as indicated in the notes appended to the work which he transmitted to the Kaiser. The woodcut preparation was forwarded to the Kaiser in even more complete and excellent form than were those for the Theuerdank. Then, from 1514 on, the work on the text of the Weisskunig lay untouched. Questions were asked of the Kaiser about many details of the text and his answers and explanations were written close to the questions in the text. However, there was much that was not clarified. In 1517 the Kaiser went to Brussels with his uncles Karl and Ferdinand. Shortly after the return from that trip he attended his last Reichstag meeting in Augsburg, and not long after that he succumbed to his last illness and died in Wels on January 12, 1519.

When young Archduke Ferdinand remembered the book in 1525, the lower-Austrian Marx Treizsaurwein was no longer assigned the task of turning Kaiser Maximilian's history and stories into a book, and no one knew where to find the books listing the questions about the Weisskunig or the other works of Maximilian. Searches for them in Innsbruck and in Freiburg, by Doctor Mennel, one of the many literary helpers of the Kaiser, proved fruitless.

They must have been found in the following year, since on March 26, 1526 King Ferdinand issued an order to Dr. Peutinger to take over all of the historical writings that had any relation to Kaiser Maximilian I and that were in the possession of Melchior Pfinzing, and to send them to Marx Treizsaurwein. At the same time, formal instructions regarding their publication were received by Marx Treizsaurwein from King Ferdinand (17).

But this venture, too, resulted in stagnation. In the years that followed there hardly seems to have been any difficulty that did not affect the works of the Kaiser, and more than two hundred years elapsed before the Weisskunig was freed from obscurity and saw the light. The manuscripts had, in the meantime, been found in Vienna. The woodblocks were found in the Duchy of Steyr, through the fortunate chance that an understanding eye happened to see them before their destruction was complete. Thus the unmerited jinx that so long operated against this book was finally overcome, and the book appeared in a painstaking and meritorious folio edition in Vienna, at the expense of Joseph Kurzböcken, in 1775. Through the diligence of the publisher, the text and the illustrations were pertinently arranged, based on the content or on the notes available in the Kaiser's own handwriting. The small amount of material for which he could not determine the proper location was included as an appendix.

The book is dedicated to the Grandduke Karl (Karl V) and the dedication appears to have been written by Treizsaurwein in 1517. The woodcut that accompanies it shows the Archduke, surrounded by knights on the right and left, standing under the canopy of the throne, with Marx Treizsaurwein before him handing him the finely bound book, to honor him and to show respect for him.

The book itself, as Treizsaurwein says in the dedication, is divided into three parts: the first part covers the marriage of the white king to his bride and how they achieved the highest crown at Rome; the second part tells of the young white king's youth, his education, his elegance, deeds and marriage; the third covers the wars and battles conducted by the young white king (18).

Coming now to the parts contributed by the individual artists to the illustration of the Weisskunig, even if none of them had born a monogram it would still have been possible to attribute the bulk of the illustrations to two masters with very different styles. The one likes tall and slender figures; with the other they are squat and the heads are disproportionately large in relation to the bodies. Similarly, their female figures are in sharp contrast. The one does everything in large scale and handles his pictures imposingly; the other is identified by his excellent handling of detail. Of these two artists, one placed his monogram on 98 illustrations and the other on one only (No. 200). The first of these is Hans Burgkmair and the other is Hans Scheifelin. In addition, there are two other monograms to be found in the Weisskunig: No. 199 bears the monogram of Hans Springinklee, and No. 78 bears that of a completely unknown artist LB.

The table that follows attempts to attribute the illustrations to their artists--but it should be understood that a number of those attributed to Burgkmair--particularly among the battle scenes--may well have been done by the painter LB. The numbers given are those that will be found at the foot of each woodcut in the 1775 edition. The illustration numbers given in that edition have two typographical errors. No's. 21 and 57 are to be found twice, while No's. 12 and 158 were omitted. Both the errors are corrected in the index, i.e., the duplicate No. 21 is given as No. 12 and the duplicate 57 is given as No. 158 in the index.

No.	Subject	Artist	Mark
1	Treitzsaurwein übergibt dem Erzherzog Karl knieend sein Buch	Burgkmair	lower left
2	Der alte Weisskunig schickt seinen Boten nach Portugal	Scheifelin	none
3	Abzug der Gesandtschaft	Burgkmair	lower left
4	Eleonora vor dem Throne des Königs von Portugal	"	"
5	Auszug des alten Weisskunig nach Italien	Scheifelin	none
6	Zusammentreffen des alten Weisskunigs mit Eleonora	"	"
7	Empfang der jungen Eheleute durch den Papst	"	"
8	Vermählung des alten Weisskunigs mit Eleonora	"	"
9	Segnung der Brautleute durch den Papst nach der Trauung	"	"
10	Krönung der Eleonora durch den Papst	"	"
11	Zug der Hochzeitsgesellschaft aus dem St. Peter	Burgkmair	lower left
12	Taufe des jungen Weisskunigs	"	below
13	Die Amme mit dem Kinde	"	none
14	Der Cardinal spricht nach der Taufe den Segen über das Kind	"	"
15	Der junge Weisskunig spielt mit Edelknaben im Grase	"	lower right
16	Leichenbegängniss des Königs vom Feuereisen	Scheifelin	none
17	Der junge Weisskunig wird von seinem Lehrer unterrichtet	Burgkmair	"
18	Der junge Prinz lernt schreiben	"	lower right
19	Der junge Prinz lernt sternsehen	Scheifelin	none
20	Der Prinz zwischen dem Papste und dem Kaiser	Burgkmair	lower right
21	Der Prinz sieht Zimmerleuten zu	Scheifelin	none
22	Der Prinz lernt die Arzeneikunde	Burgkmair	lower left
23	Der Prinz lernt die Schwarzkunst	"	none
24	Der Prinz lernt von einem Bauer Böhmisch	"	"
25	Der Prinz steht zwifchen seinen Secretairen	"	lower right
26	Der Prinz sieht einem Maler zu	"	upper left
27	Der Prinz sieht Maurern zu	Scheifelin	none
28	Der Prinz lernt Musik	Burgkmair	lower left

No.	Subject	Artist	Mark
29	Der Prinz steht zwischen den Vertretern der sieben freien Künste	Scheifelin	none
30	Der Prinz lässt einen Mummenschanz ausführen	Burgkmair	lower right
31	Der Prinz lernt kochen	"	below
32	Der Prinz sieht den Münzprägern zu	Scheifelin	none
33	Der Prinz auf der Vogeljagd	"	"
34	Der Prinz auf der Falkenbeize	"	"
35	Der Prinz auf der Hirschjagd	"	"
36	Der Prinz fängt Fische	"	"
37	Der Prinz sicht mit einem Manne Ploss	Burgkmair	"
38	Turnier	Scheifelin	"
39	Turnier	"	"
40	Der Prinz schiesst zu Pferde mit der Armbrust	Burgkmair	"
41	Der Prinz lernt die Eigenschaften der Pferde kennen	Scheifelin	"
42	Der Prinz beim Waffenschmid	Burgkmair	upper right
43	Der Prinz beim Kanonengiessen	"	below
44	Der Prinz zwischen Wagenburgen	"	lower right
45	Der König vom Feuereisen und seine Tochter	"	"
46	Zusammenkunst der beiden Könige in Trier	"	upper right
47	Die feindlichen Heere treffen am Flusse zusammen	"	none
48	Die Gesandten vor der Königin vom Feuereisen	Scheifelin	"
49	Der alte Weisskunig erlaubt seinem Sohn, gegen den grünen König zu ziehen	Burgkmair	lower left
50	Der Gesandte der Königin vom Feuereisen vor dem jungen Weisskunig	"	none
51	Vier Könige in einem Zimmer, von denen zwei mit einander sprechen, einer die Hand auf der Thürklinke hat und hinausgehen will	"	upper right
52	Der junge Weisskunig und eine Frau von Männern und Frauen umgeben in einem Säulenhof	"	"
53	Vermählung des jungen Weisskunigs mit der Prinzessin vom Feuereisen	Scheifelin	none
54	Die Bewohner einer Stadt, vor dem Stadtthore stehend, schwören dem jungen Weisskunig Treue, rechts oben eine Festung	Burgkmair 1515	upper left
55	Der junge Weisskunig sitzt mit seiner Gemahlin im Garten	Scheifelin	none
56	Turnier zu Feier der Hochzeit	Burgkmair	"
57	Der alte Weisskunig schickt seinen Sohn nach Brabant	Scheifelin	"
58	Der junge Weisskunig zwischen der Königin und der Prinzessin vom Feuereisen	"	"
59	Der junge Weisskunig lernt von Rittern Welsch	"	"
60	Fussvolk zieht aus einem Stadtthor heraus, links warten Ritter, rechts Fuss-soldaten, um in das Stadtthor einzuziehen	Burgkmair	lower left
61	Bewaffnete haben Carée gebildet und werden von zwei Seiten, auf der einen von Fussvolk, auf der andern von Reitern angegriffen	Scheifelin	none
62	Kampf vor einer einsamen Festung, ein Trommler schlägt, ein Trompeter bläst dazu	Burgkmair	lower
63	Schlacht auf einem Weinberg	"	lower right
64	Wirres Gemenge von Bewaffneten, unten Marketenderwagen und Kanonen	"	none
65	Sturm auf dem Meere in der Nähe einer Stadt. Aus den dicht besetzten Schiffen sind viele Männer über Bord gefallen	"	upper left
66	Bewaffnete ziehen zum Kampf aus, oben unter einer Palme sprechen zwei Ritter miteinander	"	lower right
67	Durchwatung eines Flusses, oben Felsen, untern Kanonen und Bäume	"	none

No.	Subject	Artist	Mark
68	Kriegsheere vor einer Stadt, unten ein Fluss und Kanonen	Burgkmair	lower right
69	Leichenbegängniss	"	upper right
70	Schlacht	"	lower right
71	Der junge Weisskunig auf dem Throne, zu jeder Seite zwei Männer, davor einer halbknieend mit einem Brief	"	upper right
72	Kampf vor einer Stadt am Meeresufer	"	lower right
73	Stadt an einem Fluss, in die Bewaffnete einziehen	Scheifelin	none
74	Schlacht in einem Engpass, der zu einer Festung hinanführt	Burgkmair	"
75	Oben Kampf vor einer Stadt, unten Reiter	"	below
76	Bewaffnete vor einer Schanze, auf der die Kreuzfahne weht, vorn Vieh	"	upper left
77	Bewaffnete vor einer brennenden Stadt	"	lower right
78	Schlacht, oben zwischen Fussvolk, unten zwischen Rittern		lower left
79	Versammlung von vier Königen, davor vier Männer	Burgkmair	none
80	Der Weisskunig spricht mit sieben Hauptleuten seiner Armee die sieben Sprachen	"	upper left
81	Schiffe fahren auf ruhiger See dahin, ein Tambour und ein Flötenbläser spielen dazu auf	Scheifelin	none
82	Schlacht zwischen orientalischen Reitern, welche die Köpfe der Erschlagenen auf ihre Lanze stecken	"	"
83	Treffen in einem Engpass, oben eine Burg, auf der die Kreuzfahne weht	Burgkmair	center
84	Belagerung einer Stadt, unten Zelte und Kanonen	"	lower right
85	Ein König sitzt, von zwei Männern umgeben, auf einem Throne, davor ein Bote mit einem Brief	"	none
86	Einzug von Rittern und Fussvolk in eine befestigte Stadt	"	lower left
87	In einem Burghof links drei Männer und ein Knabe, rechts drei Männer, die zu einer Treppe herunterkommen	Scheifelin	none
88	Eine kleine Frau, hinter welcher Ritter stehen, vor dem jungen Weisskunig	Burgkmair	lower left
89	Kriegsschiffe auf der See	"	upper right
90	Schlacht unter Vortragung der Kreuzfahne	"	upper left
91	Auszug zu einem Kampf	Scheifelin	none
92	Kampf an den Ufern eines Flusses, oben sprengen Ritter durch die Landschaft dahin	"	"
93	Ein König vor einer Stadt, dahinter Waffenträger, davor ein Mann, der einen Brief übergibt, links unten ein ummauerter Raum	Burgkmair	upper left
94	Oben Kampf von Rittern, darunter von Fussvolk, unten vier Kanonen	"	lower left
95	Die Bewohner einer Stadt schwören knieend einem auf dem Pferde sitzenden Könige Treue, dahinter Zelte und Gefolge	"	upper left
96	Schiffe, am Ufer Bewaffnete, oben ein brennendes Haus	"	none
97	Einzug in eine brennende Stadt	"	"
98	Vier Könige gehen zu den vier Thüren eines Zimmers hinaus	Scheifelin	"
99	Zu einer Festung, auf der eine Fahne weht, steigen Bewaffnete herauf, während oben Männer sich von der Mauer herunterstürzen	"	"
100	Kampf am Meeresufer, rechts unter Kanonen	Burgkmair	lower right
101	Bewaffnete vor einer brennenden Stadt	"	"
102	Ein König, hinter dem Ritter stehen, auf der Treppe eines Palastes, davor auf der untersten Stufe ein Knabe und drei Mädchen, hinter ihnen vier Männer	"	none
103	Ein König sitzt swifchen vier geharnischten Männern	"	lower right
104	Schiffskampf	"	none
105	Belagerung und Erstürmung einer Stadt, links unter drei Kanonen	"	lower left
106	Schlacht in einem Engpass unter einer Festung	Scheifelin	none

No.	Subject	Artist	Mark
107	Kampf um ein Stadtthor, ein Mann wird zur Mauer heruntergeworfen	Burgkmair	upper left
108	Heranziehendes Fussvolk und Reiterscharmützel, unten Zelte und ein Wagen	"	none
109	Kampf vor einem Stadtthor, unten ziehen Ritter und Fusssoldaten heran	"	"
110	Zwei Männer liegen geköpft am Boden, der dritte, dem die Augen verbunden sind, erwartet den Schlag des Scharfrichters, Ringsum im Kreise Lanzenträger, im Hintergrund eine Festung und Felsen, auf denen Gemsen stehen	"	above
111	Ein Bote übergibt in einem Saale einem bärtigen Könige einen Brief	Scheifelin	none
112	Kampf auf einer Anhöhe am Meeresufer	Burgkmair	"
113	Fünf Schiffe auf freundlicher See. Das erste, in dem sich nur Frauen befinden, ist gelandet und die Königin steht schon am Ufer. Der König, dem Männer folgen, ist ihr entgegen gegangen und reicht ihr die Hand	Scheifelin	"
114	Ein König mit Bewaffneten in einem Saale	"	"
115	Attacke von Bogenschützen, rechts unten ein Crucifix	Burgkmair	lower right
116	Eine Landschaft. Ein geharnischter König zeigt einem andern eine Stelle in einem aufgeschlagenen Buche, das sie beide in der Hand halten. Links Lanzenträger, rechts Bogenschützen, auf der See im Hintergrunde ein leeres Schiff	"	above
117	Vier Männer am Meeresstrande sprechen mit einem Ritter im Jägercostüm	Scheifelin	none
118	Kampf um einen Thurm, unten links ein Kreuz	Burgkmair	lower left
119	Taufe des Erzherzogs Philipp	"	none
120	Kampf, oben von Rittern, unten von Fussvolk	"	"
121	Eine reichgekleidete Frau mit zwei Knaben und mehreren Mädchen steht vor einem aus dem Throne sitzenden König	"	upper right
122	Sechs Männer sitzen um einen Tisch herum	"	"
123	Der junge Weisskunig sitzt auf dem Throne, im Kreise ringsum sieben Männer	"	none
124	Ein König sitzt unter dem Thronbaldachine. Rechts steht ein anderer König	Scheifelin	"
125	Eine Schlacht am Meeresufer unter einer Festung, rechts unten eine Kanone	Burgkmair	lower right
126	Schlacht auf einer Anhöhe, rechts unten eine Kanone	"	"
127	Männer knieen in einer Landschaft vor einer Gruppe von Lanzenträgern	"	right
128	Hinrichtung eines Mannes auf dem Markte einer Stadt	"	none
129	Ein König, von Lanzenträgern umgeben, spricht in einer Landschaft mit einem baarhäuptig vor ihm stehenden bärtigen Manne, dem ebenfalls Lanzenträger folgen	Scheifelin	"
130	Bewaffnete hinter einem prächtigen Sarge, an dem zwei Bischöfe knieen	Burgkmair	above
131	Abschied des jungen vom alten Weisskunig	"	upper left
132	Ein König mit einem Pfeile in einem Zimmer, vor ihm Lanzenkämpfer	"	none
133	Der Weisskunig neben der Königin, dahinter Männer und Frauen, davor ein Bittender	Scheifelin	"
134	Ein König auf dem Throne, davor Ritter lebhaft gesticulirend	"	"
135	Leichenbegängniss eines Königs in einer Kirche unter Fackelbeleuchtung	Burgkmair	"
136	Belagerung von Arras	"	lower left
137	Belagerung und Beschiessung einer Stadt, unten Zelte	"	none
138	Zufammentreffen des jungen Weisskunigs mit der Prinzessin vom Feuereisen	Scheifelin	"

No.	Subject	Artist	Mark
139	Leichenbegängniss, ein Bote vor einer Königin	Burkmair	upper left
140	Eine Landschaft ist dicht von bewaffnetem Fussvolk und Rittern belebt, unten acht Kanonen, die von einem Manne geladen werden	"	none
141	Der junge Weisskunig sieht zwei Männern zu, die aus eine Scheibe schiessen	Scheifelin	"
142	Vier Könige sprechen mit einander in einem Zimmer	"	"
143	Ein König ist vom Pferd gestiegen und kniet vor einem andern, der ihm die Hand reicht, links unten ein Stein	Burgkmair	lower left
144	Hinrichtung. Ein Mann liegt geköpft am Boden, ein anderer erwartet den Schlag des Henkers	"	none
145	Kampf um eine Stadtmauer, links unten eine Kanone	"	lower left
146	Kampf an einem See, links unten ein Stein	"	"
147	Männer knieen vor einer Stadt, vor der ein König und Bewaffnete stehen, rechts unten ein Schiff	Scheifelin	none
148	Ein König auf dem Markte einer Stadt, davor knieen Männer, andere werden auf das Pslafter herabgestürzt, in der Mitte das Sacrament	Burgkmair	upper right
149	Schiffe auf der See, die dicht mit Bewaffneten besetzt sind	"	lower left
150	Kampf um eine Festungsmauer. Die Angreifer suchen mit Leitern dieselbe zu ersteigen, die Vertheidiger sie durch Steinwürfe wieder herabzuwerfen	"	none
151	Einzug in eine Stadt, vorn ein Marketenderwagen	"	lower left
152	Landung in Rom	"	none
153	Feldlager und Auszug zum Kampf	"	lower left
154	Ein Kaiser zwischen einem Erzbischof und einem Cardinale, davor ein Wachtposten mit der Lanze	"	center
155	Versammlung von sechs Männern, die im Kreise in einem offenen Zimmer sitzen	Scheifelin	none
156	Ein Kaiser und ein König sitzen auf einem Throne, davor knieen drei Männer, links stehen mehrere andere, rechts einer, der ein Wappenschild hält	Springinklee	"
157	Vier Könige zu Pferde mit ihrem ritterlichen Gefolge begegnen sich in einer Landschaft	Scheifelin	"
158	Vier geharnischte Ritter sitzen rechts auf einer Bank in einem Zimmer und sprechen mit zwei vor ihnen stehenden Bogenschützen	Springinklee	"
159	Schlacht von geharnischtem Fussvolk auf einem zugefrorenen See. Die Eisdecke ist gesprungen und mehrere sind in den See gefallen	Scheifelin	"
160	Ein sterbender König auf einer Bahre, an den Seiten des Bettes acht Männer, rechts unten ein Tisch, auf dem Gefässe stehen	"	"
161	Ritter mit Stäben knieen vor einem alten auf dem Thron sitzenden König	Burgkmair	upper right
162	Vier Könige unterreden sich in einem Zimmer	Springinklee	none
163	Ein König kniet vor einem Altar, an dem zwei Bischöfe stehen, im Hintergrunde sind Bewaffnete	Burgkmair	above
164	Der junge Weisskunig und sein Gefolge in einer Landschaft, davor Ritter	Scheifelin	none
165	Der Weisskunig zu Pferde in einer Landschaft, hinter ihm Ritter, vor ihm zahlreiche Männer bittend	"	"
166	Verschwörung Ludwigs XI	Burgkmair	upper left
167	Zwei Könige gehen zu den Thüren eines Zimmers hinaus	Scheifelin	none
168	Fünf Schiffe auf stürmischer See, die Mastbäume zerbrochen, die Menschen selbst in Verzweiflung	" "	" "
169	Versammlung von sieben Männern, die auf einer Bank im Kreise sitzen, links unten ein Schreiber	"	"
170	Schlacht, oben auf dem Berge sind Kanonen aufgepflanzt	Burgkmair	none

No.	Subject	Artist	Mark
171	Kriegschiffe landen	Burgkmair	upper right
172	Ein König sieht der Hinrichtung eines Mannes zu. Zwei andere sind schon geköpft, rings herum zahlreiches Gefolge	"	none
173	Fussvolk gegen einander kämpfend, rechts ein Festung mit hohem Thurm	"	upper right
174	Zelte, Lanzenträger, eine Stadt und eine See	"	lower right
175	Gemsenjagd	Scheifelin	none
176	Der junge Weisskunig von Rittern umgeben in einer Landschaft	"	"
177	Ein König vor einer Bahre, die von Leuchtern umstellt ist, rechts die fackeltragenden Leichenträger, oben heranziehende Ritter	Burgkmair	"
178	Procession in Gent	"	lower left
179	Parlamentäre wollen in eine Stadt einreiten, deren Thor gesperrt ist und von Landsknechten bewacht wird	Scheifelin	none
180	Ein Ritter, der eine Fahne hält, steht, von Bewaffneten und Priestern umgeben, in einer Kirche und bewacht einen Sarkophag, auf dem eine Krone liegt	"	"
181	An einem Fluss kämpfen oben Bogenschützen mit Rittern, unten Lanzenkämpfer gegen einander	"	"
182	Ein König, dem seine Bewaffneten folgen, hält zu Pferde vor einer brennenden Stadt. Aus den drei Stadtthoren sind die Bewohner herangekommen, knieen vor ihm und schwören ihm Treue	Burgkmair	"
183	Ein König auf dem Throne spricht mit rings um ihn stehenden Männern	"	lower left
184	Rechts liegt ein König auf einem Bette, links steht der Weisskunig auf einer Treppe und vor ihm auf der untersten Stufe stehen einige Prinzen	"	none
185	Ein König, dem Männer folgen, steht vor einer Palasttreppe, davor ein Parlamentär	"	upper right
186	Ein König auf dem Throne, davor vier Männer mit kleinen Hüten, Kaputzen, kurzen Mänteln und Schnallenschuhen	Scheifelin	none
187	Männer knieen auf einer Brücke vor einem Stadtthor, in das Ritter einziehen wollen	Burgkmair	"
188	Versammlung von neun Bewaffneten, die in einem Zimmer auf Bänken sitzen	Scheifelin	"
189	Vier Könige in langen Mänteln, der mittlere bärtig, die anderen jugendlich, sprechen in einem Zimmer	"	"
190	Kampf an einem Flussufer hinter einer Festung	Burgkmair	"
191	Kampf vor einer Festung, unten Kanonen	"	lower right
192	Bewaffnete Ritter vor einer Festung	"	none
193	Eine Schlacht	"	"
194	Vor einem König, dem Ritter folgen, steht ein Bote mit einem Brief	Scheifelin	"
195	Kampf um einen Thurm, links unten ein Baum	Burgkmair	lower left
196	Schlacht vor einer Stadt, davor Kanonen und Zelte	"	"
197	Ein jugendlicher König sitzt, das Scepter in der Hand, unter dem Thronbaldachine. Zu beiden Seiten stehen Bischöfe und Fürsten, die seine Krone berühren. Dahinter zahlreiches Gefolge	"	lower right
198	Die Gesandtschaft des alten Weisskunigs vor dem König von Portugal	"	upper left
199	Der junge Weisskunig zwischen Geschichtschreibern und Malern	Springinklee	lower left
200	Ein bewegte Schlacht, jede der feindlichen Parteien hat drei Fahnen	Scheifelin	lower right
201	Kirchliche Feier	Burgkmair	none
202	Mehrere Männer werden auf einem Schiffe hingerichtet	Scheifelin	"

No.	Subject	Artist	Mark
203	Oben kämpfen Ritter gegen Fusssoldaten, unten Fusssoldaten gegen einander	Burgkmair	none
204	Zwei geharnischte Könige, hinter denen zu beiden Seiten mehrere Ritter stehen, sprechen zusammen in einem geräumigen Zimmer	Scheifelin	"
205	Ein Bote gibt in einem Zimmer einem König einen Brief, dahinter an den Seiten stehen andere Männer	"	"
206	Stadt in bergiger Landschaft	Burgkmair	lower left
207	Kampf vor einer Stadt, links unten eine Kanone	"	"
208	Ein Bote mit einem Brief vor dem Weisskunig	Scheifelin	none
209	Ein König, auf dem Pferde sitzend, bekommt in einem Laubwald von einem Ritter einen Brief	Burgkmair	right
210	Ein Ritter in einem Burghofe	"	upper left
211	Ein König von Rittern umgeben	"	upper right
212	Ein König, mit dem Schwerte in der Hand, sitzt auf dem Pferde, vor ihm stehen Bewaffnete	"	lower right
213	Ein Sarg von Fahnen und Leuchtern umgeben in einer Kapelle	"	none
214	Drei Schiffe, die dicht von Bewaffneten besetzt sind	"	left
215	Lanzenträger, Reiter und Bogenschützen kämpfen gegeneinander	"	right
216	Drei Männer knieen vor einem Ritter, der über ihnen die Lanze schwingt	"	upper right
217	Zelte vor einer Stadt, in der Mitte Bewaffnete	"	none
218	Der junge Weisskunig reitet durch ein Landschaft, vor ihm knieen baarhäuptige Männer	Scheifelin	"
219	Ein König mit der Krone auf dem Haupte, in prächtigem Mantel, emfängt in Audienz mehrere orientalisch gekleidete Männer, von denen die beiden ersten ihm geheftete Bücher mit Siegeln übergeben	Burgkmair	upper left
220	Vier Könige stehen in einem Zimmer	Scheifelin	none
221	Ein König, unter dem Thronbaldachin stehend, spricht mit sieben Männern	"	"
222	Ritter sprengen zum Kampfe aus, dahinter Bogenschützen und Lanzenträger. Einem Ritter geht das Pferd durch und er fällt herab	"	"
223	Ritter reiten durch eine Stadt, davor stehen Zelte und eine Hütte, rechts unten tragen zwei Landsknechte ein gebundenes Kalb an einer Stange nach dem Feuer	Burgkmair	"
224	Männer knieen vor dem Weisskunig, der von Rittern umgeben auf einer Treppe steht	Scheifelin	"
225	Raum in einer Kirche. Oben knieen drei Prälaten im Ornat an einem Altar, unten wird ein prächtig behängter Sarkophag herbeigebracht	Burgkmair	upper right
226	Männer mit langen Mänteln sprechen in einer bergigen Landschaft mit mehreren Rittern	Scheifelin	none
227	Eine Gesandtschaft vor einem König, neben dem zwei Frauen stehen	"	"
228	Der Weisskunig lernt von drei vor ihm stehenden Männern hispanisch	Burgkmair	upper right
229	Kampf in Zelten, oben Beschiessung einer Stadt	"	none
230	Eine Schlacht am Meeresufer, unten ein Gefallener	"	"
231	Sechs Männer sitzen neben einem König im Zelte	"	below
232	Der junge Weisskunig sitzt auf dem Throne, links stehen mehrere Männer, einer naht sich ihm bittend	"	lower left
233	Schlacht vor einer Festung, unten sprengen Ritter heran	"	"
234	Ein König und eine Königin stehen, von der Hofgesellschaft umgeben, in einem Raume ihres Palastes	Scheifelin	none
235	Ein todter König liegt auf einem Bett, an dessen Ecken vier Leuchter stehen, davor Männer	Burgkmair	upper left

No.	Subject	Artist	Mark
236	Männer stehen auf einer Terrasse miteinander sprechend, rechts ist an einem Thurme ein Esel angebunden	Burgkmair	none
237	Krönung des alten Weisskunigs	"	"

Judging by their style, of the 237 woodcuts in the book, about 160 were done by Burgkmair, 70 by Scheifelin, 5 by Springinklee and one by the unknown master LB. The illustrations of the Weisskunig, for the above reason, do not make as uniform an impression as did those of the Theuerdank, the illustrations for which were done by one artist.

With reference to the drawing power of the individual pictures, it is in the Weisskunig as it was with the Theuerdank. The items on which Maximilian placed the greatest value, the presentation of his battles, leave us cold, while those which the Kaiser just handled in passing, the wedding voyages of Frederick III, the younger, and of Maximilian, seem to us to be of much greater interest.

As in the 1517 edition of Theuerdank, not all the woodcuts that were made for it were used in it, and the same is true of the 1775 edition of the Weisskunig. Back in the time of Kaiser Maximilian a few proof copies of the woodcuts were run off. Three such books, with the woodcuts but not the text, have been preserved, two in Vienna and one in Dresden. They contain 13 woodcut prints in addition to those in the 1775 edition and for which the blocks could not later be found.

One additional, very beautiful woodcut by Burgkmair (250 x 88), which was originally intended for the Weisskunig, has appeared in various other Augsburg publications. It was from a first sketch of this picture that one of the Scheifelin pages in the 1775 edition was made, and the Scheifelin woodcut suffers by comparison with this one. Heinrich Steiner used this picture in his 1534 edition of Pauli's Schimpf und Ernst, as well as in Barth's Platina in 1542. It is reproduced as No. 1 in Weigel's Holzschnitten beruhmter Meister.

The third book of Kaiser Maximilian, [855] the Freydal, is of Augsburg origin only insofar as the cutting of the drawings was done there.

The Kaiser included in the Freydal the races, jousts, battles and masquerades which he held at various times and in various places, and he wished to combine all this into a poetic whole, as in his ride to Maria of Burgundy; and thus to tie all the events of his life into a poetic unit.

The first mention of the work appears in one of the Kaiser's diaries for 1502 (19). A second diary for 1505-1508 mentions the Freydal in relationship to the Theuerdank, on sheet 169, and a manuscript dated 1512 (20) outlines the way the Kaiser wanted the book arranged. The typesetting and woodcarving were being worked on in the second half of 1512, as indicated by the Kaiser's letter to Siegmund von Dietrichstein, dated October 14, 1512 in which he writes, "The Freydal is also fully half produced, with the bulk of it made in Cologne." But the completion of the woodcuts was delayed until 1516. At least, this appears to be so based on a Peutinger letter (Herberger, p. 27) which states, "that Schönsperger did not know how large the figures in the Freydal were to be painted by the artists since up to that time no instructions on this had been received." If woodcuts had been completed by that time, then Schönsperger would have known the sizes of the figures. Proofs of only five of the woodcuts were made during the lifetime of the Kaiser, and these are reproduced in facsimile in the Leitner edition.

In other respects the problems of the *Freydal* were much the same as those of the *Weisskunig*. When, in 1526, King Ferdinand made Peutinger responsible for sending all of the historical writings that related to Maximilian I to Marx Treizsaurwein, the *Freydal* had already been forgotten. The drawings were in the Ambras collection and arrived in Vienna with that collection at a later date. Since that time it has rarely been noted. Duchesne, in his *Voyage d'un iconophile*, of 1834, on p. 102, mentions this with wonder. When Herberger wrote his *Peutinger* in 1851, he knew nothing of the existence of the *Freydal*. He was of the opinion that the thing mentioned as *Freidal* in the Kaiser's writings could only refer to the book *Freidank*, which was published in Augsburg in 1513 and was an edition supplied by Sebastian Brant--a hypotheses that needs no refutation. It was not until 1881 that the beautiful first edition, published by Leitner, appeared.

The pictures total 255 and are arranged in the same order 64 times, so that there is always a race, a joust, a battle and a fancy dress ball, in that order. In the races, jousts and battles, in all cases, only the two major persons involved in the action are portrayed. The fancy dress balls are richer in figures. It would appear that, since the handling of the illustrations was quite stereotyped, there was not much freedom for variation in the woodcarving.

The man whom the Kaiser consulted with reference to the artwork of both of these books was his chief woodcarver, Martin Trummer. As far back as his diary of 1502 (21), on sheet 147, he says that Master Martin should prepare all the drawings for the fancy dress balls. This is not surprising since these required pictures of costumes primarily, and Martin Trummer, who designed the costumes, was the best person to draw them. In addition to him, Leitner, on the basis of the style, attributed the illustrations in these two works to 26 artists. Nine sheets are provided with the painter's monogram, 15· [illegible] 15., which Schönherr attributes to the Innsbruck painter Nicolaus Pfaundler. Whether one of the Augsburg artists was active in the work on *Freydal* remains undetermined. Artistically, the works are of greatly varying value. The most interesting are the fancy dress balls, in which sumptuousness and splendor could be lavishly displayed.

Thus it was an active life in this field in Augsburg, with Hans Scheifelin doing his 118 drawings for the *Theuerdank*, Hans Burgkmair, aided by other artists, supplying 250 for the *Weisskunig*, while Jost Dienecker with his ten woodcarvers was prepared to produce anything these artists drew, as well as transferring the 250 *Freydal* pictures into wood. Even at its peak period, the Koburg plant in Nuremberg must have been far behind this level of activity. It was a period of delight in creative work which had never been achieved before and was never achieved again (22).

Notes

1) Herberger, "Conrad Peutinger in his relationship to Kaiser Maximilian I." In the combined *Historischen Kreisvereins für Schwaben und Neuberg*. Augsburg, 1851; Mosel, *Geschichte der k. k. Hofbibliothek*. Vienna, 1835; *Ueber den Theuerdank Haltaus: Theuerdank*. Quedlinburg, 1836. see introduction; Goedeke, "Theuerdank, Einleitung."

In the German poets of the sixteenth century, with introduction, by Goedeke and Tittmann. v. 10. Leipzig, 1878; Lilencron, "Der Weisskunig Kaiser Maximilian I," in Riehls historischem Taschenbuche, Fifth series. III:321-358, Leipzig, 1873; "On the Freydal," in Hormayers Historischen Taschenbuch. 1820; Freydal. Des Kaiser Maximilian I..., published with the highest approval of His Majesty Kaiser Franz Joseph I, ... by ... Franz ... Leitner.

2) Old copy of Cod. Ms. 7425 in the Vienna Palace Library. The letter was first published with errors in Heinecken's Neuen Nachrichten 1:195, 1786, and then it was made available in the true text in Leitner's introduction to the Freydal.

3) Archiv des k. k. Reichs-Finanz-Ministeriums. Gedenkbuch von 1508 XVI, sheets 252 and 253. Given by Leitner in the introduction to Freydal.

4) Herberger. Anmerkungen. 99

5) Herberger. Anmerkungen. 88

6) Herberger. Anmerkungen. 94

7) Herberger. Anmerkungen. 91

8) Herberger. Anmerkungen. 95

9) Herberger. Anmerkungen. 100

10) Herberger. Anmerkungen. 96

11) Herberger. Anmerkungen. 97

12) Herberger. Anmerkungen. 83

13) The fact that payment of the balance due to woodcutters was very slow is shown in Zahns Jahrbuchern. II:244, which is based on the papers in the Basle Rathsarchiv under "letters from 1513-1519, Folio 214..."

14) Haltaus, p. 13.

15) see sheet 169.

16) Notizenblatt zum Archiv für Kunde osterr. Geschichtsquellen. 1858, p. 287.

17) Notizenblatt zum Archiv für Kunde österreichischer Geschichtsquellen. 1858, p. 268-288.

18) These woodcut proofs are described by Bartsch P. gr. VII:226-229. Also, the woodblock for No. 237 could no longer be found, so a new one was made based on the old proof in the Vienna edition.

19) Bibliog. der kunsthistor. Sammlung der österr. Kaiserhauses (formerly the Ambraer Collection). Cod. Ms. 105.

20) K. k. Hofbibliothek. Cod. Ms. 2835.

21) K. k. Haus-, Hof-und Staatsarchiv. Cod. Ms. 13, Folio 147.

22) A large part of the illustrations from the books of Kaiser Maximilian were reproduced by Hirth, in Formenschatz 1877, No. 62 and 199; in 1879 No's 51-180, 87 and in Bilderbuch I. No. 87, 137, 418, 419, 428, 429, II:600 from the Weisskunig; and from the Theuerdank in Bilderbuch I. No. 309 and 316.

Chapter XIV

HANS BURGKMAIR (1)

The deluxe editions of the works of Kaiser Maximilian were certainly by far the most artistic books produced in Augsburg around the beginning of the sixteenth century, but they are not unique. Hans Burgkmair, the first artist hired by the Kaiser, did not limit himself to this work but was active in working for all of the important printing shops in Augsburg.

Hans Burgkmair came of an old Augsburg family. Back as far as 1446 the Augsburg tax records list an Ulrich Burgkmair, and he was still included in 1454 and 1461. In 1454 they list a Thoman Burgkmair, a female Burgkmair and a Burgkmair listed without forename. In 1461 the records list a Simon and a Peter, and in 1494 a Paul and a Jörg. And the family was spread over various parts of Swabia. On a slip in the Augsburg archives, dated 1506, written and signed in Reutlingen, a Burgkmair is listed as a bailiff.

The first bearer of the name who is of interest in the history of art was Thoman Burgkmair, who was not the same as the Thoman listed above. He was, in 1460 an apprentice of the calligrapher Johann Bämler who later became a book printer. In 1471 he wrote the first list of painters found in the Augsburg archives, in which he listed the names of all the painters who lived in Augsburg in 1460; he also listed all the apprentices. Next to the name of Ulrich Wolfertzheuser he noted that this was his brother-in-law. In 1473 he lived in Kanthengasse and in 1479 he appears for the first time at Von S. Anthonio. He was listed in the same place in 1480 (folio 23a), while in 1481, 1483 and 1486 he appears under Schmidhaus, the corner house at Schmidberges and Karolinenstrasse. From 1488 on, he lived in a place called Vom Diepolt. In 1523, the owner of the house was a Mrs. Thoman Burgkmair, and in 1525 Thoman's widow, Dorothy Burgkmair, transferred it to a Colman Helmschmied (2).

Hans Burgkmair was the son, not the younger brother of Thoman, as might appear from the years the two died. This is evidenced by the tax book of 1499 in which under Thoman Burgkmair there is also listed "Hans, his son." The year of his birth has been established as 1473. In his 25th year he was a member of the Guild, as indicated in the second book listing painters, and in the following year (1499) he presented to the Guild his first apprentice, whose name is not given. In 1501 he had three apprentices: Caspar Strasso, who was born in Venice; Balthasar Kracker, of Heilbronn; and Jörg Kinig, and in 1502 he added Wilhelm Ziegler. At the beginning of the sixteenth century he lived on the east slope of Zösen mountain, which in Augsburg was called the Wall Mountain because the oldest city wall led to it.

The first book illustration by Burgkmair was due to Johannes Othmar who, along with his son Silvan, was in the forefront in Augsburg in using outstanding artists.

Burgkmair gave the first indication of his interest in book ornamentation in [856] Conrad Celtes' Rapsodia laudes et victoria de Boemannis (3), which was published by Othmar in 1505.

Burgkmair provided only the eagle, on the first page. In the same year, he provided a title page illustration, which was a portrait of Conrad Celtes with the insignia of the poet laureate (reproduced in Hirth, B. I:501), for Celtes' Romanae vetustatis fragmento in Augusta Vindelicorum et eius Dioccesi (Passavant 118), which was also published by Othmar.

The first true illustrations by the Master are [857, and Hirth, B. I: No. 295] in the 1508 edition of the Predigten deutsch und viel guter Lehren des hochgelehrten Herrn Johann von Kaisersperg published by Othmar (4). Of the three woodcuts in the book, the two before sheet 39 carry Burgkmair's monogram. The first, which is on the verso of the title page, is 80 x 140 mm. The second, which is on page 39, is 196 x 140 mm. The third woodcut, which is the same size as the second, shows little development of Burgkmair's art. Indeed, it is difficult to foresee his great individual talent from these three woodcuts.

The other illustration that he supplied in the same year was much better. It was the title page woodcut for [858, Butsch 19:1. Hirth B. II:No. 587] an Oeglin-Nadler publication of Johannes Stamler's Dialogus de diversarum gentium sectis et mundi religionibus (5). It bears his monogram below on the right.

These were followed in 1509 by more and very significant drawings. From March 1505 to November 1506 Germans made their first voyage to the Portuguese islands [859, Pl. 166-170] in ships outfitted by three German merchants, particularly the Fuggers and the Welsers. In connection with this event there appeared two books, both by Balthasar Springer, who had gone along on the voyage. The one, dated 1509 and titled Die Meerfahrt zu viln onerkannten Inseln und Kunigreichen, which may be found in the k. Staatsbibliothek in Munich, is decorated with unimportant woodcuts. The other, Geschichter des grossmächtigen Königs zu Portugal, Emanuel, und der fürtreffen Kaufherren der Fucker, Welsser, which is a short description of each of the peoples met on the trip, is found in the Baronial Archives of the Welser family (6) and contains a number of woodcuts that are characteristic of Burgkmair's hand. In five consecutive pages there are painstakingly drawn 28 x 21 cm. pictures of the peoples met in four different countries. On each of these pages there is a brief description of the particular country and its inhabitants. On the first plate the escutcheon of Balthasar Springer appears and, below it, the words "H. Burgkmair at Augsburg."

The twelve woodcuts that Burgkmair supplied for a little prayer book that Othmar published in 1510 [860, Pl. 171] under the title: Aus einem Kloster in dem Riess Kompt dieses Täschenbüchlein süss Das der Mensch soll bey jm tragen Und damit sein veind verjagen (7) present a completely different mode. They are 100 x 75 mm, and only the last one has his monogram, but the style of all of them is so much the same that there be no doubt that they were created by Burgkmair.

These illustrations are as constrained as those in the Kaiserperg Predigten of 1508. The cutting is bad. In the second edition, which Othmar [861] published in 1512, he used the same woodcuts.

In the same year (1510) there were the (72 x 25) title pages for the five sermons by Johann Geiler von Kaisersperg, which Othmar printed for the publisher Jörg Diemar [862; Hirth B. I:No. 296, and II:No. 588]. These were Das Buch Granatapfel in Latin genannt Mologranatus;

the Gaistliches Bedeutung des Ausgangs der Kinder Israel von Egypto; the Gaistlich Spinnerin nach dem Exempel der heiligen Wittib Elizabeth; the Gaistliche Bedeutung des Hesslins and Die sieben Hauptfünd (8). To this series should be added the title page (174 x 125) of [863] Geiler von Kaisersperg's sermon on the Navicula penitentiae (9), which Hans Othmar printed in 1511 for Diemar.

In 1512 there are two woodcuts in a book by Johannes Pinicianus, printed by Othmar, [864; Hirth B. II:No. 629 & 631] which contains the poems, Virtus and Voluptus; Carmen de origine ducum Austriae; and others (10). Both bear the monogram and fill a full quarto page. In style they are most like the woodcuts that Burgkmair supplied for Kaiserperg's prayers.

Johannes Othmar died in 1513 but his son, Silvan Othmar, continued to work with Burgkmair.

Among the forty woodcuts in [865] the 1513 edition of Murner's Schelmenzunft (11), only the first one, on sheet 2a, is by Burgkmair, and it bears his monogram. He portrays the author, with the superscript "Dr. Laux."

In 1513, when Burgkmair was involved in work for Kaiser Maximilian to a much greater extent, he still found time to do some private work. Indeed, he was working with all of the important printing houses in Augsburg during that year. His work for Hans Schönsperger, the younger, in 1515 had a special motive. Wolfgang Maen, Kaiser Maximilian's chaplain [866, Pl. 172-173] had done a poetic version of the Leidens Christi (12), which he dedicated to the Kaiser. The book was printed on vellum in a magnificent format. It may very well have been their consideration of the Kaiser's relationship to this book that influenced the three artists, Burgkmaier, Scheifelin and Brew, all to work simultaneously for Hans Schönsperger, the younger, when they normally avoided each other. If the escutcheon at the beginning and the repetition of the crucifixion at the end are not counted, the book had twenty-nine woodcuts, of which four bore Burgkmair's monogram. The first, on the verso of the title page, 140 x 90 mm, is of Christ on the Cross. Burgkmair's monogram is centered at the bottom. The second, the same size, depicts the raising of Lazarus from the dead. The monogram is at the bottom-right. The third, which is smaller, depicts the meal in Lazarus' house. The monogram is upper left. The fourth depicts the driving out of the money changer. The monogram is below, center (13). Burgkmair's work is not easily confused with Scheifelin's or Brew's. Fourteen of the twenty-nine woodcuts in the book: No's. 1, 2, 3, 4, 5, 6, 7, 8, 11, 19, 20, 25, 28 and 29, can unquestionably be attributed to Burgkmair. There can be no doubt that Scheifelin did twelve: No's. 10, 12, 13, 14, 15, 16, 21, 22, 23, 24, 26 and 27. Brew's contribution, if one assigns to him no's. 9, 17, and 18, may be too limitedly defined.

These were the first illustrations of religious content that Burgkmair supplied, and are the only Burgkmair illustrations to appear in a book published by Schönsperger.

His relationship with the printing plant opened in Augsburg by Johannes Miller in 1514 is much more important than his work with the younger Schönsperger.

For his very first publication [867], in 1514, Miller obtained the services of the Master. The publication was Paul Riccius' Dialogus in Apostolorum Simbolum (14). Its (160 x 120) title page bears the monogram "H. B." below, on the right.

The title page (252 x 166) which the Master prepared for Miller's 1515 edition [868, Butsch 22] of Jornandes de rebus Gothorum, Paulus Diaconus de gestis Longobardorum (15) must be counted among his most important works.

In 1516 there are two works published by Miller that include his illustrations. [869, Butsch 25] Johann Eyck's In summulas Petri Hispani explantio (16) has a title page (130 x 125) woodcut displaying the two-headed Imperial eagle. The monogram this time, HB, is a variant, but is no reason for denying that this is the work of Burgkmair. The second book published by Miller in 1516 [870] is the fourth edition of the Taschenbüchleins aus dem Riess (17), the first and second editions of which were published by Othmar in 1510 and 1512, respectively, and the third edition by Schönsperger in 1514. Of the fourteen woodcuts in Miller's edition, the first ten belong to Burgkmair and four are by Scheifelin. They appear, in general, to be copied from those in the earlier editions. The monogram appears only on the illustration of the prayer of St. Thomas Aquinas (18).

For a collection, [871] Hutten'scher Gedichte und Epigramme, which Miller published in 1519, Burgkmair provided twelve (90 x 102) illustrations, none of which bore his monogram (19).

During this period, in 1516, a remarkable pamphlet appeared without place or date. It has a superscript, [872, Hirth B. II, No. 599] Dies Kind ist geboren zu Tettnang (20). It shows a maiden with a distended stomach and a third limb on her breast. The sheet bears the Monogram "HB" and has 13 lines of prose text which state that originally Earl Ulrich of Montfort had his painter Mathes Miller, in Lindau, draw the child.

In 1518 Burgkmair could only handle private work in passing since he was working primarily on the Weisskunig. As this was completed in blocks, he was again able to divide his time for the benefit of the Augsburg printers. And starting in 1518, the newly established firm of Dr. Sigmund Grimm and Marx Würsung, kept him continuously loaded with assignments during its brief existence.

In 1518 he did the title page woodcut [873] for the Latin edition of an Italian Tractates des Marsilius Ficinus über die Pest (21), which was published by Grimm and Würsung. In the same year he did the title page woodcut for [874] the first German book on tournaments, which was printed by Würsung, Von wann und umb welcher ursachen willen das loblich ritterspiel des turniers erdacht und zum ersten geübt worden ist (22). The woodcut was 122 x 112 mm.

In 1519 he supplied the (120 x 145) title page illustration [875, Hirth B. I: No. 378] for Liber theoreticae nec non practicae Alsaharavii in prisco Arabum medicorum conventu facile principis, qui vulgo Accararius dicitur (23).

In 1520 there followed one of the most attractive products of Grimm and Würsung, [876, Hirth B. I: Nos. 8-25] the translation of the Spanish short novel entitled La Celestina, under the German title, Ain hipsche Tragedia von zwaien liebhabenden menschen (24). The material to be illustrated was quite complicated, and the book contains 26 (70 x 100) woodcuts. While the woodcuts do not bear his monogram they rank among the best of the Master's work and the book is one of the most beautiful produced in the sixteenth century. The woodcuts are executed so well, technically, that they are practically comparable to copper plates.

Also in 1520, Grimm and Würsing issued two other large illustrated works. The first was

Petrarch's De remediis utriusque fortunae, which was translated by Peter Stachel of Nuremberg, under the title Von der Artzney beider Glück, des guten und widerwärtigen. The second was translated extracts from various works of Cicero together with a general biography of Cicero. Sebastian Brant made the major contribution to the woodcut illustrations of the Petrarch, and in the case of the Cicero, Johannes von Schwarzenberg, the translator, extracted the basic maxim from each chapter, putting it in the form of a two- or four-line verse, and these verses, which formed a motto at the beginning of each chapter, served as the illustrations.

Grimm himself was involved in the completion of only a tiny fragment of these great undertakings. In 1522 he published [877, Hirth B. I, No. 490; II, No. 616] Buchlein des hochberümpten Marci Tulii Ciceronis von dem Alter, durch her Johann Neuber, Caplan zu Schwarzenberg, aus dem Latein in Teutsch gebracht (25). It had five woodcuts. After separating from Würsung, Grimm's resources were apparently too limited to permit him to carry this project any further. He was also unable to print a book by Schwarzenburg which had been turned over to him in 1520, and it was finally printed by Heinrich Steiner in 1531.

The 97 woodcuts with which Steiner's edition [878, Hirth B. I, No's. 352, 353, 366, 407, 409, 500; II, 648, 736] of Cicero's Officien were adorned had, therefore, been completed by 1520 and were originally prepared for Grimm and Würsung. Burgkmair's monogram does not appear on any of the new woodcuts prepared especially for this edition. The woodcut on page 78, which bears his monogram, was taken from Grimm's Acararius of 1519. No. 73 has the monograms "H. b. b." and "H. W." The only answer to this appears to be that the first set of initials refers to Hans Burgkmair and the second to the woodcarver. Also, there is the monogram ⊢B⊣, which is found on the lower right of the portrait of Baron von Schwarzenberg, the translator of the book, on the verso of the title page. It is probably better to attribute this to Johannes Burgkmair than to seek for any other attribution.

The second edition appeared in 1532. It still did not use the woodcuts that Burgkmair prepared for the Leben Cicero. Steiner used these in 1534, when he did a new edition of the Büchlein von Alter, which originally appeared in 1522, and he used them a third time in his "works" of Cicero. The introduction gives a biography of Cicero and is illustrated by six Burgkmair woodcuts.

As originally planned by Grimm and Würsung, there were to have been 108 illustrations in Cicero: six in the Leben Cicero, five in the Büchlein vom Alter, and 97 in the Gebürliche Werken. Steiner made a number of changes in later editions. In the second edition of the Büchleins vom Alter, on the last page, which was left blank by Grimm, Steiner inserted two completely unsuitable woodcuts. One of these was taken from Burgkmair's Glücksbuch and the other from an illustration by Scheifelin in Memorial der Tugend. On the other hand, in his 1537 edition he omitted the first five woodcuts and began with woodcuts that were supposed to appear further on in the Geburlichen Werke. In the 1545 edition, the cuts are so worn that very little of their original beauty remains. [879-885] In toto, Steiner did 1531, 1532, 1533, 1537, 1540 and 1545 editions of the above work. After him the woodcuts came into possession of Egenolph in Frankfurt whence they were transferred again to Vincenz Steinmeyer, who, in 1605, printed them again in what was termed "Newe künstliche, wohlgerissene und in Holz geschnittene Figuren."

The fate of [886, Hirth, Bilderbuch] the Petrarka (27) was much like that of the Cicero. In 1520 Burgkmair had completed the 259 woodcuts that were to go in both parts, and could happily look forward to their publication that year. But this did not happen. Grimm died without completing it. After his death, the book was "for a time laid aside and likewise forgotten" until Heinrich Steiner discovered it in organizing Grimm's estate. "I bought it at great cost as it had elegant and wonderful figures which Dr. Sebastian Brandt apparently provided for every chapter." He had Georg Spalatin arrange the text for the second part and published the whole work in 1532.

Of the 259 woodcuts contained in the Buch von der Arznei beider Glück, des guten und wider wärtigen, 125 are in the first part and 134 are in part two. Some 17 had already been used in Cicero in other contexts. While none of them bears the Burgkmair monogram, there can be no doubt of their attribution to him. Only the woodcuts for the title pages of each of the two parts do not belong with this group but were made for the 1532 Steiner edition. The last woodcut bears the date, 1520 (28), on the right side of the coffin.

In this book Burgkmair illustrated the whole cycle of human life. Steiner made maximum profit out of taking over these woodcuts. He not only used them again in a 1539 edition of the book [887] under the changed title of Das Glücksbuch; he used these same woodcuts with a new translation of Virgil. He also used them, wherever they were more or less passably usable, in practically every one of his later publications, and in the most varied combinations.

The illustrations for Cicero and for Petrarka may, along with those for the Weisskunig, be considered Burgkmair's finest work.

A title page woodcut by the Master (130 x 118), [888] in the 1522 edition of the Spiegel der Blinden, by Haug Marschalk (29), which appeared s.l. in Augsburg, has his monogram at the lower right. In 1525 the same cut was used for the title page of a small book, also published s.l., [889] Von Milterung der Fürsten gegenden aufrührerischen Bauern von Johann Brentz Ecclesiasten zn schwebischen Hall (30). The same woodcut was used as the title page [890] of Luther's Sermon von dem heyligen Creutz, which was also published s.l. in Augsburg in 1522. The monogram "H.B." is at the left and right, at the foot of the Cross.

In 1523, Othmar gave Burgkmair another assignment. Othmar was then printing [891, Pl. 176-177] the Luther translation of the New Testament and asked Burgkmair to prepare illustrations for the Apocalypse. However, Burgkmair worked too slowly to suit him, and barely six of the woodcuts were completed when Othmar sent the first edition (31) out into the world. It was not until [892-893] the next two editions (32), both of which were needed in the same year, that the full series of Burgkmair woodcuts for the Apocalypse appeared; there were now 21 of them instead of six. It was characteristic of Burgkmair that he did not simply copy the Wittemberg drawings as Holbein did for the edition that Thomas Wolff was publishing in Basel at the same time. Both the Dürer Apocalypse and the Wittemberg pages were freely metamorphosed by him. So far as possible, he made the figures more diagonal in order to make each scene more lifelike. He put his monogram on all 21 of the pages, which he had rarely done before. In spite of this, the Apocalypse can not be rated among his finest works, even though the woodcuts are not so weak that one can agree with Passavent's (III:270) attribution of them to his son.

In the 1523 publication of [894] the report on Des loblichen Fürstenthumbs Steyr Erbhuldigung in dem 1520stem Jahr bescheen (33) which Jost de Necker, "at the request of ... Sigmunden von Dietrichstein," had printed in Augsburg, on the verso of the title page and the first page of the second leaf there are two coats of arms which bear the monogram of the master.

After this, there is a seven-year period for which we have nothing by Burgkmair.

In 1530 there appeared in Augsburg, without the name of the printer, but presumably from Heinrich Steiner, a Spanish medical work, [895, Hirth B. II, No. 649] the Banqueto de nobles cavalleros by the Kaiser's physician, Ludovico di Avila (34). It contains 14 woodcuts by Burgkmair, some of which fill the whole page and some a half of the quarto. The first of these is a portrait of Dr Avila, and it bears Burgkmair's monogram. These 14 are completely comparable in style to those in Petrarka. A small woodcut in the book, which portrays a ship, is not by Burgkmair but rather is taken from an edition of the Schelmenzunft.

These are demonstrably the last woodcuts that Burgkmair supplied. When works by him appear in later publications, they are invariably taken from earlier works.

The tax records give little information about his outside activities after the beginning of the sixteenth century. He presented apprentices to the Painters Guild as follows: Bernhard Kinig in 1506, Six Forster in 1510, Heinrich Dederla in 1513, Hans Friedrich in 1517, and Hans Schiffer von Dillingen in 1520. He lived in the same street as his father did from 1509 on, and died in 1531. Thus it would appear that Burgkmair's primary interest in life was his artistic work. And, in fact, there has rarely been an artist who was as productive as he was. When one considers that the work done for book printers was only a very small part of his broad activity, one can hardly understand how he produced such an enormous amount of book illustration. He began his activity in this field in 1505 when he was first associated with Hans Othmar, and from then until Othmar's death in 1513 provided him with 40 woodcuts. Then came his large-scale undertakings for the Kaiser. He completed around 170 large paintings for the Weisskunig; then began to work with the younger Schoensperger, for whom he did 14 pictures for Leiden Christi. He started working with Johannes Miller in 1514. Thus, in the years from 1513 to 1518 he produced around 210 drawings. However, his chief activity in this field began when Grimm and Würsung opened their plant in 1518. After the title pages for Tractat über die Pest, the Turnierbuch and the Acarius, came his truly major works: the 20 woodcuts for Cölestine, the 108 for Cicero and the 240 for the Petrarka; thus he supplied 370 illustrations for a single printing office. After Grimm and Würsung closed down, there followed a period of rest for Burgkmair. He supplied only a pair of title page illustrations for Silvan Othmar's Apokalypse and provided Heinrich Heiner, who came to Augsburg in 1530, with 14 pictures for his 1533 edition of Avila's Banqueto. The total of illustrations that were unquestionably provided by him came to 650. Omitted from this count are his sequences of large woodcuts as well as many that were not attributable with certainly, even though there were many that could be attributed to him with reasonable probability. It would appear, therefore, that Burgkmair was a Master who deserves, much more than many others, monographic treatment by a professional.

Notes

1) Of the many artists who were shabbily treated in historical writings, Hans Burgkmair is in the van. The biographic particulars about him and his family are, to be sure, well reported in a paper by Huber, "Die Malerfamilie Burgkmair von Augsburg," in the Zeitschrift des historischen Vereins für Schwaben und Neuburg. I:310-320, Augsburg, 1874. But our knowledge of his works is very incomplete. Sandart gives only passing notice to Burgkmair's wide-ranging activity in book illustration. What Bartsch, in the seventh volume of his Peintre graveur and Nagler, in his Künstlerlexikon II:24, say about him leaves very much to be desired. Heller in his Zusätzen zum Peintre graveur, p. 35-38, adds little. In 1856 Wiechmann-Kadow gathered the data in Weigel's art catalogs, Panzer's Annalen and various specialized bibliographies in the special field and published them in the Archivs für die zeichnende Künste II:152-168. Nagler's new summary in the Monagrammisten is based on this. However Wiechmann's is not conclusive. Since he saw only a few of the books illustrated by Burgkmair, he could not differentiate between the works the artist actually illustrated and those in which old woodblocks, prepared by him earlier, were arbitrarily assembled by the publisher. Worthless Steiner publications, in which woodblocks are printed for the fifth or sixth time, are therefore named by Wiechmann as books illustrated by Burgkmair; these too are enumerated incompletely.

2) For the related Burgkmaiers, see the tax records for 1446, Folio 9; 1454, Folio 7, 9 & 13; 1461, Folio 5 & 6; 1494, Folio 7 & 17; For Thoman Burgkmair, see the tax records for 1493, Folio 24; 1494, Folio 27; 1495, Folio 26; 1502, Folio 35 & 36; 1513, Folio 36.

3) Panzer VI:135, No. 33; Zapf, p. 18.

4) Panzer I, No. 603; Zapf II, p. 32; Ebert, No. 8264; Weigel, No. 18360; Heller, Suppl., p. 36.

5) Zapf II:38. Folio; Hummel, Bibliothek seltener Bücher II:47-54; Illustrations in Butsch, Bücherornamentik der Renaissance I:Plate 19.

6) J. M. Frhr. von Welser, "Beiträge zur Augsburger Kunstgeschichte," in the Zeitschrift des historischen Vereins für Schwaben und Neuburg II:120. 1875.

7) Weller, No. 620.

8) Panzer I:317, No. 667; Zapf II:45; Ebert, No. 8232; Weigel, No. 13368.

9) Panzer VI:139, No. 58.

10) Weigel, No. 21115.

11) Panzer I:360, No. 764 & 797. Quarto; Zapf II:65 and 71; Ebert, No. 14530; Lappenberg, Murner's Ulenspiegel 1854. No. 397; Panzer I:372. 1514 reprint.

12) Panzer I, No. 804; Zapf II:78; Ebert, No. 12892; Nagler 15:110; Weigel, No. 10924; Wackernagel, Bibliographie der Kurchenliedes. ed. 2, No. 78.

13) The woodcut was later reused in the 1524 edition of a booklet published in Augsburg, without place of publication. The title was Fünfzig und vierzig wee; Weller, No. 3210.

14) Zapf, p. 68; Weigel, No. 8231 & 20766.

15) Schelhorn, Ergötzlichkeiten III:2231. Folio; Zapf II:79; Weigel, No. 20765; Bartsch, Der Holzschnitt, No. 63, reproduced by Butsch, Bücherornamentik I:Plate 22.

16) Zapf II:88; Heller, Geschichte der Formschneidekunst, p. 100; Nagler II:242; reproduced in Butsch I:Plate 25.

17) Panzer I, No. 973. Octavo; Zapf II:132; Weigel, No. 18771.

18) How anyone can attribute the six woodcuts in the Leben, Verdienen und Wunderwerk der Heiligen, Ausburger Bisthums Bischofen Sant Ulrichs und Symprechts, auch der sel Martyrerin sant Aphre, published by Silvan Othmar in 1516, to Burgkmair is incomprehensible to me. I am convinced that neither Wiechmann-Kadow nor Nagler could have seen the book. Metzger, who did see the book, had no notion to ascribe the woodcuts to Burgkmair.

19) Boecking, Ulrich von Hurten's Schriften I:34-35.

20) Weller, No. 1002; in Butsch's collection.

21) Panzer VI:150, No. 121. Quarto; Zapf, p. 106.

22) Panzer I:419, No. 914. Quarto; Ebert, No. 24046; Weller, No. 1158.

23) Panzer VI:154, No. 149. Folio.

24) Panzer I:445, No. 1003. Quarto; Zapf II:133; Ebert, No. 3865; Heyses, Bücherschatz, No. 2126 & 2127; Nagler (Künstlerlexicon 15:112) erroneously ascribes it to Scheifelin.

25) Panzer II:121, No. 1579.

26) Ebert, No. 4690; Heller, Leben und Werke Dürer's II:1029-1031; Heller, Supplement to Bartsch, p. 37; Weigel, No.'s 1877, 3496, 9935, 18364, 18365, 20069; Nagler, Kunstlerlexikon II:243.

27) Ebert, No. 16476; Weigel, No.'s 1875, 3499, 6776-77; 7780-81; & 18376.

28) Profuse illustration proofs from the Petrarka are in Hirth's Bilderbuch I, No.'s 139-53, 297-99, 349-51, 354-360, 364, 369-72, 385-86, 388-91, 398-401, 404-06, 410-11, 465-83, 488-89, 494-99; II, No.'s 597-98, 615, 618, 630, 632, 694-97, 732-33, 735, 740.

29) Panzer II:107. Quarto.

30) German. Museum.

31) The New Testament. s. l. e. a. & without printer. Folio; Panzer (p. 91, No. 3) sketched out a history of the Luther translation of the Bible. Description of the Augsburg Bibles, p. 74, No. 27; Annalen der älteren deutschen Literatur II, No. 1614; Muther, Deutsche Bilderbibeln. No. 42.

32) Both were in folio. The one, which appeared on March 21, 1523 is in Panzer, Annalen II, No. 1615; Beschreibung der Augsberger Bibeln, p. 76, No. XXVIII, rough sketch on p. 92, No. 4; Zapf, Augsburger Buchdruckergeschichte II:163 ff; Weigel, Kunstlagerkataloge, No. 6775; Muther, Bilderbibeln, No. 43. The other edition appeared on June 21, 1523. It is in Panzer, Annalen II, No. 1616; Beschreibung der Augsberger Bibeln, p. 77, No. XXIX with a rough sketch on p. 93, No. 5; Muther, Bilderbibeln, No. 44.

33) Panzer II, No. 2077. Folio; Zapf II:160.

34) Weigel, No. 12857. Quarto.

Chapter XV

HANS SCHEIFELIN (1)

The second great artist who supplied the Augsburg printers with illustrations was Hans Scheifelin. Whether or not he was born in Augsburg, he was a member of a family that was widespread in that city. The Augsburg tax record for 1461 lists a Conrad Scheifelin, that for 1493 a Caspar Scheifelin, that for 1494 an Ulrich Scheifelin, that for 1502 a Martin Scheifelin, etc. Little more is known of Hans' origin than is reported by Doppelmayr: his father was Franz, a wool merchant who lived in Nordlingen and settled in Nuremberg in 1476, and Hans was born there soon after; in any event, before 1492. Everything we know about his activities until 1512 is as uncertain as the facts about his birth.

In 1505 [896] Dr. Ulrich Pinder's Beschlossner Gart des rosenkranz marie (2) was published in Nuremberg. This book was ornamented by an incredible number of woodcuts from the most varied sources and times. Scheifelin's earliest book illustrations appeared in this book; at least, many of the drawings, while they do not bear his monogram, have the style characteristics of later works attributed to the Master. The woodcut that most agrees with this later style is the illustration on sheet 229b of the second volume, at the beginning of the eleventh book. It is 125 x 160 mm, and is divided into three parts. On the left there is a level landscape; in the middle an apple tree, under which Adam stands at the left and Eve at the right, with the snake above them. In addition, many of the 90 x 70 mm woodcuts may be his, such as those on leaves 107, 182 and 185 in volume I, and on leaves 87, 94 and 183b in volume II. Of the smaller ones (65 x 48), those attributed to him are on leaf 226 of volume I, and on leaves 16 and 262 in volume II. The Nagler attributions in the Monagrammisten, which are the same as those of Caspar Rosenthaler, have become untenable since the research by Schoenherr (3). The only one who could be considered a likely source is Dürer.

Not only the two large crucifixion pictures but also many of the medium and smaller woodcuts were used [897] two years later, in 1507, in Pinder's Speculum passionis domini nostri Jesu Christi (4), which is commonly termed the first book illustrated by Scheifelin. The large woodcuts, which fill the full page, give the customary scenes from the entry into Jerusalem to Judgment Day. The artist's monogram appears on two woodcuts, which may be attributed to Scheifelin without reservation; they show that the artist had already achieved greatness. The number of the other large woodcuts drawn by Scheifelin is uncertain. The fact that Egenolph, in Frankfurt, when he compiled the Doctrina vita et passio Jesu Christi in 1537, reprinted the Scheifelin woodcuts from the Evangelienbuch, which Anselm printed in 1516, together with reduced copies of the large ones from the Speculum..., putting the monogram of Scheifelin on the title page of his Doctrina..., strengthens the attribution of these to Scheifelin. Only one, the cursing of the fig tree, is omitted by Egenolph, and that illustration is certainly attributable to some other Master. One medium sized illustration (162 x 125), which covers half a page in the Speculum..., is difficult to attribute to Scheifelin. Some of the small (90 x 75) woodcuts had been used in the 1505 Rosenkranz and have already been attributed to Scheifelin. In any event, the majority of the woodcuts in the 1507 Speculum... are clearly attributable to Scheifelin.

This is all that we know about his youth. After illustrating two large books in 1505 and 1507, he seems to have disappeared from the scene completely for five years (1507-1512). His biography becomes clearer from the time he was chosen by Kaiser Maximilian, in 1512, to illustrate his deluxe books. He worked along with Burgkmair and executed his great task famously. The work for the Kaiser seems to have made it essential that he live in Augsburg and he appears to have moved there in 1512. Even though his name does not appear in the tax records, a letter from Jost Dienecker to the Kaiser establishes his abode in Augsburg quite definitely.

In 1512, also, he began his private work for Augsburg printers. While he had many disputes with Hans Schoensperger, the elder, regarding his work as illustrator of the Kaiser's books, he became connected, during this same year, with Hans Schoensperger, the younger.

The younger Schoensperger, in 1512, [898] printed an Evangelienbuch (5), in which four large (230 x 160) woodcuts bear Scheifelin's monogram. A fifth large woodcut appears not to have been ready when Schoensperger completed the work in 1512, since the picture of the resurrection, in this 1512 edition, was taken from a fifteenth century book. The [899] 1513 edition (6) had the same illustrations as the 1512 edition, except that a beautiful new picture of the resurrection replaced No. 5 of the 1512 edition. It bears Scheifelin's monogram in the lower right portion and is the same size as the other four. Scheifelin had no part in the smaller (90 x 65) illustrations in both editions of the Evangelienbuch.

A German prayer book that was richly illustrated by Scheifelin [900, Pl. 178-183] was published by Schoensperger in Augsburg in 1513, under the title Via felicitatis (7). The printer is not named in the book, the format of which is octavo. Each page is framed with border decorations recurring in the same order. The initial letters are decorated with foliage and masks. The book has thirty full-page woodcuts, of which six are repeated. All have Scheifelin's monogram. There are no vigorous-looking faces in this prayer book, but the whole work is of the highest, purest, smoothest charm. It reveals an artist who does not innovate, but who has absorbed and could use the work of the trailblazing Masters.

Scheifelin began working with Hans Othmar in 1513, also, by illustrating [901] the Heiligenleben (8) which Othmar printed for the publisher Johann Rynmann. The woodcuts in this book are less attractive than those in the prayer book. This was not the fault of the artist, but resulted from the monotonous material. Neither the size nor the finish of the title page, which was used for both parts, were of his characteristic achievement, but his monogram appears in the lower center. The 251 small (85 x 68) text woodcuts, of which 130 relate to the summer part and 121 to the winter part, while none carries his monogram, all appear to have been produced by him. The artist had undertaken the thankless task of illustrating a Heiligenleben, and, for better or for worse, he got it done. The lives of the female Saints are given special preference. In the presentation of the many martyred male Saints the same woodcuts were used from the beginning.
The woodcuts were used again in [902] the Dritt Tail christenlicher Predigten which was printed

by Ecks von Weissenhorn in 1533.

In 1514, Scheifelin provided [903] eighteen woodcuts for the edition of Taschenbüchleins aus dem Riess (9), which was published by Hans Schoensperger, the younger. This had the usual representations, which had been used by Burgkmair in 1510 for the Othmar edition. All eighteen woodcuts carry the monogram.

In 1514 Scheifelin, for the first time, had the satisfaction of being entrusted with an assignment from outside Augsburg. In this year, [904-907] Adam Petri of Basel asked him to illustrate his edition of Plenarium (10), of which he published a second edition in 1516, a third in 1518 and a fourth in 1522. The five large woodcuts, all of which bear the Master's monogram, are the same in content as those he supplied for the Schoensperger editions of 1512 and 1513. However, they differed in size (these being 198 x 130 mm) and were quite different in composition. On the bottom of the first one we have not only the monogram of the artist but, at his left, the monogram of the woodcarver is also given HF and the same is done in Number four. In addition to these five large woodcuts bearing his monogram, the 54 smaller (90 x 65) woodcuts in the Basel edition of the Plenarium may also be attributed to Scheifelin with certainty.

The years from 1512 to 1514 were thus a time of brisk activity for Scheifelin. He moved to Augsburg where the work on the deluxe editions of Kaiser Maximilian called him. Since he was not overloaded by the work on the illustrations of the Theuerdank and the Weisskunig, he took on a whole series of private projects. He supplied four large woodcuts for the 1512 Plenarium produced by Hans Schoensperger, the younger, and a fifth for the 1513 edition. He supplied 24 lovely woodcuts for a charming little prayerbook in the same year, presumably also published by Schoensperger. He prepared a large title page illustration and 251 smaller text woodcuts for Othmar's 1513 edition of the Heiligenleben and illustrated a prayer booklet for Schoensperger in 1514. He became known and he did five large and 54 small woodcuts for Adam Petri's Plenarium, which was printed in Basel. Thus, these three years in Augsburg are among the most fruitful of his life.

From 1515 on Scheifelin lived in his home city of Nördlingen where, because of his large painting of "Judith and Holofernes" for the City Hall which was then being built, he was given citizenship. In 1516 he brought his young wife, Afra Tucher of Nuremberg, there and they lived in his father's house at the Eichbrun.

Even after he moved, the Augsburg printing houses maintained their contacts with him. In 1515 he illustrated [908] the Historie und wunderlich Legend Katharinae von Senis (11), which Sylvan Othmar printed for Rynmann. He supplied 42 (90 x 65) woodcuts for this work, two of which bear his monogram. These woodcuts are not very dramatic, but they are all chastely conceived and demonstrate Scheifelin's predilection for things feminine. They are more similar to the illustrations in Othmar's Heiligenleben than they are to other works.

In the same year, with Hans Burgkmair and Jorg Brew, he worked on the illustrations of [909] Leidens Jesu Christi (12), the book compiled by Wolfgang Man and printed by Hans Schoensperger, the younger. There have been unnecessary arguments about which part of the illustration of this book was done by Scheifelin. His woodcuts were a few mm. smaller than those by Burgkmair or Brew, specifically, only 85 x 60 mm, and they do not fill their boundaries. One does not, therefore, need any great knowledge of style, only a mm. ruler, to identify Scheifelin's part in the illustration of this work. Counting from the dedication page, those attributable to Scheifelin are numbers 10, 12, 13, 14, 15, 16, 21, 22, 23, 24, 26 and 27; thus, not a majority, but 12 (13). His illustrations for this book were not as good as those by Burgkmair.

In 1516, he worked with Burgkmair in illustrating the [910] fourth edition of Taschenbüchleins aus dem Riess, published by Hans Miller. Scheifelin produced only four of its fourteen woodcuts, with numbers 11-14 bearing his monogram.

In the same year Scheifelin had another major assignment from a distant city. Thomas Anshelm in Hagenau was preparing to print [911, Pl. 184-185] an Evangelienbuch (14) and asked Scheifelin to supply the 58 woodcuts. Forty-seven include his monogram, but it is quite different from his normal one ( ). It does not have the "S" set within the "H" and the shovel next to it; instead, as shown in the monogram that follows, the "J" is set within the "S" and this unit is placed within the shovel ( ). He surpassed all of his earlier work in these woodcuts. They exhibit highly artistic ingenuity and a diversity that he had not previously displayed; the figures are refined and of a grandeur that at times makes one think of the forcefulness of Burgkmair. When one considers his earlier, squat, large-headed men and bony women and then sees these towering male figures and sensual women, one may well wonder whether these two extremes could be the product of a single artist. Also, the variant monogram which is in this Alsace product had never before been used by the master in a book.

Nine of these woodcuts were reused by Anshelm in a book that he printed for Johann Koburger, [912] the Decachordum Christianum (15), by Marcus Vigerius. Only the picture of the Annunciation, the first picture in this book, is not reproduced from the Evangelienbuch, and it does not bear the monogram.

At a later time, Egenolf, in Frankfurt, published [913-915] Doctrina vita et passio Jesu Christi, containing a new edition of the woodcuts, among which he used the Annunciation first used by Anshelm in 1517 in his Decachordum... as well as reduced copies of the illustrations in Pinder's Speculum passionis of 1507. A second edition of the Doctrina... appeared in 1542 (16) and a third in 1550.

The year 1517 brought the artist another large assignment for Silvan Othmar. He illustrated [916, Pl. 186-189] Hans von Leonrodt's Hymelwag auf dem, wer wohl lebt und wohl stirbt, fährt in das Reich der Himmel. Hellwag auf dem wer übel lebt und übel stirbt, fährt in die ewige Verdammnis (17). The book includes 21 woodcuts. Four (Nos. 1, 9, 13 and 21) are 150 x 95 mm and fill the page; the others (105 x 95) cover about two-thirds of the page. They all bear the monogram . In the second edition [918] of the book, which was published in 1518, they were used anew.

One, the peasant [919] was reused by Silvan Othmar as the title page illustration in Von dem Wucher (18) in 1520, using it in a different sense and with a different superscript.

A second, "Doomsday," is used again as the last page of [920] Abrecht von Eybe's Ob ainen sey zu nehmen ein eelich weib (19) which Silvan Othmar printed in 1517, as well as on the last page of Silvan Othmar's 1520 edition of [921] Trostbüchleins Doctor Martini Luthers, Augustiner, in aller widerwärtigkeit eines jeden Christglaubigen Menschen gedeutsch durch Georgium

Spalatinum (20). He also used the same illustration in his 1530 printing [922] of Luther's Sermon von guten Werken.

There is an unimportant woodcut by Scheifelin (100 x 63) in Johannes Miller's 1518 edition [923] of Hortulus animae (21). This bears his monogram HSI but this time without the shovel.

In 1523 he worked for Hans Schoensperger, the younger, by supplying eleven of the 27 woodcuts [924, Pl. 190-198] in the reprint of the Wittenberg edition of the Lutherischen neuen Testament (22). These are close to the Wittemberg originals and all of them bear his monogram.

In this period, again, Scheifelin produced a large number of woodcuts, and he did more for Othmar than for any other printer. For Othmar books he provided 42 for the Legende der Katharina von Siena and 21 for Leonrodt's Himmelwagen. He continued to work with Schoensperger, providing 12 woodcuts for his Leiden Christi and 10 for his 1523 edition of the New Testament. Another Augsburg printer with whom he worked was Johannes Miller; providing four woodcuts for his Taschenbüchlein of 1516 and one for his Hortulus of 1518. In 1518, in addition, he did the 58 woodcuts for Anshelm's Evengelienbuch, in which we find the monogram that he had not theretofore used.

After this period of intensive work there followed a period of rest from 1523 to 1533, during which we can not attribute any woodcuts to Scheifelin with certainty. It was not until 1533 that another woodcut bore his monogram.

During this period things changed considerably in Augsburg. The younger Hans Schoensperger, Silvan Othmar and Johann Miller were no longer active, and their place had been filled by Heinrich Steiner and Alexander Weissenhorn. Scheifelin worked with these two during the last seven years of his life.

In [925] Boner's Uebersetzung des Thukydides (23) his monogram appears on three woodcuts.

He was especially productive in 1534. The first woodcut of this year that bears his monogram is the (275 x 190) title page illustration in [926] Steiner's Biblia beider Alt und Neuen Testaments deutsch (24). Aside from the title page illustration Scheifelin produced the (98 x 180) woodcut on the verso. He had nothing to do with the other illustrations in this book.

On the other hand 40 of his most beautiful woodcuts appeared in 1534 in Steiner's edition [927, Hirth B. I:Nos. 302, 481] of Memorial der Tugend, by Johann von Schwarzenberg. This, as was Steiner's custom, was not a book in which the illustrations formed a unity. He put the 40 Scheifelin pages in the first half of the book, but even in this part he included No. 22, which he took from the Wittenberg edition of the New Testament. No. 28 had been used in the Theuerdank and the small woodcuts in the second half of the book (Nos. 60, 61, 93, 94 and 99) were taken from Burgkmair's Cicero and Petrark, and others are from unknown sources. The 40 woodcuts that Scheifelin prepared for this work all bear his monogram, and they all convey the meaning, in wonderfully charming scenes, of biblical and other stories. Here we find Scheifelin at his height of achievement; here he is in his element and we see the essence of the basic art of one of the most charming artists of the sixteenth century.

There are three new (155 x 145) woodcuts by Scheifelin in Steiner's 1534 edition [928] of

Plutarch. This volume includes five illustrations that bear his monogram, but two had been used in earlier works.

Scheifelin did his first work for Alexander Weissenhorn, the other major printer in Augsburg at this time, in 1538, for [929, Pl. 199-201] his publication Lieblich auch kurtzweylig gedichte Lutti Apuleij von einem goldnen Esel (25). His contributions to this book may be differentiated from the woodcuts in the first 35 pages simply by their difference in size. In this case he did not start the illustration of the book, but only completed it, and he had to compete with a great rival. The woodcuts on the first 35 illustrated pages, which were 110-115 x 150 mm, were far superior to his (26). The female illustrations call to mind those in the Weisskunig and can be assumed to have been prepared by Burgkmair for a book that was published after his death. Scheifelin's pages, which were the last 41, were the same width but were only 105 mm high. In these later days Scheifelin's work took on a completely different character. His drawing was not nearly as carefully executed and the illustrations seemed more like freehand sketches. His monogram, with the shovel, appears only on sheet 39.

Towards the end of the 1530's Steiner started to do an edition of the works of Boccaccio, for which Scheifelin did the illustrations. But they must have run into difficulties since the Compendium de praeclaris mulieribus did not appear until 1541, after Scheifelin's death, and the Decameron never was published.

The [930] Historibuch von den führnehmlichsten Weibern (27), which Steiner published in 1541 and again in 1543, has an illustration of three young women sitting behind a table under a canopy (135 x 140). They are viewed from in front. The second woodcut, after the index, again shows the three young women, but they are viewed from the side and there are a few other differences. A number of Scheifelin woodcuts are reprinted from older works, and many are from the original Ulm edition. On the other hand there appears to have been another woodcut that was originally prepared for this book but was not put to use until Steiner used it [931] in Ludovico Vives' Unterweisung einer christlichen Frauen, in 1544. Both in style and size it is comparable to those in the Compendium....

Scattered parts of the Decameron edition that was never completed are found in later works published by Steiner and by Egenolf.

The (175 x 160) woodcut on leaf 4 of [932, Hirth B. I: No. 300] Scherz mid der Wahrheit, Frankfurt, 1550 (28), according to Weigel, on page 39 of his Holzschnitten berühmter Meister, was intended as the title page for the Decameron. A second woodcut in this book, that was clearly intended for the Decameron, shows a marriage ceremony in a church, and bears Scheifelin's monogram, including the shovel, at the lower left. The illustration showing girls catching fish for King Karl appears in the various editions of Lonicer's [933] Kräuterbuch, which was first published in Frankfurt in 1557. Others, with slight variations in size, are included in [934] Steiner's edition of Christoph Bruno's Historien und Fabulen, which was published in 1541, and are used as title pages of the excerpts from the Decameron that are included therein.

It may have been Scheifelin's death that kept Steiner from publishing his Decameron. According to Doppelmayr, Scheifelin died in Nördlingen in March 1540 (29). Woodcuts on which his monogram appears were published in much later books, especially by Steiner, but they are always taken from books published before 1540.

Scheifelin is in no way comparable with Burgkmair. Burgkmair kept himself free of all external influences and soared to his great heights by his own genius. Scheifelin's greatness developed from the influences he absorbed in Nuremberg and from the Dürer circle. He is the assiduous worker who let the influence of the great master work fully upon him, without developing this further in any way. It is surprising that his productivity was among the highest. His work for Pinder in Nuremberg and for Kaiser Maximilian, Schoensperger, Othmar, Miller, Steiner and Weissenhorn in Augsburg, for Petri in Basel and Anselm in Hagenau has to date revealed a count of drawings which almost equals the total produced by Burgkmair, and this is why his importance in the history of book illustration is second only to his great compatriot's.

Notes

1) We lack a basic work on Scheifelin, just as for Burgkmair. The material on him in Nagler's Monogrammisten is based on too little examination; for example, it does not differentiate between books for which the woodblocks were provided especially, and those that reused old woodblocks that had been prepared for earlier works. What Rosenberg says in his paper in Dohme's collection, Kunst und Künstler Deutschlands und die Niederlande, rests mostly on error. The spelling of his name varies. Ordinarily it is Schäufelein or Schaifelin but he is always entered in the Augsburg tax records as Scheifelin.

2) Weigel, No. 18339. Folio.

3) Mittheilungen der Wiener Centralcommission X:xxiv; the hypothesis of Caspar Rosenthaler, a painter, was included in the Stuttgarter Kunstblatt v. 25, No. 29 and 30, by Count Eschenburg, and since then has made the rounds in all reference books.

4) Panzer VII:446, No. 48.

5) Weigel, No. 13361. Folio.

6) Weigel, No. 20074. Folio.

7) Lacking in Bartsch and in Nagler. First referred to by Kraenzler in the Kunstkronik of 1878, No. 1. It is identical with Weigel, No. 21121.

8) Panzer I:352.

9) Weller, No. 856.

10) Panzer I:361, No. 767; Weigel, No. 1869; Stockmayer & Reber, p. 139, No. 15, also p. 140, No. 25 for the 1516 edition, also p. 141, No. 35 for the 1518 edition; Weller, No. 1070, lists a 1517 edition also.

11) Weigel, No. 10923. Folio.

12) Weigel, No. 10924. Quarto.

13) Rosenberg, "Even though only 3 of the 30 woodcuts in the book bear Scheifelin's monogram, the majority of the illustrations is attributable to him."

14) Panzer I:385, No. 831.

15) Weigel, No. 22775 and 8510. Folio.

16) Weigel, No. 20077. Quarto; Bartsch, No. 35.

17) Panzer I:401, No. 868. Quarto.

18) Panzer, Suppl:171, No. 973.

19) First printed in 1472, cf. Panzer I:68; The edition of 1517 is lacking in Panzer.

20) Panzer, Suppl:182, No. 974. Quarto; Rottermund, No. 58.

21) Weller, No. 1115.

22) Panzer, Beschreibung der Augsburger Bibeln, No. 26. Folio; same in Annalen II:132, No. 1612; Muther, Deutsche Bilderbibeln, No. 40.

23) Folio.

24) Panzer, Beschreibung der Augsburger Bibeln, No. 65; Muther, Deutsche Bilderbibeln, No. 100.

25) Weigel, No. 20076. Folio.

26) This has already been pointed out by Wiechmann-Kadow in Naumann's Archiv I:129.

27) Koch, Compendium der deutschen Literatur 2:294 (incorrectly dated 1501.) Folio; Lappenburg, Murner's Ulenspiegel. 1854, p. 375ff; Heyse, Bücherschatz der altdeutschen Literatur, No. 1800; Ebert, 15999; Weigel 13358.

28) Wiechmann-Kadow, in Archiv für die Zeichnenden Künste 2:135.

29) Heller & Jaeck. Beiträge zur Literatur- und Kunstgeschichte. No. 3.

Chapter XVI

MINOR AUGSBURG ARTISTS

In addition to Burgkmair and Scheifelin, there were a number of artists preparing book illustrations in Augsburg during the first 30 years of the sixteenth century. To be sure, none of them matched the two masters in quantity or in the artistic quality of their works; nevertheless they always provided proficient works.

One painter, "H. F.," illustrated [935, Pl. 202] the Layenspiegel von rechtmässigen Ordnungen in pürgerlichen und peinlichen Regimenten (1), by Ullrich Tengler, which Hans Othmar printed in 1509 for the publisher Rynmann. It had 29 (190 x 133) woodcuts, of which nine (nos. 7, 8, 12, 13, 20, 23, 24, 25 and 27) were repeated, leaving a total of 20 woodcuts. While this artist uses the monogram "H. F.," his identity is uncertain. In any event he cannot, as supposed by Brulliot, be the same artist HF, who was active in illustrating for Basel and Strassburg printers and whose works are written up in Bartsch VII:452. It may possibly have been Hans von Freiburg, who appeared in the tax records of Augsburg frequently during this period; however, the tax records always listed him as a woodcarver and not as an artist. Another option has been to ascribe these woodcuts to Burgkmair, crediting the unknown artist only with number 18, on which the monogram "H. F." appears.

The artist whose monogram was HWS provided a quite oldfashioned title page illustration for [936] Loblichen Tractat von Beraitung und Brauchung der Weine (2), by Arnoldus de Nova Villa, which was published by Johann Sittich in Augsburg in 1512. His monogram is on the left of the vat.

The same letters appeared on the large woodcuts of [937] a Plenarium (3) that appeared in Augsburg in 1515, without the name of the publisher, but it is not certain whether the drawings were independently done or whether they were copies of the drawings that Scheifelin prepared for the Schoensperger Plenarium of 1513. As in the latter, they are 230 x 155 mm. On one of the pictures, which covers the adoration of the Child, there is the monogram HWS; and on the second, Christ on the Cross, it is somewhat changed as it is on the illustration of the resurrection. The small woodcuts of the book (90 x 66) are, in any event, reversed copies of those that appeared in the 1512 Schoensperger edition. The first of the larger ones (205 x 130) is, to be sure, without a monogram but it must be attributed to the artist "H. W. S." It is singular that three years later, and published in the same city, the artist dared to put a different monogram on the work of some one else, omitting the original monogram.

The artist LB has already been discussed in the coverage of the Weisskunig, in which this monogram is found on leaf 78. Aside from this he is known only from a (245 x 160) title page woodcut that appeared in Hans Othmar's [938] 1514 edition of Geiler von Kaisersperg's Schiff der Penitenz und Busswürkung (4). The woodcut is divided into four parts, with the monogram at the foot of one of the columns in the fourth part.

Daniel Hopfer, who was important in the history of book ornamentation, experimented with presentation of figures. As stated in the Record of Citizens: "Item: On the Saturday before St. Gall's day, in the year 1493, Daniel Hopfer from Kaufbeuren, painter, purchased his citizenship." During the same year he took an apprentice, as the legal record of painters, leaf 75b, attests, stating, "Item: Meister Daniel Hopfer has presented a young man whose name is Michael Maistettern and whose work showed good promise. 1493." According to the tax records (Folio 25) he lived at St. Antonio in 1493, at "Schmidhaus No. 37" in 1502 and, from 1505, at "Unserer Frauen Bruders." According to the tax records of 1530 he had another house in addition to his dwelling (apparently in the St. Annagasse) and he paid ownership and income tax of eight Gulden, in addition to the regular tax. He must have been a highly respected man, since a record dated 16 June, 1533 indicates that on that date he served as a judge. He died in 1537, as is indicated by the fact that in that year Mrs. Daniel Hopfer paid the taxes.

Hopfer never achieved the level at painting figures that he achieved in book ornamentation.

One of his title page woodcuts, (253 x 173), appears in [939; Butsch 20] the 1514 Johannes Miller edition of *Chrysopassus*, by Johann Eck (5). A second of his title page illustrations (250 x 165) appeared in [940; Butsch 21] *Chronicon Abbatis Urspergensis a Nino Rege Assyriorum usque ad Fridericum secundum Romanorum imperatorem* (6). The composition in both these title pages is meaningless and the figures are squat and insignificant.

Georg Brew was a much more important illustrator, if the "J. B." monogram, which is found on one of the woodcuts [941] in Maen's *Leiden Christi*, is his. This book was printed by Schoensperger in 1515 and the rest of it was illustrated by Burgkmair and Scheifelin. This monogram appears at the lower left of the seventeenth woodcut. It is noteworthy that Brew, who was certainly very active in his work for book printers, made his mark on just this one page.

The large title page woodcut [942] of the 1516 Othmar edition of the *Leben verdienen und Wunderwerk des heiligen Augsburger Bisthums Bischofen St. Ulrichs und Symprechts aud der heiligen Martyrerin St. Apher* (7) is in some curious way attributed by Nagler to Hans Burgkmair, even though the style is quite old and is completely different from Burgkmair's and the monogram ⊦ is very clear in the work. Next to the artist's monogram we find the letters "F. S. W.," which refer to the woodcarver. In addition to the title page woodcut, the book has a woodcut before each biography and these agree in style with that of the title page. Altogether, the illustrations give the impression of work of an older period. (8)

The monogram F$, is a puzzling phenomenon since it was used by an artist in both Augsburg and Leipzig publications during the period 1514-1530.

The first book that he illustrated [943, Pl. 203] is Marcus von Waida's *Spiegel der Bruderschaft des Rosenkrans* (9), which was published in Leipzig in 1514 without indication of its printer. It has a (140 x 92) title page illustration and 14 (162 x 103) text woodcuts, three of which are used twice. The fact that the artist is of the Augsburg school is indicated by the completely Swabian Madonna-style.

Another work that he did for Leipzig is the (120 x 80) title page woodcut [944] of Luther's *Sermo de virtute excommunicationis* (10), which was published by Valentin Schumann in 1518.

His other pages are in Augsburg books, and chiefly in those printed by Hans Miller.

Miller's 1515 [945] edition of the *Passional* (11) contains a number of fair woodcuts by him and his monogram is on the title page.

In 1518 there appeared a title page illustration (70 x 57) in [946] Miller's *Hortulus animae,* with the following monogram at the base of a column and there are many smaller woodcuts in the text (usually 25 x 18) that are attributable to him. Just two large woodcuts in this book bear Scheifelin's monogram.

This is followed by a title page woodcut bearing his monogram (115 x 115), in [947] Miller's printing, in 1519, of *Vita Johannis Capistrani* (12).

The most familiar works of this artist are the nine large woodcuts in [948] Sigmund Meisterlin's *Chronographie Augsburgs* (13), which was printed by Melchior Ramminger in 1522. The title page woodcut, which fills the entire page, bears his monogram at the lower left.

His last woodcut appears as the title page [949] of *Bekenntniss des glaubens Doct. Martin Luther's mit kurzen glossen D. Hieronymi Dungersheim.*

Attempts to attribute the monogram have been made in many ways. The earlier unfortunate attempts to attribute it to Hans Scheifelin have been completely abandoned. On the other hand a second artist has met with enthusiastic support. The identical monogram is found on the colophon of Heinrich Steiner's edition of *Xenophon* of 1540. As a result of this some have claimed that all works bearing this monogram should be attributed to Heinrich Steiner. Brulliot maintained that all woodcuts bearing this monogram were the property of the publishing house of Heinrich Steiner, and as such were his colophon. However Brulliot's interpretation is untenable since it can be pointed out that this monogram does not occur on a single woodcut published by the Steiner press. Thus it will be necessary to continue to search for the identity of the master .

The great Burgkmair's son was also active in book illustration. He clearly belongs to a later generation and he is named here simply because a number of his works are often attributed to his father.

In 1534 Alexander Weissenhorn produced a new [950] edition of Hieronymus Brunschwig's *Chirurgia,* which was published by Grüninger in Strassburg in 1497. It has 17 woodcuts, of which a number are frequently repeated, and of which 15 bear the monogram H. B. The idea that they are posthumously published works of the elder Burgkmair is ruled out because the woodcuts are copies of the woodcuts in the original edition and are copied in a fairly craftsmanlike manner, a process that would have been completely unacceptable to the old master. A few other woodcuts by Hans Burgkmair, the younger, are found in [951] H. Steiner's edition, in 1542, of Platina's *Von der ehrlichen ziemlichen auch erlaubten Wollust des leibs in essen und trinken.* Steiner included a number of woodcuts from *Petrarka* and from the *Weisskunig.* His woodcuts in this book show the younger Burgkmair to be an able and skilled artist. His three woodcuts in this book are 75-85 mm. high and 112 mm. wide and they bear the monogram "H. B." These are capable works and show a certain similarity with his father's.

The most important of these minor painters are and H. F. The artists identified by the monograms HWƧ have not freed themselves of the style of the fifteenth century, and too little is known of the work of Georg Brew and the artist LB to justify an opinion of their work. Daniel Hopfer achieved little fame in drawing figures and was far more outstanding as a painter of ornamentation. The younger Burgkmair, finally, was a fine artist who never, however, approached the greatness of his father.

Notes

1) Ebert, No. 11781. Folio; Panzer I:307, No. 645; Weigel III, No. 348, the other 1512. Folio. The 1511 edition, Panzer I:333; 1512 ed., Panzer I:342.

2) Panzer I:345.

3) Panzer I:374.

4) Brulliot I:1050; Nagler lists an edition published without place or date; Panzer I:364, No. 774.

5) Reproduced in Butsch I:20.

6) Reproduced in Butsch I:21; Zapf I:83; Panzer VI:144, No. 84.

7) Panzer I:388.

8) Panzer I:388, No. 838. The book was also published in Latin, under the title, Gloriosorum Christi confessorum Udalrici et Symperti nec non beatissimae martyris Afrae Augustanae sedis patronorum historia. Burgkmair also illustrated these same situations.

9) Panzer, Suppl.:128, No. 772b. Quarto.

10) Panzer VIII:205, No. 668; Rotermunde, No. 16.

11) Weller, No. 906. Folio; Weigel, No. 17888.

12) Panzer VI:153, No. 140.

13) A lovely tale of the origins of the warlike Germans after Noah's flood, and also the imperial city of Augsburg. Panzer II:117. Folio.

Chapter XVII

AUGSBURG ILLUSTRATIONS BY UNKNOWN ARTISTS (1)

In addition to the great artistic productivity of Burgkmair, Scheifelin and the minor Augsburg artists, there are many Augsburg books in existence for which the illustrations can not be attributed to any particular artist.

The printer Hans Schoensperger, the younger, became more interested in publishing than in book printing, and produced few illustrated books except those illustrated by Burgkmair and by Scheifelin. Their works have already been discussed, and there are relatively few to be added.

Reyman's [952-56] 1511 (2) and 1514 editions of Wetterbüchleins (3); his Rossarzneibüchlein (4) and his 1513 (5) Büchlein von Complexion der Menschens, reissued in 1515, have minor title page illustrations only.

In 1520 Walter Isenberg's [957] Wie die Machtige Reich Hispania, Ungarn und Geldern an Oestereich und Burgund gekommen sein (7) has a (170 x 128) title page illustration and 23 (100 x 130) text woodcuts. The best of the lot is the title page illustration, which appears to have been done by an artist.

The little book [958] by Albrecht von Eybes, Vom ehelichen Stand (8), which was printed by Schoensperger in 1520 and issued in a new edition in 1522, has a decorative title page which is 45 x 35 mm.

An elegant small publication [959] is Gilgengart einer yetlichen Christlichen Sel (9), which first appeared in 1520 and was published in a new edition in 1521. It is printed on parchment, with every page having a broad border decoration. It has nine woodcuts (85 x 60).

The title page of [960] Joseph Grünbeck's Nützlicher Betrachtung aller Trübsalen, die über alle Stande des Christenheit in kurzen Tagen gehen werden (10), which was printed by Schoensperger in 1522, has a title page illustration.

The title page woodcut for the little book that he printed s. l. e. a., [961] Eberlin's Wie gar gfarlich sey, so ain Priester kain Eeweyb hat (11) is 112 x 125 mm. On the rostrum shown in this illustration is the date 1522. In [962] the Frauenspiegel of 1522 (12), and in [963] Luther's Christlicher Vorbetrachtung und bekanntniss in Gott of 1523 (13) there are only unimportant small woodcuts.

There is a very charming book of this period [964], printed by Erhard Ratdolt in 1516, the Breviarium constantiniense (14). It has five full page woodcuts which can, with great probability, be attributed to Burgkmair. Unfortunately it does not bear a monogram.

Johannes Othmar moved his printing plant to Augsburg and began there in 1502 [965, Butsch I:18] with the Pomerium de tempore et Quadragesimale (15). The title pages of this two-part book are decorated with a single excellent woodcut (180 x 125). The technique is that used in ancient times, in which outlines are white and the background is black. The handling of the landscape is especially interesting.

An equally important [966] title page woodcut appears in the 1502 Stellarium coronae benedictae Mariae virginis (16).

The large (180 x 135) title page illustration in the [967] Oratio Theodorici Rysichei in laudes sancti Hyvonis (17), which was printed by Johannes Rynmann in 1502, was taken from a Grüninger publication of the fifteenth century.

The woodcuts in the following contribute nothing new: [968] In the Seelenwurzgarten of 1504 (18) the illustrations are repeated from earlier editions. [969] Those in both the Plenarien which Othmar published in 1506 and [970] 1509, which are 82 x 60 mm, are from the fifteenth century editions of Schöensperger, which were published around 1480.

The 108 woodcuts in [971] Othmar's Deutscher Bibel of 1507 (19) are reduced copies of those in the Cologne Bible, which had already been used by Schönsperger in his 1487 Bible. Since Othmar's edition had wider columns than were in the Schönsperger edition, he had to add ornamental borders along the sides of the woodcuts to make them fill the columns. Othmar reused these same woodcuts again [972] in his 1518 Bibel (20). The woodcuts in Othmar's [973] Heiligenleben (21) were likewise from much earlier works.

Those in his [974] 1508 (22) publication of the third German edition of Ulricus Molitoris' Tractatus de laniis et phitonicis mulieribus are the same as those first used by Cornelius von Zürichsee in his first Cologne edition of 1489, which Othmar had himself reused in the s. l. e. a. edition that he had published in Reutlinger.

Also, the woodcuts in [975] the 1508 edition of the large Hortus Sanitatis (23), which he printed at Rynmann's expense, and which was the 22nd edition of this book, were the same as those used from the beginning. In [976] Kayssersperg's Achtzehn Eigenschaften eines Christenpilgers, which he printed in 1508, he repeated on leaf 136b the illustration which Burgkmair had supplied for use in the same year in Kayssersperg's Predigten....

He supplied new illustrations again starting with the books he produced in 1510.

His 1510 printing for Rynmann of an edition [977] of Lanzkranna's Himmelstrass (24) has a full page title page illustration.

The 1510 edition of the [978] booklet Von warer Erkanntnuss des Wetters (25), which was printed three times that year, has a studying astrologer on the title page.

In 1511 he printed for Rynmann [979] the Spiegel der Sitten im Latein genannt Speculum morum, übersetzt von Albrecht von Eybe (26). The woodcut on the verso of the title page is 213 x 143 mm. Under the woodcut it states: Albrecht von Eybe, Doctor.

In the same year, Othmar printed [980] Ulbertinus Pusculus' Duo libri Symonidos de Judaeorum perfidia, quo modo Jesum Christum cruxifixerunt (27). The Othmar edition had three woodcuts, and the title page illustration is 90 x 75 mm.

The [981] Tractat von der edlen reinen unbefleckten Jungfrauschaft Mariae (28), which Othmar issued in 1511, had a good title page. Othmar's 1511 edition of [982] Bonaventura's Psalter Mariae (29) had a woodcut illustration on the verso of the title page.

The 21 woodcuts in [983] the edition of Seussen (30), which Othmar printed in 1512 for Rynmann, present the same situations as are presented in the fifteenth century Sorg edition, but there is variation in treatment and one can, almost with certainty, attribute the reworked woodcuts to Burgkmair.

Ueberling's [984] Practica deutsch (31) of 1513 has only a title page woodcut and [985] the Wurzgärtlein de andachtigen Uebung (32), published in the same year, has a woodcut at the end only.

The last illustrated printing by Johannes Othmar appeared in 1514 [986-988]: Die Passion zu singen in des Regenbogen Brief weis (33) which had a title page illustration; the Passio Jesu Christi (34), with eight woodcuts; and Geiler von Kaisersperg's Predigt über das Schiff der Penitens und Busswirkung (35), in which he reused the woodcut of Christ on the Cross that Scheifelin had prepared for the Heiligenleben.

Sylvan, Hans Othmar's son, followed worthily in the footsteps of his father. His first publication to have a title page woodcut was [989] Grammatica cum praeceptis moralibus ad inventutem (36) by Pinicianus, which he published in 1513.

This was followed, in 1515, by [990] Wurzgärtlein der andächtigen Uebung (37), in which he repeated Burgkmair's woodcut of Christ on the Cross from the Taschenbüchlein of 1510, on the verso of the title page. In 1518 there appeared [991] the booklet Complexion des Menschen (38) and Luther's Sermon von der Betrachtung des heiligen Leidens Christi (39), each of which had title page illustrations only.

In his 1520 edition of [992] of Auslegung der fünf Zeichen so zu Wien geschehen sind (40) he had five woodcuts, and the title page illustration was 108 x 100 mm.

Also in 1520 he printed [993-994] three of Luther's writings: Sermon von der Bereitung zum Sterben (41); Trostliches Büchlein, deutsch von G. Spalatin (42); and Erklärung der 10 Gebote (43), each of which had Scheifelin's "Last Judgment" at the close. In 1522 [995-997] he published the pamphlets, Wie der heilige Vater Adrianus zu Rom eingeritten ist (43); Dialogus von einem rechtschaffenen Christmenschen (45); and Sendbrief der Kanzlers von Rodis (46), each of which had a single woodcut.

In Luther's translation [998] of the Neuen Testamentes (47), which he reprinted three times in 1523 and a fourth time in 1524, he reused as the title page the Scheifelin 1512 Heiligenleben woodcut, "Christus und die Vertreter des Alten und Neuen Testamentes."

[999] The Alte Testament, deutsch (48), the first part of which he issued in 1523, the second in 1524 and the third in 1525, has little in the way of new illustration, and all the illustrations in all three parts were copies of woodcuts in earlier publications.

In his later years Silvan Othmar no longer placed any great weight on illustration. The ten woodcuts in his 1525 printing [1000] of Erklärung und gründlichen Unterweisung alls Nutzes so in dem Edlen Instrument Astrolabium begriffen find (49) provide illustrations for mathematical theorems only.

The first illustrated book published by Oeglin-Nadler was issued in 1507. It was [1001] Conrad Celtes' edition of Gunther Ligurinus' De gestis Friderici I. On the title page appears Dürer's woodcut of Apollo on Parnassus. From 1508, we have [1002, Pl. 204] the Mortilogus, by Conrad Reiter from Nördlingen. The woodcuts are well drawn and excellently translated into wood. Oeglin soon separated from Nadler and thereafter each went his independent way.

In 1507 Oeglin [1003-1005] printed a Deutschen Kalender, with 80 woodcuts (50); in 1508 he produced a Büchlein die Liebe Gottes (51), with a title page illustration; and in 1510 he produced Pfefferkorn's Von des Kaisers Vollmacht den Juden ihre Bücher zu nehmen (52), with a title page woodcut.

Also in 1510, Oeglin [1006] printed Liber vagatorum der Bettlerorden (53), which has a title page illustration, and his little booklet [1007], also printed in 1510, Reinigung Seel und Leibs mit Erwerbung Gnad und Ablass (54) which has eleven competently done (90 x 60) woodcuts; they have great similarity to Burgkmair's early work.

The 24 illustrations [1008] issued by Oeglin in his 1512 edition of Passio oder Leiden unseres heren Jesu Christi (55) are, on the other hand, unimportant: as are those in his 1512 [1009] Brunn der durstigen Seel (56).

Johann Böschenstein von Esslingen's book [1010] Neu geordnet Rechenbüchlein (57), which he printed in 1514, has a woodcut in each of the two parts.

Jacob Köbel's [1011] Neu geordnet Rechenbüchlein (58) has a similar title page woodcut.

Of the illustrated books that Nadler printed alone [1012-1013], he had a title page woodcut and four more in the text in Pfefferkorn's Büchlein von der Judenbeicht (59), which he printed in 1508. The 24 woodcuts that appeared in his 1515 edition were repeated in his 1517 edition of Passio unseres Herrn Jesu Christi (60). These are 60 mm x 40-48 mm and are not as important as those in the Passion... printed by Oeglin. The first one in Nadler's edition shows that his come from an older book.

In 1520 he published five of Luther's sermons. In [1014] the Sermon von der Bereitung zum Sterben (61), there are three woodcuts on the title page. In the [1015] Sermon von dem Wucher (62) there is a title page woodcut. There is one woodcut [1016] in the Sermon von dem Sacrament der Busse (63). [1017] The Sermon von dem Bann (64) has a woodcut on its title page. His [1018] Sermon vom Sacrament der Taufe (65) has one woodcut.

Nadler's [1019] edition of Fussfad zur ewigen Seeligkeit (66) has a crude title page and 24 equally worthless small woodcuts in the text. It was published in 1521.

In addition to the Burgkmair products of the Miller Press, which have already been discussed, there should be added their 1515 printing of [1020] Ritterlich und lobwürdig Reis des gestrengen Ritters Hern Ludovici Vardomans nach Aegyptien, Syrien, Arabien, etc. (67). It has a (130 x 97) title page woodcut and 45 smaller (97 x 70) text woodcuts.

The title page [1021] of Nicolaus Faber's Musicae rudimenta (68) of 1516 has a (100 x 100) woodcut. The woodcuts in Miller's [1022] Evangelienbuch of 1517 (69) are taken from earlier editions. In 1518 he printed [1023] the Kalender by Johann Küngsperg (70).

He published, undated, [1024] Hutten's »Οὖτις *Nemo*« with a very important (160 x 111) title page woodcut.

While the very productive plant of Dr. Sigmund Grimm and Marx Würsung (1518-24) always kept Burgkmair busy, they also produced a number of illustrated books by unidentifiable artists.

Their 1520 publication [1025, Pl. 170-171], Devotissimae meditationes de vita, beneficiis et passione Salvatoris Jesu Christi cum gratiarum actione (71), is first class. It has 37 woodcuts, some of which fill the entire octavo page of the booklet, with the others taking half a page. They are in the Burgkmair tradition but are hastily sketched. The interpretation of the textual message is mostly original, elementary, clear and interpretive. They are somewhat short of being distinguished, yet in many of the presentations a certain spiritual consecration appears undeniable. The carving is exceedingly skillful.

After Grimm separated from Würsung, in 1522, he printed for two years on his own.

In the [1026] Evangelia der vier Evangelisten verdeutscht (72), issued in 1522, there are pictures of the four evangelists.

Grimm's [1027] 1523 printing of the Psalter des göttlichen Propheten Davids, gedeutscht von Caspar Amman (73) has two woodcuts.

In [1028-1030] Böschenstein's Gebet Salomonis, in 1523 (74), there is a woodcut on the second-last page; in 1524 (75), in Othmar Nachtigall's Psalter der Königs David (70) there is one on the title page; and the Erasmus, Paraphrases in Evangel. Matthaei, of 1523 (77), has five woodcuts. It is practically incomprehensible that, in the time of Burgkmair and Scheifelin, such poor woodcuts could be used as are found in the works issued by many of the smaller printing plants.

Johannes Froschauer, who played an unimportant part in book illustration in the fifteenth century, did no better in his later years.

[1031] The Histori von Orendel un unseres Herrn Rock zu Trier (78), printed in 1512, has a title page illustration and 32 bad text woodcuts.

There is a crude title page woodcut in [1032] Kaisersperg's 1513 edition of Trostspiegel, so dir Vatter mutter kind oder freundt gestorben sind (79).

The title page illustration [1033] in Tallat's Margarita Medicinae of 1514 (80) is the same as that in the 1507 edition.

The woodcuts in [1034] his Passion of 1514 (81) are all from much earlier sources.

The title page in [1035] Michael Schrick's Von den ausgebrannten Wassern (82), which Froschauer printed in 1514, is bad. Unimportant woodcuts appear in [1036] his Unterweissung der Chirurgie, issued in 1515 (83). Indeed, Froschauer did not blush at using, in the 1520's, woodcuts that were prepared around 1470.

[1037-1044] He published editions of Verzückungen des Tondalus in 1515 and in 1521 (84); of the Historie St. Brandon's in 1517 (85) and 1521 (86); of the Historie des Königs Apollonius (87) in 1516 and 1521; and the Meister Elucidarius (88) in 1519, and in all of these books woodcuts used in publications issued in the 1470's were reused. His Teutscher Kalender (89), issued in 1522, reused the woodcuts that Schoensperger had used back in 1480.

Melchior Ramminger's publications were quite as unimportant in artistic value. [1045-1048] The books that he printed that had title page woodcuts were: Der gulden Paradeys in 1520 (90); Alphabet Gott zu ehren in 1521 (91); the Heilig ewig Wort Gottes in 1523 (92); and the Schöne Unterweisung wie allein im Glauben und guten Werken Seligkeit erfunden wird, of 1526 (93).

In 1511, Joh. Sittich printed [1049] Andreas Proles' Lehre von der Taufe der Kinder (94), which he provided with unimportant woodcuts.

The woodcuts in some of the books issued without indication of the printer are better than the above. The 1509 Augsburg edition [1050] of Fortunatus (95) has a good title page but the woodcuts in the text are bad. The 1509 edition of Pfefferkorn's [1051] Wie die Juden ihr Ostern halten

(96) has a title page woodcut illustration, as does his [1052] Der Judenfeind (97) which was published in the same year.

[1053] The Büchlein von dem ganzen Geschlecht St. Anna (98), published in Augsburg in 1510, has a large woodcut on the verso of the title page.

The 1518 edition [1054] of Zwei Comödien des sinnreichen Poeten Plautus, gedeutscht durch Albrecht von Eybe (99) was more richly illustrated.

A little book [1055], Die Ständ des römischen Reichs mit sammt allen Kurfürsten und Fürsten, so auf dem Augsburger Reichstag erschienen (100), was published in 1518 without the name of the printer but "at the cost of Hans Haselberg," of Reichenau. Its title page woodcut was 105 x 105 mm.

A book that certainly was published in Augsburg, and apparently with a woodcut provided by Burgkmair [1056], came out in 1520 without location. This was the Krönung Kaiser Karls zu Aachen (101). The title page illustration is 157 x 110 mm. The woodcut in [1057] the 1520 publication, Werbung an Herrn Carln römischen König (102), is similar.

An Augsburg publication issued in 1521 without the name of the printer [1058], by Erasmus Amman (103), has an unimportant (120 x 100) title page woodcut.

The last of the great Augsburg printers was Heinrich Steiner, who presumably came there from Switzerland around 1522 and started printing in Augsburg in 1523. In the years that followed his was destined to become Augsburg's largest and one of the richest printing houses of that time. Little popular pamphlets, great editions of Bibles, and works of historical or moralistic content went hand in hand with classical works, and practically all of these books were freely illustrated. Unfortunately, the quality of the woodcuts that Steiner used did not always match their quantity. Steiner was the first Augsburg printer who misused woodcuts that were originally intended for other books, putting them in books he published for which they were not suitable. One may extoll him as the chief employer of Burgkmair and Scheifelin; nevertheless, in most cases, it is not possible to say how he came by the woodcuts he used. One is astonished by the mass of illustrations that he provided for all his publications, but examination of the individual books shows that the same woodcuts or some of the same woodcuts were repeated in the great majority of them.

Steiner began [1059-1060] his activity quite modestly. In 1523 he published Unüberwintlich Beschirmbüchlein von Hauptartikeln der göttlichen Schrift (104), with an unimportant woodcut on its last page, and Christlich und nutzbarlich Betbüchlein in 1524 (105), with an unimportant woodcut on the verso of its title page.

On the verso of the title page [1061] of the Psalter deutsch Martinus Luthers of 1524 (106) the same woodcut is used as Grimm had used in his Ammann Psalter of 1523. There is a second illustration on the first side of the last leaf. Steiner's first richly illustrated book [1062] is the Betbüchlein und Lesbüchlein Martin Luthers (107), which includes 14 large and 17 smaller woodcuts. The last 1524 book published by Steiner is [1063] a reprint of Rösslin's Rosengarten der Schwangern Frauen und Hebammen (108), which was first published by Martin Flach in Strassburg in 1513. Most of its woodcuts are badly recut after the original illustrations, some in reversal, and at least one, that on leaf 15b, is a bad recutting of the one in the 1522 Flach edition.

In 1526 Steiner issued an edition [1064] of Pauli's Schimpf und Ernst (109), which was first published in Strassburg in 1522. He has in this a combination of woodcuts which include some made by Burgkmair for Grimm's edition of Petrarka (which was first brought to fruition by Steiner himself in 1532). The first of these illustrates the 23rd chapter; the second is in chapter 71 of book 1; no. 8 is in book two for chapter 115; No. 9 is in chapter 5, etc. Only the title page illustration (142 x 155) is not found in the Petrarka or in the Cicero. The carving is good and would not have been unworthy of Burgkmair.

His second book, in 1526, Widmann's Behende und hübsche Rechnung auf allen Kaufmannschaften (110), also has illustrations. Except for the first one (75 x 70), the other woodcuts are of little significance.

The title page woodcut in Steiner's 1527 edition of Alten Testament, deutsch (111), which he reran in 1529, is a copy of that in the original Wittenberg edition. This is followed by twelve small woodcuts in the text and, in the third part, another large one which is taken from Gerssdorf's Feldbuch der Wundarznei, which was published in Strassburg in 1517.

The title page woodcut of [1065] the Neuen Testaments recht gründlich teutscht (112), which was published in the same year (1527) and then again in 1528 and 1531, is the one used by Knoblouch in Strassburg in his 1524 and 1525 editions of the Old Testament. At the beginning of each book there is either a small woodcut to start it or a small woodcut separate from the letter. The Apocalypse has the customary 21 woodcuts (100 x 67).

The title page woodcut of [1066] his 1528 edition of Rechnung auf der Linien und Feldern auf allerlei Handtierung gemacht durch Adam Rysen shows two men who are calculating. In the same year he followed this with the second edition of [1067] Der schwangeren Frauen und Hebammen Rosengarten (113) which used the same illustrations that had been used in 1524.

In 1529 [1071] he issued his edition of Vier Bucher der Ritterschaft des Flavius Vegetius Renatus (114). Its title page comes from Burgkmair's Cicero. The knight on page 2 was often used by Scheifelin, but the painter of this one is not known. In addition the book has the familiar 109 full page illustrations of siege and other war machinery. [trans. note: references [1068-1070] were omitted in the original.]

He did a number of books in 1530. The woodcuts in [1072] Steiner's Altem Testament deutsch (115) are the same as those in the Wittenberg edition except that Steiner adds just one; it appears before the first book of Moses.

The 1530 [1073] edition of Margarita. Der ganz jüdisch Glaub mit sammt einer gründlichen Anzeig aller Satzungen und Ceremonien (116) has six (107 x 98) woodcuts.

The third book [1074] published in 1530 was Luftgärten und Pflanzungen (117); it has an 80 x 106 mm title page woodcut.

The fourth book printed in 1530 [1075] was Johannes Tallat's Arzneibüchlein der Krauter (118). The title page woodcut (105 x 102) gives the impression of having come from a book at least thirty years older.

The last of his 1530 books, [1076] Von allen Speisen und gerichten allerhand Art künstlich und wol zu kochen, einmachen und berayten. Durch den hochgelehrten Platinam Pii II Hofmeister (119), likewise has a title page woodcut (75 x 120) which Steiner later used in his 1542 work by Platina.

In 1531 [1077] Steiner completed the Cicero which Grimm and Würsung had prepared. The Burgkmair woodcuts supplied for this work in 1520, which Steiner obtained from Grimm's estate, served him from then on as an inexhaustible supply for illustrating various types of works. Even as early as his 1531 edition [1078] of Herodian (120) he used one of the Burgkmair woodcuts for its title page. Similarly [1079] the woodcuts in Justin's Wahrhaftigen Historien (121), which Steiner published in that same year, 1531, were almost entirely from the Burgkmair hoard.

After these he issued only smaller works in 1531.

[1080] Hans Hörburger's Nützlich Büchlein, darin alle Ständ der Menschen begriffen (122), has an 80 x 70 mm title page woodcut. [1081] Die Meisterlichen Stuck von Bayssen und Jagen auch wie man Habich und andere Vögel auch Hunde dazu erziehen soll. Waidleuten und Jagern ganz nützlich und dienlich (123) has two 95 x 95 woodcuts; one as the title page illustration and the other on leaf 22b.

The (160 x 110) title page woodcut for [1082] Bartholomäus Vogther's Arzneibüchlein für den gemeinen Menschen (124), was taken from Burgkmair's Petrarka, and the last of his 1531 books [1083] was Michael Krautwadel's Ein nützlich Regiment der Gesundheit (125). In addition to the two Burgkmair woodcuts which were taken from the original edition, this book has four other unimportant woodcuts. Why Steiner did not use the other Burgkmair illustrations from the first edition is not known.

The major achievement of 1532 was the issuance of [1084] the Petrarka (126), for which Burgkmair supplied even more illustrations back in 1520 than he had done for Cicero. It is a fact that, after 1532, practically no publication issued by Steiner, regardless of its authorship, lacked one or more of the Petrarka woodcuts.

In his 1532 edition of [1085] Propheten, teutsch, Dr. Martin Luther's (127), Steiner used the title page woodcut that he had used before, e.g., in his Old Testament of 1527; in his Propheten of 1528, etc.

Hans Busteter's [1086] Ernstlicher Bericht, wie fich eine fromme Obrigkeit in und nach gefährlichen Kriegsnöthen verhalten soll (128) has a (120 x 110) title page woodcut that was taken from Burgkmair's Cicero.

The title page woodcut for Raymundus Lullus' [1087] Künstlicher Eroffnung aller Verborgenheiten und Geheimnisse der Natur (129), likewise published in 1532, was 110 x 105 mm. The [1088] booklet by Johann Boschenstein (130), Gegen das Tanzen, printed in 1533, had a title page woodcut (67 x 97).

His [1089] Cronika, by Johann Carion (131), also printed in 1533, has two good woodcuts that are in the style of Scheifelin. The first is 88 x 50 mm and the second is 112 x 69 mm.

In 1533 he also printed [1090] Des allerstreytbarsten und theuersten Fürsten und Herrn Georgen Castrioten genannt Scanderbeg ritterliche Thaten von Marinus Barletius in Latin beschrieben und von Johann Pinicianus verdeutscht (132). The 115 woodcuts it contains were mostly prepared for the book and are very poor. They could only have been done by a low-grade artist. There are a few woodcuts from Burgkmair's Cicero, which can be distinguished from the others by their difference in size alone.

The woodcuts [1091] in Thukydides, which Boner supplied in a German edition in the same year, are closely related to the woodcuts in the Scanderberg... Only Nos. 15, 26, 28 and 38 are by Burgkmair. Nos. 2, 30, and 46 are by Scheifelin. The other illustrations are partly taken from the Scanderbeg and the rest were produced by the same unknown and unimportant artist.

The year 1534 was especially fruitful in new illustrations, which Steiner printed in three moralistic texts by Johannes von Schwarzenberg.

The woodcuts in [1092, Pl. 205] Büchlein wider das Zutrinken included some attributed to Scheifelin without full evidence. Aside from the title page, four of the woodcuts were taken from Burgkmair's Glücksbuch. The title page woodcut in the second booklet by Schwarzenberg [1093], Wider das Morlaster des Raubens, shows a robber in the woods near a city, with a man on the left tied to a tree, and on the right, another man with Satan behind him.

The [1094] Memorial der Tugend, for the first part of which Scheifelin provided the woodcuts, is an especially beautiful production; and the artist who provided the woodcuts for the second part must have been particularly well qualified.

Another small [1095] book done in 1534 is the Wohlgeordnet und nützlich Büchlein, wie man Bergwerke suchen und finden soll (133). The title page woodcut (70 x 75) is very bad and the text has a number of crude woodcuts representing mines.

There is a remarkable collection of woodcuts in Steiner's 1534 edition of the Worms Bible, under [1096] the title, Biblia beider, Alt und Neuen Testaments (134). The title page woodcut has already been discussed under Scheifelin's works. The second, which appears before Genesis, is attributable to him also. Then, up into the middle of the third book, there are small, exceedingly bad woodcuts which are followed by an unillustrated portion that extends to the Apocalypse. Those in the Apocalypse are larger, but just as bad as the others, and are equally bad copies of those in the Worms Bible.

[1097-1099] Der Teutsch Cicero, 1534 (135), 1535 and 1540 (published by Johann von Schwarzenberg), had primarily woodcuts that were available in the plant. The Scheifelin series from the Memorial der Tugend was reused (Bartsch, Nos. 55-94). The woodcut on leaf 111a had previously been used in various editions of Gersdorff's Feldbuch der Wundartznei. The presentation of the satyr on leaf 92a is related to a similar sheet from the Cranach school, as is described in Heller, Cranach, ed. 2, No. 595.

Steiner's 1534 edition of [1100] Johann Pauli's Schimpf und Ernst (136) contains the familiar Burgkmair woodcuts from Petrarka as well as two charnel houses, with dead bodies, which had been taken from Scheifelin's Memorial der Tugend.

He also did a second edition of [1101] Grimm and Würsung's 1520 Tragödie von Calixt und Melibea and his 1534 edition had the title, Ain recht liebliches Büchlein und gleich ain traurige Comedi von schaden und gefar flaischliche lieb und untreu der dirnens (137). The illustrations in this second edition came from the Cicero and Petrarka woodcuts.

The 99 small woodcuts in Steiner's 1534 edition of [1102] Andreas Alciatus' Emblematum liber (138) are French in their characteristics and were taken from a Parisian edition of the book.

The five woodcuts which Steiner uses in the introduction to [1103] the second edition (1534) of the Flavius Vegetius Renatus, Vier Büchern der Ritterschaft (139), are from Burgkmair and Scheifelin.

Also Steiner's [1104-1105] *Biblia* of 1535 (140), which he repeated in 1539, adds nothing new to book illustration. It is a copy of the 1534 Wittenberg edition, including the woodcuts.

In the same year (1535) Steiner printed [1106] his *Neues Testament, wiederum fleissig corrigirt* (141), which in addition to a title page woodcut has a portrait of the compiler before each book. The Apocalypse has 21 woodcuts of the same size as the earlier editions.

His 1535 edition [1107] of Boner's German text of *Herodot* (142) is fitted with an assembly of the woodcuts from the *Cicero* and from his 1533 *Scanderbeg*.

The last book he printed in 1535 is an edition [1108] of Riederer's *Spiegel der waren Rhetorik*. It contains six woodcuts taken from *Petrarka*, *Cicero* and *Alsaharavius*.

In 1536 there followed [1109] his *Kosnitzer Concilienbuch* in which he used the same illustrations as in the Sorg edition of 1484, but had all the woodcuts modernized and recut to bring them up to the 1530 period style.

On the other hand, [1110] another publication that he issued in 1536, *Wahrhaftigen Histori von dem Troianischen Krieg--Durch Dictyn Cretensem und Darem Phrygium--newlich durch Marcum Tatium aus dem Latein ins Teutsch vewandelt mit durchaus schönen Figuren* (143), has woodcuts from Burgkmair's *Cicero* and *Petrarka*, Scheifelin's *Theuerdank* and the *Scanderbeg*. Eighteen of the figures are Burgkmair's. These are Nos. 1, 3, 5, 8, 16, 18, 19, 21, 22, 23, 24, 29, 32, 44, 48, 49, 51, and 57. Six are by Scheifelin: Nos. 25, 40, 46, 47, 53, and 59, some of which are from the 1533 *Thukydides* and No. 61 from the *Theuerdank*. All the others are from the *Scanderbeg*.

A few of Burgkmair's woodcuts for the *Petrarka* are also found in [1111] *Translationen oder Deutschungen des Nicolaus von Weil* (144), published in 1536.

In 1537 he did a third edition of *Theuerdank* with the original 118 woodcuts, which he apparently obtained from the younger Hans Schoensperger in 1532.

In the same year he printed a German edition [1112] of Polydorus Virgilius' *Buch von der Erfindung der Ding* (145). It has 118 woodcuts, of which 68 came from Burgkmair and four are from Scheifelin's *Memorial der Tugen* of 1534. Nos. 23, 73, 74, 75, 98, 99, 104 and some others must be attributed to an unknown illustrator. Steiner also included some 15th century woodcuts. As compared with those of Burgkmair and Scheifelin, these others show a rapid decay in style.

The two woodcuts [1113] in *Germaniae Chronikon*, by Sebastian Frank, which Steiner printed cooperatively with Alexander Weissenhorn in 1538, had been used in the *Scanderbeg*.

In Steiner's edition of Boner's translation [1114] into German of *Xenophonausgabe*, in 1540, the title page illustration is the same woodcut that Scheifelin used in 1534 for the biography of Alexander in the *Plutarch* (146). Similarly, for the birth of the Persian King, Steiner used a woodcut prepared by Burgkmair twenty years earlier, which had also been used in the 1534 edition of *Cicero*. At the end there is a modification of Scheifelin's monogram .

In addition, in 1540 Steiner printed [1115] *Zwei schöne auch lustige Historien und Geschichtbücher, der Römerkrieg wider Carthaginienser-Durch L. Aretinum beschrieben und newlich inn das Teutsch durch Marcum Tatium gemacht* (147). Among the many woodcuts, some sheets reproduce those by Scheifelin.

In his edition of [1116] Albertus Magnus' Buch der Heimlichkeiten Steiner repeated the title page woodcut that Burgkmair had provided for Avila's Banqueto of 1530.

The woodcuts in [1117] the 1541 printing of the translation of Petrarch's De rebus memorandis, which Stephanus Vigilius supplied under the title, Gedenkbuch aller der Handlungen, die sich fürtrefflich vom anbeginn der Welt wunderbarlich begeben Haben (148), at least show uniform character since they, with the one exception of the three women sitting at the table, have all been taken from Burgkmair's Glücksbuch. This was also true of Steinhowel's translation [1118] of Boccaccio's Compendium de claris mulieribus, which Steiner printed in 1541. The numerous small woodcuts are free reworkings of those in the original Ulm edition of 1472. The two larger woodcuts are taken from Scheifelin's works.

Christoph Bruno's [1119] Historien und Fabulen (140) of 1541 (which were translations of selections from Ovid and Boccaccio) had a title page that was taken from Burgkmair's Tragoedie von zwei liebenden Menschen, published in 1520. In addition, many small woodcuts are basically those that Scheifelin supplied for the Decameron.

Christoph Bruno's translation of [1120] Boccaccio's Romischer Geschichte, published in 1542 (150), is once again a remarkable mixture of woodcuts. The bulk of the illustrations dealing with siege weapons, etc., came from the Scanderbeg of 1533, and had been reused in the 1540 Xenophon. Nine woodcuts, Nos. 1, 12, 14, 15, 16, 20, 21, 22 and 23, came from various works illustrated by Burgkmair. Two bear Scheifelin's monogram; these come from the 1533 Thukydides and from the Memorial der Tugend of 1534. It is utterly incomprehensible how anyone (151) could attribute the 23 illustrations that Steiner assembled from his stock of woodblocks, as all having the characteristics of Scheifelin's illustrations.

Platina's book [1121] Von der eerlichenn ziemlichen und erlaubten Wollust des leibs in essen und trinken (152) was also published in 1542. One woodcut comes from the Weisskunig and many others come from Burgkmair's Petrarka. Three, which are 75 to 85 mm high and 112 mm wide, are by the younger Burgkmair. The many small (70 x 60 or 80 x 66) illustrations belong to the Scheifelin school.

In the 1543 edition of Boner's [1122] translation of Demosthenes, the title page illustration comes from the Theuerdank and the second from Burgkmair's Cicero, with only a change in the inscription.

In the same year Steiner printed the book compiled by Veit Traut [1123] on Türkischer Kaiser Ankunft, Krieg und Sieg wider die Christen. Most of the 14 smaller woodcuts are taken from the 1540 Xenophon while the last one, which is large, originally appeared in the Theuerdank.

The third book printed by Steiner in 1543 was [1124] Schöne chronica vom Königreich Hispanien (153), which was compiled by Jacobus Bracellus and Johannes Jovianus. It has 45 woodcuts. The two knights in armor on the verso of the title page appeared first in the Flavius Vegetius of 1529. Nos. 2, 3, 4, 23, 24, 30, 33, 34, 37 and 45 come from the Theuerdank; No. 17 is from Memorial der Tugend of 1534; No. 35 is from the Plutarch of 1534, as is No. 41. No. 20, which bears Scheifelin's monogram, first appeared in the 1533 Thukydides. All the above were by Scheifelin. From Burgkmair's Cicero and his Petrarka there are No. 19, (with some question, No. 21), and Nos. 25, 26, 29, 32, 36, 38, 39, 43 and 44. All the rest come from the Scanderbeg, and there is not a single new woodcut in the book.

A more uniform treatment is found in the 1544 edition of Ludovico Vives' [1125] Von gebührlichem Thun und lassen eines Ehemannes (154). In this case all thirteen of the woodcuts came from Burgkmair's Glücksbuch.

The book by Ludovico Vives [1126], also printed in the same year, Unterweysung einer christlichen Frauen (155), had 24 woodcuts. Fifteen of these: Nos. 3-6, 10-14, 17 and 19-23, came from Burgkmair's Glücksbuch. No. 24 came from the Theuerdank and No. 2 is attributable to Scheifelin. Nos. 1, 7, 15, 16 and 18 appear to be new.

In 1545 he published Hieronymus Ziegler's German translation [1127] of Boccaccio's Fürnehmsten Historien und Exempel von widerwärtigem Glück grossmächter Kaiser (156). Most of the illustrations came from Burgkmair and from Scheifelin. The only new woodcuts in the book are the coat of arms of Beckh von Beckhenstein and, possibly, that on leaf 186.

The woodcuts [1128] in Colloquia Erasmi, also published in 1545, were largely taken from Burgkmair and Scheifelin.

Those in the 1547 edition [1129] of Melusine (157) are new, but worthless.

Steiner's last illustrated book, which appeared in 1548, was [1130] Von den adelischen Tugenden--Ritter Pontus und Sidonia, which has mostly old Scheifelin woodcuts.

This ended Steiner's activities. He died in 1548. Much of his printing apparatus as well as his woodblocks went to Frankfurt, to the plant of Chr. Egenolphs, who used Burgkmair's and Scheifelin's woodblocks countless additional times.

Thus, after 1535 book illustration in Augsburg came to a halt and the new illustrations produced were worthless. The art rested on the great achievements of the past and on Heinrich Steiner, who in one sense brought Augsburg to its high point in printing, but who also built the basis for its rapid decline.

Notes

1) Zapf, Augsburgs Buchdruckergeschichte nebst den Jahrbüchern derselben. Part II, From 1501-1530. Augsburg, 1791; Panzer, Ausführliche Beschreibung der altesten Augsburgischen Ausgaben der Bibel. Nuremberg, 1780.

2) Panzer I:335.

3) Weller, No. 849.

4) Weller, No. 799.

5) Weller, No. 760.

6) Weller, No. 881.

7) Panzer, Suppl:195, No. 995e. Folio.

8) Weller, No. 1369. The 1522 edition is not listed in Weller; German. Mus. 1274.

9) Weller, No. 1708, the edition of 1521; Panzer I:435, No. 972, the edition of 1520.

10) Lacking in Panzer and in Weller.

11) Panzer II:176. Quarto.

12) Weller, No. 2067.

13) Weller, No. 2591. Octavo.

14) Panzer VI:145, No. 88.

15) Panzer VI:132, No. 10; Reproduced in Butsch, Bücherornamentik. V. 1, Plate 18.

16) Panzer VI:132, No. 12.

17) Panzer VI:132, No. 13.

18) Panzer I:266.

19) Panzer, Beschreibung der Augsburger Bibeln, No. 19; Panzer, Annalen I:275; Vogt, 135.

20) Panzer, Beschreibung der Augsburger Bibeln, No. 20; Panzer, Annalen I:410.

21) Weller, No. 395.

22) Weller, No. 464.

23) Panzer, Suppl. 109; Zapf II:36; Choulant, p. 254, No. 22; Weller, No. 4074.

24) Panzer I:320.

25) Weller, No. 611, 612 and 613.

26) Ebert, No. 1238. Folio; Panzer I:327, No. 689.

27) Panzer VI:139, No. 57.

28) Weller, No. 634.

29) Panzer, No. 687.

30) Panzer I:338, No. 710.

31) Weller, No. 806.

32) Weller, No. 761.

33) Weller, No. 847.

34) Weller, No. 848.

35) Panzer I:364.

36) Weller, No. 795.

37) Panzer I:376.

38) Weller, No. 1098.

39) Weller, No. 1233.

40) Weller, No. 1322.

41) Weller, No. 1554.

42) Panzer, Suppl:182, No. 974kk; Rotermund, No. 58.

43) Panzer, Suppl:179.

44) Weller, No. 2086.

45) Weller, No. 2096.

46) Weller, No. 1522.

47) Panzer II, No. 1614, 1615 and 1616. Folio; Panzer, Beschreibung der Augsburger Bibeln, No. 27, 28, 29 and 40; Panzer, Entwurf einer Geschichte der Luther schen Bibelübersetzung, p. 91-93. Zapf II:163ff; Weigel, No. 6775.

48) Panzer, Beschreibung der Augsburger Bibeln, No. 30, 41 and 43. Folio.

49) Weller, No. 3366.

50) Weller, No. 391.

51) Weller, No. 442.

52) Panzer I:321.

53) Lacking in Panzer.

54) Weller, No. 535.

55) Weller, No. 730.

56) Panzer I:339, No. 711.

57) Panzer I:373.

58) Weller, No. 1003.

59) Panzer I:293, No. 613.

60) Weller, No. 1067.

61) Weller, No. 1552; Panzer, Suppl:172.

62) Panzer, Suppl:171.

63) Panzer, Suppl:169.

64) Panzer, Suppl:177.

65) Panzer, Suppl:176.

66) Weller, No. 1706.

67) Panzer I:381.

68) Becker, Lit. p. 277. Quarto; Panzer VI:146, No. 94.

69) Weller, No. 1060.

70) Panzer I:422.

71) Panzer VI:157, No. 181.

72) Panzer II:58; Panzer, Beschreibung der Augsburgischen Bibeln, No. 23.

73) Panzer II:131; Panzer, Beschreibung der Augsburgischen Bibeln, No. 24.

74) Weller, No. 2673.

75) Weller, No. 3122.

76) Weller, No. 3109.

77) Lacking in Panzer.

78) Weller, No. 701.

79) Weller, No. 778.

80) Weller, No. 857.

81) Panzer I:363.

82) Panzer I:368.

83) Panzer, Suppl:133, No. 817c. Quarto.

84) Weller, No. 1954.

85) Weller, No. 1040.

86) Weller, No. 1704.

87) Weigel, No. 20085. Quarto.

88) Weller, No. 4086.

89) Weller, No. 2107.

90) Weller, No. 1393.

91) Weller, No. 1687.

92) Weller, No. 2610.

93) Weller, No. 4104.

94) Panzer I:329, No. 691.

95) Panzer I:316.

96) Panzer I:303.

97) Panzer I:304. Quarto.

98) Weller, No. 537.

99) Panzer I:421.

100) Panzer I:419, No. 915. Quarto.

101) Panzer, Suppl:194, No. 995d. Quarto.

102) Panzer, No. 995. Quarto.

103) Weller, No. 1610. Quarto.

104) Weller, No. 2442.

105) Weller, No. 2786. Octavo.

106) Panzer II:242, No. 2116. Octavo.

107) Weller, No. 2979. Octavo.

108) Weller, No. 3126.

109) Veith, Karl, Ueber den Barfüsser Joh. Pauli und das von ihm verfasste Volksbuch, "Schimpf und Ernst," nebst 46 Proben aus demselben. Vienna, 1839. Octavo.

110) Weller, No. 4030.

111) Panzer, Beschreibung der Augsburger Bibeln, No. 47 and 48.

112) Panzer, Beschreibung der Augsburger Bibeln, No. 49. Folio.

113) Choulant, "Die botanischen und anatomischen Abbildungen des Mittelalters." In Naumanns Archiv III:277, 1857.

114) Folio.

115) Panzer, Beschreibung der Augsburger Bibeln, No. 61. Quarto.

116) Germ. Mus. Quarto.

117) Germ. Mus., No. 3366. Quarto.

118) Germ. Mus., No. 11847. Quarto.

119) For an example of this in Stuttgart, see: Pfeiffer, "Altdeutsche Kochbücher." Serapeum IX:280.

120) Ebert, No. 9536. Folio.

121) Ebert, No. 11169.

122) German Mus., No. 2504. Quarto.

123) German Mus., No. 29022.

124) German Mus., No. 6500. Quarto.

125) Weigel, No. 19438, cf. No. 12857. Quarto.

126) Ebert, No. 16476; Weigel, No. 1875, 3499, 1776, 6777, 7780, 7781, 18376.

127) Panzer, Beschreibung der Augsburgischen Bibeln, No. 63. Folio.

128) Germ. Mus., No. 786. Quarto.

129) Germ. Mus., No. 9660.

130) Not listed in bibliographical tools. Germ. Mus., No. 618.

131) Not listed in bibliographical works. Germ. Mus., No. 830.

132) Weigel, No. 18792.

133) Not listed in bibliographical works. Germ. Mus., No. 1063.

134) Panzer, Beschreibung der Augsburger Bibeln, No. 65. Large folio.

135) Ebert, No. 4680. Folio; Heller's Albr. Dürer II:1031; Heller's Supplement to Bartsch, p. 38; Weigel, No. 17894 and No. 20787b; Nagler XV:111.

136) Weigel, No. 13357, 19441, 20768; Lappenberg, Murner's Ulenspiegel, p. 369-375; Ebert, No. 15997; Heinecken, Dict. des artistes. III:461; Steiner published nine editions of the book: 1526; 1534; 1535; 1536; 1537; 1542; 1544; and 1546; and s.a.

137) Quarto.

138) Weigel, No. 10927. Octavo.

139) Ebert, No. 23457. Folio; Weigel, No. 17893.

140) Panzer, Beschreibung der Augsburger Bibeln, No. 66.

141) Panzer, Beschreibung der Augsburger Bibeln, No. 67. Octavo.

142) Ebert, No. 9563; Heyse, Bücherschatz, No. 244.

143) Ebert, No. 5778. Folio; Weigel, No. 3496 and 20095b; Nagler, XV:111 (second edition 1540).

144) Heyse, Bücherschatz, No. 1794. Folio.

145) Ebert, No. 23519; Weigel, No. 8509 and 18383; Nagler, XV:111 (second edition 1544)

146) Der hochgelörtesten Philosophen und Hauptmanns Xenophontis Commentaria und Beschreibung von dem Peloponnenskrieg, übersetzt, von H. Boner; Ebert, No. 24147. Folio; Weigel, No. 19436.

147) Weigel, No. 13365. Folio; Nagler XV:112.

148) Ebert, No. 16477. Folio; Weigel, No. 7781, 8508, 20071 and 20769.

149) Quarto.

150) Weigel, No. 18374; Nagler XV:112.

151) "Rosenberg" by Dohme. In Kunst und Künstler Deutschlands u. d. Nederlande. I.

152) Weigel, No. 17898. Folio.

153) Nagler XV:112. Folio.

154) Weigel, No. 9937 and 18387. Folio. Nagler XV:111.

155) Weigel, Same as note 154.

156) Clement, Biblioth curieuse IV:243; Weigel, No. 19437; Nagler XV:112. Folio.

157) Weigel, No. 19439. Quarto.

Chapter XVIII

NUREMBERG (1)

As compared with the large scale production of book illustrations in Augsburg, Nuremberg's seems almost meager. The minor Nuremberg artists who lived contemporaneously with Dürer were not nearly as zealous as those of Augsburg, and none of them produced enough to be compared with Burgkmair or Scheifelin. All these artists applied their skill to book illustration only rarely, and practically by chance.

Hans Springinklee, who next to Dürer was the most significant of the artists who worked for the Nuremberg printers, did his first book illustrations in 1515, when he made some of the illustrations for the _Weisskunig_.

His private work for the Nuremberg printers began in 1516.

Wilhelm Schaffner published the first edition of the beloved prayer book, _Hortulus animae_, in Strassburg in 1498. The publication of such _Hortuli_ became the speciality of the Nuremberg publisher Johann Koburger from 1516 on. He had some of them done by Nuremberg printers and some by Johann Clein in Lyon. In 1516 [1131-1132] Johann Stüchs in Nuremberg completed a German edition (2) and Johann Clein did one in Latin (3).

The woodcuts are the same in both these editions; there are 83 of them in three different formats. The largest are 90 x 67 mm, the medium size 75 x 57 mm, and the small ones are 60 x 48 mm. Only the large and the small ones are new; the medium-size group had previously been used in a _Hortulus_ that Johann Clein had printed on his own in 1513, and these were done by an artist who had not yet freed himself of the fifteenth century style. Of the large illustrations, three bear Springinklee's monogram and one bears the monogram of another artist. Since the remaining large illustrations agree completely in style with the three that bear his monogram, the rest of the large illustrations may be attributed to Springinklee.

With regard to the small woodcuts, Springinklee's monogram, to be sure, does not appear on any of them, but they match his large ones so precisely in style that one is forced to the conclusion that he did them. In addition to the large and small illustrations, the title page woodcut should also be attributed to him. It is reproduced in Weigel's _Holzschnitten berühmter Meister_. In this book Springinklee appears as an artist who has not yet developed his own individual style; there is a good deal in his work that reminds one of Scheifelin. The 1517 [1133] edition reuses the same woodcuts (4).

In 1517 Springinklee [1134] worked on illustration of the _Eichstaedter Missale_. The woodcut that is most clearly attributable to him is one that was earlier attributed to Dürer. It is the 285 x 200 mm full figure of Saint Willibald in standing position. In addition to this one, the large and figure-filled initial letters appear to be attributable to him.

Two years later we see his splendid illustrations [1135, Pl. 206-207] for the Latin _Hortulus_ that Koburger had printed by Friedrich Peypus in Nuremberg (5). This Hortulus, revised by Neudorffer, was supplied by Springinklee with its figures and decorations. He prepared a total of 37 new woodcuts, all bearing his monogram, for this work. They were 118 x 83 mm, but are primarily differentiated from other woodcuts in the book, aside from their size, by the fact that they all bear his large monogram and that the base is part of the woodcut. All the (90 x 67) woodcuts that merely have border ornaments and have no base, as well as the smaller ones, (60 x 48), are taken from the 1516 edition; thus, some of these are by Springinklee. A few that are still smaller come from Schoen's Hortulus of 1517, which will be described later. The last illustration does not belong to this work but was taken from a fifteenth century book.

Nagler's very complex question on which of the illustrations in the Nuremberg and Lyon editions of the Hortulus can be attributed to Springinklee, really solves itself very easily. There were two Hortuli for which Springinklee prepared illustrations. The first of these appeared in 1516, printed by Stüchs in Nuremberg in German, and in Latin by Clein in Lyon. Each of these contains the same 53 woodcuts by this artist. Of these, one is 90 x 67 mm and the others are 68 x 48 mm. For a second Latin Hortulus, which Koburger had printed by Friedrich Peypus, he supplied 37 new woodcuts (118 x 83), all of which bear his monogram, and which are of much greater artistic merit than those done for the 1516 edition. Thus the grand total of drawings he did for the Hortuli was 90. The other editions of the Hortulus that were produced in Nuremberg in 1517, 1518, 1519, and 1520 contain no other new woodblocks--just the 90 done by Springinklee, those in Schön's Hortulus of 1517, and those from the old Lyon Hortulus of 1513, in varying combinations.

The question of Springinklee's Bible woodcuts is just as confused as was that of the ones he did for the Hortuli.

The first Bible that has a title page illustration bearing his monogram is [1136, Pl. 208-210] the Lyon Bible of 1520 (6). This woodcut is 250 x 162 mm. Aside from his large woodcut, some of the smaller ones (60 x 87) appear to be his and some of these had previously been used in the 1518 Lyon Bible.

None of the settings or scenes is particularly original, all having come from the 1511 Venetian edition of the Vulgate. The intention was merely to follow the series of illustrations therein done by Leonardus Lauredanus, reproducing these on a somewhat larger scale. This artist was supposed to follow the circumstances illustrated in the Venetian edition for the 1520 Lyon edition, but handling them in his freer and more attractive style. This cycle, supplied by Springinklee, was reused in all the later Lyon Old Testament Vulgate editions until Holbein, later, received an assignment from the Trechsel Brothers to develop a completely new series of illustrations.

The 1521 edition of the Vulgate, printed in Lyon by M. Jac. Sacon at the expense of A. Koburger, still bears Springinklee's monogram on the title pages of both the Old and the New Testaments, that for the Old Testament being 137 x 180 mm, and that for the New Testament 207 x 175 mm. The former bears his monogram on the tree trunk to the right and the latter has it on the stone slab at the left. The woodcut for the New Testament is one of the artist's most important works, and it was the last one he did for a printer in Lyon (8).

When, in 1524, Peypus in Nuremberg [1137] printed his Bibel, das alte Testament mit Fleiss verdeutscht mit Vorrede M. Luthers (9), he reassembled these Springinklee illustrations, adding eight of the small woodcuts that were not used in the Lyon Bible. It is apparent that these eight woodcuts were prepared for the Lyon edition but for some unknown reason were omitted. The number of small woodcut illustrations prepared for the Old Testament by Springinklee totalled 88.

The Hortulus animae and the Bibel are the only two books for which Springinklee made substantial contributions.

We have only one other woodcut that he prepared in this period, a relatively unimportant title page illustration [1138] in the Perornata eademque verissima D. Christophori Descriptio Theobaldo Billicano Autore (10). This book appeared s. l. e. a. His monogram appears on a column at the right.

The series of the 12 Apostles in a 1539 book [1139] titled, Zwellf hauptartikel des christlichen Glaubens, genannt der 12 Apostel Symbolus sammt drei anderen Symbolis für die Leyen und Einfältigen, "Printed at Nuremberg by Milchthaler, 1539," does have some Springinklee woodcuts, but there is nothing new in it; all of his woodcuts come from the Hortulus animae.

The total of Springinklee woodcuts for book illustration is some 200; with a small, indeterminate number in the Weisskunig, 90 in the Hortulus and 91 in the Bibel.

The second Nuremberg artist, Erhard Schön, is as little known biographically as is Springinklee.

He did his earliest wood carving [1140, Pl. 212] for the Hortulus animae. Here, too, there has been confusion because later editions were cited as those for which Schön provided his first woodcuts. The first Hortulus that Schön illustrated was the one in twelvemo which was produced by Clein in Lyon in 1517 (11). To be sure, not all the illustrations in this edition were by Schön. The woodcuts in the 1517 edition that fill the full width of the page are taken from Springinklee's Hortulus of 1516; and those that fill the full page come from Clein's Hortulus of 1513. However, these represent only a small percentage of the total. The 58 woodcuts that are 65 x 55 mm are all by Schön. Six of the woodcuts bear his monogram. These woodcuts, in somewhat smaller numbers, were repeated in practically every later edition. The Lyon Hortulus of 1518 has three illustrations bearing Schön's monogram and the Peypus edition of 1519 has five.

After a long interlude he completed the (260 x 165) large title page woodcut for the second part of Peypus' [1141, Pl. 211] Bibel of 1524 (12). It bears his monogram on the lower right.

These 59 illustrations make up the total of Schön's contribution to book illustration that is extant. The architectural drawings that Schön did in the closing years of his life (1538-1547) cannot be considered book illustration.

The third artist in this circle was Sebald Beham, who like the others, did not, in his Nuremberg period (to 1530), do very much in the way of book illustration.

The first woodcut signed with his monogram is the title page illustration [1142] in the poem by Hans Sachs, Ein Gespräch zwischen St. Peter und dem Herrn von der jetzigen Welt lauf (13).

In 1526 he illustrated [1143, Pl. 213] Das Babstum mit seynen gliedern gemalet und beschryben, gebessert und gemehrt (14), which was published by the Nuremberg printer Hans

Wandereisen. After his title page illustration of the Pope, each following page had two pictures of men who are either spiritual leaders or members of the various Orders, and each illustration is accompanied by a brief description and a few verses. In all there are 74 figures. The fact that the verses are sharply polemical and the whole thing is a satire on the Papacy is not indicated in any way by the illustrations.

This is all we have of Sebald Beham's work in book illustration during his Nuremberg period. He concentrated on the study of proportions and in 1528 he issued the famous [1144] Buchlein von dem mass oder den proporcion der Ross nutzlich jungen gesellen, malern und goltschmied (15) which originally was alleged to be plagiarism from manuscripts stolen from Dürer.

His next work did not appear until 1530, in [1145] Auslegung der Evangelien, which was published by Eck in Ingolstadt. He shared the 41 drawings for this book with Ostendorfer and the artist L. B.

Aside from these three artists of Dürer's circle, there were few who were involved in book illustration in Nuremberg.

The lettering artist Hans Guldenmundt, who carried on a lively business in letters, documents and pictures, also got involved in book printing, and he published Hans Sachs' [1146] Wunderliche Weissagung von dem Papsthum (16), which is tinged with strong feeling for reform. It is illustrated with 30 (110 x 75) woodcuts which are all simple yet capably done.

The wood carver Wolfgang Resch printed, during his later years, a number of poems by Hans Sachs, with title page illustrations. In the poem by Sachs, published in 1530, [1147] All römisch Kaiser nach ordnung von dem ersten bis auf Kaiser Karl (17), the first illustration is a (130 x 110) bust of Kaiser Karl, which is on the title page. The woodcut on the last page (140 x 102) has the monogram "W. R. F."

In 1531 Resch printed [1148] Sachs' Klagred der Welt ob yhrem verderben. The title page woodcut is 138 x 120 mm.

The third poem by Sachs to be published by Resch [1149] is undated but it was also issued around this same time. It was the Nachred das greulich Laster. It has a very attractive title page woodcut that is 138 x 142 mm.

The calligrapher Niclas Meldemann prepared one title page woodcut to go with [1150] a poem by Hans Sachs published in 1531, Klag Antwort und urteyl zwischen Fraw Armuth und Pluto der Gott der Reichthumb, welches unter yhm das pesser sey (18).

There are few monograms of other artists to be found in Nuremberg publications. Nagler gives the monogram "W. T." as referring to Wolfgang Traut. This occurs next to the monogram of the wood carver in the Missale Pataviense (19), which was published in 1514 by Jobst Gutknecht. The woodcut is in Dürer's style, and perhaps it was modelled after one of his.

The monogram "o Wo" is found in the medium size woodcut at the end of the 1513 folio Kalender, which was published by Wolfgang Huber. The monogram appears on the saddle blanket of a horse being ridden by a Knight. Since the title page woodcut is very similar to this one in style, it may, therefore, also be attributed to this artist, "W."

As in other cities the majority of illustrations can not be given any definite attribution.

The printing plant of Georg Stüchs, which he founded in 1484, was operated by him and then by his son, Johann, up to 1520.

Grünpeck's [1151] Spiegel der Trübsalen (20), which Georg Stüchs printed in 1508, had a title page woodcut illustration as well as a woodcut illustration at the head of each of the twelve chapters.

The title page woodcut in Peycht's [1152] Spiegel des Sünders (21), which he published in 1510, was the only illustration in that book. In 1514, Stüchs printed for the publisher Caspar Rosenthaler, in Schwaz in Tirol, [1153] Das Leben unseres erledigers Jesu Christi mit beilaufung des Lebens der Jungfrau Maria (22). On the verso of the title page there is a portrait of St. Francis; then there are 63 small and relatively unimportant woodcuts. The first of these is 62 x 47 mm; the second, 70 x 45 mm, and the rest are only 50 x 35 mm. Only two of these bear monograms; one has the letters "RV" and the other "RH."

The 1518 edition of [1154] Johannes Aventinus' Historia non vulgaris Otingae (23) has a small (60 x 43) woodcut on its title page. Also published in 1518 was [1155] Henricus Grammateus' Kaufmannsschaftsbuch (24), which Johann Stüchs printed for Lucas Alantsee, bookseller and citizen of Vienna. Not counting the well executed escutcheon of Johann Tscherte on the verso of the title page, the book has four (100 x 66) woodcuts.

In 1520 and 1521 there followed [1156-1161] poems by Hans Folz, with woodcut illustrated title pages. These included: the Frauenkrieg (25); Pfarrer im Loch (26); and Praktika (27) in 1520; and in 1521, the song Von einem Wirthsknecht und der Hausmagd (28); Von dem König Salomon und Marcolpho (29); and the Fast abenteuerlich klopfen auf meerlei art (30).

One of the first publications of the printing plant of Hieronymus Hölzel, which was started in 1500, was the [1162] Reformation der Kaiserlichen Stadt Nürnberg (31). The title page woodcut (255 x 180) does not indicate anything new since it was based on the one in the appendix to Koburger's original edition of 1484.

This was followed, in 1506, by [1163] an edition of Johann Andreae's Arbor consanguineitatis (32). Of its many woodcuts, the only one of any artistic interest is the (175 x 125) title page illustration which is in the old-fashioned tradition.

In 1512 Hölzel printed [1164] for the publishing house of Kaspar Rosenthaler, Bonaventura's Legende des heiligen Vaters Francisci (33). It has 54 woodcuts which, with the exception of a few larger ones, are 80 x 100 mm. There is no artist's monogram anywhere, but the dates 1511 and 1512 appear on a few illustrations. The title page woodcut is 137 x 113 mm and the second illustration is even larger (150 x 120). The woodcuts are competent works but they seem to be the result of routine handicraft rather than the work of an artist.

In 1514 Hölzel printed two other works with title page illustrations. One was the [1165, Pl. 213] Historie des Lebens, Sterbens und Wunderwerks S. Sebalds (34), the (175 x 125) title page woodcut of which was at one time attributed to Dürer. The other 1514 publication was the Türkenschlachts (35), the title page illustration of which is not important.

In a later period Hölzel printed [1166] Von den sieben Geistern oder Engeln (36), by Johann von Trittenheim (Trithemius). The title page woodcut (125 x 105) gives a bust of Karl V. The woodcut is attractive and it could have been the work of a major artist.

In 1523 there followed [1167] L. Rynmann's Practica über die grosse Conjunction der Planeten (37), which had a title page woodcut illustration.

More illustrated books were published by Friedrich Peypus, who began printing in 1512, than were done by Stüchs and by Hölzel.

In 1514 he produced [1168] Lehre und Vermahnung Gott zu dienen (38), which has a woodcut illustration on the verso of the title page, as well as the Walfahrt der Pilgerin (39), which has an illustration on the verso of the title page.

In 1515, Peypus published [1169] Vierzig lateinische Sendbriefe aus dem Latein in deutsch gezogen von Chr. Scheurl (40), with two woodcuts. The one that is 170 x 120 mm was attributed to Dürer in earlier times, but Bartsch disagrees and Heller lists it as doubtful. The smaller woodcut, on the last page, is 125 x 100 mm. This one too appears to have come from Dürer or his circle.

Leonhard Reynmann's [1170-1172] Strass zu Glück und Heil (41) was printed by Peypus in 1515 with an illustrated title page, as was Tallat's Margarita Medicinae of 1516 (42). His Wurzgärtlein (43), issued in 1516, was somewhat more richly illustrated.

His edition of [1173, Pl. 214] Nutzbarliches Büchlein von endlicher Erfüllung göttlicher Fürsehung (44), by Johann Staupitz, which he printed in 1517, had a handsome (110 x 85) title page woodcut.

In [1174] a Latin Hortulus animae which he issued in 1519 (45), Peypus provides as assembly of earlier woodcuts. Those that are 60 x 50 mm came from Springinklee for Stüchs' Hortulus of 1516; those with interlaced ornaments (64 x 55) were done by Schoen for Clein's Hortulus of 1517; those that are 70 x 50 mm come from Clein's first Hortulus of 1513. Among the larger woodcuts are the (90 x 70) ones by Springinklee for Stüch's Hortulus of 1516, and the 120 x 80 mm illustrations were done by Springinklee for the Peypus Hortulus of 1518. There is nothing new in the 1519 Latin edition. Among the 75 woodcuts there are three that have Springinklee's monogram and five which have Schoen's monogram.

In [1175] the German Hortulus of 1519 the same woodcuts are used as were used in the Latin edition of 1518.

The [1176] Hortulus of 1520 also offers nothing new.

In 1520 Peypus [1177-1178] printed Luther's Sermon vom Neuen Testament (46), which has a representation of the Mass on the last page; and his sermon, Von Guten Werken (47), which has a representation of Christ on the Cross on its title page.

In his 1522 publication [1179] Biblia sacra utriusque testamenti cum praef. Andr. Osiandri (48) he used on the fifth sheet (Genesis) the woodcut of the Creation of Eve that Springinklee prepared for the Lyon Bible of 1521.

His 1523 new edition of this [1180] Bibel (49) has on its title page the Hieronymous that Springinklee did for the Lyon Bible of 1520.

The 1523 edition [1181] of Chistenlich nutzbarlich Betpüchlein mit dem auszug der heiligen Evangelien (50) contains two Springinklee woodcuts that have been reused from his illustrations for the Hortulus... (see Bartsch No. 8).

Peypus' [1182] 1524 Bibel (51) is likewise illustrated by an assembly of old woodcuts, with the exception of the eight small Springinklee woodcuts which have already been noted. In the Old Testament the Springinklee Hieronymus, which had been used in the 1520 edition, is on the title page; his 1521 "Creation of Eve" is repeated here at the beginning of Genesis. Sixty-two of the small (60 x 87) woodcuts are reused from the Lyon Bible of 1521, and the third part of the 1524 Bibel uses a number of woodcuts from Springinklee's Hortulus group. The illustrations on folios 82, 122, 123, 126, 132 and 134 bear his monogram.

In [1183] the Psalter deutsch zu singen (52) the fourth page repeats the woodcut of David praying.

The [1184] Biblia Sacra utriusque Testamenti (53) of 1530 uses the rest of the small woodcuts originally prepared by Springinklee or Schoen, and, in addition, has repeated Dürer's large woodcut from the Reformation Nürnberg's.

In 1531 Peypus printed [1185] Johannes Schoener's Conjectur über die Planeten (54), and, finally, in 1532 he issued [1186] Die Propheten alle deutsch (55), with a title page illustration.

Among the smaller printers, there was Wolfgang Huber, who practically never went beyond a title page woodcut in illustrating a book. His first book [1187] was issued in 1505 under the title, Von der Region der neuen Welt (56).

The title page illustration of the book he published [1188] in 1509, Versehung von Leib, Seel, Ehre und Gut (57), was 130 x 85 mm and is the same as that in earlier editions.

In 1510 he issued [1189-1194], with title page woodcuts, the songs: Maria Zart (58); Contz Zwerg (59); Fronika, wie sie von Hyerusalem gen Rom ist kommen (60); Ritter Gottfried, wie er sein Weib Sträft (61); Königin von Frankreich (62); as well as the booklet, Der Segen des starcken Poppen, dadurch er selig ist worden (63).

The little book Ecken Ausfahrt, of 1512 (64), is richly supplied with woodcuts, while the other products of the year [1195-1198] have only title page woodcuts. These other works are: Lied von dem Kauffmann, der dem Jüden ein pfundt Schmerbs aus seiner seytten versetzet (65); as well as the booklet, Rosenkranz unsrer lieben Frauen (66); and Scheidung unserer lieben Frauen (67).

In 1513 [1199-1200] Huber produced the Lied von dem Kunig Lasla (68) and in 1514 the Lied von den schnoden Mannen, die do sitzen in brass und wollen nit dannen (69). These, too, had only title page woodcuts.

Adam Dyon, who later moved to Breslau, issued [1201-1202] three publications which he supplied with title page woodcut illustrations. These were: Lied von der Kröte (70) in 1509; Graf von Rom (71) and the Krämer Christi (72) both of which were published in 1510.

Johann Weissenburger, who later moved to Landshut, produced two richly illustrated books that have survived. These are the [1203-1204], Büchlein vom Sterben (73), which had twelve woodcuts, and the Tractätlein vom sterbenden Menschen, with five woodcuts. Both of these were published in 1509.

His other products have title page illustrations only. These include the 1509 edition [1205] of Manuale parrochialium sacerdotum (75) which has a 127 x 97 mm title page woodcut, and the 1510 publications: [1206-1209] Betrachtung der Stunden des Tods (76); the Traum des Aeneas Silvius, dass er in das Reich der Kunigin Frawgluck kommen (77); and the 1512 publications:

Lied von dem Leben der heiligen Jungfrau Katharina (78); and Ordnung und Unterweissung, wie sich ein Jeder soll halten vor dem Rechten (79).

In the 1512 edition [1210] of Wahrhaftiger Sag von dem Rock Jesu Christi zu Trier, which was printed by Johannes Adelphus, there is a 92 x 92 mm title page woodcut. In the same year, he printed [1211, Pl. 214] Strabus' Hortulus nuper apud Helvetios in S. Galli monasterio repertus (80), which has a title page illustration by an important painter (99 x 127).

Ulrich Pinter printed [1212] the Rosenkranz Mariae in 1505; the Speculum passionis in 1507 and the Bruderschaft St. Ursulä (81) in 1513. There is a woodcut on the verso of the title page and one at the close.

Pinter's [1213] Ursulaschifflein of 1515 (82) has four woodcuts in the text in addition to its title page woodcut.

A whole series of brochures, each supplied with a title page woodcut, was issued by Jobst Gutknecht. In 1515 [1214-1221] he issued: the song of Grafen von Rom (83); the Ablassbüchlein (84); the Historia von Phyloconio (85); Kolb's Neujahrsbüchlein (86); the Lied vom edlen Moringer (87); Vom Tannhauser (88); Ritter von Steyermark (89); and the Segen des Poppens (90).

The 1516 [1222-1227] edition of Sphera materialis, by Joh. von Sacrobusco (91), has 26 woodcuts of astronomical subjects. The Brandenburgische Halsgerichtsordnung (92), of the same year, is a reprint of the Bamberg edition of 1507 including the title page woodcut. In 1517 there followed the Franciscan Nicolaus Wankel's Vermerkung der Städte des heiligen Landes (93); Sibillä Weissagung (94); Tallat's Margarita medicinae (95) and H. Langenstain's Spiegel der Seele (96); and, in 1518, the Tractat von Herzog Gottfried (97).

The year 1519 was especially rich. The title page illustration of the book by Wenzeslaus Link, [1228] Wie der grobe Mensch unsers Herrn Esel sein soll (98), is 62 x 50 mm. In the octavo [1229] Exercitium spirituale hominis ecclesiastici (99), a woodcut illustration on the verso of the title page bears Springinklee's monogram. However, the woodcut is not new, but is copied from Peypus' 1518 Hortulus animae, and the cutting is very crude.

Other title page woodcuts occur in [1230-1232] the Geistlich arztbüchlein vom fünften Psalm Maria (100); the Briefsteller wie man einem jeglichen Fürsten schreiben soll (101) and the song, Von einem Apfel und dem Leiden Christi (102).

The year 1520 [1233-1252] was even richer in such small brochures. These included a Briefsteller (103); the Geistliche Hausmagd (104); the Histori vom Grafen Alexander zu dem Pflug (105); Nunnenpeck's Meistergesang von der Zerstörung Troias (106); as well as a whole series of songs: about Leiden Christi (107); Königin von Asion (108); Nero (109); Reichen Bauer (110); Uppigen Bauer (111); Bauernwunsch (112); Bauernkalender (113); Aergerniss (114); of Evangelischer Lehre (115); Maienzeit (116); Graffen von Saffoy (117); of a Hausmagd (118); Hildebrand (119); of a Kaufmann (120); Falschen Marschall (121); Falscher Buhlschaft (122); and so forth.

A very interesting book followed in 1521 [1253] with the superscript: Die geystlich Strass bin ich genannt, Im Leyden Christi wohl bekannt (123). The woodcuts that represent the seventeen stations are all a full page in size and, characteristically, the figures are all in decorated surroundings and stand on decorated wall columns. They are 160 mm high and the pedestal always uses two-thirds of this space, with the figure only one-third of the height.

In addition, in 1521, there were many booklets with title page illustrations [1254-1256] such as: Folz's Frauenkrieg (124); the Historie von Weyda (125); Wenck's Lied von den bosen Weyben, wie man die ziehen soll (126); and others.

[1257] Folz's Fastnachtsspiel (127) of 1521, includes a title page illustrating a farmer's wedding and the final achievement of the bedding of the pair. Bonaventura's Psalter Maria (128), published in the same year, has an illustration on the verso of the title page. From 1522 we have only one book with an illustrated title page, [1258] Historie von Griselde (129).

The woodcuts in [1259] Gutknecht's Plenarium (130) are 62 x 50 mm and were not originally intended for this book. The first illustration in the book is only 50 x 50 mm. The drawings are quite unimportant and the carving is crude.

The last books printed by Gutknecht [1260-1262] were Schrick's Abhandlung von den gebrannten Wassern (131) in 1523 and the two books printed in 1526: Das Lied von Gott (132) and Luther's Tedeum (133).

The 1523 edition of [1263] Form und Gestalt der 23 Schloss, so der schwäbische Bund hat eingenommen und verbrannt (134), which was printed by Hans Wandereisen, had 23 illustrations (325 x 210). These illustrations are very crude and are of historical interest only, rather than of artistic interest.

The series of illustrated books issued by Hans Hergott began in 1524 [1264] with his reprinting of Das neue Testament, deutsch Martin Luther (135). The title page illustration is a woodcut occupying the entire page. There is a small woodcut at the beginning of Matthew. There is one at the end of the Apostles and one on the verso of this sheet which represents Peter and Paul. The Apocalypse has the usual 21 individual octavo-page-filling figures; they were not, however, copied from the original Wittenberg edition, but from some later one.

In 1525, Hergott printed [1265] Johannes von Schwarzenberg's Beschwerung der alten teuflischen Schlangen mit dem göttlichen Wort (136). It has ten (95 x 95) woodcuts, which are not bad.

Luther's [1266] Prophet Jona ausgelegt, which Hergott printed in 1526, in octavo, has only a woodcut of four angels holding an escutcheon.

In 1526 Hergott did another octavo edition of [1267] the Neuen Testamentes (137). The title page woodcut and the other illustrations are the same as those in the 1524 edition, as are the 21 full-page woodcuts for the Apocalypse.

After Hans Hergott's death his wife, Frau Kunigund Hergottin, continued the printing operation.

In 1531 she printed [1268] an octavo edition of Das Alt Testament, deutsch mit viel schönen Figuren (138). The woodcuts, which are spoken of very highly in the preface, are most unimportant and could not make any artistic impression because of their small size.

In addition we must mention a few books that can not be attributed to any known printer.

In a book that appeared in Nuremberg in 1512, [1269] Albrecht Hochmeisters von Preussen Vorstellung an päpstliche Heiligkeit den künstigen Schaden zu ermessen (139), there is a woodcut illustrated title page.

In the case of the poems of Hans Sachs, there are still some illustrations that require attribution. Included are: the (118 x 112) title page woodcut which appeared in [1270] Disputation zwischen einem Chorherrn und einem Schuhmacher (140), which was published in 1524 without place of publication; also, the title page woodcut (105 x 105) in [1271] Gesprach von den Scheinwerken der Gaystlichen, also published in 1524 without location; the title page woodcut of [1272] the Dialogus und Argument der Romanisten; the poem Frau Keuschheit, which has an illustration on the first leaf; and, finally [1273] the Lieder fur die Laien zu singen, published s. l. in 1526 and the (likewise s. l.) 1530 edition of the Lobspruch der Stadt Nürnberg.

The last great typographer of Nuremberg was Johann Petrejus, who only published one book within our period, the 1527 edition [1274] of Biblia sacra utriusque testamenti (141), which had only a title page woodcut.

Thus, Nuremberg was never as important as Augsburg in the development of book illustration. The old master of the Nuremberg painters, Albrecht Dürer, rarely applied his skill to book illustration, and then chiefly when he wished to befriend the author. Springinklee worked practically only for Koburger, for his books printed in Lyon as well as in Nuremberg. He supplied some ninety illustrations for the Hortulus animae and another ninety for the Vulgate. Erhard Schön's activities were tied mostly to the Lyon printer, Johann Clein, for whom he supplied 58 illustrations. He did only one title page for Friedrich Peypus in Nuremberg. Sebald Behan really began working in this field in 1530, when he left Nuremberg. What he supplied here was the title page for Sachsen's Gesprach der Herrn mit St. Peter and the 74-leaf illustration cycle for Wandereisen's edition of Papstthum mit seinen Gliedern; and these were not in his usual style. Of the other artists of this period, Guldenmundt, Resch, Meldemann and Wolfgang Traut may be named, but there was a large number of book illustrations by unfamiliar artists, none of whom was very important artistically.

Notes

1) For the minor Nuremberg artists there is a little information in Joseph Baader's "Beiträge zur Kunstgeschichte Nürnbergs." In Jahrbüchern für kunstwissenschaft I:221 and II:73, 1868. For Hans Sebald Beham, see Rosenberg, Barthel und Sebald Beham. Leipzig, 1875.

2) Panzer I:387, No. 835. Octavo.

3) Panzer VII:457, No. 121. Octavo. As early as 1513 Clein had printed a Hortulus with 80 woodcuts, for Koburger; Weller, No. 782.

4) Weigel, No. 4889. Octavo; Panzer I:387, No. 835.

5) Weller, No. 1193; Panzer I:412, No. 892.

6) Biblia impressa Lugduni per Marion Exp. n. v. Antonii Koberger Nurembergensis 1520. Panzer, Annales typogr. VII:434.

7) Biblia cum concordantiis veteris et novi testamenti. Panzer VII:330, No. 447. Folio; Weigel III, No. 15477.

8) Die Lyoner Bibel von 1522. Folio; Panzer VII:332, No. 460 states that it has the same number of illustrations as the 1521 edition.

9) Ebert, No. 2172. Folio; Panzer II:240, No. 211.

10) See Weigel and Panzer.

11) The edition is very rare. There is a copy in the Munich State Museum, but it is not listed in Panzer VII:316ff.

12) Ebert, No. 2172. Folio. Panzer II:240, No. 211.

13) Not in Panzer; German. Museum.

14) Weller, No. 3730. Quarto; Weigel, No. 6785.

15) Heller, Beiträge p. 93-94; Weigel, No. 12246.

16) German. Museum No. 32691.

17) Weigel, II No. 12866 d. a. Frf. 1535. Quarto. The woodcut of Emperor Max was incorrectly described in Brulliot II, No. 2759.

18) Weigel, No. 12788. Quarto.

19) Panzer VII:455, No. 108.

20) Panzer I:289.

21) Panzer I:317, No. 966.

22) Printed in Nuremberg by Joh. Stüchs in C. Rosenthaler's shop; Panzer I:362, No. 768; Weigel IV, No. 17885.

23) Panzer VII:459, No. 137. Quarto.

24) Weller, No. 1114. Octavo. Repeated as No. 1528.

25) Weller, No. 1377.

26) Weller, No. 1380.

27) Weller, No. 1381.

28) Panzer II:51.

29) Panzer II:51.

30) Panzer II:52.

31) Panzer I:262, No. 539. Folio. Will I(2):5, No. 955.

32) Panzer VII:443, No. 29.

33) Panzer I:341, No. 717. Octavo. Weigel III, No. 16354; Hummel, Neue Bibl. I:1ff.

34) Panzer I:366, No. 777. Octavo. Bartsch, App. No. 19 und Heller, No. 53 (2023); also Dürer 3. Abthlg. p. 1021, No. 8 (58); Weigel, No. 18779.

35) Weller, No. 852.

36) Germ. Mus. No. 6305. Quarto.

37) Panzer II:234. Quarto.

38) Weller, No. 4077.

39) Panzer I:365, No. 775.

40) Panzer I:377, No. 810. Quarto; Heller 44:766 and 1022.

41) Panzer I:385, No. 829.

42) Panzer I:393, No. 849.

43) Weller, No. 987. Octavo.

44) Panzer I:340, No. 873.

45) Panzer VII:461, No. 148.

46) Panzer, Suppl:182.

47) Panzer, Suppl:181.

48) Panzer, Geschichte der Nürnbergischen Ausgaben der Bibel. Quarto.

49) Ibid. Quarto.

50) Panzer II:138, No. 1628. Small octavo.

51) Old Testament. Ebert 2172. Folio; Panzer II:240, No. 211; New Testament. Panzer II:245, No. 2129; Weigel II, No. 8525.

52) Panzer II:349, No. 2610.

53) Weigel, No. 8825. Folio.

54) Germ. Mus. No. 9888. Quarto.

55) Panzer, Geschichte der Nürnbergischen Ausgaben der Bibeln. Octavo.

56) Weller, No. 335.

57) Panzer, Suppl:111, No. 635e. Quarto.

58) Weller, No. 577.

59) Weller, No. 583.

60) Weller, No. 588.

61) Weller, No. 590.

62) Weller, No. 592.

63) Weller, No. 616.

64) Weller, No. 681. Octavo.

65) Weller, No. 706.

66) Weller, No. 734.

67) Weller, No. 736.

68) Weller, No. 787.

69) Weller, No. 840.

70) Weller, No. 501.

71) Weller, No. 567.

72) Weller, No. 571-572.

73) Weller, No. 478.

74) Weller, No. 513.

75) Panzer VII:447, No. 58. Quarto.

76) Weller, No. 533.

77) Weller, No. 618.

78) Weller, No. 713.

79) Weller, No. 727.

80) Panzer VII:451, No. 83. Quarto.

81) Panzer I:354, No. 752.

82) Panzer I:379, No. 812.

83) Weller, No. 569.

84) Weller, No. 875.

85) Weller, No. 896.

86) Weller, No. 902.

87) Weller, No. 916.

88) Weller, No. 919.

89) Weller, No. 920.

90) Weller, No. 944.

91) Panzer, Suppl:140, No. 860b. Quarto.

92) Panzer I:392.

93) Panzer I:406, No. 879.

94) Panzer I:404, No. 875.

95) Panzer I:407, No. 881.

96) Panzer I:401, No. 866.

97) Weller, No. 1153.

98) Panzer, p. 929. Quarto.

99) Not in Panzer VII:460ff.

100) Weller, No. 1162.

101) Weller, No. 1173.

102) Weller, No. 1206.

103) Weller, No. 1338.

104) Weller, No. 1398.

105) Weller, No. 1400.

106) Weller, No. 1607.

107) Weller, No. 1460.

108) Weller, No. 1462.

109) Weller, No. 1464.

110) Weller, No. 1466.

111) Weller, No. 1467.

112) Weller, No. 1468.

113) Weller, No. 1469.

114) Weller, No. 1470.

115) Weller, No. 1471.

116) Weller, No. 1472.

117) Weller, No. 1473.

118) Weller, No. 1475.

119) Weller, No. 1477.

120) Weller, No. 1481.

121) Weller, No. 1483.

122) Weller, No. 1484.

123) Panzer II:3. Quarto; Meusel, Neue Miscellaneen artist. Table of contents 12 and p. 476ff.

124) Weller, No. 1765.

125) Weller, No. 1783.

126) Weller, No. 1964.

127) Panzer II:51.

128) Panzer II:6.

129) Weller, No. 2240.

130) Panzer II:137, No. 1625.

131) Weller, No. 2679.

132) Weller, No. 3849.

133) Weller, No. 3867.

134) Panzer II:229, No. 2075. Folio.

135) Panzer, Geschichte der Nürnbergischen Ausgaben der Bibel. Octavo.

136) Panzer II:407, No. 2895. Quarto; Weller, No. 3637 and 3638.

137) Panzer, Geschichte der Nürnbergischen Ausgaben der Bibel.

138) Panzer, Geschichte der Nürnbergischen Ausgaben der Bibel.

139) Panzer I:343.

140) Weller, No. 3134; Heller. Dürer II:790.

141) Panzer VII:472, No. 236. Large octavo; and Geschichte der Nürnbergischen Ausgaben der Bibel.

Chapter XIX

URS GRAF (1)

Along with Augsburg and Nuremberg, Basel was also an important printing center in the sixteenth century. The first important artist who supplied the Basel printers with illustrations was Urs Graf, who was born in Solothurn, sometime between 1485 and 1490. It appears likely that he lived in Strassburg in his youth since his first book illustrations were done for printers in that city.

The first book he illustrated was published around 1506 by Joh. Knobloch, in Strassburg. It was [1275, Pl. 215-217] Text der passions oder leidens Christi aus den vier Evangelisten zusammen in ein syn brach mit schönen Figuren (2). Among the 25 woodcuts that the book contains, one recognizes the unskilled first work of the beginner, while individual pages show remarkable improvement. It is apparent, therefore, that completion of the work took a relatively long time, during which Graf developed his skill. This is also indicated by the fact that certain of the leaves are dated 1503, although the book was not published until 1506. The woodcuts range from 215 to 220 mm in height and from 153 to 158 mm wide. The monogram on the second illustration is a letter "V" surrounded by florid ornamentation.

In 1507 Knobloch published a Latin edition of the Passion under the title [1276]: Passio domini nostri Jesu Christi ex evanelistarum textu atque accuratissime deprompta additis sanctissimisexquisitissimisque figuris (3). The series of woodcuts is the same except that the last one is omitted. There was [1277] a second German edition in 1509 (4).

Graf's Passion illustrations, considered as a whole, show his fundamental weakness: the tendency towards realism for the common man. Technically, the sheets show wide variations. The one that shows the repentance of Judas, which is dated 1503, is among those produced earliest in the series, and is among the most inferior. The handwashing of Pilatus shows improvement; also, in the "Ecce Homo..." sheet, there are some relatively well drawn figures. The most successful illustration is "The resurrection of Lazarus," in which the composition is richer, the grouping more reasoned, the perspective more correct, the figures better drawn, and the background landscape handled with especial care.

Another book that Graf illustrated for Knobloch in 1508 [1278, Pl. 218] is the Leben Jesu Christi (5), in which six of the (190 x 157) illustrations from the Passion are reused.

Graf was in Zurich from 1507-1508, where he worked for the goldsmith, Leonhard Tüblin. The only illustrating he did in Zurich was [1279] for the 1508 Kalender (6), which had woodcut illustrations of various sizes. The first four of these had Graf's monogram.

The year 1509 or 1510 may have seen the production of the fourteen woodcuts in [1280] the booklet entitled Händel des Bruders Hans Jetzer zu Bern (1507-1509) (7). These fourteen woodcuts, which range in height from 56 to 60 mm and in width from 99 to 100 mm, were supplied by Graf. In addition to being used in the above book, they were used in two other books (8, 9).

Graf appears to have settled in Basel in 1509; at least his connection with printers of that city dates from that time.

The first Basel book printer who engaged him was Adam Petri, who had him illustrate [1281] Guilielmus' Postilla super epistolas et evangelia (10). The title page woodcut is 120 x 92 mm, and his monogram is on the bottom center of the illustration. The 94 small (43 x 33) text illustrations all bear his monogram, and have been used in many other books since that time. Petri himself reused them in all later editions of the Postille. Johann Froben [1282] used 74 of them in the edition of this same book that he published in 1512 (11). Thirty-nine of them appear in [1283] Petri's Plenarium of 1514 (12), which had one additional woodcut. Michael Furter had copies made for [1284] his 1511 Passion (13).

Graf finished the 95 illustrations for Petri in 1509. In the following year he worked with Johann Amerbach, for whom he produced 21 woodcuts for the 1510 publication of [1285, Pl. 219] Statuta ordinis cartusiensis a domino Guignone priore cartusie edita (14). The first one is 230 x 161 mm. The second, a geneological portrayal of the family tree of the Saints of the Carthusian order, is 170 x 107 mm. The 17 portraits of the Popes are on separate small woodcuts (35 x 35), some of which are repeated as the woodcuts at the beginning of chapters. The twentieth, one of the large woodcuts (150 x 110), portrays Guilielmus Rinaldi giving the Order new statutes. The 21st and last woodcut is also large (214 x 142) and is similar in composition to the preceding one. While there is no monogram on any of these woodcuts, there can be no doubt that they were produced by Graf.

The year 1511 was an especially productive one for Graf. First, he prepared a different series of 57 similar though larger illustrations of the life of Christ (77 x 53), which were published by Michael Furter [1286] in his Postille des Guilielmus (15).

The woodcuts that he prepared for Adam Petri's 1511 edition [1287] of Leben des heiligen bychtigers und einsidlers sant Batten, des ersten apostel des Oberlandes Helvetiae are far superior to his previous illustrations. They are 112 x 87 mm and, except for the last illustration, relate to the life of Saint Beatus (16). All of these illustrations bear his monogram and they are masterful, particularly in their presentation of landscapes.

No less important, even though it belongs to a completely different range, is the title page he prepared for three 1511 publications of the combined firm of Johann Amerbach, Petri and Froben. These were [1288-1290, Pl. 220]: the Clementis Quinti Constitutiones in concilis vienensi edite (17); Sextus decretalium liber a Bonifacio VIII in Concilio Lugdunensi editus (18); and Gregorii IX Decretalium liber accuratissime emendatus cum concordantiis annotationibus et additionibus marginalibus (19). The woodcut is the same in all three title pages, even though it had to present a different Pope on each. Graf's monogram is found on the roof of the canopy.

Comparable with this woodcut is the (230 x 190) woodcut for the title page of [1291] Decretum Gratiani (20). Aside from this one, the other two illustrations are not new but are based on earlier works by the same publishers. Graf's woodcuts were reused later in the 1519 edition in Lyon.

In 1512 he had more works to illustrate. Graf supplied two woodcuts to Adam Petri for [1292] Geiler von Kaissersperg's Christlich Bilgerschaft zum ewigen Vatterland (21). The first of these is 65 x 47 mm and the second 62 x 57 mm. His monogram appears on the border of the first one and on the upper left of number 2.

Two other woodcuts by Graf appeared in the summer section of [1293] the 1512 edition of Breviarium Augustanum (22), which was printed by Jacob von Pforzheim. The very industriously worked title page illustration is 113 x 87 mm. The second, which is next to the first page of text, is 126 x 81 mm, and the monogram appears in border decoration.

Graf also made connections with Strassburg in 1512. Mathias Hupfuff published [1294], in the above place and year, Murner's Narrenbeschwerung (23) for which he needed 97 woodcuts. For 78 he used the illustrations from Brant's Narrenschiff; one came from Marner; the remaining 17, as well as the title page illustration, were contracted with Graf. The title page illustration by Graf was 168 by 112 mm. His 17 text illustrations (64 x 72-78) illustrate chapters. These woodcuts are of varying artistic value. The title page illustration and the first nine text woodcuts are sketchily drawn and partially crudely cut, while the remaining eight are first rate.

Of Graf's outside life during this period, all we know is that in 1512 he achieved citizenship of Basel, since there is a record of his borrowing from his father-in-law the money necessary to buy citizenship.

A more attractive woodcut by him (163 x 103) appears in [1295] Petri's 1514 edition of Henricus Glareanus' Panegyricon in laudatissimum Helvetiorum foedus ad divum Maximilianum Aemilianum Romanorum imperatorem semper augustum (24). This woodcut shows the coat of arms of the Swiss Confederation.

In the same year he produced the woodcut (109 x 186) for the Winter portion of Jacob von Pforzheim's [1296] Breviarium Basiliense (25), which had originally appeared in 1505. Above the coats of arms there is the date, 1514, and his monogram.

We have nothing to show that he produced anything in the next four years. When, in 1519, Petri printed [1297] Luther's Predig von der wyrdigen Bereitung zu dem hochwürdigen Sacrament (26), Graf supplied one (52 x 44) woodcut for it. Luther's [1298] Predig oder unterrichtung wie sich ein Christenmensch mit Freuden bereiten soll zu sterben, which was published by Petri in 1520, contains two (57 x 44) woodcuts by Graf. These do not bear his monogram.

Also the four (75 x 97) woodcuts in Erasmus [1299] Enchiridion oder Handbüchlein eines christlichen ritterlichen Lebens durch J. Adolphus gedeutscht (27), which was also published by Petri in 1520, are by him and bear no monogram.

These are the last works that can be attributed to Graf. The date of his death is uncertain, but it appears that he did not live beyond 1529. He was one of the most productive artists who worked on book illustration. His activity in this field began in 1506 and the total of his book illustration comes to 268.

Notes

1) Archiv für die zeichnenden Künste I:81-92, 1865; Jahrbüchern für Kunst-Wissenschaft VI:150-174, 257-262, 1873.

2) Panzer I, No. 577. Folio.

3) Ebert, No. 15933. Folio; Panzer VI:38, No. 100.

4) Weigel, No. 2080. Folio.

5) Weigel, No. 19445. Small folio; Panzer, p. 285, No. 601.

6) Fully described by Vogelin, in Züricher Neujahrsblatt of 1868.

7) Weigel, No. 18355; described by His.

8) His, p. 162.

9) Historia mirabilis quator heresiarcharum apud Bernem combustorum. His, p. 162.

10) Not in Stockmeyer und Reber. Basel. N. A. VI:42.

11) Not in Stockmeyer und Reber. Baseler Bibliothek N. A. VI:5a.

12) Panzer I:361, No. 767. Folio; Weigel, No. 1869 is for the 1516 edition.

13) Stockmeyer und Reber, p. 84, No. 41. Quarto.

14) Stockmeyer und Reber, p. 47, No. 34. Folio.

15) Stockmeyer und Reber, p. 84, No. 43. Quarto.

16) Not in Stockmeyer und Reber. Quarto; Baseler Bibliothek. F. O. V 13e.

17) Stockmeyer und Reber, p. 48, No. 39. Folio.

18) Stockmeyer und Reber, p. 48, No. 38. Folio.

19) Stockmeyer und Reber, p. 48, No. 36. Folio.

20) Stockmeyer und Reber, p. 48, No. 42. Folio.

21) Stockmeyer und Reber, p. 138, No. 8. Folio.

22) Panzer VI:188, No. 102.

23) Panzer I:347.

24) Not in Stockmeyer und Reber; Panzer VI:195, No. 150.

25) Not in Stockmeyer und Reber. Folio. Baseler Bibliothek N G I 19.

26) Stockmeyer und Reber, p. 142, No. 45; Weller, No. 1228.

27) Panzer I:436, No. 976. Quarto; Stockmeyer und Reber, p. 143, No. 55; His, No. 260-264; Weller, No. 1357.

Chapter XX

THE FLOWERING OF BASEL BOOK ILLUSTRATION (1)

The finest period in Basel book illustration began around 1515 when the Holbein brothers moved to the city; along with them there were a number of other important artists working for the printing plants.

To be sure Hans Holbein rarely undertook book illustration. While he did his first work, an ornamental border, for a book printed by Froben in 1516, another seven years passed before he really appeared as an illustrator. Even if he did the beautiful sheets listing the patrons and the Freiburg escutcheon, which Adam Petri published in 1520 in [1300] the Freiburger Stadtrechte (2), these can not be considered true book illustrations.

The first opportunity to supply book illustrations as such came to Holbein in 1522 when the printers Adam Petri and Thomas Wolff were both reprinting editions of the Lutheran Bible translation.

The Wittemberg edition of Luther's Bible appeared as the first folio edition of the New Testament in September 1522. In December of 1522 Petri issued his reprint, under the title [1301] Das Neu Testament, yetzund recht grüntlich teutscht. Welchs allein in Christum unser Seligkeit recht und klärlich leret. Mit gar gelerten und richtigen Vorreden und der schwersten Oertern kurz, aber gut, Auslegung. Folio (3). Holbein composed the beautiful title page. As title pages for the various books (80 x 66) he repeated the illustrations found in the Wittemberg edition, but only the one of Matthew at the pouring of the Holy Spirit shows any resemblance to the Wittemberg Bible. All the others were completely newly done by Holbein.

Just as he was finishing the woodcuts for Petri, he accepted the second task, the reproduction of the illustrations of the Apocalypse for Thomas Wolff, who published it in 1523 in its first octavo edition, under the title [1302, Pl. 221-225] Das gantzs neuw Testament yetz klärlich aus dem rechten Grundt teutscht. Auch die Offenbarung Joannis mit hüpschen Figuren, auss welchen man das schwerest leichtlich verston kann (4). For the title page Wolff used a bad reversed copy of one of Holbein's older works and he used the Urs Graf woodcuts for Peter and Paul on the verso of the title page. Before each of the books was a minor portrait of the author. For the Apocalypse he had Holbein copy the 21 illustrations from the Wittemberg edition of 1522. Here too Holbein, while externally following the originals, was left enough latitude for the free play of his own genius. It is interesting to note that in the pictures in which he was most free in his rendition he approaches most closely to the Dürer Apocalypse, with which he does not appear to have been familiar. After these, both Petri and Wolff reprinted in 1523 Luther's Old Testament which was published by Melchior Lotter; and they drew Holbein into its illustration.

Thomas Wolff published his first quarto reprint in 1523, under the title [1303] Das Allt Testament yetzt recht grüntlich aus dem Ebreischen teutscht und auf ein rechten verstant bracht.

Und an vil örtern erklärt und bessert, welchs in vorigen gar schwer, tunkel und falsch gewesen ist (5). Here too, Holbein's assignment was to reduce the pictures in the Wittemberg folio edition to the customary octavo format (123-124 x 75). Thomas Wolff did not complete the publication of the Old Testament but turned it over to Petri, who likewise had Holbein do the illustrations; however, the requirement that these be copies of the Wittemberg illustrations was changed to use of the reduced copies of the Cologne Bible of 1480, which had been done for Schoensperger's 1487 edition by the artist Hb and which both Othmars had used in their Bibles of 1507 and 1518. Holbein undertook the reworking of the woodcuts for the first part of the [1304] Alten Testaments, which did not get printed until 1523.

This is all that the Basel printers received from Holbein during this period. In 1523 he made a trip to southern France and there he received a commission from the Brothers Melchior and Caspar Trechsel, in Lyon, to redo the cycle of illustrations of the Catholic version of the Old Testament. This cycle had been static since the 1511 edition except for some reworking by Springinklee in 1518. This is how it happened that his famed "Icones historiarum veteris testamenti" came into being. It had been started by Lutzelburger, who died in 1526, with some of the illustrations already cut in wood, some drawn and some just in the form of sketches. Some of these were used in Froschauer's Bible of 1531 but the whole cycle was included first in the 1538 Lyon edition issued by Melchior and Caspar Trechsel, under the title [1305, Pl. 226-227] Biblia utriusque Testamenti iuxta vulgatam translationem (7) and a second time in a separate issued by the Brothers Trechsel [1306] under the title, Historiarum veteris Testamenti Icones ad vivum expressae.

Finally, the crown of all illustrations, [1307] Holbein's Dance of Death, in the same period, is so well known that a mere mention of it here will suffice.

Towards the end of his activity in Basel, Holbein supplied, as a headpiece for Dr. Copp's [1308] Evangelischen Wandkalender (8), the well-known woodcut known as "Christ, The True Light." This work was published by Froschauer in Zurich. A substantial period must have elapsed between the drawing and its publication in 1527 as a wall calendar, since by that time Hans Holbein was long gone from Basel.

His older brother, Ambrosius, arrived in Basel contemporaneously with Hans. At first Ambrosius worked with the painter Hans Herbster. As early as September 24, 1516 he was called as witness in a case at law, and on June 14, 1518 he bought his citizenship in the town. He will not be treated fully in this book since all of his work that we have is in the short period of 1517-1519. We find him working with book printers: Pamphilus Gegenbach, Johannes Froben and Adam Petri, and can attribute only 23 illustrations to him.

He provided seventeen woodcuts to Pamphilus Gegenbach for use in [1309] the comedy, Nollhard, Dies sind die prophetien sancti Methodii und Nollhardi (9), and these illustrations were attractive and lifelike.

For Johannes Froben he supplied the two woodcuts for [1310, Pl. 228-229a] for Thomas More's booklet, De optime reip. statu deque nova insula Utopia (10), which was published in 1518.

For Petri, Ambrosius Holbein undertook the illustration of Murner's [1311, Pl. 229b-230]

Geuchmatt (11). When the book was published in 1519 it had only four of his woodcuts (120-125 x 96-98). Apparently he died suddenly, since his series of illustrations breaks off at this point and Petri had to find another artist. The artist who finished off the work after A. Holbein's death used the monogram "C. A." and maintained the same format for the remaining 51 illustrations for the book. No artist with the initials "C. A." has been identified. His initials appear on six woodcuts.

In addition to the two Holbeins and "C. A.," there was one more artist who should be named; the initials in his monogram were "V. C." He has, in the past, been identified by some as associated with Urs Graf, and he supplied Johann Froben with the woodcuts for his undated Erasmus. He also prepared the illustrations [1312] for Johann Bebel's 1523 edition of Precatio Dominica in septem portiones distributa (12). The eight handsome illustrations he supplied (85 x 65) were outstanding in drawing, composition and ideas. In view of the fact that the initials "V" and "C," which form his monogram, have no relation to Urs Graf, this artist has been the subject of further research.

In addition to these illustrations which are by attributable artists (even if only by initials in their monogram) there were a large number of other artists who were working in Basel at this time to whom no specific works can be attributed.

Michael Furter, whose press produced so many illustrated books in the 15th century, produced only a few small things in the sixteenth. Around 1514 he published [1313] Unterweisung, wie sich die Chirurgici halten sollen (13), which had a title page woodcut and seven text illustrations. In 1515 he printed [1314] a German Hortulus animae (14), with 79 colored woodblocks, and as a supplement to this he issued Sant Brigitten gebettly (15) with a colored woodcut illustration on the title page and on its verso. His last illustrated book is Johann Gerson's [1315] Sermo de passione domini (16), which was published in 1515.

Jacob von Pfortzheim printed, in 1515, at the expense of Henrici Reitzmann, [1316] the Historia de festo nivis gloriosissimae deigenitricis et virginis Mariae (17). The title page illustration is made up of four separate woodcuts.

In 1518 he printed [1317] Der ewigen Weisheit Betbüchlein (18), with a number of small (some 62 x 45 and some 50 x 35) woodcuts.

Adam Petri, in addition to Urs Graf and the two Holbeins, used some unknown painters. In 1518 he printed [1318] Engelbrecht's Lehre von dem hochwürdigen Sacrament (19), with a title page woodcut illustration. In 1520 there followed a number of [1319] smaller writings of Luther; of which the outstanding example is Kurze Erklärung der 10 Gebote (20). The title page woodcut is 115 x 120 mm. The ten other woodcuts (68 x 46) illustrate the individual commandments. The woodcut for Luther's [1320] Predigt von zeitlichem Amt (21), which he published in 1520, shows two people at a table with an account book; and that (60 x 100) for his [1321] Predigt von der Gnade Gottes und dem freien Willen (22) shows Peter with the key and Paul with a sword.

In 1521 there followed [1322] the Zwo wunderbarlichen Historien von Olwier und Orso (23), with many illustrations.

In Luther's [1323] Auslegung der Episteln und Evangelien (24), which he published in 1522, he repeated the woodcuts that Scheifelin provided for his 1514 Plenarium. In 1523 he printed

Luther's [1324] Sermon am Tag unser Frawen lichtmess (25) and his Predich wie sich ein Christmensch mit Freuden bereiten soll zu sterben (26), providing only a title page illustration for the former and a title page illustration plus thirteen text woodcuts (which are small and of no importance) for the latter.

After 1523, Petri's chief occupation was reprinting Luther's translation of the Bible. His first one, the New Testament, for which Holbein prepared the illustrations, was reprinted by him no less than seven times. His second folio edition (27) appeared in March, 1523 [1325] and is a simple reprint of the edition of 1522, with the same illustrations.

Also in March, 1523 he issued [1326] an octavo edition of the New Testament (28), with the reduced title page illustration by Holbein, based on the folio edition.

[1327-1329] The fourth reprint in octavo followed in December, 1523 (29), the fifth in December, 1524 (30), and the sixth in February, 1525 (31). In all of these we find Holbein's original drawings, with the exception, in all, of the illustration of Saul's conversion.

The only others that appear to have been issued from Petri's printing plant are [1330-1331] a new folio edition, which was printed without indication of the publisher, only stating on the last page, "Printed for the third time at Basel, 1525" (32); and the quarto edition, which appeared without place, publisher, or date and has, at the end, the statement: "End of the New Testament" (33). The woodcuts in both of these are from the first folio edition, with the exception of Saul's conversion.

Petri's reprint of the [1332] Alten Testamentes (34) which was issued in three parts, with part one coming out in 1523, the second in 1524 and the third in late 1524, has been treated under the Holbein contributions to part I. All 97 leaves of the Cologne Bible are presented here except for the book of Jude and illustrations 81-84, since Luther had not, at that time, completed translation of this part. Petri used a large number of artists. Some of these were very good, but there is no record of who they were.

Petri worked until 1528. A few of his last publications [1333-1334] are Des türkischen Kaisers Thaten (35) in 1526, and Sebastian Munster's woodcut illustrated Calendarium Hebraicum (36) in 1527. In 1528 his son took over the printing company.

There is now very little remaining of the work of Thomas Wolff, who has already been mentioned in reference to the publication of the Old and New Testaments.

In 1520 he printed [1335] a German Hortulus animae (37) of which he printed [1336] a new edition in 1523 (38). He used various Basel artists for this work, because there are many woodcuts.

In [1337] Kaiser Sigmunds Reformation (39), which he printed in 1521, the title page illustration is a woodcut of Kaiser Maximilian.

In the years after 1523 there followed his editions of the Bible. There was his first octavo reprint of the New Testament, for which Holbein prepared the 21 woodcuts for the Apocalypse, and he repeated this in [1338] a quarto edition in the same year (40). The title page illustration for the quarto was prepared especially for it by Holbein and it is excellent; however, the original illustrations for the octavo edition were used here and their size is not suitable for a quarto publication.

Still another edition, which is not listed in Panzer, [1339] appeared in 1523 in Basel, under the title Das newe Testament klerlich auf dem rechten grundt teutscht (41). Its title page layout is architectural, which is reminiscent of Urs Graf. The text is printed on 240 leaves.

A [1340] fourth edition in large octavo which, according to the title page, was printed in 1523, appeared after the last part of August, 1524; it is listed by Panzer (42). Here too the Holbein woodcuts of the Apocalypse are reused. In 1524, there followed [1341-1342] the fifth (43) and sixth (44) octavo editions, in which the same woodcuts were also reprinted.

Otherwise, only small publications came from Wolff's press: in 1523 he issued [1343] Neu wunderbarlichen Beichtbüchlein (45) with a woodcut to illustrate the title page. Also, in the same year [1344] he issued Luther's Zehn nutzliche Sermones von der Messen, Bildnussen, beiderlei Gestalt des Sacraments (46). This had an illustration at its close.

In the [1345-1346] Sermon gepredigt vom Pawren zu werd bei Nurnberg (47), which was printed in 1524, and in the Auslegung des Propheten Maleachi (48) by Oecolampadius, printed in 1526, each has an unimportant title page.

Nicolaus Lamparter's first illustrated book was a reprint in 1509 of Brant's Narrenschiff. He later printed only booklets with title page illustrations. Among these are [1347-1352] his Cato of 1515 (49); the Schönen Betrachtung des Leidens Jesu (50) and the Büchlein, wie sich ein Christenmensch schicken soll (51) of 1518; the Guldin schleslin (52) of 1519 and the Recept guiacum (53) of the same year; as well as the Offenbarung geschehen Sigismundo zu Pressburg (54) of 1520.

Johann Bebel is known for little except his Erasmus, Precatio dominica, in which he has eight pages by the artist "C. V."

In 1523 he printed the [1353] Narragonia monachorum (55) with two woodcuts. In 1524 this was followed by [1354] Claudius Catinucula's German translation of More's Von der wunderbarlichen Insel Utopia genannt (56), which reprinted the two woodcuts by Ambrosius Holbein.

In 1524 he either bought or borrowed from Wolff the woodcuts of the Apocalypse by Holbein and he printed them in his 1525 French edition of the New Testament, which he printed under the title [1355] Les choses contenues en ceste partie du nouveau testament etc. Imprime a Basle l'an MDXXV (57).

Andreas Cratander issued only one illustrated book of which we have any record. It was [1356] his 1524 Spruch von der evangelischen Lehre und von dem Wort Gottes (58), which has an illustration on the title page and one on its verso.

The poet Pamphilus Gengenbach, while his work is not comparable with the large Basel houses in output, used woodcuts in his various small publications which are of especial interest. The dated works that bear his name come between 1517 and 1522. Goedeke attributes 36 of these to him, practically all of which have title page woodcuts.

The poem [1357] Der welsch Flusz (59), which was published in 1513, has a title page woodcut and the next three pages of text have illustrations.

The 1514 poem [1358] Der alt Eydgenoss (60) has six figures beneath the title and a larger woodcut on the last leaf.

The title page and its verso in [1359] Der Bundschuh (61) are illustrated by woodcuts.

In the poem [1360] Tot, Teufel und Engel (62) a title page woodcut illustrates the three in the title.

The title page woodcut in the poem [1361] of the Funf Juden (63) is larger than the others.

In [1362] Zehn Altern dieser Welt (64), which was published in 1515, the drawing for the title page is good but the cutting is crude. Each chapter is preceded by an old woodcut (80 x 105).

Gengenbach's [1363] Gouchmatt, gespielt durch etlich geschichkt Burger einer löblichen stat Basel (65) has unimportant woodcuts.

[1364] Die Todtenfresser (66) has a title page illustration and his [1365] Practica deutsch auf 1515 (67) has two 10 mm high calendar woodcuts on the title page. In his [1366] Pfaffenspiegel (68) the title page illustration is taken from the Gouchmatt.

The [1367] Layenspiegel (69) has reproductions of two elegant woodcuts. In the poem [1368] Der Ewangelisch Burger (70) the title page woodcut has the inscription, "Unum deum adorabis et illi soli servies." On the verso of the title page and repeated on the last page there is a woodcut of Christ on the Cross.

The [1369] 1523 edition of the poem Von dreien Christen (71) has one woodcut illustration. The [1370] Hübsch lesen von dem heiligen Zwölfboten St. Jacob (72) has three woodcuts. The subject matter of the small illustration on the title page is repeated but in a different execution, and at the end of the poem there are two escutcheons.

Gengenbach's [1371] Novella (73) has seven large figures and woodcuts taken from the Gouchmatt....

The title page woodcut in [1372] Frischen Combiszt (74) portrays Hexes brewing an unusual drink in a large kettle.

In his [1373] Neuen Bileamsesel (75) there is a woodcut showing how Christ shoved the Pope off the donkey.

The most familiar of all is [1374] his Bettlerorden (76), the woodcut of which is repeated in most later editions.

The two woodcuts in [1375] his Räbhänslin (77) are unimportant. His [1376] Regiment der Gesundheit (78), which appeared in 1513, has a woodcut on the title page, which is also dated 1513.

In the [1377-1378] Kalender of 1514 (79) and in that for 1521 (80) there are three large and six smaller woodcuts and, in one part, some one to two-inch woodcuts.

[1379-1381] In 1522 he printed the Gesprach nit weit von Trient (81); and in 1523 the Kurzen Begriff vom Schultheiss und der Gemein des Dorfes Fridhusen (82) and the History von einem Pfarrer und einem Geist (83), some of which had title page illustrations and others had text woodcuts.

All of the illustrations in the above publications by Gengenbach received great care and they showed a significant advance in quality from the earlier works to the later ones. It would appear that Gengenbach himself worked with the artists in the preparation of the drawings.

Thus, until the end of the 1520's there was a spirited activity in this field in Basel. From 1509 to 1520 Urs Graf worked for the various printers there. In 1515 the two Holbeins began their activity in this field, with Hans supplying 45 illustrations to the Basel printers and Ambrosius supplying 23. The artist "C. A." was not unworthy to stand alongside Ambrosius Holbein, and the artist "C. V." excelled him in his sheets dealing with "Our Father."

As in Augsburg and Nuremberg, the time of this flowering was not very long, and later decades saw the decline of book illustration here too.

Notes

1) What Woltmann wrote in Holbein und seine Zeit, p. 213ff, about Hans Holbein's work as an illustrator, is outdated by Voegelin's "Ergänzungen und Nachweisungen zum Holtzschnittwerk Hans Holbein des Jüngern," in Repertorium für Kunstwissenschaft V:182ff, 1879. Nothing more has been learned about Ambrosius Holbein since the research by His, as reported by Woltmann on p. 207ff. For additional information on Gengenbach, see Goedeke, Pamphilius Gengenbach. Hannover, 1856.

2) Panzer I:442, No. 994.

3) Panzer, Entwurf einer vollständigen Geschichte der deutschen Bibelübersetzung Luther's. No. 1, Nurenberg, 1783; Stockmeyer und Reber, Baseler Buchdruckergeschichte, p. 144, No. 75.

4) Panzer, Entwurf... No. 5; Weller, No. 2712; Muther, Bilderbibeln, No. 55.

5) Small quarto or octavo; Weller, No. 2709; Panzer, Annalen II:130, No. 1609; Metzger, Geschichte der deutschen Bibelübersetzung in der schweitzerisch-reformirte Kirche von der Reformation bis zur Gegenwart. Basel, 1876, p. 48.

6) Das Alte Testament deutsch. Basel, Petri. Folio; Weigel, No. 17891; Stockmeyer und Reber, p. 145, No. 80; Panzer, Entwurf... p. 175; Panzer, Annalen II:130, No. 1607.

7) Weigel, No. 18335.

8) Weller, No. 3757.

9) Goedeke, Gengenbach, p. 77, 460, 605; Weller, No. 1051; Panzer I:410, No. 887.

10) Panzer VI:205 and IX:296, No. 222.

11) Panzer I:432, No. 965; Stockmeyer und Reber, p. 142, No. 41.

12) Weigel, No. 9931. Octavo; Rumohr, Holbein, p. 112-113; Brulliot I:1497.

13) Weller, No. 904.

14) Weller, No. 898.

15) Weller, No. 899.

16) Stockmeyer und Reber, p. 84, No. 50.

17) Germ. Mus., No. 5210. Folio.

18) Weller, No. 1094.

19) Weller, No. 1108.

20) Weller, No. 1535. Quarto; Rotermund, No. 55; Panzer, Suppl:179, No. 974p.

21) Panzer, Suppl:172; Weller, No. 1538; Stockmeyer und Reber, p. 143, No. 59.

22) Panzer, Suppl:187, No. 974^{xxx}; Rotermund, No. 70; Stockmeyer und Reber, p. 144, No. 61.

23) Weller, No. 1709; Stockmeyer und Reber, p. 144, No. 71.

24) Panzer II:62, No. 1284. Folio.

25) Weller, No. 2550.

26) Weller, No. 2535; Panzer, Suppl:172.

27) _Das neuw Testament recht grüntlich teutscht._ Basel, Petri, 1523; Panzer, _Entwurf..._ No. 2. Folio.

28) _Das ganz Neuw Testament..._ ; Panzer, _Entwurf..._ No. 3. Octavo.

29) Panzer, _Entwurf..._ No. 4. Octavo.

30) Panzer, _Entwurf..._ No. 10. Octavo.

31) Panzer, _Entwurf..._ No. 11. Octavo.

32) Panzer, _Entwurf..._ No. 12. Folio.

33) Vogelin, p. 4 (des Separatabdrucks) No. 8.

34) Weigel, No. 17891. Folio; Stockmeyer und Reber, p. 145, No. 80; Panzer, _Entwurf..._ p. 175, 177-178; Panzer, _Annalen_ II:130, No. 1607, and II:239, No. 2109.

35) Weller, No. 4009.

36) Panzer IX:402 and 655.

37) Weller, No. 1402. Octavo.

38) Weigel, No. 16351.

39) Panzer II:47, No. 1231. Quarto.

40) Panzer, _Entwurf..._; No. 6; Weigel, No. 1867.

41) Vogelin, p. 6 (des Separatabdruck) No. 3. Small folio.

42) Large octavo. Panzer, _Entwurf..._ No. 7. Large octavo.

43) Panzer, _Entwurf..._ No. 8. Octavo.

44) Panzer, _Entwurf..._ No. 9.

45) Weller, No. 2703.

46) Weller, No. 2585.

47) Weller, No. 3093.

48) Weller, No. 3941.

49) Weller, No. 886.

50) Weller, No. 1095.

51) Weller, No. 1099.

52) Weller, No. 1171.

53) Weller, No. 1262.

54) Weller, No. 1613.

55) Weller, No. 2621.

56) Not in Weller.

57) Panzer, <u>Annales typogr.</u> VI:283, No. 602.

58) Weller, No. 3174.

59) Goedeke, p. 3, 435, 529.

60) Goedeke, p. 12, 436, 543; Weller, No. 832.

61) Goedeke, p. 23, 438, 546.

62) Goedeke, p. 32, 441, 557.

63) Goedeke, p. 39, 442, 557; Weller, No. 686.

64) Goedeke, p. 54, 442, 559.

65) Goedeke, p. 117, 503, 615.

66) Goedeke, p. 153, 505, 619.

67) Goedeke, p. 160, 505, 627; Weller, No. 934.

68) Goedeke, p. 167, 506, 628; Weller, No. 2037.

69) Goedeke, p. 167.

70) Goedeke, p. 198, 512, 629; Weller, No. 2084.

71) Goedeke, p. 214, 513, 629; Weller, No. 2434.

72) Goedeke, p. 231, 513, 629; Weller, No. 1005.

73) Goedeke, p. 262, 514, 658.

74) Goedeke, p. 292, 514, 658.

75) Goedeke, p. 310, 515, 667.

76) Goedeke, p. 343, 515, 678.

77) Goedeke, p. 519, 681; Weller, No. 561.

78) Weller, No. 796.

79) Weller, No. 833.

80) Weller, No. 1774.

81) Weller, No. 2084.

82) Weller, No. 2433.

83) Weller, No. 2436.

Chapter XXI

STRASSBURG ARTISTS (1)

At about the same time that Urs Graf and the two Holbeins were active in Basel, Strassburg also underwent great development in book illustration. While at the turn of the century Sebastian Brant was the leader whose great publications set the pace, now it became Geiler von Kaisersperg, whose primary position was as a clergyman in Munster, through whom the printers and book illustrators were able to put forth a claim to fame. Of course he was not the only one who required book illustration; there was also Murner who could not get along without illustrations in his books. As in the previous century Hieronymus Brunschwig could not get along without anatomical and botanical illustrations, so now there were the Doctor Hans von Gersdorf and the botanist Otto Brunfels who could not do without such illustrations in their books.

In the beginning, there did not appear to be sufficient local talent to meet these requirements, since they called on outside beginners such as Urs Graf back in 1506 and 1508.

The position that Urs Graf achieved in Basel was achieved in Strassburg by Hans Wächtlin. Very little is known of his life. He was the son of a priest, of the same name, and became a citizen of Strassburg on St. Gallen's Day, 1514. Two years later he became a member of the guild of artistic handicrafts and became a Leading Master in the battle against the bungler Hans Hage. And, indeed, among the artists who at that time formed the group of Masters, he was ranked fourth (2). A year later, when he appeared in the controversy the members of the Guild were having with Hans Hage, he was named second among the four Masters who appeared for the guild. He appears again in 1519, listed with three other men of his guild in a disagreement about debts between the artists and the goldsmiths. After this his name does not appear in the source records.

His works are few in number. Among the known book illustrations that he prepared are 43 (215 x 165) sheets for [Pl. 231-234] the Leben Christi (3). These 43 woodcuts were used in selected fashion with other woodcuts and were never reused as a whole unit.

One of these, No. 35, was used by Knoblouch as early as 1506 in the [1382] Passion (4) that was illustrated primarily by Urs Graf.

The earliest edition that was dated and that contained the bulk of these illustrations was [1383] Das Leben Jesu Christi, gezogen aus den vier Evangelisten. Darzu vil schöner Figuren bedeutung, Strössburg bei J. Knoblouch 1508. Small folio (5). Of the 36 woodcuts in this book, 30 are attributable to Wächtlin and the others to Urs Graf.

Again, many of the illustrated leaves attributable to Wächtlin, and indeed, giving his name, are found in the Passion published in Latin s. l. e. a., with the Latin version by Benedicturs Chelodonius, under the title [1384] Passio Jesu Christi salvatoris mundi vario carminum genere P. Benedicti Chelodonii cum figuris artificiosissimis Joannis Vuechtelin.

Numbers 2, 4, 10, 11, 12, 14, 16, 31, 37 and 38 were used in the 1514 edition of Geiler von Kaisersperg's [1385-1386] Postill uber die vier Evangelia, printed by Johann Schott, and were also reused by him in the second edition, published in 1522 (6). In addition to the ten above, Schott used in both editions of the Postill another series of 30 small (80 x 105) woodcuts that are apparently attributable to Wächtlin.

In a third book another aspect of Wächtlin's work is shown than appeared in the series for the Life of Christ. Hans von Gerssdorf, an outstanding physician, prepared the much used textbook [1387] titled Feldbuch der Wundarznei (7). It was first published in an illustrated edition by Johann Schott, who had Wächtlin supply the drawings. It is certain that the three anatomical sheets are attributable to Wächtlin. The other illustrations, even though there is no record of his having done them, may also be ascribed to Wächtlin (8). They are, on the average, 150 x 115 mm and are all scenes of surgery. While a few of the sheets have illustrations that are slightly broader (see 16b), nevertheless they have characteristics that, taken together, indicate Wächtlin as the artist. The second edition [1388-1392] of the Feldbuch... was issued in 1528 (9), the third in 1530, the fourth in 1535, the fifth in 1540, and the sixth in 1542. Grüninger had also issued a medical book in 1518, by Laurentius Phrys (10), and he reprinted the woodcuts with somewhat revised text type.

The years in which Wächtlin appears in book illustration are, therefore: 1508, with 30 large sheets for the Life of Christ; 1514, with 30 smaller illustrations for the Postille; 1517, with the surgical-anatomical illustrations for the Feldbuch.... His last known original illustration, his last dated work, the hand drawing in the Brauschweig Museum, comes in 1519. We do not know how long after that he was alive.

He was an artist who had not completely freed himself from the style and concepts of the old times. In his scenes illustrating the life of Christ he distinguishes himself primarily through his skillful handling of landscapes. In the anatomical pages of the Feldbuch... it is the well done presentation of nudes that makes him a member of the artistic movement of his times.

Wächtlin, in his later days, must have worked with the younger artists' group which was centered on Hans Baldung Grün. Baldung was born between 1470 and 1480 in Swabia. His name frequently appeared in Augsburg and in Strassburg archives, and a letter in the Augsburg Archives, dated January 30, 1512, indicates that the Master Hans Baldung died around this time and left an heir, Dr. Hieronymus Baldung.

The first evidence of Baldung's residence in Strassburg appears in the city records of 1509; soon thereafter, and before October, 1510, he was married. The first book woodcut that has his monogram HG appears in [1393] the 1509 edition of Johannes Gerson's Sermo de passione domini nuper e Gallico in Latinum traductus, published without identification of publisher. The monogram is in the lower center of the title page (110 x 90). A new edition of this book appeared in 1510.

In 1510 Grüninger printed [1394, Pl. 235] Geiler's Buch Granatapfel, which consisted of prayers on various subjects. Hans Baldung did a title page woodcut (172 x 135) for each of these.

From this one sees immediately that Baldung must have contributed his six woodcuts, in cooperation with Burgkmair, to the Othmar edition of the book shortly before (11). Nevertheless, they show some very significant differences.

When, in 1511, Knoblouch published an edition of [1395] Buches Granatapfel, of which he did [1396] a new edition in 1516, he had Hans Baldung do the illustrations with minor changes. However, these were not as original as were those in the Grüninger edition.

The third printer in Strassburg for whom Baldung did some work was Martin Flach. While Flach used only earlier woodcuts in his [1397, Pl. 236-237] *Hortulus animae* of 1510, in the edition for 1511 he had Hans Baldung supply the 46 small (52-62 x 47-68) woodcuts that he used. The illustration of the Annunciation, at the beginning of the book, is not by Baldung but was taken from Knoblouch's *Hortulus* of 1507.

When Martin Flach did another [1398] edition of the *Hortulus* (13) in 1512, Baldung replaced some of the old illustrations with new woodcuts; supplying nine woodcuts to this edition, not 28 as Eisenmann says. Comparison of Baldung's pictures with the old ones in the book shows the tremendous development of the art during these years. Baldung's sensual, voluptuous women contrast sharply with the spiritual-aesthetic appearance that they were given in the fifteenth century.

While Baldung left Strassburg in the first half of 1511 and went to Freiburg, he remained in close and unbroken contact with Strassburg, as is indicated by official sources which listed his name in 1518.

In 1513 Mathias Schürer issued a book, [1399] *Die welsch Gattung* (14), which had two (115 x 85) woodcuts. On the first of these the monogram HGB appears on the upper right. The second one, which appeared at the end of the book and is also astronomical in content, has the same monogram on the lower right.

Three years later he illustrated [1400, Pl. 238-247] the *Auslegung der 10 Geboten* (15), which was published by Johann Grüninger in 1516. The woodcut for the first commandment is 132 x 104 mm (16). The woodcut for the third commandment is reproduced in Geiler (17); that for the fourth is also reproduced in Geiler (18); that for the fifth is in Pauli (19); that for the sixth is in Geiler (20); and those for the first, ninth and tenth are in Pauli (21). Altogether the woodcuts are 103-105 mm x 133-135 mm. Whether Baldung knew the illustrations in the earlier editions of the ten commandments is uncertain. In any event, his very rich illustrations are independently developed.

From 1522 we have a title page by him in a book printed by Johann Schott, [1401] *Die Kunst der Chiromantzey* (22), by Joh. Indagine. It is a bust picture of the author (190 x 150).

After 1522 there were a few occasional illustrations by Baldung. When, in 1531, Peter Schöffer, in Strassburg, printed [1402, Pl. 248a] Ulrich Kern's *New kunstliches wohlgegrunds Visierbuch,* Baldung supplied the (132 x 135) printer's mark. It bears the monogram HGB.

In Caspar Hedions' 1543 edition of [1403] *Chronik von Strassburg,* Baldung supplied the bust portrait of the author. This is the last book illustration by Hans Baldung that has been found. He died in 1545 (23).

Next after Baldung there is the artist HF who worked on the illustration of Grüninger's edition of [1404, Pl. 248b-249] Geiler's *Brösamlin uffgelesen von Frater Johann Paulin* (24), which was published in 1517. The first prayer has a 95 x 140 mm woodcut. The second prayer has six large woodcuts, which are all by the artist HF. The corner post on the first of these illustrations has the date and monogram 1516. HF . The second, smaller, woodcut is 80 x 104 mm; the third is 112 x 142 mm and the fourth is 97 x 104 mm. The other woodcuts are unimportant.

After these two prayers there follows the Brösamlin proper, in which there are six (95 x 140) sheets by the artist HF

In addition to these sixteen woodcuts in the Brösamlin the artist HF provided [1405] ten leaves of illustrations for Geiler's Buch der Sünden des Munds (25), which was published by Grüninger in 1518. These illustrations do not bear his monogram. However, they are so similar in size (96 x 142) and style to those in the Brösamlin that they may be attributed to this artist.

This artist is not particularly important. His figures are not very attractive. His people are small and squat. The head and throat are too large in relation to the body. His women are equally crudely done; they have tremendously full bosoms and unnaturally thick legs; wherever possible these are nudes. The name of this artist is unknown. Nagler has guessed that he may have been Hans von Frankfurt; others have postulated that he may have been Hans, the son of Hieronymus Greff, who called himself Hieronymus von Frankfurt. These, however, remain hypotheses; the only thing that is certain is that the artist who used this monogram has not been positively identified.

Erhard Schlitzoc, who was named in learned sources before Hans von Frankfurt, is deemed by Nagler to have used the monogram which is found on four woodcuts between 1516 and 1519. The first two (90 x 142) are in Geiler's 1516 [1406] Buch von der Ameisen (26), which was printed by Grüninger. The one on sheet 41a has the monogram on a rock in the lower right. The second woodcut is on leaf 51b and it has the monogram on the wall of the house at the right, along with the date. The two other sheets by this artist appeared three years later. One is on the title page of [1407] Hutten's Von der wunderbarlichen artznei des Holz Guiacum (27), which was printed by Grüninger in 1519. The other is the very attractive title page woodcut (85 x 98) in [1408] Laurentius Phries' Tractat über di Wildbäder (28), which was printed by Grüninger in 1519. No other works by this artist are known.

There is only one known sheet of the work of the artist . This appeared in [1409] Geiler's Buch der Sünden der Munds, which was printed by Grüninger. The woodcut was 115 x 97 mm and it appeared on page 66. It was hardly justiable for the artist to inscribe his in broad strokes, since the drawing and the cutting were bad and the composition was borrowed from the corresponding drawing by Dürer.

The artist is equally unimportant. His monogram appears on four woodcuts [1410] in Geiler's Alphabet in 23 Predigten, which was printed by Grüninger in 1518. These woodcuts give the impression that the artist is still working completely in the style of the fifteenth century. Various people have tried to determine the name of this artist. At first it was attributed to Hans Baldung Grün; then to Hans Grüninger, and finally Nagler did research in attempting to attribute it to Hieronymus Greff. However, it is doubtful that Greff was still alive at this time and, furthermore, he used a different monogram in illustrations that are known to be by him.

An artist who is really transitional to the later period is Heinrich Vogther of Augsburg, whose only work that falls into our period is the 1527 Grüninger edition of the Neue Testament [1411, Pl. 250-251]. The title page woodcut is 205 x 160 mm, with the monogram HVH on the bottom. In the many text woodcuts (210 x 160) which fill entire pages there is great variation in artistic value.

At the same time that painting of figures reached new heights through the work of Hans Baldung, illustrations of plants, which had heretofore been available in the old sheets from the Hortus, appeared in a new realistic rendition. The groundbreaking work in this field was Otto Brunfel's [1412] Krauterbuch (29), first issued by Johann Schott in 1530. The artist who prepared the illustrations for this edition was Hans Weiditz, who dated the title page woodcut with the year 1529.

The German edition [1413] of the Krauterbuches, which was published in Strassburg in 1536, also indicated that Hans Weyditz of Strassburg did the illustrations. There were [1414-1416] Latin editions in 1531 and 1532 and a German edition in 1537. The studies by Wigand and Treviranus evaluate the scientific value of these illustrations.

Thus there was no shortage of artists in Strassburg. From 1506 to 1519 Hans Wächtlin was active and 43 large sheets in the Leben Christi, as well as 30 small ones in Kaisersperg's Postille and the anatomical drawings for Gersdorf's Feldbuch der Wundarznei may be attributed to him.

Hans Baldung Grün, who began his activity in 1510 with the sheets for Geiler's Buch Granatapfel, which was printed by Grüninger, surpassed him. He followed in 1511 with 46 small presentations for Martin Flach's Hortulus animae, to which he added another nine for the new edition in 1512. In 1513 he did the two woodcuts for Schürer's Welsch Gattung. In 1516 he supplied ten highly significant ones for Grüninger's Erklärung der 10 Gebote. After that he supplied only individual illustrations. In 1522 he did the title page for Indagine's Chiromanzey, which was printed by Schott; in 1531 he provided the coat of arms for Kern's Visierbuch; and in 1543 the bust illustration of Hedion for his Chronik.

While he did not continue to provide as much in this later period, there were still many minor artists doing book illustration. In 1517 the artist HF illustrated Geiler's Brösamlin with 16 woodcuts and the Buch der Sünden des Munds with 10 leaves. The artist GH supplied two sheets for Geiler's Buch von der Ameise and decorated other of Gruninger's publications with title pages. The artist [illegible] supplied a bad page to Geiler's Buch der Sunden des Munds in 1516, while the artist [illegible] supplied Geiler's Alphabet with four woodcuts. Heinrich Vogtherr was really transitional to a later period, but in 1527 he supplied the illustrations for Grüninger's Neuen Testament. Finally, drawing of plants was raised to new heights by Hans Weiditz.

While a number of important Strassburg artists have been identified, a still larger number who supplied illustrations are unknown.

Notes

1) Woltmann, Geschichte der deutschen Kunst in Elsass. Leipzig, 1876. Chapters 12 & 13; For Hans Wächtlin, see Loedel. Des Strassburger Malers und Formschneiders Johann Wächtlin gen. Pilgrim Holzschnitte in Clairobscur. Leipzig, 1863; Schneegans in Naumann's Archiv für die zeichnenden Künste II:148-152, 1856; Choulant, Geschichte und Bibliographie der anatomischen Abbildungen. Leipzig, 1852; Choulant in Archiv für die zeichnenden Kunste. VII:272; For Hans Baldung Grün see: "Eisenmann" in Meyer's Künstlerlexicon. No's 20 and 21; For his illustrations of the ten commandments, see Geffcken. Der Bilderkatechismus der 15ten Jahrhunderts. Leipzig, 1835; For Hans Weiditz see Flückiger in Brunsel's Archiv für Pharmacie. Halle, 1878; Choulant

in Naumann's Archiv III:228, 1857; Wigand, Wetzlar'sche Beitrage für Geschichte und Rechtsalterthümer I:227ff; Treviranus in Archiv für die zeichnenden Künste 1:139ff; Treviranus, "Ueber Pflanzenabbildungen durch den Holzschnitt." Druckschriften der k. bair. bot. Gesellschaft zu Regensburg III, 1841.

2) Stated by Schneegans in another source.

3) Reproduced in Weigel, Holzschnitte berühmter Meister. Part IV, No. 28 and text pages 18-19.

4) Panzer I, No. 577. Folio.

5) Weigel, No. 19445. Small folio.

6) Ebert, No. 8245. Folio; Panzer II:62, No. 1280; Weller, No. 2072.

7) Weigel, No. 18777; Choulant, "Botan. und anatom. Abbildungen" in Naumann's Archiv III:272-273, 1857.

8) A reduced copy of one of the woodcuts is in Choulant's Geschichte und Bibliographie der anatomischen Abbildungen. Leipzig, 1852, see p. 26 and text on pages 25-27.

9) Weller, No. 3794.

10) Panzer I:417, for the 1518 edition; Panzer I:425, for the 1519 edition.

11) Woltmann, on p. 282, names a 1508 edition that was illustrated by Baldung and published by Knoblouch and designates the mass of Burgkmair's drawings as copies; however no such edition could be located.

12) Weller, No. 997.

13) Weller, No. 702. Octavo; Weigel, No. 9926 and 1513; Panzer I:352, No. 747.

14) Panzer I:357, No. 761.

15) Weller, No. 995; Panzer I:386.

16) Copied in Geiler von Kaisersperg's Buch der Sünden des Munds on sheet 18b and in Pauli's Schimpf und Ernst in 1533.

17) Copied in Geiler's Alphabet in 23 Predigten, issued by Grüninger in 1518, on leaf 13.

18) Copied in Geiler's Alphabet in 23 Predigten on leaf 34 and in Pauli's Schimpf und Ernst of 1533.

19) Copied in Pauli's 1533 Grüninger edition of Schimpf und Ernst on leaf 61b.

20) Copied in Geiler's Alphabet in 23 Predigten, leaf 6, published by Grüninger in 1518.

21) Copied in the 1533 Pauli's Schimpf und Ernst on leaf 37b.

22) Panzer II:232, No. 2084. Folio.

23) Eisenmann reproduces two illustrations by him without giving the title of the book in which they appeared. The first one bear the initials "H. B. G." I have not been able to locate either of these in any book.

24) Ebert, No. 8227. Folio; Panzer I:400, No. 865; Weigel III, No. 13361; Weigel IV, No. 18360.

25) Weller, No. 1049; Ebert, No. 8228; Panzer I:413, No. 894.

26) Ebert, No. 8229; Panzer, Suppl:136, No. 834c; Weigel III, No. 13361; Weigel IV, No. 18360.

27) Weller, No. 1199. Quarto.

28) Weller, No. 1225. Quarto; Panzer I:825, No. 938.

29) Weigel 14, No. 12862. Folio; Schott, Strassburg 1530, 1531, 1532; Weigel 15, No. 13356.

Chapter XXII

STRASSBURG ILLUSTRATIONS BY UNKNOWN ARTISTS (1)

Johann Grüninger continued his wide scale activity in publishing illustrated books in the sixteenth century; however, he did not continue to lavish the high level of care that he had earlier given his book illustrations. He owned so many woodblocks that he used them for dissimilar works, using practically everything in his stock. He only rarely had new drawings made.

The first illustrated book that he published in 1509 [1417] was a Beschreibung der Weltkugel (2). This was followed by [1418] Boccaccio's Decameron (3). The title page woodcut is 100 x 148 mm. The 65 text woodcuts, which are 80-85 mm high and 135-140 mm wide, are assembled from square blocks which frequently do not relate to each other.

Of the many woodcuts in [1419] the 1509 edition of Murner's Logica memorativa (4), the first one (160 x 100), with the superscript "Typus logices," is taken from the Margarita philosophica by Gregor Reisch, which was printed by Johann Schott in 1504. The other 49, which are new, illustrate the various theorems of logic in fantastic ways.

The four woodcuts (120 x 96) that illustrate [1420] the little 1509 booklet Saget wie Fernandus König von Castilien und Emanuel König zu Portugal haben das weite mer ersucht un funden viel inseln und eine neue Welt (5) belong to an entirely different field. As a group the woodcuts are well done, though not comparable to the illustrations for the same voyage that Burgkmair supplied at about the same time.

The fifth book printed in 1509 is Geiler's [1421] Passion in Form eines Gerichtschandels (6), which had 22 woodcuts. Of these, the first five were taken from older works. Of the other seventeen, two were used twice and the group was clearly the work of a number of different artists. These same illustrations were used in a second edition of the Passion in 1514.

The last of the group printed in 1509 was [1422] the Prognosticatio, by Jacob Henrichmann (7), which had only a small and unimportant (60 x 60) title page woodcut.

In 1510 Grüninger issued a new edition of the [1423] Heiligenlebens (8) which he had issued in 1502. He also printed [1424] Geiler's Navicula fatuorum, using the original woodcuts that had been used in Brant's Narrenschiff, and reissued it in 1511.

In 1512 there followed Hermann von Sachsenheim's tale [1425] of Die Mörin (10), which first appeared in Worms in the same year. Here, too, many of the woodcuts are old, with one of the old illustrations being from the title page of the 1496 Terenz.

The illustrations in the edition of [1426] Reisch's Margarita Philosophica nova (11), published by Grüninger in 1512, were partly from the Johann Schott edition of 1504, with numbers 1-5 and 9 being taken directly from that source; the other mathematical and astronomical illustrations are also from that source.

In the same year, 1512, Grüninger printed [1427] Geiler's Schiff des Heils (12), which is a

German abstract of the Navicula penitentiae. It had nine woodcuts (usually 105 x 135) portraying ships, and some larger ones.

Geiler's [1428] Predigt von der Himmelfahrt Maria (13), which was also published in 1512, has three woodcuts. The first one is 210 x 140 mm and the other two are smaller.

In 1513 Grüninger [1429-1431] published a new edition of the Evangelienbuches (14), as well as the Heiligenlebens (15), and he printed, without his imprint, Geiler's Predigt an Bischof Albrecht von Strassburg (16). The first of the three important woodcuts in these is 200 x 155 mm, the second is 122 x 134 mm, and the third 147 x 95 mm.

In 1514 [1432] he issued Murner's Geistliche Badenfahrt (17). The woodcuts (113 x 80) are just as curious as the text. The book itself is designed, like the Narrenschiff, so that the woodcuts, in order to explain the events, are always placed on the left-hand page. First there is a superscript and then a four-line verse to explain the woodcut, followed by the woodcut itself and, finally, text on the other half page. The second illustration is taken from Geiler's Predigt.

In addition to this there followed in 1514 a whole series of works by Geiler. His [1433] Passion des Herrn Jesu aus dem latin gebracht, by Joh. Adelphus (18), has many large woodcuts which are of low artistic value. His [1434] Irrig Schaf of 1514 (19) consists of seven tracts, each of which has a (84 x 75) title page woodcut. The one with the three-cornered mirror has the large letters "H G" on the sides, which may perhaps refer to the artist HG. There are six very important Dance of Death scenes in [1435] Geiler's Sermones de tempore et sanctis (20), which was first published in 1514. The first woodcut is 162 x 130 mm; the next is 75 x 65 mm and the third is 160 x 130 mm. The last three are 85 x 110 or 100 x 110 mm. These too are very similar to the works of the artist HG.

The final book printed in 1514 by Grüninger is [1436] Der weis Ritter, wie er so getruwlich beistund ritter Leuwen, des Herzogen Sun von Burges, das er zuletzt ein Künnigreich befass (21). The woodcuts are by various artists and some of them are new. The large (160 x 130) title page woodcut appears to have come from the same artist whose monogram is given above. Then come carefully prepared (80 x 130) illustrations in the first part of the book. The illustrations in the second part of the book are assembled from various woodblocks and mostly are from the Hug Schapler of 1500 and from the 1502 Virgil.

There is nothing new in the 33 illustrations in [1437] Historie von Kaiser Karls Sohn Lothar (22). The many (120 x 145) woodcuts come from the Geschichte des Hug Schapler. Some come from Virgil. The source of those on sheets 28b, 42b, 81b, 94a and 95 is unknown.

The edition of [1438] Virgil's Dryzehn Aeneadische Bücher von Trojanischer Zerstorung und uffgang des Römischen Reichs durch Doctor Murner tutst (23), which appeared in 1515, had the woodcuts of the Latin edition of 1502. Aside from this the only other 1515 item is the reprint [1439] of Geiler's Evangelienbuch (24).

Starting with 1516, [1440-1442] there was the Histori von eines reichen Burgers son uss der schönen inseln Cypern geboren (25), with four woodcuts; and a new edition of Der Altväter Leben (26); followed by a reprinting, in 1517, of Geiler's 1516 book with the supplement Herr der Kung ich diente gern attached to his Buch von Ameisen (27). The 28 illustrations in this are of various different types. All of the larger woodcuts were various scenes from the Passion, used here in a different sense.

Geiler's [1443] *Brösamlein* of 1517 (28) is not as complicated. It has a total of 34 woodcuts. The title page was previously used in the 1513 *Predigt an Bischof Albrecht.* Sheets 4 to 18, 20, 21, 23, 24, 27 and 29 are attributable to the artist HF. Numbers 31 and 32 were used before in the *Buche von der Ameise.* Figures 19 and 26 are taken from the *Geschichte von Hug Schapler* of 1500. Nos. 2 and 3 were taken from the 1502 *Vita sanctorum.* Of the remaining ones that appear to be new, namely 22, 28, 30, 33 and 34, the last three are the most important.

Geiler's 1517 [1444] *Buch der Sünden des Munds* has 18 woodcuts from a number of sources. No. 1 is the one used in the edition of 1513. Numbers 2-5, 8-11, and 14-16 were done by the artist HF. No. 7 is by Hans Baldung Grün and number 13 by the artist [monogram]. No. 6 is from the 1498 *Horaz* and number 17 is from Brunschweig's *Chirurgia* of 1497. No. 18 comes from the 1517 *Brösamlein* and No. 12 is from Geiler's *Passion.*

The three woodcuts in [1445] Geiler's 1518 *Sermones et varii tractatus* (30) appear, however, to be attributable to the artist [monogram] because of their large heads, small bodies and long slitted eyes.

In Geiler's 1518 [1446] *Alphabet in 23 Predigten,* each section is illustrated by a woodcut. Numbers 4, 7, 8 and 21 are by Hans Baldung Grün; sheets 2, 5, 13, and 18 by the artist HF, and Nos. 3, 10, 14, 15, 22 and 23 are by the artist [monogram]. Nos. 9 and 20 come from the 1500 *Geschichte des Hug Schapler.* No. 17 is taken from an old *Hortulus.* The new illustrations appear to be the title page and numbers 6, 11, 12, 16 and 19.

In 1519 Grüninger, in addition to a small piece [1447] by Laur. Phries on *Synonymae* (31), did Murner's [1448] *Ulenspiegel* (32), which had 88 illustrations. In the 1520 edition [1449] of the *Frag und Antwort der zehn Gebot* (33), Baldung's illustrations were repeated. Kaisersperg's 1520 edition of [1450] *Predigt von den drei Marien am Grabe* (34) has a large title page illustration and five text woodcuts. In 1520 Gruninger also printed [1451] Amandus Farckal's *Historie von Flos und Blank Flos* (35), in which the woodcuts are a reprinting of those that appeared in Kaspar Hochfeder's original Metz edition of 1499.

The 1520 edition of [1452] *Lebendsgeschichte Barbarossa,* by Joh. Adelffus (36), has artistically unimportant illustrations.

Geiler's [1453] *Narrenschiff us latin in tütsch gebracht von Johan Pauli* (37), which was published by Grüninger in 1520, has the familiar (115 x 82) woodcuts that were originally in Brant's *Narrenschiff,* and which Grüninger had already used in Geiler's *Navicula fatuorum.* Only the first text woodcut (100 x 93), in which the initial "T" is on the left of the cripples at the entrance to the temple, is from an earlier Grüninger edition.

This was followed in 1521 by [1454] Geiler's *Arbore humana von dem menschlichen Baum* (38), with five woodcuts.

Also in 1521, there was an edition of [1455] Marsilius Ficinus' *Buch des gesunden und langen Lebens aus Latein in Deutsch gemacht* (39) with the same woodcuts that were used in the 1505 *Medicinarius,* and which even at that time were taken from the 1497 edition of Brunschweig's 1497 *Chirurgia* and from the 1502 *Virgil.* The woodcuts in the new 1521 editions [1456-1457] of *Der*

Altväter Leben (40) and Brunschwig's Destillirbuch are equally old.

In 1522 [1458-1459] Grüninger printed Geiler's Plenarium und Postil (41), but the best known publication of this year was Murner's Von dem grossen lutherischen Narren (42). It has 52 woodcuts (115 x 95) which are not very important. However the book gladdens one because it is one of the few Grüninger publications of that period for which the illustrations were newly prepared.

Laurentius Phries' [1460] Bericht zur Stärkung des Gedächtnisses (43) has Phries' portrait on the title page. In the [1461] Ordnung des Hofgerichts von Rotweil (44), of the same year, there is a large woodcut on leaf 3.

In 1524 (45) and 1525 (46) there were new editions [1462] of the Buchs des Weisheit, using the old woodcuts. In 1525 he printed [1463] Altensteig's Büchlein über die Füllerei (47), and in addition, at the expense of Johann Koburger, the Pirkheimer edition of Ptolomaeus (48) for which Dürer provided the drawing.

The 1527 [1464] Evangelia mit Auslegung des hochgelehrten Doctor Kaisperspergs (49) had an assembly of woodcuts of varying ages, including some from Scheifelin's Geburt Christi and some works by the artist HF which are among the most important of those included.

Grüninger's last 1527 book [1465] is Hieronymus Gebweiler's Kaiserlicher und Hispanischer Majestät Erzherzoge und Herzoge von Oesterreich alt Herkommen (50), which has the imperial escutcheon (49 x 45) on the title page and pictures in the text showing the progenitors of the House of Austria from Noah on.

Grüninger's edition [1466] of the large Hortus sanitatis (51) of 1529 is the 26th in the series of editions of this book. It includes a title page woodcut and badly cut text woodcuts. The bad woodcuts in the first four books are mostly newly cut; the 21 in the fifth book are old blocks.

The 1531 edition of Geber's [1467] De alchimia libri III (52) has a small title page illustration, followed by two important woodcuts in the style of Wächtlin. The first of these is 105 x 131 mm and the second is 100 x 128 mm. The rest of the illustrations are small renditions of chemical apparatus.

The stock of woodblocks that Joh. Grüninger accumulated later became the property of B. Grüninger. The way the latter used them is shown by his 1557 edition of [1468] Johann Pauli's Schimpf und Ernst (53) in which he used eleven from one old artist, two from another and the rest from a miscellany of other books.

What Johannes Grüninger contributed in his last years is really very little; he lived off the woodcuts of the great publications that he produced around the turn of the century.

In terms of the number of publications produced, the other printers who were working in Strassburg at this time cannot be compared with Grüninger.

Mathias Hupfuff continued in the 16th century, as in the fifteenth, to produce popular writings: tales, legends, songs, calendars, books of advice, etc., all richly supplied with woodcuts. These, however, continued to be as worthless artistically as his earlier ones, and were mostly borrowed from older books.

In his 1510 edition [1469] of Brandon's Meerfahrt (54) there is a (108 x 74) title page woodcut and a 50 x 75 mm woodcut on the verso of the title page. The other 22 (50 x 70) are the same as those in the earlier editions but have been done in the Alsace style.

The many illustrations that were printed in the 1510 edition of [1470] Tengler's Layenspiegels, which was issued in a new edition in 1511 (55), are copies of those that decorated the Othmar edition issued in Augsburg in 1509.

His [1471] Seelenwurzgarten (56) of 1511 has 95 woodcuts, all of which were taken from earlier books. There is not a single newly cut woodblock in Hupfuff's edition.

His [1472-1476] Lucidarius of 1511 (57) has the customary old woodcuts; the Kalender of the same year (58), which he repeated in 1513 (59), has the 18 large and 37 smaller calendar illustrations that present the planets and the fixed stars, the four seasons and bloodletting; in the Büchlein von der Complexion des Menschens (60) as well as the Donatus minor (61) there are only title page illustrations.

In 1512 he issued an edition [1477-1483] of the Narrenschiffes (62) with the original woodcuts; one of the Sieben weisen Meisters (63); one of the Evangelienbuches and one of Arnold de Villanova's Tractat von der Bereitung der Weins (64). Of the 97 woodcuts in Murner's Narrenbeschwörung of 1512, seventy are from the Narrenschiff, two are from old books and 17 were done by Urs Graf. The 1512 edition of Murner's richly illustrated Schelmenzunft (65) was likewise printed by Hupfuff. The last book printed by Hupfuff in 1512 was Johann Adelphus' Sage vom Rock zu Trier (66).

In 1513 he issued [1484-1489] an edition of Lebens des Altväters (67); of the Evangelien (68); of the Heiligenlebens (69); and he printed a Canzleibüchlein (70); Folzen's Lied von der göttlichen Weisheit und menschlichen Thorheit (71); a Lied vom Sacrament (72); and a reprint of the Passion (73) with the 25 Urs Graf illustrations. The edition of the Heiligenlebens was particularly characteristic of Hupfuff's work. Of the 272 woodcuts--of which 140 related to the summer part and 132 to the winter part--many were taken from the 1470's. A Strassburg artist then filled in the few that were missing.

In 1514 he published [1490-1492] a new edition of Brandon's Meerfahrt (74); Meister Elucidarius (75); and the Historie der grossen Alexander (76).

Many illustrated books were issued in 1515 [1493-1502]: Die vier Angeltugenden (77); Die Problemata des Aristoteles (78); Das Lied von den sieben Worten unser lieben Herrn (79); the Monch, der zwei zusammengekoppelt ohn sein Wissen (80); Der Bruder Rausch, was er wunders geschrieben hat in einer Kloster (81); Murner's Muhle von Schwindelsheim (82); Talat's Arzneibüchlein (83); and Das Mirakel von einem Geist (84). Also, the Sellenwurzgarten of 1511 was issued in a new edition (85); and Geiler's Auslegung des Pater noster (86) was printed with a (182 x 135) title page woodcut which had been reused frequently.

The woodcuts in [1503] Brant's Richterlich Klagspiegel (87) of 1516 were taken from Tengler's Layenspiegel.

Thus Hupfuff is independent in practically none of his publications; his woodcuts are worthless duplications of earlier works.

The third printer of this period, Johann Schott, is of much greater importance. The edition of Ptolemaus, supplied with maps by Jakob Oessler and Georg Ueberlin, which he published in 1513 and again in 1520, is among the best produced by Strassburg typography. Its merits are comparable to those of Gehler's Postill of 1514, with its admirable portrait of the preacher; the Wächtlin illustrations of the Passion; Gerdsorf's Feldbuch der Wundarznei; and Brunsel's Krauterbuch, with its plant illustrations by Hans Weiditz.

In 1518 he issued a German edition of Petrus de Crescentiis' Liber ruralium commodorum, which had appeared in illustrated editions five times in the fifteenth century, under the title [1504] Von dem Nutz der Ding, die in Aeckern gebaut werden (88). The (215 x 165) woodcut after the table of contents is in the style of Hans Baldung. The 157 smaller (usually 85 x 70) woodcuts in the text follow those in earlier editions. The genre paintings are reproduced carefully but the illustrations of the individual plants are not as good in drawing or as well cut as those in the 1493 edition.

Schott's 1519 printing of the booklet [1505] Carolus V Romanorum rex electus (89) has a 142 x 100 title page woodcut.

The Gallianus [1506] Practica auf drei Jahr (90), which was published in 1521, had two large and six small woodcuts; the [1507] Epistel an die Römer (91), published in 1522, had only a title page illustration.

Also in 1522 he printed a first octavo edition [1508] of Luther's New Testament, with a portrait of each evangelist before his section and, before the treatment of the apostles, a large group woodcut showing the apostles all together. After the apostles there is a picture of the Savior with a legend. Also, before each epistle there is a woodcut of its author. The woodcut on the last leaf shows Christ on the Mount of Olives, and above him the legend "Christ Prevails."

In 1523 he printed [1509] Luther's 27 Predigten (93). It has an illustration on the verso of the fourth leaf. In the same year Schott published [1510] Johan Indagine's Die Kunst der Chiromantzey which, in addition to the bust illustration of the author, which was discussed under H. B. Grün, had a number of well done (75 x 130) woodcut illustrations of the planets.

In 1524 he printed [1511] Concordanz des neuen Testaments deutsch (94). It has an attractive border around the title.

Schott's second edition [1512] of Gersdorf's Feldbuch der Wundarznei, which was issued in 1526, has on the title page a picture of a burning city which is not in the 1517 edition. The other illustrations, which are all chirurgical, are the same as the earlier ones except that they are in a smaller format.

Schott lived until 1545, but was not active in his later years.

Johann Knoblouch, from Zofingen in Switzerland, printed in Strassburg from 1504 to 1528, but the quality of his publications was not up to that of Schott's, even though he was a very active printer. There are available some 200 Latin and 70 German works printed by him and they are in all fields from theology and classical literature to cookbooks. He not only printed for other publishers but, since his presses did not always suffice even for his own requirements, he had some of his printing done by Heinrich Gran of Hagenau and by other Strassburg printers. The many illustrations in his books, with the exception of the few that Urs Graf and Hans Baldung did for him, were mediocre and were mostly taken from books of the fifteenth century.

Two of his attractive little books were his editions [1513] of the Hortulus animae in 1507 (95) and 1509 (96). The 73 woodcuts are of varying sizes and by various artists.

His 1507 edition [1514] of Montevillas Reise (97) had the customary worthless woodcuts of this book.

The 24 illustrations in von Passau's [1515] 24 Alten (98), published in 1508, were those that Johann Schott had prepared (140 x 142) for his 1500 edition. The one for the title page (150 x 110) is new.

The [1516] 1508 Moretus (99) has only a title page illustration. The 1509 edition [1517] of Spiegel christlicher Walfahrt (100) is much more interesting. It was by Johannes Schottus Argentinensis and presents the ten commandments in words and pictures. At the end there is a woodcut of the drowning of the Egyptians in the Red Sea. The illustrations are quite old-fashioned and are not comparable to those prepared by Baldung in 1516 (101).

[1518-1521] The many woodcuts in Knoblouch's 1510 edition of Histori von der Zerstörung der Stadt Troy (102) are reused from earlier editions. In the same year there appeared the small books Ein Narr gab seinem Herrn guten rat (103), Vom König Salomon (104), and Vom Habicht (105). The title page woodcut and the 46 text illustrations in the Salomon book are taken from earlier editions and the booklet about Habicht has only a title page woodcut.

In 1511 he printed an edition of [1522] Geisler's Rhetorik (106) and then there is a gap until 1515 when he issued [1523] Reisebeschreibung des Ludovico de Barthemia (107). This last-named had 45 (67 x 97) woodcuts which were copied from the ones in the Augsburg edition. The most important of its illustrations is that on the title page.

Knoblouch's output in 1516 was rich. His [1524] Türkische Chronika (108) had the title page illustration and the 25 woodcuts in the text from the Flach edition of 1508. In the small cookbook [1525], which he published under the title Kuchenmeisterei (109), there is a 150 x 100 mm title page woodcut.

The woodcuts in [1526-1528] Murner's Schelmenzunft (110) of 1516, as well as those in Riederer's Spiegel der Rhetorik (111) and in the Büchlein von Complexion (112) were, again, taken from earlier editions. The same is true of the 51 illustrations in his 1518 edition of [1529] Brant's Vom Anfang der heiligen Stadt Jerusalem (113). These are all worthless and some had already been used in the Strassburg Bible of 1485.

In 1518 he also published [1530-1532] Murner's Narrenbeschwerung (114) in which he re-used the woodcuts in Hupfuff's edition of 1512; Brandon's Leben (115) in which the 26 old woodcuts were reused; as well as an edition of Versehung von Leib, Seel, Ehre und Gut (116) with its old title page.

In 1519 [1533-39] there followed an Evangelienbuch (117) as well as a new edition of the Ritters von Thurn (118) which was first published by Furter in Basel in 1492; the Tondalus (119); the Küchenmeisterei (120); and the Lucidarius (121). Also Schrick's Von den gebrannten Wassern (122) and Novavilla's Tractat von der Bereitung der Weine (123) were printed again with the old title pages.

In the 1519 edition [1540] of Luther's Sieben Busspsalmen (124) the title page woodcut shows the praying David with the harp.

The many woodcuts in his 1519 edition [1541] of Historie vom Ritter Wigoleis vom Rade (125) are little changed copies of the original Schoensperger edition of 1493. The [1542] Canzleibüchlein of 1520 (126) likewise used much older woodcuts.

In 1524 he printed [1543] Luther's Altes und neues Testament in folio. In the Old Testament the woodcuts of the first part are reworkings of the Othmar Bible of 1518, and the second part has reduced copies of those in the original Wittemberg edition, while the third part has true copies of the Wittemberg illustrations.

In his 1524 folio edition [1544] of the Neuen Testamentes (127) the border of the title page has a variety of biblical scenes. The 16 (115 x 68) woodcuts for the apocalypse are new but worthless.

Knoblouch's second folio edition [1545] of the Neues Testamentes repeats the woodcuts used in the earlier edition for the evangelists and the epistles. It has 20 (100 x 65) woodcuts for the apocalypse, instead of 16, but these do not add much to those in the 1524 edition.

He reprinted the second part of the Old Testament again in 1526 (128).

Thus, Knoblouch, with the exception of the woodcuts supplied by Urs Graf, also provided very little that was new.

Mathias Schürer published [1546] Geiler's Seelenparadies (129) in 1510. It has a very significant landscape on the title page, (130 x 130) which shows the wall around Paradise, the tree of knowledge with the snake wound around it, with Adam and Eve on the right and God on the left talking to them, and the gate to Paradise guarded by an angel bearing a sword.

Carben's [1547] Tractat von der unbefleckten Empfängnis (130), which Schürer printed in 1519, has only the title page illustration that had been used in earlier editions.

Martin Flach, the younger, the son of the like-named printer of the fifteenth century, started printing in Strassburg in 1501. He did not use many illustrations in his books and, aside from the large woodcut by Urs Graf in the Catalogus sanctorum of 1513 and the Hortulus illustrations by Hans Baldung, his illustrations were of little value.

Wintperger's [1548-1553] Badenfahrt of 1507 (131) and the Himmelfahrt Mariae (132); the Klage eines weltlichen sterbenden Menschen (133); the Lied von der Katharine (134); the Brunn des Rates (135); and the Bruder Rausch (136) of 1508, all have unimportant title pages.

In 1509 he printed the [1554] Historie des grossen Alexander (137), with the woodcuts that Kistler had had cut for his edition of 1503, as well as the [1555] Historie von Pontus und Sidonia (138) with reworked woodcuts from the first Augsburg edition of 1485.

In 1510 he did an edition of [1556] Hortulus animae in twelvmo, in which he reused mostly the woodcuts that Knoblouch used in his Hortulus of 1507.

In 1512 there followed [1557] Talat's Arzneibüchlein (139), using the customary title page woodcut; and a new edition of Wintperger's Badenfahrt (140).

In 1513 he printed [1558] Adolphis' Türkisch Cronika von ihrem Ursprung, Anfang und regiment bis auf dise Zeit (141), with eighteen (130 x 130) woodcuts. In preparing these woodcuts the model was the 1496 edition of Caorusin's work published in Ulm. Some of the reduced copies are from the Ulm pages. The newly prepared ones differ from the Ulm woodcuts in that while they show skill they also show carelessness. They have thick outlines and little shading.

A supplement to the Türkisch Cronika, [1559] the Historia von Rhodis (142), was also published in 1513, and this likewise was a new reworking of the fifteenth century Ulm edition of Caorusin's Opera ad Rhodiorum historiam spectantia. The title page is a woodcut of a Maltese knight and the text woodcuts repeat those in the Türkische Cronika.

In 1513 Flach printed the work of Doctor Eucharius Rosslin, [1560] Der schwangeren Frawen und Hebammen Rosengarten (143). One woodcut has the monogram . The others are by a different artist. The larger text woodcut, which is 125 x 95 mm, is quite worthwhile and the 19 smaller woodcuts are skillfully done even if they are not up to the quality of the large one, the chief illustration of the artist whose monogram is given above.

In 1519 Flach printed [1561] the Büchlein von der Complexion (144), and in 1520, a Frauenspiegel (145) as well as the Rede eines Ackermanns und des Tods (146); all of these had title page illustrations.

The title page of [1562] Luther's Sermon von dem Wucher (147), which Flach printed in 1520, is different from that found in other editions of this work.

In 1521, there followed [1563] his Heiligenleben (148). The full page Passion scenes are all taken from Urs Graf's Passion of 1506. The smaller woodcuts, which either filled the width of the entire page (80 x 148) or of only one column (70 x 74) are Strassburg works and are similar to those of the artist .

The woodcuts in [1564] the Evangelienbuch, which Flach printed for Knoblouch in 1522, are likewise highly variable. Most are 80 x 60 mm and are made broader by added borders, some of which are attributable to a skilled artist of the fifteenth century. Their original source is uncertain. The other works Flach prepared in 1522 were [1565-1566] the book Von einer Gräfin von Anhalt (150) and a new edition of Rosslin's Rosengarten. In the latter the title page woodcut shows the book being handed to the princess; the rest of the illustrations are the same as those in the earlier editions except that they are cut in reverse and are somewhat better.

Of the two printers, Reinhard and Balthasar Beck, there are only a few church publications and natural science publications that can be listed. In the [1567] Missale speciale (151), which was printed by Reinhard Beck in 1512, there is a fine large woodcut that is completely in the style of Wächtlin and is identified by the highly skilled handling of costume.

The two editions [1568] of the larger Hortus sanitatis which he printed in 1515 and 1521 are the 23rd and 24th in the series of editions of this work. The first part of the 1515 edition (152) is based on that of the Joh. Prüss edition of 1507-1509. The rest of the illustrations, except for the plant pictures in Part 2, which are redone either in reversal or the same direction, reuse the old woodblocks from Pruss' edition. The [1569] 1521 edition (153) is quite different in many respects and the full page woodcut before the table of contents is taken from Gersdorf's Feldbuch der Wundarznei of 1517. The 25th edition in the series, [1570] which Balthasar Beck produced in 1527 (154), has the same woodcuts except that they appear more worn.

In 1529 he printed [1571] Laurentius Phries' Spiegel des Arznei (155). The title page woodcut is 230 x 160 mm.

A later printer, Wolff Köpphl, is known primarily through his [1572] 1530 folio edition of the Gantze Bibel Alt und Neuw Testament verteutsch durch D. Mart. Luther. Item auch mit zweihundert Figuren mehr dann vor hier nie im Truck aussgangen seind. It is divided into six parts. The woodcuts of the first part, which comprises the five books of Moses, are 65 x 55 mm. The second part has the same title page as the first, and a couple of text woodcuts. The third part has just one illustration and the section on prophets has none. In the apocrypha the woodcuts are 48 x 66 mm and there are not many of them. In the New Testament there are handsome pictures (80 x 65) of Matthew, Luke and John before their text, and only Mark is out of this series, being represented in a smaller and less important picture. There is one illustration at the beginning of the Apostles, and the epistles are preceded by woodcuts of their authors, but here the illustration of Paul is taken from the Knoblouch edition of 1524.

Thus, in the first quarter of the sixteenth century Strassburg was second to Augsburg in terms of the number of illustrated books produced. The largest printers, including Hans Grüninger, Mathias Hupfuff, Johann Schott, Johann Knoblouch, Mathias Schurer, Martin Flach and the two Becks, could hardly produce the workload themselves and had at times to call on other printers to help out. While Grüninger used his old stock of woodblocks very freely, nevertheless he called on a whole series of artists to prepare woodcuts for him, including not only Hans Baldung and Heinrich Bogtherr, but many others, including the artists [illegible] The smaller printers eagerly competed with him. Mathias Hupfuff got illustrations from Urs Graf and made boundless use of woodcuts from earlier books. Johan Schott had Reich's Margarita Philosophica illustrated by the artist [illegible] and Geller's Postille and Gersdorf's Wundarzneibuch illustrated by Hans Wächtlin, Otto Brunfel's Krauterbuch illustrated by Hans Weiditz, and published many handsome books whose decoration can not be attributed to any particular artist. Johann Knoblouch, also, was so varied in the form of his publications, that he may not be scorned. While most of his books had worthless reproductions of fifteenth century woodcuts, yet he also engaged artists like Urs Graf, Hans Wächtlin and Hans Baldung to prepare illustrations for his books. To do Martin Flach justice we need only call attention to the Hortulus of 1511 which he had Hans Baldung illustrate. There are three names that stand out like bright stars from the fullness of materials in Strassburg in this period: Geiler von Kaisersperg, Hans Grüninger and Hans Baldung.

Notes

1) Schmidt, Zur Geschichte der ältesten Bibliotheken und der ältesten Buchdrucker zu Strassburg. Strassburg, 1882.

2) Weller, No. 521. Quarto.

3) Panzer I:315, No. 661.

4) Ebert, No. 14534. Quarto; Panzer VI:46, No. 146.

5) Weller, No. 520. Quarto.

6) Panzer, Suppl:127, No. 769b. Folio.

7) Lacking in bibliographical works; German. Mus. No. 16030.

8) Weller, No. 566.

9) Panzer VI:50, No. 202.

10) Panzer I:346, No. 735.

11) Germ. Mus. No. 28071; Not in Panzer VI:55ff.

12) Ebert, No. 8240. Folio. Panzer I:337, No. 708; Weigel IV, No. 18360; Weller, No. 684.

13) Weller, No. 685.

14) Panzer I:351.

15) Panzer I, No. 750.

16) Weller, No. 777. Folio.

17) Panzer I, No. 798.

18) Weller, No. 827.

19) Panzer I:364, No. 773.

20) Panzer VI:64, No. 317.

21) Weller, No. 850.

22) Panzer, Suppl:1129, No. 728c. Folio.

23) Panzer I:384.

24) Weller, No. 894.

25) Weller, No. 1000.

26) Panzer I:388.

27) Ebert, No. 8229; Panzer, Suppl:136, No. 834c; Weigel III, No. 13361, IV, No. 18360; Weller, No. 996 for the 1517 edition; Weller, No. 1050.

28) Ebert, No. 8227. Folio; Panzer I:400; No. 865; Weigel III, No. 13361, IV, No. 18360.

29) Ebert, No. 8228. Folio; Panzer I:413, No. 894; Weller, No. 1049.

30) Panzer VI:86, No. 502.

31) Weller, No. 1256.

32) Weller, No. 1252.

33) Weller, No. 1384.

34) Weller, No. 1392.

35) Lacking in Panzer and Weller.

36) Barbarossa, Eine wahrhafte Beschreibung des Lebens Friedrich I. Folio; Panzer I:443, No. 998. Folio.

37) Ebert, No. 8236. Folio; Panzer I:434, No. 968; Weigel IV, No. 17887.

38) Weigel, No. 23787. Folio.

39) Weller, No. 1170. Folio.

40) Weller, No. 1804. Folio; Weigel, No. 9929.

41) Weller, No. 2071 and No. 2072.

42) Panzer II:112. Quarto; Waldau, _Nachricht von Th. Murner's Leben und Schriften._ New ed. Kurz. p. 99; Reviewed by Naumann in _Serapeum_ IX:265.

43) Weller, No. 2428.

44) Weller, No. 2627.

45) Weller, No. 2800.

46) Weller, No. 3335.

47) Weller, No. 3262.

48) Ptolomaeus, Claudius. _Geographicae Enarrationis libri ed. Bilipaldus Berkheymer_; Becker in _Naumann's Archiv_ IV (Thausing's _Dürer_) p. 447-448.

49) Weller, No. 2071.

50) Germ. Mus. No. 1785.

51) Choulant, p. 256, No. 26. Folio.

52) Germ. Mus. No. 1786. Folio.

53) Ebert, No. 15996. Folio.

54) Weller, No. 823.

55) Panzer I:322 re the 1510 edition; Panzer I:332 re the 1511 edition.

56) Weller, No. 633.

57) Panzer I:334.

58) Weller, No. 647.

59) Panzer I:361, No. 766. Quarto.

60) Panzer I:334.

61) Weller, No. 636.

62) Panzer I:347, No. 736.

63) Weller, No. 703.

64) Panzer I:345, No. 730.

65) Panzer I:349, No. 738; Weller, No. 726.

66) Weller, No. 735; Panzer I:340, No. 715. Quarto.

67) Panzer I:352.

68) Weller, No. 775.

69) Weller, No. 785.

70) Weller, No. 762.

71) Weller, No. 790.

72) Weller, No. 800.

73) Weller, No. 802.

74) Weller, No. 823.

75) Panzer I:369.

76) Panzer I:369.

77) Weller, No. 955.

78) Weller, No. 882.

79) Weller, No. 908.

80) Weller, No. 921.

81) Weller, No. 940.

82) Panzer I:384.

83) Panzer I:380.

84) Weller, No. 927.

85) Panzer I:367, No. 807. Folio.

86) Panzer I:375, No. 806.

87) Panzer I:390.

88) Ebert, No. 5443. Folio; Weller, No. 1103; Panzer I:417, No. 908; Choulant, p. 285, No. 7.

89) Panzer IX:370, No. 544b. Quarto.

90) Weller, No. 1929.

91) Weller, No. 2046.

92) Panzer II:136, No. 1623.

93) Panzer II:163, No. 1798.

94) Panzer II:251, No. 2156.

95) Panzer I:277, No. 580.

96) Hortulus animae denuo diligenter castigatus; Weigel, No. 6801. Small octavo.

97) Weller, No. 408; Panzer I:285.

98) Weller, No. 430.

99) Weller, No. 453.

100) Weller, No. 512.

101) Geffken. Der Bilderkatechismus des 15. Jahrhunderts. Leipzig, 1885. p. 179-188.

102) Panzer I:324, No. 684.

103) Weller, No. 599.

104) Weller, No. 4076.

105) Weller, No. 534.

106) Panzer I:334.

107) Panzer I:381.

108) Weller, No. 991.

109) Panzer, Suppl:107, No. 597d. Quarto; Weller, No. 1004.

110) Panzer I:396, No. 858.

111) Panzer I:406.

112) Weller, No. 988.

113) Panzer I:418, No. 912. Folio; Weller, No. 1096.

114) Panzer I:421.

115) Weller, No. 1097.

116) Weller, No. 1156.

117) Weller, No. 1180.

118) Panzer I:430, No. 957.

119) Weller, No. 972.

120) Weller, No. 1204.

121) Weller, No. 1217.

122) Panzer I:274, No. 571. Quarto; p. 345, No. 730-731.

123) Weller, No. 1253.

124) Panzer, Suppl:152.

125) Panzer, Suppl:164.

126) Weller, No. 1341.

127) Panzer II:240, No. 2112 re Part I; No. 1524 re Part II; Panzer II:240, No. 2113 re Part 3, 1525; Panzer II:347, No. 2953.

128) Panzer II:422, No. 2953.

129) Panzer I:319, No. 669.

130) Weller, No. 1175.

131) Panzer I:283.

132) Weller, No. 437.

133) Weller, No. 440.

134) Weller, No. 443.

135) Panzer I:288.

136) Weller, No. 457.

137) Panzer I:313.

138) Panzer I:313, No. 658.

139) Panzer I:344.

140) Panzer I:345; Weller, No. 751.

141) Panzer I:356; Weigel, No. 20082. Folio.

142) Panzer I:355, No. 759.

143) Panzer I:355, No. 755. Quarto; Brulliot I, No. 1391; Choulant, in _Naumann's Archiv_ III:1857.

144) Weller, No. 1168.

145) Weller, No. 1386.

146) Weller, No. 1631.

147) Panzer, Suppl:157.

148) Weller, No. 1803.

149) Weller, No. 2062.

150) Weller, No. 2095.

151) Panzer VI:58, No. 270.

152) Panzer I:379. Folio; Pritzel, No. 11896; Choulant, p. 254, No. 23.

153) Bibl. Rivin. No. 5685. Folio; Pritzel, No. 11897; Choulant, p. 255, No. 24; Weller, No. 1710; Weigel, No. 20087.

154) Trew Catal. II, No. IV, 11-12; Pritzel, No. 11899-11900; Choulant, p. 255, No. 25; Weller, No. 3810.

155) Germ. Mus. No. 19939. Folio.

Chapter XXIII

WITTEMBERG (1)

Wittemberg achieved its position in the history of book illustration by virtue of Martin Luther and Lucas Cranach.

Johann Grünenberg opened his printing shop in 1509 and one of his first publications was [1573, Pl. 252-253] Cranach's *Heiligthumsbuch* (2), which he printed in 1509. It has 44 leaves with 119 woodcuts to present the religious relics preserved in Wittemberg. After this there was a long period of quiescence until 1516 when he issued [1574] Luther's first German work, the *Geistlich edle Büchlein von rechter Unterscheyd und verstand, was der alt und new mensche sey*. It had a title page woodcut.

Starting in 1520 a number of new printing plants became active in Wittemberg. Melchior Lotther was active from 1520 to 1529; Georg Rhaw printed his first work in 1520; in 1525 Hans Lufft took the place of Johann Grünenberg, who died in 1522; and Joseph Klug started printing in 1524. And they all found enough work to do in the printing of Martin Luther's writings.

Practically all of the small publications of the Reformer were supplied with title page woodcuts.

The 1519 edition of [1575] *Sermon von dem Wucher* (3) had a title page illustration and [1576] the two printings of the *Sermon von dem Hochwürdigen Sacrament* (4), which were issued in this same year, each had a different title page illustration.

In 1520 [1577-1580] Grünenberg reprinted the *Sermon von dem Wucher* (5), with the same title page; Lotther printed the *Sermon von guten Werken* (6), with a woodcut on the title page; the *Sermon von der Betrachtung des Leidens Christi* (7), which was published without the name of the publisher, but with a title page illustration; as well as the *Sermon von der Freiheit eines Christenmenschen* (8), also with a title page woodcut.

In 1521 [1581] there appeared the *Unterricht für die Beichtkinder* (9) with a title page woodcut. However, the important publication of the year was [1582, Pl. 254-255] Grünenberg's edition of Cranach's *Passional Christi und Antichristi* (10, 11). The illustrations, which are counterposed left and right, maximize the contrasts. One of the woodcuts, however, is taken from [1583] the undated (but certainly published in 1521 in Wittemberg) *Clag und Bitt der deutschen Nation an Gott um Erlos aus dem gesenckniss der Antichrist* (12).

In 1522, in addition to [1584-1590] *Auslesung der Episteln und Evangelien* (13), there were again many smaller writings. In *Welche Personen verboten sind sich zu ehelichen* (14) there is a title page woodcut. In the *Sermon am Sonntag Quasimodogeniti* (15); the *Sermon von der Auffahrt Christi* (16); *Von dem heiligen Kreuz* (17); and the *Passio Christi* (18) each has a title page woodcut. In the *Sermo de sancto Anthonio Heremita* the (90 x 67) woodcut bears the monogram HD.

The [1591-1592] *Taufbüchlein* of 1523 (19) has a picture of a christening and the title page of the *Unterricht dem Rath zu Stettin zugeschickt* (20) shows a council meeting.

Luther began to translate individual parts of the Bible quite early. In 1521 Grünenberg issued [1593] the *Auslegung des 67ten Psalms* (21) with David and the harp on the title page.

This was followed [1594-1598], without the name of the printer, by *37te Psalm Davids* (22), with a picture of Mary and Child on the verso of the title page; and by the *Magnificat verdeutscht und ausgelegt* (23), with a woodcut on the last page. The first reprint in Wittemberg of the *Evangelium am zweiten Adventsonntage*, which was first published in 1521, appeared without date and with a woodcut illustration of the Judgment Day on its title page. Luther put his 1520 edition of *Kurze Form der zeehn Gepott* into his *Betbüchlein und Lesbüchlein*, which did not have any woodcuts until its second edition, published in 1523.

The beginning of the large scale publication of Luther's Bible translations was the 1532 folio edition of the New Testament which Melchior Lotther printed under the simple title [1599, Pl. 256-257], *Das Newe Testament. Deutzsch, Vuitennberg* (24) . It has woodcuts for the initial letters of the evangelists, followed by two heterogeneous, worthless, woodcuts, and the 21 illustrations in the Apocalypse, which are all 230 x 160 mm and fill the entire folio sheet. These latter are the most important illustrations. They were the first drawings of the Apocalypse since Dürer's and are based closely on his illustrations. The 21st of these is a reversed copy of the corresponding half of Dürer's sheet and it has the monogram HB. This monogram does not resolve the argument over the artist or artists who did the illustrations. It appears certain that in 1527 the woodblocks were in the possession of Cranach since there is a record of his having made them available, for 40 Thaler, to the Catholic theologian Emser for use in his translation of the New Testament, which was published by Stoeckel in Dresden in 1527. It also appears that they were produced in Cranach's workshop, with the basic work being done by his apprentices and the final corrections made by himself. This would explain the varying excellence of the individual sheets.

By December, 1522, Melchior Lotther issued [1600] the second folio edition (25) with the same illustrations except for minor variations in numbers 11, 16 and 17.

These slightly changed illustrations appeared in all later folio editions: [1601-1603] the third in 1523; the fifth in 1524, printed by the brothers Melchior and Michel Lotther; and the tenth, which Michel Lotther issued in 1526 (26).

When octavo editions of the New Testament were published it was no longer possible to use these large woodcuts, and new ones had to be prepared. The first edition in large octavo (27), which according to Panzer was the sixth in the series of editions of the New Testament [1604, Pl. 258], was published by Melchior Lotther, the younger, and the illustrations were prepared by the artist "G L" (Gottfried Leigel). For the title page the woodcut was a reduced (150 x 100) copy of the one that appeared first in the fifth folio edition of 1524. The other woodcuts were 145 x 95 mm.

It is doubtful that the woodcuts in the Apocalypse are attributable to the artist "G L"; in any event, they are less important than those in the *Evangelists* and the *Epistles*. The total num- of illustrations including the title page is 45, of which 24 are in the Evangelists, the Apostles and the Epistles, and 21 are in the Apocalypse. One bears the date 1523 and the eighth figure in the Apocalypse is the number XXII. These woodcuts were reprinted in [1605-1607] all subsequent large octavo editions of the New Testament: the fifth, which Melchior Lotther, the younger, printed in 1524; the sixth, which he printed in 1525; and the ninth, which was published by Michel Lotther in 1527 (28).

A number of the illustrations in the Lotther folio and large octavo editions are found in the small octavo editions [1608-1611] that were printed by Hans Luft. His first, which was the ninth in the total series, appeared in 1526 and had only the 21 illustrations of the Apocalypse. The second, number 14 in the total series of editions, followed in 1530 and had 13 illustrations for the four Evangelists and for the Apostles and the Epistles, and 26 in the Apocalypse. The new woodcuts in this edition are the eighth, ninth, tenth, eleventh and 25th. The third octavo edition (15th in the series) uses the same woodcuts, which here fill the page since the page is smaller. The same is true of the 1533 edition published by Lufft, which is the 17th octavo edition (29).

No sooner had Luther completed the translation of the New Testament in 1522 than he turned his skill to translation of the Old Testament. He started by translating the first three parts which he permitted to be published individually in Wittemberg.

The first part of the Alten Testamentes, including the five books of Moses, [1612, Pl. 259] was issued by Melchior Lotther in 1523 in its first folio edition, under the title, Das Allte Testament deutsch. M. Luther (30). It has eleven woodcuts which range in height from 220 to 232 mm and in width from 130 to 160 mm, thus filling the entire folio page. These woodcuts were reused in all later folio editions [1613-14] from the second by the Brothers Melchior and Michel Lotther in 1523, through the third to the sixth editions (31). The only difference is that they are not each done on a separate leaf as heretofore, but are printed on the versos.

The artist "G L" was again called upon to illustrate the [1615] large octavo editions which were initiated by Melchior Lotther, the younger, in 1524. The first of these editions has 13 woodcuts that fill the full page and are printed on the verso, and they have the date 1523 and the initials of the artist "G L." They were reused [1616] in Michel Lotther's 1525 fifth edition and in his [1617] 1528 large octavo edition (32).

The third group of illustrations is in [1618] the Hans Lufft 1523 edition, which was the third edition in small octavo (33). It has fifteen woodcuts which fill the page and are printed on the versos.

In the same year (1523) in which the first part of the Old Testament was printed three times in Wittemberg, Luther completed the second part and turned it over to the printer in time for publication early in 1524. This included the Old Testament from Joshua to Esther. The first edition bore the title [1619] Das Ander teyl des alten Testaments. Gedruckt zu Vuittemberg. In Folio (34). It was published at the beginning of 1524 by Melchior Lotther. The title page woodcut shows Joshua sitting on a rock, dressed in armor and holding the tablet of the commandments in his right hand and his helmet in his left hand. This woodcut was copied by Edward Schoen in his leaf for the Peypus Bible of 1524. The edition had a total of 24 figures, of which three were full page in size and the others were 105 x 160 mm. The woodcuts are of highly variable quality in drawing and in cut, and appear, like those of the New Testament, to have been done by various apprentices in Cranach's plant.

The illustrations of the second edition [1620] in large octavo that Melchior Lotther published in 1524, were supplied by the artist "G. L." The woodcut on the verso of the title page differs from that of the other editions in that Joshua, dressed in armor, has a large sword on his left and the tablet of commandments on his right; he is not sitting on a rock, as in the folio edition, but is standing and talking with the elders of the people. The 24 text illustrations, each of which fills a full page, are very skillfully modeled on those of the folio edition. Michel Lotther [1621] repeated then in the fourth of the large octavo editions (35), which he published in 1527.

By September, 1524, Luther had completed the third part of the Old Testament (from Job to Solomon). The first folio edition was published by Melchior Lotther [1622] under the title, Das Dritte teyl des alten Testaments. Wittemberg 1524 (36). The title page woodcut is 260 x 160 mm and, aside from this, on the verso of the preface to Job there is a full page woodcut that is 225 x 165 mm.

For [1623] the second large octavo edition (37) of 1525, which was apparently done by Michel Lotther, the artist "G. L." prepared both of the woodcuts.

Quickly as other parts of the translation had followed one another up to this point, the translation of the Prophets was delayed for an equally long time. The beginning of their publication was made in 1526 when Michel Lotther published [1624] Prophet Jona, with a full page title page illustration (Panzer No. 2964). He also published [1625] Propheten Habakuk, with Cranach's title page woodcut of the prophets (Panzer No. 2971).

In Michel Lotther's 1528 edition of [1626] Prophet Zacharia there is a large title page woodcut by Cranach.

In 1528 there followed [1627-1629] the Jesaias (Isaiah); in 1530, Daniel; and in 1532, the first edition of the Propheten alle deutsch. All of these three were published by Hans Lufft.

The flowering that the Wittemberg printing of illustrated books achieved in the 1530's and 1540's through Hans Lufft's first complete edition of Luther's German Bible in a magnificent edition, and when Georg Rhaw distinguished himself with his editions of the Hortulus animae, fall outside the time period covered in this book.

Notes

1) Panzer, Entwurf einer vollständigen Geschichte der deutschen Bibelübersetzung D. Martin Luther's vom Jahr 1517 an bis 1581. Nuremberg, 1783; Vogelin, "Ergänzungen und Nachweisungen zum Holzschnittwerk Hans Holbein des Jüngeren." In Repertorium für Kunstwissenschaft. 1879. 182ff; Schuchardt, Lucas Cranach des Aeltern Leben und Werke. Leipzig, 1851; Muther, Die ältesten deutschen Bilderbibeln. Munich, 1883.

2) Panzer, Suppl:114, No. 664. Quarto; A splendid facsimile was produced by Georg Hirth in his Liebhaberbibliothek alter Illustratoren. No. 6.

3) Panzer, Suppl:157.

4) Panzer, Suppl:160.

5) Panzer, Suppl:171.

6) Panzer, Suppl:181.

7) Panzer, Suppl:174; Weller, No. 1590.

8) Panzer, Suppl.

9) Panzer, No. 1060.

10) Ebert, No. 15938. Quarto; First, but rare, edition which is lacking in Panzer; Weigel II, No. 8518; For later editions, see Schuchardt, p. 244.

11) Schuchardt II:240ff.

12) Germ. Mus. No. 148. Quarto.

13) Panzer, p. 62.

14) Panzer, p. 75.

15) Panzer, p. 77.

16) Panzer, p. 77.

17) Panzer, p. 83.

18) Panzer, No. 1430.

19) Panzer, p. 145.

20) Panzer, p. 166.

21) Panzer, No. 1037; draft p. 36.

22) Panzer, No. 1036; draft p. 43.

23) Panzer, No. 1084.

24) Panzer, No. 1254.

25) Muther, Deutsche Bilderbibeln, No. 17.

26) Muther, Bilderbibeln, No. 18 & No. 19.

27) Muther, Deutsche Bilderbibeln, No. 20.

28) Muther, Deutsche Bilderbibeln, No. 21-23.

29) Muther, Deutsche Bilderbibeln, No. 24-27.

30) Muther, Deutsche Bilderbibeln, No. 28.

31) Muther, Deutsche Bilderbibeln, No. 29-30.

32) Muther, Deutsche Bilderbibeln, No. 31-33.

33) Muther, Deutsche Bilderbibeln, No. 34.

34) Muther, Deutsche Bilderbibeln, No. 35.

35) Muther, Deutsche Bilderbibeln, No. 36-37.

36) Muther, Deutsche Bilderbibeln, No. 38.

37) Muther, Deutsche Bilderbibeln, No. 39.

Chapter XXIV

THE REST OF GERMANY (1)

As in the fifteenth century, the other cities played a secondary role as compared with Augsburg, Nuremberg, Basel, Strassburg and Wittemberg in the first quarter of the sixteenth century.

George Erlinger, form cutter and printer, who was apparently born in Erlangen, was first active in Augsburg in 1516 and then worked in Bamberg. Aside from [1630] Johann Schöner's Aequatorium astronimicum of 1521, which was supplied with astronomical figures, there are extant only two illustrated books by this printer. In one, [1631] Türken heymlichkeit. Von der Türken Ursprunge und Gebräuchen (2), there is a title page woodcut. In the second, which appeared in 1528, [1632] Libellus Fratris Bartholomaei de Usingen Augustiniani de invocatione et veneratione Sanctorum (3), there is also a title page illustration.

Cologne has no important illustrations to show until 1520, when Anton von Worms started to work for Peter Quentel.

Martin von Werden's 1507 publication, [1633] Gemma gemmarum, had only a title page woodcut (4).

Johann Pfefferkorn printed a [1634] Büchlein über die Judenbeicht (5) in 1508.

In 1508 and 1511 Johann von Landen published [1635] a Historia von St. Ursula (6).

Heinrich van Nuyss supplied all his small publications [1636-1646] with title pages. In 1509 he published the Historie von den drei Königen (7) and the booklet Von Arnolt Boschmann (8); in 1510 a text Van dem Begyngyn von parisz (9) and the Katherinen Passie (10); in 1511, the Historie von S. Ursel (11); in 1513 the Sybillenboich (12) as well as the Barbaren und Margareten Passie (13); in 1514 the Anselmus Frage (14), the Margareten Passie (15) and the Marienklage (16); and in 1515 a reprinting of the Sybillenboich (17).

Arnt von Aich [1647-1649] printed the Chirurgenbuchlein (18) in 1515, with eight woodcuts; and in 1519 the Histori von S. Anna (19) as well as Johannes Sacrobusto's Sphera materialis (20), with a title page woodcut and 26 text illustrations.

Extensive activity started, however, only when Anton von Worms started to work for the Cologne establishments. One of his earliest products was the title page for [1650] the Divi Hieronymi Epistolae tres ab Erasmo Roterodamo regognite, Cöln, Johannes Gymnicus 1518 (21). Above a recess there is the date 1518, and the escutcheon of the City of Cologne is above, with the letters "J. G." (Johannes Gymnicus) in the upper corners.

The second press with which Anton von Worms worked was that of Eucharius Cervicornus. In 1526 he completed the title page for [1651] Catalogus Hereticorum by Bernardus Lutzenburg (22), which appeared without the name of the printer, but was apparently by Cervicornus.

The title page of Cervicornus' 1527 edition of [1652] Lutzenburg's De ordinibus militaribus et armorum militarium libellus utilis (23) shows St. George slaying the dragon.

In 1528 he did the title page [1653] for Haymonis episcopi Halberstattensis in divi Pauli epistolas omnes interpretatio (24), which was printed by Cervicornus. His last work that was printed by Cervicornus in this period is the title page in the 1530 folio edition of [1654] Biblia juxta Hieronymi translationem (25).

Anton von Worms did a great deal more for Peter Quentel during this period. In 1527 Peter Quentel printed his folio [1655, Pl. 260-261] Biblia sacra utriusque testamenti juxta Hebraicam et Graecam veritatem (26), for which Anton von Worms supplied 27 woodcuts.

Shortly after 1527 Quentel published an undated quarto booklet, [1656] Nova quomodo Anno 1527 urbs Roma capta sit (27), with a title page illustration.

In 1528 there followed Peter Quentel's new edition of [1657] Lichtenberger's Pronosticatio, which he did in German under the title, Die weyssagunge Johannis Lichtenbergers deutsch tzugericht mit vleyss, and in Latin under the title, Pronosticatio Johannis Lichtenbergers jam denuo sublatis mendis quibus scatebat pluribus, quam diligentissime excussa. While the subject matter of the earlier illustrations was retained, they were reworked into the modern style.

In 1528 Peter Quentel also published, in octavo, the third edition [1658] of Emser's Neuem Testament (28) with 32 woodcuts by Anton von Worms.

The fourth octavo edition [1659] of Emser's translation of the New Testament, which was printed s.l. in 1529 under the title Das New Testament (29), appears to be attributable to Quentel. The title page shows Emser kneeling, as in the previous edition, but aside from this there are no illustrations.

In the same year, however, Quentel printed [1660], under the title, Das gantz New Testament, the sixth edition in folio (30). The Cologne City coat-of-arms is on the title page, with the inscription "O felix Colonia." The four large sheets of the Evangelists (135 x 90) are repeated from the Latin Bible of 1527. At the beginning of the Epistles and in the Apocalypse are the woodcuts that Anton von Worms prepared for the octavo edition of 1528.

Apparently the folio edition [1661] of the Biblia integra veteris et novi Testamenti (31), which appeared in Cologne in 1529, is also attributable to Quentel.

Dresden is of interest primarily because the first edition of Emser's translation of the New Testament was published there by Wolfgang Stoeckel in folio in 1527, under the title [1662] Das new testament nach lawt der Christlichen Kirchen bevertem text corrigirt un wiederumb zu recht gebracht (32). Its title page woodcut is divided into several fields and it bears the year 1527 at the left and the initials "G. L." at the right. Since Emser wanted to make his edition appear as much like Luther's as possible, he wrote to Cranach at Wittemberg offering him 40 Thaler for the use of the original woodblocks prepared for the Apocalypse (33) in Luther's edition and he used some of these. It is difficult to understand Emser's fondness for the Wittemberg woodblocks since Duke Georg, in his mandate against the Luther translation, was specific in mentioning the small illustrations therein (34). Emser used them all with the exception of the fifth and sixth plates, which he replaced with the small sheets (145 x 114) by the artist "G. L."

In Dutenstein Wilhelm Schaffner printed [1663] an Evangelienbuch (35), using the usual woodcuts.

In Erfurt in 1511 Mathes Maler printed the second edition [1664] of Flavius Vegetius' Vier Büchern der Ritterschaft.

In 1516 Mathes Morssheim printed [1665-1672] Spiegel des Regiments in der Fürsten Höse da Fraw untreue gewaltig ist (36), with twenty small woodcuts; and Schwarzenberg's Gesetze der Zutrinker und Prasser (37). In 1517 he followed these with a Kalender (38) with woodcuts; in 1518 an edition of Meister Elucidarius (39) and a richly illustrated book, Von König Etzel's Hofhaltung (40); and Copp's Regiment wie man sich halten soll (41) in 1521, with a number of woodcuts. Schreiber's Rechenbüchlein of 1523 (42) and Riese's Rechnung auf der Linie (43), of 1525, had only title page illustrations.

Michael Buchführer, who stayed in Erfurt just a short time before moving to Jena, has only one book to be listed: [1673] the Dialogus zwischen Petrus und einem Bauern (44), which has a title page illustration.

In Frankfurt am Main Beatus Murner, in 1509, printed [1674-1675] Schifffahrt von diesem elenden Jammerthal (45), which he supplied with woodcuts. In 1512 and 1513 he produced editions of Th. Murner's Schelmenzunft (46).

There is only one Frankfurt a. M. publication by Johannes Hanau to be listed. It is [1676] Summarius, wie Paul Fromm das Sacrament zu Knobloch gestohlen (47); its woodcuts are unspeakably bad.

Johann Wörlin [1677-1679] worked in Freiburg im Breisgau, producing Mennel's Heiligenbuch in 1522 (48); Preiing's Lied von der göttlichen Majestat in 1525 (49), with a title page woodcut; and, also with a title page illustration, Galienus Büchlein wie sich ein jeder Mensch halten soll das ganze Jahr mit Essen und Trinken (50).

The J. Mennel [1680] Hübsche Chronik von heidnischen und Christenkönigen der Franken (51) has the coat-of-arms on the title page and then 48 smaller (40 x 40) bust pictures of the Frankish kings. The edition of Emser's translation of the New Testament [1681], which was published in octavo by Johannes Fabrus Juliacensis, belongs to a later period, 1534.

Hagenau, which entered into the history of book illustration back in the fifteenth century, also produced some works in the first quarter of the sixteenth century.

Heinrich Gran, Hagenau's first printer, has left us only a 1513 edition of [1682] Rösslin's Rosengarten der schwangeren Frauen und Hebammen (52), in which he reused the woodcuts that had been used by Martin Flach.

In 1516 Thomas Anshelm made the city his permanent residence, after having lived in Strassburg from 1488, in Pforzheim from 1500, and in Tübingen from 1511.

One of his first Hagenau publications, the Evangelienbuch of 1516, contained 58 fine Scheifelin woodcuts, of which he repeated ten in the Decachortum of Marcus Vigerius in 1517.

In 1518 he printed [1683] a Missale for the Bursfeld Benedictine Congregation (53) and in 1520 he did one [1684] for the Strassburg Diocese (54). Both of these were large and handsome volumes with illustrations which belonged to quite a different school than the Alsace school.

Anshelm's successor in 1523 was Johann Secer. In 1530 he published [1685] the Epitome regii ac vetustissimi ortus Sacrae Caesareae Catholicae Majestatis Ferdinand (55), duplicating the illustrations that Grüninger used in his edition of 1527.

Halberstad is important chiefly because of the [1686, Pl. 262] Biblia dudesch (56), published by Ludwig Trutebul, which has some illustrations by a talented but unknown artist, "C. G." In addition to his illustrations there are included the 108 original woodcuts from the 1480 Cologne Bible. This was the last Bible in which these old woodcuts are found.

In Halle there appeared [1687] the Vorzeichnuss und zceigunge des hochlöbl heilighthums der Stiftkirchen zu Halle (the Heiligthumsbuch of that place). It contains on 122 quarto leaves pictures of the costly and ancient things with which the Archbishop Albrecht von Brandenburg decorated the church that he built in Halle in 1518 (57).

In Hamburg, Hans Borchard published an illustrated book [1688] in 1510, under the title De veer utersten (De quator novissimis) (58).

In Jena, Michael Buchführer, who earlier was active in Erfurt, printed [1689] Stanberger's Epistel von der Lieb des Nächsten (59). It was published in 1523 and had a title page woodcut.

From Ingolstadt came the earliest illustrated book by Johann Stabius. It appeared s. a. [1690] under the title Descriptio quator Labyrinthorum (60), and had three illustrations.

In 1519 Andreas Lutz printed [1691] Aventinus' Des Stifts Altenötting loblichem Herkommen (61), with a title page woodcut.

In 1530, G. Krapf and J. Focker published [1692] Johann Eck's Opera contra Ludderum (62), with a large title page illustration.

Johann Eck's 1530 edition of [1693] Auslegung der Evangelien is more richly illustrated and its illustrations are divided among the artist "L. B." and Sebald Beham and Michael Osterdorfer.

In Krakau in 1514 there appeared [1694] a Passio Jesu Christi Salvatoris mundi vario carminum genere F. Benedicti Chelidonii musophili doctissime descripta (63), printed by Florian and Wolfgang de Pfaffenhofen.

Johann Weyssenburger moved his activity from Nuremburg to Landshut in 1515. The [1695] Leben St. Wolfgangs (64), which he printed in Landshut, had 20 woodcuts.

Simon Brabant de Quercu's [1696] Opusculum Musices (65) was published in 1516. It has a very attractive (80 x 117) title page woodcut.

In 1519 there followed the [1697] Histori von Kaiser Friedrich (66), with a title page illustration and five woodcuts in the text; and in the same year [1698] the Lied von der Ausschaffung der Juden aus Regensburg (67), which has a woodcut on the title page and one on its verso.

The year 1520 was especially productive, with Weyssenburger publishing [1699-1701] the Auslegung des Vaterunsers (68), with a title page illustration; the Büchlein von dem Sterben (69), with a title page illustration and three woodcuts in the text; and the St. Christofs Geburt und Leben (70), with 32 woodcuts. The woodcuts are gifted and some of the landscapes are very good. It appears that they came from a Nuremberg artist.

Weyssenburger's 1520 edition of [1702] Geiler's Predigt uber die Passion (71) has a number of small woodcuts. The first one, which is the largest, is about 75 x 105 mm and the following twenty are 45 x 30 mm.

The last book published by Weyssenburger in 1520 is [1703] Alexander Sytz's Tractat vom Adlerlassen (72), which has a (120 x 73) title page illustration.

The new edition, in 1522, of the [1704] Leben des St. Wolfgang (73) has 51 (104 x 70) woodcuts instead of the 20 that were in the 1515 edition, and everything that was in the 20 woodcuts in the old edition is covered in the new edition. The woodcuts are all somewhat stiff and old-fashioned, but they were made with care, with the landscapes being the best of the group; the figures, with their long slit-like eyes, are not up to the times.

Eck's [1705] *Enchiridion locorum communiorum adversus Lutheranos* (74), which was printed in Landshut in 1525 without the name of the printer, may also be attributed to Weissenburger. It has a very important (106 x 80) title page woodcut, which bears the initials "G. A." and the date 1525.

In [1706] the second edition, 1527, of Seitz's *Tractat vom Aderlassen* the title page illustration is different from that of the 1522 edition.

As with Wittemberg, Leipzig became important only after the first fifteen years of the sixteenth century. A [1707] *Hortulus animae* appeared in Leipzig in 1513 without the name of the printer. Its illustrations, some of which are 60 x 40 mm and some full page woodcuts, appear to have been taken from an Alsatian Hortulus. The woodcut of David with harp and a few others came from Knoblouch's 1507 edition. All the others originated long before 1513 and have the darkness and the haziness of the Strassburg school.

Conrad Kachelofen printed [1708-1711] a *Kalender* (75) in 1516, with a title page woodcut and the conventional calendar woodcuts. In 1516 Melchior Lotther printed Bonaventura's *Marial unserer lieben Frauen* (76), with twelve woodcuts; in 1519 Luther's *Sermon von der Betrachtung des heiligen Leidens Christi* (77), with a title page woodcut; and in 1520 the *Sermon von der Bereitung zum Sterben*.

Wolfgang Stoeckel, also, did only works by Luther during 1520. [1712-1715] The *Sermon gepredigt zu Leipzig* (78) has a title page woodcut; the *Sermon von Gebet und Prozession* (79), the *Sermon vom Sacrament der Taufe* (80) and the *Sermon von dem Leichnam Christi* (81) also all have title page woodcuts.

In 1521 Stoeckel [1716-1717] printed a *Historia von Weyprecht* (82); and in 1522 he printed Carion's *Prognosticatio* (83), with a title page woodcut.

In 1519 Jacob Thanner printed [1718] Luther's *Sieben Busspsalmen* (84). Valentin Schumann did practically nothing but works by Luther, for the illustration of which he used the artist HS almost exclusively.

He did two editions of [1719] Luther's *Auslegung des Vaterunsers* (85). The first has, on the verso of the title page, an illustration of Christ washing Peter's feet; the second, published in 1518, has a handsome large woodcut at the end and another on the last side.

In Luther's [1720] *Auslegung des 109 Psalmen* (86) there is a title page woodcut. In the [1721] *Sermon von der Wucher* (87), published in the same year, the title page illustration is the customary one for this publication.

Two additional 1519 publications of Luther's works that appeared in Leipzig, without the name of the printer, appear to be attributable to the Schumann press. These were: [1722-1723] the prayer for the *Bereitung zum Sacrament* (88), with an illustration on the title page and its verso; and the *Sermon von der Betrachtung des Leidens Christi* (89), with a title page illustration.

In 1520 Valentin Schumann printed [1724] *Sermon von dem Sacrament* and his [1725] *Predigt* von dreierlei Gerechtigkeit (90), both with title page woodcuts. However, in his later days he printed publications against the Reformation.

In 1528 he printed an octavo edition of [1726] Emser's Uebersetzung des neuen Testament (91). The title page woodcut is divided into two parts and the full page (112 x 85) woodcut after the preface is copied from the title page of the original edition which was issued by Stoeckel in Dresden the year before. The woodcuts before the Evangelists, the Apocalypse and the Epistles and the Romans are also full page (112 x 70). The 21 woodcuts in the Apocalypse are reduced copies (90 x 65) of those in Luther's New Testament.

In the fifth edition of [1727] Emer's translation of the Neuen Testamentes, which Schumann printed in octavo in 1529, the same woodcuts were repeated.

In Lübeck, in the first decade of the sixteenth century, the printing plant of Steffen and Hans Arndes developed further and made principal use of the woodcarver ⟨ W, who distinguished himself by his originality in presentation and at times approaches the artist of the Grüninger plant.

Among his woodcuts are those in [1728] Nyge Kalender (92), printed by Hans Arndes in 1519, in which his monogram appears on several sheets. The woodcut on sheet Bjb gives one of the oldest pictures of a spinning wheel.

He appears also to have provided the illustrations for Steffen Arndes' lower-Saxon edition of 1520 of [1729] Hortus sanitatis (93) since his peculiar monogram ⟨W appears on the last page with the Arndes colophon. The woodcuts of the natural bodies are very good and appear, at least in part, to be modeled after those in the original Schöffer edition of 1485.

In Mainz, Johann Schöffer developed his extensive productivity from 1502 to 1532, entering into the field of book illustration in 1505 with his edition of Livius.

The 22 woodcuts in his 1510 reprint of [1730] the Bambergischen Halsgerichtsordnung (94), which originally appeared in Bamberg in 1507, follow the original illustrations except that they are smaller, and with the further exception that when he had Livius woodblocks that appeared suitable, he used them instead of copying the originals. It also often happens that he uses both the woodcut of the Bamberg artist and the Livius woodcut together.

In 1512 he printed [1731] the Abschied des Reichstags zu Cöln (95) with a title page woodcut.

In [1732] Schöffer's 1514 Hortulus animae, the title page woodcut (62 x 47) is quite different in subject matter than is customary and the text woodcuts (53 x 42) are artistically highly varied. The presentation of the Trinity is important, while the various pictures of the saints are quite unskilled.

Schöffer's 1515 edition of Johannes Trithemius' [1733] Compendium sive Breviarium primi voluminis Annalium sive Historiarum de Origine Regum et gentis Francorum (97) has a full page woodcut illustration on the second sheet.

The woodcut on the first leaf of [1734] the 1516 Psalterium (98) displays a standing Bishop before whom a Benedictine has thrown himself prone. Hutten's [1735] De guaiaci medicina et morbo gallico (99) has a 155 x 110 mm illustration on its last leaf. It was printed in 1519.

The [1736] 1520 edition of Hortus deliciarum (100) has many woodcuts.

The illustrations in the 1521 edition of [1737] Collectanea antiquitatum in urbe et agro

Moguntino repertarum (101), which was printed by Johannes Huttichius, is a collection of sarcophagi and stones with inscriptions, as well as a gland-like rock, which are of great interest as the first archeological-antiquarian reproductions.

The 1526 [1738] Abschied des Reichstags zu Speier (102) has only a title page illustration; while the 1527 edition [1739] of 4 Bücher Sexti Julii Frontini von den guten Raethen. Onexander von den Kriegshandlungen (103) has a number of woodcuts.

These were followed in 1530 [1740] by Schöffer's German edition of Cäsarausgabe (104), with 112 woodcuts. The eleven large ones (227 x 150): Nos. 4, 16, 22, 27, 34, 44, 49, 62, 71 and 97, are taken from Grüninger's Caesar of 1508. The new illustrations have varying formats. The large ones are battle scenes which always fill a full page. The smaller ones, which are in the text, are 145 mm wide and vary in height from 30 to 120 mm; however, with the exception of those which are 30 mm high, they are all built up from three to six blocks, which reduces their artistic value, even though the work is often as careful as that in Grüninger's printing.

Schöffer's last illustrated book [1741] is his 1531 Abschied des Reichstags zu Augsburg (105), with a (160 x 140) title page woodcut.

In Metz, during this period, there was the firm of Caspar Hochfeder, which printed the Geschichte von Flos und Blankflos in 1499.

The first edition of Ennen's [1742] Medulla gestorum Trevirensium, which Hochfeder published in 1514 (106), had a title page illustration and 11 text woodcuts; while the second edition, which he published in 1515 (107), had only three small woodcuts.

Hans Schobser, who had been printing in Augsburg from 1485 to 1498, moved to Munich around the turn of the century. After he published the woodcut-illustrated [1743] 7 Tagzeit vom Frohnleichnam Christi (108), in 1506, there is nothing available for several following years. Not until 1518 did he print [1744] the Passion so der durchlauchtig Herr Johann Geyler von Kaisersperg Doctor und Predicant der loblichen Stadt Strassburg seinen Kindern daselbst hat gepredigt in Form eines Gerichtshandels (109). The woodcuts vary. The three large ones belong to the Swabian-Alsace school and the 14 smaller ones, which appear to be much older, are apparently by a Munich artist.

His 1518 edition of [1745] Gengenbach's 10 Altern (110) has the eleven woodcuts that are customary in this book.

In the 1519 edition of [1746] Von der Chur des Königs Karl zum Kaiser (111), the title page illustration is the familiar one from the Augsburg edition.

His other 1519 book, [1747] Alofresant's Prophezeihung (112), likewise has just a title page illustration.

In 1520 [1748-1749] he published Der dreien Glauben Juden, Haiden und Christen (113) with 36 woodcuts; a new edition of the 7 Tagzeiten (114), and the Histori von Melibeo und Prudentia, the last of which had a 105 x 85 mm title page woodcut.

His 1521 publications, [1750-1751] the Amt der Messe (115) and the Psalter Mariae (116), had only title page illustrations.

In 1523 he printed Caspar Schatzger's [1752] Von der lieben Eernung und Anrueffung (117), with a 90 x 58 mm title page woodcut that is taken from a much older work.

The same is true of the title page in [1753-1754] Schatzger's 1524 Erklärung (118) and in his 1525 Vom Sacrament des Fromleichnams Christi.

The last of Schobser's publications to bear a woodcut is [1755] a Missal of 1526. (119)

Johann Locher worked at the same time as Schobser, but only his 1525 edition [1756] of Sendbrief des Bauernveinds an Karsthansen (120) had a title page woodcut.

Three books published in Munich without indication of printer had much more important woodcuts. The [1757] Buch des gemeinen Landpot, Landsordnung, Satzung und Gebrauch des Fürstenthums im Ober- und Niederbaiern im Jahr 1516 aufgericht (121) has a title page woodcut that is 140 x 180 mm. Following this book in 1518 is [1758] the Reformation des bairischen Landrechts 1518 aufgericht (122). The title page woodcut (140 x 185) is the same in content as the one above but is very different in style. The third woodcut occurs in [1759] the Gerichtsordnung im Fürstenthum Ober- und Niederbaiern Anno 1520 aufgericht (123). The title page illustration is, again, the same in general content, with the year date 1520. However, on a stool next to the table there are the initials "C. C." Nagler I:993, interprets these initials to mean Caspar Clofligl, or Clofigl, who was the chief artist for Duke Wilhelm IV. He lived in Munich and until 1529 was listed in guild records as a court painter. Since the woodcuts are fully in keeping with the style of the period it is possible to attribute the three sheets to Caspar Clofigl.

Jacob Kobel printed in Oppenheim for an extended period. In 1505 he printed [1760] the Antwort auf ein schmähliches Gedicht (124) with a title page; and he also printed the Gedicht von einem Hasen (125) which has a woodcut showing a remarkable animal with three eyes, two stomachs and eight feet.

In 1511 he followed these with [1761-1763] a poem, with a title page woodcut, titled Fledermaus (126) and the Geistliche Regiment gegen die Pestilenz (127), with four woodcuts. In 1512, in addition to a Kalender (128) with four large and 33 small woodcuts, he also printed Schwarzenberg's Gesetze der Zutrinker und Prasser. The three woodcuts (160 x 100) are the same in content as those which Heinrich Steiner used in Augsburg at a later date. In addition to these, the book contains a number of small bust illustrations of men and women with glasses in hand.

Köbel's [1764] Neu geordnet Rechenbüchlein (129), of 1514, has only a title page woodcut, while [1765] Petrarch's Neuw geteutscht Büchlein (130) inhaltend grosse erbermliche Klagen der Sinnlichkeit und des Schmertzes, of 1516, is decorated with fine small woodcuts.

The [1766-1768] Evangelisch A. b. c. of 1517 (131) has a title page illustration; the two editions, 1517 (132) and 1518 (133), of Köbel's Rechenbüchlein have three small woodcuts. The J. Stöffler Calendarium Romanum (134) of 1518 is more richly illustrated.

Kobel's last publications [1769-1774] are Andreae's Baum der Sippschaft of 1519 (135); a new edition of Rechenbüchleins of 1520 (136); Virdung's Auslegung of 1520 (137), with 36 woodcuts, and his Practica (138) of 1521, with 41 woodcuts; the Gerichtsordnung of 1523 (139), with three; and the Legende von St. Rupprecht of 1524 (140), with four illustrations.

At the same time as Johann Köbel, Johann Hasselberger was working in Oppenhem and in 1515 he published [1775] Johann Trithemius' Liber octo quaestionum ad Max. Caes. (141), with a fine title page illustration (120 x 105).

Regensberg, where Paul Kohl was printing, achieved its significance through the work of

Michael Ostendorfer, the painter, who worked there from 1519 to 1559. His first book illustration was brought about by the building of the church loft. In 1519, when Kohl printed [1776] the Marienkirche, Ostendorfer supplied the illustration. It is not certain whether the title page illustration in the small, undated, book [1777] Wie die newe Capell zu der schönen Maria in Regenspurg erstlich auffkummen ist, nach Christi geburt 1519 jar (143), was attributable to him or to Altdorfer.

Likewise, it is not possible to attribute to him with certainty the title page woodcut that appeared in Kohl's edition of [1778] Lied von der schönen Maria (144).

On the other hand the title page woodcut in the 1522 Kohl booklet, [1779] Wunderbarliche Czaiche vergangen Jar beschehen in Regensburg czu der schönen Maria der mutter Gottes Hyein begriffen (145), is definitely attributable to Ostendorfer.

In 1530 he worked with Sebald Beham and the artist "L. B." in the illustration of Eck's [1780] Christenlicher Auslegung der Evangelien, which was printed in Ingolstadt. Even though his monogram appears only on the woodcut of Christ on the Cross and on that of the four evangelists at the end of the table of contents of the first part, nevertheless the major portion of the illustrations in the book were done by him. He later worked for the Nuremberg printers as well as for those in Regensberg.

There is available only one edition of Brant's Narrenschiff (146) of 1519, and one Kalender for 1522 (147) from the printing plant of Ludwig Diez in Rostock.

In Aedibus Thuriis in Rostock there appeared, [1781-1782] in 1517 and 1520, Nic. Marschalk's Historia aquatilium latine ac grece (148), with many woodcuts; and in 1522, an Auszug aus der Mecklenburgischen Chronik (149), with one woodcut only.

A city that was unimportant up to this time moved into the history of book illustration in 1530. This was Simmern, in which many richly illustrated books were printed by Hieronymus Rodler in 1530. In that year there appeared [1783] Georg Rixner's Turnierbuch (150) which, in addition to large escutcheons, had 125 woodcuts of various sizes. These woodcuts were by the artist "H. H.," whose work is reminiscent of Scheifelin's, and who appears also to have illustrated the other books published by Hieronymus Rodler. The 1531 edition [1784] of Schön nützlich Büchlein und Unterweisung der Kunst des Messens mit dem Zirkel (151) has 51 full page (212 x 142) woodcuts.

The [1785] Geschichte des spanischen Riesen Fierrabras (152) has twenty woodcuts of varying sizes, each assembled from three woodblocks.

From Speier we have only [1786-1788] Jacob Schmyed's 1514 edition of Virdung's Auslegung (153) and Anastasius Nolt's edition, in 1523, of Practica (154), each with only a single woodcut; and Hans Eckart's edition, in 1525, of the 4 Evangelisten (155), with eight woodcuts.

In Tubingen, Thomas Anshelm published [1789] Ave preclara getutscht durch Sebastian Brant (156), in 1512.

Ulrich Morhart, who later settled in Strassburg, published [1790] the Beschreibung der göttlichen Muhle (157) in 1521, with two woodcuts.

In 1532 there appeared the eighth folio edition [1791] of the Emser'schen Uebersetzung des Neuen Testamentes, which was a true reprint of the Cologne edition of 1529.

Ulm, which fostered book illustration in the fifteenth century, had no illustrated books to show for the first quarter of the sixteenth century except [1792-1793] Mathis Hoffischer's publication in 1522 of the Unterweisung über das höchst Amt (158) and his 1524 edition of Liedes von der Sündfluth (159), each of which had a title page illustration.

The monogram, which is found on the second woodcut in Rösslin's [1794] Rosengarten der schwangeren Frauen und Hebammen, which was printed by Martin Flach in Strassburg in 1513, was attributed by Nagler to the Ulm artist Conrad Merkel, but this is still moot.

In Vienna [1795-1796] Johann Singriener produced Himmelserscheinungen (160) in 1520 and Hans Judenkönig's Unterweisung im Lautenspiel (161), each of which had one woodcut.

In Worms [1797-1799] Peter Schöffer produced the Morin, by Hermanns von Sachsenheim. In 1513 he produced a Hortulus animae (162) with a title page illustration and 72 colored text woodcuts. In 1529 he published the Beyder Allt und Newen Testaments Teutsch (163), in folio, with 46 woodcuts by Anton von Worms. Most of these had already been used by Peter Quentel in Cologne in 1527 in his Latin Bible, as well as in 1528 in his octavo edition of the Emser translation of the New Testament. The 21 woodcuts for the Apocalypse were reproduced from the Cologne Bible of 1528.

The first illustrated book produced in Zurich [1800] was a 1508 Kalender published by Hans am Wasen, which has been noted above because of its woodcuts by Urs Graf.

From the same period there is an eight-page pamphlet, [1801] Der Psalter oder Rosenkranz von unserer lyeben Frowen, which has a handicraft type illustration.

Of much greater significance is a Zurich folio sheet (265 x 210) which was described by Vogelin [1802], and which was issued around 1514. It deals with the relationships of the Pope, Emperor and King of France in the form of a card game in which each displays his powers in a lifelike manner in the broadside, Das Spiel. The sheet achieved acclaim and widespread imitation, among which the most significant was the (150 x 160) sheet entitled [1803] Ludus Novus.

Another field was represented by the Zurich picture book of 1519, with verses accompanying the pictures. However, the chief turning point of Zurich book illustration came about in 1521 when Christoph Froschauer started his printing plant there.

His [1804] 1521 edition of Erasmus' Nutzliche Unterweisung eines christlichen Fürsten wohl zu regieren (164) has a title page illustration that is taken from an Augsburg publication.

The 1523 edition of Erasmus, translated by Leonhard Jud, [1805] Paraphrases aller Episteln Pauli, Petri, Joannis, Jude, Jacobi (165), has a title page drawn with childlike awkwardness. The small woodcut at the end of the preface is far better.

Zwingli's 1523 edition of [1806] Von Gerechtigkeit (166) has a title page illustration.

After 1524, when he broadened the scope of his printing operations, Froschauer had a xylographic studio in which he appears to have used chiefly students of Holbein.

In 1524 he reprinted [1807] the Luther Neue Testament twice. In the first reprint, which was octavo (167), the illustrations in the first part are very bad. In the second part of the book, which begins with the Epistles of Paul, there is an illustration of Paul with the initials "C. V." at his feet, and the same initials appear later at the feet of Peter; so it is possible that these illustrations were done by the same artist who did the eight handsome sheets for Froben's edition of

Erasmus' Precatio.

The folio edition [1808] of the Neuen Testamentes (168), which also appeared in 1524, used as the title page illustration the woodcut that Froschauer had procured for the Leo Judae translation of the Erasmischen Paraphrasen... The pictures of the authors used in the octavo edition were reused here except that the picture of Paul by the artist "C. V." is omitted and one from another source is inserted.

The only other Froschauer publication in 1524 is Zwingli's Von gottlicher und menschlicher Gerechtigkeit, which had a title page woodcut.

In 1525, Froschauer continued with [1809] his three-part folio edition of the Alten Testamentes (169). The illustrations of part 1 are slightly reduced copies of the eleven Wittemberg edition illustrations. At the beginning of part 2 there is a (270 x 400) map of the beloved land indicating the places at which the events described took place. The text woodcuts of part 2 (70 x 70) are few in number and illustrate temples, etc. They are, in part, reprints of those found in Othmar's 1523 Augsburg edition. Part 3 has three woodcuts, with the last one appearing to be by one of Holbein's students. There are a number of initial character illustrations that are 48 x 48 mm.

In addition, Froschauer also printed, in 1525, some writings [1810-1811] by Zwingli. One was Von dem Nachtmahl Christi, and it had only an unimportant title page illustration. In the booklet Welche ursach gebind zu ufrüren, welches die waren ufrürer syginds (171), on the contrary, there is a (60 x 73) woodcut that is so fine that it is practically like a copper engraving.

Another 1525 publication was [1812] the Züricher Wandkatechismus (172) on which a grotesque woodcut is overprinted. The one copy of a Wandkatechismus was in the Sotzmann Collection but it has been lost.

Copp's 1526 edition of [1813] the Evangelischer Wandkalendar for the year 1527 has been discussed under Holbein.

In 1530 [1814] he printed Zwingli's Ad Carolum Romanorum regem imperatorem Germaniae comitia Augustae celebrantem fidei ratio (173), which has on its title page the bust portrait of Carl V, which had already been used in 1521, and, additionally, has an illustration with Holbein's initials.

The Bibles after 1525 had only ornamentation. It was not until the folio edition in two parts appeared in 1531, [1815] Die gantze Bibel der ursprunglichen Ebraischen und Griechischen waarheyt nach auffs aller treuwlichest verteuschet, that a Bible was adorned with pictures to excel all the others (174). At the beginning of Genesis there is a full page wide (132 x 175) woodcut which is not very important. Aside from this, there are three groups of woodcuts in the book. In the first group Froschauer used the woodcuts that had been used in the 1525 edition. For the second group he had 69 illustrations of scenes prepared, of which 41 were reversed copies of Holbein's Icones Veteris Testamenti. Not satisfied with this rich and attractive display, he had another 45 scenes cut in the same (60 x 87) format. In doing these the artist used two sheets of Holbein's illustrations of Petri's Altem Testament (Woltman 173, 175) and two others from the Lyons Vulgate, doing the remaining woodcuts independently. On two of his compositions he included his monogram, which was an interlaced S and V.

For the New Testament, Froschauer used the illustrations of his earlier editions and also borrowed from Thomas Wolff in Basel the Holbein woodblocks for the Apocalypse. Thus Froschauer's Bible is one of the most richly and profusely illustrated Bibles ever published.

Simultaneously with Froschauer, Hans Hager worked in Zurich and his dated works came in the 1520's.

He began in 1522 with [1816-1817] three small pieces by Zwingli: *Von Klarheit und Gewissen* (175); *Erkiesen und Freiheit der Speisen* (176); and his *Vermahnung* (177), all of which had title page woodcuts.

In 1524 he produced his [1818] quarto edition of the *Neuen Testamentes,* which contributed nothing new.

In his 1525 edition of [1819] *Antwurt Zwinglis an Valentin Compar über die vier Artikel* (178) there is a title page woodcut that appeared to be by a student of Holbein, and which was reused in the 1525 edition of Zwingli's booklet [1820] *Von dem Touff, vom Widertouff und vom Kindertouff.* It is uncertain whether Luther's [1821] *Von den geistlichen und Klostergelübden*, which was published in Zurich in 1522, is attributable to Froschauer or to Hager. It has a title page illustration. Also, attribution to either of these is not possible in the case of Zwingli's [1822] *Lehrbüchlein wie man die Knaben christlich unterweisen und erziehen soll* (180), which was published without location in 1524. The title page woodcut (125 x 110) shows a teacher at a table, offering a book to a lad, and in front of the table are three men, one of whom is bringing two books to the teacher.

The art continued to flower in Zurich through the 1550's.

Summary

Book illustration never again had such a flowering as it had in the first quarter of the sixteenth century. Whereas in the fifteenth century it was zealously pursued as a handicraft, in this later period it was done by the best artists. Albrecht Dürer gave it its artistic inauguration. Kaiser Maximilian I spent a substantial part of his busy life in forwarding his illustrated deluxe editions and inaugurated a school of illustrators and woodcarvers in Augsburg under the direction of the artistically qualified and interested Peutinger. Artists such as Burgkmair and Scheifelin supplied their illustrations for the *Theuerdank*, *Weisskunig* and *Freydal*; and woodcarvers like Jost Dienecker transferred these into wood.

In addition to the deluxe editions sponsored by the Kaiser, a series of other worthwhile publications were produced in Augsburg by the younger Schoensperger, the two Othmars, Johannes Miller, and Grimm and Wirsung. In addition to Burgkmair and Scheifelin there was a whole series of minor artists working on book illustration in Augsburg.

In addition to Augsburg, the art blossomed in Nuremberg where Hans Springinklee produced many illustrations for the Hortulus and the Vulgate for the publisher Johann Koburger; Erhard Schon was equally active and Sebald Beham was making his start in developing his artistic skill. During this period they had the calligrapher Hans Guldenmund and Niclas Meldemann; and the great printers Georg and Johann Stuchs, Hieronymus Holzel and Friedrich Peypus kept many woodcutters working.

In Basel there were the printers Johann Amerbach, Johann Froben, Adam Petri and Thomas Wolff, whose initial attempts to produce illustrated books were greatly aided by Urs Graf, until 1515 when Hans and Ambrosius Holbein moved there from Augsburg and began their rich activity.

In Strassburg, Geiler von Kaisersperg had his many writings printed with the helping hand of the printer Grüninger, who provided an array of productive artists, some of them not particularly important. For him as well as for the other printers, including Hupfuff, Schott, Knoblouch and Flach, there were the artists Hans Wächtlin, Hans Baldung Grün, Heinrich Vogtherr and Hans Weiditz.

In Wittemberg Lucas Cranach's Heiligthumsbuch was published early, but it was not until Luther that the illustrated book achieved its great success, with Cranach supplying the ideas for the artistic forms and the printing plants of Johann Grünenberg, Melchior Lotther, Nickel Schyrlentz, Georg Rhau and Hans Lufft.

In addition to the illustrations produced in these five major printing cities, there was a whole series of printers of illustrated books all over Germany. In Bamberg there was Georg Erlinger. In Cologne the place of the smaller printers became less important when Peter Quentel enlisted the services of Anton von Worms, towards the end of the 1520's. In Dresden there was Wolfgang Stöckel; in Erfurt there was Mathes Maler; in Freiburg Johannes Wörlin; in Hagenau Heinrich Gran, Thomas Anshelm and Johann Secer; in Ingolstadt there were the richly illustrated works of Johann Eck. The Nuremberg printer Johann Weissenburger moved to Landshut; small works by Luther were published in Leipzig; Steffen and Hans Arndes worked in Lübeck; there was Johann Schöffer in Mainz; Hans Schobfer in Munich, and Jacob Köbel in Oppenheim. In Regensburg Paul Kohl was greatly helped by Michael Ostendorfer and Simmern became an important printing center through the work of Hieronymus Rodler. All these smaller cities were surpassed by Zürich, where Christoph Froschauer collected a group of Holbein's students and printed many sumptuous books.

The art of drawing and of woodcarving had been transformed, over a fifty year period, from the crudest beginnings to the highest achievement, and one can hardly believe his eyes when he compares a book of the 1530's with one of the year 1470. To be sure, as we have seen, the major impetus to the development of book illustration had already been given in the fifteenth century. As early as 1490, as a result of the extensive activity of the great illustrators Reuwich and Wohlgemuth, the outlines had lost their earlier crudeness and stiffness, and shading had been added. Nevertheless, the figures were wooden and without proper proportion and the landscapes lacked perspective. The change in this, and thus the final step in making book illustrations true works of art, first appeared at the beginning of the sixteenth century. Thus, the first quarter of the sixteenth century may truly be considered the time of the flowering of book illustration in Germany.

By the middle of the sixteenth century book illustration started to take new directions. Copper engraving, an art which Dürer had brought to highest achievement, replaced woodcuts in book illustration to an increasing extent. To be sure, woodcuts were still produced on a large scale during the second half of the sixteenth century. There were skilled artists, such as V.

Solis, J. Amman, Stimmer, and Maurer who supplied numerous drawings for this purpose and there were still skilled woodcarvers (181). However, increasingly woodcuts were limited to popular literature, while artistic works tended more to the use of copper engravings. Later they even left blank spaces in the text for imprinting of the vignettes or for pasting these in after printing them on thin paper. It was not until our century (the nineteenth) that they were again recognized as twins in bookprinting, and one saw with astonishment the excellence with which they could be jointly emplaced.

In England as well as in Germany the idea of the woodcut illustration reawoke simultaneously, and after Ludwig Richter and Adolpf Menzel gave it artistic direction, there came a new period of development of woodcut book illustration in Germany, albeit it was quite different from the first period.

Notes

1) Heller, Georg Erlinger; Rudolphi. Christoph Froschauer. Zürich, 1869; Voegelin, "Die Holzschneidekunst in Zürich im 16. Jahrhundert." Neujahrsblatt der Staatsbibliothek in Zürich 1879-1882. Zürich, mit sechs Kunstbeilagen; Merlo, "Anton Woensam von Worms, Maler und Xylograph zu Cöln. Sein Leben und seine Werke." In Naumann's Archiv. X:129-275, 1864. Also in a separate reprint; Panzer, Versuch einer kurzen Geschichte der römisch-katholischen deutschen Bibelübersetzung. Nuremberg, 1781.

2) Panzer II:230, 2079. Quarto; Heller, Leben Georg Erlingers, Buchdruckers und Formschneiders von Bamberg. Bamberg, 1837.

3) Heller. Octavo.

4) Weller, No. 423.

5) Weller, No. 454.

6) Weller, No. 643.

7) Weller, No. 495.

8) Weller, No. 523.

9) Weller, No. 529.

10) Weller, No. 603-604.

11) Weller, No. 645.

12) Weller, No. 952.

13) Weller, No. 808.

14) Weller, No. 816.

15) Weller, No. 845.

16) Weller, No. 846.

17) Weller, No. 801.

18) Weller, No. 4078.

19) Weller, No. 1192.

20) Weller, No. 1270.

21) Panzer, Annales XI:398, No. 306b; Merlo, No. 294. Quarto.

22) Merlo, No. 395.

23) Merlo, No. 366.

24) Merlo, No. 373. Octavo.

25) Merlo, No. 367 and 522. Folio.

26) Merlo, Nos. 266, 267, 270-280, 285-290, 338-341, 374, 477-487, 515, 520, 541. Folio.

27) Merlo, No. 407.

28) Panzer, Versuch einer Geschichte der römisch-katholischen Bibelübersetzung, p. 58-60, No. 3; Muther, Deutsche Bilderbibeln, No. 105; Merlo, Leben des Anton von Worms does not list this edition.

29) Panzer, Versuch..., p. 60-62, No. 4; Muther, Deutsche Bilderbibeln, No. 106.

30) Panzer, Versuch..., p. 64-67, No. 6; Muther, Deutsche Bilderbibeln, No. 108.

31) Cologne, 1529; Merlo, No. 266-267. Folio.

32) Panzer, Versuch..., p. 34-40. Folio.

33) Kraft, Hist. Nachricht von ersten vollständigen Bibeln Luthers, p. 67.

34) Luthers Werke. Walch edition. Pt. XIX, p. 592; Muther, Deutsche Bilderbibeln, p. 62.

35) Panzer I, No. 564.

36) Weller, No. 1021.

37) Panzer, Suppl. 25, No. 104d. Small quarto; Koch I:130, No. 13; Weller, No. 1029.

38) Weller, No. 1055.

39) Weller, No. 1107.

40) Weller, No. 1110.

41) Weller, No. 1718.

42) Weller, No. 2678.

43) Weller, No. 3628.

44) Panzer, No. 2087.

45) Panzer, Suppl. No. 635c.

46) Panzer, No. 712 and 738.

47) Panzer, No. 695.

48) Weller, No. 2218.

49) Weller, No. 3473.

50) Octavo.

51) Panzer II:224, 2053. Quarto.

52) Weller, No. 797 and 798.

53) Missale Monachorum Bursfeldensium; Panzer, VII:84, No. 141.

54) Lacking in Panzer VII:87ff; see Schmidt.

55) Panzer VII:106, No. 314.

56) Muther, Deutsche Bilderbibeln, No. 15.

57) Michaelis, Catal. libror; Clement Bibliothek I:122; Freytag Analecta, p. 1047; Vogt, Catalogus, 1753, p. 414; Bauer, Bibliotheka libror. rar., IV:249; Panzer, Annalen I, No. 999 and Suppl:196; Widekind, Verzeichniss von raren Büchern, p. 48; Ebert II, No. 23883; Heller, Lucas Cranachs Leben und Werke, ed. 1., p. 258, No. 354 and ed. 2, p. 48, Nos. 195 and 199; Heller, A. Dürers Leben und Werke II:508ff; Merkel, Die Minaturen zu Aschaffenburg, p. 11; Schwetzke, Vorakademische Buchdruckergeschichte der Stadt Halle II:12; Wiechmann-Kadow, in Naumann's Archiv für die zeichnenden Künste, I:196-209; Nagler, Monogrammisten IV:568ff; Weller, No. 1653.

58) Panzer, Suppl., No. 673b.

59) Weller, No. 2695.

60) Weigel, No. 19432. Folio.

61) Weller, No. 1163.

62) Folio.

63) Panzer VI:456, No. 66.

64) Weller, No. 905.

65) Panzer VII:133, No. 12. Quarto; Becker, Lit. pag., p. 301.

66) Weller, No. 1190.

67) Weller, No. 1207.

68) Weller, No. 1520.

69) Weller, No. 1335.

70) Weller, No. 1347.

71) Panzer, Suppl:166, No. 968c. Quarto.

72) Weller, No. 1640. Small quarto.

73) Weller, No. 2118.

74) Panzer VII:134, No. 22. Quarto.

75) Lacking in bibliographical works; German. Museum.

76) Weller, No. 986.

77) Panzer, Suppl:159.

78) Panzer, Suppl:157.

79) Panzer, Suppl:161 and 176.

80) Panzer, Suppl:174-175.

81) Panzer, Suppl:176.

82) Weller, No. 1782.

83) Weller, Nos. 1999-2000.

84) Panzer, Suppl:152.

85) Panzer, No. 896b.

86) Panzer, Suppl:152.

87) Panzer, Suppl:157.

88) Panzer, Suppl:154.

89) Panzer, Suppl:159.

90) Panzer, Suppl:181.

91) Muther, _Deutsche Bilderbibeln_, No. 104.

92) Lacking in Panzer and in Weller. _See_ Wiechmann-Kadow in _Naumann's Archiv._

93) Bibl. Rivin, No. 5684. Folio; Pritzel, No. 11903; Deecke, _Nachrichten von dem in 15. Jahrhundert zu Lübeck gedruckten niedersächsischen Büchern_, Lübeck, 1834, p. 17; Choulant, p. 258, No. 31.

94) Ebert, No. 9226. Folio; Panzer I:323, No. 677.

95) Weller, No. 665.

96) Weller, No. 835.

97) Schaab I:555, No. 110. Folio.

98) Schaab I:558, No. 111. Large folio.

99) Panzer VII:411, No. 30. Quarto.

100) Weller, No. 1403.

101) Schaab I:584, No. 205.

102) Weller, No. 3699.

103) Weigel, No. 3497.

104) _Caii Julii Caesaris des grossmächtigen ersten römischen Kaisers Historien vom Gallier-_

Römer und Bürgerkrieg, so er selbst geschrieben und geführet hat. German. Mus., No. 17461.

105) Germ. Mus., No. 5161. Folio.

106) Weller, No. 826.

107) Weller, No. 893.

108) Weller, No. 372.

109) Lacking in Panzer and Weller; Germ. Mus. Folio.

110) Weller, No. 1113.

111) Panzer, Suppl:102, No. 947. Quarto.

112) Weller, No. 1394.

113) Weller, No. 1394.

114) Weller, No. 1641.

115) Weller, No. 1691.

116) Weller, No. 1923.

117) Panzer II:221, No. 2041. Quarto.

118) Panzer II:417, No. 2915. Quarto; Weller, No. 3154.

119) Weller, No. 3929.

120) Panzer, No. 2777.

121) Ebert, No. 11701. Folio; Panzer I:390, No. 843.

122) Ebert, No. 18753. Folio.

123) Ebert, No. 8374. Folio.

124) Weller, No. 325.

125) Weller, No. 329.

126) Weller, No. 641.

127) Weller, No. 642.

128) Weller, No. 704.

129) Weller, No. 837.

130) Weller, No. 1027.

131) Weller, No. 1056.

132) Weller, No. 1057.

133) Weller, No. 1123.

134) Panzer VI:491, No. 21. Folio.

135) Weller, No. 1164.

136) Weller, No. 1442.

137) Weller, No. 1652.

138) Weller, No. 1961.

139) Weller, No. 2437.

140) Weller, No. 2941.

141) Panzer VII:489, No. 14.

142) Weller, No. 1305.

143) Weigel, No. 18351. Quarto.

144) Weller, No. 1205.

145) Panzer, No. 1551.

146) Panzer, No. 964.

147) Panzer, No. 2099.

148) Weigel, No. 17890. Folio.

149) Weller, No. 2213.

150) Anfang, Ursprung und Herkommen des Turniers in deutscher Nation; Weigel, No. 15774. Folio; A number of reproductions in Hirth, Kulturgeschichtlich Bilderbuch.

151) Folio.

152) Eine schöne kurzweilige Histori von einen mächtigen Riesen aus Hispanien; Folio. Ebert, No. 7593.

153) Weller, No. 863-864.

154) Panzer, No. 2098.

155) Weller, No. 3337.

156) Weller, No. 677.

157) Weller, No. 1743.

158) Weller, No. 2289.

159) Weller, No. 2948.

160) Weller, No. 1323.

161) Weller, No. 2460.

162) Weller, No. 783.

163) Panzer, Entwurf, p. 275; Muther, Deutsche Bilderbibeln, No. 99.

164) Lacking in bibliographical works; German. Mus., No. 21004. Quarto.

165) Rudolphi, No. 73; Weller, No. 2416.

166) Weller, No. 3244.

167) Rudolphi, No. 88; Vögelin, Holzschneidekunst in Zürich I:18.

168) Das ganz Nüw Testament recht gründlich vertütsch; Weller, No. 3192; Rudolphi, No. 87; Vögelin, Holzschneidekunst in Zürich, p. 21; Muther, No. 81 and No. 82.

169) Das Alt Testament dütsch der ursprünglichen Ebreischen Waarheit nach uff das allertrüwlichiest verdütschet. 3 Parts. Folio.

170) Weller, No. 3691.

171) Panzer II:411, No. 2915. Quarto.

172) Weller, No. 3676; publicized by Geffcken, Der Bilderkatechismus des 15. Jahrhunderts. Leipzig, Weigel, 1855.

173) Panzer VIII:310, No. 36. Quarto.

174) Compare with the Zürich editions of the Bible in Muther, Deutsche Bilderbibeln, Nos. 81, 82 and 102.

175) Weller, No. 2308.

176) Weller, No. 2309.

177) Weller, No. 2314.

178) Weller, No. 3685.

179) Panzer II:67, No. 1306. Quarto.

180) s. l. 1524; Not listed in Voegelin; German. Mus.

181) A large number of examples of this very interesting later blossoming of German book illustration by woodcuts appears in Hirth's Kulturgeschichtliches Bilderbuch, Volumes I and II. See, especially, the introduction to Volume II of this work.

Artist Index

1. Please note that the arrangement is by first name or first letter of the monogram. Titles are listed chronologically, with reuse of illustrations following the original, with one of the pertinent terms below.
2. The citations--in the right margins--do not refer to page numbers or footnotes. They refer to the numbers in square brackets which are in the text and which are listed at the top-center of the text.
3. Abbreviations and common terms used to characterize the entries:

Abgedruckt =	reproduced
Blatt =	leaf or sheet
Blätter =	leaves or sheets
Copiert =	copied
d. A. =	the elder
d. J. or D. J. =	the younger
Druckerzeichen =	colophon
Einzelne Blätter =	individual sheets
Fol. =	folio
gr 8° =	large octavo
kl. Fol. =	small folio
8° =	octavo
4° =	quarto
s. a. =	undated
s. l. =	no place of publication
s. l. e. a. =	no place or date
Teilweise wiederholt =	partly reproduced
Titelblatt =	title page
Wiederholt =	reproduced

AH AMBROSIUS HOLBEIN.

1. 17 Blätter zu Gengenbach, Nollhart, Basel, Gengenbach 1517 1309
2. 2 Blätter zu: Morus, Thomas, De optimo reipublicae statu deque nova insula Utopia, Basel, Froben 1518 1310
   Wiederholt in: Morus, Von der wunderbarlichen Insel Utopia deutsch von Catinucula, Basel, Bebel 1524 1354
3. 4 Blätter zu: Murner, Thomas, Geuchmatt, Basel, Petri 1519 1311

ALBRECHT PFISTER.

1. 61 Blätter zu: Buch der 4 Historien von Joseph, Daniel, Esther und Judith, Bamberg, Pfister 1462 1
2. 101 Blätter zu Boners Edelstein, Bamberg, Pfister 1461 2
3. 34 Blätter zur Biblia pauperum s. l. e. a 3
4. 24 Blätter zum Rechtstreit des Menschen mit dem Tode s. l. e. a. 4

ANTON VON WORMS.

1. Titelblatt zu: Epistolae Hieronymi ab Erasmo Rot. recognitae, Cöln, Joh. Gymnicus 1518 1650
2. Titelblatt zu: Lutzenburgus, Catalogus Hereticorum, Cöln, Cervicornus 1526 1651
3. Titelblatt zu: Lutzenburgus: De ordinibus militaribus et armorum militarium libellus, Cöln, Cervicornus 1527 1652
4. Titelblatt zu: Haymonis episcopi Halberstattensis in divi Pauli epistolas interpretatio, Cöln, Cervicornus 1528 1653
5. Titelblatt zu: Biblia iuxta Hieronymi Translationem, Cöln, Cervicornus 1530 1654
6. 27 Blätter zu: Biblia sacra utriusque Testamenti, Cöln, Quentel 1527 Fol. 1655
   2 Blätter wiederholt in:
   Biblia integra, Cöln 1529 Fol. 1661
   Biblia Teutsch, Worms, P. Schöffer 1529 Fol. 1799
7. Titelblatt zu: Nova. Quo modo anno 1527 urbs Roma capta sit. Cöln, Quentel um 1527 1656
8. 38 Blätter zu Lichtenbergers Pronosticatio, Cöln, Quentel 1528 1657
9. 32 Blätter zu: Neues Testament, deutsch von Emser, Cöln, Quentel 1528 8° 1658
   Wiederholt in:
   Das New Testament, 1.1. 1529 8° 1659
   Das gantz New Testament, Cöln, Quentel 1519 Fol. 1660

C. A. IN BASEL.

51 Blätter zu: Murner, Thomas, Geuchmatt, Basel, Petri 1519 1311

C. A. IN STRASSBURG.

1 Blatt zum Virgil, Strassburg, Grüninger 1502 557
   Wiederholt in: Marsilius Ficinus, Buch des Lebens, Strassburg, Grüninger 1509 1417
   Wiederholt in: Virgil deutsch von Murner, Strassburg, Grüninger 1515 1438

C. C. CASPAR CLOFLIGL.

1. Titelblatt zu: Gerichtsordnung im Fürstenthum Ober- und Niederbaiern 1520 aufgericht Fol. 1757
2. Titelblatt zu: Das Buch der gemeinen Landboth, Landsordnung Satzung und Gebräuche in Ober- und Niederbaiern, 1516 aufgericht 1758
3. Titelblatt zu: Reformacion der bayrischen Landrechte, 1518 aufgericht 1759

1520 C O

2 Blätter zu Biblia dudesch, Halberstadt 1520 Fol. 1686

CM CONRAD MERKEL?

1 Blatt zu: Rösslin, Eucharius, Rosengarten der schwangeren Frauen und Hebammen, Strassburg, Flach 1513 1794

VF

1. 8 Blätter zu: Erasmus Roterodamus, Precatio dominica in septem portiones distributa, Basel, Froben s. a. 1312
   Wiederholt in: Erasmus, Precatio dominica, Basel, Bebel 1523 1312
2. 2 Blätter zu: Neues Testament, Zurich, Froschauer, 1524 8° 1808
   Ein Blatt wiederholt in: Neues Testament, Zürich, Froschauer 1524 Fol. 1809

DANIEL HOPFER.

1. Titelblatt zu: Eck, Joh., Chrysophassus, Augsburg, Miller 1514 939
2. Titelblatt zu: Chronicon Abbatis

Urspergensis a Nino rege Aissyriorum usque ad Fridericum II, Romanorum imperatorem, Augsb., Miller 1515 940

ERHARD REUWICH.

Die Blätter zu: Breidenbach, Bernhard v., Opusculum sanctarum peregrinationum in Montem Syon ad venerandum Christi sepulchrum, Mainz, Reuwich 1486 639

Wiederholt in:

1. Breidenbach: Die heyligen Reysen gen Jherusalem, Mainz 1486 640
2. " Heilige bevaerden tot dat heylige grafft, Mainz 1488 641

Copirt in:

1. Breidenbach's Reise, Speier, Peter Drach 1490 756
2. -- -- Augsburg, Sorg 1490 181

ERHARD SCHLITROC?

1. 2 Blätter zu: Geiler v. Kaisersperg, Buch von der Ameisen, Strassburg, Grüninger 1516 1406
2. Titelblatt zu: Hutten, Holz Guiacum, Strassburg, Grüninger 1519 1407
3. Titelblatt zu: Phries, Tractat über die Wildbäder, Strassburg, Grüninger 1519 1408

ERHARD SCHOEN.

1. 58 Blätter zu: Hortulus animae, Lyon, Clein 1517 12° 1140

   Theilweise wiederholt in:

   1. Hortulus animae, Cleyn, Lyon 1518 8° 1140
   2. -- -- (lateinisch) Nürnberg, Peypus 1518 1135
   3. -- -- Nürnberg, Peypus 1519 1174
   4. -- -- (deutsch) Nürnberg, Peypus 1519 1175
   5. -- -- Nürnberg, Peypus 1520 1176
2. Titelblatt zu: Bibel deutsch von Martin Luther, 2. Theil, Nürnberg, Peypus 1524 1141

GEORG ERLINGER.

1. Blätter zu: Schoner, Aequatorium Astronomicum 1521 1630
2. Titelblatt zu: Der Türken Heimlichkeit, Bamberg, Erlinger 1523 1631
3. Titelblatt zu: Bartholomaeus von Usingen, de invocatione et veneratione sanctorum, Bamberg, Erlinger 1528 1632

G. L. GEORG LEIGEL.

1. 13 Blätter zu: Altes Testament deutsch von Luther, Wittenberg, Melchior Lotter d. J. 1524 1615
2. 45 Blätter zu: Neues Testament, Wittenberg, Melchior und Michel Lotter 1524 Fol. 1604
3. Blätter zu: Emser, Hieron., Neues Testament, Dresden Stoeckel 1527 1662

HD

108 Blätter zu der deutschen Bibel, Augsburg, Schoensperger 1487 287

Wiederholt in:

Deutsche Bibel, Augsburg, Schoensperger 1490 288

-- -- Johannes Othmar 1507 971

-- -- Silvan Othmar 1518 972

HB

1. Blatt zu: Neues Testament, deutsch von Luther, Wittenberg, Lotter 1522 Fol. 1599

H. G. HANS BURGKMAIR.

1. Titelblatt zu: Celtes, Conrad, Maximiliani rhapsodia, laudes et victoria de Boemannis, Augsburg, Hans Othmar 1505 856
2. 3 Blätter zu: Geiler von Kaisersperg, Predigten deutsch und viel guter Lehren, Augsburg, Hans Othmar 1508 857

   1 Blatt wiederholt in: Geiler, 18 Eigenschaften eines Christenpilgers, Augsburg, Hans Othmar 1508 976
3. Titelblatt zu: Stamler, Joh., Dialogus de gentium sectis, Augsburg, Oeglin-Nadler 1508 858
4. 5 Blätter zu: Springer, Balthasar, Beschreibung der Fahrt nach den portugiesischen Inseln, s. l. e. a. (1509) 859
5. 12 Blätter zum: Taschenbüchlein aus dem Riess, Augsburg, H. Othmar 1510 860

   Wiederholt in: Taschenbüchlein aus dem Riess, Augsburg, H. Othmar 1512 861

   1 Blatt wiederholt in: Wurz-

gärtlein der andächtigen Uebung, Augsburg, Silvan Othmar 1515 990

6. 5 Blätter zu: Geiler von Kaisersperg, das Buch Granatapfel, Augsburg, H. Othmar 1510 862
7. Titelblatt zu: Geiler von Kaisersperg, Navicula penitentiae, Augsburg, H. Othmar 1511 863
8. 2 Blätter zu: Pinicianus, Joh., Virtus et voluptas, Augsburg, H. Othmar 1512 864
9. Titelblatt zu: Murner, Thomas, Schelmenzunft, Augsburg, Silvan Othmar 1513 865
10. 160 Blätter zum Weisskunig, 1512-1518 854
11. Blätter zum Freydal 855
12. 14 Blätter zu: Man, Wolfgang, Leiden Christi, Augsburg, H. Schoensperger d. J. 1515 866
    1 Blatt wiederholt in: Fünfundvierig Wee s. l. e. a. 866
13. Titelblatt zu: Ricci, Paul, Dialogus in Apostolorum Simbolum, Augsburg, Miller 1514 867
14. Titelblatt zu: Jornandes de rebus Gothorum, Augsburg, Miller 1515 868
15. Titelblatt zu: Eck, Joh., Explanatio in summulas Petri Hispani, Augsburg, Miller 1516 869
16. 10 Blätter zu: Taschenbüchlein aus dem Riess, Augsburg, Miller 1516 870
17. 12 Blätter zu: Huttenii Epigrammata, Augsburg, Miller 1519 871
18. Flugblatt: Das Kind zu Tettnang, s. l. e. a. (Augsburg 1516) 872
19. Titelblatt zu: Marsilius Ficinus, Tractatus de epidemia Augsburg, Grimm und Wirsung 1518 873
20. Titelblatt zu: Turnierbuch, Augsburg, Grimm und Wirsung 1518 874
21. Titelblatt zu: Alsaharavii liber theoreticae et practicae, Augsburg, Grimm and Wirsung 1519 875
    Wiederholt in:
    1. Petrarka, Glücksbuch, Augsburg, Steiner 1532 868, 1084
    2. Riederer, Spiegel der wahren Rhetorik, Augsburg, Steiner 1535 1108
22. 26 Blätter zu: Tragoedie von Calixt und Melibea, Augsburg, Grimm und Wirsung 1520 876
    Wiederholung des Titelbildes in Bruno, Christoph, Historien und Fabulen, Augsburg, Steiner 1541 930, 1118
23. 5 Blätter zu: Cicero, Büchlein vom Alter, deutsch von Johann Neuber, Augsburg, Grimm und Wirsung 1522 877
24. 97 Blätter zu einer von Grimm und Wirsung 1520 vorbereiteten Ausgabe von Cicero's Officien, deutsch von Schwarzenberg
    Abgedruckt in:
    Cicero, gebührliche Werke, Augsburg, Steiner 1531 878
    -- -- 1532 879
    -- -- 1533 880
    -- -- 1535 881
    -- -- 1537 882
    -- -- 1540 883
    -- -- 1545 885
25. 242 Blätter zu einer von Grimm und Wirsung 1520 vorbereiteten, von Steiner 1532 vollendeten Ausgabe von Petrarka, De remediis utriusque fortunae 886
    Wiederholt in: Petrarka, Glücksbuch, Augsburg, Steiner 1539 887
    Wiederholungen einzelner Blätter für den Cicero und Petrarka kommen in folgenden Steiner'schen Publicationen vor:
    1. Pauli, Johann, Schimpf und Ernst, Augsburg, Steiner 1526 1064
    2. Flavius Vegetius Renatus, 4 Bücher der Ritterschaft, Steiner 1529 1071
    3. Herodian, Augsburg, Steiner 1531 1078
    4. Justin, Wahrhaftige Historien, Augsburg, Steiner 1531 1079
    5. Vogther, Bartholomaeus, Arzneibüchlein 1531 1082
    6. Busteter, Hans, Bericht, wie sich die Obrigkeit in Kriegsläufen verhalten soll 1532 1087
    7. Marinus Barletius, Thaten des Scanderbeg 1533 1090
    8. Thukydides 1533 1091
    9. Schwarzenberg, Büchlein wider das Zutrinken 1534 1092
    10. Pauli, Schimpf und Ernst 1534 1100
    11. Schwarzenberg, Memorial der Tugend 1534 1094
    12. Tragoedie von Calixt und Melibea 1534 1101
    13. Flavius Vegetius Renatus, Bücher der Ritterschaft 1534 1103
    14. Dictys Cretensis, Histori vom trojanischen Krieg 1536 1110
    15. Weil, Nicolaus von, Translationen 1536 1111

16. Polydorus Virgilius, von der Erfindung der Ding 1537 1112
17. Xenophon, deutsch von Boner 1540 1114
18. Petrarka, De rebus memorandis, deutsch von Vigilius 1541 1117
19. Boccaccio, Römische Geschichte, deutsch von Bruno 1542 1120
20. Platina, Von der Wollust des Leibs in Essen und Trinken 1542 1121
21. Demosthenes, deutsch von Boner 1543 1122
22. Bracellus und Jovianus, Chronik von Spanien 1543 1124
23. Vives, Ludovico, Von gebührlichem Thun und Lassen eines Ehemannes, deutsch von Bruno 1544 1125
24. Vives, Ludovico, Unterweisung einer christlichen Frauen 1544 1126
25. Boccaccio, Fürnehmste Historien und Exempel von widerwärtigem Glück grossmächtiger Kaiser 1545 1127
26. Colloquia Erasmi 1545 1128

26. Titelblatt zu: Marschalk, Haug, Spiegel der Blinden s. l. 1522 888
    Wiederholt in: Brentz, Johann, Von Milterung der Fürsten gegen den aufrühreischen Bauern, s. l. 1525 889
27. Titelblatt zu: Luther, Sermon von dem heiligen Kreuz, s. l. 1522 890
28. 21 Blätter zu: Neues Testament, Augsburg, Silvan Othmar 1523 881-893
29. Titelblatt zu: Steyrs Erbhuldigung, Augsburg 1524 894
30. 14 Blätter zu: Avila, Luys de, Banqueto de nobles cavalleros, Augsburg 1530 895
    Wiederholungen einzelner Blätter in:
    Avila, Luys de, Regiment der Gesundheit, Augsburg, Steiner 1531 1083
    Albertus Magnus, Buch der Heimlichkeiten, Augsburg, Steiner 1540 1116

H. B. HANS BURGKMAIR D. J. ?

1. 17 Blätter zu: Brunschwig, Hieronymus, Chirurgia, Augsburg, Weissenhorn 1534 950
2. 3 Blätter zu: Platina, Von der Wollust des Leibs in Essen und Trinken, Augsburg, Steiner 1542 951

HD

Titelblatt zu: Luther, Sermo de Sto. Antonio Heremita, Wittemberg 1522 1590

HF IN BASEL.

Schneidet die Blätter zu: Das Plenarium oder Ewangelibuoch, Basel Petri 1514, Fol. 904
    Wiederholt in den folgenden Ausgaben des buches
    von 1516 905
    " 1518 906
    " 1522 907

HF HIERONYMUS FORMSCHNEIDER IN NURNBERG.

Schneidet das Titelblatt zu: Missale Pataviense cum additionibus Benedictionum, Nürnberg, Jobst Gutknecht 1514 Fol. 1150

HF IN STRASSBURG.

1. 16 Blätter zu: Geiler von Kaisersperg, Brösamlin, aufgelesen von Johann Pauli, Strassburg, Grüninger 1517 1404
2. 10 Blätter zu: Geiler von Kaisersperg, Buch der Sünden des Munds, Strassburg, Grüninger 1518 1405

H. F. IN AUGSBURG.

20 Blätter zu: Tengler, Ulrich, Laienspiegel, Augsburg, Johannes Othmar 1509 935

HIERONYMUS GREFF.

16 Blätter zur Apokalypse, Strassburg Greff 1502 634

HG HIERONYMUS GREFF?

4 Blätter zu: Geiler von Kaisersperg, Alphabet in 23 Predigten, Strassburg, Grüninger 1518 1410

HG HANS BALDUNG GRUN.

1. 6 Blätter zu: Geiler von Kaisersperg, Buch Granatapfel, Strassburg, Grüninger 1510 1394
2. 6 Blätter zu: Geiler von Kaisersperg, Buch Granatapfel, Strassburg, Knoblouch 1511 1395
    Wiederholt in:
    Geiler von Kaisersperg, Buch

Granatapfel, Strassburg, Knoblouch 1516 1396
3. 46 Blätter zu: Hortulus animae, Strassburg, Flach 1511 1397
Wiederholt in: Hortulus animae, Strassburg, Flach 1512 1398
4. 9 Blätter zu: Hortulus animae, Strassburg, Flach 1512 1398
5. 2 Blätter zu: Die welsch Gattung, Strassburg, Schürer 1513 1399
6. 10 Blätter zu: Auslegung der zehn Gebote, Strassburg, Grüninger 1516 1400
7. Titelblatt zu: Indagine, Kunst der Chiromantzey, Strassburg, Johann Schott 1522 1401
8. Druckerzeichen zu: Kern, Visierbuch, Strassburg, Peter Schöffer 1531 1402
9. Titelblatt zu: Hedion, Chronik von Strassburg 1543 1403

H. G. HANS GULDENMUNDT.

30 Blätter zu: Sachs, Hans, Wunderliche Weissagung von dem Papsthum, Nürnberg, Guldenmundt 1527 1146

H. H.

1. Die Blätter zu: Rixner, Georg, Turnierbuch, Simmern, Rodler 1530 1783
2. 50 Blätter zu: Unterweisung der Kunst des Messens mit dem Zirkel, Simmern, Rodler 1531 1784
3. 20 Blätter zu: Geschichte des Fierrabras, Simmern, Rodler 1533 1785

H. H. HANS HOLBEIN.

1. Acht Bilder zum Neuen Testament (Passavant 17-24, Woltmann 184-191) angefertigt für: Das new Testament, Basel, Petri Christmond 1522 Fol. 1301
Wiederholt in:
Neues Testament Basel, Petri März 1523 Fol. 1325
-- -- 8° 1326
-- -- Christmond 1523 8° 1327
-- -- Brachmond 1524 8° 1328
-- -- Hornung 1525 8° 1329
-- -- 1525 Fol. 1330
-- -- s. l. e. a. 4° 1331
Copirt in:
Biblia beider alt und neuen Testaments, Worms, Peter Schöffer 1529 1799
2. 21 Bilder zur Apokalypse (Passavant 149, Woltm. 150-170) angefertigt für: Das gantz neuw Testament, Basel, Wolff 1523 8° 1302
Wiederholt in:
Neues Testament Basel, Wolff 1523 4° 1338
-- -- 1523 kl. Fol. 1339
-- -- Wolff August 1524 gr. 8° 1340
-- -- 1524 8° 1341
-- -- 8° 1342
Le nouveau Testament, Basel, Bebel 1525 1355
Die gantze Bibel, Zürich, Froschauer 1531 1815
3. 11 Bilder zum Pentateuch (Voegelin p. 21-25) Altes Testament, Basel, Wolff 1523 gr. 8° 1303
4. 5 Bilder zum Pentateuch (Pass. 7. Woltmann 171-175) Altes Testament, Basel, Petri Christmond 1523 Fol. 1304
5. 91 Illustrationen zur Vulgata (Pass. III p. 359 ff.; Woltmann Nr. 1-91) 1305
Abgedruckt in:
Biblia utriusque Testamenti, Lugduni 1538 1305
Copirt in:
Die gantze Bibel, Zürich, Froschauer 1531 1815

HS HANS SCHEIFELIN.

1. Eine unbestimmte Anzahl von Blättern zu: Pinder, Ulrich, der beschlossene Gart des Rosenkranz, Nürnberg 1505 896
2. Die Blätter zu: Pinder, Ulrich, Speculum passionis Jesu Christi, Nürnberg 1507 897
Wiederholungen in: Doctrina vita et passio Jesu Christi, Frankfurt, Egenolph 1542 897
3. 4 Blätter zu: Evangelienbuch, Augsburg, Schoensperger d. J. 1512 898
4. 1 Blatt zu: Evangelienbuch, Augsburg, Schoensperger d. J. 1513 899
5. 24 Blätter zu: Via felicitatis, Augsburg 1513 900
6. 252 Blätter zu: Leben der Heiligen, Augsburg, H. Othmar 1513 901
Der Titelholzschnitt wiederholt in:
1. Geiler von Kaisersperg, Schiff der Penitenz und Busswirkung, Augsburg,

H. Othmar 1514 938, 988
2. Neues Testament, Augsburg, Silvan Othmar 1523 891
-- -- 1523 892
-- -- 1523 893
-- -- 1524 998
Die Textholzschnitte wiederholt in:
Eck, Christl. Predigten, Augsburg, Weissenhorn 1533 902
7. 18 Blätter zu: Taschenbüchlein aus dem Riess, Augsburg, Schoensperger d. J. 1514 903
8. 5 grosse und 54 kleine Blätter zu: Evangelienbuch, Basel, Petri 1514 904
Wiederholt in:
Evangelienbuch, Basel, Petri 1516 905
" " " 1518 906
Luther, Auslegung der Evangelien, Basel, Petri 1522 907
9. 42 Blätter zu: Historie der Katharina von Siena, Augsburg, Silvan Othmar 1513 908
10. 12 Blätter zu: Maen, Wolfgang, Leiden Christi, Augsburg, Schoensperger d. J. 1515 909
11. 4 Blätter zu: Taschenbüchlein aus dem Riess, Augsburg, Miller 1516 910
12. 58 Blätter zu: Evangelienbuch, Hagenau, Anshelm 1516 911
Wiederholungen in:
Marcus Vigerius, Decachordum christianum, Hagenau, Anshelm 1517 912
Doctrina vita et passio Jesu Christi, Frankf., Egenolf 1537 913
-- -- 1542 914
-- -- 1550 915
13. 118 Blätter zum Theuerdank, Nürnberg, Schoensperger 1517 845
Wieder agbedruckt in:
Theuerdank, Augsburg, Schoensperger 1519 846
-- -- Steiner 1537 847
-- Ulm, Schulthes 1679 852
-- Augsburg, Schulthes s. a. 853
Einzelne Blätter wiederholt in folgenden Steiner'schen Drucken:
1. Dictys Cretensis, Historie vom trojanischen Krieg 1536 1110
2. Xenophon, deutsch von Boner 1540 1114
3. Aretinus, Krieg der Römer wider die Carthaginienser 1540 1115
4. Boccaccio, Historibuch von den fürnehmsten Weibern 1541 930, 1118
5. Demosthenes, deutsch von Boner 1543 1122
6. Bracellus und Jovianus, Chronik von Spanien 1543 1124
7. Boccaccio, fürnehmste Historien und Exempel von widerwärtigem Glück grossmächtiger Kaifer, deutsch von Ziegler 1545 1128
8. Von den adelischen Tugenden Ritter Pontus und Sidonia 1548 1130
14. 21 Blätter zu: Leonrodt, H. von, Himmelwag und Hellwag, Augsburg, Silvan Othmar 1517 916
Neue Ausgabe des Buches 1518 918
Einzelne Wiederholungen in folgenden Drucken des Silvan Othmar:
1. Eybe, Ob einem sei zu nehmen ein ehelich Weib 1517 919
2. Luther, Sermon von dem Wucher 1520 920
3. -- Trostbüchlein in aller Widerwärtigkeit 1520 921
4. -- Sermon von guten Werken 1520 922
5. -- Sermon von der Bereitung zum Sterben 1520 993
6. -- Erklärung der zehn Gebote 1521 994
15. I Blatt zu: Hortulus animae, Augsburg, Miller 1518 923
16. 11 Blätter zu: Neues Testament, Augsburg, Schoensperger d. J. 1523 924
17. 3 Blätter zu: Thukydides, deutsch von Boner, Augsburg, Steiner 1533 925
Wiederholungen in:
1. Dictys Cretensis, Historie vom Trojanischen Krieg, Augsburg, Steiner 1536 1110
2. Boccaccio, römische Geschichte, deutsch von Bruno, Augsburg, Steiner 1542 1120
3. Bracellus und Jovianus, Chronik von Spanien, Augsburg, Steiner 1543 1124
18. 2 Blätter zu: Bibel, Augsburg, Steiner 1534 926
19. 40 Blätter zu: Schwarzenberg, Memorial der Tugend, Augsburg, Steiner 1534 927
Einzelne Blätter wiederholt in folgenden Steiner'schen Drucken:
1. Boccaccio, Historibuch von den fürnehmsten Weibern 1541 930, 1118
2. Teutsch Cicero 1534 1097
" " 1535 1098
" " 1540 1099
3. Pauli, Schimpf und Ernst 1534 1100
4. Flavius Vegetius Renatus, 4 Bücher der Ritterschaft 1534 1103
5. Polydorus Virgilius, Von der

Erfindung der Dinge 1537 1112
6. Braccellus und Jovianus, Chronik von Spanien 1543 1124
7. Colloquia Erasmi 1545 1128

20. 4 Blätter zu: Plutarch, Augsburg, Steiner 1534 928

Wiederholungen in:
1. Xenophon, Augsburg, Steiner 1540 1014
2. Bracellus und Jovianus, Chronik von Spanien, Augsburg, Steiner 1543 1124
3. Von den adelischen Tugenden Ritter Pontus und Sidonia, Augsburg, Steiner 1548 1130

21. 41 Blätter zu: Apulejus goldener Esel, Augsburg, Weissenhorn 1538 929

22. Blätter zu einer von Steiner vorbereiteten aber nicht vollendeten Ausgabe der Werke Boccaccio's

Einzelne angewendet in:
1. Boccaccio, Historibuch von den fürnehmsten Weibern, Augsburg, Steiner 1541 930
2. Ludovico Vives, Unterweisung einer christlichen Frauen, Augsburg, Steiner 1544 931
3. Christoph Bruno, Historien und Fabulen, Augsburg, Steiner 1541 934
4. Pauli, Scherz mit der Wahrheit, Frankfurt Egenolph 1550 932
5. Lonicer, Kräuterbuch, Frankfurt, Egenolph 1550 933

HANS SCHROTBANK.

Praktika, Strassburg, Kistler 1502 633

HANS SPORER.

Titelblätter zu:
1. Von Kaiser Karls Recht, Bamberg, Sporer 1493 656
2. Histori vom Grafen in dem Pflug, Bamberg, Sporer 1493 657
3. Morgeners Wallfahrt nach St. Thomasland, Bamberg, Sporer 1493 658
4. Wunderzeichen des heil, Thomas, Bamberg, Sporer 1493 659
5. Vom König im Bad, Bamberg, Sporer 1493 660
6. Rosenplüt, Der Mann im Garten, Bamberg, Sporer 1493 661
7. Adams Erschaffung, Bamberg, Sporer 1493 662
8. Bauernlob, Bamberg, Sporer 1493 663
9. Gedicht vom ersten Edelmann, Bamberg, Sporer 1493 664

HS

1. 15 Blätter zu: Weida, Marcus v., Spiegel der Bruderschaft des Rosenkranz, Leipzig 1514 943
2. Titelblatt zu: Luther, Sermo de virtute excommunicationis, Leipzig, Valentin Schumann 1518 944
3. Blätter zum Heiligenleben, Augsburg, Miller 1515 945
4. Titelblatt zu: Hortulus animae, Augsburg, Miller 1518 946
5. Titelblatt zu: Vita Johannis Capistrani, Augsburg, Miller 1519 947
6. 9 Blätter zu: Meisterlin, Sigmund, Chronographie Augsburgs, Augsburg, Ramminger 1522 948
7. Titelblatt zu: Bekenntniss des Glaubens Doctor Martin Luthers mit kurzen Glossen D. Hieronymi Dungersheim, Leipzig, Schumann 1530 949

HSP HANS SEBALD BEHAM.

1. Titelblatt zu: Sachs, Hans, Gespräch zwischen St. Peter und dem Herrn von der jetzigen Welt Lauf, Nürnberg 1521 1142
2. 74 Blätter zu: Das Papsthum mit seinen Gliedern, Nürnberg, Hans Wandereisen 1526 1143
3. 41 Blätter zu: Eck, Joh., Christliche Auslegung der Evangelien, Ingolstadt 1530 1144

HSK HANS SPRINGINKLEE.

1. Blätter zum Weisskunig 854
2. 53 Blätter zum: Hortulus animae, Lyon, Clein 1516 1131

Wiederholt in:
Hortulus animae, Nürnberg, Stüchs 1516 1132
-- Lyon, Clein 1517 1133
Bibel deutsch von Luther, Nürnberg, Peypus 1524 1182
Psalter deutsch zum Singen 1525 1183
Biblia sacra, Nürnberg, Peypus 1530 1184

3. 1 Blatt zum: Missale Eystettense, Nürnberg, Hölzel 1517 1134
4. 37 Blätter zu: Hortulus animae lat., Nürnberg, Peypus 1518 1135

Wiederholt in:
Hortulus animae deutsch, Nürnberg, Peypus 1519 1175

Zusammenstellungen dieser Blätter und solcher aus dem Hortulus von 1516 in:

1. Hortulus animae lat., Nürnberg, Peypus 1519 1174
2. -- Nürnberg, Peypus 1520 1176
   12 fernere Wiederholungen in:
   12 Hauptartikel des christlichen Glaubens, genannt der 12 Apostel Symbolus, Nürnberg, Milchthaler 1539 1139
   Ein Blatt in: Exercitium spirituale hominis ecclesiastici, Nürnberg, Gutknecht 1519 1229
5. Titelblatt und 83 Vulgata-Illustrationen zu:
   Biblia sacra utriusque testamenti, Lyon, Sacon 1520 1136
   Wiederholungen in:
   Biblia sacra utriusque testamenti, Lyon, Sacon 1521 1136
   Bibel deutsch von Luther, Nürnberg, Peypus 1524 1182
   Biblia sacra, Nürnberg, Peypus 1530 1184
6. 2 Titelblätter zu: Biblia sacra utriusque testamenti, Lyon, Sacon 1520 1136
   Wiederholt in: Bibel deutsch von Luther, Nürnberg, Peypus 1524 1182
7. 5 kleine Vulgata-Illustrationen zu: Bibel deutsch von Luther, Nürnberg, Peypus 1524 1137
8. Titelblatt zu: Billicanus, Theobaldus, perornata eademque verissima Christophori Descriptio s.l.e.a. Vilae Suevorum 1522 1138

HVH HEINRICH VOGTHERR.

25 Blätter zu: Neues Testament, Strassburg, Grüninger 1527 1411

HANS WÄCHTLIN

1. 43 Blätter zum Leben Jesu. Theilweise verwendet in:
   a) Text des Passions, Strassburg, Knoblouch 1506 1382
   b) Leben Christi, Strassburg, Knoblouch 1508 1383
   c) Passio Jesu Christi vario carminum genere F. Benedicti Chelidonii s.l.e.a. 1384
   d) Geiler von Kaisersperg, Postille, Strassburg, Schott 1514 1385
   e) Geiler von Kaisersperg, Postille, Strassburg, Schott 1522 1386
2. 30 Darstellungen zu den Evangelien gefertigt für:
   Geiler von Kaisersperg, Postille, Strassburg, Schott 1514 1385
   Wiederholt in:
   Geiler von Kaisersperg, Postille, Strassburg, Schott 1522 1386
3. Die Blätter zu: Hans von Gersdorf, Feldbuch der Wundarznei, Strassburg, Schott 1517 1387
   Wiederholt in:
   Hans von Gersdorf, Feldbuch der Wundarznei, Strassburg, Schott 1528, 1530, 1535, 1540, 1542 1388
   Laurentius Phries, Arzneibuch, Strassburg, Grüninger 1518 1392

HANS WEIDITZ.

Die Blätter zu: Otto von Brunfels, Herbarum vivae icones, Strassburg, Schott 1530 1412
   Wiederholt in:
   Otto von Brunfels, Herbarum vivae icones, Strassburg, Schott 1531, 1532 1413, 1414
   Otto von Brunfels, Kräuterbuch, Strassburg, Schott 1536 1415
   -- --
   Strassburg, Schott 1537 1416

HWS

1. Titelblatt zu: Arnoldus de Novavilla, Tractat von der Bereitung der Weine, Augsburg, Sittich 1512 936
2. Die Blätter zum Plenarium, Augsburg 1515 937

JÖRG BREW.

3 Blätter zu: Man, Wolfgang v., Leiden Christi, Augsburg, Schoensperger d.J. 1515 941

F

Die Blätter zu: Leben Verdienen und Wunderwerk der heiligen Augsburger Bisthums Bischofen St. Ulrichs und Symprechts, auch der heil. Afra, Augsburg, Silv. Othmar 1516 942

K, FORMSCHNEIDER KUPFERWURM IN BASEL.

1. Schneidet Blätter zum Theuerdank 845
2. " " " Alten Testament, Basel, Petri 1583 1304

LB

1. I Blatt zum Weisskunig 854
2. Titelblatt zu: Geiler von Kaisersperg, Schiff der Penitenz und Busswirkung, Augsburg, Hans Othmar 1514 938
3. Blätter zu: Eck, Auslegung der Evangelien, Ingolstadt 1530 1145

L. C. LUCAS CRANACH.

1. Wittemberger Heiligthumsbuch 1509 4° 1573
2. Passional Christi und Antichristi 1521 1582

LUDWIG HOHENWANG.

10 Blätter zu: Wimfeling, De fide concubinarum, Ulm, Hohenwang 1501 380

MG MATHIAS GRÜNEWALD.

(Pseudogrünewald, wahrscheinlich Simon v. Aschaffenburg.)

234 Blätter zu: Vorzeichnuss und zceigunge des hochlöblichen Heiligthums der Stiftskirchen zu Halle, Halle 1520 1687

MO MICHAEL OSTENDORFER.

1. Abbildung der Marienkirche zu Regensburg, Regensburg, Kohl 1519 1776
2. Titelblatt zu: Wunderbarliche Czaiche vergangen Jars beschehen in Regensburg czw der schonen Maria, Regensburg, Kohl 1522 1779
3. Blätter zu: Eck, Johann, Christliche Auslegung der Evangelien, Ingolstadt 1530 1780

MICHAEL WOHLGEMUTH.

1. Schatzbehalter, Nürnberg, Koburger 1491 423
2. Schedel, Hartmann, Weltchronik, Nürnberg, Koburger 1493 und 1494 424, 425

XXX

15 Blätter zu: Reisch, Gregor, Margarita philosophica, Strassburg, Johann Schott 1504 635

NM NICLAS MELDEMANN.

Titelblatt zu: Sachs, Hans, Klag, Antwort und Urtheyl zwischen Fraw Armuth und Pluto dem Gott der Reichthumb, welcher unter yhn das pesser sey. Nürnberg 1531 1150

I Blatt zu: Geiler von Kaisersperg, Buch der Sünden des Munds, Strassburg, Grüninger 1518 1409

SEBASTIAN PFISTER.

4 Blätter zu: Otto von Passau, 24 Alte 6

VG URS GRAF.

1. 25 Blätter zu: Text des Passions oder Leidens Christi, Strassburg, Knoblouch 1506 1275
   Weiderholt in:
   Passio domini nostri, Strassburg, Knoblouch 1507 1276
   Text des Passions, Strassburg, Knoblouch 1509 1277
2. Titelblatt zu: Leben Jesu Christi, Strassburg, Knoblouch 1508 1278
3. 7 Blätter zu: Kalender, Zürich, Hans am Wasen 1508 1279
4. 14 Blätter zu: Histori etlicher Predigermönch, wie sie mit ein bruder verhandelt haben s. l. e. a. um 1509 1280
   Wiederholt in:
   1. Lied von der unbefleckten Empfängniss Mariae und dabei die war histori von den vier Ketzeren predigern zu Bern verbrannt s. l. e. a. um 1509 1280
   2. Historia mirabilis quatuor heresiacharum apud Bernen combustorum 1509 1280
5. 96 Blätter zu: Guilelmi Postilla, Basel, Petri 1519 1281
   Wiederholt in:
   Guilelmi Postilla, Basel, Froben 1512 1282
   Plenarium, Basel, Petri 1514 1283
   Passion, Basel, Furter 1511 1284
6. 21 Blätter zu: Statuta ordinis cartusiensis a domino Guigone edita, Basel, Amerbach 1510 1285
7. 57 Blätter zu: Guilelmi Postilla, Basel, Furter 1511 1286

8. 16 Blätter zu: Agricola, Leben des heil. Beat, Basel Petri 1511 — 1287
9. Titelblatt zu: Clementis V. Constitutiones, Basel, Amerbach, Petri, Froben 1511 — 1288
   Wiederholt in:
   Bonifacii VIII. Sextus decretalium liber, Basel, Amerbach, Petri, Froben, 1511 — 1289
   Gregorii IX. Decretalium liber, Basel, Amerbach, Petri, Froben 1511 — 1290
10. Titelblatt zu: Decretum Gratiani, Basel, Amerbach, Petri, Froben 1512 — 1291
11. 2 Blätter zu: Geiler von Kaisersperg, Bilgerschaft zum ewigen Vaterland, Basel, Petri 1512 — 1292
12. 2 Blätter zu: Breviarium Augustanum, Basel, J. von Pfortzheim 1512 — 1293
13. 17 Blätter zu: Murner Thomas, Narrenbeschwerung, Strassburg, Hupfuff 1512 — 1294
14. Titelblatt zu: Glareanus, Panegyricon in foedus Helvetiorum, Basel, Petri 1514 — 1295
15. I Blatt zu: Breviarium Basiliense, Basel, Pfortzheim 1515 — 1296
16. I Blatt zu: Luther, Predigt von der würdigen Bereitung zum hochwürdigen Sacrament, Basel, Petri 1519 — 1297
17. 2 Blätter zu: Luther, Predigt von der Bereitung zum Sterben, Basel, Petri 1520 — 1298
18. 4 Blätter zu: Erasmus, Enchiridion eines christlichen Lebens, Basel, Petri 1520 — 1299

VS

45 Blätter zu: Die gantze Bibel, Zürich, Froschauer 1531 — 1815

‹W

1. Nyge Kalender, Lübeck, Hans Arndes 1519 — 1728
2. Hortus sanitatis, niedersächsisch, Lübeck, Steffen Arndes 1520 — 1729

WILHELM PLEYDENWURF.

Schedel, Hartmann, Welchronik, Nürn, berg, Koburger 1493 — 424, 425

WR WOLFGANG RESCH.

1. 2 Blätter zu: Sachs, Hans, All römisch Kaiser nach Ordnung bis auf Kaiser Karl, Nürnberg, Resch 1530 — 1147
2. Titelblatt zu: Sachs, Hans, Klagred der Welt ob ihrem Verderben, Nürnberg, Resch 1531 — 1148
3. Titelblatt zu: Sachs, Hans, Nachred das greulich Laster, Nürnberg s. a. — 1149

W. T. WOLFGANG TRAUT.

I Blatt zum Missale Pataviense, Nürnberg, Gutknecht 1514 — 1150

Printer Index

1. Please note that the arrangement is by surname of the printer if he has one, which is generally the case. The titles printed by any given printer are given chronologically. If he has printed in more than one place that is indicated, but the titles are still given in a single chronological series. Undated titles are filed under the estimate of their probable date.

2. The citations in the right margins, as with the Artist Index, refer to numbers that are enclosed in square brackets and are included in the text.

Book Index

1. The arrangement of this index is by author, if there is one, and primarily by title, if there is no author. Large specialized groups such as "Bibles" are classified under that heading. Alphabetization of Roman names is ordinarily, but not invariably, by first name. Where there are multiple editions the subarrangement is chronological, with s.a. editions under the estimated date where possible.

2. As in the preceding indexes, the numbers in the right hand column refer to numbers enclosed in square brackets in the text.

VOLUME 2

PLATES

CONTENTS

Pl. 42-48. 12 sheets from Buch und Leben des hochberühmten Fabeldichters Aesopi, Ulm, Johannes Zainer about 1475, Text No. [100.]

Pl. 49-62. 14 pages from Geistlichen Auslegung des Lebens Jesu Christi, s. l. e. a. (Ulm about 1470), Text No. [102.]

Pl. 63. 1 sheet from Rudimentum noviciorum, Lübeck, Lucas Brandis 1475, Text No. [132.]

Pl. 64-66a. 10 sheets from ed. 5 of Spiegels menschlicher Behaltniss, Basel, Bernhard Richel 1476, Text No. [134.]

Pl. 66b. 2 sheets from Defensorium immaculatae conceptionis Mariae, s. l. e. a. (Würzburg, Georg Reyser about 1470), Text No. [148.]

Pl. 67-69. 3 sheets from Montevilla's Reise ins heilige Land, Augsburg, Anton Sorg 1481, Text No. [166.]

Pl. 70-71. 2 sheets from Heinrich Suso's Seusse, Augsburg, Anton Sorg 1482, Text No. [168.]

Pl. 72-73. 2 pages from Heldenbuch oder dem Wolfdieterich, Augsburg, Hans Schoensperger d. A. 1491, Text No. [304.]

Pl. 74. 1 sheet from Ringbüchlein, Augsburg, Hans Sittich s. a. (about 1490), Text No. [211.]

Pl. 75-78. 4 sheets from Johannes de Thwrocz, Chronica Hungariae, Augsburg, Erhard Ratdolt 1488, Text No. [329.]

Pl. 79-81. 3 pages from Buch der Weisheit der alten Meister, Ulm, Leonhard Holm 1483, Text No. [346.]

Pl. 82-84. 3 sheets from the 3d. German ed. of Melusine, s. l. e. a. (Ulm or Basel about 1485), Text No. [350.]

Pl. 85-87. 3 sheets from the Seelenwurzgarten, Ulm Conrad Dinkmuth 1483, Text No. [352.]

Pl. 88-89. 2 sheets from Thomas Lirers Schwäbischer Chronik, Ulm, Conrad Dinkmuth 1486, Text No. [354.]

Pl. 90-93. 4 pages from Terenz' Eunuchus, Ulm, Conrad Dinkmuth 1486, Text No. [356.]

Pl. 94-103. 10 sheets from Jacob Wimpfeling's work De fide concubinarum, Ulm, Ludwig Hohenwang 1501, Text No. [380.]

Pl. 104-105. 4 sheets from the s. l. e. a. (by Heinrich Quentel about 1480) Cologne Bibel, Text No. [383.]

Pl. 106-107. 4 sheets from Ulricus Molitoris work De laniis et phitonicis mulieribus, Cöln Cornelius von Zürichzee 1489, Text No. [406.]

Pl. 108-112. 5 sheets from Chronica von der hilligen Stadt Coellen, Cöln Johann Koelhoff 1499, Text No. [413.]

Pl. 113-119. 7 sheets from Schatzbehalter oder Schrein der wahren Reichthümer des Heils und ewiger Seeligkeit, Nürnberg, Anton Koburger 1491, Text No. [423.]

Pl. 120-123. 5 sheets from Hartmann Schedels Neuer Weltchronik, Nürnberg, Anton Koburger 1493, Text No. [424.]

Pl. 124-129. 6 sheets from Buch des Ritters vom Turn, von den Exempeln der Gottesfurcht und Ehrbarkeit, Basel, Michael Furter 1493, Text No. [466.]

Pl. 130-131. 2 sheets from Sebastian Brants Narrenschiff, Basel, Johannes Bergmann von Olpe 1494, Text No. [478.]

Pl. 132-134. 5 sheets from Johannes Hildeshemiensis Buch der heiligen 3 Könige, s. l. e. a. (Strassburg, Johann Prüss about 1480), Text No. [507.]

Pl. 135. 1 sheet from Terentius, Strassburg, Johann Grüninger 1496, Text No. [533.]

Pl. 136-137. 2 sheets from Hieronymus Brunschwig Buch der Chirurgia, Strassburg, Johann Grüninger 1497, Text No. [538.]

Pl. 138-143. 6 sheets from Sebastian Brant's edition of Virgil, Strassburg, Johann Grüninger 1502, Text No. [557.]

Pl. 144. 1 sheet from the German Caesar, Strassburg, Johann Grüninger 1507, Text No. [568.]

Pl. 145-147. 3 sheets from Conrad Botho's Chroneken der Sassen, Mainz, Peter Schoeffer 1492, Text No. [638.]

Pl. 148-149. 4 sheets from Bernhard von Breidenbach's Reisse nach dem heiligen Land, Mainz, Erhard Reuwich or Peter Schöffer 1486, Text No. [639.]

Pl. 150. 1 sheet from the large Hortus sanitatis, Mainz, Jacob Meidenbach 1491, Text No. [642.]

Pl. 151-153. 3 sheets from the German Livius, Mainz, Johann Schoeffer 1505, Text No. [645.]

Pl. 154-155. 2 sheets from Antichristus oder Endchrist, s. l. e. a., Text No. [782.]

Pl. 156-157. 2 sheets from the first ed. of Johann Lichtenbergers Pronosticatio, s. l. e. a., Text No. [820.]

Pl. 158-161. 8 sheets of the Stephan Arndes 1494 Lübeck Bible, Text No. [713.]

Pl. 162-163. 2 sheets by Hans Schaufelein's for Theuerdank, Nürnberg, Hans Schoensperger 1517, Text No. [845.]

Pl. 164-165. 1 sheet by Hans Burgkmair's and one by Hans Schaufelein for the Weisskunig, Text No. [854.]

Pl. 166-169. 8 illustrations by Hans Burgkmair's for Petrarka's Buch von der Arzenei beider Glück, des guten und widerwärtigen, Augsburg, Heinrich Steiner 1532, Text No. [886.]

Pl. 170-171. 8 illustrations by Hans Burgkmair for the Devotissimae meditationes de vita, beneficiis et passione Jesu Christi, Augsburg, Grimm und Würsung 1520, Text No. [1025.]

Pl. 172-175. 8 illustrations by Hans Burgkmair for Wolfgang Man's Leiden Christi, Augsburg, Hans Schoensperger d. J. 1515, Text No. [866.]

Pl. 176-177. 2 illustrations by Hans Burgkmair for Silvan Othmar's Augsburg 1523 Neuen Testament, Text No. [891.]

Pl. 178-183. 12 illustrations by Hans Schäufelein for Via felicitatis, a German prayer book published in Augsburg, Text No. [900.]

Pl. 184-185. 2 sheets by Hans Schäufelein for Thomas Anshelm's Hagenau 1516 edition of

Evangelienbuch, Text No. [911.]

Pl. 186-189. 8 Hans Schäufelein illustrations for Hans von Leonrodt's Himmelwagen und Höllenwagen, published by Silvan Othmar in Augsburg, Text No. [916.]

Pl. 190-198. 11 sheets by Hans Schäufelein for Hans Schoensperger d. J. Augsburg edition of the Neuen Testamentes, Text No. [924.]

Pl. 199-201. 6 sheets by Hans Schäufelein and an unknown artist for the Goldenen Esels by Apulejus, Augsburg, Alexander Weissenhorn 1538, Text No. [929.]

Pl. 202. 1 sheet by an unknown artist H F for Ulrich Tenglers Layenspiegel, printed by Hans Othmar in Augsburg in 1509, Text No. [935.]

Pl. 203. 1 sheet by an unknown artist in Marcus von Waida 1514 Leipzig edition of Spiegel der Bruderschaft des Rosenkranz, Text No. [943.]

Pl. 204. 3 sheets by an unknown artist for Oeglin and Nadler's 1508 Augsburg edition of Conrad Reiter's Mortilogus, Text No. [1002.]

Pl. 205. 2 sheets by an unknown artist for Johannes von Schwarzenberg Büchlein wider das Zutrinken, Augsburg, Heinrich Steiner 1534, Text No. [1092.]

Pl. 206-207. 8 illustrations by Hans Springinklee's for Friedrich Peypus Nürnberg 1518 edition of Hortulus animae, Text No. [1135.]

Pl. 208. Hans Springinklee's title page for the Lyon 1520 edition of the Vulgata, Text No. [1136.]

Pl. 209-211. 2 sheets by Hans Springinklee's and one by Erhard Schoen from Friedrich Peypus, Nürnberg 1524 Lutheran Bible, Text No. [1137 and 1141.]

Pl. 212. 4 illustrations by Erhard Schoen's for Johann Clein's Lyon 1517 edition of Hortulus animae, Text No. [1140.]

Pl. 213a. 1 sheet by Sebald Behams for Hans Sachsen's Gespräch zwischen St. Peter und dem Herrn von der jetzigen Welt Lauf, Text No. [1142.]

Pl. 213b. 1 sheet, perhaps by Dürer, for Hieronymus Hölzel's Nürnberg, 1514 edition of Historie des Lebens, Sterbens und Wunderwerks S. Sebalds, Text No. [1165.]

Pl. 214a. 1 sheet, perhaps by Dürer, for Friedrich Peypus Nürnberg, 1517 edition of Johann Staupitz's Nutzbarlichen Büchlein von endlicher Erfüllung göttlicher Fürsehung, Text No. [1173.]

Pl. 214b. Title page illustration by an unknown artist for the Hortulus nuper apud Helvetius in S. Galli monasterio repertus, Nürnberg Johann Wessenburger, Text No. [1211.]

Pl. 215-217. 3 sheets by Urs Graf's for the Johann Knoblouch, Strassburg, 1506, edition of Passion Jesu Christi, Text No. [1275.]

Pl. 218. Urs Graf's title page for the Johann Knoblouch, Strassburg, 1508, edition of Leben Jesu Christi, Text No. [1278.]

Pl. 219. 1 sheet by Urs Graf's for the Johann Amerbach, Basel, 1510, edition of Statuten des Karthäuserordens, Text No. [1285.]

Pl. 220. 1 sheet by Urs Graf's for the Amerbach, Froben and Petri, Basel, 1511, publication Gregorianischen Decretalen, Text No. [1290.]

Pl. 221-225. Hans Holbein's illustrations for the Apokalypse in Thomas Wolff's Basel 1523 octavo edition of the Neuen Testamentes, Text No. [1302.]

Pl. 226-227. 8 sheets from Hans Holbein's Icones veteris testamenti, Text No. [1305.]

Pl. 228-229a. 2 sheets by Ambrosius Holbein for Thomas Morus De optimo republicae statu deque nova insula Utopia, Basel Johann Froben 1518, Text No. [1310.]

Pl. 229b-230. 3 sheets by Ambrosius Holbein and an unknown Basel artist "C. A." for Adam Petri's Basel, 1519, edition of Murner's Geuchmatt, Text No. [1311.]

Pl. 231-234. 4 Hans Wächtlin's sheets from Johann Knoblouch's Strassburg, 1508, edition of Leben Jesu Christi, Text No. [1383.]

Pl. 235. 1 sheet by Hans Baldung Grün for Geiler's von Kaisersperg Buch Granatapfel, published by Johann Grüninger in Strassburg, Text No. [1394.]

Pl. 236-237. 8 illustrations by Hans Baldung Grün for Martin Flach's Strassburg, 1511, edition of Hortulus animae, Text No. [1397.]

Pl. 238-247. 10 sheets by Hans Baldung Grün for Johann Grüninger's Strassburg, 1516, edition of Auslegung der 10 Gebote, Text No. [1400.]

Pl. 248a. 1 sheet by Hans Baldung Grünn for Ulrich Kern's Neuen Visierbuch, published by Peter Schöffer in Strassburg, Text No. [1402.]

Pl. 248b-249. 3 illustrations by an unknown Strassburg artist HF for Geiler von Kaisersperg 1517 edition of Brösamlin aufgelesen von Frater Johann Pauli, published by Johann Grüninger in Strassburg, Text No. [1404.]

Pl. 250-251. 2 sheets by Heinrich Vogther for Johann Grüninger's Strassburg, 1527, edition of Neuen Testament, Text No. [1411.]

Pl. 252-253. 8 sheets by Lucas Cranach's from Johann Grünenberg's Wittemberg, 1509, edition of Wittemberger Heiligthumsbuch, Text No. [1573.]

Pl. 254-255. 4 sheets by Lucas Cranach's for Luther's Passional Christi und Antichristi, published by Johann Grünenberg in Wittemberg in 1521, Text No. [1582.]

Pl. 256. 1 sheet of the September 1522 Wittemberg edition of Editio princeps from Luther's Neuem Testament, Text No. [1599.]

Pl. 257. 2 sheets by Gottfried Leigel for the 1524 Wittemberg large octavo edition of the Neuen Testamentes, published by Melchior Lotter d. Junger, Text No. [1604.]

Pl. 258-259. 2 sheets of the first edition of Luther's Altem Testament, Wittemberg, Melchior Lother 1523, Text No. [1612.]

Pl. 260-261. 3 sheets by Anton von Worms for the Lateinischen Bibel, published by Peter Quentel in 1517, Text No. [1655.]

Pl. 262-263. 2 title pages by Caspar Clofigl for the München 1518 Reformation des bairischen Landrechts and for the 1520 Gerichtsordnung im Fürstenthum Ober- und Niederbayern, Text No. [1758 and No. 1759.]

O maria ein guetige mueter
cristi dein dritte freud hast
du enphangen da du dein
aingeporn sun ihesum mit
versloßen und unczerrutten
deiner Junckfrawlichen slos-
sen gepert hast das uns fi
guriert was in der verslosen
porten ezechielis durch wel
chew got der her allain aus
gangen ist O guetige mueté
ich ermane dich deiner drittu
freud das du dein kinde
fur mich pitez das er mir
mittail sein ewigkait amen.

O lieber herr ihesu criste als
du kreftigklichen pist erstan
den an dem dritten tag von
dem tode und pist erschinen
deiner lieben muter und
maria marte auch den andern
deinen lieben jungern und
sy erfrewest als du sprachst
der frid sey mit euch also
lieber herr las mich auch also
erfrewet werden an dem jün
gsten tag und gyb uns nach
disem leben in deines vater
reich das ewig leben amen

Plate 2

got macht die vestenkeit· vnd teilte die wasser die
do waren vnder der vestenkeit von dem die do wa
ren ob der vestenkeit vnnd es geschach also· Vnnd
got der hieß die vestenkeit den himel· vnd es ward
abent vnd der morgen der ander tag Wañ got der
sprach Die wasser die do sein vnder dem himel die
werden gesamelt an ein stat vnd die dürre erschein
vñ es ist geschehen also Vñ got der hieß die dürre
der erden· vnd die samnung des wessers hieß er dz
merr Vnd got der sach das es was gůt· vñ sprach
Die erde bring grünß kraut vñ mache somen· vnnd
das öpffelbömn holtz mach frücht nach seinem ge
schlecht des som sey in im selbs auff der erde Vñ es
ist geschehē also Vñ die erd bracht grünß kraut vñ
bringt den somen nach irē geschlecht· vnd das holtz
macht den wůcher vnd ein yegliche het somen nach
seinem bild Vnd got ð sach das es was gůt· vñ es
ward gemacht abent vnd ð morgen ð drit tag Vñ
got ð sprach liecht werdent gemacht in der vestenkeit des himels· vnd teilent den tag vnnd die nacht
vnd seind in zeichen vñ in zeit vnd in iare dz sy leü
chten in der vestenkeit des himels vñ erleüchten die
erde. Vnd es ward getbō also Vñ got macht zwei
grosse liecht· das merer zů leüchten das es vor wer
dē tag vnd das minner ze leüchten das es vor wer
der nacht vnd sternen· vnd saczte sy in die vestēkeit
des himels das sy leüchtent auff die erde· vnnd vor
weren dē tag vnd ð nacht vnd teilten das liecht vñ
die vinster Vnd got ð sach das es was gůt· vnd es
ward abēt vnd ð morgē der vierd tag: Jedoch got
der sprach Die wasser für fůrent kriechende dinge ei
ner lebendige sele vnd gefügel auff ð erde vnd der
vestenkeit des himels Vnd got beschůff groß wal-
visch vnd ein geleich lebendig sele· vnd sein beweg/

der mensch ward gemacht in ein lebēdige sel Wañ
ð herre got het gepflantzet ein paradeis des wollu
stes von anefang darein saczt er den menschē den
er het gebildet Vnd der herre got ließ wachssen vō
ð erd ein holcz schöner gesicht· vñ senfft zeessen· vñ
das holtz des lebens in mitten des paradeiß· vñ daz
holtz ð wissentheit des gůten vñ des übeln Vñ ein
fluß gieng auß von ð stat des wollustz zů feüchtē
das paradeise· ð darnach ward geteilt in vier teile
Der nam des einen phison Der ist der da vmbget
alles das lant euilath· da wirt geborn das gold· vñ
das golt des landes ist das best Vnd da wirt fun/
den ð wurtzbaum bedellium· vnd ð stein onichinus
Vnd der nam des anderen fluß gion· Der selb ist ð
do vmbget alles das lant ð moren Wann der nam
des dritten fluß tigris. der selb get gegen den assiri
ern Aber ð vierd fluß ist eufrates: Also nam got
der herr den menschen· vnd saczte in in das paradi
se des wollusts das ers worchte vnd es behůt· vnd
er gebot im sagend Jsse von einem yeglichen holtz
paradises· wann von dem holtz der wissenheit des
gůten vnd der übeln solt du nit essen Wañ an wel-
chem tag du issest von im du stirpst des todes Vñ
got ð herr sprach Es ist nit gůt dē menschen zesein
allein· wir machen im einen hilffen im gleich: Darumb got ð herre ð zůfürt zů adam alle die lebētige
ding ð erden· vnd alle die vogel des himels die er
het gebildet von ð erden· das er sech wie er sy hieß
Wann was adam bestimpt einer yeglichen lebendē
sel das ist ir nam· vnd adam ð hieß ir namen all le
bēnige ding ð erden vnd alle vogel des himels vñ

alle tier ð erd: Wañ adam ward nicht funden sein
geleich Darumb der herre got sant einen schlaff in
Adam. Vnd do er was entschlaffen er nam eine vō

Plate 4

Da zayget Media dem Jason eyn bild gemacht in der ere Jouis mit grosser ziere vnnd wirdigkeyt Vnd der Jason gelobt oder schwert d Media einen eyde· das er sy haben wöll zů eynem eelichen weibe·

Wie Achilles kam von dem gejayd / vnd bracht eyn geschunden leowen· vñ warff in für sein mů-ter vnd schiron· doch kant er sy nit sein můt zesein

Plate 5

¶ Hie nach volget wie paris fraw venus begabet mit dem apfel für die andern frawen die do waren.

¶ Wie paris begraben vnd geklaget ward.

Plate 6

Die ander figur ist von den fünff weißen iunckfrawen. vnd von den fünff torochten iunckfrawen die ir öl verschütt hetten.

¶ Das·xij·capitel. Von der beſchwärd· vngemach· vnd manigerley arbeyt der gemahelſchaft. Vnd vil vrſach warumb ſy widerraten wirdt:·

¶ Das·xxxv. capitel, von den zweien ersten freyē kün
sten· Gramatica vnd logca von irem vrsprung vñ
vrsach warumb sy erfunden seynd· auch von irem
lob vnd nutz·vnd zeletst von irem mißbrauch vñ
vngemach·

Plate 12

DAs seind die fürlegung vnd stuck die belial
für legt als man in der vorgeschribnen fürlegung die Moyses getan hat vnd die vorred

VNd also ward der fräuel mit fräuel angriffen
vnd mit maur vnd mit turen warff er nider
vnd vnder dem Baner eynes weyssen fanens
mit rottem creucz. Da veryaget er die tewfel vnd

¶ Erant ſigna in
ſole ꝛc. luce xxj. ca
¶ In ꝺ zeit ſprach
jhs zů ſein jūgern
Es werden geſche
hen czaichen an ꝺ
ſunnē. vnd an dē
mon an den ſtern
vnd auff der erde
ein getreng ꝺ vœl
cker von der vnge
ſtůme des gedœn
es des mœres. vñ
ꝺ flűß. vnd dorren
die menſchen von den vorchtſamē zůkünfftigen zaichen
die űbergeen werdent alle welt. wān die krefft ꝺ himel
werden bewegt. vñ dann werden ſy ſehen des menſchen

DEr künig nimpt geſtalt nach ey/
nem lebendigen künig· wann der
ſoll ſitzen in ſeinē palaſt in purpur
gekleydet. Das bedeütet dz er ſoll
ſein mit tugenden vnd mit gnadē
bekrönet vnnd bekleydet mit dem
ſoll des küngs můt vnd will ſein
geziert vnd beſſert·an den dingen ſoll er leüchtē vor
andern leüten als er in ſcheint an dem gewande·eyn
kron ſoll er haben auff ſeinem haupt·das bedeüttet
ſein hohe wirdigkeydt·wann ſein wirde iſt ſeinem
volck ein ere·wann all ſein vndertan plickent in an
vnd ſeind im gehorſam. In der gelincken hand ſoll
er haben eyn guldin apffell do mit er zeygt dz er ſey
eyn beſeher vnd eyn tegler aller ſeiner vndertan mit
imſelber oder mit ſeinen verweſern. In der gerechtē
hand ſoll er habē eyn zepter das bedeütet ſein krafft
vnd gerechtikeyt do mit er die böſen ſoll bezwingē
die mit leib noch mit gůt nit mügen gezämpt wer
den·douon ſpricht Salomon. Gerechtikeyt hat ge
ſetzt die kron des künigs. Des erſten ſoll der künig
ſein ſänfftmůtig vnd ſoll von im leüchten barmher
tzigkeyt·vō dem ſpricht Seneca hintz Neroni. Auß

Plate 16

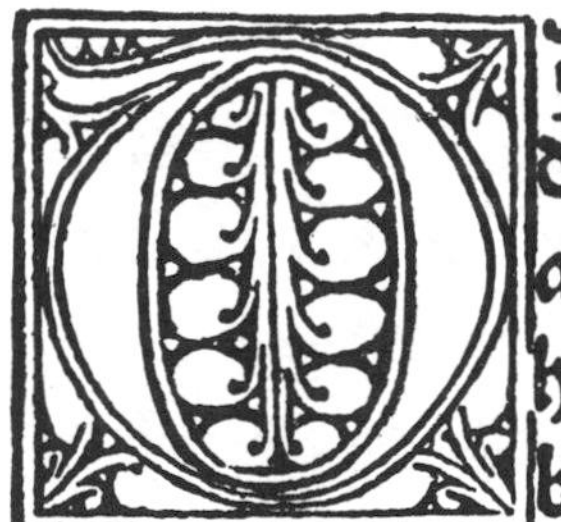

Je erst tugent ist diemütigkeit/die wi=
derstreÿtt d̕ hoffart Vñ kumpt geritten
auff einē Panteltÿer Vñ fürt auff dem
helm einē krancz võ einer grünē weinre=
ben/vñ in dem schilt zwo laitter/vnd
im dem paner einen Greÿffen.

ie ſechſt tugent dz iſt die andacht vñ
kömt geritē wider die trackheit vñ
ſitzt auf einem Gemſen vñ fürt auf
dē helm einē krantz vō rautē vñ dar
jnnen ein Nachtigal/ Jn dem ſchilt
einen vogel der heyſt Angnophilo
vnd in dem paner einen Fenix.

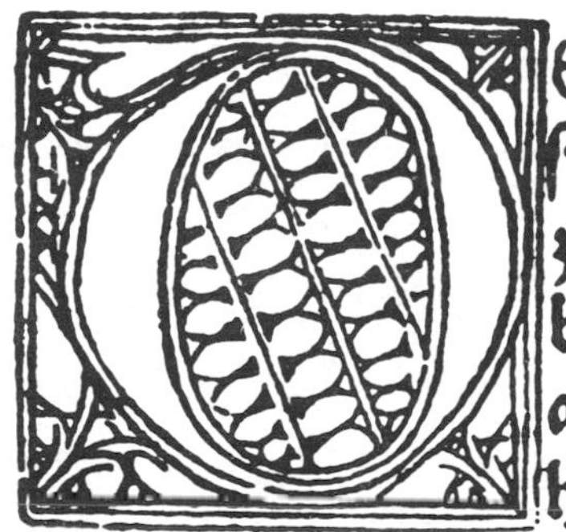

Er erſte heÿmlich ſcheinbott oder ſcherg dē d̄ teẃfel ſendt dē menſchē ze fahen dʒ iſt die hochfart/der ſelb bott kumpt geritten / vnd ſitzt auff aimē Dromedari/vñ iſt mit guldim harnaſch angelegt Vñ fürt auff dē helm eimē pfaben/im dē ſchilt einen Adler Jn dem paner eimē gekrönten Leo/vñ im d̄ hand ein braites ſchwert ·

Er and heÿmlich ſcheinbott / dz iſt die vnkeüſche Den ſelbē ſendet der teẅfel dē menſchen zů fahen Vnd kumpt gerittē auff einē Beren / vñ fürt auff dē helm einē roſen krantz / vñ darinn ein neſt mit ſchwalben Vñ fürt in dē ſchilt einen Sÿrenē / vñ in dē paner einen Baſiliſcum / dz iſt ein gifftiger wurme Vñ in der hande einē kopff vol aller vnſauberkeit / vñ ſitzt flüchtigklichē auff dē beren / vñ ſcheẅſſet hinderſich mit einē bogen Vnd hat dreÿ ſtralen angezogen.

Der dise figur eret mit einem pater noster der het
xiiij dusent iar ablas und von iij und xl bepsten ge-
gab iegklicher vi iar und von xl bischoffen von igli=
chẽ xl tag und dẽ ablas hat bestetigt bapst Clemens

darumb ward es im verkört in schand vnd laster.

¶ Wie Corbanans müter kam vnd jren sun strafft das er vnbekümert wär mit den cristen. &c.

NAch dē kam Corbanans müter zů jm traurig weinend vn̄ klagend. vnd da sÿ heÿmlich zůsamen komen do sprach die müter O du mein lieber sun vn̄ einiger trost meis alters. du einigs pfand aller meiner liebe. Jch kumb zů dir eÿlend vn̄ bin vast müd wordē vō dem verrē weg Jch was

doch nam er zů letst den gewalt vn̄ ordnung das volck gottes auff · gesegnet von dem bapst vn̄ dem gantzē cōcily ¶ O wie vil menschen jung vnd alt mächtig vn̄ gemein volck empfieng das creütz vn̄ gelopte den weg zů dem heiligen grab Da ward auß gepreyt die ere des Cōcilys Vnd kam den cristen zeoren sein loblichs gesatzte · Das geuiel in allen wol Vnd da ward gerechnet drew mal hunderttausent man die willen hetten ze ziehē Vnd die fart zevolbringen nach irem vermügen · vn̄ zugē auf die manlichen Frātzosen durch drey weg · vn̄ stritē als im willē mit dē türckē.

¶ Von dem eynsidel Petrus genannt vnnd vō dem Hertzogen Gotfrid geheissen.

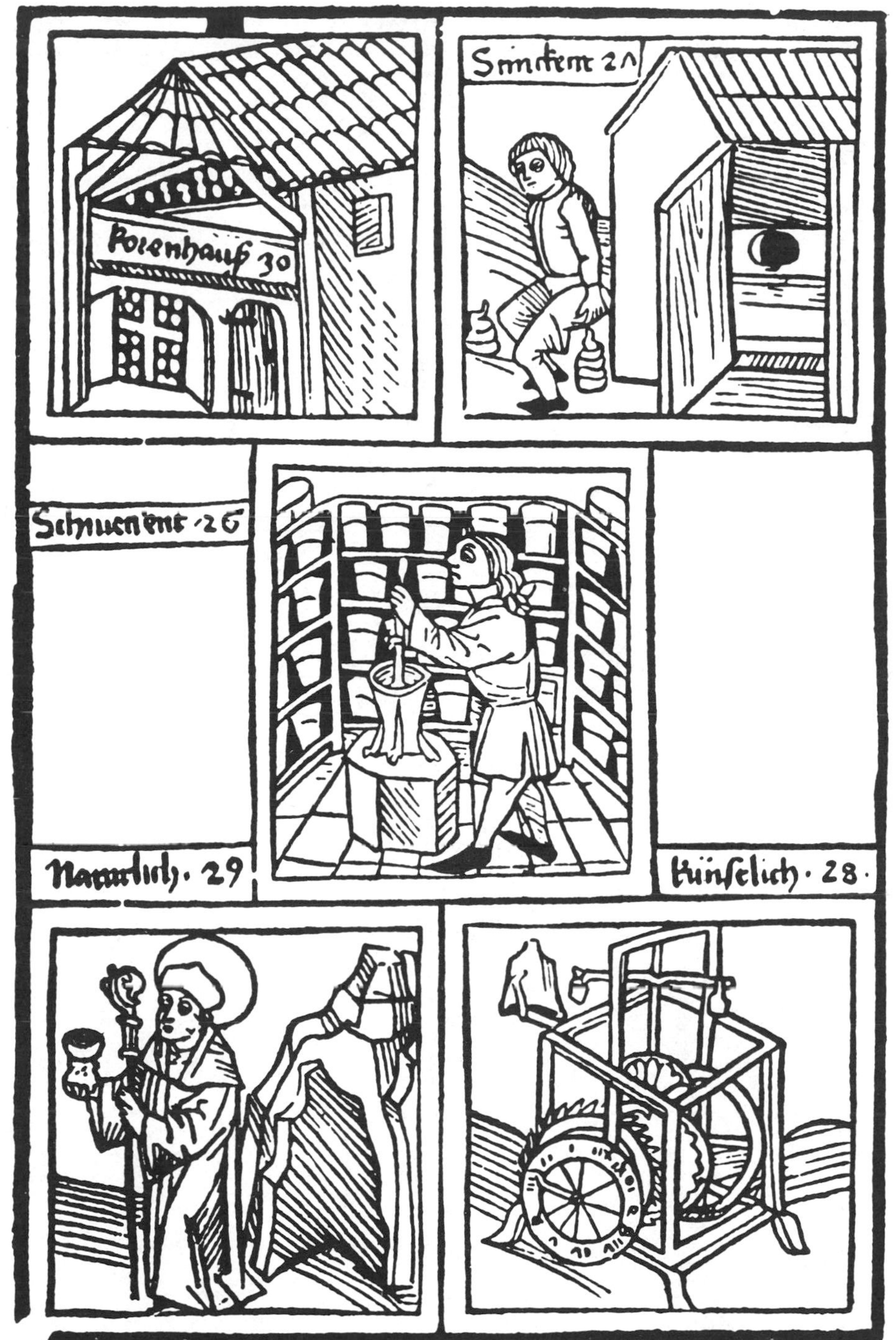
Schmeckent ·26
Naturlich · 29
Künstlich · 28 ·

Das ·cxxvi· blat
Du solt nit vnkeüsch sein

Du solt vater vnd můter eren

Plate 30

¶ Jenner byn ich genant·
Trincken vnd eſſen iſt mir wol bekamt·
In diſem monat iſt nit gůt·
Von dem menſchen laſſen das blůt·

¶ Hornűg bin ichs genant erkenn mich·
Haſt du nackendt es gereűdt dich·
In diſem monat iſt gůt laſſen·
Iſſe vnd trinck zů maſſen·

¶ Ich bin gehe̋yſſen mertz·
Den pflůg ich hie auff ſtertz·
In diſem monat laſſe keyn blůt·
Doch iſt ſchweißbaden faſt gůt·

¶ Aprill byn ich genamt
Die reben ich beſchne̋yd durch dz landt·
In diſem monat nym̄ dich nitt an·
Das du laſſeſt zů der median·

¶ Hÿe kum̄ ich ſtolczer may·
Mit klůgen blůmen mangerlay·
In diſem monat man auch baden ſol·
Tanczen ſingen ſpringen vnd leben wol

¶ Brachmonat bÿn ichs genamt·
Heü vnd korn nÿm̄ ich in die handt
In diſem monat ſol man nicht lan·
Darzů ſoll nÿemandt müſſig gan·

¶ Wölcher ochß gern zeücht den pflůg
Dem will geben heües gnůg·
Auch will ich dir mit treüen ſagen
Hůtt dich vor den hündiſchen tagen·

¶ Wol auff mit mir in die åren·
Die do ſchneÿden wöllen leren·
Siehe auch gar eben auff das bret·
Sÿ trincken weder wein noch mett·

¶ Gütes mostes hab ich vil.
Wem ich den geren geben will.
In disem monat solt du mit gan.
Vnd solt zü der leber adern lan.

¶ In gottes namen amen.
Säe ich meinen samen.
Ich bitt dich herr sant Galle.
Das er mir nützlich falle.

¶ Ich will scheÿter hawen also vil.
Seÿd das der wÿnter kömen will.
Mit seiner keltten also seren.
Das ich mich des frostes müg erneren

¶ Mit würsten vnnd mit braten.
Will ich mein hauß wol beraten
Also hat das jar ein ende.
Got vns in sein ewiges reÿch sende.

¶ Von dē vier Complexion.

¶ Melencolicus.
¶ Vnſer complexion iſt von erden weÿch
Darūb ſeÿ wir ſchwärmütigkeyt gleich

¶ Flegmaticus.
Vnſer complex iſt mit waſſer mer getan
Darum̄ wir ſubtilikeit mit mügen lan.

¶ Sanguineus.
¶ Vnſer conplexion ſind von luſtes vil.
Darumb ſeÿ wir hochmütig one zyl.

¶ Colericus.
¶ Vnſer complexion iſt gar von feüer
Schlahē vn̄ kriegen iſt vnſer abenteüer.

¶ Mercke das du nit lassest wenn sich daz neü anzündet von der sunnen· oder wenn der mon ist vol· fünff tag vor oder nach· es sey denn fast nott· zů winters zeyten so soll das eyßen grösser sein dann im sumer

¶ Du solt wissen das gesunde leüt nit söllen lassen noch kein tranck nemē sy seyen dann ettwān kranck· wann sy seind von den vier elementen geleich getemperiert Gibst du im heysse ertzney so meret sich die hytz· Gibstu im kalte so wirt er kalt

¶ Haly der meister schreibt Man sülle in keynem heyssen zeichen in die badstuben geen· Als im Lewen· zwiling· junckfrawen· vnd in dem Steinbock·

¶ Von den vier winden vnd jrer natur· Wie sy vnser natur auff enthaltent dz ist Orient· Meridian· Occident· vnnd auch Septentrio·

Das ist currus falcatus in teutsch genät streitwagen

Das ist aries in teutsch genant ain wider

Pallas

Venus
Vulcanus
Mars
Cupido

Tispe
Piramus

Nÿobe
Amphion

Von sabina popea das ·xc· capitel·

SAPHOS

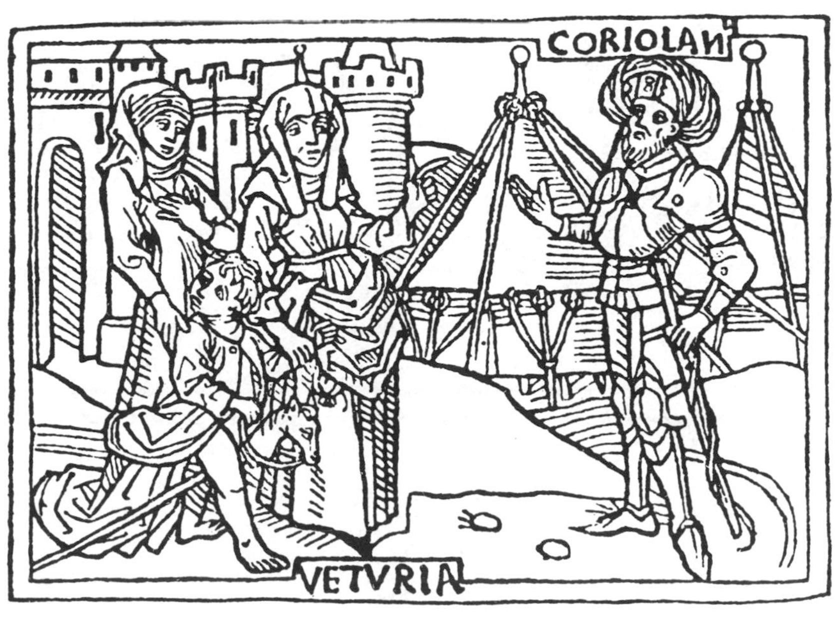
CORIOLAN
VETVRIA

Plate 42

¶ Die·xij.fabel Von zweyen meüsen

Vil besser ist ĩ armůt sicher lebē: wañ in reichtůg durch forcht vñ sorgfeltigkeit v̓schmorten: als durch dise kurtze fabel Esopi würt beweyset ¶ Ein haußmaus gieg über feld/ vñ ward võ einer feldmauß gebeten bey ir ze herberbē·Võ ď sy ward wol vñ schon in ir kleines heüßlin enpfangen vñ mit eicheln vñ gersten gespeiset·Als sy aber von dānen schiede vnd iren weg volbracht wider heim in ir hauß kerend: bat sy die feldmauß mit ir zegan vñ dz mal auch mit ir zenemē; daz beschach/ vñ giengen mit einanď in ein schön herlich hauß/ in einen keller dariñ aller hand speyß behalten was: die zeyget die maus ď maus vñ sprach·Freünd nun brauch diser gůtē speiß nach deinē willē: der hab ich täglich überflüssig·Als sy aber mangerley speiß genossen hetten do kam ď keller eylend geloffen vñ rumpelt an ď tür die meüß erschrackent vñ wurden fliehen: die haußmauß in ir erkantes loch: aber der feldmauß warend die löcher vnerkant vñ wiste nit zefliehen: wañ alleyn die wend auff vñ ab ze laffen/ vñ hette sich irs lebēs verwegē·Do aber ď schaffner auß dē keller kā vñ die tür beschlossē het· sprach die haußmaus zů ď

Die iiij. fabel von dem pfawen vnd der göttin vnd der nachtgallen.

Die viij. fabel von den hasen vnd fröschen.

¶ Die·x.fabel Võ einer bůlerin vnd einem iüngling

¶ Die·xj·fabel Von dem esel vnd wilden schwein

¶ Die·xiij·fabel vō einē listigē weib eins weīgarters

¶ Die·xiiij·fabel vō dē stelenden kind vñ seiner müter

¶ Die·xviij·fabel von dem leuwen vnd der maus

¶ Die xx·fabel vō eyner schwalbē vñ dē andern .

Plate 48

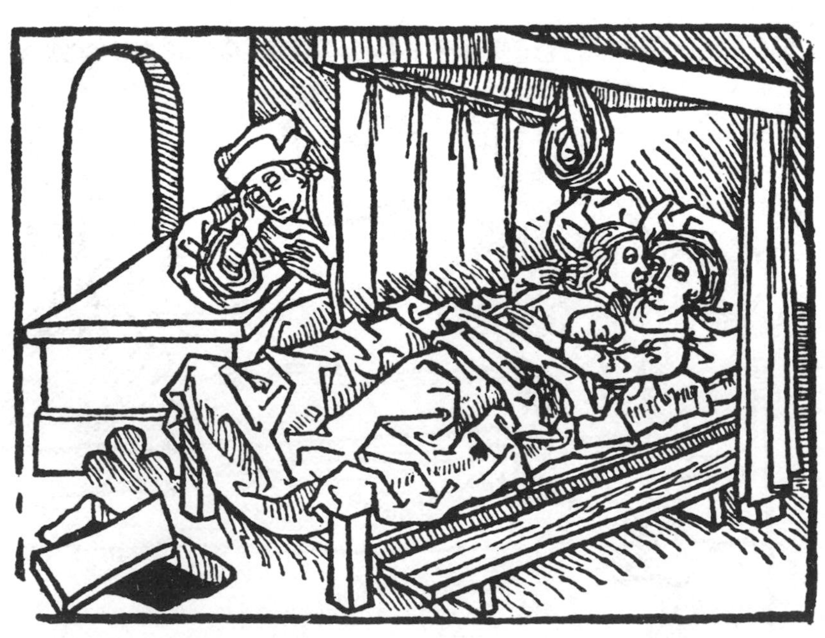

Von der enphachong xpi

ES ist vß gesent der engel gabriel von gott czu der
iūkfrowe mariā zc, Wie wol alle wort diß ewā-
gelis vol syend haimlicher mistery gaistlicher vß
legong· so syend doch die sechs wort die die iūk-
frow sprach in ir verwilgong zu dem engel vnussprechenli-
che tugend der iunkfrowe bedutten . Im ersten wort als si
sprach· Niem war· verstand ir schnelle korsamikait. In dem
anderen als si sprach. Ain dienerin· verstand ir ware demie-
tikait. Im drittenn. Des herren· verstand ir vnuermalgete
iunkfrölichhait. Im fierden. Mir· verstand ain sichere hoff
nong. Im fünfften. Geschench· verstand inbrinstige liebe Vñ
im sechsten. Nach dinem wort· verstand ieren andechtigen

Wie die mutter gotz ist kōmen zu elizabeth

Nach dem vñ ietz maria schwanger was mit dē son des lebendigen gottes· vnd noch ingedenk der wort so ir der engel hett gesagt von eliza-beth ierer mumen· stund si vff von ð selbe statt da si lang zit mit ruw in schowendem leben ge sessen was· von ierem andechtigen gebet in willen die selbe

Das guldin aue maria

AVe got grieß dich raine magt·lob vnd er sy dir gesagt·darumb das du gebard den trost· der vns von adams val erloßt aue maria

Von der beschnidong cristi

DArnach über acht tag als man das kind zů beschniden trůg· ist im gegeben ð namē ihesus zů Nach loblicher gewonhait vff disen hüttigen tag so gibt ain iettlicher fründ dem anderen ain gaub zů ainem gůten iar· also haut ouch geton ihesus xp̄s

Von der erschinong des herren den hailigen dꝛy kingen

ALs nun geboꝛē was ihesus in bethlehem iude zu den ziten herodis. Niemwar da kamend dꝛy king von oꝛient ꝛc. An dem dꝛyzehenden tag erschin dz kind ihs den hailigen dꝛy kinigen. die in suchtēd vnnd fundend in bethlehem by siner müter. da selbs si in

O muͦtter der barmherczikait Zuͦ mitliden mich berait
Gib das der bitter ſchmercz Gedrukt werd in min hercz
Das mich dins kindes hertter tod Entledige vß ewiger
not
amen

Plate 56

Wie maria ihesum fand im tempel

O nun alt was wordē das kind ihesus zwelff
iar stig er vff mit vatter vnd mütter nach gewonhait der gesaczt zů dem hochzitlichen vest
gen iherusalem in den tempel. Vnd wañ es sitt

Er ist vßgangen der da sat säen sinen somen zc

Hie wüſch pylatus ſin hend als ob er des tods criſti wölte vnſchuldig ſin

Pylatus in willē iheſum ledig zelauſſend· haut aber gerett mit den iuden vnd ſi gefrauget alſus Wöllend ir barrabam lauſſen gon· was ſol ich dañ tůn mit vwerem künig criſto·od̓ was haut er geton·ich find kain vrſach dz mā in mit recht kund tötten. Da ſi das horttend vnd ſahend wie er in gern

durch die selbe din stätmietige gedult so du warer gott vnd mensch in allen dinem liden wonderberlichen allzit haust be wisen amen

Noch von d krönög vnd menigfaltige belaidong des herrē

Complet

ZV der complet gedenk vnd sich an mit innikait vnd truren dins herczen wie sant iohanns bittend die mutter gocz wann es spaut worden ist das si den lib ihesu vergraben lauß vor vnd ingang der sabat an dem sich nit zimet die toten zeuergraben Nun also zů dem letsten die beschaiden wis iunkfrow wiewol mit grossem süffzen ieres herczen gesegnen den lib cristi hieß si hinnemen vnd vergraben den si dann vor salbotend vnd

O Du miñengliche ſel ſich iecz an den woñſamen
ſchōnē mayen·dz holcz des leben mit ſinen edlē
eſten vnd abriſender zarter pluſt·die luſtige vol-
komne frucht ewige ſpis mit ſo fil ſieſſē geſch-
mak vnd ſtarker krafft für alle gifft vnd breſten der ſel· des
füchtikait geſprengt haut ſine eſt· das iſt ſine zerſpannenn
arm·vnd die griene blöter ſiner gebenediter hend·vñ ouch
die zwen eſt zeſamē geflochten ſiner haſtige bain·dardurch
vnſere liebe vnnd vmbfauhong des gemiecz geſeſtiget vnd

t 3

Plate 62

Die beschliessong diß büchs

hic xpūs baptizat. Mat. iij° Lu. iij° Mar. j°
hic xp̄c crucifigit Mat. xx vij° Mar xv° L. xxiij° Jo x°
hic xp̄s ascendit Mar. xvi° & actu. j°
hic noua lex instituitur. L. xxij° Mat. xxvj° Mar. xiiij°
hic xp̄s sepelitur. Math xxvij° Mar. xv° Lu xxiij°
hic spūs sanctus mittit. act ij° & ps. lxvij°
hic xp̄s indicat. Math. xx vij° Mar. xv° L. xxiij. Jo. xix
hic xp̄s resurgit Mat. xx viij° Mar. xvi° Lu xxiiij°
hic apl̄i diuiduntur Math. xxviij° Mar. xvj°

Alſo keſtigeté künig dauid die burger zu rabach ſine veynde· Am anderen künig buch am·xij·capitel·

Künig pharaons ſchencke ſahe in dem traum ein rebe wachſen

Künig aſtrages ſahe ein rebe wach ſen von ſyner dochter

Hie verkuntēt die engel den hirten
die geburt christi
Dis ewangelium schribet lucas am
ij zu der crist messe

Icis si de Ilice. auernia ortum habet.
Cur vitem veram. supne virgo nõ generaret
Ag in Auernia ein eiche/võ natur tragen
wyne / Da by du jude din hertze erweiche/
Vnd glaub maria kusch fruchtbar sin.

Icit liber decimoseptimo de ꝓprieta-
tibꝰ rerũ Ilex jlicis est species quercꝰ
arbor vtiqꝫ glãdifera. q̃ ꝫm Plinĩ mi-
tas reficit nacões Nã ꝫm Isidorꝫ hꝰ arboris
fructũ hõies sibi primo ad victũ invenerunt
ꝛ elegerũt. priusq̃ frumẽta spargerent' in ter
re semina Ilex arbor est ꝓfunde ꝛ grosse ra-
dicis multe ramositatis ꝛ foliorꝫ umbrosita
tis Cuiꝰ lignũ forte est ꝛ imputribile. De q̃-
bus lignis deorum templa ꝛ regala pallacia
olim edificabant'.

I vinũ in sanguinem. ꝯversum fore claret
Cur xp̃m deũ ꝛ hõiem. virgo nõ generaret.
Art verwandelt wyn zu blute/ob tische
fur eynem hertzen/ So wolte auch ihus der
gute/ siner mutter kuschheyt nit enteren.

Alerius maximus. vinũ ponit in sanguinem mutatum. Quid hic miraculi facit stu-
por. cum scriptura dicit Exodi septimo capi
tulo. omnes aq̃s egipciorꝫ fuisse in sanguinẽ
p dies septem. tam manu dñi q̃ etiã malefi-
ciorꝫ Egipciorꝫ mutatas. Ego non habeo ad
p̃sens Valeriũ maximũ Ideo historiã clariꝰ
interpretari non valeo.

Johannes
De montevilla·

Et operatus eſt ſalutem in medio terre. Jr ſöllt wiſſen das ich hört von einē erbern mañ do ich ein knab wz der für auß nach abenteüer zeſüchen vnd zoch in der welt vmb vñ zoch in jndiam vñ durch die inſeln der ſeind wol ſechßtauſent. vñ er hört ſein ſprach in einer inſeln von einem d̕ traib ochſen an die waid/vnnd in nam wunder wie das möcht geſein. do wz er als verr gefaren über waſſer vñ über land das er wider heÿm was kōmen. aber er weßt ſein nit/vñ kert ſich wider vmb/vñ den weg den er gezogen was den zoch er wi-derumb vñ verlor manig lang tagweid. darūb ſprich ich als vor man mag die welt vmbziehen vō d̕ inſeln do ich vor von hab geſagt zeücht man in ein andre in-ſel die heÿſt ſÿmophos vnd das iſt ein groſſe inſel.

Hie wil ich euch ſagen von einem volck das iſt be-zeichnet vnder den augen mit einem eyſen.

In der jnnſelen die ich ÿetz geſagt hab. do iſt eÿn kü-nig der laßt ſei vel-ck alles bezeichnen vnnder den augen mit einem haÿſſen eÿſen das ſy söllen erkennit ſein vnder andern leütē. wēn ſy ſprechent dz ſÿe ſeyen dÿe frümſtē vnnd die edleſten vnder andern leẅten. vnd habent allzeit krieg mit den nackenden leẅten do ich euch vor von geſagt habe die nackend geend. Nit verr dauon iſt ein jnnſel die heißt Wetengle das iſt gar ein gütte jnnſel. vnnd darjnn do iſt vil wunderlichs volcks dauō lang zeſagen wär. vō der ſelbē inſeln vert man über ein wenig mörs. ſo kōt

In meinem götliche schurm will ich sy haben·
Die meine name ihu in irer begird welle trage·
Die ewig· weißhait
IHS
IHS
IHS
IHS
IHS
IHS
IHS
IHS

Der sunnē bild ist so fein· Er vbertrift der stern schein :~
David.
Salomon.
Ain anfang götlich weis-
heit ist got ewigclichen
dienē ĩ vorchtlich behütikeit
Kind meins begerest du der götlichen weißheit· So behalt die
tugent der gerechtigkait :~
Diß han ich geliebet vñ auß-
gesüchet von meinē iungen
tagen. vnd han sy mir auß-
erkorn zü ainem gemachel·
Die welt müß erlan
der die ewigen weyß-
heit ze ainem liebe
will han :~
Wer diser weisheit wil pflegen der ordne alles sein lebē·
Job:
Aristoteles
Wer seins leibs mit zart
heit will pflegen der en
darffe sich der weyßheit
lieb nymer angenemen·
Sapiencia nō ĩuenitr ĩ tra suauiter viuenciū·

Die kumbt zů hauße balde
Vnd tődt vns all geleich.
¶ Sy ligt an einer leytten
Wirt sÿ gewar der brunst
Sy kůmet im kurczen zeytten
Hand jr manheyt oder kunst
Der thůt euch aller beyder
Gegen dem weybe not
Wann ich fürcht leyder
Sÿ thů vns an den todt.
¶ Er sprach fraw sigeminne
Ich wil eüch hinnen lan
Vnd wil ich künigiñe
Hyn für die porten gan
Sihe ich sÿ gān mir kūmen
Das vngetreüe weyb
Jr wirt gar bald genūmen
Jr leben vnd jr leÿb.
¶ Er gieng gar schnelligklichen
Do spehen für den tan
Er sahe wo her gestrichen
Die wilde frawe kan
Groß waren jr die brüste
Als ichs vernūmen han
Wann sÿ lauffens gelüste
So stieß sÿ sich daran.
¶ Die wat die sÿ solt decken
Das rechte laster vaß
Die ließ sÿ do emblecken
Fürwar so wissent das
Do sÿ die burg sach brinnen
Sy dacht jres brůdern todt
Sich hůb von jrem zürnen
Groß jamer vnd groß not.
¶ Sy trůg do im der hende
Ein stang von stahel scharpff
On alle missewende
Wann sÿ die vmbewarff
Wen sÿ damit anrürte
Des ende můst es wesen
Kein ritter nichtz anfürte
Der dar vor mőcht genesen.

Hye bindet des hey

den treffan schwőster Wolfdiete
richē alle fiere zůsamen. vñ wol
te jn gehenckt han. do giengen jm
die band auff von dem regen.

Sy schoß die stāg mit kreften
Dem herzen auff den schilt
Mit rechten meysterscheften
Vnd das der tegen milt
Sich nit do kund erweren
Er strauchte auff das lant
Mit krafft fieng sÿ den heren
Alle fiere sÿ jm bant.
¶ Mit starcken riemen neüe
Das tugentlose weyb
Die sprach nun můß mich reüe
Meins lieben brůder leyb
Das du den hast verhawen
Des wirt dir hie kein frid
Man můß dich bald anschawen
Hangen an einer wid.
¶ Das můß eüch got verbieten
Sprach hugdieter ichs baren
Der wöll sich mein gemieten
Das es baß müsse faren
Hie vmb mich ellenden
Wann du mir hast beschwert
Will mir got hilffe senden

So wirt ich wol ernert.
¶ Do lieff die vil vnreine
Do von jm in den tan
Sy ließ jn ligen eine
Do auff dem grünen plan
Sy trůg do in der hende
Das liebe waffen sein
Zů einer steines wende
Do verbarg sÿ es ein.
¶ Wie es gieng dem fürstē jūgē
Das wirt eüch schier gesept
Got durch sein erbarmunge
Kein vnrecht lang vertrept
Sein genad er jm do sande
Ein starcker regen kan
Auff giengen jm seine bande
Der ritter freüd gewan.
¶ Ye doch so klagt er balde
Das liebe waffen sein
Sein klag hört in dem walde
Ein kleines zwergelein
Das sach wo sÿ das waffen
Stieß in die steines wandt
Das zwerglin kam gelaffen
Do er wolffdieterichen fandt.
¶ Es schwang jm gar behende
Ein nebelkappen an
Den edelen held ellende
Fůrt es do bald von dan
Hyn zů der steines wende
Vnd do sein schwert in was
Es bots jm in sein hende
Do ward ime mamme baß.
¶ Ozel die fraw küne
Was kůmen so man sept
Vnder die linden grüne
Mit einer wyd was brept
Sÿ kam hyn zů der linden
Vnd sůcht den werden man
Sy kund jn nyndert finden
Er was gefůret hindan.
¶ Do lieff sÿ schnelligkliche
Hyn gān der steines wand
Das sach wolffdieteriche
Er lachte do zů hand
Er gunde bald entstricken
Die nebelkappen sein
Do geriet jn aneblicken
Die übel walledein.
¶ Sy lieff jn vnder augen
Gar sturmigklichen an
Do ist es one laugen
Jr ward ein schlag getan
Hyn zů der glincken brüste
Jr do der schlag geschlach
Vnd das jr starcks gelüste
Do můste werden schwach.

Hye streyt wolffdieterich mitt des rysen schwöster. vnd schlůg sÿ zů tod.

Sy buckt sich zů der erde
Die brust sÿ balde nan
Den edelen fürsten werde
Sy werffen do began
Das jm bey was geschwunden
So fräfelich was jr můt
Doch starb sÿ zů den stunden
Das was dem fürsten gůt.
¶ Also das weyb so wilde
Jr starckes ende koß

¶ In sant Jörgen namen heb an vnd schau zů ersten Ob der man hoch oder nyder gang das ist des ringens anfang

hyſtoria ſancti
ladiſlai.

dyaconꝰ de kykullew ī eccl'ia trāſſiluana vicariꝰ ſtrigonieñ. ⁊ ſpiri
tualibꝰ gñalis: tūc licet indignꝰ ſuoꝝ ſecretoꝝ notariꝰ: poſterioꝝ
notitie duxi cōmēdādā ordine ſequētiū ꝯtinuādo ꝑ capitula ⁊ ꝑti
culas terminatas ſub certis titulis: vt i ꝓmptu īueniat̄ qđ q̄rit̄ ꝓ
legentiū vtilitate: ⁊ in q̄tuor ꝑticulas ut infra de q̄libet ꝑticula ꝑ
ſe poſita clariꝰ apparebit: diuidēdo ſeu diſtinguēdo. Siquid aūt
minꝰ recte īueniat̄ vl' incōuenienter ꝓpoſitū lector ꝓuidus ⁊ beni
gnus ſupplēda ſuppleat ⁊ corrigat queſo ſine iniuria corrigēda.

De coronatiōe ac vita ⁊ exercicijs Lodowici regis.

ipse ꝯtexuit: tū v̇o illa meis iuuenilibꝰ q̄ ī annis a viris etate parit
⁊ fide plenis: q̇ se illiꝰ ꝑiculi, ꝓcellis agitatos aiebāt: rege de p̄ta/
cto audiui āpliꝰ ꝯscribere curaui. Legas igiꝭ ⁊ discerne: exalta vl'
dep̄me: ⁊ qui hoiez ignarū īsueta angariare p̄sūpsisti sarcina: ipse
laudis ul' vituꝑij q̇cq̇d referre videboꝛ ꝑticeps esto. Me aūt ut
⁊ plāctuosū huiꝰ karoli regis vite exitū: ⁊ reginarū hūgarie flebi/
le factū: altiꝰ oꝛdinare ⁊ lōgis animū saciare q̄relis ve mutatis in
aue altissimꝰ iuuet: supplex oꝛo. Sequiꝭ exoꝛdiū narratiōis
Et pꝛimo de coꝛonatione regine Marie ⁊ de odio subsecuto.

p̄meditat⁹ē: paucos post dies mitis eū muneribꝰ (vt ip̄e sp̄abat) placatū regni hūgarie trāssiluanas traducere fecit in partes.

De electione dn̄i iohānis wayuode in gubernatorē: ⁊ de talione per eundē a drakul wayuoda exacta.

Post hāc tādē belli tēpestatē: postq̄ȝ regis wladislai lugubrem interitū: ne quis in regno in alterius offensā moueretur: per dominos prelatos ⁊ barones regni interdictum est. ⁊ nihilominus vt adueniente festo pē/

Plate 80

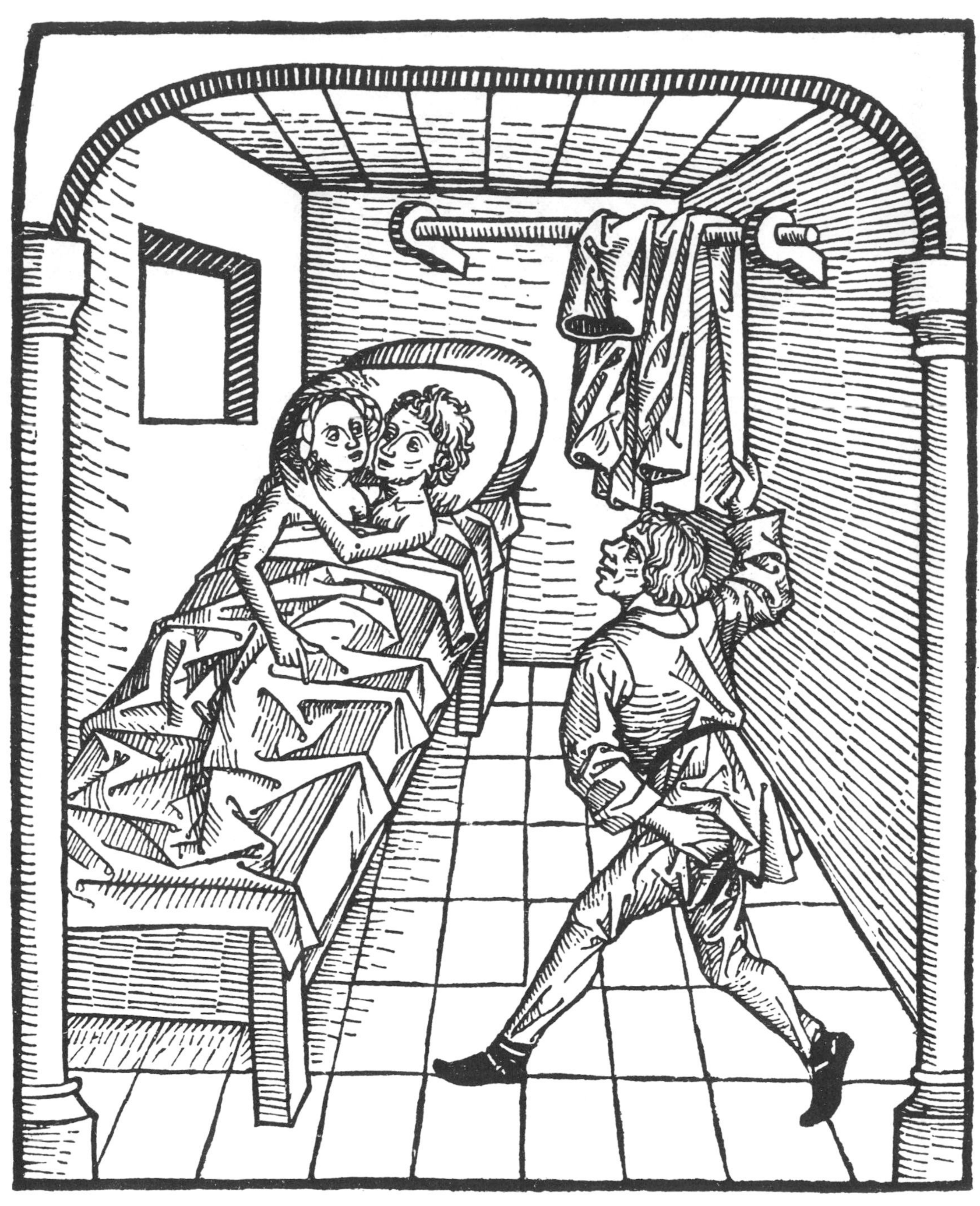

zů eym seinē rat/was beduncket dich mit disem rappē/der ant/
wurt/nicht dunckt mich besser dañ in zů tödtē/dañ er ist ei vil
wissender me dañ wir/vñ er ist einer vō dē edelsten vñ weyse/
sten dē redē des künigs d' rappen vñ sein vertilckung würt vns
grosser růw kūmen/vñ den rappē zů grossem verlust vñ scha/
den/dañ sie haben keinē me bey yn d' ynen so vernünfftige rat
geben mag/dañ es sprechen die weisen wen got grosses beradt
vñ das verleußt der findt dz selten wider/vnd welcher seinen
feindt begert zů überwindē vñ das glück schafft ym den in sein
hand/vñ er acht des nit das er yn vmb bringe dem ist nit nutz
sein weyßhait/sunder ym zůkunfftigen schaden/dañ wann er
den gern wider hett/so mag er ym nit werdē/darnach fragt d'
künig den andern rat was yn gůt bedeucht vō des rappen we
gen. der sprach mein rat ist dz du yn nit tödtest/dañ den demů/
tigen vñ armē ist barmhertzigkait zů erzaigen/vnd ob der ein
feindt wer noch ist er vō dē tod zů erledigen vñ er ist ietzt gefan
gen/darumb ist ym glaubē zů haltē. Es hat maniger hilff fun
den vō seinē feinden vnd wart damit sein fründt. Als des alten
mans weyb die yn lieb gewan do sie ym feindt was/sprach der
künig wie was dz/antwurt der rapp/man sagt es sey fast eyn
reicher kauffman gewesen/vñ fast alt/vñ d' het ein schöns iun
ges weyb vñ ward doch vō ir nit lieb gehaltē/vñ sie wolt ym
auch am bedt nit gehorsam sein/vñ wie fast er sie zů im zoch so
zoch sie wider vō ym/auff ein nacht als sie aber bey einand' la
gen do kam zů yn ein dieb vñ die frauw erwacht vō dem gang
des diebs/vñ wart sich fürchtē vñ vō forcht schmuckte sye sich
hart an dē mā biß er auch erwachte/do sprach er wannē kumpt
mir diser nüwer grůß dz du dich mir neher tůst dañ vor ye vñ
hort damit dē dieb vñ mercket dz sie vō forcht des diebs zů yme
geruckt was/vñ sprach zů dē dieb ich acht mirs für ein groß ge
nad die du mir auff dise nacht geton hast/darumb ich dir meī
lebē lang gůts schuldig bin/das du vrsach bist das mich meyn
gemahel vmbfangen hat/nym yetz was dir gefellet vnd sey dir
auß meine hauß erlaubt zů tragen was du bedarffen bist.

Plate 82

Wye ſy zů tiſchē ſaſſent vnd reymond ſelbes zů tiſch diente / Vnd ander vil ritter vnd knechte

Wye reymont vnd melusina zů samen würdent geleit / Vnd von dem bischoff geseg enet wurdent in dem bett

.Wie reymund melusʒmen Jm bàd ſach vnd er zů moll übel erſcrack vñ im groſſem zorn ſinen brůder wō yme ſchickito wan er yme argeſ von melusʒmen ſeit/das er aber nit befunden hatt

Plate 86

Plate 88

Der and tail deß fünfften vnderschaids. Chérea lieff noch im hem
ling klaid. vnd kam auff der gassen zů Thais vnd Pithias. Nach
vil worten begab sich Cherea die saittenspilerin zenemen do er hő
ret das sie ain Burgerin von Athenis was. Allso gieng er in Tha
is hauß zewarten das Cremes mit irr sengmůtt er kam ir herkom-
en ze beweisen.

Der Sibend tail deß fierden vnderschaids · Wie der Ritter mit den knechten das hauß wolt stürmen · Vnnd wie es zergieng vnd ab schieden·

Der vierd tail deß vierden vnderschaids · Phedria gieng mit den megten in sein hauß den hemling zesuchen · Da fand er den rechten hemling in seines brůders Cherea klaid · Vnd als die megt wider umb heruß lieffen · do sach sie den Cremes der was auf deß ritters hauß gangen vnd wolt in Thais hauß · Da lieff die ain diern mit den klaineten vorhin ·

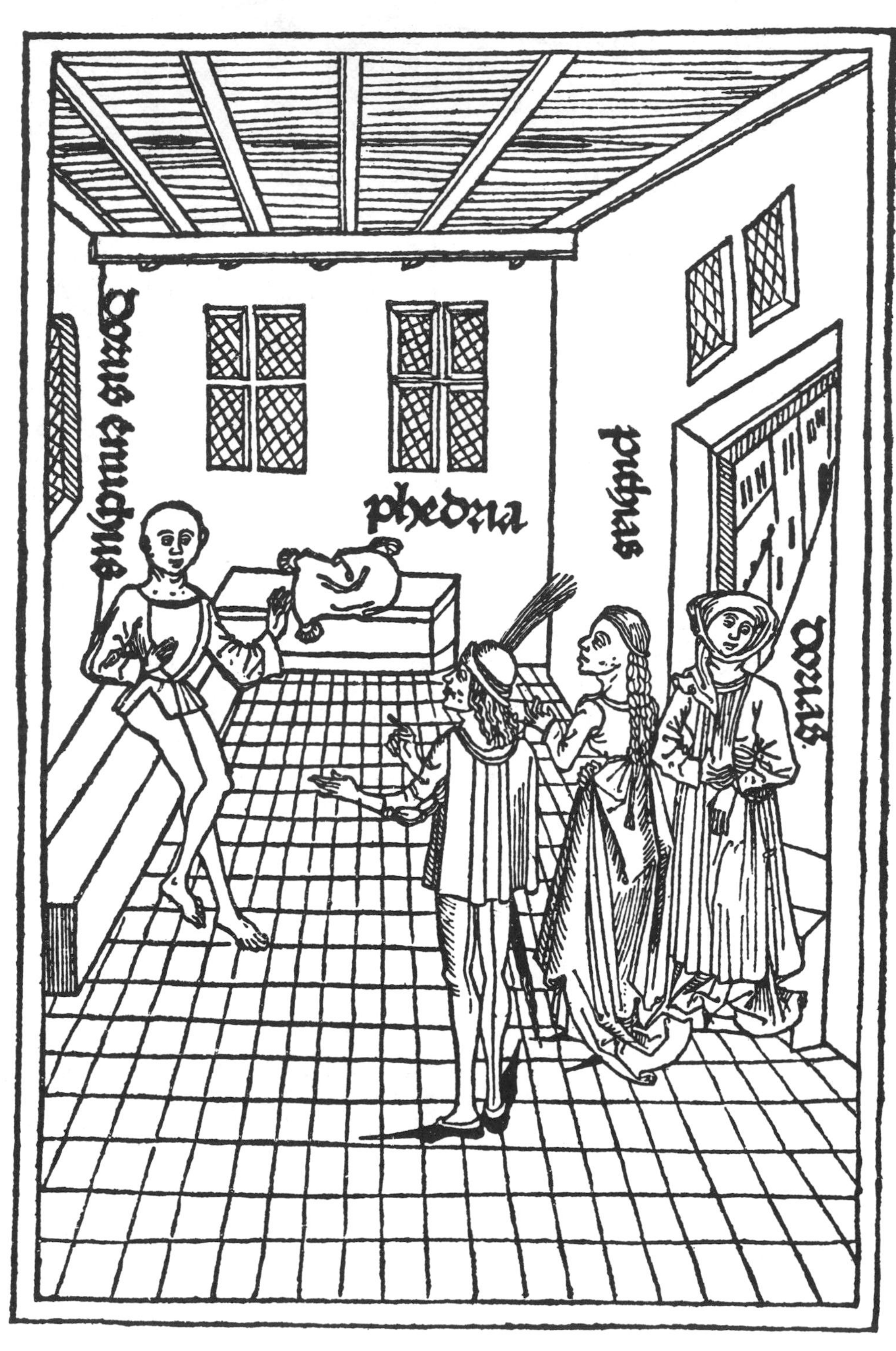

Tra. lxii

Olt ich icht dise so
merckliche smach in
mich entpfahen Gnato. ze
sterbē ist mir gnuglicher.
Simalio/Dorax/Siriste
folgend mir nach. erstlich
will ich dz hauß stürmē.
Gna. Jst recht. Tra. Jch
will die iunckfrawen mit
gwalt nemē. Gna. Frūm
klich. Tra. Jch will si üb
el slahē. Gna. hübschlich.
Tra. Dorax kum du her/
mit dē rigel enmitten in dz
geschick. du simalio in den
lingken spitz. siriste du in
den rechten. rüeff den andern. wa ist centurio ꝛc san
ga ꝛc vñ die schar der kuch
enknecht ꝛc San. Sich an
Sanga ist engegē. Tra.
Du tor wz gedenckst du

¶ Solt ich. Hie wirt
widerū deß vngeschick-
ten ritters schnōdikait
ertzaigt. ď zů seinē bůlē
als gegē sein feinden vf
gezogē ist mit bewegtē
gemüt. eilendē lauff vñ
vngeberde. Wie ain sp
ōtlich für nemē. Als ob
traso nimer so keck we
re ainig scheltung wid
die bůlerin für zenemē
er het im dann den tod
für gesetzt. ¶ Simalio
zōs. Dise wort soll man
zorniglich aussprechē.
¶ Jch will sie übel zēs.
Merk die ordnūg ainß
krigs. am erstē die stür
müg ď maur. darnach
widernemung deß ent-
werten gůtz. Zům let-
sten die pein ď rauber.
Gedenck aber den offē
barn spot vnď den wor
ten deß lobs. Dañ was
ist recht geton. in ď stür
müg deß hauß was ist
frümkait. Jn entwerūg
ď iunckfrawen. was ist
hübschs in übelslahūg
deß weibs. dann so er spricht. Jch will sie übel slahē. do maint er
Thais. ¶ Dorax kumb du her. Wunderlich sind die namen der
scharhalter zů versmehūg versamelt. wañ Dorax hat den namē
von aim ror enpfangē. als ob er snōď vñ swach sei. Simalio vō
aim affen von vnrainigkait wegē deß munds oder ď nasen. Siri
stus ist aī klains nämlin vom Siro. ¶ Kumb mit dē rigel. Gnůg
spōtlich ist es ain rigel zebrauchē wiď ain frauen. darumb stele
er in mitten in den hauffen. ¶ Du tor. Hie erscheint das der koch
durch den snellen auflauf zů gelofen wz gleich wie er sich zů seinem gescheffť in ď küchen zů gericht het mit dem fürlüch.

Plate 94

De fide concubinarum in sacerdotes
Questio accessoria causa ioci et urbanitatis in quolibeto Heidelbergensi determinata a magistro Paulo oleario heidelbergensi.

De cōcubinarijs post mortem etiam (quod
stultissimum est) in Heredam suam damnabi-
liter affectis.

Vergilio in hec item dissuadente.

Non hoc ista sibi tempus spectacula poscit
Maior agit deus atq; opa ad maiora remittit
Cura tibi diuū effigies templaq; tueri.

Doctrine experimẽtales ab inueteratis dierũ malorum: iunioribus meretricibus de dãno sacerdotũb⁹ inferẽdo date da die võ Noppenheim gen Altzeim sindt kummẽ iuuenes informando ad decipiẽdos et spoliandos sacerdotes.

Fides concubine in sacerdotẽ prima.

Concubine cum rustico in hec conducto (sacerdote cruciatam agente) crurale conuiuium ab ea in id vulgare irriso Her andres gond ir mitt dem crütz vbi plorandum vobis vnd singēt nit

b iiij

q Uestio min⁹ principalis ad me data fuit hec. Cur ceci amatores mulierꝝ easdē plus colunt venerantur et amant q̄ꝫ deum optimum et verū. Patres et domini prestantissimi protestor in primis me nō de his verbis aut dictionibus deus amor mulier locuturum/licet his verbis vsurus sim/sed de rebus per ea significatis/q̇s eiū

Amatorē arduis neglectis vt simeā pueri
libus duci et fatuis in illud Vergilianum.
Ach chorydon chorydon que te dementia cepit
Semiputata tibi frondosa vitis in vlmo est
Quin tu aliquid saltem potius: quoꝝ indiget vsus
Viminibus molliqꝫ paras detexere iunco.

f Uit insuper quedam matrona que elegit sibi studentem quēdam stolidum/alliciens eundē paruis munusculis puta mitris/ligis/pectoralibus plicatis/ zonis ex serico confectis/ et siqua sunt similia. At ille multum gauisus/ ex ea quesiuit/cur nam mihi tantum honorem exhibes/ cum tamen de te nihil bene meritus sim/

Amorẽ inquietũ inſtabilẽ ⁊ ad oia paſſionatũ nũc mu-ſicis nũc choreis quo amice placeat i hora mille mutabili-tatibus deditũ. De quo ſub noie galli in hec Vergilius.

Jam mihi per rupes videor lucoſqꝫ ſonãtes
Ire/ libet partho torquere cydonia cornu
Spicula/tanqꝫ hec ſint noſtri medicina laboris
Aut deus ille malis hominũ miteſcere diſcat.

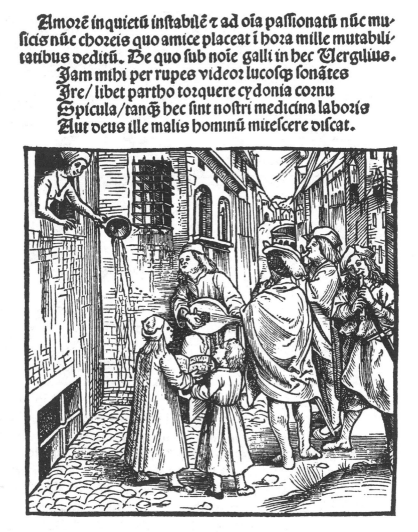

Plate 102

q Uod amoꝛ mulierũ faciat hoiem bestiã / insensatũ / seipsum nõ cognoscentẽ / imo ⁊ poꝛcũ ex certa hystoꝛia possum asseuerare. Fuit qdã amou de dit⁹ / ⁊ licet oim litteraꝝ ignar⁹ sicut stylpho / scholas tñ regẽdas assũpsit docẽs pueros ꝑ oia ex ysidonio germanico. Et pꝛimo in grãmatica in capitulo de vocalib⁹ A E J O U. Posthac in grãmatica positiua. panẽ bꝛot. caseum keß. vinum wyn offam ein supp. pira ein bier. lob⁹

T vt multa paucis cõprehendam: Amor mulie-
e rũ deũ offendit/angelos contriſtat/demones leti
ficat/ hominem excecat/ rationẽ eneruat/ viſum
obnubilat/ memoriam debilitat/ fantaſiam lacerat/mar-
ſupium euacuat/infamat/ vilem abiectum ꝛ incõſtantem
facit / anxium et ſollicitum omni tempore reddit/poda-
gram/cyragrã/ arteticam/ vertiginem generat. Amator

OOLIAP
BEZELEEL

Assuerus
·hester·

Plate 106

synen stat·dar en mach yt nicht ouer gan He schop ock dat ertricke droge
syne frucht alle·korne bome vnd crude dat yt sat an öm sulvest worde·
In dem verden dage den wy heten myddewecken·mackede got de Son=
ne dat se dem dage lyecht geue·vnd de mön vnd sterne der nacht·Vnd is
de dach mercurius Des vefften dages den wy heten donnerdach·Schopp
got allerhande vogel in der lucht vnde fyssche in dem water In dem seste
dage den wy heten frydach schop he allerhande fee queck vnd wilde dere
Vnd in der ersten stunde des dages mackede got Adame van der erde na
synem likenisse·vnd gaff öme gewalt ouer fee·ouer voggel·ouer fissche·
vnd sande öne in dat Paradis·dar mackede he Eua van Adames ribbe·
In der driddē stunde des dages diewile dat he sleyp·vnd gaff eua adame
to wiue·vñ scholde ewich leuē vñ vorbot öne frucht an eynē bome to eten

Sent Peter Patroin des Stiffts van Coellen

Plate 110

Van dē Baeswijler Strijt tusschen heren wentzelt hertzoge
zo Brabant ind zo Lutzenburch op eyn. ind hertzoch Wilhelm van Guylch
op die andere sijde.

Innocencius.v.der.Cxxiij.pays CCxl
Syffert vā Westerburch d.lij.bysschoff zo Coellen

Zacharias pays
Bertelinus der .xvij. byſſchoff tzo Collen.

Die erst figur gehort zü dem erstē gegēwurf.

Die dreizehend figur

Die ſechßvndachtzigiſt figur

Die dreyvndachtzigist figur

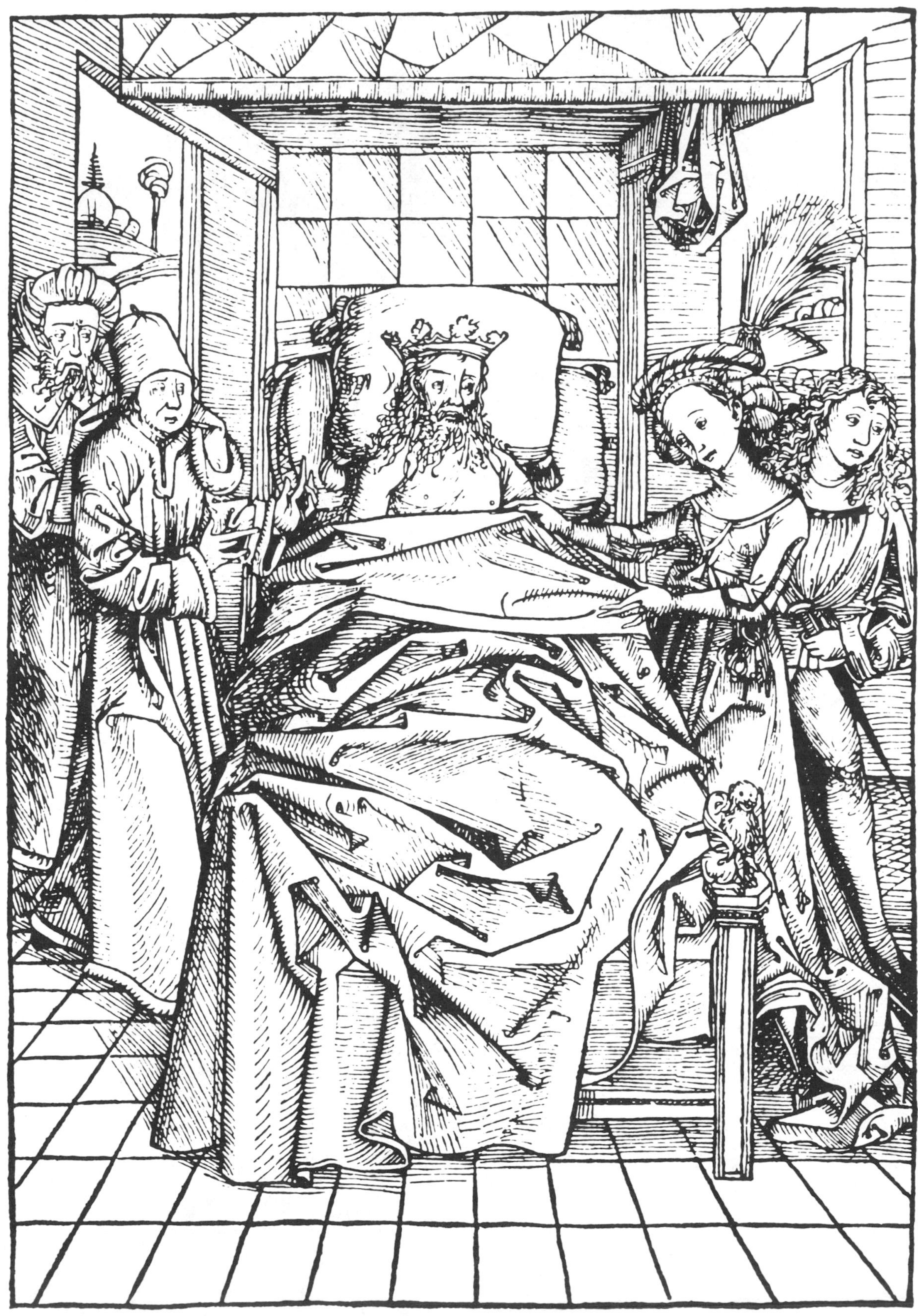

Die außlegung diser figur

Dise lxxxiij. figur. von der schönen abisag ist hieher gesetzt zu einer anzeigüg. wie zartlichen. vñ eerlichen den künigen d iudē gedient ist wor den. als der anfang des dritten puchs der künigen setzt. von künig dauid. das er (da man yn deckt mit vil deckenn) nit warm würd. da sprachē sein diener. Lasset vns vnserm herrē ein iunge iunck frawenn suchenn. das sy vor dem künig stand. vnnd schlaff in seiner schoß. vnd werm vnsern herrē den könig. Vñ steet darnach geschribē. Also süchten sy ein schöne iunckfrauenn an allen orten des lands israhels. vnd funden abysag von suna vnd fürtē sy zu dein könig. vñ sy schlieff bey dem könig vñ dienet ym. vñ was fast ein schöne iunckfraw. Vñ ist da zeuersteen. das sie der könig zu ey ner eelichen haußfrawenn nam. wiewol er sy nit bekant oder beschlieff als hernach geschriben steet. Auß diser hystorien merck den vnterschayd zwischē vnserm herren vñ andern iüdischen königen. Da dauid der iuden künig. alt vñ kalt ward. da deckt man yn mit menger ley decken. da dasselb nit halff da sucht man ym ein schöne iunckfrawenn dy yn mit irem zartē leib wermete. Künig da uid lag. vnser herr must hāgē. König da uid lag in einē waichen herrlichen kostbern pett. darumb dz er alt vñ schwach was. Vnser herr was aller königen könig. aller herren herr. vnnd was ye kein mensch als müd vñ schwach als er. dar zu was er in dem grösten wee. dennoch must er an dē lesterlichē verleümten her ten mördergalgen hangen. vñ dz ym de ster wirß gescheh. so must er an hēdē vñ füssen hangen. vnd das ym noch wirser beschech so must er an den nagelen hange. Man bedeckt könig dauid mit men gerley waychen vnd köstlichen tüchern. mit purpur. mit seyden. vnnd puntwerck oder ir gleichen. oder vilkercht mit weyt kostlicherm gewant denn man yetz hat. So zoh man vnserm herrē sein arme vñ demütige wat ab. vnd entplösset seinen zerschlagenen verwundten zitternden leib. vñ schlug yn nackend on dz creütz. Man besah könig dauid. vmb ein zarte schöne außerwelte iunckfrawen. in d arm vnnd schoß er schlief. dy yn mit irē zarten leib erwermte. das er senfft rwe te. Da bereit man dē zarten leib des her ren. scharpf gertenn vnnd geyseln. seinē hohwirdigen haubt scharpf dörnn. sey nen guttetigen milten henden. vnd demütige füssen hert nageln. seiner adelichen seytten vñ dem allerzertestē gütig sten hertzē ein scharpfs greulichs sper. Dise historie ist hieher gesetzt. nit das yemants nach dem buchstaben ein ebē pild dar auß sölk oder getürr nemē. des gleichen zethun so sölche ding nit zu ey nem ebenpild dein nach dem puchstabē nach zefolgen sey geschriben seyen. sun der zu einer figur vnd bedeütung geist licher ding. als sant Jeronimus dise hy storien von der weißheit außlegt. doch so sie nach dem buchstaben ergangē ist. vnd ist zu der zeit in einer sölchen sach. in sölchen personen. denē es zimlich wz keüschlich vnd erberlich beschehen. So bedenck die hertigkeit des leidēs vnnd creützhangēs vnd sterbens cristi gegen disem geschiht. vnd sih wie vngleich mā dem herrenn. vnnd seinen knechtenn ge dient hab.

Die dreyvndfunfftzigiſt figur

Die sechßtzigist figur

Plate 120

Coreizantes per annum

Vltima etas mundi

Numbered by Muther as two plates.

Von eyner edlen frowen wie die vor eym spiegel stůnd/ sich mutzend/ vnnd sy jn dem spiegel den tüfel sach jr den hyndern zeigend/

EJn ander exẽpel will ich üch aber sagẽ/ vff die meynũg võ eyner frowen/ die den vierden teil des tags haben műst sich an ze thůnde vñ zů mutzen/ Dero huß wz nun etwz wyt võ der kylchen/ deßhalb jr der kylchherr vnd syne vndertanẽ zů manchen malen mit dẽ ampt wartẽ műsten/ deß sy zů mal grossen vnwillen vñ verdrieß hattẽ/ Also begab sich eins sonnentags das sy gar lang vß bleib/ vnd vil lüten jn der kylchen warten machet/ Die selben sprachen/ sy mag sich dysen tag nit gnůg strelen noch spieglen/ So redten dañ etlich heymlich ein vngesunds strelen vnd spieglen thůge jr got zů senden/ vmb das sy vnnß so manch mal alhie warten machet/ Also jn der selben stund da sy sich also spieglet/ ward sy den tüfel jn dem spiegel sehen/ so gar grusamer gestalt/ vnnd jr den hyndern zeigende/ das sy so hart dar ab erschrack/ dz sy schyer võ synnẽ komen were/ vñ lange zyt mit schwerer kranckheit wart beladẽ/ doch vlech jr got wyder gesũtheit vñ strafft sich selbst darumb gröslich/ vñ stalt söllich jr wesẽ mit dem zieren ab/ Vñ sagt mit demůtigẽ hertzẽ got dẽ hern siner straffen lob vñ danck

Schlůg er mit der hand vff das bůch vñ vermeynt sy zů geschweigen/ aber
etlich wolten es darumb nit myden/ Da batt er got das er sy schwygen ma
chte/vnd jnen jr torheit zů erkennen geben wölte/ Also vff dz da fiengen frowen vnnd man an die also geschwatzt hetten/ vnnd gelachet/ mit kleglicher
stymen zů schryen/wie dann lüt die tüfelhaftig synd/vnnd lyttent so grossen
schmertzen das es ein erbermde was zů hören/ Da nun die meß geschehen
was/sagt jnen der heilig man/wie er den tüfel vff jnen gesehenn hette/vmb
jrs geschwetzs vnnd böser geberden wyllen/so sy hynder der meß gehandelt
hetten/ Vnd sagt jnen dar by wz grossen schadens daruß keme/ Deß glich
die gnad vnnd den lon so sy hyn wyder mit jrem andacht hynder der messe
verdienen möchten/ Darumb sy sich fürbas flyssen vnd demütiklichen got
bytten vnd lieb haben solten/ Darnach durch bytt vñ anrůffung deß heiligẽ
mans/komen sy all wyder zů jren synnen/vnnd aller pyn vnd schmertzens
entladen/vnnd hůten sich dar nach vor söllichem/ Darumb dyß eyn gůtt
byspel/ist das nyeman hynder der meß söllich geschwetz vnd gelachter ůben
sonder ernsthaft vnnd andechtig syn sol/

Wie der tufel hynder der mesz

die klapperig edicher frowen vff schreib/vnd jm das berment zů
kürtz wart/vnnd ers mit den zenen vß eynander zoch/

Wie eyn edle junckfrow vff eyner hochzyt eyner edlē frowē mit eym stecken die nasen zer schlůg vmb das sy sy jrs mans bezech/

Vch will ich üch sagen eyn exempel wie sorglich vnd böse es ist / das eyn frow jrs mans jn yferung vnd forchten stat/ Es ist gewesen eyns edelmans husfrow/ die hat den selben jren hußwirt so üb ermessicklichen lieb/ das sy syn vor allen denē die mit jm redten/ jn grossen forchtē was/ Darumb sy dañ der herr offt vnd dick gůtlichen straffet/ vnd vmeynt sy dar vō zů wysen/ Es wz aber an jr vnuerfencklich/ Vnd vnder andern forcht sy syn aller meist vor eyner hochmůtigen stoltzen junckfrowen deß landes/ Mit deren fieng sy an vff eyn zyt zů zürnen / vnnd wart sy jrs mans bezyhen/ Das vantwurt die junckfrow so best sy mocht/ vnd sagt dz sy jr vnrecht thete/ Die frow wolt aber darumb nit ablassen/ vnd vermeynt ye es wer wor/ Begundē also eynander beidersyts mit gar bösen wortē handlen/ ye dz zů letst die junckfrow so gröslich erzürnt wart/ Das sy die frowen mit eynem steclen über die nasen schlůg / mit eym so grossen streich/ das sy jr die nasen als hart zerschlůg/ dar vō sy all jr tag eyn krumbe vngestalte nasen habē műste/ vñ sy dañ so vngestalt machte/ dz jr der man abhold vnd

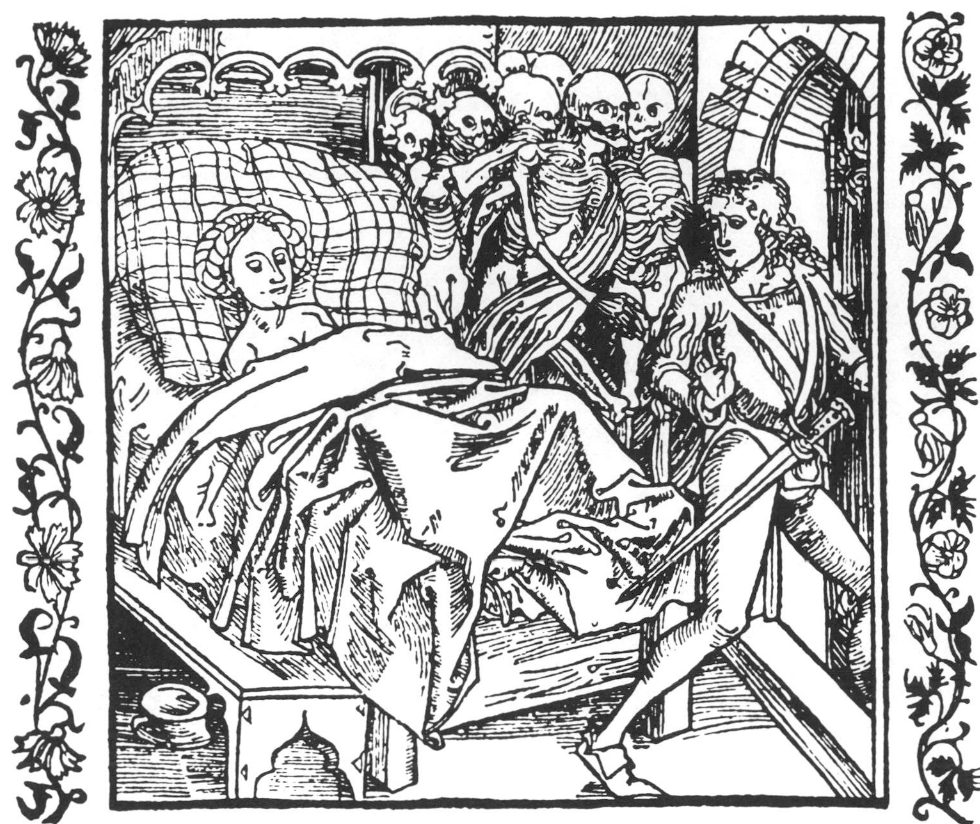

ZU cōstantinopel wz vff eyn zyt eyn keyser/der hatt zwo gar hüpscher döchtern/Under denen dañ die junger gar eyns frōmen gotsforchtenden gemütz vñ grunds was/In sonderheit dz sy gern bat für die todtē wañ sy nachtz erwachet/Die selben zwo döchtern lagent nun nachtz by eyn ander/Vñ wañ die elter die junger also hort betten/spottet sy jr/vñ sagt sy solt sy schlaffen lassen/Also begab sich durch jr jugēt/vñ wol essende spyß/dz sy in fleischlicher liebe angefochtē/vñ zweyē jungē Rittern gebrüdern hold wurdē Der massen/dz sy denē vff eyn zyt ein stund beschieden/jn der nacht heymlich zü jnē zü komē Als aber der Ritter der zü der jungern dochter gon wolt/nahent gegen jrem bet kam/Beducht jn/wie dz er vmb vnd by jr sehe/eyn grosse menige geist vnd selen/jn wyssen tüchern verwunden/Dar ab er eyn söllich forcht vnnd schrecken nam/dz er vnbesynnet wyder dannan floch/Vnnd ward mit schwerer kranckheit/vnnd dem kalten siechtagen beladen/Als man nun morndes/syner kranckheit jnnen vnnd dar von sagen ward/Sonders vor der junckfrowen von deren wegen jm söllichs was begegnet/fügt sy sich zu jm/jn zü besehen/vñ zü fragē/vß was vrsach vñ wie jm sölliche kranckheit zü gestandē were Da sagt er jr/als er zü jrē bet wölte gangē syn/dz er die geist/wie ob stat/also gesehen hett/vñ dar vō jn sölliche kranckheit vō schrecken wer gefallē Da die jünckfrow dz horte/hatt sy dar ab ouch groß erschrecken/vñ verwundern/vñ gar demütecklich sagt sy got lob vñ ere vnd

Der Ritter vom Turn
von den Exempeln der
gotsforcht vñ erberkeit

Wie der Beyler eyn münich by glast eyns fliers vnd syn wyb by eynander mit eym schwert durch stach vnnd tödtet.

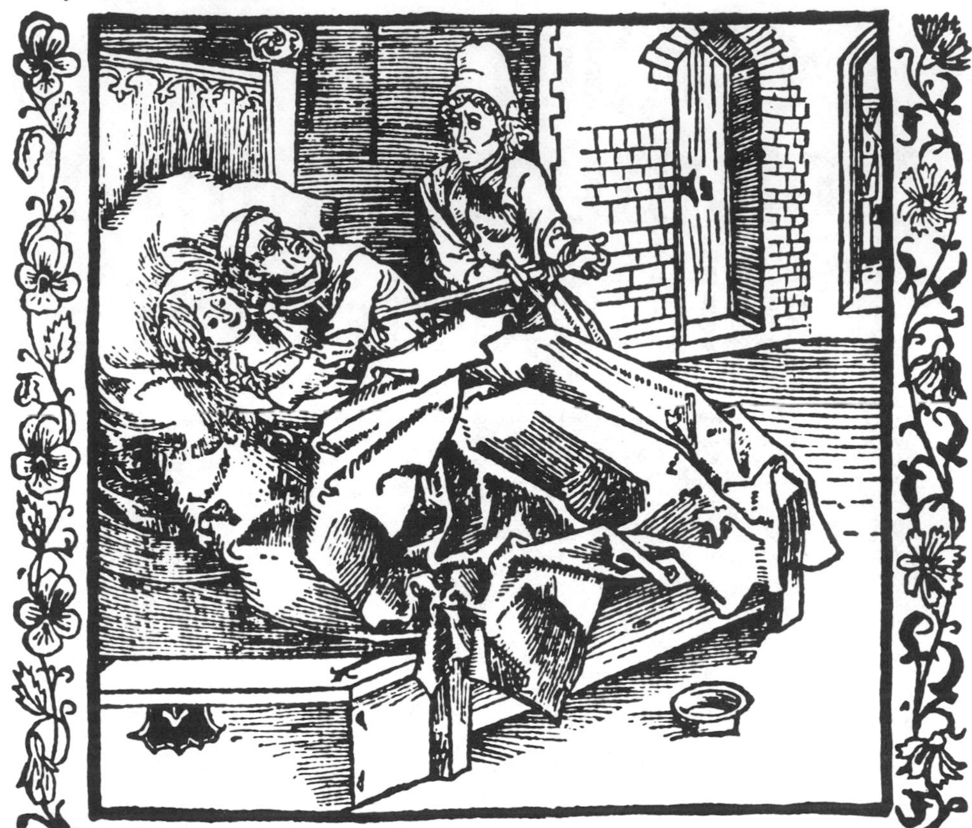

ALs er nun sach vnd marckte dz die sach wor wz/ Wart er so schwerlichen erzürnet/ dz er all syn gedechtnyß verlor/ Vnd heymlich eyn langes schwert vß zoch/ mitt dem selben stro jn das für werffent/ dz er gesehen könde/ Vnd stach dz schwert durch sy beyd vß hyn/ Vnd ertödt sy jn söllichen sündē/ darnach berüfft er syne nachburen vnd vil lüten jnen söllichs zü zeigen/ Vnd ließ berüffen eyn gericht sich zü entschuldigen/ Dar ab mengellich groß wunder nam/ das die frow den pryor lieb gehept hatt/ der doch eyn feyster grosser schwartzer man wz/ Vñ jr man der Seyler hüpsch jung vñ rich/ Aber es synd etliche frowen die sich der wölfyn gelichen/ die selb erwölt allweg den vngestaltestē vnder allen wolfen/ Also thünd ouch die torechten frowen/ mit jren sünden vñ anfechtungen deß tüfels/ Vñ als vil die sünd schwerer ist als vil hat der tüfel mer gewaltz über sy/ Dañ ist es eyn eewyb/ vnnd er ein ordens man/ ist die sünd so vil dest grösser als man dañ dz durch etlich geschafften vñ sunst wol sehen mag/ wañ eyn frow mit jrē gesyptē fründ oder gefattern vnluterkeit handlet/ ye neher er jr dañ zü gehörig ist/ ye mer sy angefochten vnd entzündt würt/ deßglich ist es ouch

Wer durch keyn ander vrsach me
Dann durch gůts willen grifft zůr ee
Der hat vil zancks/leyd/hader/we/
wibē durch gutz willē
Wer schlůfft jnn esel/vmb das schmär
Der ist vernunfft/vnd wißheyt lär
Das er eyn alt wib nymbt zůr ee
Eyn gůtten tag/vnd keynen me

Wer artzeny ſich nyemet an
Vnd doch keyn preſten heylen kan
Der iſt eyn gůtter gouckelman

Von narrechter artzny

Der gat wol heyn mit andern narrn
Wer eym dottkrancken bſycht den harn
Vnd ſpricht/wart/biß ich dir verkünd
Was ich jn mynen bůchern fynd

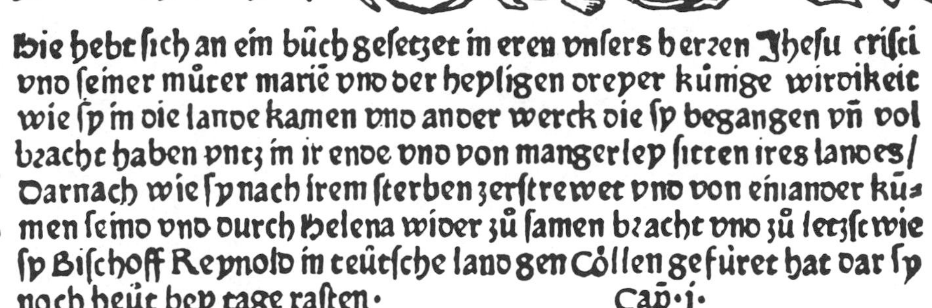

Hie hebt ſich an ein bůch geſetzet in eren vnſers herren Jheſu criſti vnd ſeiner můter mariē vnd der heyligen dreyer künige wirdikeit wie ſy in die lande kamen vnd ander werck die ſy begangen vñ volbracht haben vncz in ir ende vnd von mangerley ſitten ires landes/ Darnach wie ſy nach irem ſterben zerſtrewet vnd von einander kü-men ſeind vnd durch Helena wider zů ſamen bracht vnd zů letzſt wie ſy Biſchoff Reynold in teütſche land gen Cöllen gefüret hat dar ſy noch heüt bey tage raſten. Cap̄. j.

LOb ere vñ wirdikeit ð heyligen dreyer künigē hant erfüllet die criſtenheit vō auf gange ð ſunnen vncz do ſy nyð gat/die eccleſia in oriente iſt gezieret vō dem das ſy die erſten warent von ð heidenſchafft dz die ir opffer brachtent vnſerm herrē jheſu criſto vñ im bekantē got vñ menſch Die eccleſia vō occidēte hant ſy gezieret vñ zie-rent ſy noch heüt diſes tags mit irē heiligē leibhaft gē wonnūgen wañ ſy leibhaftig in dē lande begrabē ligēt wie ſy aber in diſe lant kümen ſeind vñ ander ire werck die ſy begangen hant vnd wie ſy ir ende nament dz iſt hie zů lande nit wol kuntliche

Von Balaams prophecie oder weyssagunge.

Figura Principalis

Das ander capitel diß tracretlins leret erkēnē die zeichen des todes von einer ietlichē wun den nach dē sybendē bůch Rasis / vnd die zeichē die vnß ypocras beschriben

Plate 137

Hie fachet an der erste tractat dis bůchs mit
hilfe deß Almechtigē gottes on den kein gůt werck angefangen oder vollent
mag werdē. Das würt dich lerē/wyssen vñ vndrichtē wz einē yedē wūdartzt ī
sittē vñ wessen not ist/warnūg prenosticatio erkenūg des franckē/vñ d wūdē

Publij Virgilij marõis opera.

Argumēta Aeglogæ Primæ.

Publij Virgilij Maronis Mantuani opera
cū cōmētariis Seruii Mauri honorati grāmatici: Aelii Donati: Christofori Landini: Antonii Mancinelli & Domicii Calderini.

Argumentum egloge prime: que Tytirus dicitur.
A patria fugiens Melibeus forte sub vmbra.
Tytrion inuenit cantantem carmina amice.
Quapropter miratus ei sua damna recenset:
Auctoremq; sui declarat Tytirus oci.

SEBASTIANVS BRANT

Sub fagi recubans Melibeum Tytirus vmbra
Solatur profugum: collataq; munia laudat.

Georgicoꝝ Liber.I. XXXIIII

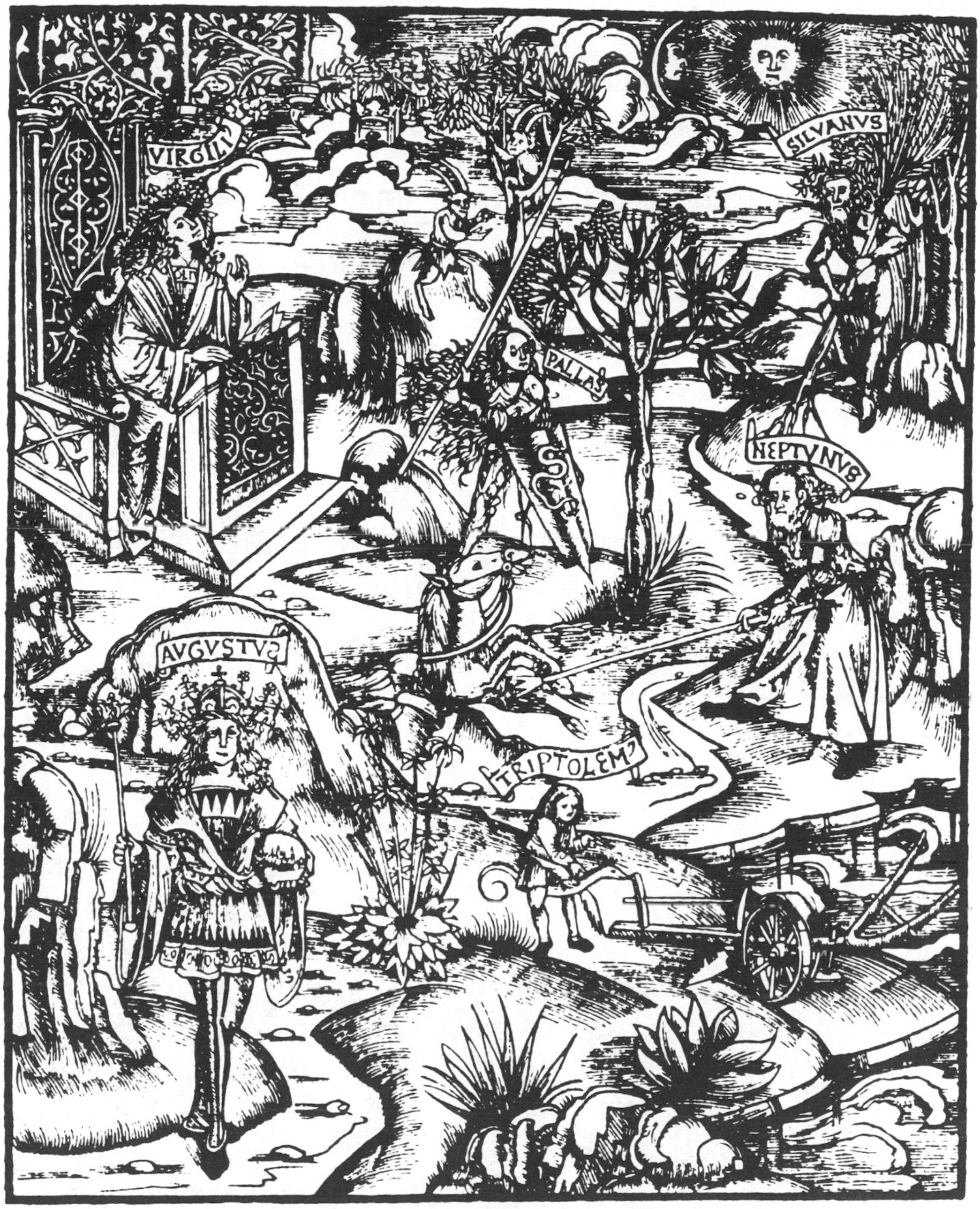

Argumentū Sebastiani brant.

primus aratra docet telluri infindere: semen
proijcere: & messem matura falce legendam
Obseruanda etiam quę sidera/tempora/signa.
Ne ver: ne sit hyems: ęstas ve ignaua colono.

P. Virgilij Maronis Georgicorum
liber primus ad Mœcenatem.

Virgilius in Eneide secut⁹ est Homerū: licet longo interuallo In bucolicis Theocritum: a quo non longe abest. In Georgicis Hesiodū: quē longe reliquit. Hesiodus ex Ascręa ciuitate natus scripsit ad Persen fratrem librū quē appellauit ἔργα καὶ ἡμέραι id est opera & dies. Hic liber continet quō & quo tpere agri sint colēdi. Nō tn̄ trāstulit titulū vt bucolicoꝝ trāstulit: Sicut cu⁹ titulū transferre noluit: eneiden appellauit

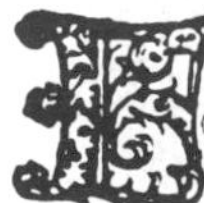

De operibus Virgilij Sebastianus brant

Vita magis nulli est sua cognita: docta Maronis
Quam mihi musa: canens pergama: rura: capras.

Tetrasticon eiusdem

post nemora atq greges culturam ruris: & vuas:
disce & equos lector: mellificas q feras.
Grandior oblectat si te hinc tuba parthenopea:
Diuigenum poteris perlegere arma ducum.

Eneidos

Que secũdo eneidos libro cõtineãt. ouidi⁹.
¶ Cõticuere omnes: tũc sic fortissimus heros
Fata recensebat troię. casusq; suorum:
Fallaces graios: simulataq; dona mineruę
Laocontis pœnã. et laxantem claustra sinonẽ⁹
Somnũ quo monit⁹ acceperat hectoris atrũ:
Iam flãmas cœli: troum patrięq; ruinas.
Et regis priami fatum miserabile semper:
Imposituq; patrẽ collo: dextraq; prehensũ
Ascanium: frustra tergum comitante creusa.
Ereptã hanc fato. sociosq; in monte reptos.

Eneidos

auctor. l Se se attol. i auras. S. Ostendit neqꝫ hūilioribꝰ: neqꝫ maioribꝰ illā parcere. m Ingre-diturqꝫ solo. S. nec hūili parcit fortunę: nec supio-ri. n Parēs. S genera-tr oim rerū. o Irritata. S. Amphibolon est: vtrū sua ira ꝓpter extinctos gigantes: an ira deorū q extinxerāt gigantes.

p Extremā. S. Post oēs gigantes: Nā ad illorū vltionē nata ē. Vl' extremā. pessimā. Nam qui de medicina tractant: dicūt in-utiliores esse q nascūt vl-timi. q Vt ꝑhibēt. S. cum fabulosum aliquid refert: dicit vt fama est: nunc de fama loq̄ns mi-re dixit. vt perhibent.

r Pedibus ce. S. Conuertit epithera: nā pedū est pernix: vt ꝑnicibus ignea plantis. Celeritas penna-rū. vt. Celerisqꝫ fuga sub sydera lapsę. s Cor-

Extemplo lybię magnas it fama per vrbes:
Fama malum: quo non aliud velecius vllum
Mobilitate viget: viresqꝫ acquirit eundo:
parua metu primo: mox se se attollit in auras:
Ingrediturqꝫ solo: & caput inter nubila condit:
Illam terra parens: ira irritata deorum
Extremam (vt ꝑhibent) cęo enceladoqꝫ sororē
progenuit: pedibus celerem: & ꝑnicibus alis:
Mōstrū horrēdū ingēs: cui q̊t sunt corꝑe plu-
Tot vigiles oculi subter (mirabile dictu) (mę
Tot ligue: totidē ora sonāt: tot surrigit aures:
Nocte volat cœli medio: terręqꝫ ꝑ vmbram
Stridens: nec dulci declinat lumina somno:

pore plu. S. Non ipsiꝰ: sed omniū: Est enim exaggeratio: ac si diceret: q̊t sunt arenę. t Oculi subter. S. aduerbiū: ac si diceret: Non sub plumis: sed sub ipsa. v Tot linguę. S. Quot em̄ sunt homies in quibꝰ fama est. tot ora habet quę sunt hominum. x Surrigit. C. Nā bruta cū attente audiunt: aures erigunt. y Nocte vo. cœli. S. Nam q̄nto magis celatum: tanto magis cō-querit: et certe incipiēs fama semꝑ obscura est: q̄ deuulgata ꝯquiescit: vnde. luce sedet. z Custos. S. Speculatrix.

a Summi culmie tecti. S. per domos nobilium. b Turribꝰ. S. ꝑ domos regū. c Magnas vr. S. Magnos pplos: & dicit plebeios d Ficti prauiqꝫ. C. Nam multa sunt ficta q̄ nō sunt praua: vt. Poemata ficta sūt

Des erſten bůchs Figur

Brandenborch·
margreta
albrecht
Anna
hans
wulfgäck
Anna
frederick
sigmunt
barbara
elizabeth
elizabeth
dorothea
Anna

krich·

Vſſe keyſer luder de krigede mit ſynē broderen vmme de lant vnderlan ges Jn duſſem vnfrede de denen vnder breken de freſen vnder ere tribut vnde ſchepeden vp dem ryn vnde beleydē Collen vnde do ſe to hus wolden varen do togen ſe vpp de elue vor hamborch vnde wunnen de ſtade vnde breken den nygen dom in de grunt ſo dat de ſtadt vnde dat ſtiffte hamborch gruntlick vorſtöret wart· vnde de leue ſunte anſcharius mit ſynen clereken wunderlike vorſchuchterde·

Otheberne·

N dem lande to stade was eyn hußman efte ein torne man· de heyt otheberne eyn wanschapen kerle de vndermatede sick dat he don wolde vele teken vnde heylt sick vor eyn hilligen Dût ruchte kam in de lant dat volck begunde to dwalen vnde menden all wars· do lepẽ se dar hen vñ brachten ôm opper· vnde wan dat volck dar kam so gingk he sitten vpp eynen koniges stol de was gestrauwet mit rosen vnde he sat naket sunder eynen slichten rock Vnde wan dat volck kam so gaff he ône einẽ lude mit eynem horne Hyr lepp to manigh mynsche vt allen landẽ de ôm opper brachten vnde worden bedroge so dat de heren vnde forsten de brachten den torne man vt dem wege dat ône nemet konde wedder vindẽ.

Yn sollicher maß rythen die Turcken zů frydsammer zytt wan sie ettwas truumph oder sust freud vnd lust wollen gebruchen vnd haben Aber zů kriegs zytten bruchen sie gar by sollich gewandt doch ettlich ander gewere·

Die sarraceni bruchen arabisch zung vnd litter·welche litter hye vnden steet yn rechter form getruckt·

Von den Abbasinen oder jndianen die sich auch cristen gloryren.

Von den juden werren auch eyn gůt teyl zů diser zytt
zů Jherusalem wonen.

us synen eltern brůder/Numitorem von dem rych/Der selb Numitor verließ ein tochter Rhea vnnd ouch Ylia genant die machet ein closter frowen in dem Tempel der abgöttin Vesta genant/dar in sie ewige küscheit geloben vnd halten můßt/vff das kein frucht von syns brůders geschlecht/geborn würd/die in rechen vnd Amulium oder syn nach komen wider von dem Rych stossen möcht Es fügt sich aber anders.

Wie Rhea Ilia gebare Romulũ vnnd Remum zwyling vnnd wurden die selben kynde an die tyber getragen.

d

An Ilia ward dar nach swanger in dem sybenden iar vnwissent von wem vnd gebar zwyling/Romulũ vnd Remũ/dar vmb sie von dem küng Amulio lebendig vergrabẽ vnd ire kind für fündling an das wasser Tyber vßgesetzt wurdẽ die fand ein hyrt/Faustulus genãt/der sie von Miniglicher schön wegẽ der kind heym trůg/die wurden von syner hußfrowen Laurentia gesögt/vnd vfferzogen/die selb frow/was ouch lupa geheissen/das ist zů latin souil gesprochen als ein wölfin/Da her die fabel entsprungen ist/das die kind von einer wölfin gesögt vnnd ernert syen.

Wie die romer mit gewalt yrer nachburen wieber namen vnnd tochter raubten.

S ſollicher gutten ordnung vnd geſatzt· mert
v ſich die ſtatt. großlich an mannē. Aber nit ſo vil an frowen/ Alſo das die burger an wieben mangel vnnd gebrechen hetten/ vnnd wie wol ſie von den nachburen durch bitt vnnder ſtůnden ſollichs zů erlangen/ vnd vmb ir kynder wurben/ ſo wurdē ſie doch (als ein neüwes weſen) verachtet/ vñ móchten es mit willen/ nit bekommen/ Nun kund Romulus ouch wol ermeſſen/ wa von den eltern nit tüglich kynd geporn wurden/ die ir vetter vñ můtter nach irem ſterben erſatzten/ dz Rom ein vergencklich ſtatt ſyn würde/ darumb do er des mit lieb nit bekomē mocht/ Erdacht er einen fund/ vnd ließ ein ritterſpil/ mit geſtech turnieren vnd andren kurtz wiligen dingen zůrichten/ dar zů ladet er die anſtóſſer vñ nachburen/ die kamen mit iren wieben vnnd kynden emſigklich dar zů/ in ſonder die Sabini/ Da nůn das ſpil im beſten was/ vnnd nyemant ſich des verſach. ließ Romulus die ſynen mit gewalt die frómbden frowen vñ iunckfrowen roubē/ vñ in die ſtatt Rom füren/ die ſie dar nach teylten/ vñ für eelich frowen hielten Der was an der zal ſechßhundert vnd dry vnd achtzig/ vnder den die aller ſchónſt Herſilia genant Romulo zů geteilt wardt/ wie das zuuerantwurtten ſy/ waiß ich nit es ſye dan das die notturfft romulū als einē heyden. (der noch der keyſerlichen geſatz ſyderher gemacht vnwiſſen was.) entſchuldigen müg.

Wie die iungfraw Cloelia die mit etlichē andern dem küng Porſenna zu merher ſicherheit der rachtung vnd des frydens geben warē/ by nacht vff der ſynd pferd über die Tyber ſchwemmet vnd gen Rom kam/darab der küng aber mals groſſe verwundern hett vñ geurſacht wardt mit dem höre vñ leger von Rome ab zuziehen/vnd mit den Römern ein ewig frűntſchafft zů machen.

Vn was gewonheit wan man ein richtung

n traff das man zů beyden ſyten ettlich der beſten an einer zal zů gyſel gab/ die ſolten pfand ſyn biß die richtung volſtreckt ward/vnnd waren von den Römern ettlich Jungling vnd Junckfrowen Porſenne zů gyſel ge/ ben/vnder denen iunckfrowen/was eine Cloelia genāt die berett etrlich ander iunck frowen mit ir/das ſie vnderſtůnden ſich ſelber zu ledigen/vñ namen der ſynd pferd die in dē hör ſtůnden /ſaſſen daruff vnd ſchwempten by nacht über die tyber/vñ ka/ men alſo an morgen gen Rom ingeritten Als das morgens frů dem küng Porſen/ na geſagt ward/verwundert er ſich vnnd ſprach/ Für war es iſt nit allein manheit in den mannen zů Rom Sonder ouch in dem weiblidhen geſchlecht/vnnd ſendet ein bottſchafft gen Rom begert das man im die gyſel wider ſchickte/Mer das er die Junckfrowen recht ſehe / Wan das ſyn gemůt ſtůnde icht arges zů zefůgen./

Hye sytzet des Endcrist vatter vnd würbt vmb syn lyplich toch
ter in üppigkeit· die im der werck verwylliget Vnnd empfachet
von irem eygen vatter den antchycrist.

Der anthyrrist berüffet alle ffürsten herren Crysten heyden judẽ vnd alle dye an im geloubentt Vnd heiset sy kommen zü dem perg Olivueti/vnd sprycht er welle gen hymmel varen

Ptolomeus Ariſtoteles Sibilla Brigida Reynhardus

Hic Imperator ingreditur Romā cū seuitia ⁊ eiꝰ timore fugiunt Romani clerici ⁊ laici ad petras ⁊ siluas ⁊ multi detruncabantur.

aaron

Plate 161

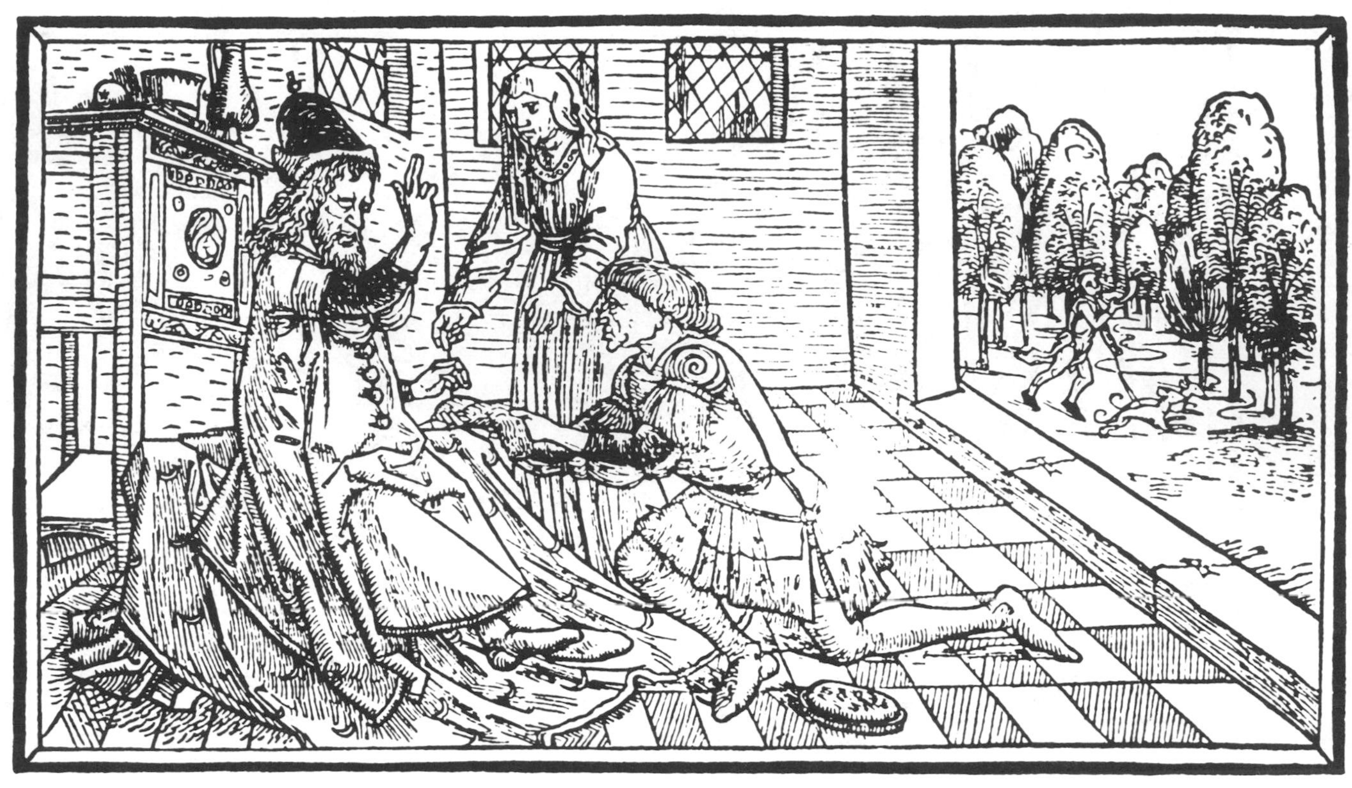

26

Unfalo nach lanngem bedacht
Den Er het gehabt tag vnnd nacht
Thet Er gar ein grosse schalckhait
Tewrdannck dem Helden vnuerzeit
Nit weyt ein hoher thuren was
Darinn ein schneck gelaubet das
Gemachet von eim gůten stein
Drauf zůhöchst ein hültzens stieglein

Bracht Er den Helden in ein schiff
Wie sich dasselb weyter verlieff
Steet hernach geschriben gar klar
Dasselbig lest/dann es ist war.

Wie der Edel Tewrdannck durch die gröss eines Vegels ein gross not laid daruon Er sich vnd die andern durch vnerschrockenlichait erlediget.

32 E iiij

Plate 165

Rumorum cupidus, mendacia multa necesse est
Mann sagt mir offt viel newer Mehr/
Die sind doch aller Warheit lär.

Audiat, est fallax fama, rotunda, levis.
Wer newer Mehr will glauben han/
Der muß allzeit im zweiffel stahn.

N iij

Bey diser gleychnus man vernympt/
Was sich im kauff zů öffen zympt.
On waren nutz ist der gewynn/
Da man gebrauchet falschē synn.

Als wilde pferd/ dauō man spricht/
Durch arbeit werden abgericht.
Dē gleich/ wen thumer můt verkert/
Vil gůter vbung tugent lert.

Vlyxes/darumb als man spricht/
Sich selbst für einen thoren dicht.
Das er im frid daheimen lebt/
Vnd seinen pflichten widerstrebt.

Wer wil dz höchst auff wollust machē/Der krönt ein schwein in wüster lache

Quid frustra exultas clarorum nomine avorum,
Ein frembdes lob vnd scheltens wert/
Der lob von seinem gschlecht begert.
Et falsum nomen nobilitatis habes.
Starcks gműt vnd tugentsam/
Macht klar vnd edel einen man.

Wer sich lest halten/solche bandt/
Die dyse gleychnus/macht bekant/
Im rechten weg/hat nit Bestandt.

Armůt/ Kranckheit/ Wollust/ Tod.

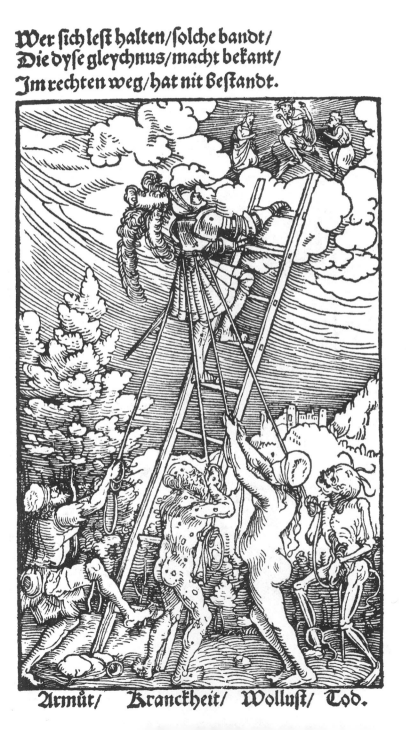

D 4

Plate 171

Martha ergo vt audiuit q: Jhesus venit rc. Jois.II.

Plate 173

Tunc apprehendit Pilatus
Ihesum. et flagellauit. Et milites plectentes coronā
de spinis imposuerunt capiti eius zc. Johannis.19.

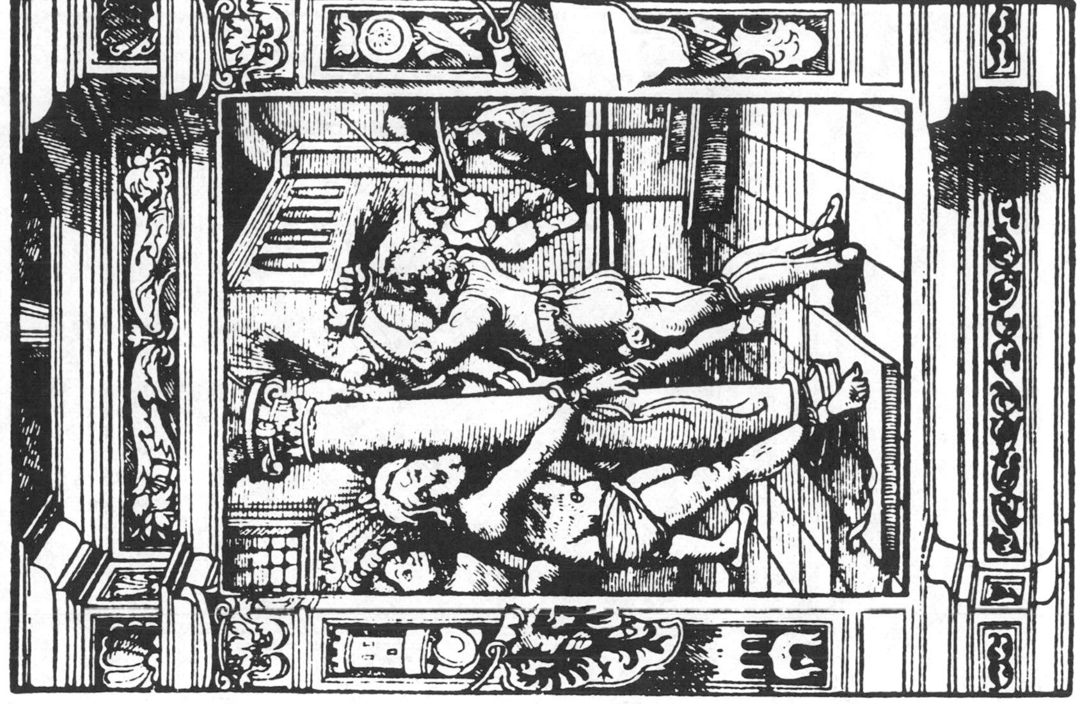

Vespere autē Sabbati que
lucescit in prima Sabbati ꝛc. Mathei.28.

HB

Plate 177

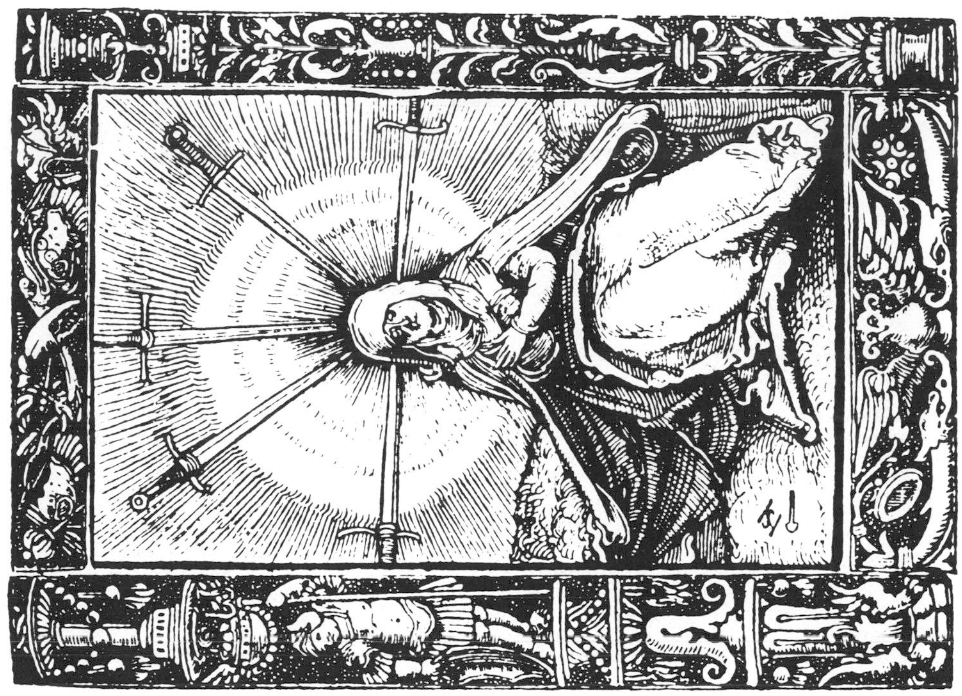

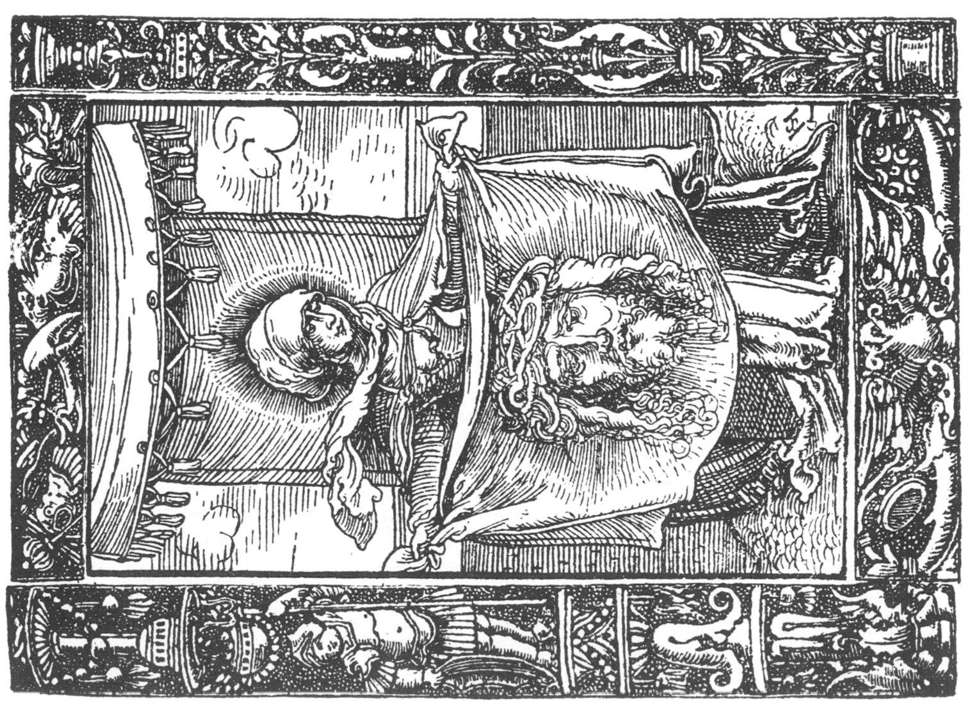

CVI

XXXII

alle tag ain mal zu beeten zů starckmůti-
gem vestem glauben/hoffnung vnd lie-
be/auch zů behůtung seel vnd leibs gar
nutzlich sein. Deßgleichen dem der nit
lesen kan/vñ das in solcher mainũg bey
im tregt vñ sich vor todtsünden behůt.
Der an.✝ fang des hai ✝ ligen ewan
✝ gelij sancti Johannis (Gloria tibi
In de an fa- ng wz dz w ort vñ dz w ort
was bey gott/vnnd gott was das wort.

E

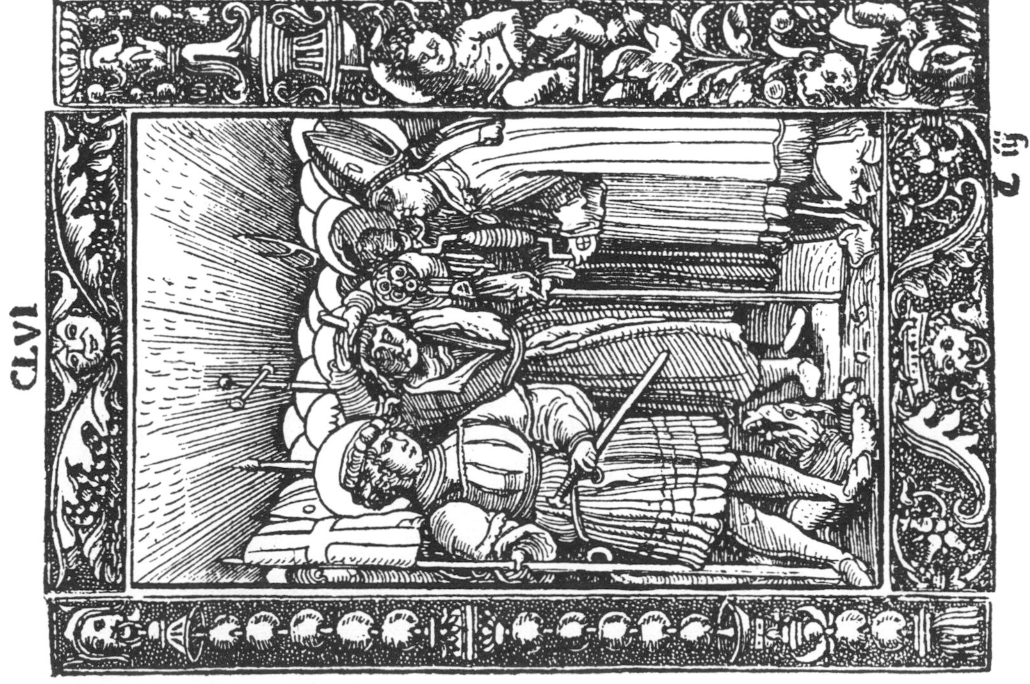
CLVI

C iij

Am Andern Suntag Inn Der Vasten

Ewangelium

¶ In illo tempore. Egressus Jesus secessit in partes Tyri et sidonis/ et ecce mulier quedam chananea ꝛc. Mathei xv. cap.

Inn Der Zeit: Gieng Jesus vß vnnd keret inn die gegendt Tyri vnnd Sidonis/ vnnd nempt war do begegnet im ain haidnische fraw/ die was gegangen von der selben gegent/ vñ rüfft in an sprechend zů im. Herr ain sun dauid erbarm dich über mich. Mein tochter wirt übel gepyniget von dem deuffel/ Do antwurt er ir kain wort/ Do giengen die iünger zů im/ vnnd batent in sprechende. Herr hilff ir/ wan sie schreyt nach vnß. Do antwurt Jesus vnd sprach. Ich bin allein gesendt zů den scheflin die do verloren waren des hauß Israel. Vnd die fraw kam vnd betet in an sprechẽt Her hilff mir/ Do antwurt ir Jesus vnd sprach/ Es ist nit gůt das man nimpt das brot den kinden/ vnnd gibt es den hunden. Do sprach das frewlin/ Ja herr/ aber die hündtlin essent auch die brosamen die do vallent von dem tisch irer herren. Do antwurt der herr Jesus vñ sprach zů ir/ O weib groß ist dein glaub/ dir geschehe nach deinem begeren. Vnnd ir tochter ist gesundt worden zů der selben stund.

Glosa vnnd vßzlegung über das hailig Ewangelium.

Das ist das hailig ewãgelium/ darinnẽ wir mercken sollen drey ding. Zům ersten was vns die haidnisch fraw bedeut/ das ist die cristenhait die vnser her Cristus in seinem vßgang des väterlichen schöpffers findẽ hat/ vnd die gesamlet hat von Chananea dz ist die haidẽschafft die erst můter/ die fraw ist gewesẽ vß Judea/ da von vns der vrsprung des glaubens kummen ist. Die můter hat ain tochter/ dz ist die sündig sel/ die besessen ist mit dẽ teuffel viler sünd/ die rüfft zů gott/ Dauids sun erbarm dich mein. Warũm nent sie in dauids sun vñ nit gótes/ darũb man lißt also Reg. i. Do saul wz besessen mit dẽ teufel/ do nam dauid sein harpffen vñ harpffet/ zůhãdt floch ꝺ teufel võ saul/ wan man nun sprach/ Dauid sun/ so begeret die fraw das er würcket vnnd erzaiget das werck Dauids seins vaters/ vnd solt hin weg treiben den teufel von ir tochter. Nun sollen wir wissen dz er warlichẽ

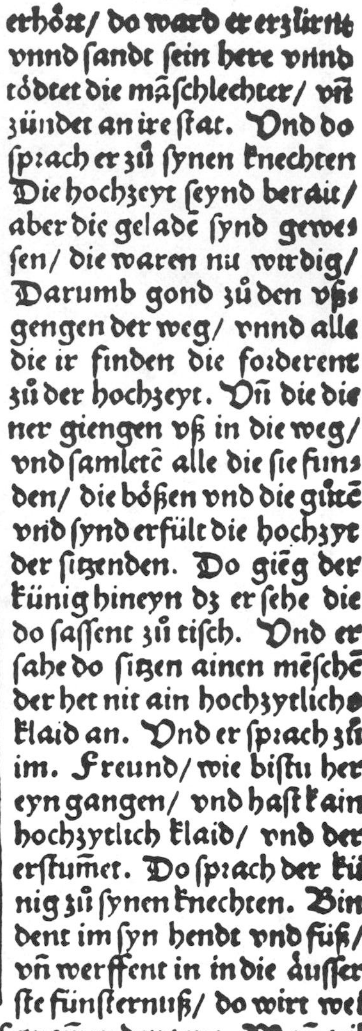

JN der zyt. Redt der herr Jeſus mit ſynen iüngern ain gleichnuß. Gleich iſt worden das reich der himel ainē menſchen ainē künig der do hat gemacht hochzyt ſynē ſun. Vñ hat vßgeſandt ſein diener zů berůffen die geladen zů der hochzyt/ vnd ſie wolten nit kūmen. Widerumb hat er vßgeſendet ander diener vnd ſprach. Sagēt den geladē nement war/ myn mal hab ich bereit/ myne ochßen vnd huß gevögel ſeynd getödt/ vnd alle ding die ſynd berait/ kūment zů d' hochzyt. Aber die verſeumpten es/ vñ giengen ab/ ainer in ſein dorff/ vnd der ander zů ſeinem geſchefft. Vnd die anderen hieltent ſein knecht vnd peynigeten ſie mit laſter/ vnd tödtē ſie. Vnd do das der künig erhört/ do ward er erzürnt vnnd ſandt ſein here vnnd tödtet die mā ſchlechter/ vñ zündet an ire ſtat. Vnd do ſprach er zů ſynen knechten Die hochzeyt ſeynd berait/ aber die geladē ſynd gewesen/ die waren nit wirdig/ Darumb gond zů den vßgengen der weg/ vnnd alle die ir finden die forderent zů der hochzeyt. Vñ die diener giengen vß in die weg/ vnd ſamletē alle die ſie funden/ die böſen vnd die gůtē vnd ſynd erfült die hochzyt der ſitzenden. Do giēg der künig hineyn dz er ſehe die do ſaſſent zů tiſch. Vnd er ſahe do ſitzen ainen mēſchē der het nit ain hochzytlicho klaid an. Vnd er ſprach zů im. Freund/ wie biſtu her eyn gangen/ vnd haſt kain hochzytlich klaid/ vnd der erſtumet. Do ſprach der künig zů ſynen knechten. Bindent im ſyn hendt vnd füß/ vñ werffent in in die äuſſerſte fünſternuß/ do wirt wel nen vnd grißgramen der zene. Mañ vil ſynd berůfft/ aber wenig vßerwelet.

¶ Gloſa.

¶ Jn diſem ewangelio leßen wir wie ain künig machet ſynē ſun ain wirtſchafft vñ lůd darzů vil leut. Jn diſen worten ſollen wir mercken dē wolluſt himeliſcher wirtſchafft/ in der man findt wz man begert.

¶ Zum erſten/ findt man da ſüeſſikait die man inn der welt nit findt. Als man liſt in Moyſes bůch von den kinden von Jſrael/ die litten groſſen durſt vnnd waren nahent verdorben von des durſtes wegē. Exodi an dem xvij. cap. Do kamen ſie zů letſt an ain waſſer das was gar bitter dz ſie es vor bitterkait nit trincken mochten/ aber den ſüeſſen geſchmack findt man in dem ewigen vatter landt/ der in ſůche.

werd dein hertz leib vnd seel hertigklich vnd schwärlich
vergifftet/vnd gedenck das kain kranckhait am leib
herter zů vertreiben vnd zů artzneyen ist dann die von
gifft kumpt/Wann dem menschen mag nit geholffen
werden von der kranckhait/es werd dan das gifft von
jm getriben. Also will ich mir fürnemen/sey es auch
vmb vnrecht gůt/es vergifft/vnd laßt sich hart vnnd
gantz vngern wider geben/So würt die sünd doch nit
vergeben es werd dañ das vnrecht gůt widerkert/Dar

D

DEr fürman ſoll ſein die hailig ewig vngetailt trifaltigkait/got vater/vnd got ſun/ vñ got hailiger gaiſt/ain warer got Abrahams/Yſa acks/vnd Jacobs/got Jſrael der da alle ding vermag/waißt/vnd ſicht/vnnd iſt ewig/der anfang/ mittel/vnd end aller ding/Jn jm ſelbs gantz volkom= men/dem nichts gebricht/kain mangel hat. in dem/vñ durch den/vnd auß dem alle ding entſpringen/flieſſen

Von dem tod in ſonderhait zu gedencken

VErgiß nit des nachuolgenden deines treüwen dieners/der dein auch on allen zweyfel nit ver= gißt. O du grauſamer. O du erſchrockenlicher. O du bitrer. O du herter. O du ſtarcker. O du ſtrenger. O du ſorgklicher. O du laid ger. O du betrüber. O du vnbarmhertziger. O du grimer. O du vnaußbleiblicher vnzweifenlicher. O du ängſtlicher tod. O du martrer. O du peinlicher. O du nemer meines leibs vnd lebens.

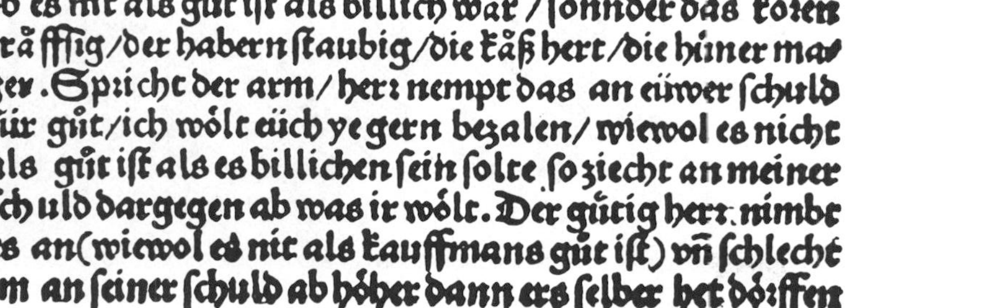

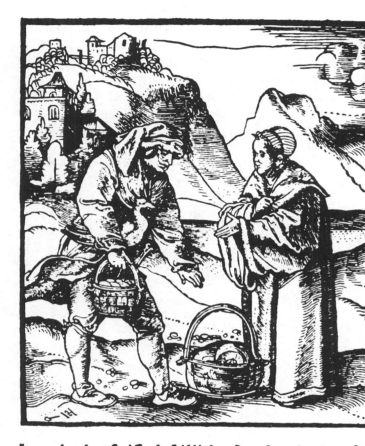

ob es nit als gůt ist als billich wär / sonnder das koren
träffig/der habern staubig/die käß hert/die hüner ma-
ger. Spricht der arm/ herr nempt das an eüwer schuld
für gůt/ich wölt eüch ye gern bezalen/ wiewol es nicht
als gůt ist als es billichen sein solte so ziecht an meiner
schuld dargegen ab was ir wölt. Der gůtig herr nimbt
es an(wiewol es nit als kauffmans gůt ist) vñ schlecht
im an seiner schuld ab höher dann ers selber het dörffen

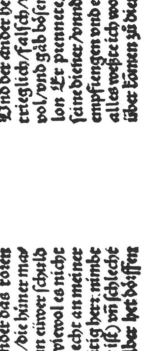

Und der ander herr wär vngetreüw/lugenhafftig/be-
trieglich/falsch/vngerecht/ vnd gantz aller boßhait
vol/vnd gäb bösen falschen nutz vnd gar bösen sold vnd
lon Er prennete/er schmeltzte/er röschte/er peinigte/
seine diener/vnnd für die schäden die sy in seinem dienst
empfiengen vnd erlitten näm er jn das ir dartzů/Das
alles weßte ich wol an baiden herren / vnd ich bin darüber kömen zů dienen den vngetrewen bösen lugenhaff

D U solt an dich nemen die aigenschafft des pfawen/der hat die art/so er sein federn auffpraitt vnd sy ansicht so hat er gar ain groß wolgefallen an seiner schöne/wenn er aber die füß ansicht/die so schwartz/vngestalt/vnd vnsauber seind/so erschrickt er das im die hochfart alle vergeet/vnnd laßt denn seinen schwantz widerumb nider
Also solt du auch thůn wenn du ain wolgefallen hast

M ij

N It vergiß alle tag getreüwlich zů loben vnd zů eeren das hailig/wirdig/wunnesam/vnd überfröwdenreich angesicht vnsers lieben herrn Jesu christi/darein alle Engel vnd alle hailigen stätigs on vnderlaß begern zů sehen in dem ewigen lebñ/darinnen alles himmelisch höre ymmer vnd ewig erfröwet würt/ Weliches begirlich/ergötzlich angesicht/der hailigen frawen Veronica võ christo jesu in rechter lieb zů ainer letz eingedrucket ist worden in ain schneeweiß tůchlin/

Die Epistel sanct Pauli zů den Römern. I

Das Erst Capitel.

Vnter schrifft

Paulus ein knecht Jesu Christi: berůffen zum Apostel/außgesündert zů predigen das Euangelion gottes (welchs er zůuor verheyssen hat/durch seine propheten/in der heyligen schrifft/võ seinem sun/der jm geborn ist von dem samen Dauid/nach dem fleysch/vnd krefftigklich erweyset ein sun gottes/ª nach dem geyst der do heyliget/sint der zeyt er aufferstanden ist von den todten/nemlich/Jesus Christ vnser her/durch welchen wir haben empfangen gnad vnd Apostel ampt vnter alle heyden/dem gehorsam des glaubens auffzůrichten/vnter seinem namen/welcher jr zum teyl auch seyt/die da berůffen seind von Jhesu Christo)

ª (Nach dem geyst ꝛc.) Der geyst gottes ist gebẽ nach Cristus auffart/võ da an heiliget er die Cristẽ vñ verkleret Christũ in aller welt/das er gotes sun sey/mit aller macht/um wortten/wunder vnd zeychen.

Vber schrifft

Allen die zů Rom sind/den liebstẽ gottes/vñ berůffnẽ heyligen.

Grus

Gnad sey mit eüch vnd fride von got vnserem vater vnnd dem herrn Jhesu Christo.

Erbietũg

Auffs erst/danck ich meinem got/durch Jesu Christ/ewr aller halben/das man von ewrem glauben inn aller welt sagt. Deñ got ist mein zeüge/welchem ich diene iñ meynem geyst/am Euangelio von seinem sun/das ich on vnterlaß ewr gedenck/vnd alle zeyt

Plate 193

Plate 195

Hie ſierdt der pferdt mayſter hinweck / was gůtes im hauß was/floch dauon/forchtendt den newen er=
ben/kamen für em frätlin wolten aldo herberg vber nacht haben/wolte man ſich nicht ein laſſen/
ſtanden bey nacht in ſorgen vnd forchte der grauſamen wölfe des ortes.

Alda

Hie freſſen vnd ſauffen eins tails die rauber/die anderen faren auß etlich verſteckt taub im holtz zehol/
In dem dem ſie es holen/erwiſchen ſie hie den ellenden eſel ſampt der Junckfraw flüchtige/
treibens wider an haim/haltens ſeer vbel.

Hie begert Lucius iñ eſels geſtalt roſen zů freſſen in einem luſt garten/kam der baur vber jn/beret jm die haut wol/aber als er den bauren mit ſeinem klawen auch troffen het/vnd zů boden geſchlagen / macht ſein weib ein geſchrey/lauffen die bauren zů ſamen/hetzen den gůten eſel mit hunden.

Hie kompt der ain geferte Apuleÿ zů dem ellenden Socraten/der ſagt im wie Meroe die zauberin iren bůlen zů ainem Biber verzaubert/auch iren nachbauren ainen Wirt zů ainem froſch der vnden im faß die geſt empfacht/auch ein Juriſten der wider ſie geredt zů ainem bock/vnd der ſolches von jr außpracht hauß vnd hoff in die lüfft hingefiert habe.

Hie fleügt Cupido Psyches man in die lüfft do hyn/stürtzt sich Psyche vor layde vom gestat in den nechste bache/erhelt sie dennocht der bach Cupidini zů liebe/trest sie Pan der gaiß got/mit lieblichen worten.

Hie sůchet Psyche jren man Cupidinem/der lage schwach vor prunst der liebe in seiner můtter bette Veneris/sach sie/wie sich Venus jm möre tauchet vnd badet/vnd bey jr ein weissen schwanen mit jr redende.

·H·F

Die warheit vber win det alle zeit

Plate 205

Groß lüg võ höl kümpt jtz vf erd
Dz füllerey gehandhapt werd
Darümb von heilger engel kö:
Ain yder dise warnüng hör.
Ich bin ain engel von Gott gesandt/
Meins ampts ain gütter pott genandt.
Jr hoch teütschen secht di Figur/
Si zaygt weinuollerleüt natür.'
Tracht hi das kind on aller zier/
Der Eheren kron entpfält jm schier.
Di reyset dasch verderben deüt/
Vnd di hörner/gantz vyhisch leüt.
Der degen bloß/krieg mord/vnd zanck/
Dj todtenpar/kürtz leben/kranck.
So helt der Teüffel auch gar fest/
Wj hj das kind gleich sein weingest/
Fliecht solch geloch/das ist das päst.

Oncede quesumꝰ omipotēs deꝰ Dñō
vt nos vnigeniti tui noua per carnem
natiuitas liberet : quos sub peccati
iugo vetusta seruitꝰ tenet. Per eundē do. rē.

Eodem die de tribus regibus. Añ.
Ex Caspar: rex Balthasar: rex mel
chior. Rogo vos per singl'a noia ve-
stra. Rogo vos p sanctā trinitatē.

Dominica in ramis palmarum.
Passio domini nostri Jesu chri
sti: sm Math. Cap. xxvi.

qui memor fit tui : in inferno
aūt qs cōfitebit tibi. Labo-
raui in gemitu meo: lauabo p.

Plate 207

De sancto Paulo. An.
Gloriosum lumen omniū ec-
clesiarum: sole splendidius.
O vere apostolicum sydus al

De sancto Ambrosio episco-
po et doctore ecclesie. Aña.
O presul beatissime Ambrosi:

peccatꝫ meis. Insup obsecro te pre-
clarū atq̄ deco- summe diuinitatꝫ
ministrū: vt in nouissimo die beni-
gne suscipias aiam meā in sinu tuo

nerant: precioīs tue auxilio a morbo
caduco liberent. Per dn̄m no. Je. ꝛc.
De sancto Georgio milite
et martyre. Aña.

Diui eximijq; doctoris Eusebij Hieronymi Stridonensis Aepistolarum libri: plurimis quidem quibus minoribus excusæ formis, & mendis & mutilationibus squalebant: solutarum.

Das Erst buch Mose. I

Das Erst Capitel.

AM anfang schuff Gott himel vnnd erden/vnd die erde war wüst vnd leer/vñ es war finster auff der tieffe/vnd der wind Gottes schwebet auff dem wasser.

Vnd Gott sprach/Es werde liecht/ Vnd es ward liecht/ vnnd Gott sahe das liecht für gut an / Da scheydet Gott das liecht vom finsterniß/vnd nennet das liecht/Tag/vñ die finsternis/Nacht/Da ward auß abend vñ morgẽ der Erste tag

Vnd Gott sprach/ Es werde eine feste zwisschen den wassern/vñ die sey eyn vnterscheyd zwisschen den wassern/Da machet Gott die feste/vñ scheydet das wasser vnter der festen/von dem wasser über der festen/ vñ es geschach also/vñ Gott nennet die festen hymel. Da ward auß abend vñ morgen der Ander tag

Vnd Gott sprach/Es samle sich das wasser vnter dem hymel/an söndere örtter das man das trucken sehe/vñ es geschach also/ Vnd Gott nennet das trucken/Erde/ vnd die samlung der wasser nennet er/Meere/vnd Gott sahe es für gut an.

Vnd Gott sprach/Es lasse die erde auffgehen graß vñ kraut / das sich besame/ vnd fruchtbare bewme/ da eyn yeglicher nach seiner art frucht trage/vnd hab seinen eygen samen bey im selbs / auff erden/vnd es geschach also/Vnd die erde ließ auffgehen/graß vnd kraut/das sich besamet/eyn ygliches nach seiner art/vnd bewme die da frucht trugen/vnd jren eygen samen bey sichselbs hätten/ ein yglicher nach seyner art. Vnd Gott sahe es für gut an / Da ward auß abend vnd morgen der Dritte tag.

Vnd Gott sprach/Es werden liechter an der feste des himels/vnd scheyden tag vnd nacht/vñ seyen zu zeichen/zeyttungen/tagen vnd iaren/ vnd seyen liechter an der

Das Newe Testament mit fleyſs verteutſcht.

M.D.XXIIII.

Das Ander teyl des allten Testaments mit fleyſs verteutſcht. M.D.XXIIII.

DEus q̇ affluētiſſime bonitatꝫ tue pru
dētia ḃtiſſimā Urſulā cū vndecim mi
lib⁹ ꝟginū triūpho martyꝝ coronare digna
tus es: ꝯcede ꝓpiti⁹: vt eaꝝ ꝑcib⁹ et meritis

¶ De ſancto Juda apoſtolo. Añ.
SAncte iuda apoſtole per illū qui te ſibi
in amicum aſciuit: deprecor te: vt a con
ſuetudine peccatorꝫ meorum tuis meritis

¶ Oratio ante faciem chriſti di-
cenda: alias ante Ueronicam.
SAlue ſancta facies noſtri redēptoris:
in q̄ nitet ſpecies diuini ſplēdoris: im-

·1·5·1·6·
¶ In feſto Aſſumptionis btē Marie.
VIrgo prudētiſſima quo ꝓgrederis q̄ſi
auroꝛa valde rutilās: filia ſion tota fo-
moſa ꝛ ſuauis es: pulchra vt luna: electa vt

Ein gesprech zwischen Sanct Peter vnd dem Herren/ von der jetzigen Weldt lauff.

Mehr ein gesprech zwischen eim Waldtbru der vñ eim Engel/von dẽ heimlichen gericht Gottes.

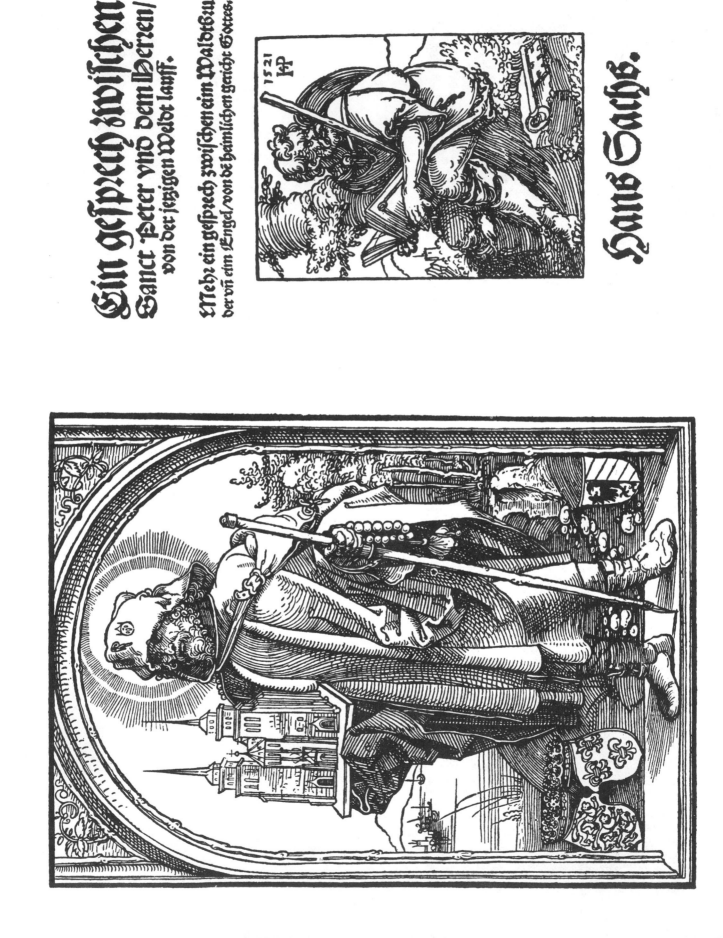

Hans Sachs.

Strabi Fuldensis mo
nachi Poete suauissimi. quondã Rabani
Mauri auditoris Hortulus nuper apud Heluetios in. S. Galli monasterio
repertus. qui Carminis elegantia tam est delectabilis. q̃z doctrine cognoscen=
darum quarundam herbarum varietate vtilis. Ad Grymaldũ Abbatem.

¶ Item Psalmus. 41. Sicut ceruus desiderat ꝛc. et Psalmus. 112. Lau=
date pueri ꝛc. per Venerabilem Bedam. sono Heroico decãtanti.

Ein nutzbarliches
büchlein | von der entlichen volzie=
hung ewiger fürsehung / Wie das der wirdig vatter Joan
nes von Staupitz / Doctor / vnd der reformirten Augusti=
ner Vicarius / Das heilig Aduẽt das 1516 Jars / zu Nürm
berg / got zu lob vnd gemeiner wolphart gepredigt hat.

15 Jesus. 17.
Dein bin ich / mach mich selig.
S. J. V. S.

Lazarus
Judas
Maria Mag
dalena

θάτωμ φὶτώμ χοίμα
VG

Plate 217

Das leben Jesu Christi gezogen auſz den vier Euangelisten: Mit kürtzer beyleer und christ licher underweisung: Darzu vil schoner figurẽ bedeütung

Plate 219

Gregorius nonus

Plate 223

Plate 225

IVDAS dux Iſraëlitarum expugnat Chananæos. Adonibezec cæſis manuum ac pedum ſummitatibus, in Ieruſalem captiuus ducitur.

IVDICVM I.

CHRISTVS ſedet ad dexteram patris. Deus pater filio ſuo ſacerdotalem dignitatem in æternum duraturã ex paſſionis præmio tradit.

PSALM. CIX.

IOSIAS quartadecima luna primi menſis, in Ieroſolymis immolat phaſe.

III. ESDRAE I.

AMOS contra Damaſcum, Philiſthæos, Tyrum, Idumæam, & filios Ammon prophetat.

AMOS I.

IOIADA pontifex, Athalia occisa, constituit Ioas regem super Israël. Mathan sacerdos Baal coram altari interficitur.

IIII. REGVM XI.

ELIMELECH Bethlehemita cum uxore Noëmi & duobus filijs peregrinatur in regione Moabitide, & ibi moritur.

RVTH I.

E iij

ASSVERVS, celebrato conuiuio, potentiam & gloriã suam ostentat. Vasthi uxore repudiata, Esther regina efficitur.

ESTHER I. & II.

PSALTES contra Iudæos excandescit, ac eos qui CHRISTVM Messiam deum in lege promissum infideliter & impiè abnegant, insipientes uocat.

PSALM. LII.

K

Amaurotũ vrbs.
Fons Anydri.
Ostium anydri
Hythlodaeus.

Cantzler.

Welch im feld geuch fahen wellen
Die müssendt geuch zü locken stellen
Darumb das ich wol locken kan
Handt sy mich gestellet vornan dran
Guck guck/fah ich züm ersten an

Von der geuch wegen

Io.Clemens. Hythlodæus. Tho.Morus. Pet. Aegid.

SERMONIS QVEM RAPHAEL HYTHLODAEVS · VIR EXIMIVS, de optimo reipublicæ statu habuit, liber primus, per illustrem uirū Thomam Morum inclytæ Britanniarū urbis Londini & ciuem, & uicecomitem.

VVM NON EXIGVI MOmenti negocia quædam inuictissim⁹ Angliæ rex HENRICVS eius nominis octauus, omnibus egregij principis artibus ornatissimus, cū serenissimo Castellæ principe CAROLO controuersa d nuper ha

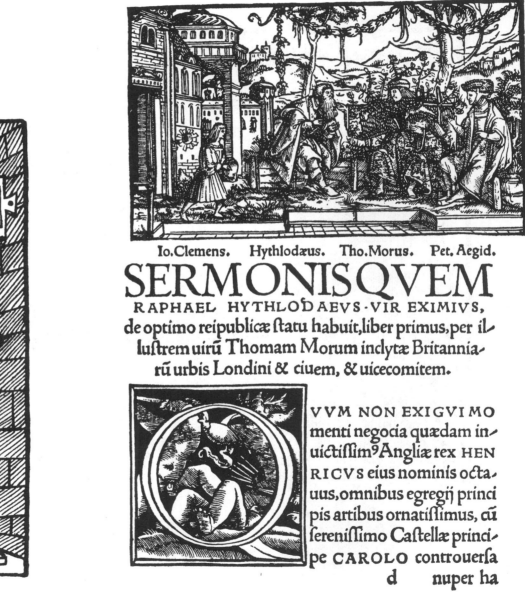

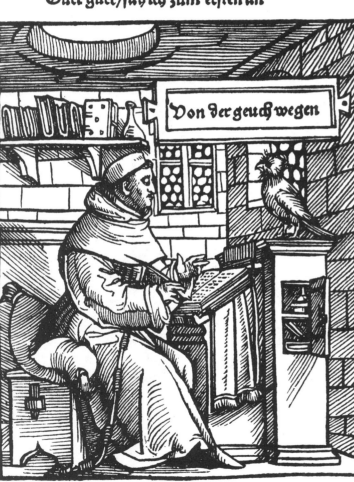

Vorred der geuchmatten.

Die geuch ein schlechtlichs liedlin handt
Darff weder baß noch ein discant
Weñ er nur guck guck singen kan
Für einen gouch nim ich jn an

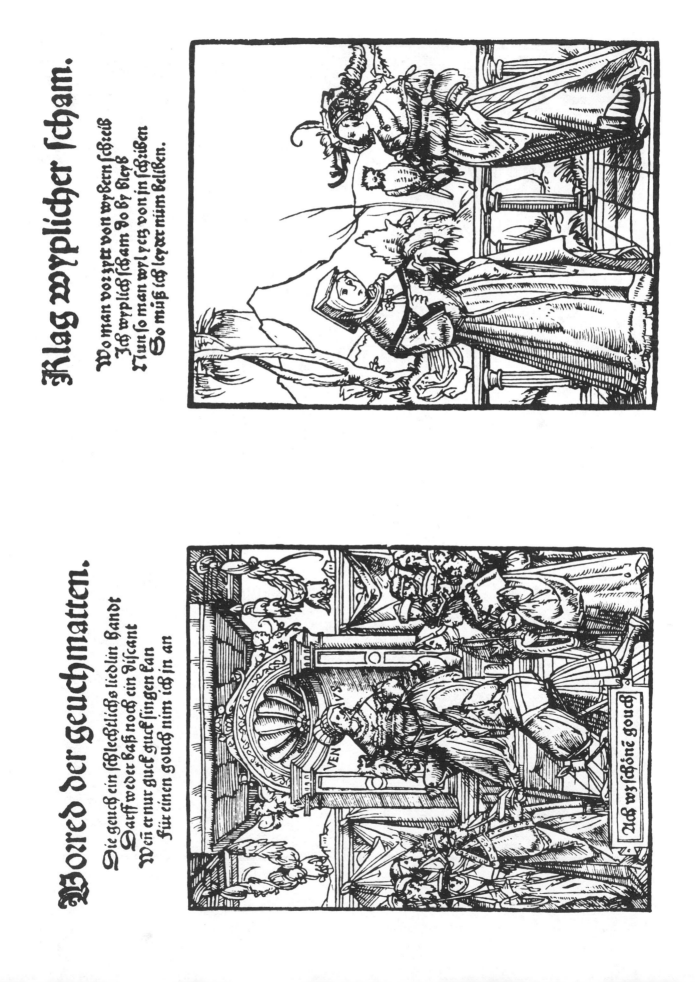

Klag wyplicher scham.

Wo man vor zytt von wybern schreib
Ich wyplich scham do by bleyb
Nun so man wyl yetz von jn schriben
So müß ich leyder nüm beliben.

Plate 231

¶Per Lazarum a morte reſuſcitatum/peccator/quem dominus ad peniten
tiam vocat/deſignatur. Per Martham exterioribus obſequijs occupatã
actiua vita ſignificatur. Per Magdalenam que verba domini re//
ſidens audiebat/cõtemplatiua vita exprimitur/Lazarus ſu//
ſcitatur/Martha nõ reprehẽditur/Magdalena laudatur.
Suſcitatio penitentis magna eſt/maiora ſunt acti//
ue vite merita/contemplatiue potiora.

Salue dies sanctitatis/ leticie et felicitatis: q̄ es celsior cūctis sanctis: sanctior oībus: dulcior vniuersis. Salue dies misericordie ⁊ liberationis: que es viuis gaudium ⁊ defunctis refrigeriū. Salue dies preclara: angelis ⁊ hoībꝫ chara: in qua nos jesus redemit: ⁊ planctū nostrū in gaudiū conuertit. Salue dies festa: in q̄ cōsolantur corda mesta. Salue gl'ia dierū: in q̄ dn̄s ī paradisum restituit hoīez reū. Per isti⁹ diei sacratissimi merita gl'iosa ⁊ p tuā le

q ij

singl'r: oēs ꝑcoꝛ parit: vt p meis excessibus oretis boīs oībꝫ. Oēs scti apl'i: mei vos mīremini: vr̄a sctā memoria: me colloce in gl'ia. Uos mūdi de tumultibꝫ: elegit pi⁹ dn̄s: q meruistis cernere: dn̄m nr̄m ī corpe. Uos estis mūdi lumīa: sup solē lucētia: p q̄s fulget eccl'ia: vt sol ⁊ luna splēdida Cū filio vos boīs: hūc mūdū iudicabitis: me p vos saluū pero extremo in iudicio. Amen.

Sequūtur nūc orōnes de martyribꝫ: ⁊ pmo de sctō Sebastiano Añ. O magne fidei sctissime sebastiane miles

m vj

veni coronaberis Aue barbara serēa pulchra q̄si luna plena: singulari cantilena: spōsum agnum sequeris. aue barbara beata: q̄ cū spōso ꝑparata: nuptiaꝝ adoptatu: tra nsiuisti gaudia. Aue fulgens margarita: i corona ihū sita: tā in morte q̄s in vita: sis nobis ꝓpicia. ℣. Specie tua et pulchritudine tua. Intēde ⁊c. Oratio.

INtercessio nos q̄s dn̄e btē barbare ꝟginis ⁊ martyris sp adiuuet: vt nō subito moriamur: sed ante diē mortis nr̄e sctissimi corpis ⁊ sanguinis: sacreꝗ

p vj

mortuoꝝ. ℣. Tecū pncipiū in die ꝟtutis tue. In splēdoribꝫ sctōꝝ ex ⁊c. Oratio.

DEus q̄ nobis nati saluatoris diē ꝯcedis celebrare octauū: fac nos qm̄s ei⁹ ppetua diuinitate muniri: cui⁹ sum⁹ carnali cōmertio repati. Qui cū deo patre ⁊ spiritu sancto viuis ⁊ regnas ⁊c.

In die epiphanie domini.

Tribꝫ miraculis ornatum diē sanctum colimus hodie stella magos duxit ad ꝑsepium. hodie vinum ex aqua factū ē ad

p viij

ta securior Amen. ℟. Dif
fusa est gratia in labiis ꝛc. Oratio.
Omnipotens ꝛ mitissime deus: te humilit im-
ploro: vt me miserum peccatorem. A. non permit
tas perire propter peccata mea: quia tua creatura sum
sed per gratiam sancti spiritus: ꝛ per intercessionem sanctissi
me dei genitricis virginis marie: ꝛ per orationem
beatissime margarethe virginis ꝛ martyris tue
concede mihi spacium viuendi: ꝛ peccata mea plan

gendi: vt
ante diem ex
itus mei
per veram
contritio-
nem ꝛ pu-
ram confessi
onem tibi
omnipotenti
deo pla-
cere me-
rear. per.
De sanctã
Maria
magda-
lena.
p ij

impēdis: adesto supplicationibus nostris
vt illa que ad salutē mētis ꝛ corporis minus
sufficere vident beate sophie ꝛ filiarum eius
fidei spei ꝛ charitatis suffragantibus meritis
celerius condonentur. Per dominum nostrum.
De sancta Margaretha.

Aue stel
la radio
sa: sol lu
ce clari-
or: mar-
garitha
preciosa
gemmis
auro ca-
rior vir-
go carne
genero-
sa: fide
spectabi
lior: pas-
siōe glo-
riosa: me
ritis pre
stantior: nobis mater gratiosa: patrona
clementior sis: ad regna gaudiosa semi-

Hodie
christus
natus est:
hodie
saluator
apparu-
it: hodie
i celo ca
nunt an
geli: letā
tur arch
angeli:
hodie ex
ultāt in-
sti dicen
tes gloria
in excel-
sis deo alleluia. ℟ Verbū caro factum
est. Et habitauit ꝛc. Collecta.
Concede quesumus omnipotēs deus: vt nos
vnigeniti tui noua per carnem natiuitas li
beret: quos sub peccati iugo vetusta seruitus tenet. Per eundē dominum nostrū ihesum christū.
In festo sanctorum innocentū Añ.
Ambulabūt mecum in albis quoniam di
q vij

Impressum Argentine per Marti
num Flach, secunda feria post
festum Purificatiōis Ma
rie virginis. Anno do
mini. M.D.xj.

Das erst gebot VII

Das ist das erst gebot du solt nit frembd göt anbetten.

Du solt nicht frömbde gött anbettē owee lieber iunger wy vil sein frömbder göt te/in manigē menschē Du solt wissen was der mensch wider gott liebet oder lieb hatt/das das syn abgott ist/was auch ynbilt in den mē schen mit irem willen stand die in got nitt in lüchtent/das seind alles abgöt Nun spricht sanctus Augustinus/daz man einen got anbetten sol mitt dreier lei weiß.

Zů dem ersten mitt gantzem glau/ ben. Also das der mensch an die heili/ gen kirchen glaub / vnd iren gebotten gehorsam sei vnd kein ding glaub das die heilig kirch verwürffet / vnd auch

Die X gebot

Das.II.gebot.Du ſolt got nit üppiklichē nennē.

Er meiſter ſager. Du ſolt wiſſen das zů dem anderen mal der allmechtig gewaltig gott ſprach alſo. (Exodi.xx.capitulo. Non aſſumas nomen dei tui invanum).

Das iſt. Du ſolt den namen deines gottes nicht vppigklichen nennen vnnd hiemitt ſpricht ſanctus Auguſtinus. Alſo ſo ſeind dir alles freuel ſchweren/vnnd alle meineide verbotten. Hiebei ſolt du wiſſen/das man gebunden iſt in dreierlei weiß/dis gebott zehaltende.

Die erſt weiß die iſt / das man ſoll on ſach nicht ſchweren.

Die ander weiß iſt/das man keinen ſchwůr noch gelůbde brech.

Die dritt ſach iſt/das man den götlichen nammen nicht flůche/vnd das du die erſt ſach oder weiß verſtandeſt

Nun ſo ſolt du verſton oder wiſſen das zů einem rechten götlichen ſchwůr drü ding gehören. Das erſt iſt warheit des ſchwůres. Das ander iſt das mã

gotes In in ē gewirdiget vn̄ erhöcht all
zeit on vndlaß/wā sie den namē gotes
liebend/in irē grund vn̄ vßwēdig mit
aller eerwirdikeit/als wir lesen dz d̓ de/
mūtig heilig sant Franciscus die brief
lin vō dem weg vffhūb/vn̄ als forcht
dz d̓ edel nam iesus darā stūnd geschri/
ben/vn̄ etwar darauff tret. Also trůg
auch gar in eerwirdikeit d̓ heilig Igna
cius den namē gottes in seinem hertzē/
das man den namen iesu christi mitt
guldinen bůchstaben fand nach seiner
tod geschriben in seinē hertzen. Hiebei
merckstu wol wie gar vnd In hoher wy
se die frūnd gottes dis gebot haben ge
haltē/vn̄ dz vorgenāt vn̄ so gar mit er
wirdikeit alle zeit habē seinē namē geer
et. Dis wolt got auch habe vō allē mē
schē. Darūb d̓ heilig Moyses hie vor/
got fragte/wie er in dēvolck/nennē sol
te/da wolt sich gott nit and̓s genēt las
sen werdē/dā dz er sprach zů Moyses.
Ego sum qui sum Exodi in ca. Ich bī
d̓ ich bin/spricht d̓ da ist d̓ hat mich zů
euch gesant. Hie mit wolt er sein bloß
abgescheidēvngenāte natur zů bekēnē
de gebē/vn̄ alle mēschē manē/dz sie nit
leichtlichē in soltē nennē. Der iūg. Nū
sag mir fürbas von dem dritten gebot.

Der meister antwurt dem iunger.

Das drit gebot ist. Du solt die feirtag heiligen.

Die .x. Gebott

als er ſich gebreitet hatt in alle ding. Diſer breite ſolt du folgen mitt einer lidigen weiten gemüte/ vnd dich ſeiner gegenwirtigkeit ergeben/ wañ hierinn würde dir vberweſenliche genad gegeben inn einem erheben deines gemütes vber alle bild vnd formen. Aber die lenge gottes iſt die ewigkeit die ſtill vnnd vnwandelbar iſt.

Hieran ſolt du dich hencken mit einem ſteten vnwandelbaren gemüt/ alſo halteſt du dann dis gebott/ mit den volkommenen fründen gotes/ die den heiligen feiertag mitt heiliger betrachtung vnd inniger ůbung vertreibent. Nun wil ich dir auch ſagen/ von dem fierden gebott gottes.

Das vierd gebott. Du ſolt vatter vnd muoter in eeren halten.

Die .X. Gebot

in dẽ götlichẽ willẽ/vñ das die vnüst alle zeit war nimpt gottes willẽ in allẽ sachẽ vnd dẽ lebet. Zů dem fierden so würt der mensch behüt vor teglichẽ sünden/so er alle ding ordinieret nach massen/wañ wer in allen seinen wercken maß rürt/der geůbet nymer keinen gebresten/vnd ist das darumb/wã gebrestẽ kommẽ von vnordenung dz mã ettwañ zů vil oder zů lützel thůt/vñ in d' vbergreiffung od' veesumniß/so ůbt man gebrestẽ. Aber wer thůt dz er nitt thů sol/vñ laßt dz er nit lõ sol/dẽ antwurt alwegẽ got. Zů dẽ.v.mal/so würt d' mẽsch behüt vor teglichẽ sündẽ so er willig arm ist/võ vssen vñ innen vñ ist dz darũb/wã arme lüt stõd alwegẽ in lidẽ/vñ mit dẽ dz ein gebrest salt an ein armẽ menschẽ/so ist leidẽ davõ vertilget in dz sein nit mer ist. Vñ danõ sprach christus/mã sol armẽ lütẽ iren gebrestẽ vbersehẽ/wã was die vnitugent verschuldet/dz verschwẽmet d' offen des armütes. Dz.vi.ist/das den menschẽ behüt vor teglichẽ sünden/dz des mẽschẽ hertz durchbrant ist mit dẽ liebendẽ feur des heilgẽ geists/wã das verschwẽdet al müglicheit am mẽschẽ vñ macht in rein on all sünd/vñ wer allweg in dẽ liebẽ feur brinet/d' lebt alweg on sünd/wã liebin vñ haß mögen nit miteinand' gestõ/vñ davon so der mensch liebet/so můß er alles das lassen das hessig ist/vnd das sünd ist

Das fünfft gebott ist. Du solt niemandt tödten.

Die .X. Gebot

Das ſechſt gebot das iſt. Du ſolt nicht vnkü ſch ſein/vnd dein ee nitt brechen.

U ſolt wiſſē zů dem.vi.mal / das der ewig gott ſprach. (Non Mechaberis. Exodi.xx.capitulo.) Du ſolt nicht vnküſch ſein/od dein ee brechen/vnd hierin hat got alle lüſt verbotten die vnküſch ſeind/vnd alſo hatt dis gebot/als die lerer ſchreibent auch drei ſynn.

Der erſt ſyñ iſt/das man nit ſol leip lichen verfallen. Darumb verſchulden ſich vil lüt in diſem gebot. Zů dem erſten ſo thůn todſünd/alle die/die da leiplich verfallent/vnd nicht in der ee ſitzen/vnd dz meint ſant Paulus (Ad epheſeos.v.capi.) Zů dem andn alle die/die gelobt haben keuſch zůſein/ſie ſeien in orden oder nit/wa die verfallē das iſt todſünd/vnd ſunderlich ob dy ſelben oder die erſten küſchen lüt iunck frawen machen verfallen/ das iſt gar ein ſchwere todſünd. Zů dem dritte alle die/die in der ee ſitzen mit vnrecht wiſſentlich/als die/die einander anhö ren/oder des gleichen. Zů dem fier den mal/alle die/die in der ee recht ſitz en/vnd darüber mit ander lüten ver-

Die .X. Gebot

Das sibent gebot ist Du solt nicht stelen.

U solt wissē das der ewige Gott sprach zů dem sibenden mal. (Non furtum facias). Du solte nicht stelen/vnd hiemit als sanctus Augustinus spricht. So ist verbotten alles vnrecht gůt/vnnd alles frembd gůt/das des menschen nicht ist. Doch so mag man on sünd frembd gůt nemen in dreierlei weiß.

Zů dem ersten so es gebotten würt/von einem obersten/der das mit recht gebieten mag/als gott der hieß die iuden in Egypten nemmen den leuten yr gůt. Nun zů dem andern so mā es durch gůt thůt. Als so man einem töbigen menschen ein schwert stilt/vñ es behaltet/das er im selber kein schaden mög thůn oder ander lüten. Oder so man einem menschen der vnnützlich sein gůt verthůt/nimpt/vnd man seinen nutz dariñ meint. Zů dē drittē so leibs not darzů zwinget/so mag mā and̄ menschē gůt mit recht angryffen/wā in der letstē not des lebens sein alle ding gemein. Nun hat dis gebot auch drei synn. Der erst ist/das

Die .x. Gebot

en wercken/das ist das sie sich entblöset von allen geschaffnen bilden / vnd mit einem vngeschaffnen liecht ynuringet/in die finsterniß der verborgenen gotheit/vnd dauon würt sie bekentloß vnd von lieben liebloß/das ist das sie niemant bekēnet nach natürlicher weise/vnd nit liebet nach liebin/mer nach gottes liebe. Vnd darūb sprach sanctus Paulus.(Ad galathas.ii.ca. Ich leb nit mer/cristus lebt in mir. Nū wil ich dir fürbaß sagē vō dē.viii.gebott.

Das achtest gebott ist. Du solt nicht falsch gezügniß geben.

O Er ewig Got sprach zū dē.viii.mal.(Exodi.xx.capi. Nō falsum testimoniū dices). Du solt nicht falsch gezügniß gebē/vnd hiemitt als sanctus Augustinus spricht/so ist verbottē aller schad den mā gethūn mag dem neben menschen/mitt worten od mit wercken/vnd kein falsch gezügniß in worten oder in wercken treiben/ vn̄ also hat dis gebot auch drei sin̄. Der sin̄ ist/dz mā nicht sol blößlich vnwarheit fürbringē/vn in die weiß sünden dreierlei menschē. Zū dē erstē alle dy die betrachtigklich etwz mit ernst wid

Die .x. Gebott

ſo mag man ſie nit bekennē/wañ alles
dz ſie habē das iſt in worden in einer lu
ter ſtillen weiſe oder rüwe vnd wer no
ch vnluter vnd vnrüwig iſt dem ſeind
ſie verborgen. Zů dem ſechſten mal
ſo ſeind ſie darumb vnbekant/wañ ſie
haben kein ſunderliche weiß an in. Vñ
dauon wer noch mit ſunderlicher weiß
vmb gat/der weiß nit vmb die weiß/
loſen menſchen vnd dauon ſeind dy al
ler beſten menſchen. Die alle vngeileb
ten menſchen/wañ was man nit bekē/
net das mag man nitt gelieben ſpricht
ſanctus Auguſtinus. Zů dē.vii.mal
ſo ſein ſie auch vnbekāt/wañ wz ſie ha
bē dz iſt vber alle wort vnd vber alles
ſprechē/vñ danō wer die ding liebt na
ch den wortē/d würt dick betrogē vnd
danō iſt dz die höchſt weißheit die ein
mēſch mag habē gůte menſchē zů bekē
nende vñ die weißheit ſtudiert mā nitt
zů Paris. Wer in dē leiden chriſti/vnd
wer ſein vernunfft daryn keret der lert
alle götliche weißheit vñ niemā kan ſi
ch vor den menſchen verbergē/er werd
in bekāt/wā als criſtus het gemeiſchaf
te mit allē dingen alſo leret d mēſch al
le gemeinſchafft in chriſto/vñ alſo wer
dē im alle ding bekant. Jch wil dir nū
fürbaß ſagen von dem.ix.gebott.

Dz.IX.gebot:du ſolt nit begerē deins nechſtē gůt.

Epistula prima. iii capitulo) Der zeitlich gůt hat vnd sicht seinen brůder gebresten haben/ vnnd beschlüsset seinen kasten vor im wie mag götliche liebe da wirckẽ sein. Als sanctus gregorius spricht. Wa grosse liebe ist da ist si wirckẽ grosse werck/ vñ wirckt sie nit grosse werck. So ist es nit götliche liebe. Es mag kum bei einand̄ geston ein hertz vol liebe/ vnd ein seckel voll pfenning Wan liebe ist ein feür in dem alle zeitliche dind verschwinden vnd zů nüt werden/ vnd dauon wa rechte liebe ist da ist leidikeit der sie macht ledikeit. Vñ das feür bran in sancto Paulo da er sprach. Ich hab alle ding geschetzet als dz bacht. Nũ wil ich dir sagen für baß wõ dem zehenden gebot.

Das zehend gebot ist Du solt keines eẽ frauwen begeren.

Du solt wissen das der ewig got zů dem zehendẽ mal sprach.(Exodi. xx capitulo. Nõ cõcupisce vxorem proximi tui) Du solt deins nechsten eefrauwen nit begeren vnd diß gebot hat auch drei siñ. Der erst ist du solt nit begerẽ deines nechstẽ ee frawen also das du begird vnd willen habest mit ir zů verfallende/ das

Von Kaufmanschatz des spils welche gebrucht mö
gen/vnnd welche nit gebrucht solten werden.

Von dem Wannenkremer vnd der kaufleut hã tierung/geistlich vnd weltlich/wie man sich halten sol/vil hübscher vnderweisung/damit ein yeglicher sein seel vor ewigem verkauff bewar/zwentzig predigẽ.

Von dem himlischen Leuwen.

a Jhesus zur statt der creützigung.
Gefürt ward mit viler draurung.
Nachvolgten die frumen frauwen.
Der alt man halff sein creütz dragen.

b Essich drincken/vnd c hangen müst.
d Verspotten/spilten/was ir lust.
Vil am creütz e der herr gethon hat.
Bsich den text/wie er kam zum grab.

Von Rom die ander schrifft zů schickt.
Thimotheo/vnd in erquickt.
Paulus/seins creutzs/der brůder flucht.
Vberal der teuffel zanck sůcht.

In letsten dagen der wolff zeit.
O crist merck/was paulus enbeut.
Auch sunderlich form/gstalt/ordnung.
Cristlicher ler gibt/vnd forderung.

Der erst gang
Der Sechst gang

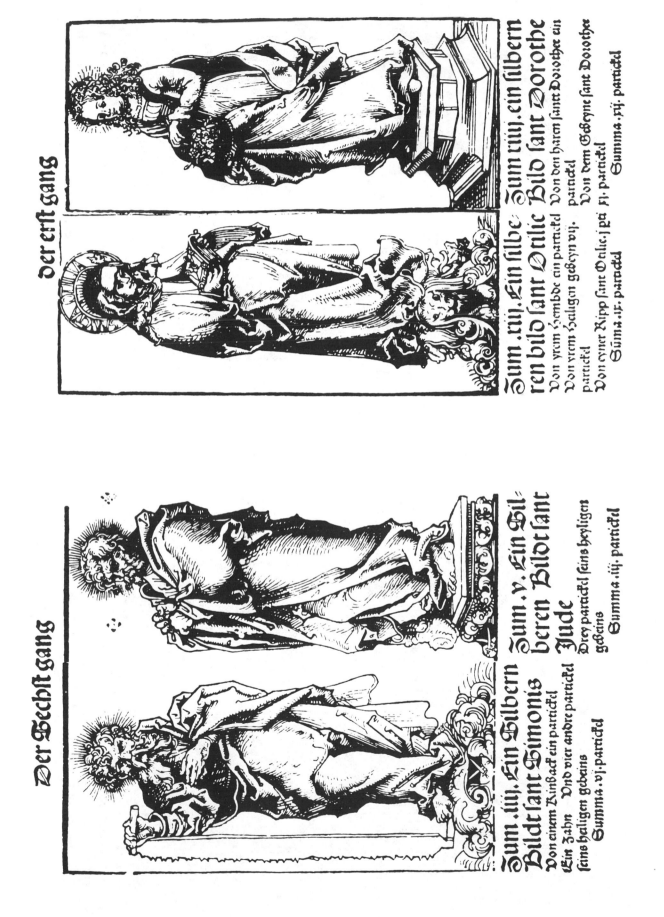

Der Sechst gang dis heiligthumbs

Zum viij. Ein Silbern
Bildt sancti Philippi.
Von seinem haligen gepein xij. ptickel.
Sūma xij. ptickel.

Zum ix. ein Silbern
Bildt des grossen sant Jacobs
Ein Zhan Vom schulterbein j. ptic. Syben andere ptickel seins heyligen gepeins
Sūma ix. partickel

Zum .ij. Ein Silbern
Bildt sant Mathei Appostoli vñ Ewangeliste
Ein Zahn Vnd .xj. andere ptickel seines heiligen gebeins
Summa .xij. ptickel

Zum .iij. Ein silbern
Bildt sant Mathie
Zehen ptickel seins haligen gebeins
Sūma .x. ptickel

h

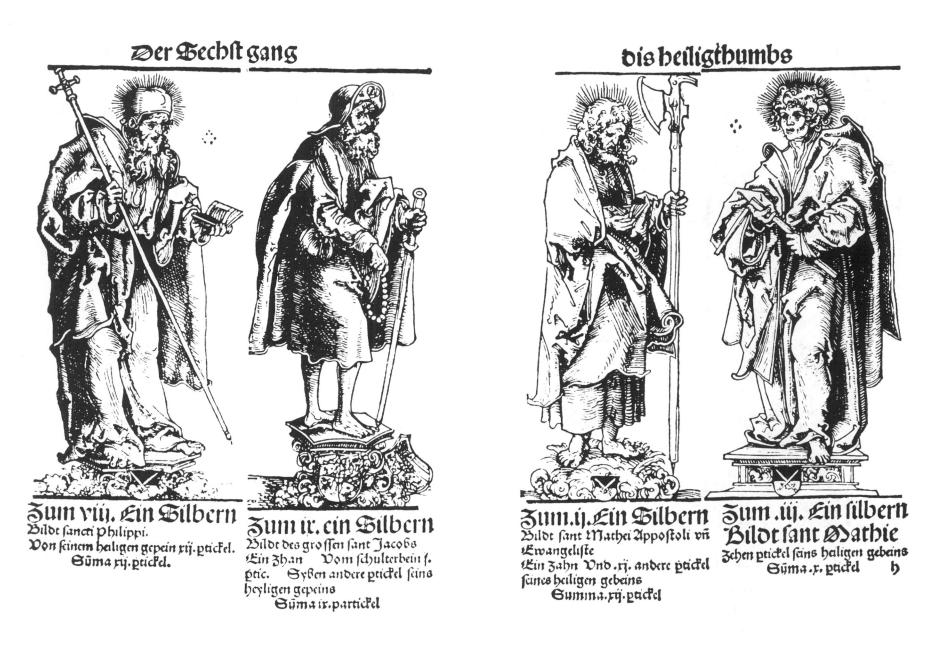

Passional Christi und

Er hat funden ym tẽpell vorkauffer/ schäff/ ochßen vñ tawbẽ vñ wechßler sitzen/ vñ hat gleich ein geyssel gemacht võ strickẽ alle schäff/ ochßen / tawben vñ wechßler außem tẽpell trieben/ das gelt verschüt/ die tzall brede vmkart/ vñ tzu den die tawben vorkaufften gesprochen / Hebt auch hin mit diessen auß meins vatern hauß/ solt ir nit ein kauffhauß machẽ. Joh. 2. Jr habts vmb sunst/ darũb gebts vmb sunst. Mat. 10. Dein gelt sey mit dir yn vordamnuß. Act. 8.

Passional Christi und

Christus.

Jr solt nicht haben golt nach silber/ nicht gelt an ewrn gorteln/ keyne taschen/ auch nit tzwen röck nach schuch/ nach eyn wanderstab Matthei. 10.

Sanct Peter sagt/ Jch habe wyder golt nach silber. Act. 3.

Ubi ist dan Patrim. onium Petri?

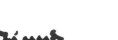

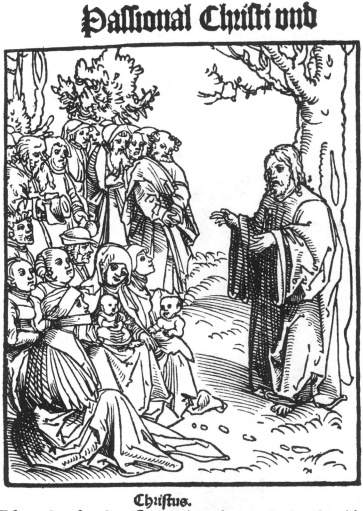

Passional Christi vnd

Christus.

Die soldner haben geflochten eyne kronen von dörner / vñ auff sein heubt gedruckt / darnach mit eynem purpur kleydt haben sie yn bekleydet. Johan. 19.

Passional Christi vnd

Christus.

Ich muß auch andern steten predigen das reych gots/ dan ich von deß wegen gesandt byn / vnd hab gepredigt in den Sinagogen durch Galileam Luce.4.

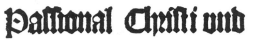

Die offinbarung

Das Ander teyl des alten testaments.

Plate 259

COLONIAE Petrus Quentel excudebat,
Anno M CCCCC XXVII.

Plate 261

Reformacion der baÿrischñ Lanndrecht nach Cristi vnnsers Hailmachers geburde Im fünftzehenhündert vnnd Achtzehendm Jar Aufgericht-

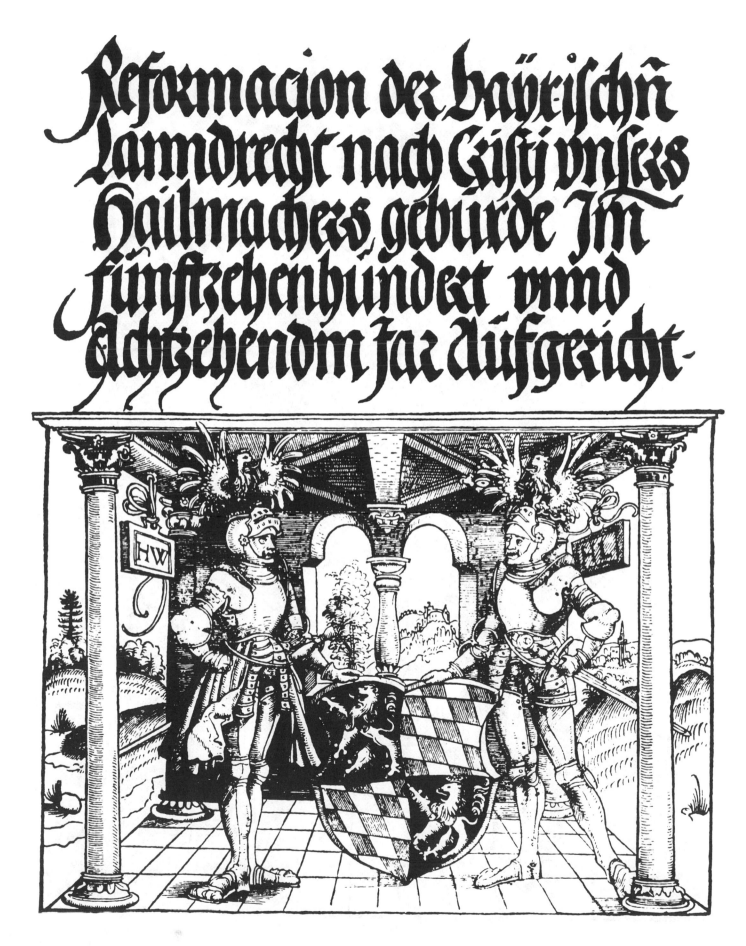

Gerichtzordnung Im fürstn=
thumb·Obern·vnd Nidern
Bayrn·Anno 1520 aufgericht